ICSE Exams 2026

AF814416

All in One®

PHYSICS

Class 9

ICSE Exams 2026

All in One®
PHYSICS
Class 9

Authors
Mansi Garg (MSc, BEd)
Jitendra Kumar (MSc, MEd)

arihant
SUCCESS AND NOTHING LESS

arihant
SUCCESS AND NOTHING LESS

ARIHANT PRAKASHAN
(School Division Series)

ADMINISTRATIVE & PRODUCTION OFFICES

Regd. Office
'Ramchhaya' 4577/15, Agarwal Road, Darya Ganj, New Delhi -110002
Tele: 011- 47630600, 43518550; Fax: 011- 23280316

Head Office
Kalindi, TP Nagar, Meerut (UP) - 250002, Tel: 0121-7156203, 7156204

SALES & SUPPORT OFFICES
Agra, Ahmedabad, Bengaluru, Bareilly, Chennai, Delhi, Guwahati, Hyderabad, Jaipur, Jhansi, Kolkata, Lucknow, Nagpur & Pune.

PO No : TXT-XX-XXXXXXX-X-XX

Published By Arihant Publications (India) Ltd.

For further information about the books published by Arihant, log on to www.arihantbooks.com or e-mail at info@arihantbooks.com

Follow us on

PRICE ₹ 320.00

PRODUCTION TEAM

Publishing Managers
Mahendra Singh Rawat & Keshav Mohan

Cover Designer
Salman Shaikh

Inner Designer
Ankit Tyagi

Project Head
Yojna Sharma

Page Layouting
Subhash Chaprana

Proof Reader
Ishan, Mansi

Index *cum* Study Planner

One Book- Endless Features

to Help you Succeed

Chapter Inside

At the start of each chapter, all the Chapter topics have been listed, so that students may know what they are going to study.

CHAPTER
01

Measurements & Experimentation

SYLLABUS

• International System of Units. • Other commonly used system of units FPS and CGS. • Measurements using common instruments. • Vernier calliper and micrometer screw gauge for length and simple pendulum for time.

Physical Quantities

All the quantities which can be measured directly or indirectly quantities can be further divided into two types i.e. **fundamental**

Fundamental Quantities

The physical quantities which are independent of other physica other physical quantities are called **fundamental** or **base quantities** luminous intensity, electric current and amount of substance a Besides these seven fundamental quantities, there are two mor **quantities**, these are plane angle and solid angle.

Simplified Theory

It contains the necessary study material well supported by Definitions, Facts, Figures, Flow Charts, etc.

Check Your Learning

A set of 3-5 Questions given in between the text, helps students to remain connected with the text while studying. They can instantly assess themselves for their understanding.

Check Your LEARNING...

1. What are the two types of physical quantities?
2. Write the name of two supplementary physical quantities.
3. Give any one advantage of SI unit over other systems of unit.
4. Convert 10 m/s to km/s. ***Ans.*** 0.01 km/s
5. Which one is largest, astronomical unit, light year or parsec?

Measurement of Length

Length is the distance of separation between two points in space. There are many instruments used to measure length like meter scale, inch tape, etc. Here, we will discuss two instruments vernier calliper and screw gauge, which are used to measure very small lengths.

Example 6. In an instrument, there are 25 divisions on the vernier scale which have length of 24 divisions of the main scale. 1 cm on main scale is divided in 25 equal parts. Find the least count.

Sol. The value of one main scale division, $x = \frac{1}{25}$ cm

The number of divisions on vernier scale, $n = 25$

$\therefore$ LC of vernier

$$= \frac{\text{Value of one main scale division } (x)}{\text{Number of divisions on vernier scale } (n)}$$

$$= \frac{(1/25)}{25} = \frac{1}{625} = 0.0016 \text{ cm}$$

Solved Examples

To explain the application of concept Solved Examples have been given in between the theory. These examples have been solved in Step-by-Step manner, so that students can learn the problem solving process completely.

One Book- Endless Features

to Help you Succeed

QUICK Revision

At the end of each chapter, QUICK Revision is given. It contains crux of the chapter in pointer form.

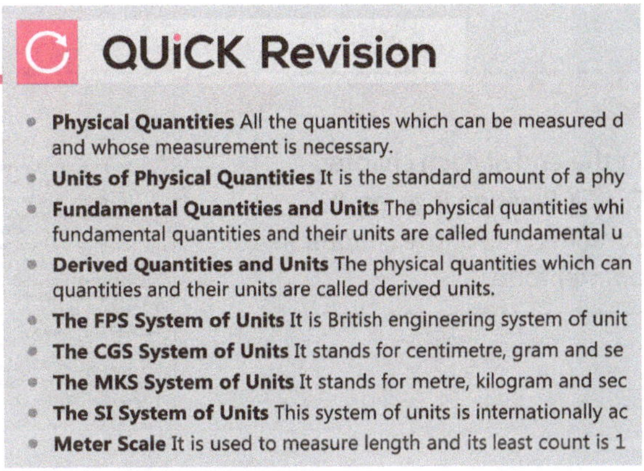
QUiCK Revision

- **Physical Quantities** All the quantities which can be measured d and whose measurement is necessary.
- **Units of Physical Quantities** It is the standard amount of a phy
- **Fundamental Quantities and Units** The physical quantities whi fundamental quantities and their units are called fundamental u
- **Derived Quantities and Units** The physical quantities which can quantities and their units are called derived units.
- **The FPS System of Units** It is British engineering system of unit
- **The CGS System of Units** It stands for centimetre, gram and se
- **The MKS System of Units** It stands for metre, kilogram and sec
- **The SI System of Units** This system of units is internationally ac
- **Meter Scale** It is used to measure length and its least count is 1

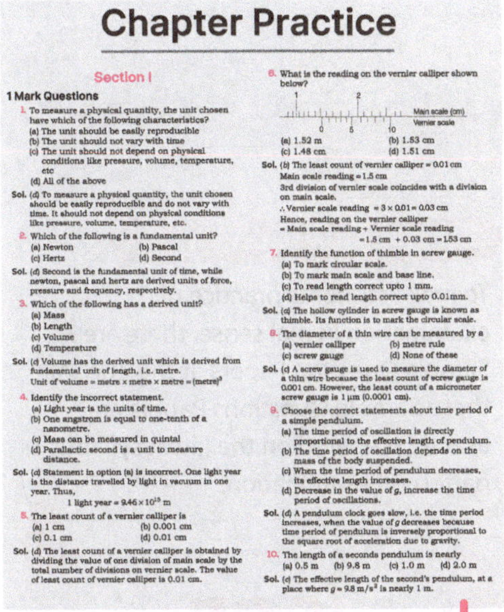
Chapter Practice

Section I

1 Mark Questions

1. To measure a physical quantity, the unit chosen have which of the following characteristics?
(a) The unit should be easily reproducible
(b) The unit should not vary with time
(c) The unit should not depend on physical conditions like pressure, volume, temperature, etc
(d) All of the above

Sol. (d) To measure a physical quantity, the unit chosen should be easily reproducible and do not vary with time. It should not depend on physical conditions like pressure, volume, temperature, etc.

2. Which of the following is a fundamental unit?
(a) Newton (b) Pascal
(c) Hertz (d) Second

Sol. (d) Second is the fundamental unit of time, while newton, pascal and hertz are derived units of force, pressure and frequency, respectively.

3. Which of the following has a derived unit?
(a) Mass
(b) Length
(c) Volume
(d) Temperature

Sol. (c) Volume has the derived unit which is derived from fundamental unit of length, i.e. metre.
Unit of volume = metre × metre × metre = (metre)^3

4. Identify the incorrect statement.
(a) Light year is the units of time.
(b) One angstrom is equal to one-tenth of a nanometre.
(c) Mass can be measured in quintal
(d) Parallactic second is a unit to measure distance.

Sol. (a) Statement in option (a) is incorrect. One light year is the distance travelled by light in vacuum in one year. Thus,
1 light year = 9.46×10^{15} m

5. The least count of a vernier calliper is
(a) 1 cm (b) 0.001 cm
(c) 0.1 cm (d) 0.01 cm

Sol. (d) The least count of a vernier calliper is obtained by dividing the value of one division of main scale by the total number of divisions on vernier scale. The value of least count of vernier calliper is 0.01 cm.

6. What is the reading on the vernier calliper shown below?
(a) 1.52 m (b) 1.53 cm
(c) 1.48 cm (d) 1.51 cm

Sol. (b) The least count of vernier calliper = 0.01 cm
Main scale reading = 1.5 cm
3rd division of vernier scale coincides with a division on main scale.
∴ Vernier scale reading = 3 × 0.01 = 0.03 cm
Hence, reading on the vernier calliper
= Main scale reading + Vernier scale reading
= 1.5 cm + 0.03 cm = 1.53 cm

7. Identify the function of thimble in screw gauge.
(a) To mark circular scale.
(b) To mark main scale and base line.
(c) To read length correct upto 1 mm.
(d) Helps to read length correct upto 0.01mm.

Sol. (d) The hollow cylinder in screw gauge is known as thimble. Its function is to mark the circular scale.

8. The diameter of a thin wire can be measured by a
(a) vernier calliper (b) metre rule
(c) screw gauge (d) None of these

Sol. (c) A screw gauge is used to measure the diameter of a thin wire because the least count of screw gauge is 0.001 cm. However, the least count of a micrometer screw gauge is 1 μm (0.0001 cm).

9. Choose the correct statements about time period of a simple pendulum.
(a) The time period of oscillation is directly proportional to the effective length of pendulum.
(b) The time period of oscillation depends on the mass of the body suspended.
(c) When the time period of pendulum decreases, its effective length increases.
(d) Decrease in the value of g, increase the time period of oscillations.

Sol. (d) A pendulum clock goes slow, i.e. the time period increases, when the value of g decreases because time period of pendulum is inversely proportional to the square root of acceleration due to gravity.

10. The length of a seconds pendulum is nearly
(a) 0.5 m (b) 9.8 m (c) 1.0 m (d) 2.0 m

Sol. (c) The effective length of the second's pendulum, at a place where $g = 9.8$ m/s^2 is nearly 1 m.

Chapter Assessment

It is the Assessment exercise for the complete chapter. With this exercise, students can assess their understanding of the chapter and can prepare for it accordingly.

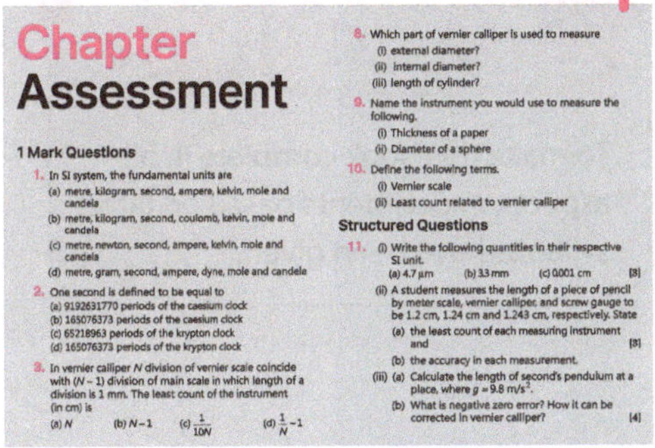
Chapter Assessment

1 Mark Questions

1. In SI system, the fundamental units are
(a) metre, kilogram, second, ampere, kelvin, mole and candela
(b) metre, kilogram, second, coulomb, kelvin, mole and candela
(c) metre, newton, second, ampere, kelvin, mole and candela
(d) metre, gram, second, ampere, dyne, mole and candela

2. One second is defined to be equal to
(a) 9192631770 periods of the caesium clock
(b) 165076373 periods of the caesium clock
(c) 65218963 periods of the krypton clock
(d) 165076373 periods of the krypton clock

3. In vernier calliper N division of vernier scale coincide with (N − 1) division of main scale in which length of a division is 1 mm. The least count of the instrument (in cm) is
(a) N (b) N − 1 (c) $\frac{1}{10N}$ (d) $\frac{1}{N} - 1$

8. Which part of vernier calliper is used to measure
(i) external diameter?
(ii) internal diameter?
(iii) length of cylinder?

9. Name the instrument you would use to measure the following.
(i) Thickness of a paper
(ii) Diameter of a sphere

10. Define the following terms.
(i) Vernier scale
(ii) Least count related to vernier calliper

Structured Questions

11. (i) Write the following quantities in their respective SI unit.
(a) 4.7 μm (b) 3.3 mm (c) 0.001 cm [3]
(ii) A student measures the length of a piece of pencil by meter scale, vernier calliper, and screw gauge to be 1.2 cm, 1.24 cm and 1.243 cm, respectively. State
(a) the least count of each measuring instrument and [3]
(b) the accuracy in each measurement.
(iii) (a) Calculate the length of second's pendulum at a place, where $g = 9.8$ m/s^2.
(b) What is negative zero error? How it can be corrected in vernier calliper? [4]

Chapter Practice

The Exercise contains questions in that format in which these are asked in the examinations. Questions have been categorised as 1 mark questions, 2 marks questions, 3 marks questions and structured based questions. All the questions given here are fully solved.

One Book- Endless Features

to Help you Succeed

Olympiad Section

At the end of each chapter, QUICK Revision is given. It contains crux of the chapter in pointer form.

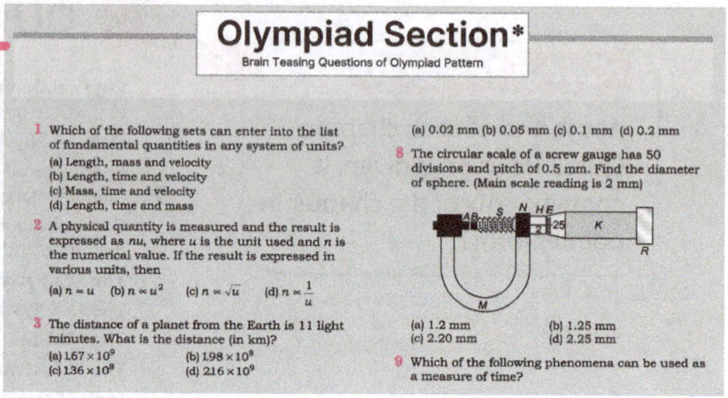

Olympiad Section*

Brain Teasing Questions of Olympiad Pattern

1 Which of the following sets can enter into the list of fundamental quantities in any system of units?
(a) Length, mass and velocity
(b) Length, time and velocity
(c) Mass, time and velocity
(d) Length, time and mass

2 A physical quantity is measured and the result is expressed as nu, where u is the unit used and n is the numerical value. If the result is expressed in various units, then
(a) $n \propto u$ (b) $n \propto u^2$ (c) $n \propto \sqrt{u}$ (d) $n \propto \frac{1}{u}$

3 The distance of a planet from the Earth is 11 light minutes. What is the distance (in km)?
(a) 1.67×10^9 (b) 1.98×10^8
(c) 1.36×10^8 (d) 2.16×10^9

(a) 0.02 mm (b) 0.05 mm (c) 0.1 mm (d) 0.2 mm

8 The circular scale of a screw gauge has 50 divisions and pitch of 0.5 mm. Find the diameter of sphere. (Main scale reading is 2 mm)

(a) 1.2 mm (b) 1.25 mm
(c) 2.20 mm (d) 2.25 mm

9 Which of the following phenomena can be used as a measure of time?

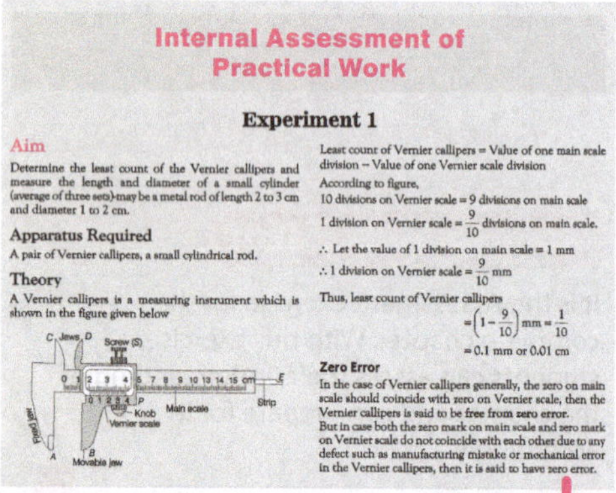

Internal Assessment of Practical Work

Experiment 1

Aim

Determine the least count of the Vernier callipers and measure the length and diameter of a small cylinder (average of three sets) may be a metal rod of length 2 to 3 cm and diameter 1 to 2 cm.

Apparatus Required

A pair of Vernier callipers, a small cylindrical rod.

Theory

A Vernier callipers is a measuring instrument which is shown in the figure given below

Least count of Vernier callipers = Value of one main scale division − Value of one Vernier scale division

According to figure,

10 divisions on Vernier scale = 9 divisions on main scale

1 division on Vernier scale $= \frac{9}{10}$ divisions on main scale.

∴ Let the value of 1 division on main scale = 1 mm

∴ 1 division on Vernier scale $= \frac{9}{10}$ mm

Thus, least count of Vernier callipers

$= \left(1 - \frac{9}{10}\right)$ mm $= \frac{1}{10}$

= 0.1 mm or 0.01 cm

Zero Error

In the case of Vernier callipers generally, the zero on main scale should coincide with zero on Vernier scale, then the Vernier callipers is said to be free from zero error.

But in case both the zero mark on main scale and zero mark on Vernier scale do not coincide with each other due to any defect such as manufacturing mistake or mechanical error in the Vernier callipers, then it is said to have zero error.

Internal Assessment of Practical Work

To make this book complete in all aspects, experiments based on latest syllabus have been given.

Sample Question Papers

To make students practice of examination in real sense, there are 3 Sample Question Papers at the end. All these Sample Questions Papers are exactly prepared on the latest syllabus & pattern of examination.

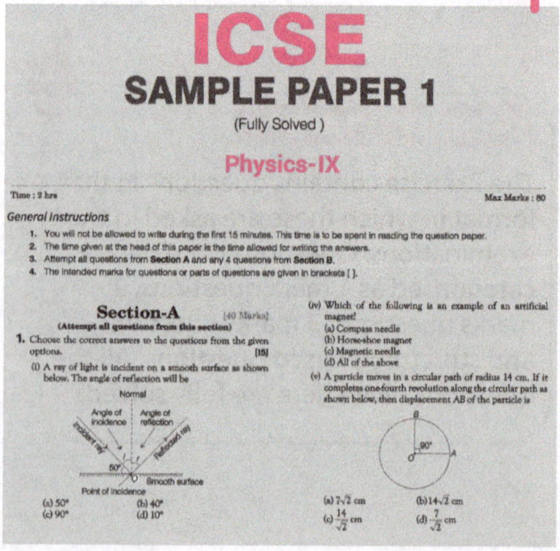

ICSE

SAMPLE PAPER 1

(Fully Solved)

Physics-IX

Time : 2 hrs Max Marks : 80

General Instructions

1. You will not be allowed to write during the first 15 minutes. This time is to be spent in reading the question paper.
2. The time given at the head of this paper is the time allowed for writing the answers.
3. Attempt all questions from **Section A** and any 4 questions from **Section B**.
4. The intended marks for questions or parts of questions are given in brackets [ ].

Section-A [40 Marks]

(Attempt all questions from this section)

1. Choose the correct answers to the questions from the given options. [15]

(i) A ray of light is incident on a smooth surface as shown below. The angle of reflection will be

(a) 50° (b) 40°
(c) 90° (d) 10°

(iv) Which of the following is an example of an artificial magnet?
(a) Compass needle
(b) Horse-shoe magnet
(c) Magnetic needle
(d) All of the above

(v) A particle moves in a circular path of radius 14 cm. If it completes one-fourth revolution along the circular path as shown below, then displacement AB of the particle is

(a) $7\sqrt{2}$ cm (b) $14\sqrt{2}$ cm
(c) $\frac{14}{\sqrt{2}}$ cm (d) $\frac{7}{\sqrt{2}}$ cm

Latest Course *Structure*

There will be one paper of **two hours** duration carrying 80 marks and Internal Assessment of practical work carrying 20 marks.

Note: Unless otherwise specified, only S I. Units are to be used while teaching and learning, as well as for answering questions.

Measurements and Experimentation

(i) International System of Units, the required SI units with correct symbols are given at the end of this syllabus. Other commonly used system of units - fps and cgs.

(ii) Measurements using common instruments, Vernier callipers and micro-metre screw gauge for length, and simple pendulum for time.

Measurement of length using, Vernier callipers and micro-metre screw gauge. Decreasing least-count leads to an increase in accuracy; least-count (LC) of Vernier callipers and screw gauge), zero error (basic idea), (no numerical problems on callipers and screw gauge), simple pendulum; time period, frequency, graph of length l vs. T^2 only; slope of the graph. Formula $T=2.\pi.\sqrt{l/g}$ [no derivation]. Only simple numerical problems.

Motion in One Dimension

Scalar and vector quantities, distance, speed, velocity, acceleration; graphs of distance-time and speed-time; equations of uniformly accelerated motion with derivations.

Examples of Scalar and vector quantities only, rest and motion in one dimension; distance and displacement; speed and velocity; acceleration and retardation; distance-time and velocity-time graphs; meaning of slope of the graphs; [Non-uniform acceleration excluded].

Equations to be derived: $v = u + at$; $S = ut + ½at^2$; $S = ½(u+v)t$; $v^2 = u^2 + 2aS$. [Equation for $S_n{}^{th}$ is not included].

Simple numerical problems.

Laws of Motion

(i) Contact and non-contact forces; cgs & SI units.

Examples of contact forces (frictional force, normal reaction force, tension force as applied through strings and force exerted during collision) and non-contact forces (gravitational, electric and magnetic). General properties of non-contact forces. cgs and SI units of force and their relation with Gravitational units.

(ii) Newton's First Law of Motion (qualitative discussion) introduction of the idea of inertia, mass and force.

Newton's first law; statement and qualitative discussion; definitions of inertia and force from first law, examples of inertia as illustration of first law. (Inertial mass not included).

(iii) Newton's Second Law of Motion (including F=ma); weight and mass.

Detailed study of the second law. Linear momentum,

$p = mv$; change in momentum $\Delta p = \Delta(mv) = m\Delta v$ for mass remaining constant, rate of change of momentum;

$\Delta p/\Delta t = m\Delta v/\Delta t = ma$ or

$\{\frac{p_2 - p_1}{t} = \frac{mv - mu}{t} = \frac{m(v-u)}{t} = ma\}$;

Simple numerical problems combining $F = \Delta p/\Delta t = ma$ and equations of motion. Units of force - only cgs and SI.

(iv) Newton's Third Law of Motion (qualitative discussion only); simple examples.

Statement with qualitative discussion; examples of action - reaction pairs, (F_{BA} and F_{AB}); action and reaction always act on different bodies.

(v) Gravitation

Universal Law of Gravitation. (Statement and equation) and its importance. Gravity, acceleration due to gravity, free fall. Weight and mass, Weight as force of gravity comparison of mass and weight; gravitational units of force, (Simple numerical problems), (problems on variation of gravity excluded)

Fluids

(i) Change of pressure with depth (including the formula $p=h\rho g$); Transmission of pressure in liquids; atmospheric pressure.

Thrust and Pressure and their units; pressure exerted by a liquid column $p = h\rho g$; simple daily life examples, (i) broadness of the base of a dam, (ii) Diver's suit etc. some consequences of $p = h\rho g$; transmission of pressure in liquids; Pascal's law; examples; atmospheric pressure; common manifestation and consequences.. Variations of pressure with altitude, (qualitative only); applications such as weather forecasting and altimeter. (Simple numerical problems)

(ii) Buoyancy, Archimedes' Principle; floatation; relationship with density; relative density; determination of relative density of a solid.

Buoyancy, upthrust (F_B); definition; different cases, F_B>, = or < weight W of the body immersed; characteristic properties of upthrust; Archimedes' principle; explanation of cases where bodies with density ρ >, = or < the density ρ' of the fluid in which it is immersed.

Relative Density (RD) and Archimedes' principle. Experimental determination of RD of a solid and liquid denser than water. Floatation: principle of floatation; relation between the density of a floating body, density of the liquid in which it is floating and the fraction of volume of the body immersed; ($\rho_1/\rho_2 = V_2/V_1$); apparent weight of floating object; application to ship, submarine, iceberg, balloons, etc.

Simple numerical problems involving Archimedes' principle, buoyancy and floatation.

Heat and Energy

(i) Concepts of heat and temperature.

Heat as energy, SI unit – joule,

1 cal = 4.186 J exactly.

(ii) *Anomalous expansion of water; graphs showing variation of volume and density of water with temperature in the 0° to 10°C range. Hope's experiment and consequences of Anomalous expansion.*

(iii) Energy flow and its importance:

Understanding the flow of energy as Linear and linking it with the laws of Thermodynamics- 'Energy is neither created nor destroyed' and 'No Energy transfer is 100% efficient.

(iv) Energy sources.

Solar, wind, water and nuclear energy (only qualitative discussion of steps to produce electricity). Renewable *versus* non-renewable sources (elementary ideas with example).

Renewable energy: biogas, solar energy, wind energy, energy from falling of water, run-of-the river schemes, energy from waste, tidal energy, etc. Issues of economic viability and ability to meet demands.

Non-renewable energy – coal, oil, natural gas. Inequitable use of energy in urban and rural areas. Use of hydro electrical powers for light and tube wells.

(v) Global warming and Green House effect:

Meaning, causes and impact on the life on earth. Projections for the future; what needs to be done. Energy degradation –meaning and examples.

Light

(i) Reflection of light; images formed by a pair of parallel and perpendicular plane mirrors; .

Laws of reflection; experimental verification; characteristics of images formed in a pair of mirrors, (a) parallel and (b) perpendicular to each other; uses of plane mirrors.

(ii) Spherical mirrors; characteristics of image formed by these mirrors. Uses of concave and convex mirrors. (Only simple direct ray diagrams are required).

Brief introduction to spherical mirrors - concave and convex mirrors, centre and radius of curvature, pole and principal axis, focus and focal length; location of images from ray diagram for various positions of a small linear object on the principal axis of concave and convex mirrors; characteristics of images.

f = R/2 (without proof); sign convention and direct numerical problems using the mirror formulae are included. (Derivation of formulae not required)

Uses of spherical mirrors.

Scale drawing or graphical representation of ray diagrams not required.

Sound

(i) Nature of Sound waves. Requirement of a medium for sound waves to travel; propagation and speed in different media; comparison with speed of light.

Sound propagation, terms – frequency (f), wavelength (λ), velocity (v), relation $v = f\lambda$. (Simple numerical problems) effect of different factors on the speed of sound; comparison of speed of sound with speed of light; consequences of the large difference in these speeds in air; thunder and lightning.

(ii) Infrasonic, sonic, ultrasonic frequencies and their applications.

Elementary ideas and simple applications only. Difference between ultrasonic and supersonic.

Electricity and Magnetism

(i) Simple electric circuit using an electric cell and a bulb to introduce the idea of current (including its relationship to charge); potential difference; insulators and conductors; closed and open circuits; direction of current (electron flow and conventional)

Current Electricity: brief introduction of sources of direct current - cells, accumulators (construction, working and equations excluded); Electric current as the rate of flow of electric charge (direction of current - conventional and electronic), symbols used in circuit diagrams. Detection of current by Galvanometer or ammeter (functioning of the meters not to be introduced). Idea of electric circuit by using cell, key, resistance wire/resistance box/rheostat, qualitatively.; elementary idea about work done in transferring charge through a conductor wire; potential difference $V = W/q$.

(No derivation of formula) simple numerical problems.

Social initiatives: Improving efficiency of existing technologies and introducing new eco-friendly technologies. Creating awareness and building trends of sensitive use of resources and products, e.g. reduced use of electricity.

(ii) Induced magnetism, Magnetic field of earth. Neutral points in magnetic fields.

Magnetism: magnetism induced by bar magnets on magnetic materials; induction precedes attraction; lines of magnetic field and their properties; evidences of existence of earth's magnetic field, magnetic compass. Uniform magnetic field of earth and non-uniform field of a bar magnet placed along magnetic north-south; neutral point; properties of magnetic field lines.

(iii) Introduction of electromagnet and its uses.

Internal Assessment of Practical Work

Candidates will be asked to carry out experiments for which instructions are given. The experiments may be based on topics that are not included in the syllabus but theoretical knowledge will not be required. A candidate will be expected to be able to follow simple instructions, to take suitable readings and to present these readings in a systematic form. He/she may be required to exhibit his/her data graphically. Candidates will be expected to appreciate and use the concepts of least count, significant figures and elementary error handling.

A set of 6 to 10 experiments may be designed as given below or as found most suitable by the teacher. Students should be encouraged to record their observations systematically in a neat tabular form - in columns with column heads including units or in numbered rows as necessary. The final result or conclusion may be recorded for each experiment. Some of the experiments may be demonstrated (with the help of students) if these cannot be given to each student as lab experiments.

1. *Determine the least count of the Vernier callipers and measure the length and diameter of a small cylinder (average of three sets) - may be a metal rod of length 2 to 3 cm and diameter 1 to 2 cm.*
2. *Determine the pitch and least count of the given screw gauge and measure the mean radius of the given wire, taking three sets of readings in perpendicular directions.*
3. *Measure the length, breadth and thickness of a glass block using a metre rule (each reading correct to a mm), taking the mean of three readings in each case. Calculate the volume of the block in cm^3 and m^3. Determine the mass (not weight) of the block using*

any convenient balance in g and kg. Calculate the density of glass in cgs and SI units using mass and volume in the respective units. Obtain the relation between the two density units.

4. *Measure the volume of a metal bob (the one used in simple pendulum experiments) from the readings of water level in a measuring cylinder using displacement method. Also calculate the same volume from the radius measured using Vernier callipers. Comment on the accuracies.*

5. *Obtain five sets of readings of the time taken for 20 oscillations of a simple pendulum of lengths about 70, 80, 90, 100 and 110 cm; calculate the time periods (T) and their squares (T^2) for each length (l). Plot a graph of l vs. T^2. Draw the best - fit straight - line graph. Also, obtain its slope. Calculate the value of g in the laboratory. It is 4p² x slope.*

6. *Take a beaker of water. Place it on the wire gauze on a tripod stand. Suspend two thermometers - one with Celsius and the other with Fahrenheit scale. Record the thermometer readings at 5 to 7 different temperatures. You may start with ice cold water, then allow it to warm up and then heat it slowly taking temperature (at regular intervals) as high as possible. Plot a graph of T_F vs. T_C. Obtain the slope. Compare with the theoretical value. Read the intercept on T_F axis for $T_C = 0$.*

7. *Using a plane mirror strip mounted vertically on a board, obtain the reflected rays for three rays incident at different angles. Measure the angles of incidence and angles of reflection. See if these angles are equal.*

8. *Place three object pins at different distances on a line perpendicular to a plane mirror fixed vertically on a board. Obtain two reflected rays (for each pin) fixing two pins in line with the image. Obtain the positions of the images in each case by extending backwards (using dashed lines), the lines representing reflected rays. Measure the object distances and image distances in the three cases. Tabulate. Are they equal? Generalize the result.*

9. *Obtain the focal length of a concave mirror (a) by distant object method, focusing its real image on a screen or wall and (b) by one needle method removing parallax or focusing the image of the illuminated wire gauze attached to a ray box. One could also improvise with a candle and a screen. Enter your observations in numbered rows.*

10. *Connect a suitable dc source (two dry cells or an acid cell), a key and a bulb (may be a small one used in torches) in series. Close the circuit by inserting the plug in the key. Observe the bulb as it lights up. Now open the circuit, connect another identical bulb in between the first bulb and the cell so that the two bulbs are in series. Close the key. Observe the lighted bulbs. How does the light from any one bulb compare with that in the first case when you had only one bulb? Disconnect the second bulb. Reconnect the circuit as in the first experiment. Now connect the second bulb across the first bulb. The two bulbs are connected in parallel. Observe the brightness of any one bulb. Compare with previous results. Draw your own conclusions regarding the current and resistance in the three cases.*

11. *Plot the magnetic field lines of earth (without any magnet nearby) using a small compass needle. On another sheet of paper place a bar magnet with its axis parallel to the magnetic lines of the earth, i.e. along the magnetic meridian or magnetic north-south. Plot the magnetic field in the region around the magnet. Identify the regions where the combined magnetic field of the magnet and the earth is (a) strongest, (b) very weak but not zero, and (c) zero. Why is neutral point, so called?*

12. *Using a spring balance obtain the weight (in N) of a metal ball in air and then completely immersed in water in a measuring cylinder. Note the volume of the ball from the volume of the water displaced. Calculate the upthrust from the first two weights. Also calculate the mass and then weight of the water displaced by the bob M=V.r, W=mg). Use the above result to verify Archimedes principle.*

Practicals

Practicals should be conducted alongside the concepts taught in theory classes

1. ALWAYS FEEL POSITIVE

Positive attitude is the key to solve many of the problems which you face in your life. During exam time, this is an important feature to have in you for success and crack your exams with flying colours. Attitude is important for all students because it reflects your personality as well as your confidence or self-confidence. It always takes you to the top of everything, whether it is for exams or interviews or for your life. Positive attitude will take you through the door of success and make you feel full of self-confidence.

2. PLAN WELL FOR STUDYING

You must make a schedule for your studies followed by strict implementation of that schedule. Make that schedule detailing days or even hours when your exams are really close or it is high time for your exam.You must interact with your teachers for the important topics or topics which need more hard work or more time than other topics. Use last years' exam papers or sample papers for making a proper schedule for your studies.

You must study more or give more attention to the topics in which you feel you are not up to the mark or which your teachers recommended you to study more. You should study these topics first during your exam preparation.

3. JUST BEFORE THE EXAM

Never try to read anything or to study or cram just before the exam time, even if your friend asks you for some topic he has missed or left during preparation for the exams. Close your book an hour before the exam starts and feel relaxed and worry free and full of self-confidence. Also get up early in the morning and take another review of the important topics and make yourself filled with confidence, as confidence is the main key to score well. The night before the exam you should sleep as soon as possible to make your brain as well as body relax a bit and to be well prepared for the exams, as our brain too needs a rest to be fresh for the exam.

4. DISCUSS WHAT YOU LEARN

Find a friend or relative who has similar interests or who would enjoy hearing about your studies and let them know what's going on in your class.

5. CHART YOUR PROGRESS

Design your map of studying and you would see a certain satisfaction coming after watching your goals being accomplished. When times get hard, you can always turn to your chart and see how far you have reached.

6. DURING EXAM TIME

Check out all the things you require during exam time i.e., pen, pencil, sketch pens, rubber, sharpener. Each and every thing, whether it is small or big, matters a lot during your exam time. Read all the instructions carefully before starting the paper and keep them in your mind during exam time. Don't make any foolish mistake regarding your exam paper instructions.

7. ATTEMPTING THE EXAMINATION PAPER

Read out all the questions carefully before writing anything on the answer sheet and always start your answering from the questions which will carry maximum marks as well as which you think are tougher or need much time to think. When you start the exam from small questions, you will always feel the problem of questions left.

So, that's why time management is very much important during exams. You can write small questions even in the last 30 minutes but you will never be able to write enough for the large questions at the end, which will eventually result in sadness.

8. WHEN YOU FEEL STUCK DURING THE EXAM

There will also come a moment in your exam when you feel stuck with some questions or a single question. You just need to be relaxed and calm, don't panic in that situation and make yourself confident and try to think about the answer with a cool mind.

If you are not feeling like giving that answer at that time, make any sign or mark that question with pen and move on to the next question and try doing that question after you finish your paper but are still left with time. Never try to think about the 'stuck' question when you are writing the answer to any other question. This will reduce your concentration and when you feel no way out, just make a guess and attempt that question. This will leave you with something in the space you left for that question.

9. SOLUTION COPY SHOULD BE NEAT & CLEAN

Handwriting matters a lot for good or highest marks during your exam, as your writing makes the first impression on the checker's mind and makes your solution copy more filled with a glow for the examiner or checker of the answer sheet.

Underline the lines you feel important and want to attract the examiner's attention towards so that he/she can be able to make a right mindset about the answer given and also reward you with the full or maximum marks.

10. AFTER COMPLETION OF EXAM PAPER

When you end the exam paper, don't feel like running out of the examination hall. Sit there and review each and every answer before depositing your answer book with the invigilator. Also, look for the questions you left during answering or in which you got stuck. Search for the mistakes you have done during writing and turn towards the hardest question you think and also feel uncomfortable in answering. Review it and look to add any other important lines you missed in that.

ART OF WRITING ANSWERS : GIVE YOUR BEST SHOT

- One can practice answering in previous test papers or sample papers to get used to the manner in which one has to write answers in the exams.
- Make sure that you answer the question asked and not answer what you hoped or wished the question would be.
- Examiners expect to the point and correct answers. Resist the temptation to write everything or writing beyond limits.
- Keep your answer stepwise. Some of you will be surprised to know that the board gives rather detailed dictates on how to evaluate the answer sheet. Try not to exceed the word limit.
- Write your answers in a logical systematic manner. Use examples, facts, figures, quotations, tables etc. wherever necessary to substantiate your answers. Give appropriate heading where necessary.
- Add a touch of class by putting extra information that indicate your being very knowledgeable and put this separately near the end, so that it is read just before giving the marks, especially in an essay type question like new trends etc.

CHAPTER

01

Measurements & Experimentation

SYLLABUS

• International System of Units. • Other commonly used system of units FPS and CGS. • Measurements using common instruments. • Vernier calliper and micrometer screw gauge for length and simple pendulum for time.

The word Physics is derived from the Greek word Physica which means nature, so physics is the branch of science concerned with the nature and laws governing it. Under the physics, we study interaction between different physical quantities along with their measurement.

Physical Quantities

All the quantities which can be measured directly or indirectly are called physical quantities. Physical quantities can be further divided into two types i.e. **fundamental** and **derived quantities.**

Fundamental Quantities

The physical quantities which are independent of other physical quantities and are not defined in terms of other physical quantities are called **fundamental** or **base quantities**. e.g. Mass, length, time, temperature, luminous intensity, electric current and amount of substance are the seven fundamental quantities. Besides these seven fundamental quantities, there are two more physical quantities known as **supplementary quantities**, these are plane angle and solid angle.

Derived Quantities

The physical quantities which can be derived from the fundamental physical quantities are called **derived quantities**. e.g. Velocity, acceleration, linear momentum, etc. All physical quantities other than the seven base quantities are derived quantities.

Measurement of Physical Quantities

The measurement of a physical quantity is the process of comparing the given quantity with a standard amount of the physical quantity of same kind, called its **unit**.

Hence, to express the measurement of a physical quantity, we need to know two parameters as given below

(i) The **unit** in which the quantity is measured.

(ii) The **numerical value** of the quantity, i.e. the number of times that unit is contained in the given physical quantity.

Thus, the magnitude of the physical quantity is expressed as

Physical quantity = Numerical value × Unit

$$\boxed{Q = nu}$$

e.g. Mass of an object can be expressed as 2 kg.

Physical Units

The standard amount of a physical quantity chosen to measure the physical quantity of same kind is called a physical unit.

As we know, unit is to be measured universally, so it should be valid everywhere.

Hence, the essential requirements of physical unit are as follows

(i) It should be of suitable size.

(ii) It should be easily accessible.

(iii) It should not vary with time.

(iv) It should be easily reproducible.

(v) It should not depend on physical conditions like pressure, volume, temperature, etc.

The unit is classified into two kinds-**fundamental units** and **derived units.**

Fundamental Units

Those physical units which can neither be derived from another unit nor be further resolved into more simpler units are called fundamental units.

The units of fundamental quantities like length, mass, time, temperature, electric current and amount of substance are called **fundamental units** or **base units.**

Derived Units

The units of measurement of all other physical quantities which can be derived from fundamental units are called derived units.

e.g. The unit of speed is derived from the units of two fundamental units length and time as given below

$$\boxed{\text{Speed} = \frac{\text{Distance}}{\text{Time}} = \frac{\text{m}}{\text{s}} = \text{ms}^{-1}}$$

Systems of Units

In mechanics, there are three fundamental quantities length, mass and time. Different systems used for units of these three basic quantities are discussed below

(i) **The FPS System** It is the British engineering system of units. It uses foot as the unit of length, pound as the unit of mass and second as the unit of time.

(ii) **The CGS System** It is based on Gaussian system of units which uses centimetre, gram and second for length, mass and time, respectively.

(iii) **The MKS System** It uses metre, kilogram and second as the fundamental units of length, mass and time, respectively.

(iv) **The International System of Units** (SI Units) The system of units which is accepted internationally for measurement is the system of International Units (French for International System of Units) abbreviated as SI.

Now, the SI system of unit is used which is a modified version of other three metric systems.

International System of Units (SI Units)

The SI with standard scheme of symbols, units and abbreviations was developed and recommended by **General Conference on Weights and Measures** in 1960 for international usage in scientific, technical, industrial and commercial work.

This system consists of seven fundamental units and two supplementary units which are abbreviated as shown in table below

Base Quantities and their SI Units

Base Quantity	SI Units		Definition
	Name	Symbol	
Length	Metre	m	One metre is the length of the path travelled by light in vacuum during a time interval of 1/299792458 a second established in the year 1983.
Mass	Kilogram	kg	One kilogram is equal to the mass of the international prototype of the kilogram (a platinum-iridium alloy cylinder) kept at International Bureau of weights and measures, at Sevres, near Paris, France in the year 1889.
Time	Second	s	One second is the duration of 9192631770 periods of the radiation corresponding to the transition between the two hyperfine levels of the ground state of the caesium-133 atom in the year 1967.
Electric current	Ampere	A	One ampere is that constant current which, if maintained in two straight parallel conductors of infinite length of negligible circular cross-section and placed 1m apart in vacuum, would produce between these conductors, a force equal to 2×10^{-7} Nm^{-1} of length in the year 1948.
Thermodynamic temperature	Kelvin	K	One kelvin is the fraction 1/273.16 of the thermodynamic temperature of the triple point of water established in the year 1967.
Amount of substance	Mole	mol	One mole is the amount of substance of system which contains as many elementary entities as there are atoms in 0.012 kg of carbon-12 established in the year 1971.
Luminous intensity	Candela	cd	One candela is the luminous intensity in a given direction of a source that emits monochromatic radiation of frequency 540×10^{12} Hz and that has a radiant intensity in that direction of (1/683) W/Sr established in the year 1979.

Supplementary Quantities and their SI Units

Supplementary Quantity	Units	Symbol
Plane angle	Radian	rad
Solid angle	Steradian	Sr

Some Examples of Derived SI Units Expressed in Terms of Base Units

Derived Quantity	Definition	Derived Units	Symbol
Area	Length × Breadth	Metre × Metre	m^2
Volume	Length × Breadth × Height	Metre × Metre × Metre	m^3
Density	$\frac{\text{Mass}}{\text{Volume}}$	$\frac{\text{Kilogram}}{(\text{Metre})^3}$	kg-m^{-3}
Speed/Velocity	$\frac{\text{Distance}}{\text{Time}}$	$\frac{\text{Metre}}{\text{Second}}$	ms^{-1}
Acceleration	$\frac{\text{Velocity}}{\text{Time}}$	$\frac{\text{Metre/Second}}{\text{Second}}$	ms^{-2}
Force	Mass × Acceleration	$\text{Kilogram}\times\frac{\text{Metre}}{(\text{Second})^2}$	kg-ms^{-2} or N
Momentum	Mass × Velocity	$\text{Kilogram}\times\frac{\text{Metre}}{\text{Second}}$	kg-ms^{-1} or N-s
Work/Energy	Force × Displacement	$\text{Kilogram}\times\frac{\text{Metre}\times\text{Metre}}{(\text{Second})^2}$	kg-m^2 s^{-2} or J
Power	$\frac{\text{Work}}{\text{Time}}$	$\text{Kilogram}\times\frac{(\text{Metre})^2}{(\text{Second})^2}$ / Second	kg-m^2 s^{-3} or Js^{-1} or W
Electric charge	Current × Time	Ampere × Second	A-s or C

Some prefixes used for different measurements

Prefix	Symbol	Value
Femto	f	10^{-15}
Pico	p	10^{-12}
Nano	n	10^{-9}
Micro	μ	10^{-6}
Milli	m	10^{-3}
Centi	c	10^{-2}
Deci	d	10^{-1}
Deca	da	10^{1}
Hecto	h	10^{2}
Kilo	k	10^{3}
Mega	M	10^{6}
Giga	G	10^{9}

e.g. 1 megaohm (MΩ) = $10^6 \Omega$

1 milliampere (mA) = 10^{-3}A

Note Advantage of SI over other unit of measurement

(i) It is easily reproducible

(ii) It has unique unit for each physical quantity.

(iii) SI is internationally accepted.

Some Important Practical Units for Length/Distance

Sub-units of metre

(i) **Centimetre (cm)** 1 cm = 10^{-2} m

(ii) **Millimetre (mm)** 1 mm = 10^{-3}m

(iii) **Micron or Micrometre** 1 μm = 10^{-6} m

(iv) **Nanometre (nm)** 1 nm = 10^{-9} m

Multiple units of metre

Kilometre (km) 1 km = 10^3 m

Non-metric unit of length

Bigger units

(i) **Astronomical Unit** It is the mean distance of the earth from the sun.

$$1 \text{ AU} = 1.496 \times 10^{11} \text{ m}$$

(ii) **Light Year** It is the distance travelled by light in vacuum in one year.

$$1 \text{ ly} = 9.46 \times 10^{15} \text{ m}$$

(iii) **Parallactic Second** It is the distance at which an arc of length 1 astronomical unit subtends an angle of 1s of arc.

$$1 \text{ parsec} = 3.084 \times 10^{16} \text{m} = 3.26 \text{ ly}$$

Smaller units

(i) **Angstrom Unit** This unit is used for inter-atomic and intermolecular separation.

$$1 \text{Å} = 10^{-10} \text{m} = 10^{-1} \text{nm}$$

(ii) **Fermi** This unit is used for measuring nuclear sizes.

$$1 \text{ fm} = 10^{-15} \text{ m}$$

Some Important Units for Mass

Sub-units of kilogram

(i) **Gram (g)** 1 g = 10^{-3} kg

(ii) **Milligram (mg)** = 10^{-6} kg

Multiple units of kilogram

(i) **Quintal (q)** 1q = 100 kg

(ii) **Metric tonne (t)** 1t = 1000 kg

Non-metric unit of mass

Bigger unit

Solar mass (M) 1M = 2×10^{30} kg

Smaller unit

1 amu (*u*) 1 *u* = 1.66×10^{-27} kg

Some Important Units of Time

Bigger units

(i) **Minute (min)** One minute is the duration of 60 s. i.e. 1 min = 60 s

(ii) **Hour (h)** One hour is the duration of 60 min. i.e. 1 h = 60 min = 3600 s

(iii) **Day** The time taken by the earth to rotate once on its own axis is called a day. One day is divided in 24 h.

Thus, 1 day = 24 h = $24 \times 60 \times 60$ = 86400 s.

(iv) **Lunar month** A lunar month is of 29.5 days and 12 lunar months are of 354.37 days.

(v) **Month** One month is considered to be of 30 days (approx) and one year 12 months or 365 days.

(vi) **Year (yr)** One year is defined as the time in which the earth completes one revolution around the sun. i.e. 1 yr = 365 days

$$1 \text{ yr} = 365 \times 86400 = 3.1536 \times 10^7 \text{ s}$$

(vii) **Leap year** A leap year is considered as the year in which the month of February is of 29 days.

1 leap year = 366 days.

(viii) **Decade** One decade has 10 years.

$$1 \text{ decade} = 3.1536 \times 10^8 \text{ s}$$

(ix) **Century** One century has 100 years.
1 century = 3.16×10^9 s

(x) **Millennium** One millennium has 1000 years.
1 millennium = 3.16×10^{10} s

Smaller units

(i) **Millisecond (ms)** 1 ms = 10^{-3} s
(ii) **Microsecond (μs)** 1 μs = 10^{-6} s
(iii) **1 shake** = 10^{-8} s
(iv) **Nanosecond (ns)** 1 ns = 10^{-9} s

Rules for Writing SI Units

(i) Small letters are used for symbols of units.
e.g. The symbol of metre is m, the symbol of kilogram is kg.

(ii) Symbols do not take plural form.
e.g. 30 kilograms in short form is 30 kg and 200 kilometres in short form is 200 km.

(iii) The initial letter of a symbol is taken in capital letter when the unit is named after a scientist.
e.g. The symbol of unit of force (newton) is N, the symbol of unit of energy (joule) is J and the symbol of unit of power (watt) is W.

(iv) The full name of a unit always begins with a small letter even if it has been named after a scientist.
e.g. Unit of force is newton not 'Newton', unit of energy is 'joule' not Joule, unit of power is 'watt' not Watt.

Some General Units (Outside from SI)

Name	Symbol	Value in SI Unit
degree	°	$1° = (\pi/180)$ rad
litre	L	$1\ dm^3 = 10^{-3}\ m^3$
carat	c	200 mg
bar	bar	0.1 MPa = 10^5 Pa
curie	Ci	$3.7 \times 10^{10}\ s^{-1}$
roentgen	R	2.58×10^{-4} C/kg
barn	b	$100\ fm^2 = 10^{-28}\ m^2$
area	a	$1\ dam^2 = 10^2\ m^2$
hectare	ha	$1\ hm^2 = 10^4\ m^2$
standard atmospheric pressure	atm	101325 Pa $= 1.013 \times 10^5$ Pa

Example 1. Write the derived unit for pressure.

Sol. $\because$ Pressure $= \dfrac{\text{Force}}{\text{Area}} = \dfrac{\text{Mass} \times \text{Acceleration}}{\text{Area}}$

Substituting the units of mass, acceleration and area in the above expression, we get

Unit of pressure $= \dfrac{kg \times ms^{-2}}{m^2} = kgm^{-1}s^{-2}$

Unit Conversion

The process of changing unit from one system to other system of unit is called **unit conversion.**

Example 2. The acceleration due to gravity is $9.8\ ms^{-2}$. Give its value in ft s^{-2}.

Sol. As, 1m = 3.28 ft

$\therefore$ $9.8\ ms^{-2} = 9.8 \times 3.28\ ft\ s^{-2}$
$= 32.14\ ft\ s^{-2} \approx 32\ ft\ s^{-2}$

Example 3. The value of gravitational constant G in MKS system is 6.67×10^{-11} N-m^2 kg^{-2}. What will be its value in CGS?

Sol. Given, $G = 6.67 \times 10^{-11}\ N\text{-}m^2\ kg^{-2}$
$= 6.67 \times 10^{-11}\ (kg\text{-}ms^{-2})\ m^2\ kg^{-2}$
$= 6.67 \times 10^{-11}\ (m^3)(s^{-2})(kg^{-1})$
$= 6.67 \times 10^{-11}\ (100\ cm)^3\ (s)^{-2}\ (10^3\ g)^{-1}$
$= 6.67 \times 10^{-8}\ cm^3\ g^{-1}\ s^{-2}$

Example 4. Calculate the number of light years in one metre.

Sol. We know that, 1 ly = 9.46×10^{15} m

or 9.46×10^{15} m = 1 ly

$\therefore$ $1\ m = \dfrac{1}{9.46 \times 10^{15}}$
$= 1.057 \times 10^{-16}$ ly

Example 5. Deduce relation between astronomical unit, light year and parsec. Arrange them in decreasing order of their magnitudes.

Sol. We know that, 1 AU = 1.496×10^{11} m
1 ly = 9.46×10^{15} m
1 parsec = 3.084×10^{16} m

$\therefore$ $\dfrac{1\ ly}{1\ AU} = \dfrac{9.46 \times 10^{15}}{1.496 \times 10^{11}} = 6.3 \times 10^4$

1 ly = 6.3×10^4 AU

Now, conversion of light year into parsec.

i.e. $\dfrac{1\ parsec}{1\ ly} = \dfrac{3.084 \times 10^{16}}{9.46 \times 10^{15}} = 3.26$

$\therefore$ 1 parsec = 3.26 ly

On comparing above results, we get
1 parsec > 1 ly > 1 AU

Check Your LEARNING...

1 What are the two types of physical quantities?
2 Write the name of two supplementary physical quantities.
3 Give any one advantage of SI unit over other systems of unit.
4 Convert 10 m/s to km/s. *Ans.* 0.01 km/s
5 Which one is largest, astronomical unit, light year or parsec?

Measurement of Length

Length is the distance of separation between two points in space. There are many instruments used to measure length like meter scale, inch tape, etc. Here, we will discuss two instruments vernier calliper and screw gauge, which are used to measure very small lengths.

Vernier Calliper

Vernier calliper is a device used to measure accurately upto $\left(\frac{1}{10}\right)$th of a millimetre. It was designed by a **French Mathematician Pierre Vernier**, hence the instrument is named so.

Construction of Vernier Calliper

Vernier calliper consists of following parts

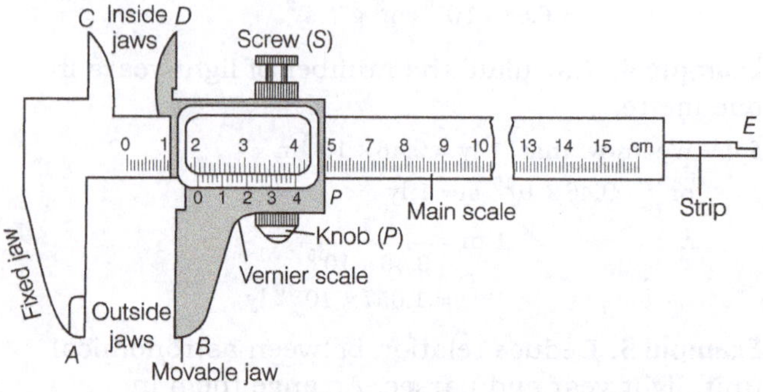

Vernier calliper and its parts

(i) **Main Scale** It is divided into division of different magnitude. The main scale is a fixed one that looks like a rectangular flat steel bar which is graduated in cm and mm. It consists of two fixed jaws *C* and *A* at right angles to the scale.

(ii) **Vernier Scale** It is also divided into division of different magnitude. This scale slides over the main scale. With the help of screw *S*, the vernier scale can be fixed at the desired position and the knob *P* is used to slide the vernier scale. The vernier scale is graduated with 10 divisions over a length of 9 mm i.e. 9 main scale divisions are equal to 10 vernier scale divisions.

(iii) **Movable Jaws** The vernier scale consists of two movable jaws *B* and *D* projecting at right angles to the scale. When the jaws of the main scale and the vernier scale touch each other, then the zero mark on the vernier scale coincides with the zero mark on the main scale, i.e. the instrument is free from zero error. The inside jaws *C* and *D* are used to measure the **internal diameter** of an object and the fixed jaw *A* and movable jaw *B* are used to measure the **external diameter** of the object.

(iv) **Metallic Strip** The thin metallic strip *E* provided at the end of the main scale is connected with vernier scale. When the two jaws *A* and *B* are in contact with each other, the strip *E* touches the edge of main scale and when the jaws *A* and *B* are separated, then the metallic strip *E* moves outward. It is used to measure the depth of a vessel.

Principle of Vernier Calliper

As, mentioned in vernier calliper construction, 10 divisions of vernier scale coincide with 9 divisions of main scale.

∴ 10 VSD (Vernier Scale Division)
= 9 MSD (Main Scale Division)

$$\therefore \quad 1 \text{ VSD} = \frac{9}{10} \text{ MSD}$$

$$1 \text{ VSD} = \frac{9}{10} \text{ mm} \qquad (\because \ 1 \text{ MSD} = 1 \text{ mm})$$

Thus, the difference between one main scale division and one vernier scale division is 1 mm − 0.9 mm = 0.1mm.

This illustrates that vernier calliper can measure length accurately upto 0.1 mm.

Least Count (LC) of Vernier Calliper

The minimum measurement that vernier calliper can take is called its least count.

The least count of vernier calliper is equal to the difference between the values of one main scale division and one vernier scale division. It is also called the **vernier constant.**

Let the value of one of the smallest division on the main scale be *x* and *y* be that on vernier scale. So, when the fixed and the movable jaws get joined, then

$$(n-1) \text{ MSD} = n\text{VSD}$$

i.e $(n-1) \times$ divisions of main scale = $n \times$ divisions on vernier scale

$$(n-1)\,x = ny$$

$$\Rightarrow \quad (x-y)\,n = x$$

$$\Rightarrow \quad (x-y) = \frac{x}{n}$$

Therefore, Least Count (LC)

$$= \frac{\text{Value of one of the smallest division on main scale}}{\text{Total number of small divisions on the vernier scale}}$$

Determination of Zero Error

If the instrument is perfect, the zero mark of the vernier scale should coincide with the zero mark of the main scale, when the jaws C and D are made to touch each other.

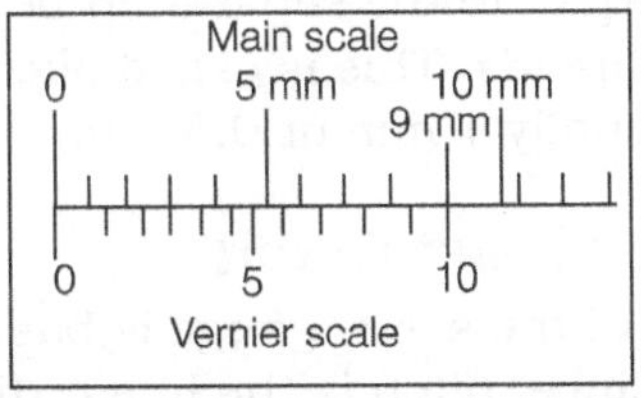

In such a situation, the instrument is free from any error.

However, in actual practice, due to wear and tear of the jaws and some manufacturing defects, zero error rises.

Zero error can be of two types

(i) **Positive Zero Error** When the zero mark of the vernier scale lies towards the right side of the zero of the main scale, when jaws C and D are made to touch each other. Then the zero error is called positive zero error. In such a situation, the measured length will be more than the actual length. It is because of this fact that the zero error is called positive zero error.

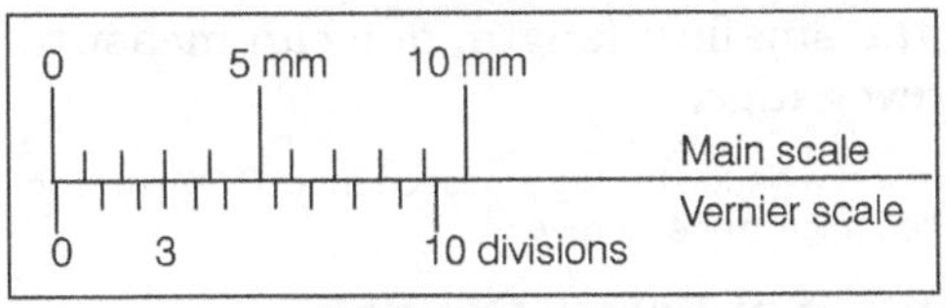

Positive zero error

Zero error = $(+)3 \times \text{LC} = +3 \times 0.01$ cm $= +\,0.03$ cm

(ii) **Negative Zero Error** When the zero mark of the vernier scale lies towards the left side of the zero of the main scale, when jaws C and D are in contact with each other, the zero error is called negative zero error.

The length of an object measured by this instrument will be less than the actual length of the object. It is because of this reason that the zero error is called negative zero error.

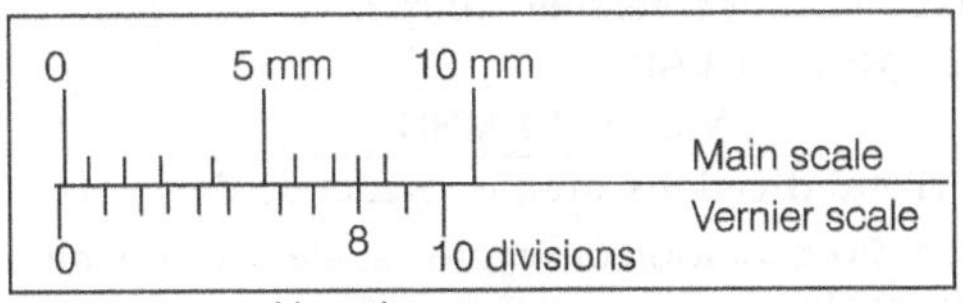

Negative zero error

Zero error = $(-)\,(0.01 \times 8)$ cm

$= -\,0.08$ cm

Measurement of Length of an Object by Vernier Calliper

The following steps are involved in measurement of length of an object with a vernier calliper

(i) First of all join both the jaws A and B of vernier calliper together.

(ii) Find the least count and zero error (if any) of the vernier calliper.

(iii) Move the jaw B away from the jaw A and place the object between the jaws.

(iv) Now, move the jaw B towards A till it touches the object and then tighten the screw S to fix the vernier scale in this position.

(v) Note the reading on main scale (MSR).

(vi) Note that division N on vernier scale which coincides with any division on main scale.

(vii) Use the formula, observed length = MSR + ($N \times$ LC).

(viii) Now, introduce the zero error correction (if any), i.e.

Correct reading = Observed reading − Zero error

True length = Observed length − Zero error (with sign)

Example 6. In an instrument, there are 25 divisions on the vernier scale which have length of 24 divisions of the main scale. 1 cm on main scale is divided in 25 equal parts. Find the least count.

Sol. The value of one main scale division, $x = \frac{1}{25}$ cm

The number of divisions on vernier scale, $n = 25$

$\therefore$ LC of vernier

$$= \frac{\text{Value of one main scale division } (x)}{\text{Number of divisions on vernier scale } (n)}$$

$$= \frac{(1/25)}{25} = \frac{1}{625} = 0.0016 \text{ cm}$$

Example 7. A vernier calliper has 1mm mark on the main scale. It has 20 equal divisions on the vernier scale which matches with 16 main scale divisions. For this vernier calliper, calculate the least count.

Sol. Least count of a vernier calliper,

$$LC = 1\,MSD - 1\,VSD$$

$$= \frac{\text{Value of 1 MSD}}{\text{Total divisions on the vernier scale}}$$

Since, 20 divisions of vernier scale = 16 divisions of main scale

$$\Rightarrow \quad 1\,VSD = \frac{16}{20}\,\text{mm} = 0.8\,\text{mm} \qquad (\because 1\,MSD = 1\,\text{mm})$$

$$\therefore \quad LC = 1\,MSD - 1\,VSD$$

$$= 1\,\text{mm} - 0.8\,\text{mm} = 0.2\,\text{mm}$$

Screw Gauge

With the help of vernier calliper, we can measure the length accurately upto 0.1 mm but screw gauge is more precise and accurate measuring instrument of length upto 0.01 mm or 0.005 mm. Thus, a screw gauge is an instrument of higher precision than a vernier calliper.

It is an instrument used for measuring very small lengths such as diameters of wires which cannot be accurately measured by vernier calliper. It is because the least count of screw gauge is smaller than the least count of a vernier calliper. A screw gauge works on the principle of a micrometer screw.

Micrometer Screw

A micrometer screw is shown in figure. There are evenly spaced threads on the screw. It means that the separation between two consecutive threads is same.

The screw can be moved forward and backward in a closely fitting nut also comprising evenly spaced threads.

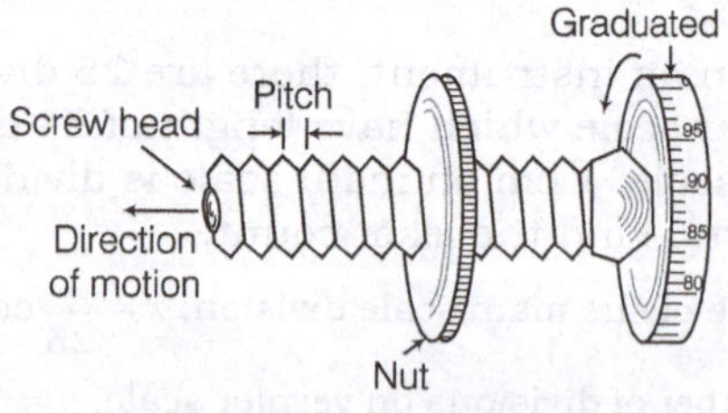

Principle of a micrometer screw

There are two types of motions associated with the micrometer screw

(i) Linear motion (ii) Circular motion

Pitch of Screw

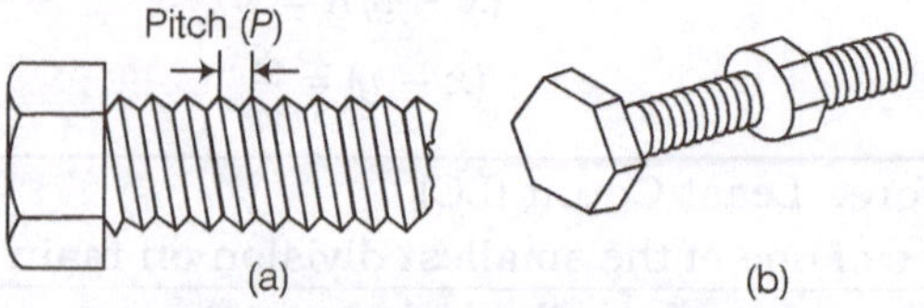

A screw (a) without nut (b) with nut

In an ordinary screw (as shown in above figures), the separation between any two consecutive threads is same, it can be moved backward and forward in its nut by rotating it anti-clockwise or clockwise. During one complete rotation, distance travelled by the screw is equal to the separation between two consecutive threads. This is called **pitch (*P*)** of the screw. It is usually 1 mm or 0.5 mm.

Principle and Least Count

The principle of the screw gauge is based on the least count. Since, pitch is the linear distance travelled by screw in one complete rotation of its head and least count of screw gauge is the ratio of pitch to the total number of divisions on the circular scale.

Therefore, pitch

$$= \frac{\text{distance moved by the screw}}{\text{number of rotations given to the screw}}$$

and least count

$$= \frac{\text{pitch of the screw}}{\text{number of divisions on circular scale}}$$

e.g. For a screw gauge with a pitch of 1 mm and 100 divisions on the circular scale,

$$\text{Least count} = \frac{1\,\text{mm}}{100} = 0.01\,\text{mm}$$

This is the smallest length, one can measure with this screw gauge.

Note The screw gauge having a least count of 0.001 mm or 10^{-6} m is called micrometer screw.

Description of Screw Gauge

The figure given below is a screw gauge. It consists of a screw *S* which advances forward or backward as one rotates the head *C* through ratchet *R* in clockwise or anti-clockwise direction. It also consists of a Linear Scale (LS) attached to limb *D* of the U-frame.

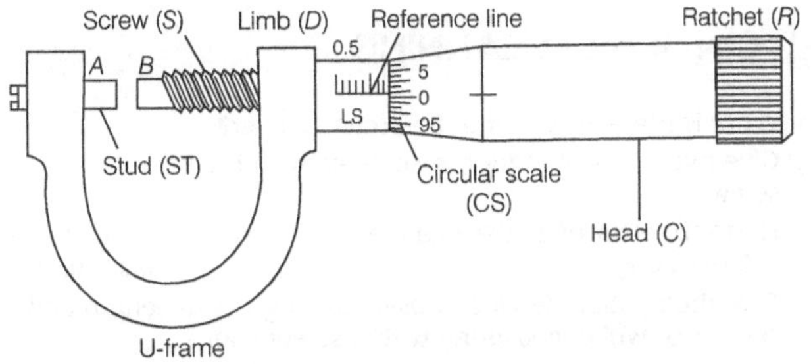

Screw gauge

The smallest division on the linear scale is 1 mm. There is a Circular Scale (CS) on the head, which can be rotated. A line parallel to the axis of screw is inscribed on the body of the screw, this line is called **reference line**. There are 100 divisions on the circular scale.

There are two studs A and B in the screw gauge. They serve as two jaws of the screw gauge. The stud A is fixed with the U-frame while stud B as the flat end of the screw is movable which can move forward and backward.

When the end B of the screw touches the surface A of the stud (ST), the zero marks on the main scale and the circular scale should coincide with each other. When both the studs touch each other or they come in contact, the ratchet itself turns on to loose the control over the screw. This in turn helps to avoid the undue pressure over the object placed between the studs.

Determination of Zero Error

In a perfect instrument, when the gap between P and Q is reduced to zero, the zero of the head scale will lie along the line of graduation and the edge of the head scale lies exactly in front of the zero of the pitch scale.

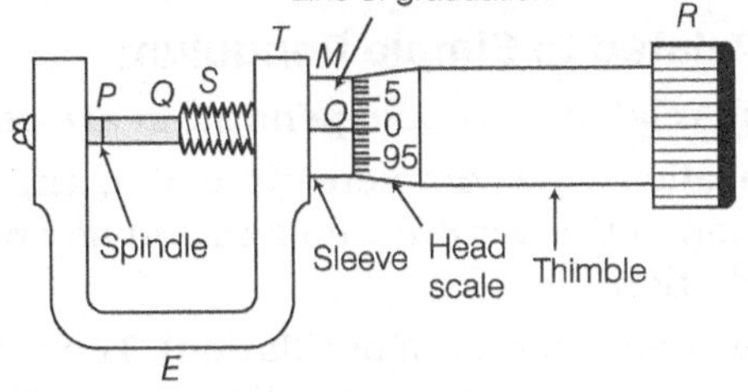

Zero error

In case, this is not so, then the instrument is said to possess an error called **zero error**. Like the zero error of vernier calliper, the zero error in case of screw gauge may also be positive or negative.

(i) **Positive Zero Error** In this case, the zero of the circular scale is below the line of graduation as the gap between P and Q is reduced to zero. Since, the zero of the circular scale lies to the right hand side of the zero of the pitch scale, the error is called positive zero error.

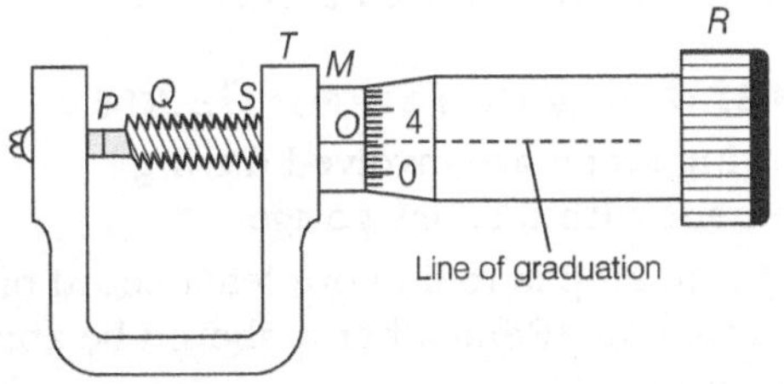

Let us determine the magnitude of this error by taking an example.

e.g. Refer the given figure (above), in which the zero line of the head scale is 4 divisions below the line of graduation.

$\therefore$ Zero error $= +4 \times \text{LC} = +4 \times 0.01 = +0.04$ mm

(ii) **Negative Zero Error** In such a case, the zero of the circular scale lies above the line of graduation, when the gap between P and Q is reduced to zero.

Under this condition, the edge of the circular scale lies to the left hand side or above the zero of the pitch scale. This is why, the zero error is called negative zero error.

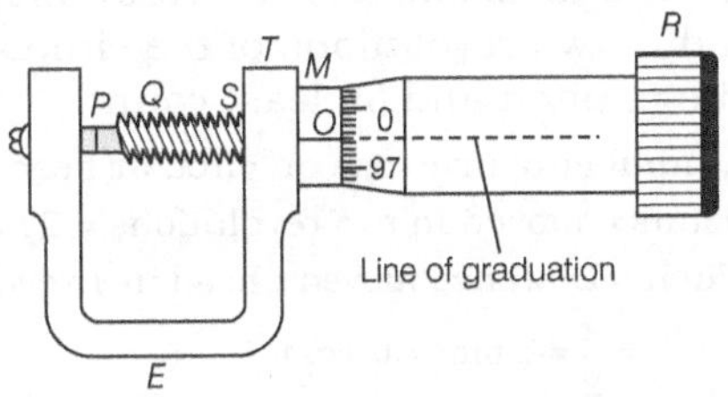

Let us determine the magnitude of this error with the help of an example.

e.g. Refer the given figure (above), Zero line on circular scale is 3 divisions (out of 100) above from line of graduation. This shows that error is negative.

$\therefore$ Zero error $= -3 \times \text{LC}$

$= -3 \times 0.01$ mm

$= -0.03$ mm

Backlash Error

When the screw is rotated very fast to measure a reading, then there is some slipping between the different tip of screw and thimble due to wear and tear or due to a loose fitting of threads which gives an incorrect reading of threads.

It is observed that on reversing the direction of rotation of thimble in screw gauge, the tip of screw remains stationary, i.e. it does not start moving in the opposite direction at once. The error due to this in observation is called backlash error.

Measurement with a Screw Gauge

The following steps are involved during measurement with a screw gauge

(i) Very first step is to find out least count of given screw gauge. (Remember it should be about 0.01 mm)

(ii) Check out, whether the screw gauge has any zero error or not. (Write it properly, along with sign)

(iii) Place the object between P and Q and turn the ratchet in clockwise direction till ratchet becomes free.

(iv) Note down the Main Scale Reading (MSR) and number of circular divisions coincide with base line called Circular Scale Reading (CSR).

(v) Observed diameter = MSR + CSR × LC

(vi) True diameter = Observed diameter − Zero error (with sign).

Example 8. The circular head of a screw gauge is divided into 100 divisions and the screw moves 2 mm ahead in two revolutions of the circular head. Calculate its (i) pitch and (ii) least count.

Sol. Given, number of divisions on circular head = 100 and distance moved in two revolutions = 2 mm

(i) ∴ Pitch = Distance moved ahead in 1 revolution

$$= \frac{2}{2} = 1\text{ mm} = 0.1\text{ cm}$$

(ii) ∴ Least count = $\frac{\text{Pitch}}{\text{Number of divisions on circular head}}$

$$\text{LC} = \frac{0.1}{100} = 0.001\text{ cm}$$

Example 9. A screw gauge gives the following reading, when used to measure the diameter of a wire. Main scale reading : 0 mm, Circular scale reading : 52 divisions. Given that, 1 mm on main scale corresponds to 100 divisions of the circular scale, then find the diameter of the wire.

Sol. Diameter of wire = MSR + CSR × LC

Given, Main Scale Reading (MSR) = 0 mm

Circular scale reading = 52 divisions

$$\therefore \text{Least Count (LC)} = \frac{\text{Value of 1 main scale division}}{\text{Total divisions on circular scale}} = \frac{1}{100}$$

$$\therefore \text{Diameter of wire} = 0 + 52 \times \frac{1}{100} = 0.52\text{ mm} = 0.052\text{ cm}$$

Check Your LEARNING...

1. What is the least count of a vernier calliper?
2. Give two types of motion associated with the micrometer screw.
3. Find zero error of a screw gauge, if zero line of the head scale is 5 divisions. *Ans.* + 0.05 mm
4. Give the relation between observed length, true length and zero error while measuring with a screw gauge.

Measurement of Time

In home and offices, we commonly use a pendulum clock to note time which depends upon time period of oscillation of a simple pendulum.

Simple Pendulum

A heavy object (bob), suspended from a rigid support, by an inextensible and light string set to oscillate freely due to gravity is called a simple pendulum.

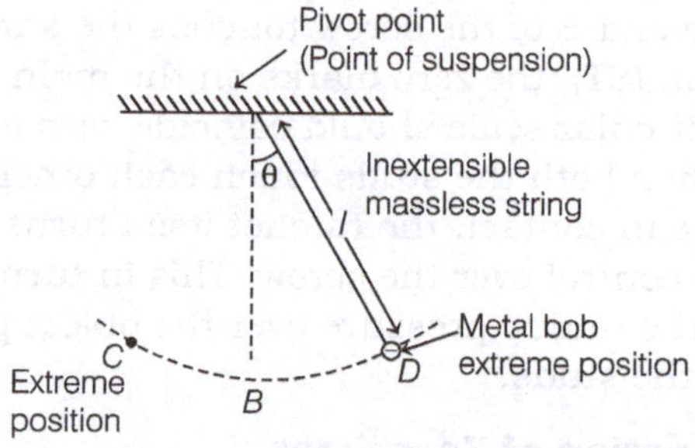

Simple pendulum

In the given diagram, B is the mean position of the pendulum bob. If bob is shifted to D from B and then released, it comes in a motion known as oscillatory motion. C and D are the extreme positions of the bob.

Terms Related to Simple Pendulum

The terms related to simple pendulum are as follows

(i) **Oscillation** One complete cycle of to and fro motion of the pendulum is known as one oscillation.

(ii) **Time Period** (period of oscillation) The time taken to complete one oscillation is called time period. It is denoted by T and its SI unit is second (s).

(iii) **Frequency of Oscillation** The number of oscillations in one second is known as frequency of oscillation. It is denoted by (f) and its SI unit is hertz (Hz).

As, $f = \frac{1}{T}$

$$1 \text{ hertz} = (1 \text{ second})^{-1}$$

$$1 \text{ Hz} = 1 \text{s}^{-1}$$

(iv) **Amplitude** It is defined as the maximum displacement of simple pendulum from its mean position. It is denoted by A and its SI unit is metre (m).

(v) **Effective Length of a Pendulum** It is a distance between the point of oscillation (i.e., centre of gravity of the bob) from the point of suspension.

It is denoted by l and its SI unit is metre (m).

Relation between l and T

Length of a pendulum (l) and its time period (T) are related to each other by the given relation $T = 2\pi\sqrt{\frac{l}{g}}$

where, g is acceleration due to gravity.

Factors on which Period of Oscillation (T) Depends

The period of oscillation depends on the following factors

(i) **Length of a Pendulum (l)**

As,

$$T = 2\pi\sqrt{\frac{l}{g}}, \quad T \propto \sqrt{l}$$

Thus, if the length of a pendulum is more, then greater will be the time period and *vice- versa.*

e.g. Suppose we have a simple pendulum which takes 4 s to complete one oscillation. i.e. $T = 4$ s.

Now, if we increase its length by four times, then time period will be doubled. It means, now a pendulum will take 8 s to complete one oscillation.

(ii) **Acceleration due to Gravity**

As, $T = 2\pi\sqrt{\frac{l}{g}}$, thus $T \propto \frac{1}{\sqrt{g}}$

i.e. Time period is inversely proportional to square root of the acceleration due to gravity. Thus, from this relation, we find that, if the acceleration due to gravity is more, then smaller will be the time period and *vice-versa*.

Measurement of Time Period of a Simple Pendulum

To measure the time period of a simple pendulum, procedure is followed as given below

(i) The bob is slightly displaced from its mean position and then released. This sets the bob into vibrations.

(ii) Now, measure the time for 20 oscillations with the help of stopwatch.

(iii) Calculate the time period of pendulum by dividing the time of 20 oscillations by 20.

(iv) The experiment is then repeated for different lengths of the pendulum and the observations are recorded in a table as given below

Length	Time for 20 oscillations	Time period
25	20	1.0
36	24	1.2
49	28	1.4
64	32	1.6

From this table, it is observed that time period of simple pendulum is directly proportional to the square root of effective length of pendulum.

Graph between Effective Length and Time Period

(i) l *versus* T^2

As, $T = 2\pi\sqrt{\frac{l}{g}}$

On squaring both sides, we get

$$T^2 = 4\pi^2\frac{l}{g} \Rightarrow T^2 = \left(\frac{4\pi^2}{g}\right)l$$

$$\therefore \quad T^2 \propto l$$

It shows that l varies linearly with T^2.

Hence, graph between l and T^2 will be a straight line starting from origin as shown below

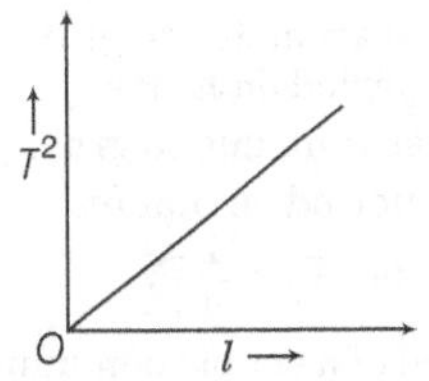

Slope of T^2 versus l Graph The slope of T^2 *versus* l graph is constant at a given place and is given by

$$\text{Slope} = \frac{T_1^2 - T_2^2}{l_1 - l_2} = \frac{4\pi^2}{g}$$

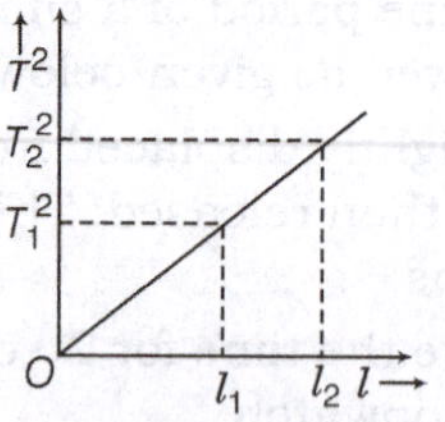

where, T_1 is the time period of the pendulum corresponding to the length l_1 and similarly, T_2 is the time period corresponding to length l_2.

(ii) $\sqrt{l}$ versus T

As, $T = 2\pi\sqrt{\frac{l}{g}} \Rightarrow T = \left(\frac{2\pi}{\sqrt{g}}\right)\sqrt{l}$

$\therefore \quad T \propto \sqrt{l}$

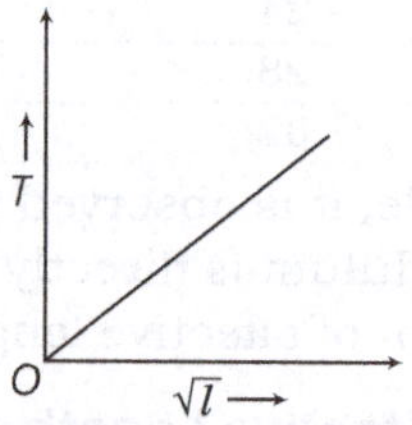

Thus, this will be a straight line starting from origin.

Example 10. Suppose we have a simple pendulum of length l. It has a time period of 4 s on Earth (provided g on Earth is 10 ms^{-2} approx). What will be the time period of a simple pendulum on any planet which has $g = 40$ ms^{-2}?

Sol. As, l is same.

Thus, $\quad T \propto \frac{1}{\sqrt{g}}$

Given, $g_e = 10\ ms^{-2}$, $g_p = 40 ms^{-2}$, $T_e = 4$ s and $T_p = ?$

$\therefore \quad \frac{T_e}{T_p} = \sqrt{\frac{g_p}{g_e}} \Rightarrow \frac{T_e}{T_p} = \sqrt{\frac{40}{10}} \Rightarrow \frac{T_e}{T_p} = 2$

where, g_e = acceleration due to gravity on Earth,
T_e = time period on Earth,
g_p = acceleration due to gravity on planet
and T_p = time period on planet.

Thus, $T_e = 2T_p$ or $T_p = \frac{1}{2}T_e$

Hence, time period of a simple pendulum on planet will be $\frac{1}{2}T_e$.

$\therefore \quad T_p = \frac{4}{2} = 2$ s

Example 11. Find the length of a simple pendulum whose time period of oscillation is 2.8 s. (Take, $g = 9.8$ ms^{-2})

Sol. Given, time period of a pendulum, $T = 2.8$ s

Acceleration due to gravity, $g = 9.8$ ms^{-2}

We know that, $T = 2\pi\sqrt{\frac{l}{g}}$

$\Rightarrow \quad l = \frac{T^2 g}{4\pi^2} = \frac{(2.8)^2 \times 9.8}{4 \times (3.14)^2} = 1.94$ m

So, length of a simple pendulum = 1.94 m

Example 12. The length of a pendulum is decreased by 5%. What effect does it have on the time period of a pendulum?

Sol. Let the length of a pendulum be l.

i.e. $\quad l_1 = l,\ l_2 = l - 5\%$ of $l = l - \frac{5}{100} \times l = 0.95\,l$

We know that, time period, $T \propto \sqrt{l}$

$\therefore \quad \frac{T_2}{T_1} = \frac{\sqrt{l_2}}{\sqrt{l_1}} = \sqrt{\frac{0.95\,l_1}{l_1}} \Rightarrow \frac{T_2}{T_1} = \sqrt{0.95} = 0.97$

$T_2 = 0.97\,T_1 = (1 - 0.03)T_1 = T_1 - 0.03\,T_1$

i.e. $\quad T_2 = T_1 - 3\%\ T_1$

So, the time period will decrease by 3%, if length is decreased by 5%.

Second's Pendulum

A pendulum which has a time period of 2 s is known as second's pendulum.

$\Rightarrow \quad T = 2$s

It is used in clocks.

Example 13. What is the effective length of a second's pendulum?

Sol. Time period of a second's pendulum is 2 s.

As, $\quad T = 2\pi\sqrt{\frac{l}{g}} \Rightarrow l = \frac{1}{4\pi^2}gT^2$

$l = \frac{1}{4\pi^2} \times 9.8 \times (2)^2 \qquad (\because g = 9.8\ ms^{-2})$

$= \frac{1}{4 \times \left(\frac{22}{7}\right)^2} \times 9.8 \times 4 \qquad \left(\because \pi = \frac{22}{7}\right)$

$= 0.99\text{ m} \simeq 1\text{ m}$

$\therefore$ The effective length of a second's pendulum is about 1 m (Taking, $g = 9.8$ ms^{-2}).

Check Your LEARNING...

1 Give the cause of motion of bob of a simple pendulum.
2 Define the amplitude of a simple pendulum.
3 If the length of a simple pendulum is increased, how will its time period vary?
4 If a simple pendulum is taken to the mars, how will its time period vary?
5 If the length of a simple pendulum is increased by 25%, then what is the change in its time period? *Ans.* 12.5% increase
6 Define a second's pendulum.

QUiCK Revision

- **Physical Quantities** All the quantities which can be measured directly or indirectly in terms of which laws of Physics are described and whose measurement is necessary.
- **Units of Physical Quantities** It is the standard amount of a physical quantity chosen to measure the physical quantity of same kind.
- **Fundamental Quantities and Units** The physical quantities which are independent of other physical quantities are called fundamental quantities and their units are called fundamental units.
- **Derived Quantities and Units** The physical quantities which can be derived from the fundamental quantities are called derived quantities and their units are called derived units.
- **The FPS System of Units** It is British engineering system of units and stands for foot, pound and second.
- **The CGS System of Units** It stands for centimetre, gram and second.
- **The MKS System of Units** It stands for metre, kilogram and second.
- **The SI System of Units** This system of units is internationally accepted form of measurement.
- **Meter Scale** It is used to measure length and its least count is 1 mm.
- **Vernier Calliper** This instrument is used to measure length accurately upto (1/10)th of a millimetre. Its least count is 0.01 cm and pitch is 0.1 cm. Also, 1 VSD (Vernier Scale Division) = 0.9 MSD (Main Scale Division).
- **Screw Gauge** This instrument is used to measure very small lengths which cannot be measured by vernier calliper. Its least count is given by

  $$\text{Least count} = \frac{\text{Pitch of the screw}}{\text{Total number of divisions on circular scale}}$$
- **Zero Error (i) For Vernier Calliper** On bringing the jaws of vernier calliper in contact with each other, the zero of the vernier scale in some instruments does not fall in line with the zero of the main scale. Such vernier callipers are said to possess zero error.
  (ii) For Screw Gauge When the gap between the two ends of the screw of a screw gauge is reduced to zero but the zero of the head scale does not lie along the line of graduation and the edge of the head scale, then such screw gauges are said to possess zero error.
- On the basis of direction of deviation of instruments from zero mark on their scale, zero errors are classified into two types i.e. **positive zero error** and **negative zero error**.
- **Simple Pendulum** This instrument is used to measure time. Time period of a simple pendulum is given by $T = 2\pi\sqrt{\frac{l}{g}}$, where l is the length of the pendulum and g is the acceleration due to gravity.

Chapter Practice

Section I

1 Mark Questions

1. To measure a physical quantity, the unit chosen have which of the following characteristics?
(a) The unit should be easily reproducible
(b) The unit should not vary with time
(c) The unit should not depend on physical conditions like pressure, volume, temperature, etc
(d) All of the above

Sol. (*d*) To measure a physical quantity, the unit chosen should be easily reproducible and do not vary with time. It should not depend on physical conditions like pressure, volume, temperature, etc.

2. Which of the following is a fundamental unit?
(a) Newton (b) Pascal
(c) Hertz (d) Second

Sol. (*d*) Second is the fundamental unit of time, while newton, pascal and hertz are derived units of force, pressure and frequency, respectively.

3. Which of the following has a derived unit?
(a) Mass
(b) Length
(c) Volume
(d) Temperature

Sol. (*c*) Volume has the derived unit which is derived from fundamental unit of length, i.e. metre.
Unit of volume = metre × metre × metre = $(\text{metre})^3$

4. Identify the incorrect statement.
(a) Light year is the units of time.
(b) One angstrom is equal to one-tenth of a nanometre.
(c) Mass can be measured in quintal
(d) Parallactic second is a unit to measure distance.

Sol. (*a*) Statement in option (a) is incorrect. One light year is the distance travelled by light in vacuum in one year. Thus,

$$1 \text{ light year} = 9.46 \times 10^{15} \text{ m}$$

5. The least count of a vernier calliper is
(a) 1 cm (b) 0.001 cm
(c) 0.1 cm (d) 0.01 cm

Sol. (*d*) The least count of a vernier calliper is obtained by dividing the value of one division of main scale by the total number of divisions on vernier scale. The value of least count of vernier calliper is 0.01 cm.

6. What is the reading on the vernier calliper shown below?

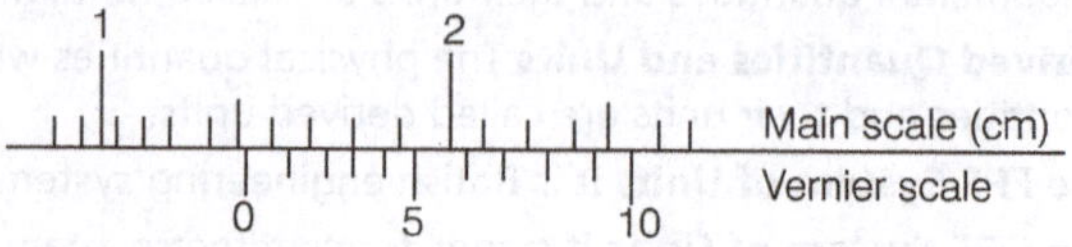

(a) 1.52 m (b) 1.53 cm
(c) 1.48 cm (d) 1.51 cm

Sol. (*b*) The least count of vernier calliper = 0.01 cm
Main scale reading = 1.5 cm
3rd division of vernier scale coincides with a division on main scale.
∴ Vernier scale reading $= 3 \times 0.01 = 0.03$ cm
Hence, reading on the vernier calliper
= Main scale reading + Vernier scale reading
$= 1.5 \text{ cm} + 0.03 \text{ cm} = 1.53 \text{ cm}$

7. Identify the function of thimble in screw gauge.
(a) To mark circular scale.
(b) To mark main scale and base line.
(c) To read length correct upto 1 mm.
(d) Helps to read length correct upto 0.01mm.

Sol. (*a*) The hollow cylinder in screw gauge is known as thimble. Its function is to mark the circular scale.

8. The diameter of a thin wire can be measured by a
(a) vernier calliper (b) metre rule
(c) screw gauge (d) None of these

Sol. (*c*) A screw gauge is used to measure the diameter of a thin wire because the least count of screw gauge is 0.001 cm. However, the least count of a micrometer screw gauge is 1 μm (0.0001 cm).

9. Choose the correct statements about time period of a simple pendulum.
(a) The time period of oscillation is directly proportional to the effective length of pendulum.
(b) The time period of oscillation depends on the mass of the body suspended.
(c) When the time period of pendulum decreases, its effective length increases.
(d) Decrease in the value of g, increase the time period of oscillations.

Sol. (*d*) A pendulum clock goes slow, i.e. the time period increases, when the value of g decreases because time period of pendulum is inversely proportional to the square root of acceleration due to gravity.

10. The length of a seconds pendulum is nearly
(a) 0.5 m (b) 9.8 m (c) 1.0 m (d) 2.0 m

Sol. (*c*) The effective length of the second's pendulum, at a place where $g = 9.8 \text{ m/s}^2$ is nearly 1 m.

2 Marks Questions

11. How will you express the result of a measurement of a physical quantity?

Sol. Result of a measurement of a physical quantity is expressed by a number accompanied by a unit. [1]
Thus, measurement of physical quantity
= numerical value × unit
i.e. $Q = nu$ [1]

12. State four characteristics of a standard unit.

Sol. (i) It must be of convenient size.
(ii) It must not change with time and place.
(iii) It must be possible to define without any doubt.
(iv) It should be easily reproduced. [1/2 × 4]

13. Define the term fundamental unit. Name fundamental units of current and temperature.

Sol. Those physical quantities which can neither be derived from other units, nor be further resolved into more simpler units are called fundamental unit. [1]
Current → Ampere (A)
Temperature → Kelvin (K) [1]

14. Write the fundamental units along with their symbols.

Sol. There are seven fundamental units as given below
(i) Metre (m) — Unit of length
(ii) Kilogram (kg) — Unit of mass
(iii) Second (s) — Unit of time
(iv) Kelvin (K) — Unit of temperature
(v) Ampere (A) — Unit of electric current
(vi) Candela (cd) — Unit of luminous intensity
(vii) Mole (mol) — Unit for amount of substance [2]

15. What are the advantages of International System of units over other systems?

Sol. The International System of units (SI) has following advantages over other system of units.
(i) **It is a Coherent System of Units** All derived units can be determined by simple multiplication or division of fundamental units by some constant.[1]
(ii) **It is a Rational System** It uses only one unit for a given physical quantity. [1]

16. How are the following derived units related to the fundamental units?
(i) newton (ii) joule
(iii) watt (iv) pascal

Sol. (i) newton (N) = kg-m s^{-2}
(ii) joule (J) = kg-m^2s^{-2}
(iii) watt (W) = kg-m^2s^{-3}
(iv) pascal (Pa) = kg-$m^{-1}s^{-2}$ [½ × 4]

17. Name the three convenient units used to measure very long distance and relate it to its SI unit.

Sol. Astronomical unit (AU), light year (ly) and parsec are three units used to measure very long distances.
$1\text{ AU} = 1.496 \times 10^{11}\text{ m}$
$1\text{ ly} = 9.46 \times 10^{15}\text{ m}$
$1\text{ parsec} = 3.084 \times 10^{16}\text{ m}$ [2]

18. Express each of the following in terms of kilogram.
(i) 1 g (ii) 1 mg
(iii) 1 quintal (iv) 1 amu

Sol. (i) $1\text{ g} = 10^{-3}\text{ kg}$
(ii) $1\text{mg} = 10^{-6}\text{ kg}$
(iii) $1\text{ quintal} = 100\text{ kg}$
(iv) $1\text{ amu} = 1.66 \times 10^{-27}\text{ kg}$ [½ × 4]

19. Name the physical quantities which are measured in the following units.
(a) ly (c) nm (c) kg (d) μs

Sol. (a) distance (b) length
(c) mass (d) time [½ × 4]

20. How can we convert the following units to m?
(i) light year (ii) Å
(iii) micron (iv) fermi

Sol. (i) $1\text{ light year} = 9.46 \times 10^{15}\text{m}$
(ii) $1\text{Å} = 10^{-10}\text{m}$
(iii) $1\text{ micron} = 10^{-6}\text{m}$
(iv) $1\text{ fermi} = 10^{-15}\text{m}$ [½ × 4]

21. The wavelength of light is 589 nm. What is its wavelength in Å and μm?

Sol. $1\text{nm} = 10^{-9}\text{m}$ and $1\text{ Å} = 10^{-10}\text{m}$
So, $1\text{ nm} = 10\text{Å}$
∴ Wavelength of light $= 589\text{ nm} = 5890\text{Å}$
$= 0.589 \times 10^{-6}\text{m}$
$= 0.589\,\mu\text{m}$ [2]

22. The size of a bacteria is 2 μm. Find the number of bacteria in 2 m length.

Sol. $1\,\mu\text{m} = 10^{-6}\text{m}$
$\Rightarrow \quad 1\text{m} = 10^{6}\mu\text{m}$
∴ Number of bacteria in 2m length $= \dfrac{2\text{ m}}{2\mu\text{m}}$
$= \dfrac{2 \times 10^6\mu\text{m}}{2\mu\text{m}} = 10^6$ [2]

23. What is meant by zero error of vernier calliper?

Sol. On bringing the jaws of vernier calliper in contact with each other, the zero of the vernier scale in some instruments does not fall in line with the zero of the main scale. Such instruments are said to possess a zero error. [2]

24. Explain
(i) Positive zero error
(ii) Negative zero error.

Sol. (i) **Positive Zero Error** The zero error is positive when the zero mark of the vernier scale lies towards the right side of the zero of the main scale when the jaws are in contact. [1]
(ii) **Negative Zero Error** The zero error is said to be negative when the zero mark of the vernier scale lies towards the left side of the zero mark of the main scale when jaws are in contact. [1]

25. How is the zero correction applied to an instrument?

Sol. Zero correction is the correction applied to a measured value on account of the zero error. It is negative of the zero error, i.e. it is negative for positive zero error and positive for negative zero error.

Corrected reading = Observed reading − Zero error (with proper sign) [2]

26. Why is screw gauge commonly known as micrometer?

Sol. Screw gauge can measure thickness of wires accurately upto 0.005 mm or 5×10^{-6} m. Since, micro means small and meter implies measurement, micrometer is commonly known as the instrument used to measure small lengths. [2]

27. State the purpose of ratchet in a screw gauge.

Sol. In a screw gauge, the circular scale is attached with a ratchet by a spring. The purpose of ratchet in a screw gauge is to advance the screw by turning it till the object is gently held between the stud and spindle of the screw.

28. Mention the relation between frequency and time period of a simple pendulum. What is the SI unit of frequency?

Sol. Frequency of a simple pendulum (f) is equal to reciprocal of its time period (T), i.e. $f \propto \frac{1}{T}$.

The SI unit of frequency is hertz (Hz). [2]

29. State the parameters on which time period of a simple pendulum does not depend.

Sol. The period of oscillation does not depend on the following parameters

(i) Mass of the material and shape of the bob [1]

(ii) Amplitude of oscillation [1]

30. What will be the frequency of oscillation of a simple pendulum in a cabin that is falling freely under acceleration due to gravity?

Sol. If a cabin is falling freely, acceleration due to gravity $g = 0$.

Since, $$f = \frac{1}{2\pi}\sqrt{\frac{g}{l}}$$

$\therefore$ $$f = 0, \text{ if } g = 0$$ [2]

31. Two pendulums P and Q of lengths 4 m and 8 m are made to oscillate. Which pendulum will make more oscillations and why?

Sol. The time period of a pendulum is given by the expression $T = 2\pi\sqrt{\frac{l}{g}}$. Since, it depends directly on the square root of length, therefore pendulum Q will have more time period than pendulum P. Hence, in the same time, pendulum P will make more oscillations than pendulum Q. [2]

32. How is the length of a simple pendulum related to acceleration due to gravity for a constant time period?

Sol. Time period of a simple pendulum is given by

$$T = 2\pi\sqrt{\frac{l}{g}} \Rightarrow T\sqrt{g} = 2\pi\sqrt{l}$$

i.e., $$\sqrt{l} = \frac{T}{2\pi}\sqrt{g}$$

As T is constant, therefore

$$\sqrt{l} \propto \sqrt{g}$$

i.e. $$l \propto g$$ [2]

3 Marks Questions

33. What is the need of measurement?

Or Why is measurement necessary?

Sol. Physics is most fundamental science, dealing with the study of nature and natural phenomena. Measurement is integral part of physics like any other scientific subject. Quantities involved in it is essential. In order to establish and verify a physical law, we have to make observations and measurements. [3]

34. Why is the International System of units (SI) developed and recommended?

Sol. MKS system of units deals with only length, mass and time. But there are some other physical quantities like current, temperature, etc., which are fundamental quantities. To express the units of these physical quantities, in 1971, SI system was accepted worldwide. [3]

35. What do you understand by the statement, the density of mercury is 13.6 g/cm^3? Convert this value into SI unit.

Sol. The above statement means that the mass volume of 1cm^3 of mercury is 13.6 g.

$$13.6 \text{ g/cm}^3 = \frac{13.6 \text{ g}}{1 \text{ cm}^3} = \frac{13.6 \times 10^{-3} \text{ kg}}{(10^{-2})^3 \text{m}^3}$$
$$= 13.6 \times 10^3 \text{ kg/m}^3 = 13600 \text{ kg-m}^{-3}$$

The SI unit of density is kg-m^{-3}. [3]

36. Draw a well labelled diagram of vernier calliper. Write the functions of

(i) main scale (ii) movable jaws

Sol. Refer to theory (Page 06).

37. Name the instrument you would use to measure the following

(i) Diameter of a ball pen

(ii) Diameter of a pencil

(iii) External/internal diameter of a calorimeter

(iv) Diameter of a metal ball (ball bearings)

(v) Internal diameter of a test tube

(vi) Width of a desk

Sol. (i), (ii) are measured by micrometer screw gauge while (iii), (iv), (v) are measured by vernier calliper and (vi) is measured by meter scale. [3]

38. Answer the following

(i) You are given a thread and a meter scale. How will you estimate the diameter of the thread?

(ii) A screw gauge has a pitch of 1.0 mm and 200 divisions on the circular scale. Do you think, it is possible to increase the accuracy of the screw gauge arbitrarily by increasing the number of divisions on the circular scale?

(iii) The mean diameter of a thin brass rod is to be measured by vernier calliper. Why is a set of 100 measurements of the diameter expected to yield a more reliable estimate than a set of 5 measurements only?

Sol. (i) The diameter of a thread is so small that it cannot be measured using a meter scale. To measure the diameter of the thread, we find a number of turns of the thread on the meter scale, so that the turns are closely touching one another. Count the number of turns n and measure the length l of the coiled thread using the meter scale.

$$\text{Diameter of thread} = \frac{\text{Length of coiled thread } (l)}{\text{Number of turns } (n)}$$ [1]

(ii) Yes, the accuracy of the gauge can be increased by increasing the number of divisions on the circular scale as the least count of the screw gauge is given by

Least count

$$= \frac{\text{Pitch}}{\text{Number of divisions on circular scale}}$$

From the formula, it is clear that by increasing the number of divisions on circular scale, least count can be decreased, hence the accuracy will increase. It is correct theoretically but practically it may not be possible because it is difficult to take the reading precisely as the resolution of human eye is not so high. [1]

(iii) The mean diameter obtained from a set of 100 measurements is more reliable than from a set of 5 measurements because the probability of making a positive random error is equal to the probability of making a negative random error. Therefore, in a set of large number of measurements, these errors cancel each other and we get a more reliable value. [1]

4 Marks Questions

39. Define the following

(i) Fundamental quantities

(ii) Derived quantities

(iii) Fundamental units

(iv) Derived units

Sol. (i) **Fundamental Quantities** Refer to theory (Page 01). [1]

(ii) **Derived Quantities** Refer to theory (Page 01). [1]

(iii) **Fundamental Units** Refer to theory (Page 02). [1]

(iv) **Derived Units** Refer to theory (Page 02). [1]

40. Precise measurements of physical quantities are a need of science. For example- To ascertain the speed of an aircraft, one must have an accurate method to find its position at closely separated instants of time. This was the actual motivation behind the discovery of RADAR in world war II. Think of different examples in modern science, where precision measurements of length, time, mass, etc., are needed. Also, wherever you can, give a quantitative idea of the precision needed.

Sol. Precise measurements of physical quantities such as length, time, mass, etc., is a basic requirement of development of astronomy, nuclear physics, medical sciences, crystallography, etc.

In the measurement of astronomical distances such as the distance of Moon from the Earth by laser beam, an accurate measurement of time is required. A very small mistake in the measurement of that time can produce a large mistake in the accurate distance of Moon from the Earth which can be a cause of failure to reach the Moon. This time is of the order of 10^{-9}s. [1]

In atomic or nuclear reactions, in nuclear weapons and in nuclear power plants a precise measurements of mass and time is required which is of the order of 10^{-9}kg and 10^{-9} s. A small mistake can be a cause of an accident, such an accident, took place in Japan in 2011. [1]

In medical sciences, a precise measurement of length is required to find location, size and mass of tumor in body (it is of the order of 10^{-9}m). [1]

A small mistake in the measurement of its location, size or mass can be a cause of a damage to any body part in laser therapy. [1]

41. Define the following

(i) MKS system of units

(ii) CGS system of units

(iii) FPS system of units

(iv) SI system of units

Sol. Refer to theory (Page 02).

42. Define the following.

(i) Solar day (ii) Sedrial day

(iii) Solar year (iv) Tropical year

Sol. (i) **Solar Day** It is the time taken by the Earth to complete one rotation about its own axis w.r.t. the Sun. [1]

(ii) **Sedrial Day** It is the time taken by the Earth to complete one rotation about its own axis w.r.t. a distant star. [1]

(iii) **Solar Year** It is the time taken by the Earth to complete one revolution around the Sun in its orbit.

1 solar year = 365.25 average solar days

= 366.25 sedrial days [1]

(iv) **Tropical Year** The year in which there is total solar eclipse is called tropical year. [1]

43. How will you measure the diameter of a wire by screw gauge?

Sol. The following steps to be taken in order to find the diameter of a wire by screw gauge

(i) Calculate the least count of screw gauge, i.e.

$$\text{Least Count (LC)} = \frac{\text{Pitch}}{\text{Number of divisions on circular scale}}$$

(ii) Calculate zero error (if any).

(iii) Place the given wire in between stud and movable screw and turn the ratchet till it becomes free.

(iv) Note Main Scale Reading (MSR).

(v) Note Circular Scale Reading (CSR).

(vi) Use the formula of diameter = MSR + CSR × LC

(vii) The correct diameter will be obtained by correcting the zero error. The correct diameter is the final measurement of the diameter of wire (given). [4]

44. How is the time period of a simple pendulum affected in the following situations?

(i) Amplitude of a pendulum is increased.

(ii) The length of a pendulum is doubled.

(iii) The brass bob is replaced with an identical aluminium bob.

(iv) The value of g is made one-fourth.

Sol. The time period of a pendulum is given by the expression, $T = 2\pi\sqrt{\frac{l}{g}}$

(i) The time period of a pendulum does not depend upon its amplitude, hence no change. [1]

(ii) The time period of a pendulum is directly proportional to the square root of its length. When length is doubled, the time period will become $\sqrt{2}$ times. [1]

(iii) The time period of a pendulum does not depend upon its mass, hence no change. [1]

(iv) The time period of a pendulum is inversely proportional to the square root of g. When g is made one-fourth, the time period will be doubled. [1 × 4]

45. What is a simple pendulum? State the factors on which time period of a simple pendulum depends.

Sol. A simple pendulum is a device which contains a heavy point mass called bob, suspended from a rigid support by an inextensible and massless string. Its effective length is taken from the point of suspension to the centre of the bob. [2]

The period of oscillation (T) is

(i) directly proportional to the square root of its length l i.e. $T \propto \sqrt{l}$. [1]

(ii) inversely proportional to the square root of acceleration due to gravity (g)

i.e. $T \propto \frac{1}{\sqrt{g}}$

$$T = \text{constant}\sqrt{\frac{l}{g}}$$

Thus, $T = 2\pi\sqrt{\frac{l}{g}}$ [1]

46. (i) A girl is swinging in a swing in a sitting position. How will the period of the swing be affected, if she stands up?

(ii) The bob of an oscillating pendulum is made of ice. How will the time period change, if the ice starts melting?

(iii) Will a pendulum gain or lose time, when taken to a mountain?

(iv) Why does simple pendulum eventually stop?

Sol. (i) Case of a swinging girl can be considered as a simple pendulum. As, the girl stands up the centre of gravity of the bob is raised up, i.e. the effective length l of the pendulum decreases. Hence, the time period T decreases, i.e. the swing moves faster. [1]

(ii) The time period will not be affected as it is independent of the mass of the bob. [1]

(iii) When a pendulum is taken to the top of a mountain, g will decrease. Therefore, T will increase i.e., the pendulum will take more time to complete one oscillation. In other words, it will lose time. [1]

(iv) Due to frictional resistance between air and bob, the amplitude of oscillation of the pendulum gradually decreases and eventually the pendulum stops. [1]

Numerical Questions

47. How many kilometres are there is 1 AU and 1 light year?

Sol. $1\text{ AU} = 1.496 \times 10^{11}\text{ m}$

$1\text{ AU} = 1.496 \times 10^{11} \times 10^{-3}\text{ km}$

$= 1.496 \times 10^{8}\text{ km}$

$\therefore 1.496 \times 10^{8}$ km are in 1 AU.

$\because 1\text{ light year} = 9.46 \times 10^{15}\text{ m}$

$= 9.46 \times 10^{12}\text{ km}$ [1]

48. Convert 25 nm in metres and micron.

Sol. $1\text{ nm} = 10^{-9}\text{ m}$

$\therefore 25\text{ nm} = 25 \times 10^{-9}\text{ m}$

Now, $1\text{ micron} = 10^{-6}\text{ m}$

$\therefore 1\text{ nm} = 10^{-3}\text{ micron}$

$\therefore 25\text{ nm} = 25 \times 10^{-3}\text{ micron}$ [2]

49. (i) Express 0.01 mm in micron.

(ii) Calculate the number of seconds in 365 days.

Sol. (i) $1\text{ mm} = 10^{-3}\text{ m}$ and $1\text{ micron} = 10^{-6}\text{ m}$

$\Rightarrow 1\text{ mm} = 10^{3}\text{ micron}$

$\therefore 0.01\text{ mm} = 0.01 \times 10^{3}\text{ micron} = 10\text{ micron}$ [1]

(ii) Number of seconds in 365 days

$\Rightarrow 365 \times 24 \times 60 \times 60$

(days) (hours) (minutes) (seconds)

$= 365 \times 86400\text{ s}$

$= 31536000\text{ s}$

$= 3.15 \times 10^{7}\text{ s}$ [1]

50. The wavelength of light of a particular green colour is 5000 Å. Express it in

(i) nanometre (ii) micrometre
(iii) metre (iv) centimetre

Sol. (i) $5000 \text{ Å} = 5.0 \times 10^{2}$ nm (nanometre) [1/2]

(ii) $5000 \text{ Å} = 5.0 \times 10^{-1}$ μm (micrometre) [1/2]

(iii) $5000 \text{ Å} = 5.0 \times 10^{+3}$ Å
$= 5.0 \times 10^{3} \times 10^{-10}$m
$= 5.0 \times 10^{-7}$m [1/2]

(iv) $5000 \text{ Å} = 5.0 \times 10^{-7} \times 10^{+2}$ cm
$= 5.0 \times 10^{-5}$cm [1/2]

51. Write the following quantities in their respective SI unit.

(i) 3.2 ly (ii) 4 parsec
(iii) 2.3 Å (iv) 1.5×10^{-3} fm

Sol. (i) $1 \text{ ly} = 9.46 \times 10^{15}$m

$\therefore$ $3.2 \text{ ly} = 3.2 \times 9.46 \times 10^{15}\text{m} = 3.02 \times 10^{16}$ m [1]

(ii) $4 \text{ parsec} = 4 \times 3.084 \times 10^{16}$ m
$= 1.232 \times 10^{17}$ m [1]

(iii) $2.3 \text{ Å} = 2.3 \times 10^{-10}$m [1]

(iv) $1.5 \times 10^{-3} \text{ fm} = 1.5 \times 10^{-3} \times 10^{-15}$ m
$= 1.5 \times 10^{-18}$m [1]

52. (i) Distance of the nearest star (other than Sun) alpha centauri is 4 light year. Express it in km.

(ii) 1 gigagram makes how many metric tonne?

Sol. (i) As we know that, $1 \text{ ly} = 9.46 \times 10^{15}$ m

$\therefore$ $4 \text{ ly} = 4 \times 9.46 \times 10^{15}$m
$= 37.84 \times 10^{15}$ m

Distance $= 3.784 \times 10^{13}$ km [1]

(ii) $\dfrac{1 \text{ gigagram}}{1 \text{ metric tonne}} = \dfrac{10^9 \text{ g}}{10^3 \text{ kg}} = \dfrac{10^6 \text{ kg}}{10^3 \text{ kg}} = 10^3$

$\therefore$ 1 gigagram = 1000 metric tonne [1]

53. A new unit of length is chosen such that the speed of light in vacuum is unity. What is the distance between the Sun and the Earth in terms of the new unit, if light takes 8 min and 20 s to cover this distance?

Sol. The speed of light in vacuum, c
$= 1$ new unit of length s^{-1}

Time taken by light to reach the Earth,
$t = 8 \text{ min} + 20 \text{ s} = (8 \times 60 + 20) \text{ s} = 500 \text{ s}$

$\therefore$ Distance between the Sun and the Earth
= Speed of light × Time
$= c \times t = 1$ new unit of length $\text{s}^{-1} \times 500$ s
= 500 new units of length [2]

54. How many protons would make 1 g, if the mass of a proton is 1.67×10^{-27} kg?

Sol. Number of protons in 1 g $= \dfrac{\text{Total mass}}{\text{Mass of one proton}}$

$= \dfrac{1 \text{ g}}{1.67 \times 10^{-27} \text{ kg}}$ [1]

$= \dfrac{1 \text{ g}}{(1.67 \times 10^{-27} \times 10^{3}) \text{ g}}$

$= 5.99 \times 10^{23}$ [1]

55. The mass of Earth is 6×10^{24} kg. Calculate the number of atoms present in Earth, if average mass of an atom of Earth is 80 u.

Sol. Mass of 1 atom $= 80 \text{ u} = 80 \times 1.6 \times 10^{-27}$kg [1]

$\therefore$ Number of atoms $= \dfrac{6 \times 10^{24}}{80 \times 1.6 \times 10^{-27}}$

$= 4.68 \times 10^{49}$ atoms [1]

56. The diagram given below shows the two scales of a vernier calliper. Calculate (i) the least count of the vernier calliper and (ii) the reading shown in the diagram.

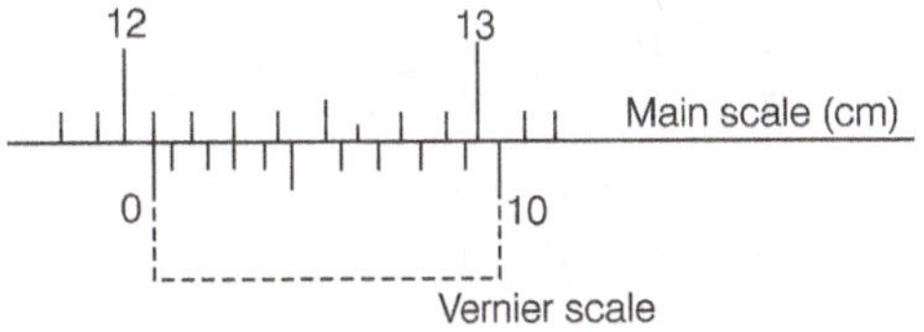

Sol. (i) There are 10 divisions in 1 cm on the main scale.

$\therefore$ The value of one main scale division, $x = \dfrac{1}{10}$ cm
$= 0.1$ cm

The number of divisions on vernier scale, $n = 10$

$\therefore$ The least count of vernier calliper
$= \dfrac{x}{n} = \dfrac{0.1}{10} = 0.01$ cm [2]

(ii) Main scale reading = 12.1 cm

Since, 3rd division of vernier scale coincides with the main scale division, so $p = 3$.

$\therefore$ Vernier scale reading $= 3 \times 0.01 = 0.03$ cm

Total reading = Main scale reading + Vernier scale reading
$= 12.1 + 0.03 = 12.13$ cm [2]

57. The pitch of a screw gauge is 2 mm and there are 200 divisions on the circular head. While measuring the diameter of a wire, the main scale reads 3 mm and the 55th division is in line with the base line. Calculate the diameter of the wire. Assuming that, the screw gauge is free from zero error.

Sol. Given, pitch = 2 mm, number of divisions on circular head = 200, main scale reading = 3 mm, number of divisions of circular head in line with base line is 55, so CSR = 55. [1]

Least count $= \dfrac{\text{Pitch}}{\text{Number of divisions on circular head}}$

$= \dfrac{2}{200} = 0.01$ mm

Diameter of wire = MSR + CSR × LC
$= 3 + 55 \times 0.01 = 3.55$ mm [1]

58. Find the time period of a simple pendulum of length 90 cm at a place, where $g = 10\ ms^{-2}$. (Take, $\pi = 3.142$)

Sol. Given, $l = 90$ cm $= 0.9$ m, $g = 10\ ms^{-2}$, $T = ?$

We know that,

$$T = 2\pi\sqrt{\frac{l}{g}} = 2 \times 3.142\sqrt{\frac{0.9}{10}}$$ [1]

$$\Rightarrow \quad T = 1.88 \simeq 1.9 \text{ s (approx)}$$ [1]

59. Time periods of two pendulums are in ratio of 1.28 : 0.32. Calculate the ratio of lengths.

Sol. Given, $T_1 = 1.28$, $T_2 = 0.32$, $l_1 = ?$, $l_2 = ?$

As, $$T = 2\pi\sqrt{\frac{l}{g}} \Rightarrow T \propto \sqrt{l}$$ [1]

$$\therefore \quad \frac{T_1}{T_2} = \sqrt{\frac{l_1}{l_2}} \text{ or } \frac{T_1^2}{T_2^2} = \frac{l_1}{l_2}$$

$$\therefore \quad \frac{l_1}{l_2} = \frac{(1.28)^2}{(0.32)^2} = \frac{16}{1}$$

$$\Rightarrow \quad l_1 : l_2 = 16 : 1$$ [1]

60. Find the length of a pendulum which completes 6 oscillations in 15 s. (Take, $g = 9.8\ ms^{-2}$, $\pi = 3.14$)

Sol. Given, $g = 9.8\ ms^{-2}$,

$$T = \frac{15 \text{ s}}{6} = 2.5 \text{ s}, l = ?$$ [1]

$$\therefore \quad T = 2\pi\sqrt{\frac{l}{g}}$$

$$\Rightarrow \quad l = \frac{gT^2}{4\pi^2} = \frac{(9.8\ ms^{-2}) \times (2.5\ s)^2}{4 \times (3.14)^2} = 1.55 \text{ m}$$ [1]

61. Length of second's pendulum is 100 cm. Find the length of another pendulum whose time period is 2.4 s.

Sol. As, $$T = 2\pi\sqrt{\frac{l}{g}} \Rightarrow T^2 = 4\pi^2\frac{l}{g}$$

Let T_1 = Time period of second's pendulum
and T_2 = Time period of another pendulum.

$$\Rightarrow T^2 \propto l$$ [1]

$$\therefore \quad \frac{T_1^2}{T_2^2} = \frac{l_1}{l_2} \Rightarrow \frac{2^2}{(2.4)^2} = \frac{100}{l_2}$$

$$\Rightarrow \quad l_2 = \frac{2.4^2}{2^2} \times 100 \Rightarrow l_2 = \frac{5.76}{4} \times 100 = 144 \text{ cm}$$ [1]

Section II

Structured Questions

62. (a) (i) Why lunar calender is short nearly by 10 days from Gregorian calender?
(ii) What is a leap year? [3]
(b) Write the rules for writing SI units. [3]
(c) Write four advantages of SI over other systems of units. [4]

Sol. (a) (i) In Hindu (Vikaram and Shak) and Muslim (Hizri) calenders, one lunar month is the time of one lunar cycle which is nearly 29.5 days. The period of 12 lunar months is 354.37 days. Thus, one year of these lunar calendars is short nearly by 10 days of Gregorian calender.

(ii) A leap year is the year in which the month of February is of 29 days, i.e.

1 leap year = 366 days [3]

(b) (i) Small letters are used for symbol of units.

(ii) The first letter of a symbol is capital only, when the unit is named after a scientist.

(iii) The full name of a unit always begins with a small letter even if it has been named after a scientist. [3]

(c) Advantages of SI over other systems of units are given below

(i) **SI is a Coherent System of Units** All derived units can be determined by simple multiplication or division of fundamental units by some constant, without introducing any numerical factor. [1]

(ii) **SI is a Rational System of Units** It uses only one unit for a given physical quantity. e.g., All forms of energy are measured in joule. On the other hand in MKS system, the electric energy is measured in watt hour, mechanical energy in joule and heat energy in calorie. [1]

(iii) **SI is a Metric System** The multiples and sub-multiples of SI units can be expressed as powers of ten.

i.e. $a \times 10^{\pm b}$ [1]

(iv) **SI is an Absolute System of Units** It does not use gravitational units. The use of g is not required. [1]

63. (a) (i) What is meant by Least Count (LC) of a measuring device?
(ii) What is the least count of vernier calliper?
(iii) What is vernier constant? [3]
(b) A screw gauge may be considered as the advancement of vernier calliper, explain. [3]
(c) (i) What do you mean by zero error of a vernier calliper ?
(ii) How do you show by a labelled diagram, the positions of the main scale and the vernier scale in case of two types of zero error? [4]

Sol. (a) (i) The least count of a measuring device is the smallest value of physical quantity which can be measured accurately by the instrument. [1]

(ii) Least count of vernier calliper,

$$LC = 1 \text{ MSD} - 1 \text{ VSD}$$
$$= 1 \text{ MSD} - \frac{9}{10} \text{ MSD}$$
$$LC = \frac{1}{10} \text{ MSD}$$

Usually, MSD = 0.1 cm

$$\therefore \quad LC = 0.01 \text{ cm}$$ [1]

(iii) Vernier constant is the least count of vernier calliper. [1]

(b) A screw gauge is an instrument used for measuring very small lengths such as diameters of wires which cannot be accurately measured by vernier calliper. It is because the least count of screw gauge is smaller than the least count of a vernier calliper. [3]

(c) (i) If zero of vernier scale does not coincide with the zero of main scale, the number of divisions between these two zeros is called zero error. [1]

(ii) Zero error is of two types

1. **Positive Zero Error** The zero error is said to be positive, if on contacting both the jaws together, the zero mark of the vernier is on the right side of the zero mark of the main scale.

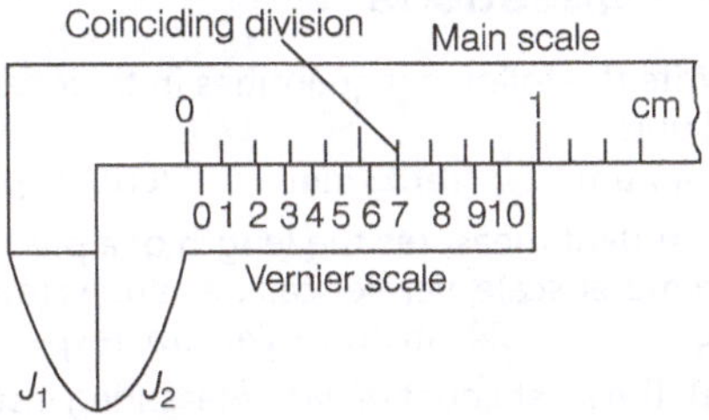

[1½]

2. **Negative Zero Error** The zero error is said to be negative, if on contacting both the jaws together, the zero mark of the vernier is on the left side of the zero of the main scale.

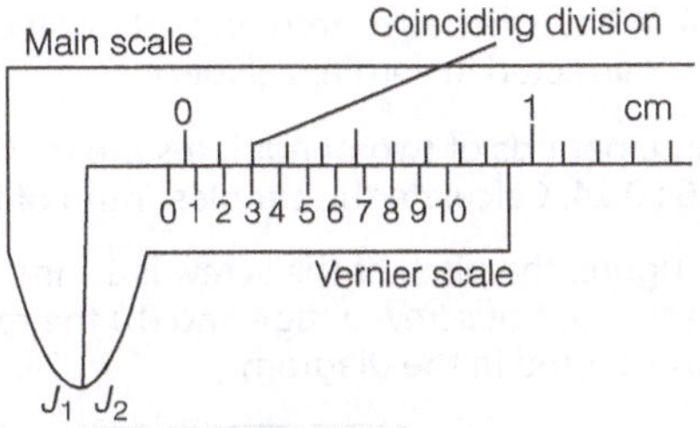

[1½]

64. (a) Answer the following

(i) Will the time period of pendulum increase or decrease, when taken to a mountain?

(ii) The bob of a simple pendulum is made of ice. How will the time period be effected, if the ice starts melting? [3]

(b) (i) What do you mean by effective length of a simple pendulum?

(ii) Draw graphs of l *versus* T^2 and l *versus* T for a simple pendulum. [3]

(c) Define the following terms related to simple pendulum. [4]

(i) Oscillation
(ii) Amplitude
(iii) Time period
(iv) Frequency

Sol. (a) (i) At the top of mountain, the value of g decreases. As $T \propto \frac{1}{\sqrt{g}}$. Thus, the time period increases, when g is decreased. [1½]

(ii) The time period of the pendulum is independent of the mass of the bob. So, the time period is unaffected, if ice melts. [1½]

(b) (i) Effective length of a simple pendulum is the distance between the point of suspension and the centre of the bob shown in diagram. [1]

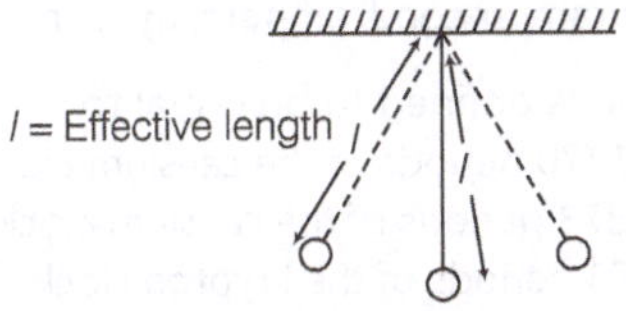

(ii) The graphical representation of l *versus* T^2 and l *versus* T are shown below

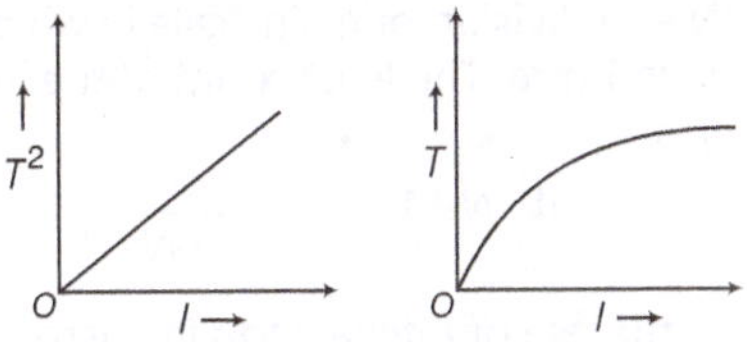

[2]

(c) (i) When the bob moves from its mean position to the extreme right, then from the extreme right to extreme left and finally back to the mean position, it completes one **oscillation.** [1]

(ii) **Amplitude** is the maximum displacement of the bob from its mean position on either side. [1]

(iii) **Period of oscillation** (or the **time period**) is the time taken to complete one oscillation. It is denoted by T and its SI unit is second. [1]

(iv) **Frequency** of oscillation of a simple pendulum is the number of oscillations made in one second. It is denoted by ν or n or f. Its SI unit is per second or hertz (Hz). [1]

Chapter Assessment

1 Mark Questions

1. In SI system, the fundamental units are
   (a) metre, kilogram, second, ampere, kelvin, mole and candela
   (b) metre, kilogram, second, coulomb, kelvin, mole and candela
   (c) metre, newton, second, ampere, kelvin, mole and candela
   (d) metre, gram, second, ampere, dyne, mole and candela

2. One second is defined to be equal to
   (a) 9192631770 periods of the caesium clock
   (b) 165076373 periods of the caesium clock
   (c) 65218963 periods of the krypton clock
   (d) 165076373 periods of the krypton clock

3. In vernier calliper N division of vernier scale coincide with $(N-1)$ division of main scale in which length of a division is 1 mm. The least count of the instrument (in cm) is
   (a) N (b) $N-1$ (c) $\frac{1}{10N}$ (d) $\frac{1}{N}-1$

4. What is the use of ratchet stop in micrometer?
   (a) Prevent motion of spindle
   (b) Provide measuring surface
   (c) Forms measuring tip
   (d) Maintain uniform measuring pressure

5. Choose the correct statement about simple pendulum.
   (a) The time period of pendulum clock, when taken from earth to artificial satellite, becomes zero.
   (b) In summer, the time period of pendulum is more than the time period of pendulum in winter.
   (c) If the acceleration due to gravity is reduced to one-fourth, the time period of pendulum will become half.
   (d) The effective length of second's pendulum is 2 m.

2 Marks Questions

6. Define fundamental units of (i) length and (ii) time.

7. Name the three convenient units used to measure very small distance and relate it to its SI unit.

8. Which part of vernier calliper is used to measure
   (i) external diameter?
   (ii) internal diameter?
   (iii) length of cylinder?

9. Name the instrument you would use to measure the following.
   (i) Thickness of a paper
   (ii) Diameter of a sphere

10. Define the following terms.
    (i) Vernier scale
    (ii) Least count related to vernier calliper

Structured Questions

11. (i) Write the following quantities in their respective SI unit.
    (a) 4.7 μm (b) 3.3 mm (c) 0.001 cm **[3]**
    (ii) A student measures the length of a piece of pencil by meter scale, vernier calliper, and screw gauge to be 1.2 cm, 1.24 cm and 1.243 cm, respectively. State
    (a) the least count of each measuring instrument and **[3]**
    (b) the accuracy in each measurement.
    (iii) (a) Calculate the length of second's pendulum at a place, where $g = 9.8\ m/s^2$.
    (b) What is negative zero error? How it can be corrected in vernier calliper? **[4]**

12. (i) Time periods of two pendulums are in the ratio of 5.6 : 0.14. Calculate the simplest ratio of lengths. **[3]**
    (ii) In figure, the pitch of the screw is 1 mm. Find (a) the least count of screw gauge and (b) the reading represented in the diagram.

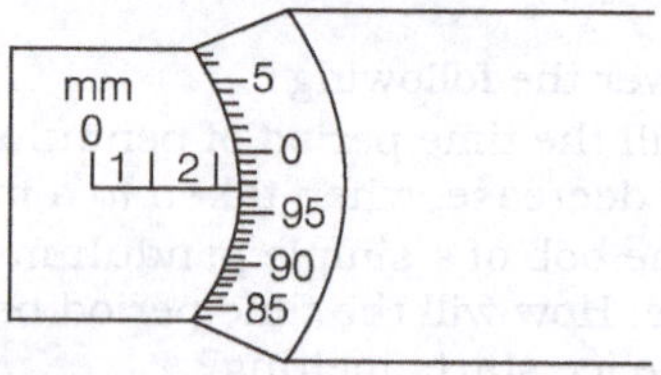

[3]

    (iii) Define the following terms related to simple pendulum. **[4]**
    (a) Second's pendulum (b) Amplitude
    (c) Effective length (d) Time period

For Solutions Scan the Code

Olympiad Section*

Brain Teasing Questions of Olympiad Pattern

1 Which of the following sets can enter into the list of fundamental quantities in any system of units?

(a) Length, mass and velocity
(b) Length, time and velocity
(c) Mass, time and velocity
(d) Length, time and mass

2 A physical quantity is measured and the result is expressed as nu, where u is the unit used and n is the numerical value. If the result is expressed in various units, then

(a) $n \propto u$ (b) $n \propto u^2$ (c) $n \propto \sqrt{u}$ (d) $n \propto \frac{1}{u}$

3 The distance of a planet from the Earth is 11 light minutes. What is the distance (in km)?

(a) 1.67×10^9 (b) 1.98×10^8
(c) 1.36×10^8 (d) 2.16×10^9

4 Why length, mass and time are chosen as base quantities in mechanics?

(a) There is nothing simpler to length, mass and time
(b) All other quantities in mechanics can be expressed in terms of length, mass and time
(c) Length, mass and time cannot be derived from another
(d) All of the above

5 A bus travels 110 km/h on an open highway. What is its speed in standard SI unit?

(a) 3.06 m/s (b) 30.6 m/s
(c) 3.06 km/s (d) 30.6 m/h

6 The mass of the Earth is 5.98×10^{24} kg. If average mass of the atoms of Earth is 40 u, then number of atoms in the Earth is

(a) 9×10^{49} (b) 10×10^{50} (c) 18×10^{50} (d) 18×10^{94}

7 A vernier calliper has 1 mm marks on the main scale. It has 20 equal divisions on the vernier scale which match with 16 main scale divisions. For this vernier calliper, the least count is

(a) 0.02 mm (b) 0.05 mm (c) 0.1 mm (d) 0.2 mm

8 The circular scale of a screw gauge has 50 divisions and pitch of 0.5 mm. Find the diameter of sphere. (Main scale reading is 2 mm)

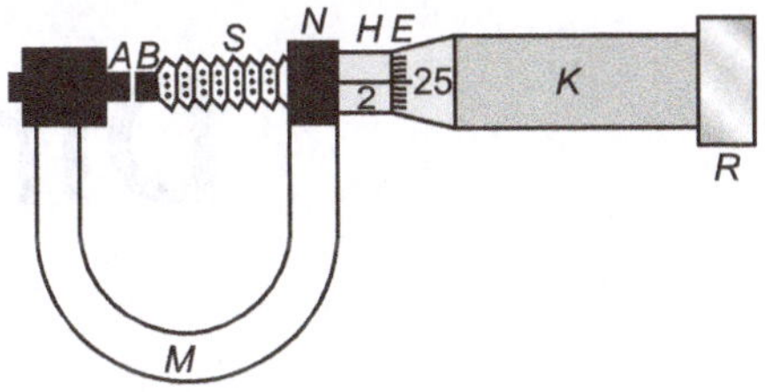

(a) 1.2 mm (b) 1.25 mm
(c) 2.20 mm (d) 2.25 mm

9 Which of the following phenomena can be used as a measure of time?

(a) Oscillation of a pendulum
(b) Rotation of Earth around its axis
(c) Both (a) and (b)
(d) Neither (a) nor (b)

10 The length of a pendulum is decreased by 10%. What will be the change in its frequency?

(a) 1.3% (b) 3.2% (c) 5.1% (d) 6.2%

11 Units of length, velocity and force in a certain system of units are double of those in SI (i.e. unit length in this system is 2 m and so on for force and velocity). Read and following statements.

(i) Unit of mass is unchanged.
(ii) Unit of time is unchanged.
(iii) Unit of linear momentum is doubled.
(iv) Unit of energy is doubled.

Among the above statements ________

(a) All four are correct.
(b) Only (i), (ii) and (iii) are correct.
(c) Ony (i) and (ii) are correct.
(d) Only (ii) and (iii) are correct.

Answers

1. (d) **2.** (d) **3.** (b) **4.** (d) **5.** (b) **6.** (a) **7.** (d) **8.** (d) **9.** (c) **10.** (c) **11.** (b)

*These questions may or may not be asked in the examination, have been given just for additional practice required for olympiads Scholarship Exams etc. For detailed explanations refer Page No. 212.

CHAPTER 02

Motion in One Dimension

SYLLABUS

Scalar and vector quantities • distance • speed • velocity • acceleration; graphs of distance-time and speed-time; equations of uniformly accelerated motion with derivations.

In everyday life, we observe several types of motions like vehicles moving on a road, flying birds, movement of needles of a watch, movement of blades of a fan, circulation of blood through veins and arteries, etc.

If a body changes its position with respect to time and its surroundings, then the body is said to be in **motion.** In the same way, if the position of an object does not change with time and w.r.t. its surroundings, then it is said to be in **rest**. Motion and rest are always relative to each other.

When the motion of a body is along a straight line, then it is said to be in **one-dimensional motion.** e.g., the motion of a train on a straight track, a stone falling vertically downwards, etc. One-dimensional motion is also known as **rectilinear** or **translatory motion.**

Scalar and Vector Quantities

The physical quantities which can be expressed only by their magnitude are called scalar quantities. e.g., mass, time, distance, speed, etc.

The physical quantities which require magnitude as well as direction for their representation are called vector quantities. e.g., weight, displacement, velocity, etc.

Various Terms Related to Motion

Various terms related to motion are discussed as follows

Position

The location of an object with respect to a particular point, is known as the position of the object. The particular point about which the position of the object is defined, is called **reference point** or **origin.**

Distance

The distance travelled by a body is the actual length of the path covered by it, irrespective of the direction in which the body travels. It is a **scalar quantity**. Its SI unit is **metre** (m).

e.g., Consider the motion of an object moving along a straight path. The object starts its journey from O which is treated as its reference point as shown in the figure below.

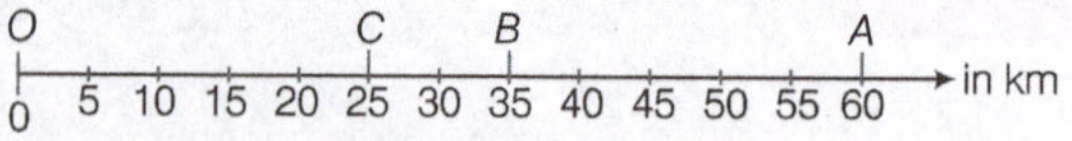

Positions of an object on a straight line path

Let A, B and C represent the positions of the object at different instants. At first, the object moves through C to B and finally reaches A. Then, it moves back along the same path and reaches C through B.

The total distance covered by the object is $OA + AC$,

i.e., 60 km + 35 km = 95 km

and this is also the total path length covered by the object.

Displacement

The displacement of an object is the change in the position of the object when it moves from a given position to another position along shortest path.

It gives the shortest path measured in the direction from the initial position to the final position of the object. It is a **vector quantity**. Its SI unit is **metre** (m).

e.g., Suppose a bus is moving in a straight path as shown in the figure below. Let O be the starting position of the bus and it reaches position A and covers a distance of 30 km.

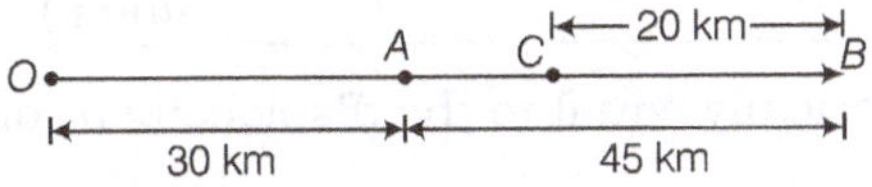

Moving forward, bus reaches the position B and travels 45 km. Now, the bus returns towards A and reaches position C. The distance covered between B and C is 20 km.

From the figure, $OA = 30$ km, $OB = 30 + 45 = 75$ km and $BC = 20$ km .

$\therefore$ The displacement of the bus

= Final position − Initial position

i.e. $OC = OB - BC = 75 - 20 = 55$ km

As displacement is vector quantity, therefore

$OC = 55$ km.

Distance *versus* Displacement

(i) Distance is a path dependent quantity while displacement is a path independent quantity.

(ii) Displacement of a moving object can never be greater than the distance travelled by it.

$\therefore$ Displacement $\leq$ Distance

$\Rightarrow \dfrac{\text{Displacement}}{\text{Distance}} \leq 1$

i.e. Ratio of displacement and distance is always less than or equal to 1.

(iii) If a body moves along a straight line (only in one direction), then distance and displacement will be equal.

(iv) The magnitude of the displacement for a course of motion may be zero but the corresponding distance covered is not zero.

(v) Displacement of the object can be positive, negative or zero while distance covered by that object is always positive.

Example 1. A Jogger jogs along one length and one breadth of a rectangular park. If the dimensions of park are 150 m × 120 m, then find the distance travelled and displacement of the Jogger.

Sol. According to the question,

Length, $l = 150$ m, Breadth, $b = 120$ m

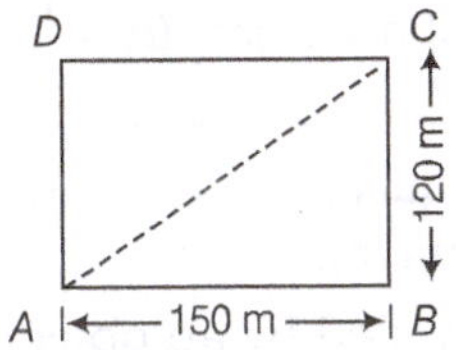

Distance travelled, s = ?

Displacement of the Jogger = ?

Suppose, the Jogger starts from point A and after covering one length and one breadth reaches at point C.

Distance, s = length of the total path covered = $AB + BC$

$s = 150 + 120 = 270$ m

Displacement = Minimum distance between initial and final position

$= AC$

From Pythagoras theorem,

$$AC = \sqrt{(AB)^2 + (BC)^2}$$

i.e. Displacement $= \sqrt{(150)^2 + (120)^2} = 30\sqrt{41}$ m

Thus, the Jogger travels a distance of 270 m and his displacement is $30\sqrt{41}$ m.

Example 2. A body moves in a circular path of radius 20 cm. If it completes two and half revolutions along the circular path, then find distance and displacement of the body.

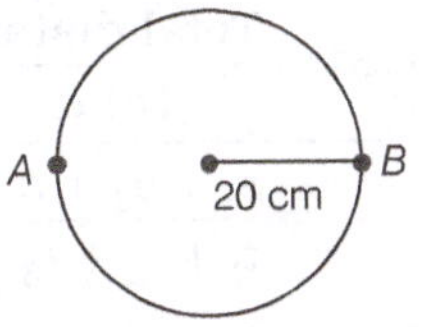

Sol. According to the question, body moves in a circular path of radius 20 cm. So, during one complete revolution the distance s moved by the body is equal to the circumference of the circular path, i.e. $2\pi r$.

where, r = radius of circular path.

So, for two and half revolutions, body covers two complete revolutions, i.e. $2 \times 2\pi r$ distance and half revolution, i.e. $\dfrac{2\pi r}{2} = \pi r$ distance.

Therefore, total distance covered by the body

$s = (2 \times 2\pi r) + \pi r = 5\pi r$

$= 5 \times 3.14 \times 20$ $(\because \pi = 3.14)$

$= 314$ cm

Now, as we know displacement d is the straight line distance between initial and final position of the body. So, after two and half revolutions, total displacement d of the body will be $2r$.

i.e. Displacement, $d = 2 \times 20 = 40$ cm.

Speed

The speed of an object is defined as the distance travelled by it per unit time.

$$\text{Speed of an object } (v) = \frac{\text{Distance}(s)}{\text{Time } (t)}$$

Speed is a **scalar quantity**. The SI unit of speed is **metre per second** (m/s).

The distance travelled by an object is either positive or zero, so the speed of that object may be positive or zero but never be negative.

The various types of speed are as given below

(i) **Uniform Speed** If a moving body covers equal distances in equal intervals of time throughout its motion, then the speed of the body is said to be uniform, i.e. constant speed.

e.g., Motion of a ball in a frictionless plane surface.

(ii) **Non-uniform (variable) Speed** If a moving body covers unequal distances in equal intervals of time, then the speed of the body is said to be non-uniform, or variable speed.

e.g., Motion of a car in a crowded street.

(iii) **Average Speed** It is defined as the ratio of the total distance travelled by a body to the total time taken. It is expressed as,

$$\text{Average speed} = \frac{\text{Total distance travelled}}{\text{Total time taken}}$$

$$= \frac{s_1 + s_2 + s_3 + \ldots}{t_1 + t_2 + t_3 + \ldots}$$

(iv) **Instantaneous Speed** The speed of an object at any particular instant of time or at a particular point of its path is called the instantaneous speed of the object.

The instantaneous speed is measured by speedometer.

Example 3. An object travels 14 m in 4 s and then another 16 m in 2 s. What is the average speed of the object?

Sol. According to question, first distance, $s_1 = 14$ m

second distance, $s_2 = 16$ m,

Time, $t_1 = 4$ s, $t_2 = 2$ s

$$\therefore \text{Average speed} = \frac{\text{Total distance}}{\text{Total time}} = \frac{s_1 + s_2}{t_1 + t_2}$$

$$= \frac{14 + 16}{4 + 2} = \frac{30}{6} = 5 \text{ m/s}$$

Therefore, the average speed of an object is 5 m/s.

Velocity

Velocity is the speed of an object moving in a definite direction. Thus, velocity of an object is defined as the displacement of the body per unit time.

It is expressed as,

$$\text{Velocity of an object } (v) = \frac{\text{Displacement } (d)}{\text{Time } (t)}$$

It is numerically equal to the displacement of a body in 1s.

Velocity is a **vector quantity**. The SI unit of velocity is **metre per second** (m/s).

Velocity of an object can be **positive, zero or negative.** Velocity of an object can be changed by changing the object's speed, direction of motion or both.

The various types of velocity are as given below

(i) **Uniform Velocity** If an object covers equal displacements in equal intervals of time without changing direction, then its velocity is known as uniform velocity, i.e. constant velocity.

e.g., Rain drops reaching on earth's surface.

(ii) **Non-uniform (variable) Velocity** If an object covers unequal displacements in equal intervals of time, then its velocity is known as non-uniform velocity, i.e. variable velocity. e.g., motion of a body in circular path.

When the body moves in a circular path with a uniform speed, it has a variable velocity because in a circular path, the direction of motion of the body continuously changes with time. Infact, its velocity changes at a uniform rate. At any instant, its velocity is along the tangent to the circular path at that point.

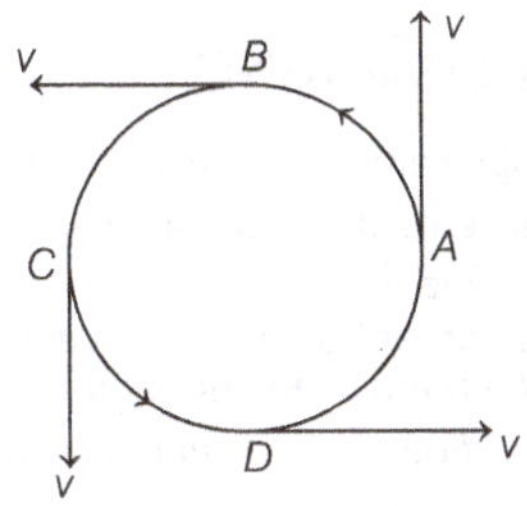

A body with a uniform speed but variable velocity.

(iii) **Average Velocity** It is defined as the ratio of total displacement of the object to the total time taken.

It is expressed as

$$v_{av} = \frac{\text{Total displacement}}{\text{Total time taken}}$$

If the velocity of an object changes at a uniform rate, then average velocity

$$(v_{av}) = \frac{\text{Initial velocity } (u) + \text{ Final velocity } (v)}{2}$$

(iv) **Instantaneous Velocity** The velocity of an object at a particular instant of time or at a particular point of its path is called its instantaneous velocity.

Note • If a body is moving in a straight line, then the magnitude of its speed and velocity will be equal.
• Average speed of an object can never be zero but the average velocity of a moving object can be zero.

Example 4. Rajeev went from Delhi to Chandigarh on his motorbike. The odometer of that read 4200 km at the start of trip and 4460 km at the end of his trip. If Rajeev took 4 h 20 min to complete his trip to Delhi, then find the average speed and average velocity in km/h as well as in m/s.

Sol. As we know that, the total distance covered,

s = final reading − initial reading of odometer

$= (4460 - 4200)$ km $= 260$ km

Total time taken, $t = 4\text{ h } 20\text{ min} = 4\text{h} + \frac{20}{60}\text{h} = \frac{13}{3}\text{h}$

$$\therefore \text{ Average speed } = \frac{\text{Total distance covered } (s)}{\text{Total time taken } (t)}$$

$$= \frac{260\text{ km}}{\frac{13}{3}\text{h}} = 60\text{ km/h} = \frac{60 \times 5}{18} = 16.67\text{ m/s}$$

$$\therefore \text{ Average velocity} = \frac{\text{Total displacement } (d)}{\text{Total time taken } (t)}$$

$$= \frac{0}{\frac{13}{3}} = 0\text{ m/s or } 0\text{ km/h}$$

Average speed of Rajeev is 16.67 m/s and average velocity is 0 m/s.

Acceleration

The change in velocity of the object during any time interval is not zero and is expressed by a physical quantity known as acceleration. Acceleration is defined as the rate of change of velocity with respect to time.

Mathematically, it is expressed as,

$$\text{Acceleration } (a) = \frac{\text{Change in velocity}(\Delta v)}{\text{Change in time}(\Delta t)}$$

If in a given time interval t, the velocity of a body changes from u to v, then acceleration a is expressed as,

$$a = \frac{\text{Final velocity } (v) - \text{ Initial velocity } (u)}{\text{Time interval } (t)}$$

$$\Rightarrow \quad a = \frac{v - u}{t}$$

or $\quad v = u + at$

This kind of motion is known as **accelerated motion.** The SI unit of acceleration is **meter per second square** (m/s^2). It is a **vector quantity**.

The acceleration is taken to be **positive** when velocity of a body increases with time and **negative** when the velocity of the body decreases with time. Negative acceleration is also called as **deceleration** or **retardation**. The acceleration is **zero** when the body is either at rest or moves with constant velocity.

The various types of acceleration are as given below

(i) **Uniform Acceleration** If an object travels in a straight line and its velocity increases or decreases by equal amounts in equal intervals of time, then the object is said to be in a uniform acceleration.

e.g.,

(a) The motion of a freely falling body.

(b) The motion of a ball rolling down on an inclined plane.

(ii) **Non-uniform Acceleration** If the velocity of an object increases or decreases by unequal amounts in equal intervals of time, then the object is said to be in a non-uniform acceleration.

e.g.

(a) The movement of a car on a crowded city road.

(b) The motion of the train leaving or entering the platform.

Example 5. Starting from a stationary position, a car attains a velocity of 6 m/s in 30 s. Then, the driver of the car applies a brake such that the velocity of the car comes down to 4 m/s in the next 5 s. Calculate the acceleration of the car in both the cases.

Sol. **Case I** Initial velocity of the car, $u = 0$

($\because$ it starts from stationary position)

Final velocity, $v = 6$ m/s, time taken, $t = 30$ s

$$\therefore \text{ Acceleration, } a = \frac{v-u}{t}$$

$$= \frac{6-0}{30} = 0.2 \text{ m/s}^2$$

Case II Initial velocity, $u = 6$ m/s

Final velocity, $v = 4$ m/s, time taken, $t = 5$ s

$$\therefore \quad \text{Acceleration} = \frac{\text{Change in velocity}}{\text{Time}}$$

$$= \frac{\text{Final velocity} - \text{Initial velocity}}{\text{Time}}$$

$$= \frac{v-u}{t}$$

$$\Rightarrow \quad a = \frac{4-6}{5}$$

$$= -0.4 \text{ m/s}^2$$

Thus, the acceleration in the two cases are 0.2 m/s^2 and – 0.4 m/s^2.

Uniform and Non-uniform Motion

Motion can be categorised as uniform and non-uniform motion which are given below

Uniform Motion

A body is said to have a uniform motion, if it travels equal distances in equal intervals of time, no matter how small these intervals may be. The distance travelled by an object in uniform motion increases linearly.

e.g., A car moving along a straight line path such that, if it covers equal distances in equal intervals of time, it is said to be in uniform motion.

Non-uniform Motion

A body is said to have a non-uniform motion, if it travels unequal distances in equal intervals of time, then no matter how small these intervals may be.

e.g., A car moving through a crowded market has non-uniform motion.

Check Your LEARNING...

1 State whether displacement is a scalar or a vector quantity.

2 What is the displacement of a satellite when it makes a complete round along its orbit?

3 Give one example of motion in which velocity of object changes but speed remains unchanged.

4 After studying the motion of a ball rolling on a straight line as shown in figure

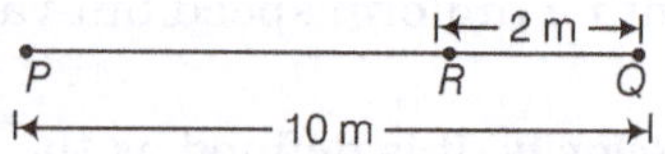

Find its distance and displacement covered when it rolls from P to Q and then to R (i.e., P to Q to R).

Ans. 12 m, 8 m

5 Which of the two can be zero under certain conditions : average speed of a moving body or average velocity of a moving body?

6 A car is moving on a road in crowded market. Name the nature of motion of car.

Graphical Representation of Motion

In order to describe the motion of an object, we can use line graphs. For graphical description of a motion, it is convenient to take time along X-axis, whereas distance, speed or velocity are taken along Y-axis.

There are mainly two types of graph which are used to represent motion of an object.

1. Distance-Time Graph

The change in the position of an object with respect to time can be represented on the distance-time graph adopting a convenient scale of choice.

To draw distance-time graph, time is plotted along X-axis and distance of the body is plotted along Y-axis. In this case, **the slope of the distance-time graph is equal to the speed of the object.**

Distance-time graphs under various conditions are explained below

Case I When the object is at rest

If the position of the object does not change with time, then the object is said to be stationary.

The distance-time graph for a stationary object is a straight line parallel to the time axis which is shown below

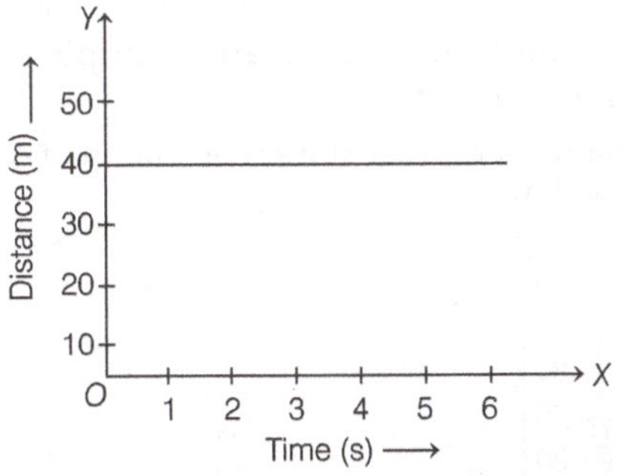

Case II When the object is moving with uniform speed or velocity If the object is moving with uniform speed, then it travels equal distance in equal interval of time. For uniform speed, a graph of distance travelled against time is a straight line as shown in the figure given below

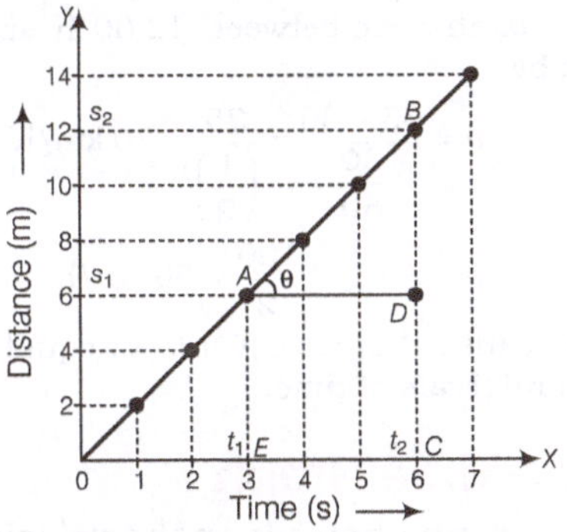

Distance-time graph for uniform motion

$$\text{Now, slope} = \tan\theta = \frac{BD}{AD} = \frac{s_2 - s_1}{t_2 - t_1}$$

Interpretation From the graph, it is clear that in equal interval of time 2 s, the object covers equal distance 4 m, so the motion is uniform and graph is a straight line.

Case III When the object is moving with uniform acceleration If the object is moving with uniform acceleration, i.e. with variable velocity, then it covers unequal distances in equal interval to time (non-uniform motion), it means graph is not a straight line but it is a curve.

This non-uniform motion due to uniform acceleration is of two types such as

(a) **When the speed of the body increases with passage of time,** then the distance-time graph will be a curve with positive slope as shown below

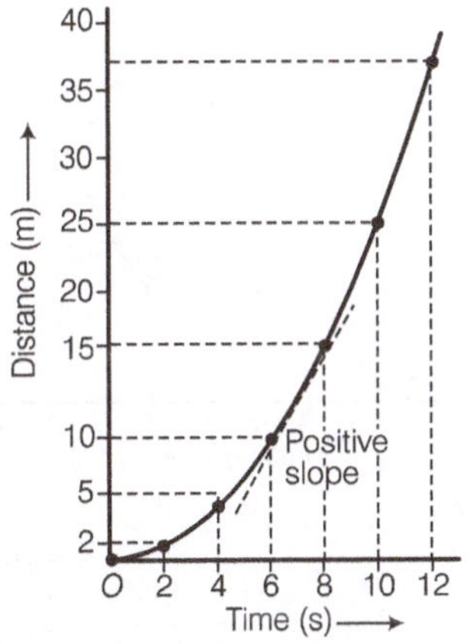

Interpretation From the graph, it is clear that in equal intervals of time of 2 s, the body is covering unequal distances and this distance goes on increasing. That means, with the passage of time, the body is covering more and more distance in equal time, i.e., the speed of the body is increasing. This graph represents uniform acceleration of the body.

(b) **When the speed of the body decreases with passage of time,** then the distance-time graph will be a curve with negative slope as shown below

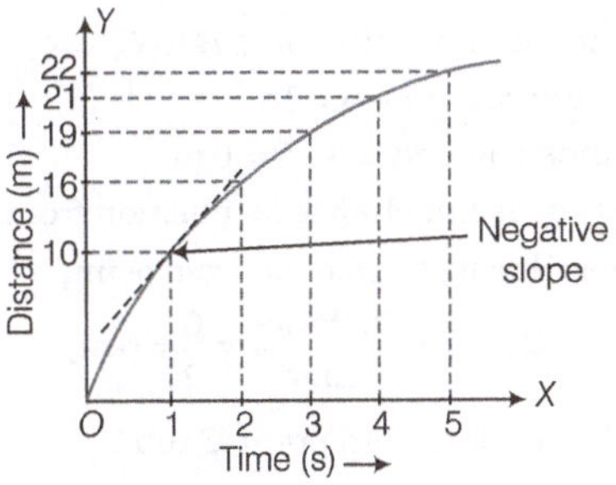

Interpretation From the graph, it is clear that in equal intervals of time of one second, the body is covering unequal distances and this distance goes on decreasing. That means, with the passage of time, the body is covering lesser and lesser distance in equal time, i.e. the speed of the body is decreasing. This graph represents uniform retardation of the body.

Note If the graph is drawn between distance or displacement and time, the slope of graph gives velocity of the object.

Example 6. The graph below shows the positions of a body at different times. Calculate the speed of the body as it moves from (i) A to B, (ii) B to C and (iii) C to D.

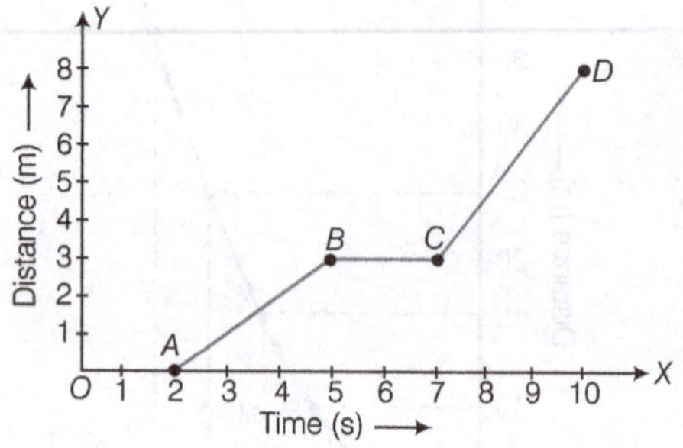

Sol.

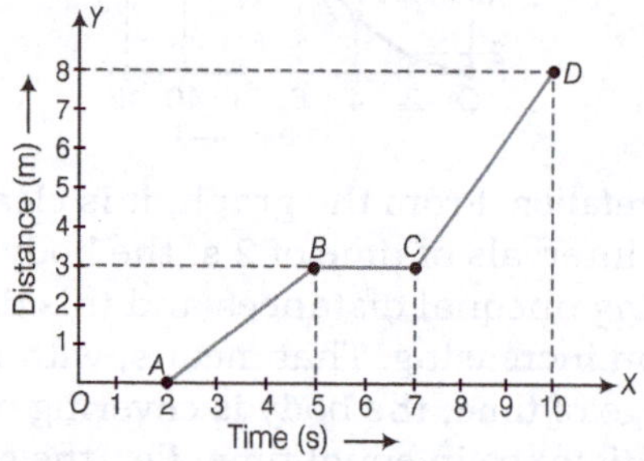

(i) For the motion from point A to B,

Time taken, $t = 5 - 2 = 3$ s

Distance covered $= 3 - 0 = 3$ m

$\therefore$ Speed during the motion from point,

$$A \text{ to } B = \frac{\text{Distance}}{\text{Time}} = \frac{3}{3} = 1 \text{ m/s}$$

(ii) For the motion from point B to C,

Time taken, $t = 7 - 5 = 2$ s

Distance covered $= 3 - 3 = 0$ m

($\because$ body does not change its position from point B to C)

$\therefore$ Speed during the motion from point,

$$B \text{ to } C = \frac{\text{Distance}}{\text{Time}} = \frac{0}{2} = 0 \text{ m/s}$$

(iii) For the motion from point C to D,

Time taken, $t = 10 - 7 = 3$ s

Distance covered $= 8 - 3 = 5$ m

$\therefore$ Speed during the motion from point,

$$C \text{ to } D = \frac{\text{Distance}}{\text{Time}} = \frac{5}{3} \text{ m/s}$$

Example 7. The following table gives the data about motion of a car

Time (h)	11:00	11:30	12:00	12:30	1:00
Distance (km)	0	20	30	65	100

Plot the graph and

(i) find the speed of the car between 12:00h and 12:30 h.

(ii) what is the average speed of the car?

(iii) Is the motion of car, an example of uniform motion? Justify.

Sol. The graphical representation of motion of car is shown below

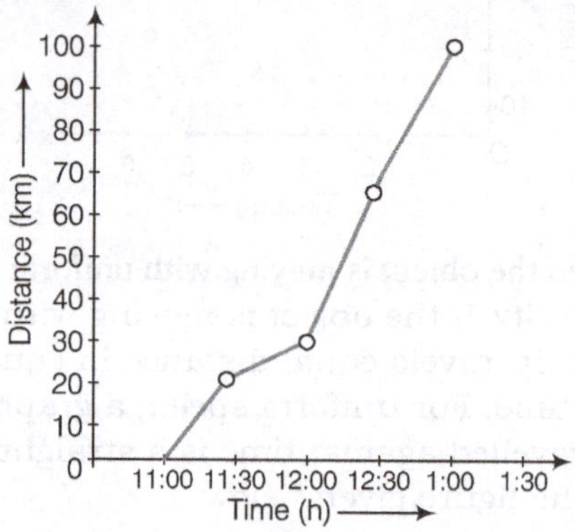

(i) Speed of the car between 12:00 h and 12:30 h is given by

$$v = \frac{65 - 30}{\frac{30}{60}} = \frac{35}{\left(\frac{1}{2}\right)} = 70 \text{ km/h}$$

(ii) Average speed, $v_{av} = \frac{100}{2} = 50$ km/h

(iii) No, because the car covered unequal distances in equal intervals of time.

2. Velocity-Time Graph

Velocity-time graph shows how the velocity of a body changes with the passage of time. To draw velocity-time graph, velocity of the body is plotted along Y-axis and the time taken by the body is plotted along X-axis.

The area under the velocity-time graph gives the distance or magnitude of displacement and the slope of velocity-time graph gives acceleration of the body.

Velocity-time graphs under various conditions are explained as below

Case I When a body is moving with constant velocity

When a body moves with constant velocity, i.e. its motion is uniform, then its velocity does not change with time.

The graph will be a straight line parallel to the time axis as shown below.

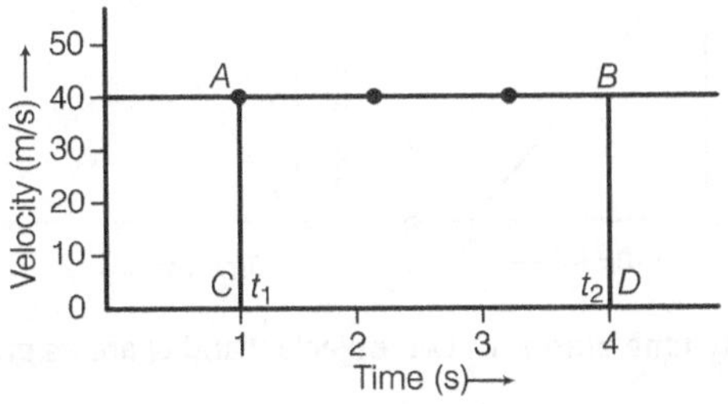

Interpretation From the graph, it is clear that with the passage of time, there is no change in the velocity, the body is moving with constant velocity.

***Case* II When a body is moving with uniform acceleration**

In uniform accelerated motion, the velocity changes by equal amount in equal interval of time. So, the velocity-time graph is a straight line.

(a) For uniform acceleration, velocity-time graph is shown below

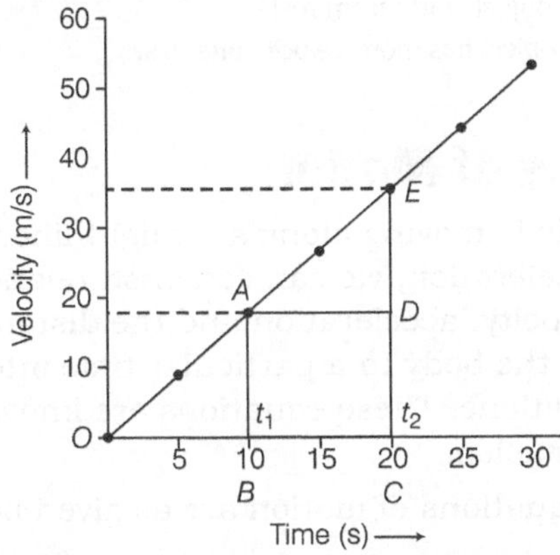

(b) For uniform retardation, the velocity-time graph is shown below

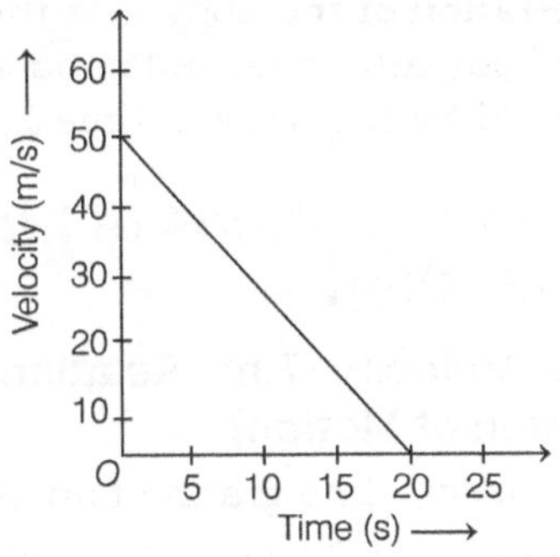

Interpretation The nature of the graph shows that velocity changes by equal amounts in equal intervals of time.

In equal interval of time 10 s, for first figure the change in velocity is 18 m/s, which remains same, that means the acceleration of the body is constant. Thus, for all uniformly accelerated motion, the velocity-time graph is a straight line.

***Case* III When a body is moving in non-uniform accelerated motion**

Velocity-time graph for non-uniform accelerated motion is given below

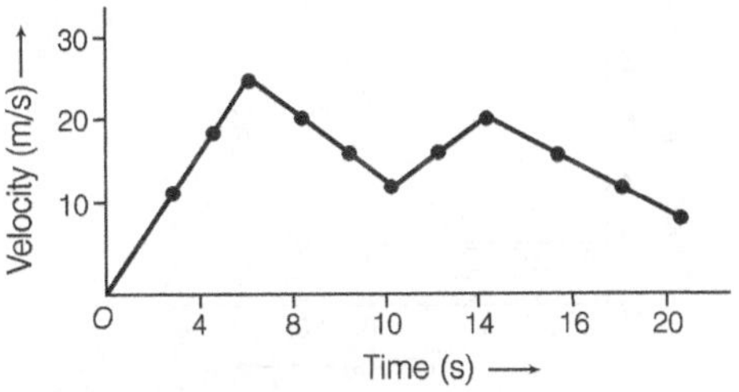

It shows that the variation of velocity of a body (or object) varies non-uniformly with time.

Example 8. The velocity-time graph of an ascending passengers, lift is shown in figure below. What is the acceleration of the lift

(i) during the first two seconds?

(ii) between 2nd and 10th second?

(iii) during the last two seconds?

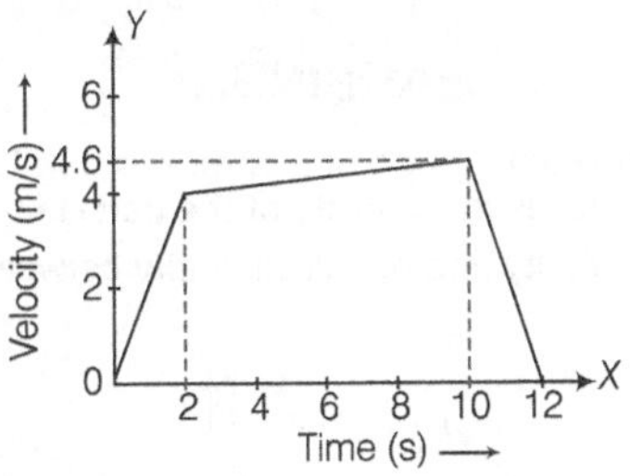

Sol. (i) ***Case* I**

$\Delta v = 4 - 0 = 4$ m/s, $\Delta t = 2 - 0 = 2$ s, $a_1 = ?$

$\therefore a_1 = \frac{\Delta v}{\Delta t} = \frac{4}{2} = 2 \text{ m/s}^2$

(ii) ***Case* II**

$\Delta v = 4.6 - 4 = 0.6$ m/s, $\Delta t = 10 - 2 = 8$ s, $a_2 = ?$

$\therefore \quad a_2 = \frac{\Delta v}{\Delta t} = \frac{0.6}{8} = 0.075 \text{ m/s}^2$

(iii) ***Case* III**

$\Delta v = 0 - 4.6 = -4.6$ m/s,

$\Delta t = 12 - 10 = 2$ s, $a_3 = ?$

$\therefore \quad a_3 = \frac{\Delta v}{\Delta t} = \frac{-4.6}{2} = -2.3 \text{ m/s}^2$

Negative sign shows retardation.

Example 9. A body moves with a velocity of 2 m/s for 5 s, then its velocity increases uniformly to 10 m/s in next 5 s. Thereafter, its velocity begins to decrease at a uniform rate until it comes to rest after 5 s.

(i) Plot a velocity-time graph for the motion of the body.

(ii) From the graph, find the total distance covered by the body after 2 s and 12 s.

Sol. (i) The graphical representation for the motion of the body is given below

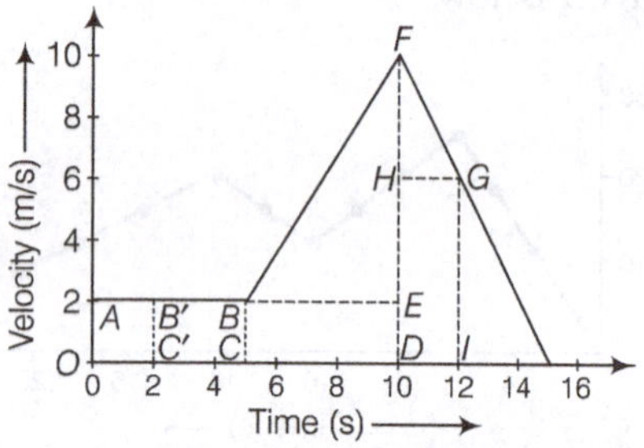

(ii) As we know, the distance moved by the body after 2 s = area $OAB'C' = 2\,m/s \times 2\,s = 4\,m$.
Again, distance covered by the body after 12 s

$= \text{Area of rectangle } OAED + \text{Area of } \Delta BEF$
$+ \text{Area of rectangle } DHGI + \text{Area of } \Delta FHG$

$= 2\,m/s \times 10\,s + \frac{1}{2} \times 5\,s \times 8\,m/s + 6\,m/s \times 2\,s + \frac{1}{2} \times 2\,s \times 4\,m/s$

$= 20\,m + 20\,m + 12\,m + 4\,m = 56\,m$

Check Your LEARNING...

1. If the distance-time graph of a particle is parallel to time axis, then how much is the velocity of the particle?
2. Give one similarity and one dissimilarity between the two graphs.

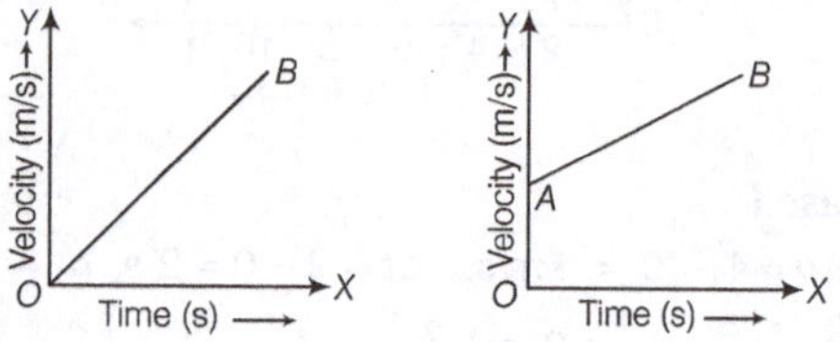

3. What is the value of acceleration in the following graph?

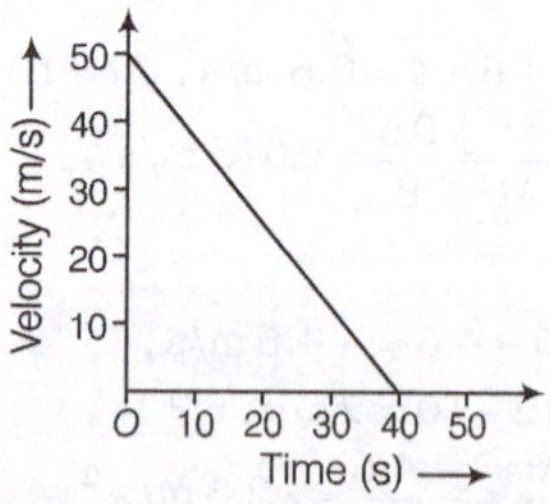

Ans. $-1.25\,m/s^2$

4. Given figures represent the motion of two objects *P* and *Q*. Which of the objects has positive acceleration and which one has negative acceleration?

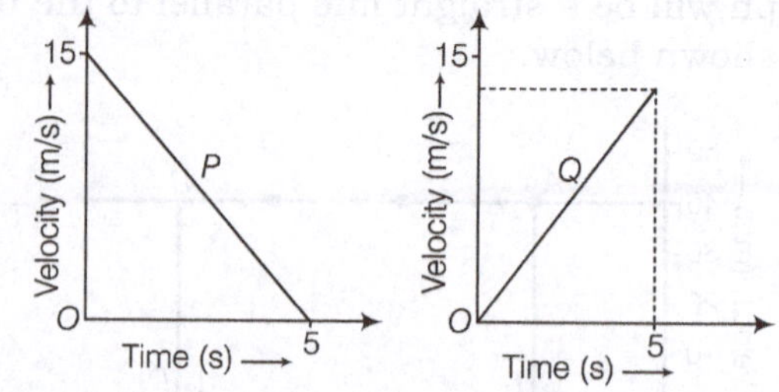

5. Velocity-time graphs of two objects *P* and *Q* are as given below

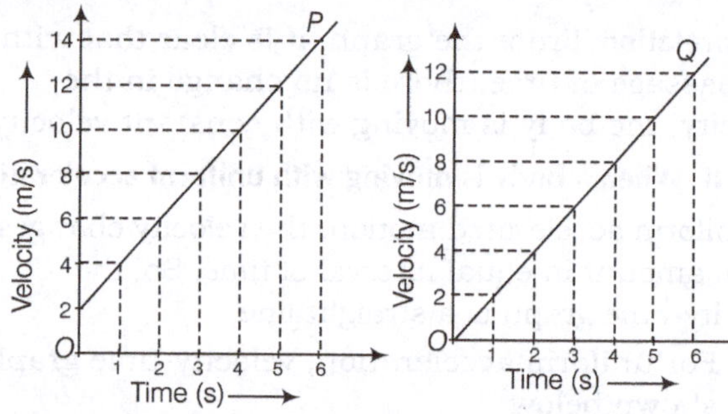

(i) Which object starts from rest?
(ii) Which object has more velocity after 5 s?

Equations of Motion

When a body is moving along a straight line with uniform acceleration, we can establish relations between velocity, acceleration and the distance travelled by the body in a particular time interval by a set of equations. These equations are known as **equations of motion.**

The three equations of motion are as given below

(i) $v = u + at$ (ii) $s = ut + \frac{1}{2}at^2$ (iii) $v^2 - u^2 = 2as$

where, u is the initial velocity of the body, a is the uniform acceleration of the body, v is the final velocity of the body after t seconds and s is the distance travelled by the body in time t.

Derivation of Equations of Motion by Graphical Method

1. Equation for Velocity-Time Relation (First Equation of Motion)

Consider the velocity-time graph of an object that moves under uniform acceleration as shown in figure.

Let the initial velocity of the object be u (at point A) and then it increases to v (at point B) in time t. The velocity changes at a uniform acceleration a.

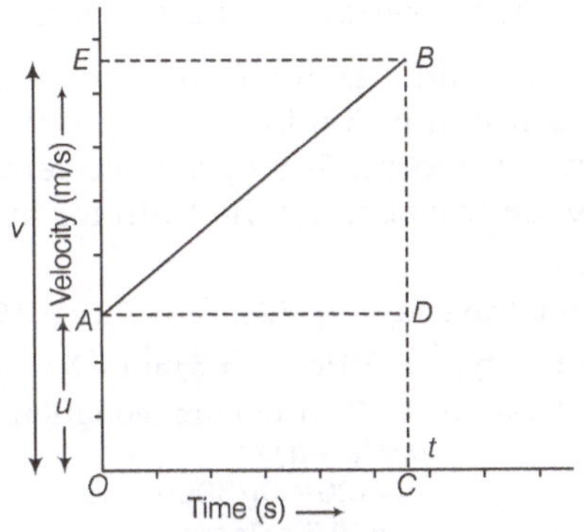

The perpendicular lines BC and BE are drawn from point B on the time and the velocity axis respectively, so that the initial velocity is represented by OA, the final velocity is represented by BC and the time interval t is represented by OC. $BD = BC - CD$, represents the change in velocity in time interval t. Let us draw AD parallel to OC.

From the graph, we observe that

$$BC = BD + DC = BD + OA \quad \text{...(i)}$$

But $BC = v$ and $OA = u$.

On substituting these values in Eq. (i), we get,

$$v = BD + u \quad \text{or} \quad BD = v - u \quad \text{...(ii)}$$

From the velocity-time graph, the acceleration of the object is given by

$$a = \text{change in velocity/time taken} = BD/AD = BD/OC$$

Substituting $OC = t$, we get

$$a = BD/t \quad \text{or} \quad BD = at \quad \text{...(iii)}$$

Using Eqs. (ii) and (iii), we get

$$\boxed{v = u + at}$$

Hence, this is the first equation of motion.

2. Equation for Position-Time Relation (Second Equation of Motion)

Let us suppose that an object has travelled a distance s in time t under uniform acceleration a. From the figure, the distance travelled by an object is obtained by the area enclosed within $OABC$ under the velocity-time graph AB.

Thus, the distance s travelled by the object is given by

$$s = \text{area } OABC \quad \text{(which is a trapezium)}$$

$$= \text{area of the rectangle } OADC + \text{area of the triangle } ABD$$

$$= OA \times OC + 1/2\,(AD \times BD) \quad \text{...(iv)}$$

But $OA = u$, $OC = AD = t$, $BD = at$ [from Eqn. (ii)]

Substituting the above values in Eq. (iv), we get

$$s = u \times t + 1/2\,(t \times at)$$

or

$$\boxed{s = ut + \frac{1}{2}at^2}$$

Hence, this is the second equation of motion.

3. Equation for Position-Velocity Relation (Third Equation of Motion)

The distance travelled by a uniformly accelerated body in time t is given by the area of the space enclosed between the velocity-time graph with time axis.

So, distance travelled, s = area of the trapezium $OABC$

$$= \frac{\text{sum of parallel sides}}{2} \times \text{(distance between parallel sides)}$$

$$\Rightarrow \quad s = \frac{(OA + BC)}{2} \times OC$$

But $OA = u$, $BC = v$ and $OC = t$

Substituting the above values,

we get, $$s = \frac{(u + v)\,t}{2} \quad \text{...(v)}$$

From equation $v = u + at$, we get

$$t = \frac{v - u}{a}$$

Substituting the value of t in Eq. (v), we get

$$s = \frac{(u + v)(v - u)}{2a}$$

$$\Rightarrow \quad s = \frac{v^2 - u^2}{2a}$$

$$\Rightarrow \quad \boxed{v^2 - u^2 = 2as}$$

Hence, this is the third equation of motion.

Mathematical Derivation of Equations of Motion

First Equation of Motion

Suppose an object starts to move with velocity u and after time t its velocity becomes v. If the acceleration in the motion is a, then

$$\text{Acceleration} = \frac{\text{Final velocity} - \text{Initial velocity}}{\text{Time taken}}$$

$$a = \frac{v - u}{t}$$

$\Rightarrow \quad at = v - u$

$\Rightarrow \quad \boxed{v = u + at}$

This is first equation of motion.

Second Equation of Motion

Suppose an object starts to move with velocity u and due to uniform acceleration a, its velocity becomes v after time t. If the distance travelled by the object in time t is s, then

Distance = Average velocity × time

$$s = \left(\frac{u+v}{2}\right) \times t \quad \text{...(i)}$$

Putting the value of v from first equation of motion, i.e., putting $v = u + at$ in Eq. (i), we get

$$s = \left(\frac{u+u+at}{2}\right) \times t$$

$$\Rightarrow \quad s = \left(\frac{2u+at}{2}\right) t$$

$$s = \frac{2ut}{2} + \frac{at^2}{2}$$

$$\boxed{s = ut + \frac{1}{2} at^2}$$

This is called second equation of motion.

Third Equation of Motion

Suppose an object starts to move with velocity u and due to uniform acceleration a, its velocity becomes v after time t. If the distance travelled by the object in time t is s, then

Distance = Average velocity × Time

$$s = \left(\frac{u+v}{2}\right) \times t \quad \text{...(i)}$$

From first equation of motion, $v = u + at$

$$\Rightarrow \quad t = \frac{v-u}{a}$$

Putting the value of t in Eq. (i), we get

$$s = \left(\frac{u+v}{2}\right)\left(\frac{v-u}{a}\right)$$

$$\Rightarrow \quad 2as = (v+u)(v-u)$$

$$2as = v^2 - u^2 \quad [\because (a+b)(a-b) = a^2 - b^2]$$

or $\boxed{v^2 = u^2 + 2as}$

This is called third equation of motion.

Some Special Points about Equations of Motion

(i) If an object starts from rest, then initial velocity is taken as zero, i.e., $u = 0$.

(ii) If an object stops after sometime, then its final velocity is taken as zero, i.e., $v = 0$.

(iii) If the velocity of an object decreases with time, then its acceleration a is taken as negative.

Example 10. A train starting from rest attains a velocity of 72 km/h in 5 min. Assuming that the acceleration is uniform, find (i) the acceleration and (ii) the distance travelled by the train for attaining this velocity.

Sol. Given, final velocity, $v = 72\text{ km/h} = 72 \times 5/18 = 20\text{ m/s}$

Initial velocity, $u = 0$, time, $t = 5\text{ min} = 5 \times 60 = 300\text{ s}$

(i) Acceleration, $a = ?$ (from first equation of motion)

$$a = (v-u)/t$$

$$\Rightarrow \quad a = (20-0)/300 = 1/15\text{ m/s}^2$$

(ii) Distance, $s = ?$ [when $u = 0$]

$s = v^2/2a$ (from third equation of motion)

$\Rightarrow s = (20)^2/2 \times (1/15) = 3000\text{ m}$

The acceleration of the train is $1/15\text{ m/s}^2$ and the distance travelled is 3000 m.

Example 11. A body is accelerating at a constant rate of 10 m/s^2. If the body starts from rest, then how much distance will it cover in 2 s?

Sol. Given, $u = 0$, $a = 10\text{ m/s}^2$, $t = 2\text{ s}$, $s = ?$

From second equation of motion,

$$s = ut + 1/2\, at^2$$

$$s = 0 \times 2 + \frac{1}{2} \times 10 \times 2 \times 2$$

$$s = 20\text{ m}$$

The body covers 20 m in 2 s.

Example 12. Brakes applied to a car produce an acceleration of 6 m/s^2 in opposite direction to motion. If the car takes 2 s to stop after application of brakes, then calculate the distance it travels during this time.

Sol. Since, car stops after applying the brakes, final velocity, $v = 0$

and $a = -6\text{ m/s}^2$, $t = 2\text{ s}$

From first equation of motion, $v = u + at$

or $u = v - at = 0 - (-6)(2) = 12\text{ m/s}$

From the second equation of motion,

$$s = ut + \frac{1}{2}at^2 = (12)(2) + \frac{1}{2}(-6)(2)^2 = 12\text{ m}$$

The distance travelled in 2 s is 12 m.

Example 13. A car starts with velocity 10 m/s and accelerates at rate 5 m/s^2. Find the final velocity when the car has travelled a distance 30 m.

Sol. Given, initial velocity, $u = 10\text{ m/s}$

Acceleration, $a = 5\text{ m/s}^2$, distance, $s = 30\text{ m}$

Final velocity, $v = ?$

From third equation of motion, $v^2 - u^2 = 2as$

$$v^2 = u^2 + 2as = (10)^2 + 2 \times 5 \times 30$$

$$v^2 = 100 + 2 \times 5 \times 30 = 400$$

$$\therefore \quad v = 20\ \text{m/s}$$

The final velocity of car is 20 m/s.

Example 14. A train accelerates uniformly from 36 km/h to 72 km/h in 20 s. Find the distance travelled.

Sol. Given, initial velocity, $u = 36$ km/h

$$= 36 \times \frac{5}{18} = 10\ \text{m/s}$$

Final velocity, $v = 72\ \text{km/h} = 72 \times \frac{5}{18} = 20\ \text{m/s}$,

Time, $t = 20$ s

From first equation of motion, $a = \frac{v - u}{t}$

$$= \frac{20 - 10}{20} = 0.5\ \text{m/s}^2$$

From third equation of motion, $s = \frac{v^2 - u^2}{2a}$

$$= \frac{(20)^2 - (10)^2}{2 \times 0.5} = 300\ \text{m}$$

The distance travelled by train is 300 m.

Check Your LEARNING...

1. A body is moving with a velocity of 10 m/s. If it starts accelerating with the rate of 2.5 m/s^2. Find out its velocity after 10 s. *Ans.* 35 m/s
2. If a car travels 50 m distance in 4 s with an acceleration of 5 m/s^2, then what was its initial speed? *Ans.* 2.5 m/s
3. A cyclist is moving with a speed of 14 m/s. He starts accelerating with a rate of 6 m/s^2 and acquire the speed of 18 m/s. Calculate, what distance did he move in acquiring that speed? *Ans.* 10.67 m
4. A bus is moving with a speed of 72 km/h can be stopped by brakes after atleast 10 m. What will be the minimum stopping distance, if the same bus is moving at a speed of 144 km/h? *Ans.* 40 m

QUiCK Revision

- If an object does not change its position with respect to time and its surroundings, then it is said to be at **rest**. If the body changes its position w.r.t. time and surroundings, then said to be in **motion**.
- **Scalar Quantities** These are the physical quantities which are completely described by their magnitude only, e.g., length.
- **Vector Quantities** These are the physical quantities which are completely described by both magnitude and direction and follow a different rule for addition called vector addition. e.g., Displacement, velocity, acceleration, force, momentum, etc.
- **Distance and Displacement** The length of the actual path covered by any body in a time interval is called distance, whereas displacement is the shortest distance covered between the final and initial positions of a moving object.
- **Speed and Velocity** The rate of change of distance with time is called speed whereas, the rate of change of displacement with time is called velocity.
- **Acceleration** The rate of change of velocity of the body with time is called acceleration.
- **Graphical Representation of Different Motion using Distance-Time Graph** It shows change in position with time.

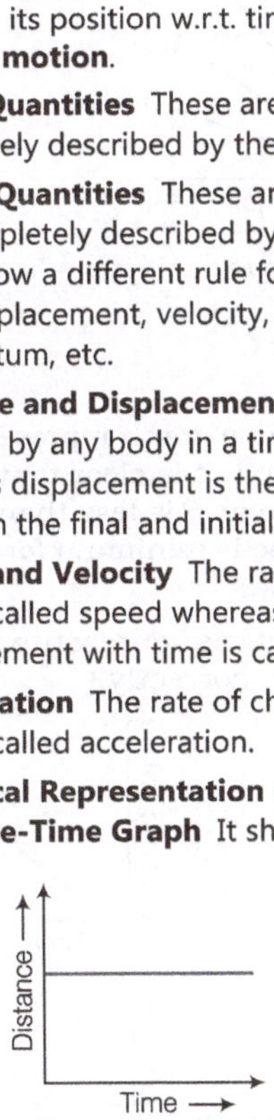

(For stationary body)

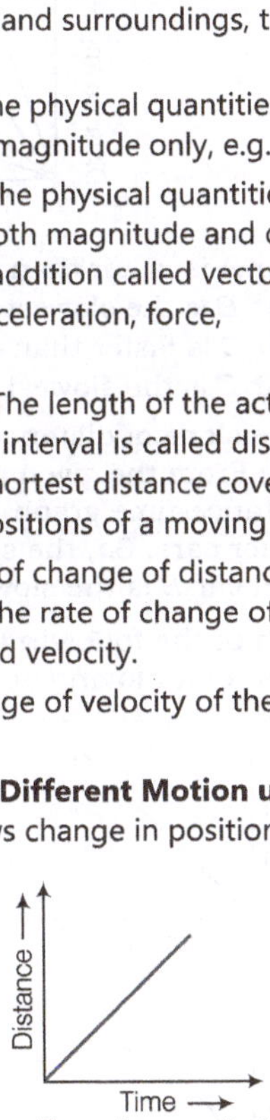

(For uniform motion)

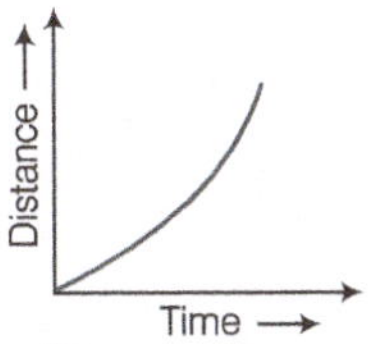

(For non-uniform motion when speed increases)

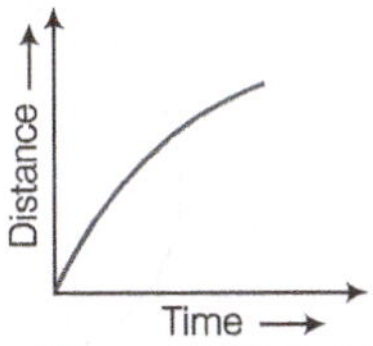

(For non-uniform motion when speed decreases)

- **Velocity-Time Graph** It shows how the velocity of a body changes with time.

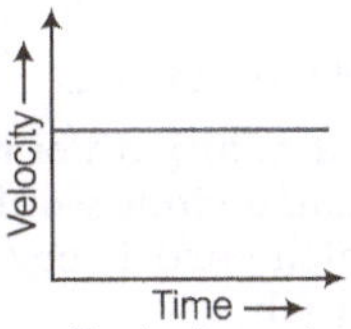

(For body moving with constant velocity)

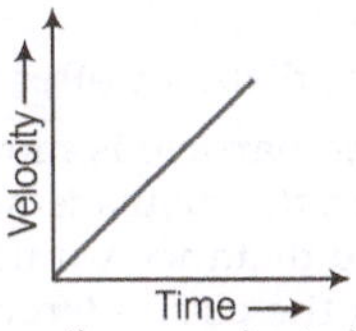

(For uniform accelerated motion with increasing velocity)

(For uniform accelerated motion with decreasing velocity)

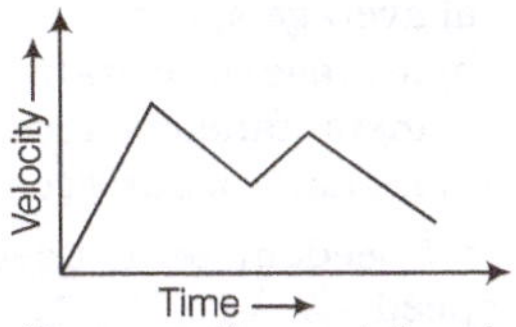

(For non-uniform variation of velocity of the object with time)

- **Equations of Motion** First equation $v = u + at$, where u = initial velocity, v = final velocity, a = acceleration and t = time.
  Second equation, $s = ut + \frac{1}{2}at^2$, here, s = distance covered by the body. Third equation, $v^2 = u^2 + 2as$.

Chapter Practice

Section-I

1 Mark Questions

1. The numerical ratio of displacement and distance for a moving object is

(a) always less than 1 (b) always equal to 1
(c) always more than 1 (d) equal or less than 1

Sol. (*d*) Displacement of an object can be less than or equal to the distance covered by the object, because the magnitude of displacement is not equal to distance. However, it can be equal to distance if the motion is along a straight line without any change in direction.

So, the numerical ratio of displacement to distance is always equal to or less than 1.

2. A particle is moving in a circular path of radius r, as shown in figure. Choose the correct statement.

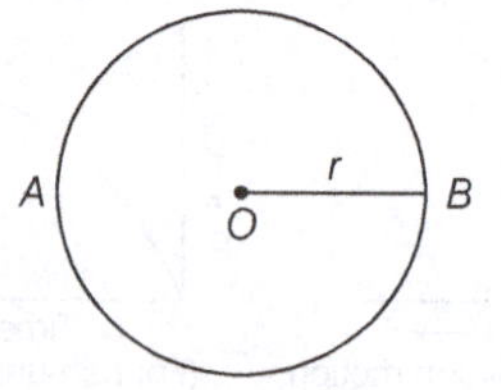

(a) The displacement after half a circle would be $2r$.
(b) The distance after completing two circles is zero.
(c) The displacement after one-fourth circle would be r.
(d) The distance after half a circle would be $2r$.

Sol. (*a*) The particle is moving in a circular path of radius r, then the displacement after half a circle would be $2r$ and distance would be πr which particle covers along the circumference of the path.

3. Speedometer is a device which is used to measure

(a) average speed
(b) average acceleration
(c) instantaneous speed
(d) instantaneous acceleration

Sol. (*c*) Speedometer is used to measure instantaneous speed.

4. When an object is thrown up with an initial velocity u goes to a maximum height h in time t and then comes back at the point of projection. Which of the following statement is correct?

(a) The average velocity of the object is $\frac{2h}{t}$
(b) The acceleration of the object is zero.
(c) The final velocity on reaching the point of projection is $2u$.
(d) The displacement of the object is zero.

Sol. (*d*) The displacement covered by the object is zero because the initial and the final points are same.

$$\text{The average velocity of object} = \frac{\text{Displacement}}{\text{Total time taken}} = 0$$

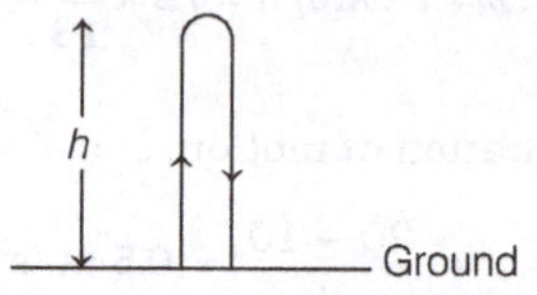

While the acceleration of the object is equal to the value of acceleration due to gravity. i.e. $g = 9.8 \text{ m/s}^2$.

On reaching the point of projection, the final velocity of the object is same as that of its initial velocity i.e. u.

5. Four cars A, B, C and D are moving on a levelled road. Their distance *versus* time graphs are shown in figure. Choose the correct statement.

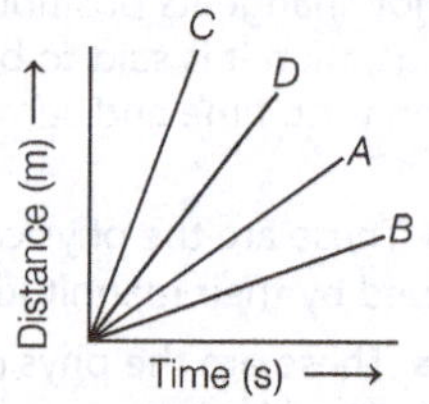

(a) Car A is faster than car D
(b) Car B is the slowest
(c) Car D is faster than car C
(d) Car C is the slowest

Sol. (*b*) The slope of distance-time graph represents the speed. From the given graph, it is clear that the slope of distance-time graph for car B is less than that of all other cars. So, the slope is minimum for car B. Hence, car B is the slowest.

6. Which of the following figures represents uniform motion of a moving object correctly?

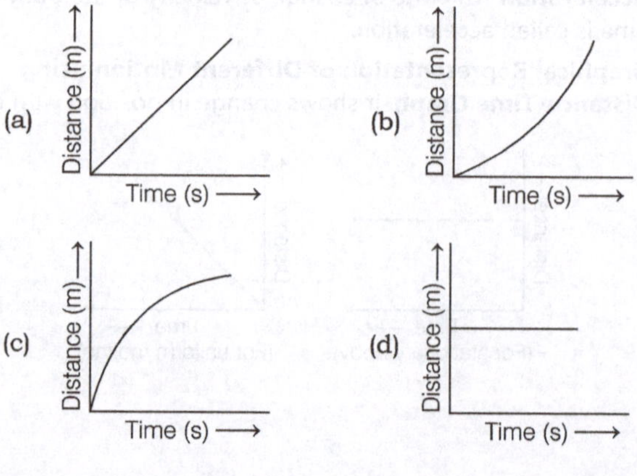

Sol. (*a*) For uniform motion, the distance-time graph is a straight line passing through origin (because in uniform motion, object covers equal distance in equal interval of time).

7. Velocity-time graph for a moving object is found to be curved line, then its acceleration is
(a) constant (b) variable
(c) zero (d) None of these

Sol. (*b*) Since, velocity-time graph for a moving object is curved line, this means that object is moving with non-uniform accelerated motion. Therefore, body is moving with variable acceleration.

8. In the following figure of velocity-time graph for the motion of the body, the total distance covered by the body from 3 s to 7 s is

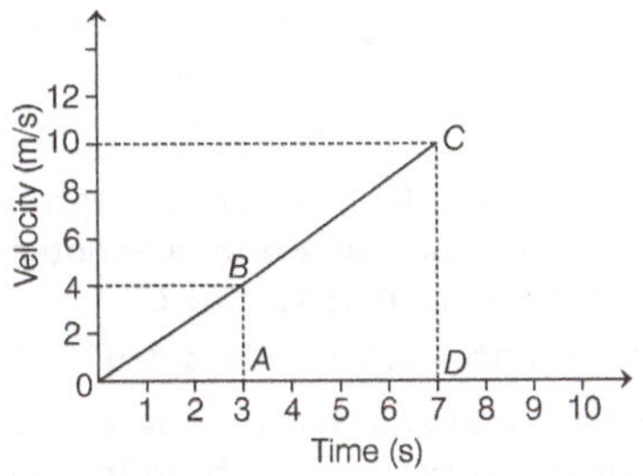

(a) 28 m (b) 56 m (c) 14 m (d) 35 m

Sol. (*a*) Total distance covered by the body from 3 s to 7 s

$$s = \text{Area of trapezium } ABCD = \frac{(AB + DC) \times AD}{2}$$

From given graph, we have

$AB = 4$ m/s

$DC = 10$ m/s

$AD = (7 - 3) = 4$ s

$$\therefore \quad s = \frac{(4+10)(7-3)}{2} = \frac{14 \times 4}{2} = 28 \text{ m}$$

9. The velocity-time graph for one-dimensional motion is shown in the figure.

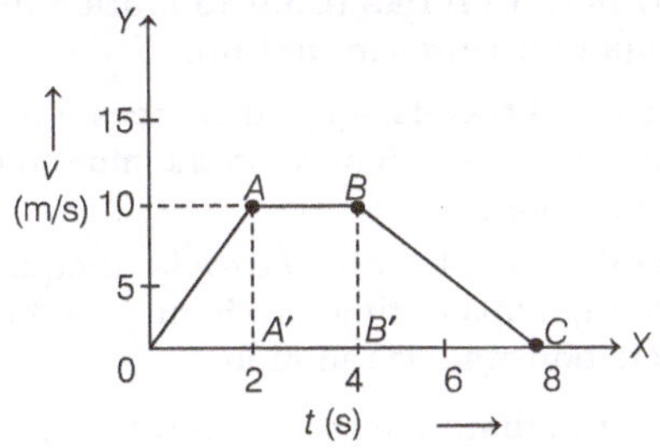

The acceleration of the body from point B to point C is
(a) -2.5 m/s^2 (b) 5 m/s^2
(c) 0 (d) 2.5 m/s^2

Sol. (*a*) From point B to C, the body undergoes uniform retardation.

Time taken by the body $= 8 - 4 = 4$ s

Now, acceleration of body = slope of line BC

$$= \frac{0-10}{4} = -\frac{10}{4} = -2.5 \text{ m/s}^2$$

10. A train starting from rest attains a velocity of 90 km/h in 2 min, then the distance travelled by the train for attaining this velocity is
(a) 1.5 km (b) 2 km
(c) 2.5 km (d) 1.2 km

Sol. (*a*) Given, initial velocity, $u = 0$,

Final velocity, $v = 90 \text{ km/h} = 90 \times \frac{5}{18} = 25$ m/s

Time, $t = 2 \text{ min} = 2 \times 60 = 120$ s

From the equation of motion,

$$v = u + at$$

$$\Rightarrow \quad a = \frac{v}{t} \quad (\because u = 0)$$

$$= \frac{25}{2 \times 60} = \frac{5}{24} \text{ m/s}^2$$

Distance covered,

$$s = ut + \frac{1}{2}at^2 = 0 + \frac{1}{2} \times \frac{5}{24} \times (120)^2$$

$$= \frac{1}{2} \times \frac{5}{24} \times 120 \times 120$$

$$= 1500 \text{ m} = 1.5 \text{ km}$$

11. If the displacement of an object is proportional to square of time, then the object moves with
(a) uniform velocity
(b) uniform acceleration
(c) increasing acceleration
(d) decreasing acceleration

Sol. (*b*) Let object starts from rest, i.e. initial velocity $(u) = 0$ and an acceleration (a) in time (t).

From second equation of motion,

$$s = ut + \frac{1}{2}at^2$$

Then, $s = 0 \times t + \frac{1}{2}at^2$

$$\Rightarrow \quad s = \frac{1}{2}at^2$$

$s \propto t^2$, if a = constant

Thus, displacement s of an object is proportional to square of time t, when the object moves with constant or uniform acceleration.

2 Marks Questions

12. How can you represent a vector quantity?

Sol. A vector quantity is represented by an arrow. The length of the arrow represents the magnitude and the arrow head represents the direction. [2]

13. How can we describe the location of an object?

Sol. To describe the position of an object we need to specify a reference point called the origin.

e.g., Suppose that a library in a city is 2 km North of the railway station. We have specified the position of the library with respect to the railway station, i.e., in this case, the railway station acts as the reference point. [1+1]

14. What do you mean by motion in one direction? Give example.

Sol. When a body moves along a straight line, then the motion of body is said to be in one direction.

e.g. A car moving on a long and straight road. **[2]**

15. Give an example when we infer the motion indirectly.

Sol. We infer the motion of air by observing the movement of dust particles or leaves and branches of trees, or simply by feeling the blowing air on our face. **[2]**

16. Give an example of a body which may appear to be moving for one person and stationary for the other.

Sol. The passengers in a moving bus observe that the trees, buildings as well as the people on the roadside appear to be moving in backward direction. Similarly, a person standing on the roadside observes that the bus (alongwith its passengers) is moving in forward direction. **[1]**

But, at the same time, each passenger in a moving bus or train observes, his fellow passengers sitting are not moving. **[1]**

17. Differentiate between distance and displacement.

Sol. Differences between distance and displacement are

Distance	Displacement
It is the length of the actual path travelled by object irrespective of its direction of motion.	Displacement is the shortest distance between the initial and final positions of an object in a given direction.
Distance is a scalar quantity.	Displacement is a vector quantity.
Distance covered can never be negative. It is always positive or zero.	Displacement may be positive, negative or zero.
Distance is always greater than or equal to the magnitude of displacement.	Displacement is always less than or equal to the magnitude of distance.

[1/2 × 4]

18. Which is smaller distance or displacement? Is the displacement of an object depends on the choice of the position of origin of the coordinate system?

Sol. Displacement of a moving object is always smaller than the distance travelled by it. No, the displacement of the object does not depend on the choice of the position of the origin. **[2]**

19. If the displacement of a body is zero, is its distance necessarily zero? Answer with a suitable example.

Sol. No, because the distance covered by an object is the length of the path covered by the object. The displacement of an object is given by the change in position between the initial position and final position. **[1]**

e.g. A boy starts from his home and moves towards market along a straight path. Then, he returns to home from the same path. Here, displacement is zero but distance is non-zero. **[1]**

20. Suppose a ball is thrown vertically upwards from a position P above the ground. It rises to the highest point Q and returns to the same point P. What is the net displacement and distance travelled by the ball?

Sol. The net displacement is zero. The distance travelled by the ball is twice the distance between position P and Q. **[2]**

21. A scooter is moving along a straight line AB covers a distance of d m in t_1 seconds and returns back from B to C and coveres d' m in t_2 seconds. Find the total path length travelled by the scooter.

Sol. From the above question, we draw the following figure.

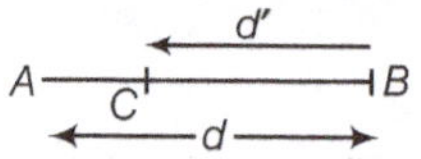

[1]

Hence, to find out the total path length it does not matter what the time taken by a scooter to reach at B and the time taken to return at C.

Total path length = $AB + BC = d + d'$ **[1]**

22. Two trains A and B start moving at the same time. The distances travelled by them in given intervals of time are shown below.

Time	Distance travelled by train *A* (in km)	Distance travelled by train *B* (in km)
6.00 pm	0	0
6.15 pm	10	15
6.30 pm	20	24
6.45 pm	30	32
7.00 pm	40	38
7.15 pm	50	42
7.30 pm	60	47

State which train has uniform motion and which train has non-uniform motion.

Sol. Since, train A travels equal distances in equal intervals of time of 15 min, so the motion of train A is uniform motion. **[1]**

On the other hand, train B travels unequal distances in equal intervals of time of 15 min, so the motion of train B is non-uniform motion. **[1]**

23. How are the distance travelled by an object related to the time taken when an object travels equal distances in equal intervals of time?

Sol. In this case, distance travelled by the object is directly proportional to the time taken. As the time increases, the distance travelled by the object also increases linearly. **[2]**

24. Suppose a boy is enjoying a ride on a merry-go-round which is moving with a constant speed of 10 ms^{-1}. What does it imply?

Sol. In merry-go-round, the speed is constant but velocity is not constant because its direction goes on changing, i.e., there is an acceleration in the motion. So, we can say that the boy is in uniform accelerated motion. [2]

25. Can an object be accelerated if it is moving with constant speed? Justify your answer with an example.

Or

Can a body have constant speed and still be accelerating? Give an example.

Or

Explain how is it possible for an object to move with a constant speed but with uniform acceleration?

Sol. An object moving with constant speed can be accelerated if its direction of motion changes. e.g., An object moving with a constant speed in a circular path has an acceleration because its direction of motion changes continuously. [1+1]

26. An object *P* is moving with a constant velocity for 5 min. Another object *Q* is moving with changing velocity for 5 min. Out of these two objects, which one has acceleration? Explain.

Sol. $\text{Acceleration} = \dfrac{\text{Change in velocity}}{\text{Time taken}}$

Since, the velocity of object *P* is not changing or change in velocity of the object is zero, therefore object *P* has no acceleration. On the other hand, there is change in velocity of the object *Q*. So, it has acceleration. [1 + 1]

27. The graph between total path length and time for a particle moving along a straight line as shown in figure is not possible. Explain why?

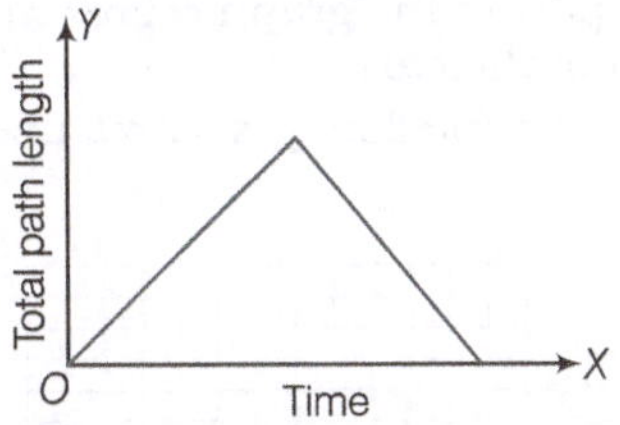

Sol. The graph shows that with the passage of time, total path length first increases and then decreases.The path length always increases or remains constant with passage of time and it cannot decrease with time as shown in given figure. Thus, this graph is not possible. [1 + 1]

28. From the given velocity-time graph (see figure), what can be concluded?

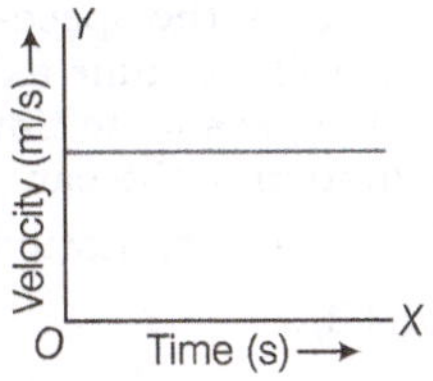

Sol. From the given velocity-time graph, it is clear that the velocity of the object is not changing with time, i.e., the object is in uniform motion. [2]

29. What do the graphs (i) and (ii) shown here indicate?

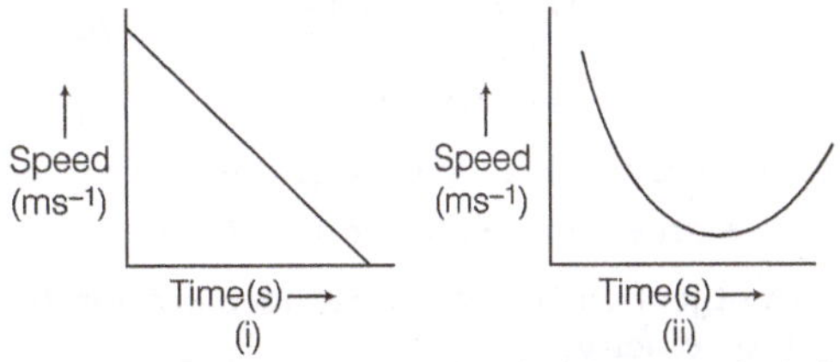

Sol. Graph (i) indicates that a body has certain initial speed and then its speed decreases to zero. [1]

Graph (ii) shows that a body first retards and then accelerates non-uniformly. [1]

30. Out of the following, identify the graph which corresponds to a motion with (i) uniform retardation and (ii) zero acceleration.

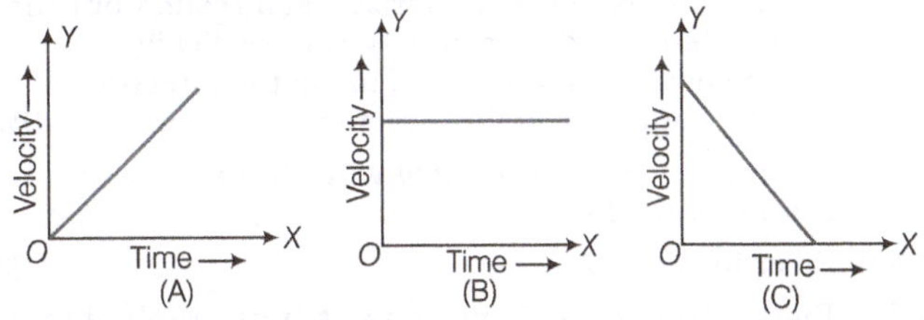

Sol. (i) The graph with uniform retardation is shown in graph (C), since in this graph, the velocity of the object decreases uniformly. [1]

(ii) The graph (B) corresponds to the zero acceleration because the velocity of body does not change with time. [1]

3 Marks Questions

31. Is motion on Earth inertial or non-inertial frame of reference?

Sol. Since, Earth revolves around the Sun and also spins about its own axis, so it is an accelerated frame of reference. Hence, Earth is a non-inertial frame of reference. [1½]

However, if we do not take large scale motion such as wind and ocean currents into consideration, we can say that the Earth is an inertial frame. [1½]

32. An insect moves along a circular path of radius 10 cm with a constant speed. It takes 1 min to move from a point on the path to the diametrically opposite point.

Find (i) the distance covered, (ii) the speed and (iii) the displacement.

Sol. Suppose the insect was at *A* initially and it moves along *ACB* to reach the diametrically opposite point *B* in 1 min.

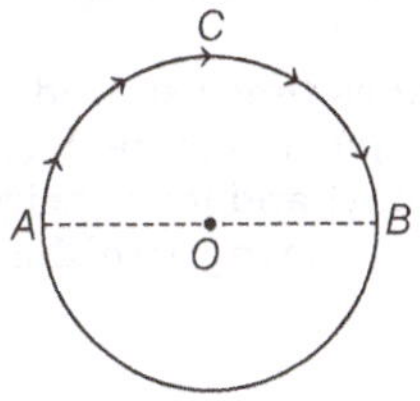

(i) $\therefore$ The distance moved in 1 min $= \pi r$

$= 3.14 \times 10 = 31.4$ cm [1]

(ii) $\therefore$ Speed $= \frac{\text{Distance}}{\text{Time}} = \frac{31.4}{1} = 31.4$ cm/min [1]

(iii) $\therefore$ Displacement, $AB = 2r = 2 \times 10 = 20$ cm [1]

33. State which of the following situations are possible and give an example for each of these.

(i) An object with a constant acceleration but with zero velocity.

(ii) An object moving in a certain direction with an acceleration in the perpendicular direction.

Sol. (i) When an object is thrown vertically upward, then at highest point its velocity is zero but it has constant acceleration 9.8 ms^{-2} (acceleration due to gravity). [1½]

(ii) An aeroplane flies in horizontal direction but the acceleration due to gravity is in vertically downward direction, i.e., along the direction perpendicular to the direction of motion. [1½]

34. What is acceleration? How will you express it mathematically?

Sol. Refer to Page 27. [3]

35. Figure shows the displacement-time graph of four children *A, B, C* and *D*. Which child has the (i) highest velocity (ii) lowest velocity?

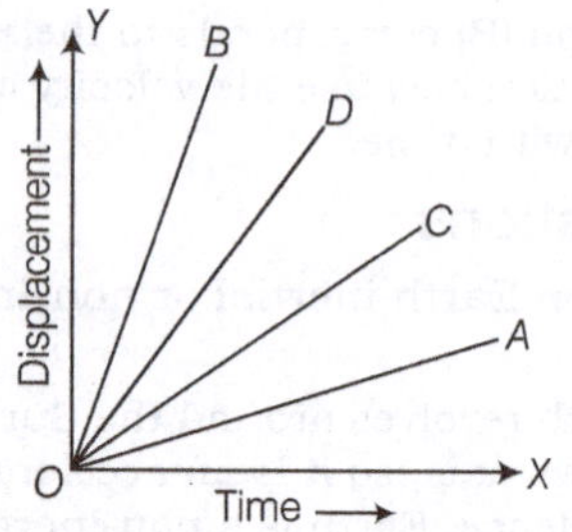

Sol. Velocity = Slope of displacement-time [1]

Since, slope of child *B* is greater than all other children. Hence, child *B* has the highest velocity. [1]

Similarly, the slope of child *A* is smallest, so it has lowest velocity. [1]

36. Draw a velocity *versus* time graph of a stone thrown vertically upward and then coming downwards after attaining the maximum height.

Sol. When a stone is thrown vertically upwards, it has some initial velocity (let u). As, the stone goes vertically upwards, its velocity goes on decreasing ($\because$ it is moving against the gravity) and at the highest point, (i.e. maximum height) its velocity becomes zero. [1]

Let the stone takes time t seconds to reach at the highest point. After that stone begins to fall (with zero initial velocity) and its velocity goes on increasing ($\because$ it is moving with the gravity) and it reaches its initial point of projection with the velocity v in the same time (with which it was thrown).

So,

Velocity	u	0	$-u$
Time	0	t	$2t$

[1]

Here, we have taken $-u$ because in the upward motion velocity of stone is in upward direction and in the downward motion, the velocity is in downward direction.

The velocity-time graph for the whole journey is shown below

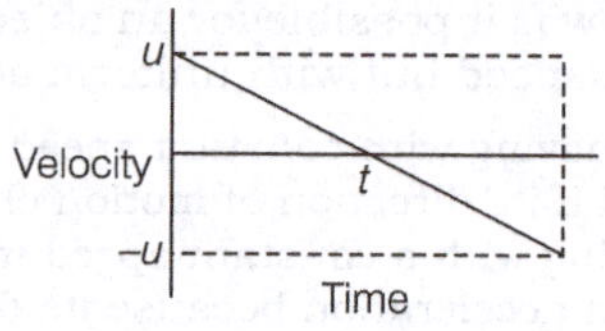

[1]

37. The speed-time graph for a car is shown in the figure.

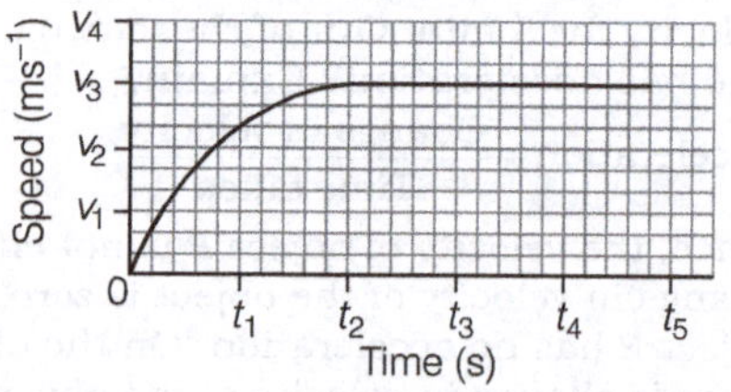

(i) Find how far does the car travel in the first t_2 s. Shade the area on the graph that represents the distance travelled by the car during the period.

(ii) Which part of the graph represents uniform motion of the car?

Sol. (i) Distance travelled in t_2, s = Area under speed-time graph

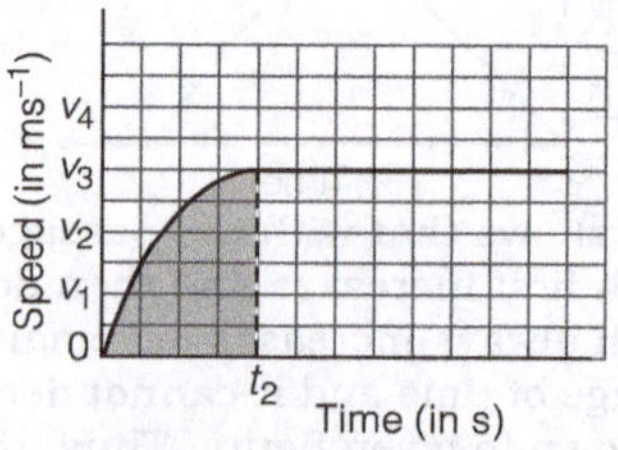

= Average speed × Time

$$= \left(\frac{v_3 + 0}{2}\right) \times t_2 = \left(\frac{v_3}{2}\right) t_2$$ [1½]

(ii) For uniform motion, the speed-time graph is a straight line parallel to time axis. So, the straight part of the curve parallel to time axis represents the uniform motion of the car. [1½]

38. Derive second equation of motion,

i.e. $s = ut + 1/2at^2$

Sol. Refer to Pages 32 and 33.

39. How will the equations of motion for an object moving with a uniform velocity change?

Sol. We know that the equations of uniformly accelerated motion are

(i) $v = u + at$

(ii) $s = ut + \frac{1}{2}at^2$

(iii) $v^2 = u^2 + 2as$

where, u = initial velocity, v = final velocity, a = acceleration, t = time

and s = distance

For an object moving with uniform velocity (velocity which is not changing with time), then acceleration $a = 0$.

So, equations of motion will become (putting $a = 0$ in above equations)

(i) $v = u$ (ii) $s = ut$ (iii) $v^2 = u^2$ **[3]**

4 Marks Questions

40. Explain clearly with examples, the distinction between

(i) magnitude of displacement (sometimes called distance) over an interval of time and the total length of the path covered by a particle over the same interval.

(ii) magnitude of average velocity over an interval of time and the average speed over the same interval.
Show in both (i) and (ii) that the second quantity is either greater than or equal to first. When is the equality sign true? (for simplicity, consider one-dimensional motion only).

Sol. Let us consider an example.

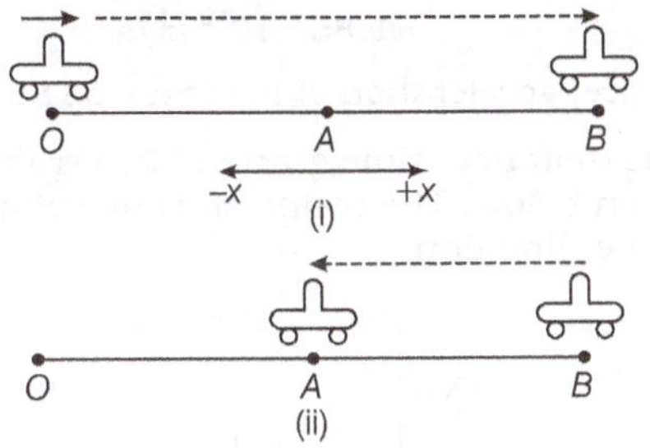

A car starts from O and moves along positive X-axis. The car stops at B and starts moving towards negative X-axis. Finally, the car reaches at A. **[1]**

(i) Magnitude of displacement of a particle in motion for a given time is the shortest distance between the initial and final position of the particle in that time, whereas the total length of the path covered by particle is the length of actual path traversed by the particle in the given time. **[1]**

(ii) Magnitude of average velocity over an interval of time is equal to the magnitude of displacement divided by time interval whereas the average speed is the total path length divided by the time interval. **[1]**

For the motion from O to B,

$|\text{Displacement}|$ = Distance covered

$|\text{Average velocity}|$ = Average speed

For the motion from $O \rightarrow B \rightarrow A$,

$|\text{Displacement}|$ < Distance covered

$|\text{Average velocity}|$ < Average speed **[1]**

41. Read each statement below carefully and state with reasons and examples if it is true or false.

A particle in one-dimensional motion

(i) with zero speed at an instant may have non-zero acceleration at that instant.

(ii) with zero speed may have non-zero velocity.

(iii) with constant speed must have zero acceleration.

(iv) with positive value of acceleration must be speeding up.

Sol. (i) True, when a body is thrown vertically upwards in the space, then at the highest point, the body has zero speed but has downward acceleration equal to the acceleration due to gravity. **[1]**

(ii) False, because velocity is the speed of body in a given direction. When speed is zero, the magnitude of velocity of body is zero, hence velocity is zero. **[1]**

(iii) True, when a particle is moving along a straight line with a constant speed, its velocity remains constant with time. Therefore, acceleration (i.e., change in velocity/time) is zero. **[1]**

(iv) False, if the initial velocity of a body is negative, then even in the case of positive acceleration, the body speeds down. A body speeds up when the acceleration acts in the direction of motion. **[1]**

42. State the three equations of motion. Which of them describes

(i) velocity-time relation? (ii) position-time relation?

Sol. For a body moving along a straight line at velocity u and accelerating uniformly at a for time t to attain a velocity v and cover displacement s. Thus, the three equations of motion are as

First equation, $v = u + at$ ...(i)

Second equation, $s = ut + 1/2at^2$ ...(ii)

Third equation, $v^2 = u^2 + 2as$ ...(iii)

[2]

(i) First equation represents velocity-time relation.

(ii) Second equation represents position-time relation. **[2]**

Numerical Type Questions

43. During an experiment, a signal from a spaceship reached the ground station in five minutes. What was the distance of the spaceship from the ground station? The signal travels at the speed of light, i.e., 3×10^8 m/s.

Sol. Speed of signal $= 3 \times 10^8 \text{ ms}^{-1}$

Time taken by the signal in reaching the Earth

$= 5 \text{ min} = 5 \times 60 = 300 \text{ s}$

Distance of spaceship from ground station

= distance travelled by the signal in 5 min

= speed of signal × time taken

$= 3\times10^8 \times 300 = 9\times10^{10}$ m **[1+1]**

44. An ant climbs up five stairs, each of width 20 cm and height 20 cm. Find the distance covered and displacement of ant.

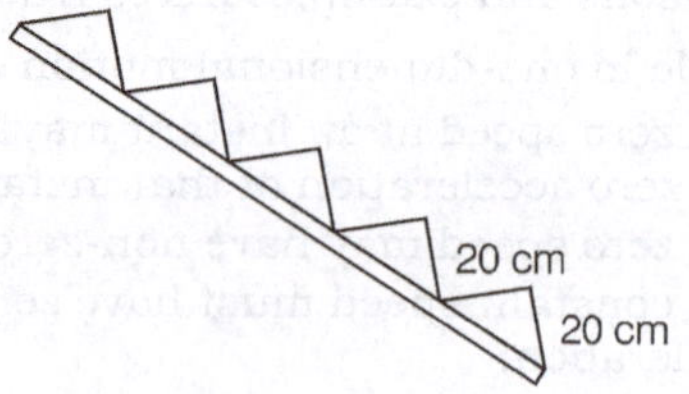

Sol. Distance covered by ant = 5× (20 cm+ 20 cm)

$= 5\times 40$ cm = 200 cm **[1]**

Displacement $= 5\times\sqrt{(20)^2+(20)^2}$

i.e., Sum of all hypotenuse of the right triangles

$= 5\times\sqrt{800} = 100\sqrt{2}$ cm **[1]**

45. A bridge is 500 m long. A 100 m long train crosses the bridge at a speed of 30 m/s. Find the time taken by train to cross it.

Sol. Total length of path covered by train

= 500 m + 100 m = 600 m

Speed of train = 30 m/s **[1]**

Time taken by train to cover the bridge

$= \frac{\text{Distance}}{\text{Speed}} = \frac{600}{30} = 20$ s **[1]**

46. An artificial satellite is moving in a circular orbit of radius 42250 km. Calculate its speed if it takes 24 h to revolve around the Earth.

Sol. Radius of the orbit, $r = 42250$ km

Distance covered in one revolution = Circumference of the orbit

$d = 2\pi r$

$= 2\times\frac{22}{7}\times 42250 = 265571.43$ km **[1]**

Time taken in one revolution, $t = 24$ h

∴ Speed of satellite

$= \frac{\text{Distance}}{\text{Time}} = \frac{265571.43}{24} = 11065.48$ kmh^{-1} **[1]**

47. A train travels at a speed of 60 km/h for 0.5 h, 24 km/h for next 0.25 h and then at 72 km/h for the next 0.75 h. Calculate the distance travelled by train and its average speed.

Sol. Total time = 0.5 h+ 0.25 h+ 0.75 h= 1.5 h **[1]**

Total distance $= v_1t_1 + v_2t_2 + v_3t_3$

= (60) (0.5)+ (24) (0.25) + (72) (0.75)

= 90 km **[1]**

Average speed $= \frac{\text{Total distance}}{\text{Total time}} = \frac{90 \text{ km}}{1.5 \text{ h}} = 60$ km/h **[1]**

48. A car moves with a speed of 30 km/h for half an hour, 25 km/h for one hour and 40 km/h for two hours. Calculate average speed of the car.

Sol. Time taken to travel,

$t_1 = 0.5$ h, $t_2 = 1$ h, $t_3 = 2$ h

$t = t_1 + t_2 + t_3 = 0.5 + 1 + 2 = 3.5$ h

Speeds, $v_1 = 30$ km/h, $v_2 = 25$ km/h, $v_3 = 40$ km/h **[1]**

Distances, $s_1 = v_1 t_1 = 30\times 0.5 = 15$ km

$s_2 = v_2t_2 = 25\times 1 = 25$ km

$s_3 = v_3t_3 = 40\times 2 = 80$ km

$s = s_1 + s_2 + s_3 = 15 + 25 + 80$

= 120 km **[1]**

Average speed $= \frac{\text{Total distance}}{\text{Total time}} = \frac{s}{t} = \frac{120}{3.5}$ **[1]**

= 34.3 km/h

49. A train starts from rest and accelerates uniformly for 30 s to attain a velocity of 72 km/h. Find its acceleration.

Sol. Given, initial velocity, $u = 0$, time taken, $t = 30$ s

Final velocity, $v = 72$ km/h $= 72\times\frac{5}{18} = 20$ m/s **[1]**

Acceleration, $a = \frac{v-u}{t} = \frac{20-0}{30} = 0.67$ m/s^2 **[1]**

50. A train starting from a railway station and moving with uniform acceleration attains a speed of 40 km/h in 10 min. Find its acceleration.

Sol. Initial velocity of train, $u = 0$

Final velocity of train, $v = 40$ km/h

$= 40\times\frac{5}{18} = 11.11$ m/s

Time taken, $t = 10$ min $= 10\times 60 = 600$ s **[1]**

Acceleration, $a = \frac{v-u}{t} = \frac{11.11-0}{600} = 0.0185$ m/s^2

$= 1.85\times10^{-2}$ m/s^2

Hence, acceleration of the train is 1.85×10^{-2} m/s^2. **[1]**

51. The distance -time graph of two trains A and B are given below. The trains start simultaneously in the same direction.

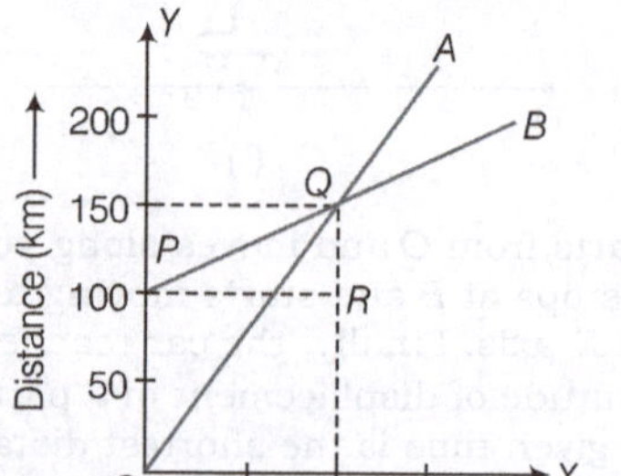

(i) How much B is ahead of A, when the motion starts?

(ii) What is the speed of B?

(iii) When and where will A catch B?

(iv) What is the difference between speeds of A and B?

(v) Is the speed of both the trains uniform or non-uniform? Justify your answer.

Sol. (i) B is ahead of A by 100 km as $OP = 100$ km **[1/2]**

(ii) Speed of B = Slope of $PQ = \frac{150-100}{2-0} = 25$ km/h **[1]**

(iii) A and B meet at Q, i.e. 150 km from origin and 2 h after the start. **[1]**

(iv) Speed of A = Slope of $OQ = \frac{150}{2} = 75$ km/h

Difference between speeds = 75 − 25 = 50 km/h **[1]**

(v) Speed of both the trains is uniform as speed-time graph is a straight line. **[1/2]**

52. A girl walks along a straight path to drop a letter in the letter box and comes back to her initial position. Her displacement-time graph is shown in figure. Plot a velocity-time graph for the same.

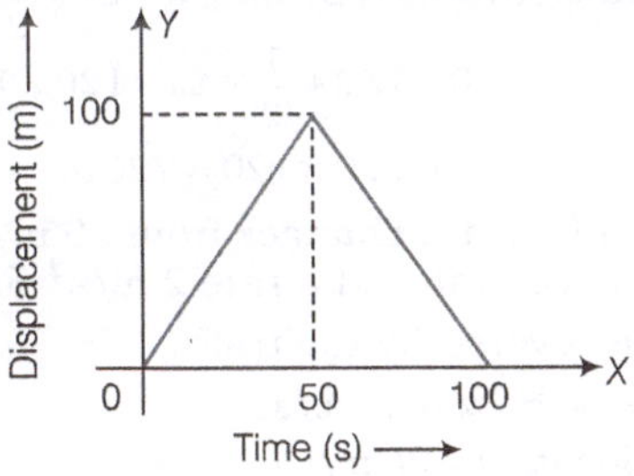

Sol. From the graph,

(i) initial velocity, $u = 0$ **[1]**

(ii) velocity after 50 s,

$$v = \frac{\text{displacement}}{\text{Time}} = \frac{100}{50} = 2\ \text{ms}^{-1}$$ **[1]**

(iii) Velocity after 100 s,

$$v = \frac{\text{displacement}}{\text{time}}$$

$$= \frac{0}{100} = 0$$ **[1]**

Therefore,

$v\,(\text{ms}^{-1})$	0	2	0
t(s)	0	50	100

Velocity-time graph plotted from the above data is shown as below

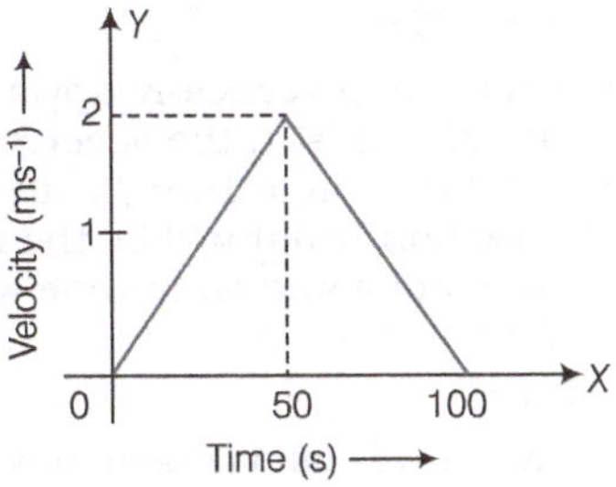

[1]

53. Make a velocity-time graph from the following displacement-time graph.

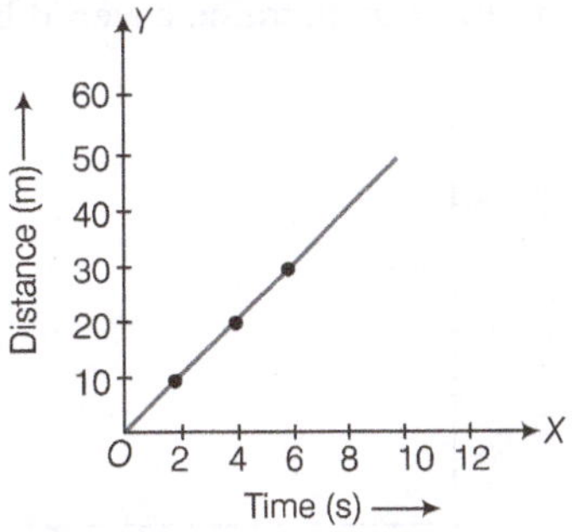

Sol. From the graph,

Velocity after 2 s = $\frac{10}{2} = 5$ m/s

Velocity after 4 s = $\frac{20}{4} = 5$ m/s

Velocity after 6 s = $\frac{30}{6} = 5$ m/s

e.g., Velocity is constant and acceleration = 0. **[1½]**

So, velocity-time graph will be drawn as

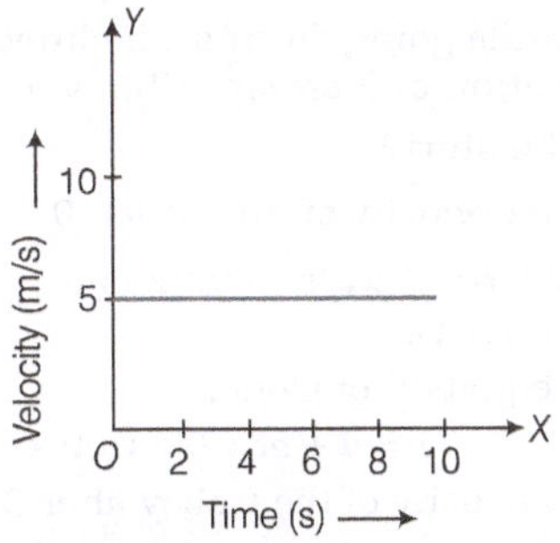

[1½]

54. Find the displacement of a body whose velocity-time graph is shown as below.

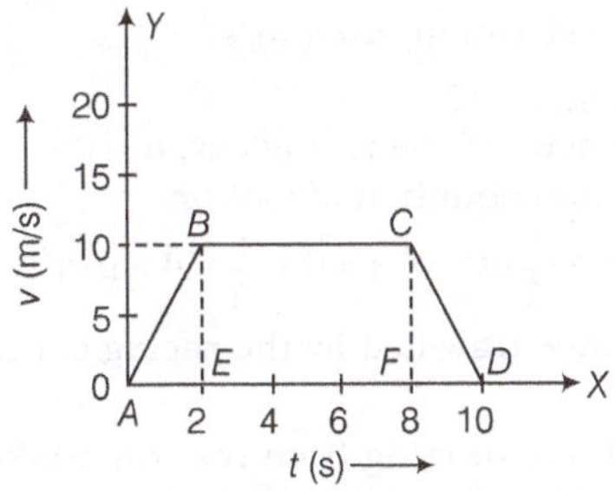

Sol. Displacement = Area under velocity- time curve

$$= \frac{1}{2}\,(\text{sum of parallel sides}) \times \text{height}$$

$$= \frac{1}{2}\,(AD + BC) \times CF$$

$$= \frac{1}{2}\,(10 + 6) \times 10 = 80\ \text{m}$$ **[2]**

55. The velocity-time graph (see figure) shows the motion of a cyclist. Find (i) its acceleration (ii) its velocity and (iii) the distance covered by the cyclist in 15 s.

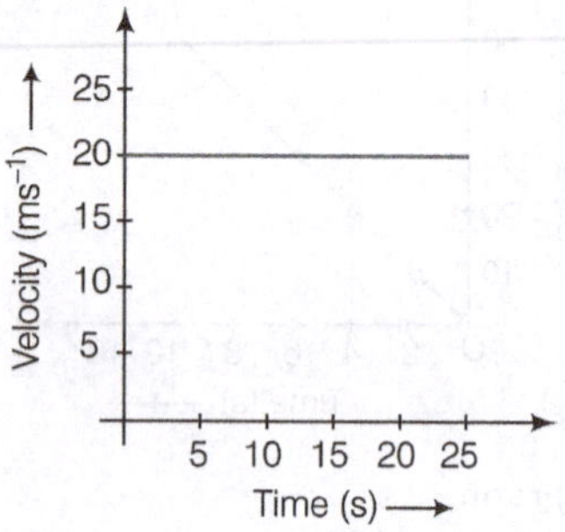

Sol. (i) From the graph, it is clear that velocity is not changing with time, i.e., acceleration is zero. [1]

(ii) Again from the graph, we can see that there is no change in the velocity with time, so velocity after 15 s will remain same as 20 ms^{-1}. [1]

(iii) Distance covered by cyclist in 15 s = velocity × time
$= 20 \times 15$
$= 300$ m [1]

56. A trolley while going down an inclined plane has an acceleration of 2 cm/s^2. What will be its velocity 3 s after the start?

Sol. Given, initial velocity of trolley, $u = 0$

Acceleration, $a = 2\ cm/s^2 = 0.02\ m/s^2$

Time taken, $t = 3$ s [1]

From first equation of motion,

$$v = u + at = 0 + 0.02 \times 3 = 0.06\ m/s$$

Hence, the velocity of the trolley after 3 s start is 0.06 m/s. [1]

57. A racing car has a uniform acceleration of 4 m/s^2. What distance will it cover in 10 s after the start?

Sol. Given, acceleration, $a = 4\ m/s^2$

Time taken, $t = 10$ s

Initial velocity of the racing car, $u = 0$ [1]

From second equation of motion,

$$s = ut + \frac{1}{2}at^2 \Rightarrow s = 0 + \frac{1}{2} \times 4 \times (10)^2 = 200\ m$$

The distance travelled by the racing car in 10 s is 200 m. [1]

58. A motorboat starting from rest on a lake accelerates in a straight line at a constant rate of 3.0 ms^{-2} for 8.0 s. How far does the boat travel during this time?

Sol. The motorboat starts from rest, so initial velocity, $u = 0$

Time taken, $t = 8$ s, acceleration, $a = 3\ ms^{-2}$

Distance covered during the given time, [1]

$$s = ut + \frac{1}{2}at^2 \quad \text{(second equation of motion)}$$

$$= 0 \times 8 + \frac{1}{2} \times 3 \times (8)^2$$

$$= \frac{1}{2} \times 3 \times 64 = 96\ m$$ [1]

59. A bus starting from rest moves with a uniform acceleration of 0.1 m/s^2 for 2 min, find
(i) the speed acquired and
(ii) the distance travelled.

Sol. Here, acceleration, $a = 0.1\ ms^{-2}$

Time, $t = 2\ min = 2 \times 60 = 120\ s$

Initial speed, $u = 0$

(i) From first equation of motion,
Speed acquired by bus,
$v = u + at = 0 + 0.1 \times 120 = 12\ ms^{-1}$ [1]

(ii) From second equation of motion,
Distance travelled by bus, $s = ut + \frac{1}{2}at^2$

$$= 0 \times 120 + \frac{1}{2} \times 0.1 \times 120 \times 120$$

$$= 0.1 \times 60 \times 120 = 720\ m$$ [1]

60. Velocity of a train changes from 20 m/s to 25 m/s when it accelerates at a rate 2 m/s^2. Find the distance covered by the train.

Sol. Initial velocity, $u = 20$ m/s

Final velocity, $v = 25$ m/s

Acceleration, $a = 2\ m/s^2$

From second equation of motion,

$$v^2 - u^2 = 2as \quad \text{or} \quad s = \frac{v^2 - u^2}{2a}$$ [1]

$$= \frac{(25)^2 - (20)^2}{2 \times 2} = 56.25\ m$$ [1]

61. A train is travelling at a speed of 90 km/h. Brakes are applied so as to produce an uniform acceleration of $-0.5\ m/s^2$. Find how far the train will go before it is brought to rest. [2]

Sol. Here, initial speed, $u = 90\ km/h = 90 \times \frac{5}{18} = 25\ m/s$

Acceleration, $a = -0.5\ m/s^2$

Train brought to rest, so final speed $v = 0$

From third equation of motion, $v^2 = u^2 + 2as$

$\Rightarrow \quad 0 = (25)^2 + 2 \times (-0.5) \times s = 625 - s$

$\Rightarrow \quad s = 625\ m$ [1+1]

62. A stone is thrown in a vertically upward direction with a velocity of 5 m/s. If the acceleration of the stone during its motion is 10 m/s^2 in the downward direction, what will be the height attained by the stone and what time will it take to reach there?

Sol. Given, $u = 5\ ms^{-1}$

$a = -10\ ms^{-2}$ (negative sign is due to upward direction)

$v = 0$ (at maximum height velocity is zero) [1]

Height attained, $s = ?$

Time taken, $t = ?$

(i) From third equation of motion, $v^2 = u^2 + 2as$

$$0 = (5)^2 + 2 \times -10 \times s$$

$$s = \frac{25}{20} = 1.25 \text{ m}$$ [1]

(ii) From first equation of motion, $v = u + at$

$$0 = 5 + (-10)t$$

$$t = \frac{5}{10} = 0.5 \text{ s}$$ [1]

Section-II

Structured Questions

63. (a) Distinguish between speed and velocity. [3]

(b) Express average velocity when the velocity of a body changes at (i) a non-uniform rate and (ii) a uniform rate. [3]

(c) Given statements show the nature of displacement-time graph of a body. Predict the nature of the motion in each case.

(i) Straight line parallel to the time axis.

(ii) Straight line inclined to the time axis with an acute angle.

(iii) Straight line inclined to the time axis with an obtuse angle.

(iv) A curve. [4]

Sol. (a) Differences between speed and velocity are given as

(i) Speed is distance travelled per second by a moving object while velocity is displacement travelled per second by a moving object.

(ii) Speed has no direction, so it is a scalar quantity but velocity has specific direction, so it is a vector quantity.

(iii) Speed can never be negative but velocity can be negative.

(b) (i) When the velocity of a body changes at a non-uniform rate, its average velocity is found by dividing the net displacement covered by the total time taken.

i.e. $\text{Average velocity} = \dfrac{\text{Net displacement}}{\text{Total time taken}}$

(ii) In case the velocity of a body changes at a uniform rate, then the average velocity is given by the arithmetic mean of initial velocity and final velocity for a given period of time.

i.e. Average velocity

$$= \frac{\text{Initial velocity} + \text{Final velocity}}{2}$$

(c) (i) Velocity is zero or body is at rest.

(ii) The displacement increases at constant rate with increase in time, so body is moving with constant velocity.

(iii) Body is returning to it initial position with constant change in displacement, so returning velocity is also constant or uniform.

(iv) Rate of change in displacement is not constant, so body is moving with non-uniform speed or velocity.

64. (a) When will you say a body is in (i) uniform acceleration and (ii) non-uniform acceleration? [3]

(b) What is the nature of distance-time graphs for (i) uniform motion and (ii) non-uniform motion of an object? [3]

(c) Give one example of each of the following situations. [4]

(i) Uniformly accelerated motion.

(ii) Motion with uniform retardation.

(iii) Accelerated motion with uniform magnitude of velocity.

(iv) Motion in a direction with acceleration in perpendicular direction.

Sol. (a) (i) A body is in uniform acceleration, when it travels in a straight path with its velocity increases or decreases by equal amount in equal time intervals.

(ii) A body is in non-uniform acceleration, when it travels in a straight path with its velocity increases or decreases by unequal amount in equal time intervals.

(b) (i) The distance-time graph for uniform motion of an object is a straight line.

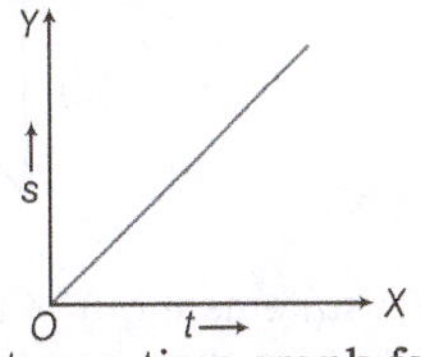

(ii) The distance-time graph for non-uniform motion of an object is a curved line.

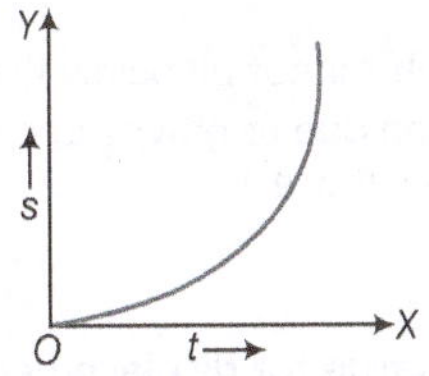

(Speed increases)

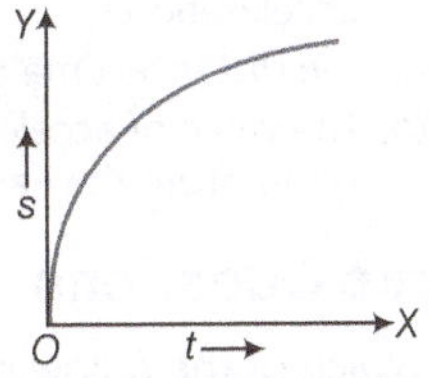

(Speed decreases)

(c) (i) Object dropped down from a height towards the surface of the Earth.

(ii) Object thrown up with a velocity, retards uniformly.

(iii) Uniform circular motion, say planetary motion.

(iv) A bullet fired horizontally from a rifle, has acceleration in downward direction (due to gravity).

Chapter Assessment

1 Mark Questions

1. If a body is moving on a circular path of radius 21 m with velocity of 2 m/s, then time taken by the body to complete half revolution is

(a) 11 s (b) 22 s (c) 44 s (d) 33 s

2. Suppose a boy is enjoying a ride on a merry-go-round which is moving with a constant speed of 10 ms^{-1}. It implies that the boy is

(a) at rest
(b) moving with no acceleration
(c) in accelerated motion
(d) moving with uniform velocity

3. Which one of the following velocity-time graph does not belong to motion in one-dimension ?

(a)
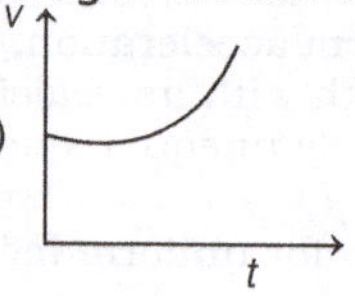

(b)
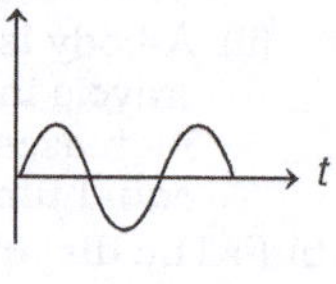

(c)
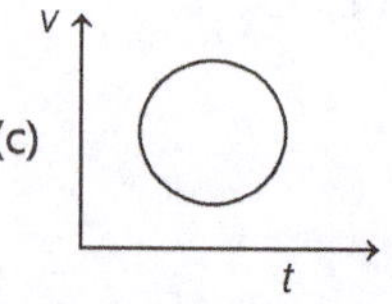

(d)
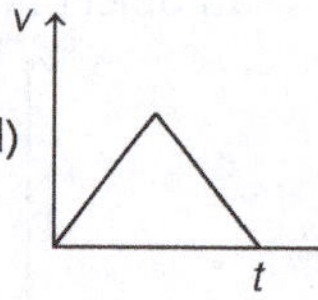

4. Find the incorrect statement out of the following.

(a) If acceleration is zero, then motion is uniform.
(b) In a velocity-time graph, area under the graph gives acceleration.
(c) The distance-time graph cannot be below the time axis.
(d) The value of acceleration due to gravity decreases with depth from the Earth's surface.

2 Marks Questions

5. Which of the following is true for displacement?

(i) It cannot be zero.
(ii) Its magnitude is greater than the distance travelled by the object.

6. Draw a diagram to show the motion of a body whose speed remains constant, but the velocity changes continuously.

7. Write the equation of motion for an object moving with a uniform velocity.

8. If the acceleration of the particle is constant in magnitude but not in direction, what type of path does the particle follow?

9. Why we cannot use equation of motion in case of acceleration varies with time?

10. Figure shows the distance-time graph of three objects *A*, *B* and *C*. Study the graph and answer the following questions.

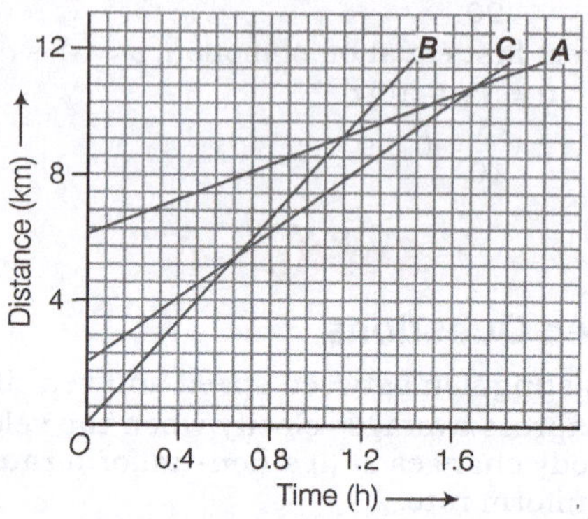

(i) Which of the three is travelling the fastest?
(ii) Are all three ever meet at same point on the road?

11. A cow and a bird both travelled from point *A* to point *B*. The cow travelled in a straight line but the bird travelled along the curved path as shown below.

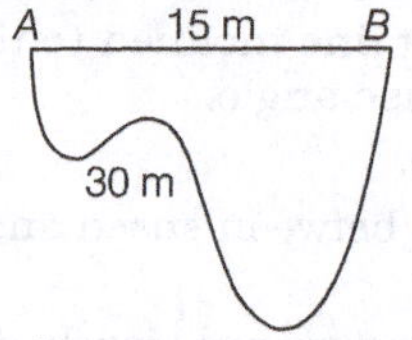

(i) What is the distance travelled by the cow and bird?
(ii) Which one of them has more displacement?

12. Give an example of motion in which average speed is not zero but average velocity is zero.

13. An object released from a certain height, bounce back to the same height after hitting ground. Show graphically the relation between velocity of the object with respect to time.

Structured Questions

14. (i) Deduce the equation for distance-time relation graphically. [3]

(ii) The graph given below is the distance-time graph of an object.

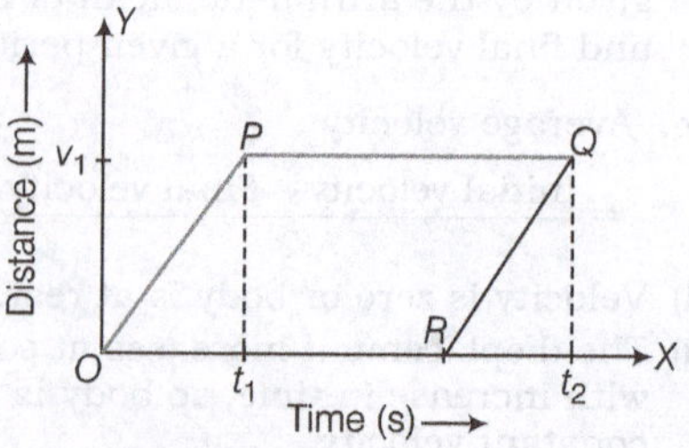

(a) Find expression for the speed of the object during first t_1 seconds of its stationary position.

(b) How long was it stationary for?

(c) Does it represent a real situation? Justify your answer. **[3]**

(iii) A particle starts to move in a straight line from a point with velocity 10 m/s and acceleration -2.0 m/s^2. Find the position and velocity of the particle at (a) $t = 5$ s and (b) $t_1 = 10$ s. **[4]**

15. (i) (a) If the velocity-time graph of an object is parallel to X-axis, then what does it mean? Can it be parallel to Y-axis?

(b) What type of motion is represented by each one of the following graphs?

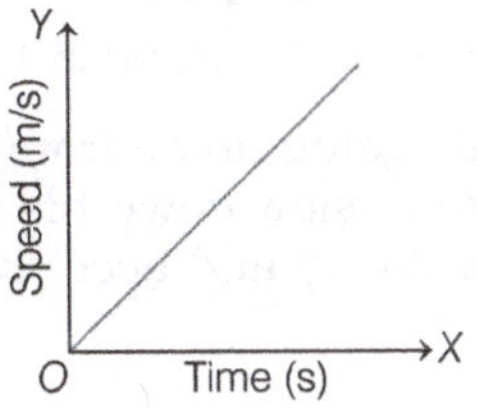

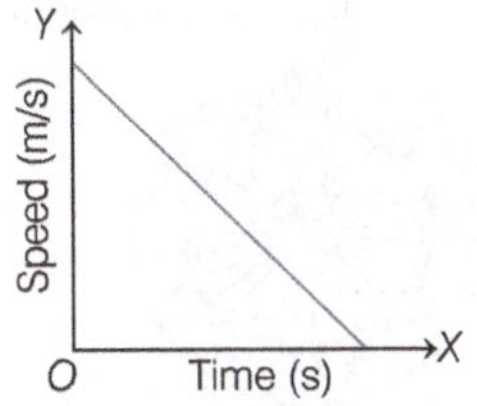

(c) A bus increases its speed from 36 km/h to 54 km/h in 10 s. Find its acceleration. **[3]**

(ii) Find the total displacement of the body from the following graph.

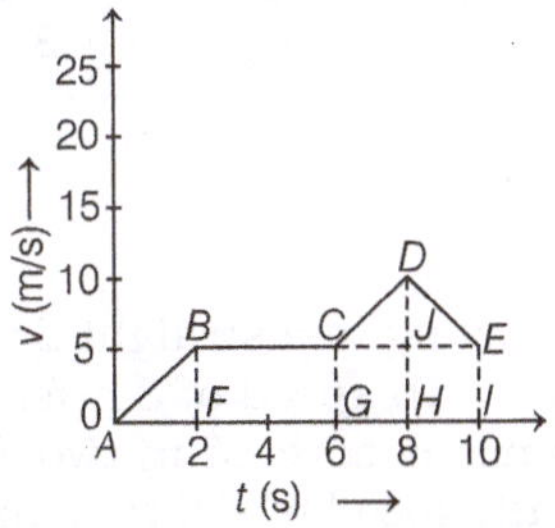

[3]

(iii) Distance travelled by a train and time taken by it is shown in the following table.

Time	Distance (in km)
10 : 00 AM	0
10 : 30 AM	25
10 : 40 AM	28
11 : 00 AM	40
11 : 15 AM	42
11 : 30 AM	50

(a) What is the average speed of the train?
(b) When is the train travelling at the highest speed?
(c) At what distance does the train slow down?
(d) Calculate the speed of the train between 10:40 AM to 11:00 AM. **[4]**

For Solutions Scan the Code

Olympiad Section*

Brain Teasing Questions of Olympiad Pattern

1 A particle moving in a straight line covers half the distance with speed of 3 m/s. The other half of the distance is covered in two equal time intervals with speed of 4.5 m/s and 7.5 m/s respectively. The average speed of particle during this motion is

(a) 4 m/s (b) 5 m/s (c) 5.5 m/s (d) 4.8 m/s

2 A bus begins to move with an acceleration of $1\ ms^{-2}$. A man who is 48 m behind the bus starts running at $10\ ms^{-1}$ to catch the bus. The man will be able to catch the bus after

(a) 6 s (b) 5 s
(c) 8 s (d) 7 s

3 A stone dropped from a balloon which is at height h, reaches the ground after t second. From the same balloon, if two stones are thrown, one upwards and other downwards, with the same velocity v and they reach the ground after t_1 and t_2 second respectively, then

(a) $t = t_1 - t_2$ (b) $t = \frac{t_1 + t_2}{2}$
(c) $t = \sqrt{t_1 t_2}$ (d) $t = \sqrt{t_1^2 - t_2^2}$

4 A bullet fired into a fixed wooden block loses half of its velocity after penetrating 40 cm. It comes to rest after penetrating a further distance of

(a) $\frac{22}{3}$ cm (b) $\frac{40}{3}$ cm
(c) $\frac{20}{3}$ cm (d) $\frac{22}{3}$ cm

5 A body is travelling in a straight line with a uniform increasing speed. Which one of the plot represents the change in distance (s) travelled with time (t)?

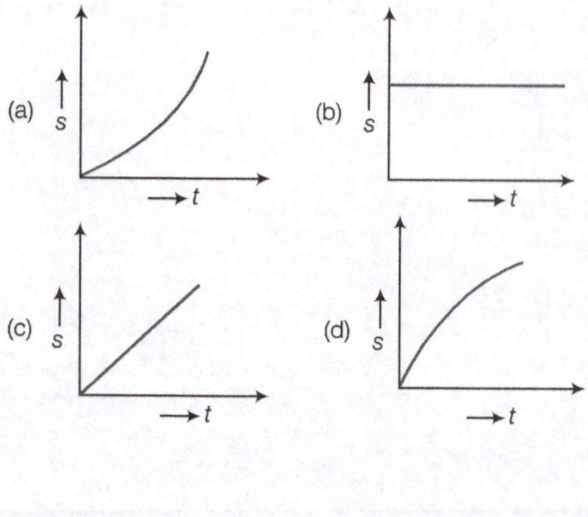

6 A scooterist sees a bus 1 km ahead of him moving with a velocity of $10 ms^{-1}$. With what speed the scooterist should move so as to overtake the bus in 100 s?

(a) $10\ ms^{-1}$ (b) $15\ ms^{-1}$ (c) $20\ ms^{-1}$ (d) $17\ ms^{-1}$

7 Madhur while going home from his school applies brake to slow down his speed. The direction of velocity and acceleration in the given case are

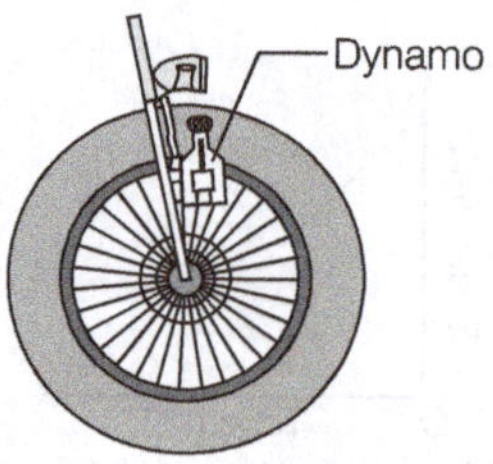

(a) opposite
(b) same
(c) perpendicular
(d) not related

8 The diagram shows a strip of paper tape that has been pulled under a vibrating arm by an object moving at constant speed. The arm is vibrating regularly making 50 dots/s.

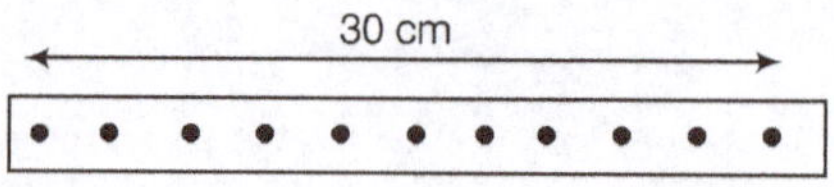

What was the speed of the object?

(a) 50 cm/s (b) 75 cm/s
(c) 100 cm/s (d) 150 cm/s

9 Two stones are thrown from the top of a building with the same speed u one in upward direction and the other in downward direction. When they reach ground, they acquire certain velocities v_1 and v_2, respectively v_1 and v_2 will be in the ratio of

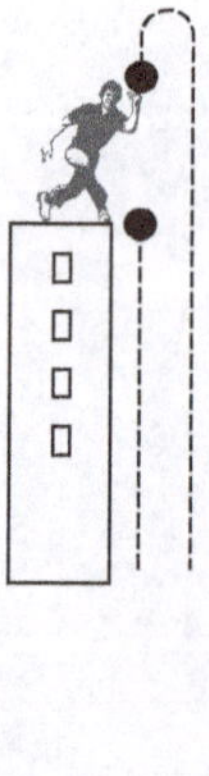

(a) 1 : 1 (b) 1 : 2
(c) 2 : 1 (d) 2 : 3

10 A car moving along straight line covers (1/5)th of total distance with speed v_1 and remaining part of distance with speed v_2. The average speed of car over entire distance

(a) $\frac{5v_1v_2}{v_2 + 4v_1}$ (b) $\frac{4v_1v_2}{5v_1 + v_2}$

(c) $\frac{5v_1v_2}{4v_2 + v_1}$ (d) $\frac{4v_1v_2}{4v_1 + v_2}$

11 A 100 m sprinter increases her speed from rest uniformly at the rate of 1 m/s^2 upto 40 m and covers the remaining distance with uniform speed. The sprinter covers the first half of the run in t_1 s and the second half in t_2 s. Then, **[INJSO 2013]**

(a) $t_1 > t_2$
(b) $t_1 < t_2$
(c) $t_1 = t_2$
(d) information given is incomplete

12 A ball is released from rest above a horizontal surface. The graph shows the variation with time of its velocity (not to scale). The scale on this graph is changed at every impact. *A*, *B*, *C*, *D* and *E* represent areas. Which of the following are correct?

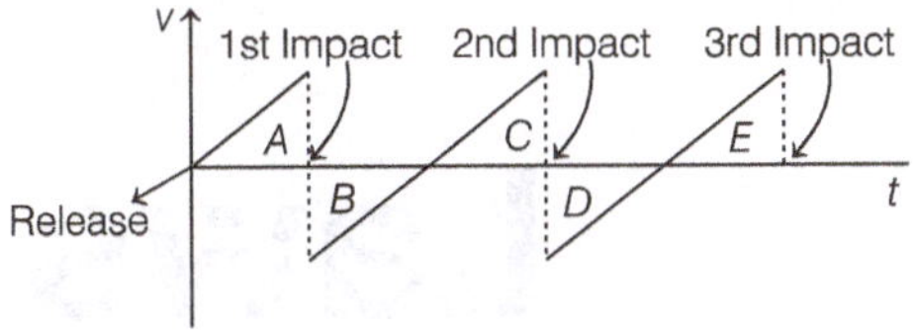

[INJSO 2011]

(a) $A = B$ and $B = C$
(b) $A = C$ and $C = E$
(c) $B = C$ and $D = E$
(d) All of the above

Answers									
1. (a)	**2.** (c)	**3.** (b)	**4.** (b)	**5.** (a)	**6.** (c)	**7.** (a)	**8.** (d)	**9.** (a)	**10.** (a)
11. (a)	**12.** (c)								

* *These questions may or may not be asked in the examination, have been given just for additional practice required for olympiads Scholarship Exams etc. For detailed explanations refer Page No. 212.*

CHAPTER

03

Laws of Motion

SYLLABUS

• Contact and Non-Contact Forces; CGS & SI units. • Newton's First Law of Motion (qualitative discussion), Introduction of the Idea of Inertia, Mass and Force. • Newton's Second Law of Motion (including $F = ma$); Weight and Mass. • Newton's Third Law of Motion (qualitative discussion only); simple examples.

In the previous chapter, we have discussed about the motion of an object along a straight line in terms of its position, velocity and acceleration. We saw that such a motion can be uniform or non-uniform. Now in this chapter, we will discuss the motion of a body by taking into consideration the cause of motion i.e. **force**.

Force

Any action which causes pull, hit or push on a body is called force. It is used in our everyday actions like pushing, pulling, lifting, stretching, twisting and pressing. It is a vector quantity and its SI unit is newton (N) and CGS unit is dyne.

e.g.

(i) A force is used, when we kick a football.

(ii) A force is used, when we lift a box from the floor.

(iii) A force is used, when we stretch a rubber band.

(iv) A force is used, when the hockey stick hits the ball forward.

Effects of Force

Force cannot be seen, it can only be judged by the effects which it can produce in various bodies around us.

A force applied on a body can produce four types of effects such as

(i) Force can start or stop a motion.

(ii) Force can change speed of an object, i.e. making it to move slower or faster.

(iii) Force can change the direction of motion of an object.

(iv) Force can change the size and shape of an object.

Types of Forces

According to the point of view of application, forces are divided into two parts.

1. Contact Forces

The forces that act between two or more bodies, when they are in physical contact with each other, are called contact forces.

Some contact forces are discussed below

(i) **Frictional Force** When a body slides (or rolls) over a rough surface, a force acts in opposite direction to the motion of body along the surface in contact, this force is known as frictional force or the force of friction.

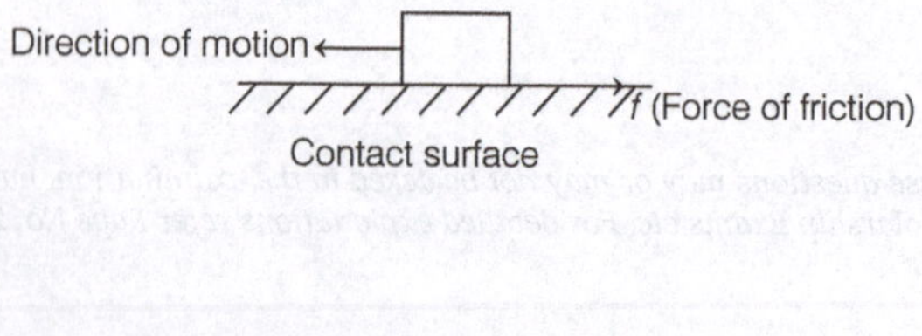

(ii) **Normal Reaction** It is a contact force between two surfaces in contact. It is always perpendicular to the surfaces of contact.
e.g. When a book is kept at a surface, weight of the book acts vertically downward and reaction force of surface is normal reaction.

(iii) **Force Exerted by a Spring** When a spring is compressed or extended by an external force, a restoring force is generated, which tries to bring the spring back to its normal position.

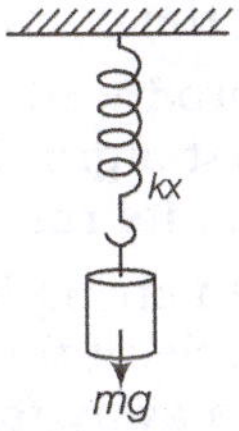

Spring force

(iv) **Tension Force as Applied Through String** When a body of mass m is suspended with the string, then the weight of the body acts downwards while a force acts just opposite to the downwards force for balancing it, this force is called tension.

(v) **Force Exerted During Collision** When two bodies A and B collide with each other as shown in the figure below, while in motion, moving body B exerts a force F_{AB} on the body A which is known as force of action. At the same instant, the body A also exerts an equal and opposite reaction force F_{BA}.

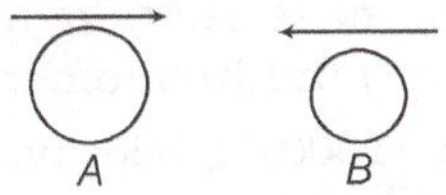

(a) Two bodies moving towards each other

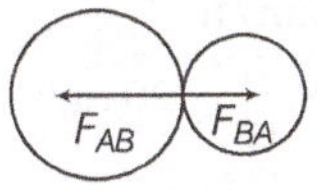

(b) Force exerted during collision

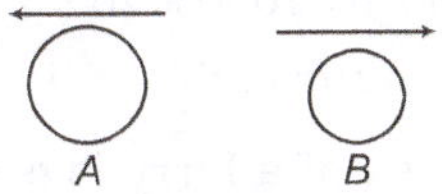

(c) After collision

As a result of these forces, the two bodies move apart after the collision.

2. Non-Contact Forces

The forces that act between two or more objects without any physical contact with each other are called non-contact forces.

Some non-contact forces are discussed below

(i) **Gravitational Force** The force of mutual attraction between any two objects (without any physical contact) because of their masses in universe is called gravitational force. This force was discovered by Isaac Newton.
It is the force of gravitation due to which Earth attracts everything towards itself.

(ii) **Electrostatic Force** The force between two charged particles is called electrostatic force. Like charges repel each other while opposite charges attract each other.
The effect of this force is evident, when we comb our hair with a plastic comb and immediately bring it close to some small pieces of paper. These pieces get attracted towards the comb as it gets charged due to friction with hair during combing.

(iii) **Magnetic Force** The force of attraction or repulsion between two magnetic poles is called magnetic force. This force acts even when these poles are at some separation. Like poles repel each other, whereas unlike poles attract each other.

General Properties of Non-Contact Forces

Following are the general properties of non-contact forces

(i) They depend upon the distance between the two objects. The magnitude of force varies inversely as the square of distance of separation.

(ii) They depend upon the medium between the two objects in case of electrical and magnetic forces but not in case of gravitational force.

(iii) These forces always act in action-reaction pair.

(iv) They are long-range forces and always act along the line joining the centres of the two bodies.

Check Your LEARNING...

1. What is the cause of motion of an object?
2. Is force needed to keep a moving body in motion?
3. A ball moving on a surface of table eventually stops. Explain the reason.
4. State one factor on which the magnitude of a non-contact force depends.
5. Given one example of non-contact force which magnitude does not depend upon the nature of medium.

Newton's Laws of Motion

Sir Isaac Newton (1642-1727) made a systematic study of motion and elaborated the views of Galileo. He then gave three laws of motion which are called Newton's laws of motion.

Newton's First Law of Motion

This law states that every body continue in its state of rest or of uniform motion in a straight line unless it is compelled by some external force to change that state.

The state of rest or uniform linear motion both imply zero acceleration. So, according to the first law of motion, if the net external force on a body is zero, its acceleration is zero. Acceleration can be non-zero only if there is a net external force on the body. Newton's first law defines force qualitatively.

Inertia

The tendency of a body to oppose or resist any change in its state of rest or of uniform motion is called inertia of the body. It is the inherent property of all the objects. Inertia of an object is measured by its mass. It is directly proportional to the mass. This means inertia increases with increase in mass and decreases with decrease in mass. A heavy object will have more inertia than lighter one.

Thus, first law defines inertia and so it is rightly inspired by the **law of inertia.**

Types of Inertia

Inertia is divided into three types as given below

(i) **Inertia of Rest** The tendency of a body to resist (oppose) any change in its state of rest is known as inertia of rest.

e.g.

(a) When a bus suddenly starts moving forward, then the passengers in the bus fall backward.

(b) The carpet is beaten with a stick to remove the dust particles.

(c) When a tree is vigorously shaken, then some of the leaves fall from the tree.

(ii) **Inertia of Motion** The tendency of a body to resist (oppose) any change in its state of uniform motion is known as inertia of motion.

e.g.

(a) The passengers fall forward when a fast moving bus stops suddenly.

(b) A person falls forward while getting down from a moving bus or train.

(c) A luggage is usually tied with a rope on the roof of a bus.

(iii) **Inertia of Direction** The tendency of a body to oppose any change in its direction of motion is known as inertia of direction.

e.g.

(a) When a fast moving bus negotiate a curve on the road, then passengers fall away from the centre of the curved road.

(b) The sparks produced during sharpening of a knife against a grinding wheel leave tangentially to its rim.

(c) A stone tied to string is whirling in a horizontal circle. If the string breaks, then the stone flies away tangentially.

Momentum

Momentum of a body is the quantity of motion possessed by the body. It is defined as the product of its mass m and velocity v and is denoted by p.

$\therefore$ Momentum, $p = mv$

Units of Momentum

SI unit of momentum = kg-m/s or kg-ms^{-1}

CGS unit of momentum = g-cm/s or g-cms^{-1}

It is a vector quantity and its direction is along the direction of velocity of the body.

Example 1. A car of mass 1000 kg is moving with a velocity of 72 km/h. Find its momentum.

Sol. Given, mass, $m = 1000$ kg, velocity, $v = 72$ km/h, momentum, $p = ?$

Velocity, $v = 72$ km/h

$$= 72 \times \frac{5}{18} = 20 \text{ m/s} \quad \left(\because 1 \text{ km/h} = \frac{5}{18} \text{ m/s}\right)$$

Momentum = Mass × Velocity

$$\therefore \quad p = m \times v = 1000 \times 20 = 2 \times 10^4 \text{ kg-m/s}$$

Thus, the momentum of the car is 2×10^4 kg-m/s.

Example 2. The mass of a lorry is 4000 kg and the mass of goods loaded on it is 20000 kg. If the lorry is moving with a velocity of 2 m/s, then what will be its momentum?

Sol. Given, velocity of lorry, $v = 2$ m/s,

Mass of lorry, $m_1 = 4000$ kg

Mass of goods on the lorry, $m_2 = 20000$ kg,

Momentum, $p = ?$

Total mass in motion = Mass of lorry + Mass of goods

i.e. $m = m_1 + m_2 = 4000 \text{ kg} + 20000 \text{ kg} = 24000$ kg

$\therefore$ Momentum = Mass × Velocity

$$p = mv = 24000 \text{ kg} \times 2 \text{ m/s}$$
$$= 4.8 \times 10^4 \text{ kg-m/s}$$

Thus, momentum of the lorry = 4.8×10^4 kg-m/s

Change in Momentum

Momentum of a body is given by $p = mv$

$\therefore$ Change in momentum, $\Delta p = \Delta(mv)$

Hence, the change in momentum can be either due to change in velocity or change in mass or both.

If the velocity of the body (v) is much smaller than the velocity of light (c), then the mass can be considered as constant, so $\Delta p = m\Delta v$.

Newton's Second Law of Motion

This law states that the rate of change of momentum of a body is directly proportional to the external force applied on it and the change in momentum takes place in the direction of the applied force.

Mathematical Formulation of Second Law of Motion

If a body of mass m moving at initial velocity u accelerates uniformly with an acceleration a for time t, such that its final velocity changes to v, then

Initial momentum, $p_1 = mu$

and final momentum, $p_2 = mv$

$\therefore$ Change in momentum = $p_2 - p_1 = (\Delta p) = mv - mu$
$= m(v - u)$

According to the second law of motion,

$$\text{Force} \propto \frac{\text{Change in momentum}}{\text{Time}}$$

$$\Rightarrow \quad F \propto \frac{\Delta p}{\Delta t} = \frac{p_2 - p_1}{t} \quad \Rightarrow \quad F \propto \frac{m(v-u)}{t}$$

$$\Rightarrow \quad F \propto ma \qquad \left(\because \frac{v-u}{t} = a\right)$$

$$\therefore \quad F = kma$$

The quantity k is a constant of proportionality.

One unit of force is defined as the amount that produces an acceleration of 1 m/s² on an object of 1 kg mass.

i.e. 1 unit of force = $k \times 1 \text{ kg} \times 1 \text{ m/s}^2$

$$\Rightarrow \quad k = 1$$

Thus, the force can be written as $\boxed{F = ma}$

This is the mathematical form of Newton's second law of motion.

As, $\quad m \times a$ = rate of change of momentum

$\therefore \quad F$ = rate of change of momentum

or $\quad \boxed{F = \dfrac{\Delta p}{\Delta t}}$

The SI unit of force is **newton (N)**.

1 newton is equal to the force which acts on a body of mass 1 kg and produces an acceleration of 1m/s^2.

i.e. $\quad 1\text{N} = 1 \text{ kg} \times 1 \text{ m/s}^2 = 1 \text{ g cms}^{-2}$

The CGS unit of force is **dyne.**

1 dyne is equal to the force which acts on a body of mass 1g and produces an acceleration of 1 cm/s²

i.e. $\quad 1 \text{ dyne} = 1 \text{ g} \times 1 \text{ cm s}^{-2} = 1 \text{ g cm}^{-2}$

Relation between newton and dyne

$$1 \text{ N} = 1 \text{ kg ms}^{-2} = \frac{1000 \text{ g} \times 100 \text{ cm}}{\text{s}^2} = 10^5 \text{ g cms}^{-2}$$

Thus, 1 N = 10^5 dyne

Graphical Representation of Second Law of Motion

According to Newton's second law of motion,

(i) The acceleration produced in a body is directly proportional to the applied force, i.e. $a \propto F$ (if mass remains constant).

The graph for this condition is shown below.

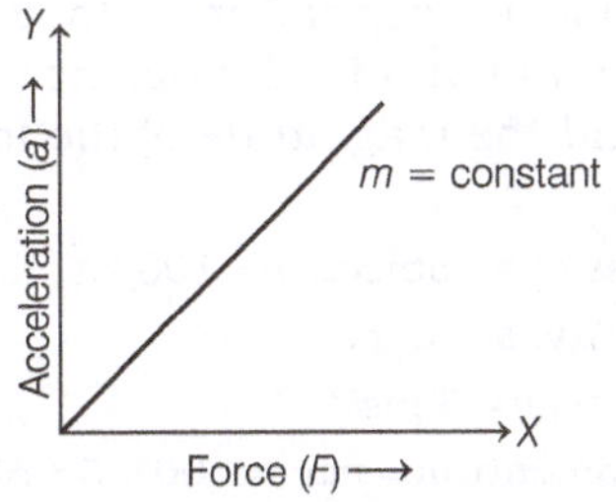

(ii) The force that is needed to accelerate the body is directly proportional to the mass of the body.

i.e. $F \propto m$ (if acceleration is constant).

The graph for this condition is shown below.

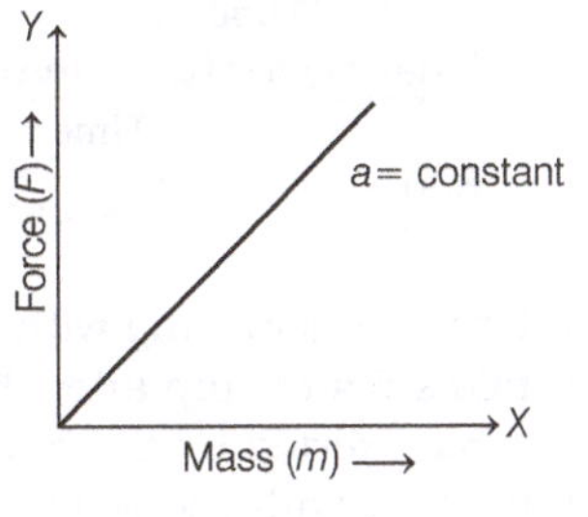

(iii) If the applied force on the body is constant, then the acceleration produced in the body is inversely proportional to the mass of that body.

i.e. $a \propto \frac{1}{m}$ (if F is constant)

The graph for this condition is shown below.

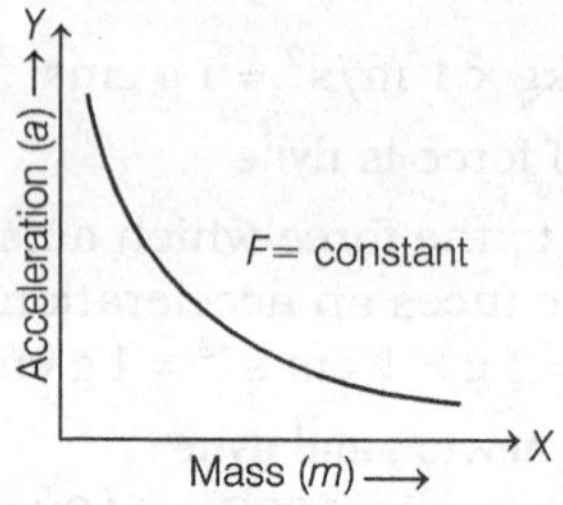

Example 3. If a force of 1000 N is applied over a vehicle of 500 kg, then in how much time the velocity of the vehicle will increase from 2 m/s to 10 m/s?

Sol. Given, force, $F = 1000$ N, mass, $m = 500$ kg

Final velocity, $v_2 = 10$ m/s

Initial velocity, $v_1 = 2$ m/s

Time, $t = ?$

From Newton's second law, $F = \frac{m(v_2 - v_1)}{t}$

$\Rightarrow \quad t = \frac{m(v_2 - v_1)}{F} = 500 \times \frac{(10-2)}{1000} = 4\ \text{s}$

Example 4. An object of mass 100 kg is accelerated uniformly from a velocity of 5 ms^{-1} to 8 ms^{-1} in 6 s. Calculate the initial and final momentum of the object. Also, find the magnitude of the force exerted on the object.

Sol. Given, mass of an object, $m = 100$ kg, time = 6 s

Initial velocity, $u = 5$ ms^{-1}

Final velocity, $v = 8$ ms^{-1}

$\therefore$ Initial momentum = mu = $100 \times 5 = 500$ kg ms^{-1}

and final momentum = mv = $100 \times 8 = 800$ kg ms^{-1}

Change in momentum = $\Delta p = (800 - 500)$ kg ms^{-1} = 300 kg ms^{-1}

From Newton's second law, force exerted on the object

= Rate of change of momentum

$= \frac{\text{Change in momentum}}{\text{Time}}$

$= \frac{\text{Final momentum} - \text{Initial momentum}}{\text{Time}}$

$= \frac{800 - 500}{6} = \frac{300}{6} = 50\ \text{N}$

Example 5. A bullet train is moving with a velocity of 180 km/h and it takes 5 s to stop after the brakes are applied. Find the force exerted by the brakes on the wheel of train, if its mass with the wagon is 2000 kg.

Sol. Given, initial velocity, $u = 180$ km/h

$= 180 \times \frac{5}{18}$ m/s = 50 m/s

Final velocity, $v = 0$, time, $t = 5$ s, mass, $m = 2000$ kg, force, $F = ?$

From first equation of motion,

$v = u + at \Rightarrow u = -at \quad (\because v = 0)$

$\Rightarrow \quad a = \frac{-u}{t} = \frac{-50}{5} = -10\ \text{m/s}^2$

Now, force exerted by the brakes on the wheel is given by Newton's second law,

$F = ma = 2000 \times (-10) = -20000\ \text{N} = -2 \times 10^4\ \text{N}$

Negative sign shows the direction of force is in opposite to motion of the body.

Example 6. A 500 kg vehicle moving with a speed of 10 m/s is brought to rest at a distance of 50 m.

(i) Find the acceleration and time.

(ii) Calculate unbalanced force acting on it.

Sol. Given, mass, $(m) = 500$ kg, initial velocity, $(u) = 10$ m/s, distance, $(s) = 50$ m, acceleration, $(a) = ?$ and force, $(F) = ?$

(i) From third equation of motion, $v^2 = u^2 + 2as$

$\Rightarrow \quad u^2 = -2as \quad (\because v = 0)$

$\Rightarrow \quad a = \frac{-u^2}{2s} = \frac{-100}{2 \times 50} = -1\ \text{m/s}^2$

Time taken to stop the vehicle is given by equation of motion.

From first equation of motion,

$v = u + at \Rightarrow u = -at \quad (\because v = 0)$

$\Rightarrow \quad t = \frac{u}{-a} = \frac{10}{-(-1)} = 10\ \text{s}$

(ii) Now, unbalanced force is given by Newton's second law.

$\therefore \quad F = ma = 500 \times (-1) = -500\ \text{N}$

Thus, acceleration, time and unbalanced force are -1 m/s^2, 10 s and -500 N, respectively.

Example 7. A force of 5 N gives a mass m_1, an acceleration of 10 m/s^2 and a mass m_2, an acceleration of 20 m/s^2. What acceleration would it give, if both the masses were tied together?

Sol. Given, force, $F = 5$ N

Acceleration in mass m_1, $a_1 = 10$ m/s^2

Acceleration in mass m_2, $a_2 = 20$ m/s^2

Acceleration produced when both the masses are tied together, $a = ?$

From Newton's second law of motion,

$m_1 = \frac{F}{a_1}, m_2 = \frac{F}{a_2}$

Total mass, $m = m_1 + m_2$

$\therefore \quad m_1 = \frac{5}{10} = 0.5\ \text{kg}, \quad m_2 = \frac{5}{20} = 0.25\ \text{kg}$

$\therefore \quad m = 0.5 + 0.25 = 0.75$ kg

Acceleration produced in combined mass, $a = \dfrac{F}{m}$

$\therefore \quad a = \dfrac{5}{0.75} = 6.67\ \text{m/s}^2$

Thus, acceleration is 6.67 m/s^2 when both the masses were tied together.

Deduction of Newton's First Law of Motion from Second Law of Motion

According to Newton's second law of motion,

$$F = ma \quad \text{or} \quad F = \frac{m(v-u)}{t}$$

If $F = 0$, then

$v = u$.

i.e. The object continues to move with uniform velocity or speed, if no force is applied on it.

If $F = 0$ and $u = 0$, then $v = 0$.

i.e. If the object is in state of rest, it will remain in this state.

Thus, a body does not change its state of rest or of motion until and unless an external force applied on it. This is the statement of Newton's first law of motion.

Some Everyday Phenomena Based on Newton's Second Law of Motion

Some common examples are

(i) Consider a light-weight vehicle, i.e. car and a heavy weight vehicle, i.e. truck parked on a horizontal road. We require a greater force to push the truck than the car to bring at the same speed in same time. Also, a greater opposing force requires to stop the truck than the car at the same time, if they are moving with the same speed. Due to heavy mass of truck as compared to car, it has greater momentum, so greater force is required.

(ii) A bullet fired by a gun can easily pierce human tissue before it stops, resulting in casuality. The same bullet fired with moderate speed will not cause much damage.

Thus, for a given mass, the greater the speed, the greater is the opposing force needed to stop the body in a certain time. With higher speed, the momentum will be higher. This is the reason that bullet with high speed applies more force, thus more damage.

(iii) If two stones, one light and other heavy are dropped from the top of a building, a person on the ground will find it easier to catch the light stone than the heavy stone. Due to more mass, heavy stone has more momentum, thus apply more force on hand, so difficult to catch.

(iv) When cricket player catches the ball, its speed becomes zero i.e., momentum changes to zero. By lowering his hand, the player increases the time of stopping the ball. By increasing the time, the rate of change of momentum of ball decreases, hence lesser force is applied on the hands of the player.

Check Your LEARNING...

1. Which type of inertia is involved in removing the dust particles from beaten carpet?
2. How is momentum related to velocity?
3. Write the SI and CGS unit of momentum.
4. Mention the type of force which can produce acceleration on a moving body with constant speed.
5. How much force is required to produce an acceleration of 2 m/s^2 in a body of mass 0.8 kg? *Ans.* 1.6 N
6. Why is it preferred to land on sand instead of hard floor while taking a high jump?

Newton's Third Law of Motion

Newton's third law states that for every action, there is always an equal and opposite reaction.

In simple terms, the third law can be stated as follows

Force in nature always occur in pairs. Force on body *A* by body *B* is equal and opposite to the force on the body *B* by body *A*.

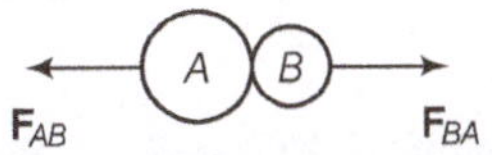

Forces acting on bodies *A* and *B*

As shown in figure, if F_{BA} is the force exerted by body *A* on body *B* and F_{AB} is the force exerted by body *B* on body *A*, then according to Newton's third law, $F_{AB} = -F_{BA}$

Force on body *A* by body *B* = – Force on body *B* by body *A*

The condition is shown in figure.

Some important implications of the Newton's third law of motion are

(i) **Newton's Third Law of Motion is Applicable Irrespective of the Nature of the Forces** The forces of action and reaction may be mechanical, gravitational, electrical or of any other nature.

(ii) **Action and Reaction Always Act on Two Different Bodies** If they act on the same body, the resultant force would be zero and there could never be an accelerated motion.

(iii) **The Force of Action and Reaction cannot Cancel each other** This is because action and reaction, are equal and opposite forces, which always act on different bodies and so cannot cancel each other.

(iv) **No Action can Occur in the Absence of a Reaction** In a tug of war, one team can pull the rope only if the other team is pulling the other end of the rope. No force can be exerted, if the other end is free.

One team exerts the force of action and the other team provides the force of reaction.

Applications of Newton's Third Law of Motion

(i) **Collision of Two Persons** If two persons walking or running in opposite directions collide with each other, then both feel hurt because they apply force on each other. Two opposing forces are action and reaction pair.

(ii) **Walking of a Person** A person is able to walk because of the Newton's third law of motion. While walking, a person pushes the ground in backward direction which is the action. The ground also pushes the person with equal magnitude of force but in opposite direction which is the reaction. This enables him to move in forward direction against the push.

(iii) **Recoil of Gun** When bullet is fired from a gun, then the bullet also pushes the gun in opposite direction with equal magnitude of force. Thus, gunman feels a backward push, i.e. recoil force from the butt of gun. Since, the gun has a greater mass than bullet, acceleration of the gun is much less than the acceleration of the bullet.

(iv) **Propulsion of a Boat in Forward Direction** Sailor pushes water with oar in backward direction resulting water to push the oar in forward direction. Consequently, the boat is pushed in forward direction. Force applied by oar and water are of equal magnitude but in opposite directions.

(v) **Rocket Propulsion** The propulsion of rocket is based on the principle of action and reaction. The rapid burning of fuel produces hot gases which rush out from the nozzle at the rear end at a very high speed. The equal and opposite reaction force moves the rocket upward at a great speed.

Check Your LEARNING...

1. Why do we need fuel to ride a motorcycle even after attaining a particular speed?
2. Explain (in brief), how rocket moves up?
3. Why do we feel ourself more heavier, when we go upward in a lift?
4. Why does the shaft of a canon come back after firing?
5. How can climbing a tree by a monkey through a rope be an example of Newton's third law of motion?

QUiCK Revision

- **Force** is an external agency (a pull or a push) which changes or tends to change the state of rest or of uniform motion or the direction of motion of a body. Its SI unit is newton(N).
- Forces are of two types
  (i) **Contact force** (ii) **Non-contact force**
- A **contact force** on an object arises due to physical contact between the two boides.
- **Non-contact force** is the force experienced by an object even without any physical contact with any other object.
- **Inertia** The tendency of a body to oppose or resist any change in its state of rest or of a uniform motion is called inertia of the body.
- **Sir Isaac Newton** (1642-1727) made a systematic study of motion and proposed three laws of motion.
- **Newton's first law of motion** states that every body continue in its state of rest or of uniform motion until and unless it is compelled by some external force to change that state.
- **Momentum** is the quantity of motion possessed by the body. It is equal to the product of its mass (m) and velocity (v).
  $$p = mv$$
  Its SI unit is kg-m/s.
- **Newton's second law of motion** states that the rate of change of momentum of a body is directly proportional to the external force applied on the body and the change in momentum takes place in the direction of the applied force.
  $$F = \frac{\Delta p}{\Delta t} = ma$$
- **Newton's third law of motion** states that for every action, there is always an equal and opposite reaction.
  $$F_{AB} = -F_{BA}$$

Chapter Practice

Section I

1 Mark Questions

1. Which of the following force is non-contact force?
   (a) Force of reaction (b) Force due to gravity
   (c) Tension in string (d) Force of friction

Sol. (*b*) Force due to gravity is non-contact force. Gravitational force of attraction acts between the two objects due to their masses.

2. The inertia of an object tends to cause the object to
   (a) increase its speed
   (b) decrease its speed
   (c) resist any change in its state of motion
   (d) decelerate due to friction

Sol. (*c*) Inertia is the property of an object by virtue of which it resist any change in its state of motion.

3. An athlete often runs before taking a long jump, which of the following reason?
   (a) Running help to apply more force
   (b) With running action and reaction forces will increase
   (c) He gains energy to take him through the long distance
   (d) By running, he gives himself large inertia

Sol. (*d*) An athlete often runs before taking a long jump because by running he brings his whole body in the state of motion. Due to inertia, when the body is in motion, it becomes easier to take a long jump.

4. Two forces F_1 and F_2 are acting on a body as shown in the figure, then acceleration in the body is

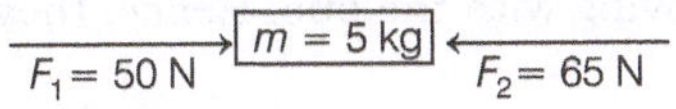

   (a) 23 m/s^2 (b) 3 m/s^2
   (c) 2 m/s^2 (d) 22 m/s^2

Sol. (*b*) Resultant force on a body,

$$F = F_2 - F_1 = 65 - 50 = 15 \text{ N}$$

By Newton's second law of motion,

$$F = ma$$

$$\Rightarrow \quad 15 = 5a$$

$$\Rightarrow \quad a = 3 \text{ m/s}^2$$

5. A truck is moving with a speed of 54 km/h. Truck driver applies brakes suddenly and brings the truck to rest in 5 s, then the average retarding force on truck, if mass of the truck and driver is 400 kg, will be
   (a) 1200 N (b) 600 N
   (c) 800 N (d) 500 N

Sol. (*a*) Given, $u = 54 \text{ km/h} = 54 \times \frac{5}{18} \text{ m/s} = 15 \text{ m/s}$

$$v = 0 \text{ and } t = 5 \text{ s}$$

$\therefore$ Retardation, $a = \frac{v-u}{t} = \frac{0-15}{5} = -3 \text{ m/s}^2$

Average retarding force, $F = ma = 400 \times 3 = 1200 \text{ N}$

6. If the acceleration of a body is doubled, then the force on the body will become
   (a) half
   (b) same
   (c) twice
   (d) one-fourth

Sol. (*c*) According to Newton's second law of motion, force on an object is directly proportional to its acceleration, if mass remains constant.
Therefore, if acceleration of the body is doubled, then the force will also become twice.

7. Which of the following is the correct form of Newton's second law of motion?
   (a) $F = p_2 - p_1$ (b) $F = mv$
   (c) $F = \frac{\Delta p}{\Delta t}$ (d) All of these

Sol. (*c*) According to Newton's second law of motion, force is defined as the rate of change of momentum, i.e.

$$F = \frac{\Delta p}{\Delta t}$$

8. Which of the following graph is not explained in Newton's second law of motion?

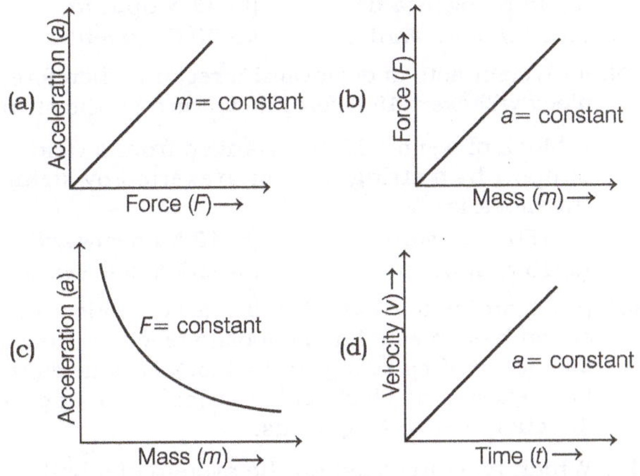

Sol. (*d*) According to Newton's second law of motion,
$F = ma$ or $a \propto F$ (if m = constant)
$F \propto m$ (if a = constant)
$a \propto \frac{1}{m}$ (if F = constant)

Here, velocity-time graph with constant acceleration in option (d) is not explained by Newton's second law of motion.

9. According to the third law of motion, action and reaction
(a) always act on the same body
(b) always act on different bodies in opposite directions
(c) have same magnitude and direction
(d) act on either body at normal to each other

Sol. (*b*) According to third law of motion, action and reaction always act on different bodies in opposite directions.

10. Consider two spring balances hooked as shown in the figure below. We pull them in opposite directions. If the reading shown by *A* is 1.5 N, the reading shown by *B* will be

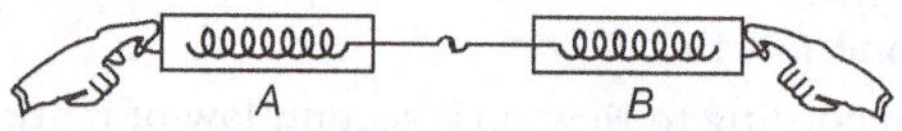

(a) 1.5 N (b) 2.5 N
(c) 3.5 N (d) zero

Sol. (*a*) According to Newton's third law of motion, every action has equal and opposite reaction. Hence, force (action) exerted by *A* on *B* and force exerted by *B* on *A* are equal hence reading shown by *B* will be 1.5 N.

11. In the given figure, a block of weight 45 N is hanging from a rigid support by a string.

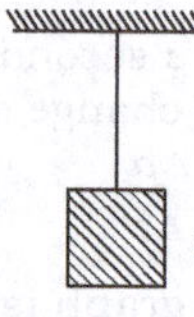

The force exerted by block on the string is
(a) 45 N downward (b) 45 N upward
(c) 90 N downward (d) 90 N upward

Sol. (*a*) Weight acts in downward direction. Therefore, the block will exert 45 N force downward on the string.

12. A block of weight 15 N is hanged from a rigid support by a string. The force exerted by string on the block is
(a) 150 N upward (b) 15 N downward
(c) 15 N upward (d) 150 N downward

Sol. (*c*) According to Newton's third law of motion, every action has an equal and opposite reaction. Hence, force exerted by string on the block is same as that of force exerted by block on the string but in opposite direction, i.e. 15 N upwards.

13. Which two forces act on the system of a ball hanged from roof using a string?
(a) Weight and friction
(b) Friction and tension
(c) Tension and normal reaction
(d) Tension and weight

Sol. (*d*) The forces acting on the system are action-reaction forces. Action force is due to the weight of the ball in downward direction and reaction due to the action force in string, in the form of tension.

14. Which of the following is incorrect about Newton's third law of motion?
(a) The action and reaction are equal in magnitude
(b) The action and reaction both act simultaneously
(c) The action and reaction act on different bodies in opposite direction
(d) The action and reaction cancel each other

Sol. Statement in option (d) is incorrect.
The force of action and reaction cannot cancel each other because both the forces are equal in magnitude but opposite in direction and always act on different bodies.

2 Marks Questions

15. Define inertia and write its types.

Sol. The tendency of a body to oppose or resist any change in its state of rest or of motion is called inertia of the body. [1]
Inertia can be classified as follows
(i) Inertia of rest
(ii) Inertia of motion
(iii) Inertia of direction [1]

16. Why do you fall in the forward direction, when a moving bus applies brakes to stop and fall backward, when it accelerates from rest?

Sol. When the moving bus applies brakes to stop, the passengers due to inertia of motion, oppose a change in their state. However, the lower portion of their body comes to rest with the bus. So, they fall forward. [1]
When the moving bus accelerates from rest, the passengers due to inertia of rest, oppose a change in their state. However, the lower portion of their body starts moving with the bus. Hence, they fall backward. [1]

17. Why is it advised to tie the luggage kept on the roof of a bus with a rope?

Sol. It is advised to tie any luggage kept on the roof of a bus because, when the bus stops suddenly, then bus comes in the state of rest but the luggage remains in the state of motion. So, due to inertia of motion, the luggage moves forward and falls down from the roof of the bus. [1]
If the bus starts suddenly, then bus comes in the state of motion but luggage remains in the state of rest. Due to inertia of rest, the luggage moves in the backward direction and falls down. [1]

18. A person driving a car suddenly applies the brakes on seeing a child on the road ahead. If he is not wearing seat belt, he falls forward and his head hits against the steering wheel. Why?

Sol. When a person driving a car suddenly applies the brakes, the lower part of the body slows down with the car while upper part of the body continues to move forward due to inertia of motion. If driver is not wearing seat belt, then he falls forward and his head hits against the steering wheel. **[2]**

19. Why does a coin thrown vertically upward in moving bus come back to the thrower's hand?

Sol. Coin thrown vertically upward in moving bus comes back to the thrower's hand due to inertia of motion of bus and thrower simultaneously in the direction of moving bus. **[2]**

20. Why do bodies of larger mass require larger initial effort force to bring them into motion?

Sol. The inertia of a body is directly proportional to mass, larger is mass, greater is inertia. So, larger mass needs larger initial force to bring it into motion. **[2]**

21. When we shake the branch of a mango tree, the mangoes fall down. Why?

Sol. Because due to shaking, the branches come into motion but due to inertia, the mangoes continue to remain at rest and get detached. **[2]**

22. Which will have greater inertia amongst three balls *A*, *B* and *C* filled with same volume of mercury, water and air, respectively? Give reasons to support your answer.

Sol. Mercury has more inertia than water and air because mercury has greatest density and hence greatest mass. If a body has more mass, it has more inertia that's why heavier body have more inertia than the lighter body.

A mercury ball *A* has more inertia than water ball *B* and air ball *C*. **[2]**

23. State Newton's first law of motion and give one example.

Sol. Newton's first law states that, an object will continue to remain in its state of rest or in uniform motion along a straight line path unless an external force acts on it. e.g., A person standing in a moving bus falls forward, if driver applies brakes suddenly. **[2]**

24. Define momentum. Give its SI and CGS unit.

Sol. Momentum is defined as the product of mass and its velocity. It is denoted by p.

As, momentum = mass × velocity

$$p = mv$$

SI unit of momentum is kg ms^{-1} and CGS unit of momentum is g cms^{-1}. **[2]**

25. Two similar vehicles are moving with same velocity on the road, such that one of them is loaded and the other one is empty. Which of the two vehicles will require larger force to stop it? Why?

Sol. A larger force is required to stop the loaded vehicle. It is because loaded vehicle has greater momentum than the empty vehicle as the mass of loaded vehicle is more than that of the empty vehicle. Thus, it requires a greater force to stop. **[2]**

26. State Newton's second law of motion. Write its mathematical formulation.

Sol. According to Newton's second law of motion, the rate of change of linear momentum is directly proportional to the force applied on (or by) the object.

Mathematically, it is expressed as **[1]**

$$F \propto \frac{\Delta p}{\Delta t}$$

$$\therefore \quad F = k\frac{m(v-u)}{t} \text{ or } F = kma \qquad \left(\because \frac{v-u}{t} = a\right)$$

As, $k = 1$, $F = ma$ **[1]**

27. When the glass vessels fall on a hard floor, they break, but when they fall on a carpet (or sand) they do not break. Why?

Sol. When a glass vessel falls from a height on a hard floor, it comes to rest almost instantaneously (i.e. in a very short time), so the floor exerts very large force and thus vessel breaks down. **[1]**

But if it falls on carpet (or sand), the time duration (for it to come to rest) increases, so force decreases. Thus, vessel does not break. **[1]**

28. How can a small mass such as a bullet kill a person when fired from a gun?

Sol. The mass of the bullet is small, it moves out of the gun with a very high velocity, due to which the momentum produced is very high ($p = mv$). This high momentum of the bullet produces a large force which is enough to kill a person. **[2]**

29. Why a cricket player, while taking a catch always moves his hands backward?

Sol. When the cricket player catches the ball, the speed of the ball becomes zero in a few seconds. Hence, its momentum is reduced to zero. The player moves his hands backward to increase the time of stopping the ball. This decreases the rate of change of momentum of the ball and less force will be applied on the hands of the player. **[2]**

30. Draw a graph showing the relationship between acceleration and mass for a constant force.

Sol. Force is given by, $F = ma$

For a constant force (F), $a \propto \frac{1}{m}$

i.e. Acceleration is inversely proportional to mass. **[1]**

Hence, the graph of a *versus* m is

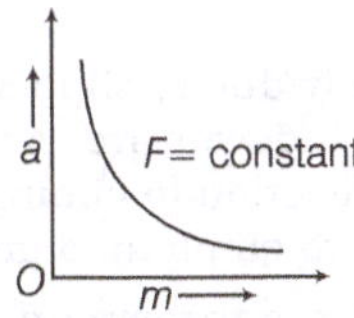

[1]

31. Glass wares are wrapped in straw during their transportation. Justify giving reason.

Sol. During transportation, the glass wares may break, if they collide with each other in the event of jerks. When they are wrapped in straw, the force of jerk is transmitted to them through the pieces of straw in a longer period of time. [1]

Thus, the change in momentum of the glass wares takes place in a longer period of time. Therefore, a very small force is experienced by them in the event of jerks and hence they do not break. [1]

32. According to the third law of motion, when we push an object, it pushes back with an equal and opposite force. If the object is a massive truck parked along the roadside, it will probably not move. A student justifies this by answering that the two opposite and equal forces cancel each other. Comment on this logic and explain, why the truck does not move?

Sol. The logic given by the student is not correct because two equal and opposite forces cancel each other only if they act on the same body. According to Newton's third law, action and reaction force always act on two different bodies, so they cannot cancel each other. [1]

When a massive truck is pushed, then the truck may not move because the force applied is not sufficient to move the truck. [1]

33. Two children stand on wheel-carts facing each other. One student throws a heavy mass towards the other who catches it. What will be the direction of motion of both the children? Give reason for your answer.

Sol. The child who throws the mass towards the other and the one who catches it, both move backwards. [1]

Reason : Thrower moves due to backward reaction of mass pushed forward. Catcher moves backwards due to forward reaction of mass. [1]

34. Two identical bullets are fired one by one by a light rifle and another by a heavy rifle with the same force, which rifle will hurt the shoulder more and why?

Sol. As both the bullets are identical and are fired with the same force. So, according to Newton's third law of motion, same force will be applied on both the rifles. With the application of same force, the light rifle will move more quickly in the backward direction, so it will hurt more to the shoulder. [2]

35. Why is it difficult to climb up a greasy pole?

Sol. A man climbing up a pole presses the pole downward with his feet to give action, the pole in turns gives reaction force in upward direction to the man with an equal force. [1]

If the pole is greasy due to slippery surface man is not able to press it downward. As there is no action, there will be no reaction to climb up. Therefore, it becomes difficult to climb up a greasy pole. [1]

36. On a sail boat, air is thrown on the sail from an electric fan attached to the same boat. Will the boat start moving?

Sol. The boat will not start moving because action and reaction should act on two different bodies. Here, resultant force is zero. [2]

37. Write any two applications of Newton's third law of motion.

Sol. Refer to page No. 56.

3 Marks Questions

38. Define force. Write any three effects produced by force.

Sol. Any action which causes pull or push on a body is called force.

Effects produced by force on a body are as follows

(i) Change in position

(ii) Change in rest or motion

(iii) Change in shape [1+1+1]

39. Which of the following has more inertia?

(i) A stone and a rubber ball of same size

(ii) A bicycle and a train

(iii) A five rupees coin and a one rupee coin

Give reason for your answer.

Sol. Inertia of an object is due to quantity of matter possessed, thus it is the measure of its mass.

(i) A stone of same size as that of rubber ball will have greater mass, so the stone will have more inertia. [1]

(ii) A train has much greater mass than that of a bicycle, so the train will have more inertia. [1]

(iii) A five rupees coin has more mass than a one rupee coin, so five rupees coin will have greater inertia. [1]

40. Interpret force in terms of momentum. Represent the following graphically

(i) Momentum *versus* velocity, when mass is fixed.

(ii) Momentum *versus* mass, when velocity is constant.

Sol. As we know, force = rate of change of momentum per unit time [1]

$$\Rightarrow \quad F = \frac{\Delta p}{\Delta t}$$

(i) Graph of momentum *versus* velocity

As, $p = mv$

if $m =$ constant

$\Rightarrow$ $p \propto v$

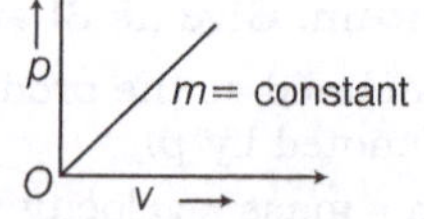

[1]

(ii) Graph of momentum *versus* mass

As, $p = mv$

if $v =$ constant

$\Rightarrow$ $p \propto m$

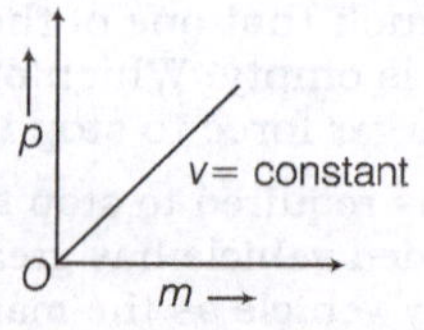

[1]

41. Derive Newton's first law using second law of motion.

Sol. According to Newton's second law, $F = ma$

where, F = external force applied,
m = mass of the body
and a = acceleration of the body.

$$F = m\left(\frac{v-u}{t}\right) \quad \left(\because a = \frac{v-u}{t}\right)$$

$$F = \frac{m}{t}(v-u)$$ **[1]**

If force applied is zero, then $F = 0$

$$\therefore \quad \frac{m}{t}(v-u) = 0$$

$$v - u = 0$$

$$\therefore \quad v = u$$ **[1]**

It shows, initial velocity = final velocity.

i.e. The object continues to move with uniform velocity or speed, if no force is applied on it.

If $F = 0$ and $u = 0$, then $v = 0$

i.e. if the object is in the state of rest, it will remain in this state.

Thus, the object does not change its state of rest or of motion until and unless external force is applied on it.

It verifies the law of inertia. **[1]**

42. A truck of mass M is moved under a force F. If the truck is then loaded with an object equal to the mass of the truck and the driving force is halved, then how does the acceleration change?

Sol. Mass of truck = M, force = F

$\therefore$ Acceleration = a

So, $$a = \frac{F}{M} \quad \text{... (i)}$$

Now, truck is loaded with mass M. **[1]**

$\therefore$ Total mass of truck (loaded) = $2M$

Driving force $= \dfrac{F}{2}$

$$\therefore \quad a' = \frac{\frac{F}{2}}{2M} \Rightarrow a' = \frac{1}{4}\left(\frac{F}{M}\right) \quad \text{... (ii)}$$ **[1]**

From Eqs. (i) and (ii), we get

$$a' = \frac{a}{4}$$

Thus, acceleration is reduced to its one-fourth of previous value. **[1]**

43. A stone when thrown on a glass window pane, it smashes the window pane into pieces, but bullet from the gun passes through it making a clean hole, why?

Sol. Speed of stone is small, so it remains in contact with window pane for a longer time. Due to this, it transfers its momentum to window pane and breaks it into pieces. But the particles of window pane near the hole are unable to share the fast momentum of the bullet in short interval of time and so remains undisturbed due to inertia of rest. **[3]**

4 Marks Questions

44. (i) Two balls of the same size but of different materials, rubber and iron are kept on the smooth floor of a moving train. The brakes are applied suddenly to stop the train. Will the balls start rolling? If so in which direction? Will they move with the same speed? Give reasons for your answer.

(ii) Give two applications of inertia in daily life.

Sol. (i) When the train is stopped suddenly, then it comes in the state of rest but the balls remain in the state of motion. So, due to inertia of motion, the balls move in the forward direction.

As the balls are of same size but of different materials that means their mass will be different. So, both the balls will move with different speeds. **[2]**

(ii) Applications of inertia in daily life are given below

(a) A carpet is beaten with stick, so that dust particles fall down.

(b) Branches of tree are shaken, so that fruits fall down. **[2]**

$$F = ma = 0.01 \times (-5000) = -50 \text{ N}$$

45. Write four important implications of Newton's third law of motion.

Sol. Refer to page No. 55 and 56.

Numerical Based Questions

46. An automobile vehicle has a mass of 1500 kg. What must be the force between the vehicle and road, if the vehicle is to be stopped with a negative acceleration of 1.7 ms^{-2}?

Sol. Given, mass, $m = 1500$ kg,

Acceleration, $a = -1.7 \text{ ms}^{-2}$

From Newton's second law of motion,

$$F = ma = 1500 \times (-1.7)$$
$$= -2550 \text{ N}$$

Negative sign indicates that force between the vehicle and road is type of friction. **[2]**

47. Two persons manage to push a motorcar of mass 1200 kg at a uniform velocity along a level road. The same motorcar can be pushed by three persons to produce an acceleration of 0.2 ms^{-2}. With what force does each person push the motorcar? (Assume that all persons push the motorcar with the same muscular effort.)

Sol. Given, mass of motorcar, $m = 1200$ kg

Acceleration produced, $a = 0.2 \text{ ms}^{-2}$

$\therefore$ Force applied on the car by three persons,

$$F = ma = 1200 \times 0.2$$
$$= 240 \text{ N}$$ **[1]**

Force applied by each person

$$= \frac{F}{3} = \frac{240}{3} = 80 \text{ N}$$ **[1]**

48. A hockey ball of mass 200 g travelling at 10 ms^{-1} is struck by a hockey stick, so as to return it along its original path with a velocity at 5 ms^{-1}. Calculate the change in momentum occurred in the motion of the hockey ball due to the force applied by the hockey stick.

Sol. Given, mass of hockey ball, $m = 200$ g $= 0.2$ kg

Initial velocity, $u = 10\ ms^{-1}$

Final velocity, $v = -5\ ms^{-1}$

($\because$ final velocity of the ball is in the direction opposite to the direction of initial velocity) [1]

Change in momentum of the ball

$= $ Final momentum − Initial momentum

$= mv - mu = m(v - u) = 0.2(-5 - 10)$

$= 0.2 \times (-15) = -3$ kg ms^{-1} [1]

49. A bullet of mass 10 g travelling horizontally with a velocity of 150 m/s strikes a stationary wooden block and comes to rest in 0.03 s. Calculate the distance of penetration of the bullet into the block. Also, calculate the magnitude of the force exerted by the wooden block on the bullet.

Sol. Given, mass of bullet,

$$m = 10\ g = \frac{10}{1000}\ kg = 0.01\ kg$$

Initial velocity, $u = 150$ m/s

Final velocity, $v = 0$ (since, bullet comes to rest)

Time, $t = 0.03$ s

From Newton's first law of motion, $v = u + at$

$$0 = 150 + a \times 0.03$$

$$\Rightarrow \quad a = \frac{-150}{0.03} = -5000\ m/s^2$$

Distance covered by the bullet before coming to rest is given by $v^2 = u^2 + 2as$

$$0 = (150)^2 + 2(-5000)s$$

$$\Rightarrow \quad s = \frac{(150)^2}{10000} = 2.25\ m$$ [1½]

Magnitude of the force applied by the bullet on the block,

$$F = ma = 0.01 \times (-5000) = -50\ N$$ [1½]

50. The distance-time reading of an object is given as follows.

Time (in s)	Distance (in m)
0	0
1	1
2	8
3	27
4	64
5	125
6	216
7	343

(i) What conclusion can you draw about the acceleration? Is it constant, increasing, decreasing or zero?

(ii) What do you infer about the force acting on the object?

Sol. (i) Here, $u = 0$

Using $s = ut + \frac{1}{2}at^2$,

$$\Rightarrow \quad s = \frac{1}{2}at^2 \quad (\because u = 0)$$

We get, $a = \frac{2s}{t^2}$

Time (in s)	Distance (in m)	$a = 2s/t^2$
0	0	0
1	1	2
2	8	4
3	27	6
4	64	8
5	125	10
6	216	12
7	343	14

Thus, acceleration is increasing. [2]

(ii) Since, acceleration is increasing, so net unbalanced force is acting on the object. [1]

51. How much momentum will a dumb-bell of mass 10 kg transfer to the floor, if it falls from a height of 80 cm? Take its downward acceleration to be 10 ms^{-2}.

Sol. Given, mass of dumbbell, $m = 10$ kg

Initial velocity, $u = 0$ ($\because$ it falls from rest)

Distance covered, $s = 80$ cm $= 0.8$ m

$a = 10\ ms^{-2}$

From equation of motion, $v^2 = u^2 + 2as$

$$v^2 = 0 + 2 \times 10 \times 0.8 = 16$$

$$v = \sqrt{16} = 4\ ms^{-1}$$ [1]

Momentum of dumb-bell just before it touches the floor,

$$p = mv = 10 \times 4 = 40\ kgms^{-1}$$

When the dumb bell touches the floor, its velocity becomes zero and hence the momentum also becomes zero. Thus, the total momentum of the dumbbell is transferred to the floor.

$\therefore$ The momentum transferred to floor is 40 kg ms^{-1}. [1]

52. A truck starts from rest and rolls down a hill with a constant acceleration. It travels a distance of 400 m in 20 s. Find its acceleration. Find the force acting on it, if its mass is 7 tonne. (Take, 1 tonne = 1000 kg)

Sol. The truck starts from rest, so initial velocity, $u = 0$

Distance, $s = 400$ m

Time, $t = 20$ s

Mass, $m = 7$ tonne

$= 7 \times 1000 = 7000$ kg

From second equation of motion,

$$s = ut + \frac{1}{2}at^2$$

$$\Rightarrow \quad 400 = 0 \times 20 + \frac{1}{2} \times a \times (20)^2$$

$$\Rightarrow \quad 400 = 200\,a$$

$\Rightarrow \quad a = 2\ ms^{-2}$ [2]

From Newton's second law of motion, force acting on the truck,

$$F = ma$$
$$= 7000 \times 2 = 14000\ N$$
$$= 1.4 \times 10^4\ N$$ [1]

53. A stone of size 1 kg is thrown with a velocity of $20\ ms^{-1}$ across the frozen surface of a lake and comes to rest after travelling a distance of 50 m. What is the force of friction between the stone and the ice?

Sol. Given, mass of stone, $m = 1$ kg

Initial velocity, $u = 20\ ms^{-1}$

Final velocity, $v = 0$ ($\because$ the stone comes to rest)

Distance covered, $s = 50$ m

From third equation of motion,

$$v^2 = u^2 + 2as$$
$$(0)^2 = (20)^2 + 2a(50)$$
$$100a = -400$$

$\Rightarrow \quad a = -4\ ms^{-2}$ [2]

Here, negative sign shows that there is a retardation in the motion of stone.

Force of friction between stone and ice

= Force required to stop the stone

$= ma$

$= 1 \times 4 = 4$ N [1]

54. A force acts on a body at rest of mass 200 kg for 10 s. When the force stops acting, the body moves through a distance 100 m with a constant velocity in 5 s. Calculate the force.

Sol. When the force is acting, then

initial velocity, $u = 0, m = 200$ kg, $t = 10$ s

When force stops

$$s = 100\ m, \quad t = 5\ s$$

$v = \dfrac{s}{t} \Rightarrow v = \dfrac{100}{5} = 20\ ms^{-1}$ [1½]

v is the final velocity attained by object due to acceleration given by force.

From first equation of motion, $v = u + at$

$$20 = 0 + a \times 10$$

$\Rightarrow \quad a = 2\ ms^{-2}$

$\therefore \quad F = ma = 200 \times 2$

$= 400$ N [1½]

55. A body of mass 0.5 kg is resting on a frictionless surface. When a force of 2000 dyne acts on it for 10 s, then calculate the distance travelled by it in 10 s.

Sol. Given, mass, $m = 0.5$ kg

$$F = 2000\ \text{dyne} = 2000 \times 10^{-5}\ N$$
$$= 0.02\ N \quad t = 10\ s \quad u = 0$$

$\therefore \quad F = ma$

$$0.02 = 0.5 \times a$$

$\Rightarrow \quad a = \dfrac{0.5}{0.02} = \dfrac{50}{2} = 25\ m/s^2$ [1]

$\therefore$ Distance, $s = ut + \dfrac{1}{2}at^2 = 0 \times 10 + \dfrac{1}{2} \times 25 \times 10 \times 10$

$\Rightarrow \quad s = 1250$ m [1]

56. A force of 10 N produces an acceleration of $5\ ms^{-2}$ in mass m_1 and $20\ ms^{-2}$ in mass m_2. What will be the acceleration by this force, if both masses m_1 and m_2 are tied together?

Sol. Given, force, $F = 10$ N, $m = m_1, a_1 = 5\ ms^{-2}, a_2 = 20\ ms^{-2}$

$$m_1 = \frac{F}{a_1} = \frac{10}{5} = 2\ kg$$

$m_2 = \dfrac{F}{a_2} = \dfrac{10}{20} = \dfrac{1}{2}$ kg [1]

Therefore, $M = m_1 + m_2 = 2 + \dfrac{1}{2} = 2.5$ kg [1]

When both m_1 and m_2 are tied together, $a = \dfrac{F}{M} = \dfrac{10}{2.5}$

$= 4\ ms^{-2}$ [1]

57. A bullet of mass 0.04 kg is moving with speed of $90\ ms^{-1}$ enters a heavy wooden block and stopped after a distance of 60 cm. What is the average resistance exerted by the block on bullet? How much time is taken by bullet to stop in block?

Sol. Given, mass of bullet, $m = 0.04$ kg

Initial velocity of bullet, $u = 90\ ms^{-1}$

Distance, $s = 60\ cm = 0.6$ m, final velocity, $v = 0$,

$$t = ?, F = ?$$

From second equation of motion,

$$v^2 = u^2 + 2as$$
$$0 = 90 \times 90 + 2 \times a \times 0.6$$
$$0 = 8100 + 1.2a$$

$\Rightarrow \quad a = -\dfrac{8100}{1.2}\ ms^{-2}$ [1]

$\therefore$ Retardation $= \dfrac{8100}{1.2}\ ms^{-2}$ [1]

$\therefore$ Retarding force, $F = ma = 0.04 \times \dfrac{8100}{1.2}\ N = 270$ N [1]

From first equation of motion, $v = u + at$

$$0 = 90 - \frac{8100}{1.2} \times t$$
$$t = \frac{90}{8100} \times 1.2 = \frac{1.2}{90} = \frac{1}{75}\ s$$
$$t = 0.013\ s$$

Time taken by bullet to stop in block is 13 ms. [1]

58. A 8000 kg engine pulls a train of 5 wagons, each of 2000 kg, along a horizontal track. If the engine exerts a force of 40000 N and the track offers a friction force of 5000 N, then calculate

(i) the net accelerating force

(ii) the acceleration of the train and

(iii) the force of wagon 1 on wagon 2.

Sol. (i) ∵ Net accelerating force
= Force exerted by engine – Friction force
(here, frictional force is subtracted because it opposes the motion)
$= 40000 - 5000 = 35000$ N
$= 3.5 \times 10^4$ N **[1]**

(ii) From Newton's second law of motion,
Accelerating force
= Mass of the train × Acceleration of train
$\Rightarrow \quad a = \frac{F}{m}$
Mass of train = Mass of engine + Mass of all wagons
$= 8000 + 5 \times 2000$
$= 8000 + 10000 = 18000$ kg
$\therefore$ Acceleration $= \frac{35000}{18000} = \frac{35}{18} = 1.94$ ms^{-2} **[1]**

(iii) Force of wagon 1 on wagon 2
= Mass of the engine × Acceleration
$= 8000 \times 1.94 = 15520$ N **[1]**

59. A car is moving with a uniform velocity 30 ms^{-1}. It is stopped in 2 s by applying force of 1500 N through its brakes. Calculate
(i) the retardation produced in car
(ii) mass of car
(iii) change in momentum of car.

Sol. Given, initial velocity, $u = 30$ ms^{-1}
Final velocity, $v = 0$ (stopped), $t = 2$ s
(i) From first equation of motion, $v = u + at$
$\Rightarrow \quad 0 = 30 + a \times 2$
$a = -15$ ms^{-2}
(Negative sign shows retardation) **[1]**

(ii) As, $F = ma$
$1500 = m(15)$
Mass of car, $m = \frac{1500}{15} = 100$ kg **[1]**

(iii) Change in momentum of car,
$\Delta p = p_f - p_i = mv - mu = m(v - u)$
$\Delta p = 100(0 - 30)$
$\Delta p = -3000$ kg ms^{-1}
(Negative sign shows decrease in momentum) **[1]**

60. A bullet of mass 50 g moving with an initial velocity 100 ms^{-1}, strikes a wooden block and comes to rest after penetrating a distance of 2 cm in it. Calculate
(i) initial momentum of bullet
(ii) final momentum of bullet
(iii) retardation caused by the block and
(iv) resistance offered by the wooden block.

Sol. Given, mass, $m = 50\text{ g} = \frac{50}{1000}\text{ kg} = 0.05$ kg
Initial velocity, $u = 100$ ms^{-1}, final velocity, $v = 0$,
$s = 2\text{ cm} = 0.02$ m
(i) ∴ Initial momentum of bullet, $p_i = mu$
$= 0.05 \times 100 = 5$ kg ms^{-1} **[1]**

(ii) Final velocity of bullet is zero, $v = 0$
So, final momentum, $p_f = mv = 0.05 \times 0$
$= 0$ kg ms^{-1} **[1]**

(iii) From second equation of motion, $v^2 = u^2 + 2as$
$0 = (100)^2 + 2a \times 0.02$
$a = -\frac{100 \times 100}{2 \times 0.02} = -2.5 \times 10^5$ ms^{-2}
Negative sign means there is retardation.
∴ Retardation $= 2.5 \times 10^5$ ms^{-2} **[1]**

(iv) Retarding or resistive force,
$F = ma = 0.05 \times 2.5 \times 10^5$
∴ Resistive force = 12500 N **[1]**

Section II

Structured Questions

61. (i) State reason for the following questions.
(a) Road accidents occurring due to high speeds are much worse than accidents due to low speeds of vehicles.
(b) When a motorcar makes a sharp turn at a high speed passengers tend to get thrown to one side. **[3]**

(ii) Look at the diagram below and answer the following questions.

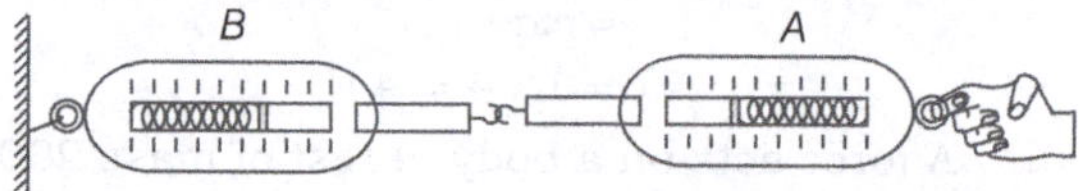

(a) When a force is applied through the free end of the spring balance A, the reading on the spring balance A is 15 g-wt. What will be the measure of the reading shown by spring balance B?
(b) Write reasons for your answer.
(c) Name the force which balance A exerts on balance B and the force of balance B on balance A. **[3]**

(iii) Obtain the formula, $F = ma$ from Newton's second law of motion. In the formula, the symbols have their usual meanings. **[4]**

Sol. (i) (a) Road accidents occurring due to high speeds are much worse than accidents due to low speeds of vehicles. This is because the momentum of high speed vehicles is more than that of the low speeds of vehicles. **[1½]**

(b) When a motorcar makes a sharp turn towards left or right at a high speed, the lower portion of their passengers turns suddenly along with the motorcar but their upper portion does not turn due to inertia.
So, this portion of passenger moves forward and the passenger tends to get thrown to one side or other side. **[1½]**

(ii) (a) 15 g-wt. [1]

(b) From Newton's third law, the force exerted by B on A and force exerted by A on B are equal. [1]

(c) Force of reaction and force of action. [1]

(iii) According to Newton's second law of motion, the rate of change of linear momentum is directly proportional to force applied and takes place in the direction of force. [1]

Let m is mass of the body. Initial and final velocity are u and v, respectively.

Let t is the time taken to change the velocity from u to v.

$\therefore$ Initial momentum, $p_i = mu$

Final momentum, $p_f = mv$

$\therefore$ Change in momentum, $\Delta p = p_f - p_i$

$$\Delta p = mv - mu \quad \text{...(i)}$$ [1]

Now, rate of change of momentum $= \Delta p / t$

As, $$F = \frac{\Delta p}{t}$$

$$F = \frac{m(v-u)}{t} \quad \text{... (ii)}$$

By first equation of motion, $v = u + at$

$$\Rightarrow \quad a = \frac{v-u}{t} \quad \text{...(iii)}$$ [1]

From Eqs. (ii) and (iii), we get

$$F = ma$$ [1]

62. (i) Give reasons for the following.

(a) Water sprinkler used for grass lawns begins to rotate as soon as water is supplied.

(b) Water drops are removed from wet clothes by giving tight jerk to the cloth. [3]

(ii) (a) If F and F' are balanced forces, then what will be the magnitude of F_2?

(b) Using a horizontal force of 200 N, we intend to move a wooden cabinet across a floor at a constant velocity. What is the friction force that will be exerted on the cabinet? [3]

(iii) Give reasons.

(a) Why are the mudguards provided over the wheels?

(b) Why do the sparks produced during sharpening process of a knife fly off tangentially?

(c) When a train starts or stops suddenly, sliding doors of some compartments may open or shut. Explain.

(d) Why does the electric fan continue to rotate for sometime after the current is switched OFF? [4]

Sol. (i) (a) When water is pushed out of sprinkler with a force, it exerts reaction force on the sprinkler causing it to rotate. [1½]

(b) Water drops have inertia of rest. They do not move with the cloth as it is jerked and comes out. [1½]

(ii) (a) As per question, F and F' are balanced forces.

So, $F = F'$

$\Rightarrow \quad 15 + F_2 = 25$ N

$\therefore \quad F_2 = 10$ N [1½]

(b) The cabinet will move across the floor with constant velocity, if there is no net external force applied on it. Here, a horizontal force of 200 N is applied on the cabinet, so for the net force to be zero, an external force of 200 N should be applied on the cabinet in opposite direction.

Thus, the frictional force = 200 N

[frictional force always acts in the direction opposite to the direction of motion] [1½]

(iii) (a) The rotating wheels of cycle throw out mud sticking to it tangentially due to inertia of direction. This is why mudguards are provided over the wheels to protect the clothes of the cyclist. [1]

(b) When a knife is sharpened against a grinding stone, sparks produced fly off tangentially due to inertia of direction. [1]

(c) When a train starts or stops suddenly, sliding doors of some compartments may open or close due to inertia of rest and motion. [1]

(d) The electric fan continues to rotate due to inertia of motion, until the friction in bearings and that of air brings it to state of rest after sometime. [1]

Chapter Assessment

1 Mark Questions

1. A water tank filled upto $\frac{2}{3}$ of its height is moving with a uniform speed. On sudden application of the brake, the water in the tank would

(a) move backward

(b) move forward

(c) be unaffected

(d) rise upwards

2. A bus of mass 500 kg is moving with a velocity of 5 m/s and is acted upon by a forward force of 500 N due to engine and retarding force of 200 N due to friction velocity of bus after 20 s will be

(a) 15 m/s (b) 17 m/s

(c) 19 m/s (d) 21 m/s

3. Trolley *X* and trolley *Y* are joined with stretched spring. Trolley *X* has twice the mass of trolley *Y*.

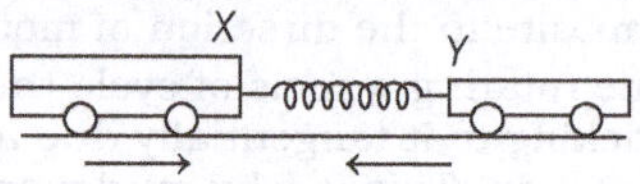

When the trolleys are released, the acceleration of *X* is 2 m/s^2 to the right. What is the initial acceleration of trolley *Y* to the left?

(a) 1 m/s^2 (b) 2 m/s^2

(c) 3 m/s^2 (d) 4 m/s^2

4. A goalkeeper in a game of football pulls his hands backwards after holding the ball shot at the goal. This enables the goalkeeper to

(a) exert larger force on the ball

(b) increase the force exerted by the ball on hands

(c) increase the rate of change of momentum

(d) decrease the rate of change of momentum

5. Two objects *A* and *B* exert force on each other, the whole system is in equilibrium.
Which of the following is the correct expression of forces on *A* and *B*?

(a) $F_{AB} = F_{BA}$ (b) $F_{AB} = F_{BA}$

(c) $F_{AB} = -F_{BA}$ (d) $F_{AB} > F_{BA}$

2 Marks Questions

6. Make a pile of similar carrom coins on a table, then remove the lower coin without touching the other coins. With your fingers, you may give a sharp horizontal hit at the bottom of the pile using striker.

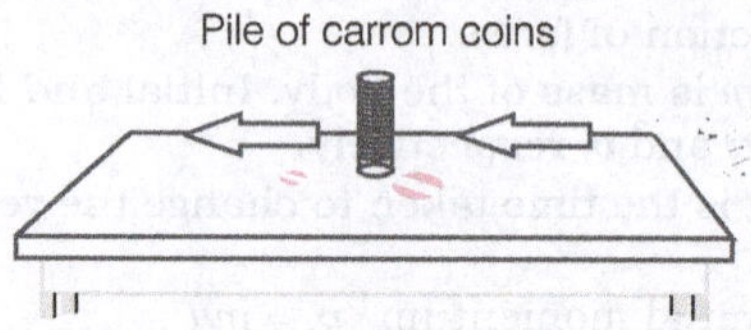

(i) What will happen, if the hit is strong enough?

(ii) What will happen to the remaining coins once the lower coin is removed?

7. Why do you prefer to fall on a mattress or sand after high jump rather than cemented floor?

8. What will be the change in acceleration of a sliding block, if its mass is doubled while a constant force is acting on it?

9. Why does a boat tend to leave the shore, when passengers are alighting from it?

10. Explain the mechanism of rocket propulsion using Newton's third law of motion.

11. Two bodies *A* and *B* of same mass are moving with velocities *v* and 2*v*, respectively. Compare their inertia and momentum.

12. (i) What are non-contact forces?

(ii) How does the distance of separation between two bodies affect the magnitude of the non-contact force between them?

13. When a body is placed on a table top, it exerts a force equal to its weight downwards on the table top but does not move or fall.

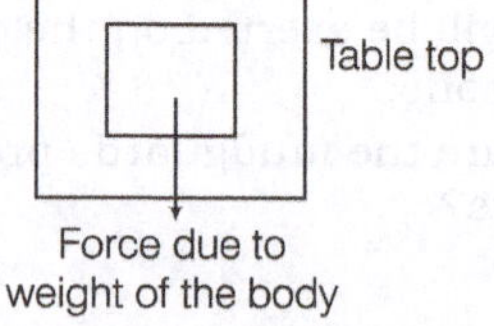

(i) Name the force exerted by the table top.

(ii) What is the direction of the force?

14. For how much time should a force of 200 N acts on an object having mass 5 kg, so as to increase its velocity from 50 m/s to 100 m/s?

Structured Questions

15. (i) An object experiences a net zero external unbalanced force. Is it possible for the object to be travelling with a non-zero velocity? If yes, state the conditions that must be placed on the magnitude and direction of the velocity. If no, provide a reason. **[3]**

(ii) The motion of a body of mass 5 kg is shown in the velocity-time graph.

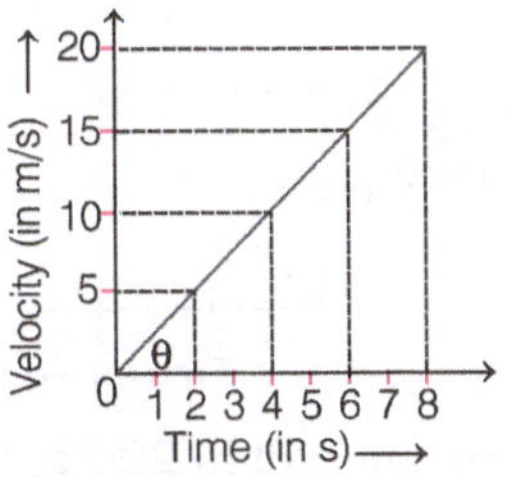

Find from the graph.

(a) Its acceleration.

(b) The force acting on the body.

(c) The change in momentum of body in 2 s after start. **[3]**

(iii) In the following example, try to identify the number of times the velocity of the ball changes.

A football player kicks a football to another player of his team who kicks the football towards the goal. The goalkeeper of opposite team collects the ball and kicks it towards a player of his own team.

Also, identify the agent supplying the force in each case. **[4]**

16. (i) Explain, why is it difficult for a fireman to hold a hose-pipe, which ejects large amount of water with a high velocity? **[3]**

(ii) (a) If action is always equal to the reaction, then explain how a horse can pull a cart?

(b) Velocity-time graph of a moving particle of mass 1 kg is shown in figure.

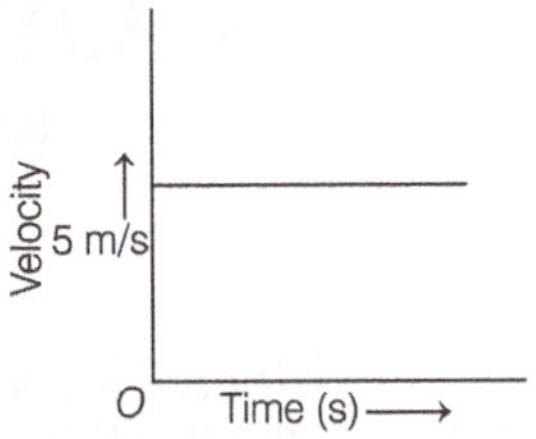

Is any force acting on the body? Justify your answer. **[3]**

(iii) A car was travelling at 30 m/s. The driver applies brakes suddenly by seeing a running dog. The velocity-time (v-t) graph and its corresponding table during the time of applying brakes is shown below

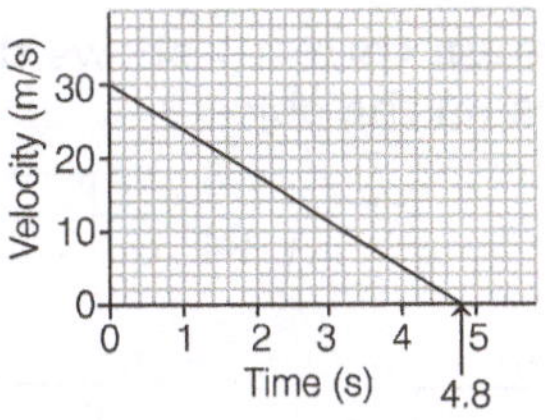

Velocity-time (v-t) graph

Time (s)	Velocity(m/s)
0	30
1	23.5
2	17
3	11
4	5
4.8	0

(a) Calculate the rate at which the velocity of a car decreases (deceleration).

(b) Calculate the braking force, if the mass of the car is 900 kg.

(c) Calculate the distance travelled by the car in 4.8 s.

(d) Why the driver of car applies brakes suddenly? **[4]**

For Solutions Scan the Code

Olympiad Section*

Brain Teasing Questions of Olympiad Pattern

1 A block of metal weighing 2 kg is resting on a frictionless plane. It is struck by a jet releasing water at the rate of 1 kgs^{-1} and with a speed of 5 ms^{-1}. The initial acceleration of the block is

(a) 2.5 m/s^2 (b) 5 m/s^2
(c) 10 m/s^2 (d) 5.9 m/s^2

2 An object of weight w is pulled along a rough horizontal surface by a force P. The force of friction is F.
Which diagram correctly shows the direction of these forces on the object?

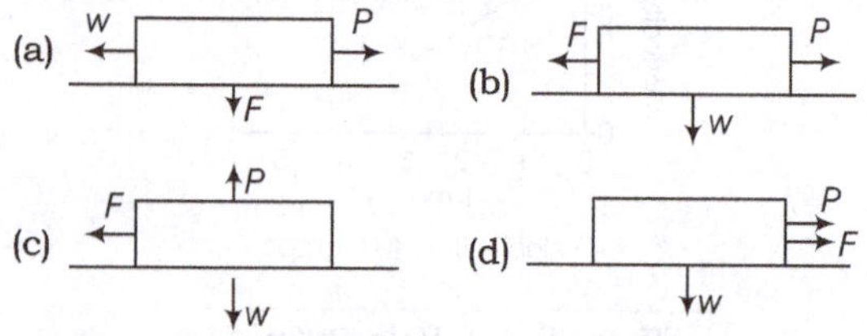

3 A man is drawing a bucket of water out of well. Suddenly, bucket falls back, when the rope snaps. This is because of

(a) law of gravitation
(b) first law of motion
(c) Newton's second law of motion
(d) Newton's third law of motion and gravitation

4 Three blocks A, B and C of masses 4 kg, 2 kg and 1 kg respectively, are in contact on a frictionless surface as shown.

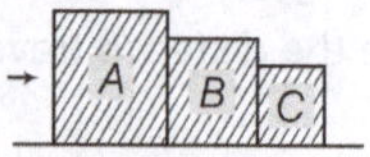

If a force of 14 N is applied on the 4 kg block, then contact force between A and B is

(a) 6 N (b) 8 N
(c) 18 N (d) 2 N

5 A person just supports a mass of 20 kg suspended from a rope.

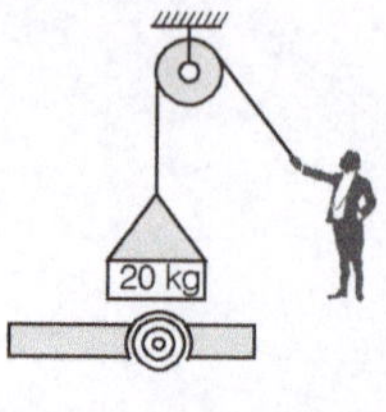

What is the resultant force acting on the mass?

(a) Zero (b) 10 N
(c) 20 N (d) 200 N

6 The velocity-time graph of a ball moving on the surface of a floor is given below

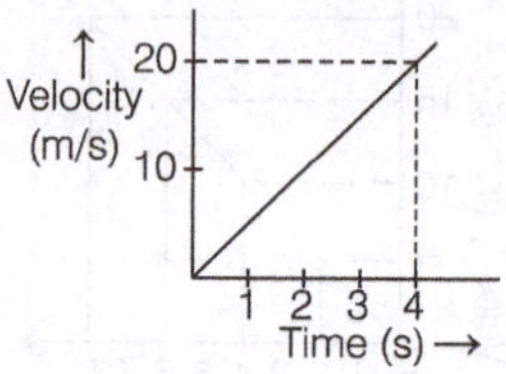

If the mass of the ball is 200 g, then the value of force on the ball is

(a) 1 N (b) 2 N
(c) 5 N (d) 7 N

7 A cricket ball of mass 120 g is moving with a velocity of 12 m/s. It turns back and moves with a velocity of 20 ms^{-1} when hit by a bat. Find the force, if the force acts for 0.02 s.

(a) 192 N (b) 190 N
(c) 20 N (d) 110 N

8 Study the diagrams given below.

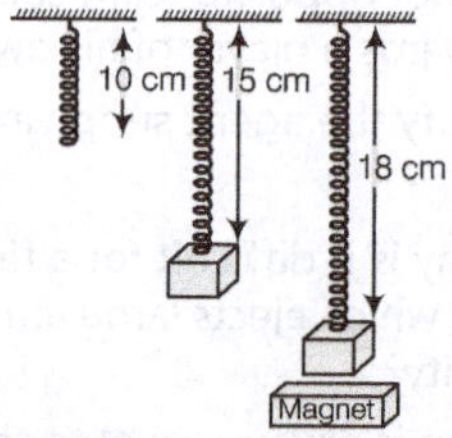

Which type(s) of forces cause(s) the spring to extend most?

A. Elastic force exerted by the spring
B. Magnetic force acting on the iron box
C. Gravitational force acting on the iron box
D. Frictional force acting between the iron box and the magnet

(a) Only B (b) Both B and C
(c) A, B and C (d) A, C and D

9 Figure shows the displacement of a particle going along the X-axis as a function of time.

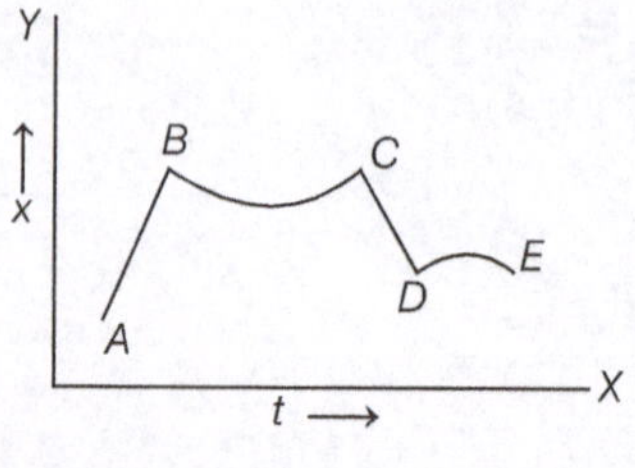

The force acting on the particle is zero in the region

(i) *AB* (ii) *BC* (iii) *CD* (iv) *DE*

Choose the correct option.

(a) i, iv (b) i, iii
(c) iii, ii (d) iv, iii

10 The masses of 10 kg and 20 kg, respectively are connected by a massless spring. A force of 200 N acts on the 20 kg mass. At the instant shown,

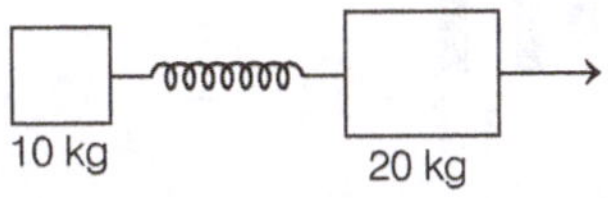

The 10 kg mass has an acceleration of 12 m/s^2, what is the acceleration of 20 kg mass?

(a) 12 ms^{-2} (b) 4 ms^{-2}
(c) 20 ms^{-2} (d) None of these

11 A truck and a car moving with the same kinetic energy are brought to rest by application of brakes which provide equal total retarding force for both. The truck has 8 tyres, and weighs 4 times more than the car which has 4 tyres. What can you say about the distance in which the two vehicles stop?

(a) The car will stop at a shorter distance.
(b) The truck will stop at a shorter distance.
(c) They will stop at the same distance.
(d) Not enough information is given.

12 A variable force is exerted on a body of constant mass. The body, initially at rest, moves in a straight line. The following graph shows how the force varies with time. All frictional forces are ignored.

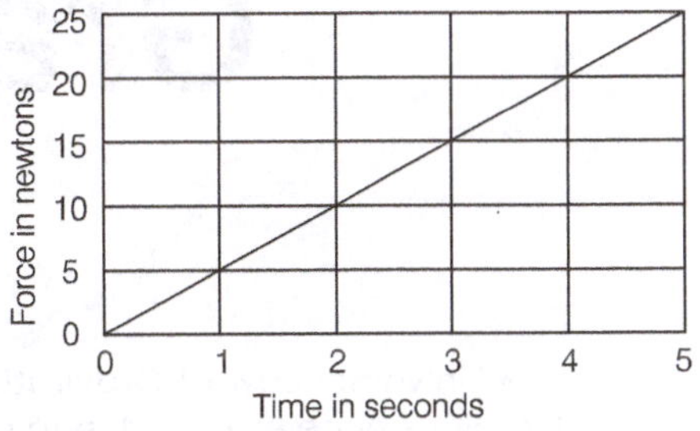

If the velocity of the object is 7.0 ms^{-1} after 2.0 s, the velocity after 3.4 s will be approximately

(a) 11.9 ms^{-1}
(b) 17.0 ms^{-1}
(c) 20.2 ms^{-1}
(d) 28.9 ms^{-1}

Answers									
1. (a)	**2.** (b)	**3.** (d)	**4.** (b)	**5.** (a)	**6.** (a)	**7.** (a)	**8.** (a)	**9.** (b)	**10.** (b)
11. (c)	**12.** (c)								

* *These questions may or may not be asked in the examination, have been given just for additional practice required for olympiads Scholarship Exams etc. For detailed explanations refer Page No. 214.*

CHAPTER

04

Gravitation

SYLLABUS

• Universal Law of Gravitation. (Statement and equation) and its importance Gravity • Acceleration due to gravity free fall • Mass and Weight • Weight as force of gravity • Comparison of mass and weight • Gravitational units of force (simple numerical problems).

It has been observed that an object dropped from a height falls towards the Earth, i.e. Earth pulls everything towards itself. Newton generalised this idea and said that not only the Earth but every object in the universe attract every other object. This phenomenon of attraction between two objects is called **gravitation.**

In this chapter, we shall learn about gravitational force and universal law of gravitation.

Gravitational Force

Gravitational force is the non-contact force of attraction between any two bodies in the universe. The Earth attracts (or pulls) all objects lying on or near its surface towards its centre. The force with which the Earth pulls the objects towards its centre is called the **gravitational force of the Earth** or **gravity of the Earth**.

Universal Law of Gravitation

This law was given by Isaac Newton. According to this law, the attractive force between any two objects in the universe is directly proportional to the product of their masses and inversely proportional to the square of distance between them.The direction of this force is along the line joining the centres of two objects.

Consider two spherical bodies A and B having masses m_1 and m_2, whose centres are at a distance d from each other as shown in figure.

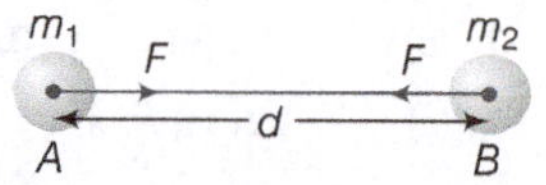

Direction of gravitational force between two spherical bodies

Then, according to Newton's law of gravitation, the gravitational force between the two bodies is directly proportional to the product of their masses.

i.e. $$F \propto m_1 m_2 \quad \text{...(i)}$$

and the force between the two bodies is inversely proportional to the square of the distance between them, i.e.

$$F \propto \frac{1}{d^2} \quad \text{...(ii)}$$

Combining Eqs. (i) and (ii), we get

$$F \propto \frac{m_1 m_2}{d^2}$$

or $$\boxed{F = G\frac{m_1 m_2}{d^2}}$$

where, $G = 6.67 \times 10^{-11}$ N-m^2/kg^2 is the **universal gravitational constant.**

This law is universal because

(i) the value of G does not depend on the medium between the two bodies, masses of the bodies or the distance between them, nature of particle, temperature, etc.

(ii) it is applicable to all bodies, whether the bodies are big or small, whether they are celestial or terrestrial.

Suppose, the two bodies having masses 1 kg each and the distance d between them is 1 m, then

$$F = G \qquad (\because m_1 = m_2 = 1 \text{ kg and } d = 1 \text{ m})$$

Hence, **the universal gravitational constant is defined as the gravitational force between two objects of unit mass each separated by a unit distance from each other placed anywhere in space.** The value of G was found out by Henry Cavendish (1731-1810) by using a sensitive balance.

Example 1. The mass of the Earth is 6×10^{24} kg and that of Moon is 7.4×10^{22} kg. If the distance between the Earth and the Moon is 3.84×10^5 km, then calculate the force exerted by the Earth on the Moon. (Take, $G = 6.7 \times 10^{-11}$ N-m^2/kg^2)

Sol. Given, mass of the Earth, $M_e = 6 \times 10^{24}$ kg

Mass of the Moon, $M_m = 7.4 \times 10^{22}$ kg

Distance between the Earth and the Moon,

$$d = 3.84 \times 10^5 \text{ km} = 3.84 \times 10^8 \text{ m}$$

Universal gravitational constant,

$$G = 6.7 \times 10^{-11} \text{ N-m}^2/\text{kg}^2$$

Force exerted by the Earth on Moon, $F = ?$

We know that, $F = G\dfrac{M_e \times M_m}{d^2}$

$$= \frac{6.7 \times 10^{-11} \times 6 \times 10^{24} \times 7.4 \times 10^{22}}{(3.84 \times 10^8)^2} \text{ N}$$

$$= 2.01 \times 10^{20} \text{ N}$$

Thus, force exerted by the Earth on the Moon is 2.01×10^{20} N.

Example 2. A sphere of mass 40 kg is attracted by a second sphere of mass 60 kg with a force equal to 4 mgf. If G is 6×10^{-11} N-m^2/kg^2, then calculate the distance between them. Consider acceleration due to gravity is 10 m/s^2. (Take, $G = 6.67 \times 10^{-11}$ N-m^2/kg^2)

Sol. Given, $M = 40$ kg, $m = 60$ kg,

$$F = 4 \text{ mgf} = 4 \times 10^{-6} \times 10 = 4 \times 10^{-5} \text{ N}$$

$$G = 6.67 \times 10^{-11} \text{ N-m}^2/\text{kg}^2, g = 10 \text{ m/s}^2$$

According to the universal law of gravitation, $F = \dfrac{GMm}{r^2}$

$$\Rightarrow \quad r = \sqrt{\frac{GMm}{F}} = \sqrt{\frac{6.67 \times 10^{-11} \times 40 \times 60}{4 \times 10^{-5}}}$$

$$= 0.062 \text{ m} = 6.2 \text{ cm}$$

Importance of Universal Law of Gravitation

The universal law of gravitation successfully explained several phenomena given as below

(i) The force that binds us to the Earth.

(ii) The motion of the Moon around the Earth.

(iii) The motion of planets around the Sun.

(iv) The tides due to the Moon and the Sun.

(v) The flow of water in rivers is also due to gravitational force of the Earth on water.

Note The gravitational force of attraction is highly significant between heavy mass objects but it is insignificant between small mass objects, because of small magnitude of universal gravitational constant.

Check Your LEARNING...

1 Why G is called as universal gravitational constant?

2 What is the ratio of gravitational forces acting between two objects placed 2 m apart in air and then in water? *Ans.* 1:1

3 Does gravitational force depend upon medium between the two particles?

4 If suddenly the gravitational force between the Sun and the Earth becomes zero, what will happen to the Earth?

Free Fall

When an object falls towards the Earth under the Earth's gravitational force alone, then it is called **freely falling object** and such a motion is called **free fall.**

e.g. A ball is dropped from some height.

Force due to Gravity (Gravity)

According to Newton's law of gravitation, the Earth attracts all other objects around it, towards its centre. The force of attraction with which it attracts other objects is called the force due to gravity (gravity). It always acts in vertically downward towards the centre of the Earth.

From the universal law of gravitation, $F = \dfrac{GMm}{r^2}$

If M is mass of Earth ($= 5.96 \times 10^{24}$ kg), r is radius of Earth (6.37×10^6 m) and m is object (say 1 kg), then the force of gravity becomes

$$F = \frac{(6.67 \times 10^{-11})(5.96 \times 10^{24}) \times 1}{(6.37 \times 10^6)^2} = 9.8 \text{ N}$$

Thus, the Earth attracts the body of mass 1 kg towards its centre with the force of 9.8 N.

As we know, gravitational force acts in action-reaction pair, so if the Earth attracts an object towards it, then the object also attracts the Earth towards it by an equal and opposite force. But the mass of the object is negligibly small as compared to the Earth, so it starts moving towards the Earth while Earth does not move towards the object because of its large mass. That is why, it is seen that a falling apple is attracted towards the Earth but we do not see the Earth moving towards the apple.

Acceleration due to Gravity

When an object falls freely towards Earth's surface, then its velocity increases continuously till it reaches the Earth's surface, it means that there is an acceleration in the motion of object, this acceleration is called acceleration due to gravity.

Acceleration due to gravity can be defined as the acceleration produced in the motion of a freely falling object due to gravitational force of Earth.

It is denoted by g. The SI unit of g is ms^{-2}.

Relationship between g and G

Suppose the mass of Earth is M and its radius is R. If an object of mass m is falling freely towards Earth, then from Newton's law of gravitation, force of attraction between Earth and the object is

$$F = \frac{GMm}{R^2} \quad \text{...(i)}$$

The distance between Earth and the object can be considered as equal to the radius of Earth.

But according to Newton's second law of motion, force applied on object of mass m is given as

$$F = mg \quad \text{...(ii)}$$

where, g is the acceleration produced in the object due to force of gravity.

From Eqs. (i) and (ii), we get

$$\frac{GMm}{R^2} = mg$$

$$\Rightarrow \quad \boxed{g = \frac{GM}{R^2}}$$

From this formula, it is clear that acceleration due to gravity does not depend on the mass of falling object. It depends only on the mass and radius of Earth or any other planet towards which the object is falling.

Value of Acceleration due to Gravity (g) at Surface of Earth

The value of g at the surface of Earth can be calculated as follows

Mass of Earth, $M_e = 6 \times 10^{24}$ kg

Radius of Earth, $R_e = 6.4 \times 10^6$ m

Universal gravitational constant,

$$G = 6.67 \times 10^{-11} \text{ N-m}^2/\text{kg}^2$$

$$\therefore \quad g_e = \frac{GM_e}{R_e^2} = \frac{6.67 \times 10^{-11} \times 6 \times 10^{24}}{(6.4 \times 10^6)^2} = 9.8 \text{ m/s}^2$$

The value of acceleration due to gravity decreases with height and depth from the surface of Earth and it become zero at the centre of Earth.

Acceleration due to gravity (g) is also affected due to rotation and shape of the Earth. It is minimum at equator and maximum at poles.

Note • Though, the value of g is independent of freely falling mass, a feather falls much slower than a coin, when released from a height. This is due to the resistance offered by air to the falling mass. If both the bodies were released at the same time in vacuum, they would reach on the Earth's surface within the same duration of time.

Example 3. Calculate the acceleration due to gravity on the surface of Moon whose mass is 7.4×10^{22} kg and radius is 1.74×10^6 m. Also, find the ratio of acceleration due to gravity of Earth to the Moon.

Sol. Mass of Moon, $M_m = 7.4 \times 10^{22}$ kg

Radius of Moon, $R_m = 1.74 \times 10^6$ m

$$G = 6.67 \times 10^{-11} \text{ N-m}^2/\text{kg}^2$$

The acceleration due to gravity at the surface of Moon,

$$g_m = \frac{GM_m}{R_m^2} = \frac{6.67 \times 10^{-11} \times 7.4 \times 10^{22}}{(1.74 \times 10^6)^2}$$

$$= 1.63 \text{ m/s}^2$$

Now, the ratio of acceleration due to gravity at the surface of Earth to the Moon is

$$\therefore \quad \frac{g_e}{g_m} = \frac{9.8}{1.63} \approx \frac{1}{6} \quad \text{(approx)}$$

$$\Rightarrow \quad g_e : g_m = 1 : 6$$

Equations of Motion of Object under Free Fall

The equation of motion for an object moving in a straight line with uniform acceleration can be used for freely falling objects, as the acceleration in this case i.e., acceleration due to gravity is uniform throughout the motion.

So, the three general equations of motion can be applied for the motion of bodies under free fall as follows

General equations of motion	Equations of moiton of a body under free fall i.e., $a = g$
(i) $v = u + at$	(i) $v = u + gt$
(ii) $s = ut + \frac{1}{2}at^2$	(ii) $h = ut + \frac{1}{2}gt^2$
(iii) $v^2 = u^2 + 2as$	(iii) $v^2 = u^2 + 2gh$

where, h is the height from which the object falls, t is the time of fall, u is the initial velocity and v is the final velocity, when the body accelerates with g.

In solving numerical problems, we should remember the following points.

(i) If an object falls vertically downwards, then acceleration due to gravity is taken as positive, since its velocity increases while falling.

(ii) If an object is thrown vertically upwards, then acceleration due to gravity is taken as negative, since its velocity decreases as it moves upward.

(iii) If an object is dropped freely from a height, its initial velocity u is zero.

(iv) If an object is thrown vertically upwards, its final velocity v becomes zero at peak/highest point.

(v) The velocity of an object with which it falls on the ground is always equal to the velocity of the object at the time of projection.

Example 4. A ball is thrown vertically upwards with a velocity of 25 m/s. If g is 10 m/s^2, then calculate

(i) height that it reaches,

(ii) time taken to return back.

Sol. Given, initial velocity, $u = 25$ m/s, final velocity, $v = 0$.

If a body is thrown upwards, then its velocity becomes zero at the maximum height.

Acceleration due to gravity,

$$g = -10 \text{ m/s}^2$$

(i) $\because$ Height, $h = \frac{v^2 - u^2}{2g}$

$$= \frac{0 - (25)^2}{2(-10)}$$

$$= \frac{-625}{2 \times (-10)}$$

$$h = 31.25 \text{ m}$$

(ii) $\because$ Time, $t = \frac{v - u}{g} = \frac{0 - 25}{-10} = 2.5$ s

Time taken to return back,

$T =$ Time of ascending + Time of descending $= 2t$

$\therefore$ Time taken to return back, $T = 2 \times 2.5 = 5$ s

Mass and Weight

Mass

It is the total content of the body which measures the inertia of a body. It is a scalar quantity and its SI unit is kilogram. In other words, mass is the quantity of matter contained in a body. Irrespective of the position of the body in the universe, mass always remains constant everywhere. The mass of the body cannot be zero. It is an intrinsic property of the body.

Weight

The weight of an object is the force with which it is attracted towards the centre of the Earth.

Weight of an object, $w = mg$

where, m = mass and g = acceleration due to gravity.

or $$\boxed{w = \frac{GMm}{R^2}} \qquad \left[\because g = \frac{GM}{R^2}\right]$$

Here, M = mass of the Earth and R = radius of the Earth.

- From the above formula, it is clear that weight of an object will change on a planet other than Earth.
- Spring balance is used to measure the weight of a body and pan balance is used to measure the mass of a body.

Important points regarding weight are as follows

(i) Weight is a vector quantity, it acts in vertically downward direction and its SI unit is newton (N). Weight of 1 kg mass is 9.8 N. (i.e., 1 kg - wt = 9.8 N).

(ii) Weight of an object is not constant, it changes from place to place.

(iii) In the space, where $g = 0$, weight of an object is zero. This phenomenon is called weightlessness.

(iv) At the centre of the Earth, weight becomes zero. This is due to the fact that on going below to the surface of Earth, the value of g decreases and becomes zero at the centre of Earth.

Comparison of Mass and Weight

Mass	Weight
Quantity of matter contained in an object.	Force with which an object is attracted towards centre of the Earth due to gravity.
Constant everywhere.	Changes from place to place.
It is a scalar quantity.	It is a vector quantity.
Its SI unit is kg.	Its SI unit is N.
Mass is never zero.	Weight is zero at the centre of the Earth or in free space.
It is measured by physical or beam balance.	It is measured by spring balance.

Example 5. What is the weight of a body of mass 12 kg? What is the force acting on it? (Take, $g = 10\ ms^{-2}$)

Sol. Given, $m = 12$ kg, $g = 10\ ms^{-2}$

$\therefore$ Weight of the body, $w = mg = 12 \times 10 = 120$ N

Force acting on the body is the force of gravity, which is equal to the weight of the body.

Example 6. Mass of an object is 20 kg. What will be its weight on the Earth and mass on the Moon? (Take, $g = 9.8\ ms^{-2}$)

Sol. Given, $m = 20$ kg, $g = 9.8\ ms^{-2}$

$\therefore$ Weight of the object on Earth, $w = mg$
$= 20 \times 9.8 = 196.0$ N

Mass of the object on the Moon will remain the same i.e., 20 kg as mass does not change from place to place.

Gravitational Units of Force

The gravitational units of force are kgf (kilogram force) and gf (gram force) in MKS system and CGS system, respectively.

Kilogram force (kgf) is the force exerted by one kilogram of mass in the gravitational field of Earth ($g = 9.8\ ms^{-2}$).

$$1\text{kgf} = \text{Mass} \times \text{Acceleration due to gravity}$$
$$= 1\text{kg} \times 9.8\ ms^{-2} = 9.8\ kgms^{-2} = 9.8\ N$$

Gram force (gf) is the force exerted by a mass of 1g in the gravitational field of Earth.

$$1\text{gf} = 1\text{g} \times 980\ cms^{-2} = 980\ g\ cms^{-2} = 9.8\ mN$$

$\therefore$ 1 gf = 980 dyne

and 1 kgf = 1000 gf

kgf and gf are not accepted in SI system of units. It is used in the gravitational unit system, where length, mass and force are the base units.

Check Your LEARNING...

1. How are g and G related?
2. What do you mean by the term force due to gravity?
3. Explain the meaning of weightlessness.
4. What is the weight of a body of mass 2 kg on the Moon? (Take the value of g on Moon as 1.63 ms^{-2}). *Ans.* 3.26 N
5. Write the two gravitational unit of force.

QUiCK Revision

- **Gravitation** is the force with which two massive bodies attract each other.
- **Gravitational force** is the non-contact force, which is inversely proportional to the square of distance between the bodies and directly proportional to the product of their masses.
- According to **Newton's law of gravitation**, the force between two bodies is given by, $F = \frac{Gm_1m_2}{d^2}$. Here, G is called **universal gravitational constant** and its value is 6.67×10^{-11} N-m^2kg^{-2}.
- **Acceleration due to gravity** is given by, $g = \frac{GM}{R^2}$, which is independent of the mass of falling object. At the surface of Earth, $g = 9.8\ ms^{-2}$.
- The ratio of acceleration due to gravity (g) on Earth and Moon is 6:1.
- Equations of motion of an object under free fall is
  (i) $v = u + gt$
  (ii) $h = ut + \frac{1}{2}gt^2$
  (iii) $v^2 = u^2 + 2gh$
- **Weight** is the force with which an object is attracted towards the Earth, i.e. $w = \frac{GMm}{R^2}$.
- **Weightlessness** is the situation, when a body falls freely under the effect of gravity alone, i.e. $a = g$.
- The gravitational units of force are **kgf** and **gf.**

Chapter Practice

Section-I

1 Mark Questions

1. The force of attraction between two unit point masses separated by a unit distance is called
(a) gravitational potential
(b) acceleration due to gravity
(c) gravitational field strength
(d) universal gravitational constant

Sol. (*d*) Force of attraction between two masses.

$$F = \frac{Gm_1m_2}{r^2}$$

If $m_1 = m_2 = 1$ kg and $r = 1$ m
Then, $F = G$. Hence, universal gravitational constant is equal to the force of attraction between two unit point masses separated by a unit distance.

2. Gravitational force between two objects is 10 N. If masses of both objects are doubled without changing distance between them, then the gravitational force would become
(a) 2.5 N (b) 20 N
(c) 40 N (d) 10 N

Sol. (*c*) Given, $F = 10$ N

Now, mass of two objects are doubled, then force of attraction between them,

$$F' = \frac{G(2M)(2m)}{d^2}$$

$$F' = \frac{4GMm}{d^2} = 4 \times 10 \qquad \left(\because F = \frac{GMm}{d^2}\right)$$

$$\Rightarrow \quad F' = 40 \text{ N}$$

3. In the given figure, there are two protons.

What will be the gravitational force between them? (Take, 1 fm $= 10^{-15}$ m and mass of proton $= 1.67 \times 10^{27}$ kg)
(a) 1.86×10^{-34} N (b) 5.86×10^{-34} N
(c) 2.8×10^{-34} N (d) 4.86×10^{-34} N

Sol. (*a*) The gravitational force between two protons is given by

$$F = \frac{GM_pM_p}{d^2}$$

where, $m_p = 1.67 \times 10^{-27}$ kg, $d = 10^{-15}$ m

and $G = 6.67 \times 10^{-11}$ Nm^{2}kg^{-2}.

$$\therefore \quad F = \frac{6.67 \times 10^{-11} \times 1.67 \times 10^{-27} \times 1.67 \times 10^{-27}}{10^{-15} \times 10^{-15}}$$

$$\Rightarrow \quad F = 1.86 \times 10^{-34} \text{ N}$$

4. The value of acceleration due to gravity
(a) is same on equator and poles
(b) is least on poles
(c) is least on equator
(d) increases from pole to equator

Sol. (*c*) On equator, the value of g is slightly less as compared to that at poles.

5. A car falls off a ledge and drops to the ground in 0.9 s. If the value of g is 10 m/s^2, then speed of car on striking the ground is
(a) 6 m/s (b) 8 m/s (c) 9 m/s (d) 18 m/s

Sol. (*c*) Initial velocity, $u = 0$
Acceleration due to gravity, $g = 10$ m/s^2
$\because$ v be the speed of car on striking the ground, then

$$v = u + gt = 0 + 10 \times 0.9 = 9 \text{ m/s}$$

6. An object is thrown vertically upwards and it rises to a height of 20 m, then the velocity with which the object was thrown upward is
(Take, $g = 10$ m/s^2)
(a) 15 m/s (b) 25 m/s
(c) 10 m/s (d) 20 m/s

Sol. (*d*) Given, height, $h = 20$ m, $g = 10$ m/s^2
At highest point, final velocity, $v = 0$
From equation, $v^2 = u^2 - 2gh$,

$$0 = u^2 - 2 \times 10 \times 20$$

Initial velocity, $u = \sqrt{400} = 20$ m/s
Thus, object was thrown upward with velocity 20 m/s.

7. The atmosphere is held to the Earth by
(a) Earth's magnetic field (b) Earth's rotation
(c) gravity (d) Earth's electric field

Sol. (*c*) The atmosphere is held to the Earth by gravity.

8. The magnitude of weight of a body at the centre of Earth is
(a) zero (b) equal to mass of the body
(c) greater than g (d) less than g

Sol. (*a*) The value of gravitational acceleration (g) at the centre of Earth is zero, hence weight,

$$w = mg = m \times 0 = 0$$

9. At the surface of a certain planet, acceleration due to gravity is one quarter of that on Earth.
If a ball of brass is transported to this planet, then which one of the following statements is not correct?
(a) The mass of the brass ball on this planet is quarter of its mass as measured on Earth.
(b) The weight of the brass ball on this planet is quarter of the weight as measured on Earth.

(c) The brass ball has the same mass on the other planet as on Earth.

(d) The brass ball has the same value on the other planet as on Earth.

Sol. (*a*) Statement in option (a) is incorrect.

As we know that, mass is constant for a body and it does not change with the change of place. So, the mass of brass ball is same on the planet as that on the Earth.

10. Choose the incorrect graph.

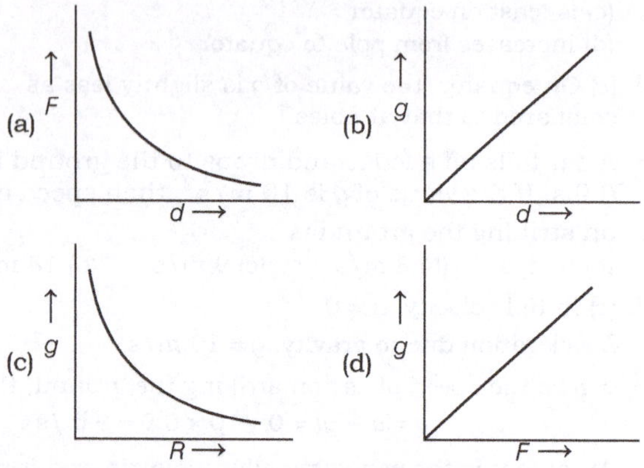

Sol. (*b*) The graph in option (b) is incorrect.

As we know that, $g \propto \frac{1}{d^2}$

So, the correct graph is

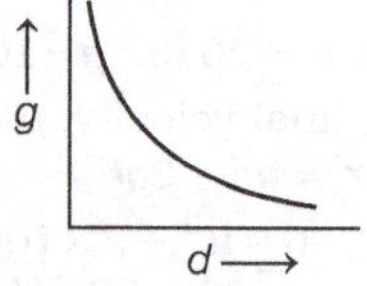

2 Marks Questions

11. How is the gravitational force between two masses affected, if the masses are separated by twice of earlier distance?

Sol. Let initially the distance was d.

Now, distance is $2d$.

As, $F \propto \frac{1}{d^2}$

$\therefore \quad \frac{F_1}{F_2} = \frac{d_2^2}{d_1^2}$

$\therefore \quad \frac{F_1}{F_2} = \frac{(2d)^2}{d^2} = \frac{4}{1} \qquad (\because d_2 = 2d)$

$\Rightarrow \quad \frac{F_2}{F_1} = \frac{1}{4} \Rightarrow F_2 = \frac{F_1}{4}$

Force reduced to one-fourth of earlier case. [2]

12. Draw the graph between the gravitational force and distance between masses.

Sol. Let F is the force and d is distance between the masses.

As we know that, $F \propto \frac{1}{d^2}$

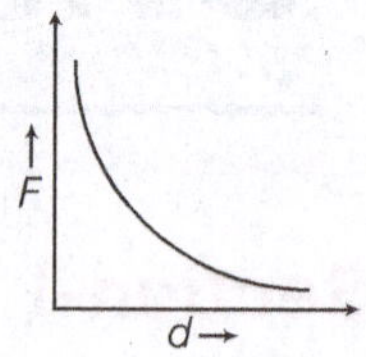

[2]

13. What is the source of centripetal force that a planet requires to revolve around the Sun? On what factors does that force depend?

Sol. The motion of the planet around the Sun is due to the centripetal force. This centripetal force is provided by the gravitational force between the planet and the Sun. This force depends on the mass of the Sun and mass of the planet and the distance between Sun and planet. [2]

14. Imagine what would happen, if the value of g becomes

(i) 100 times of its present value?

(ii) $\frac{1}{100}$ times of its present value?

Sol. (i) Earth's attraction would be so large that you would be crushed to the Earth. [1]

(ii) We can easily jump to the top of a multi-storey building from the ground. [1]

15. Is it possible to shield a body from gravitational effects?

Sol. No, it is not possible to shield a body from gravitational effects because gravitational interaction does not depend upon the nature of the intervening medium.

16. If the Moon attracts the Earth, why does the Earth not move towards the Moon?

Sol. Moon and Earth both attract each other with equal force. But, as force = mass × acceleration

Lighter mass has greater acceleration. Moon is lighter than the Earth. Therefore, Moon is more accelerated. [1]

This acceleration is centripetal acceleration, hence Moon is revolving around the Earth. [1]

17. Amit buys few grams of gold at the poles as per the instruction of one of his friends. He hands over the same, when he meets him at equator. Will the friend agree with the weight of gold bought? If not, why?

Sol. No, his friend will not agree with the weight of gold bought because the acceleration due to gravity at poles is greater than that of at equator.

Thus, weight at pole > weight at equator. [1+ 1]

18. Why at the centre of Earth, value of g is zero?

Sol. At the centre of Earth, g becomes zero because in all directions forces are equal in magnitude but opposite in direction which cancel each other.

19. Write the value of g on surface of the Earth,

(i) in SI unit (ii) in CGS unit

Sol. (i) $g = 9.8 \text{ ms}^{-2}$ (in SI unit)

(ii) $g = 980 \text{ cm s}^{-2}$ (in CGS unit) [1+1]

20. It is known to us that acceleration due to gravity on the Earth is six times greater than that of Moon. How does it affect the weight of an object on both the surfaces?

Sol. As, weight = mass × acceleration due to gravity

i.e. $w = mg$

$\therefore$ $w \propto g$ (because m is always constant)

So, weight of an object on Earth is six times greater than that on the Moon. [2]

21. Write equations of motion of objects under the influence of gravitational force of Earth.

Sol. (i) $v = u + gt$ (ii) $h = ut + \frac{1}{2}gt^2$

(iii) $v^2 = u^2 + 2gh$ [2]

3 Marks Questions

22. (i) Two particles are placed at some distance. If the mass of each particle is doubled, keeping the distance between them unchanged, what will be the value of gravitational force between them?

(ii) An apple falls from a tree because of gravitational attraction between the Earth and apple. If F_1 is the magnitude of force exerted by the Earth on the apple and F_2 is the magnitude of force exerted by apple on Earth, then find the relation between F_1 and F_2.

Sol. (i) Gravitational force, $F_1 = G\frac{Mm}{r^2}$

If mass of each particle is doubled, then

$$F_2 = G\frac{(2M)(2m)}{r^2}$$

or $$F_2 = 4G\frac{Mm}{r^2}$$

or $$F_2 = 4F_1 \quad \left(\because F_1 = G\frac{Mm}{r^2}\right)$$ [1½]

(ii) From third law of motion, to every action, there is an equal and opposite reaction and they act on two different bodies, so magnitudes of F_1 and F_2 are equal. [1½]

$\Rightarrow$ $F_1 = -F_2$

23. Why does a body reach the ground quicker at poles than at the equator, when dropped from the same height?

Sol. The acceleration due to gravity is more at the poles than at the equator. The time taken for a body is smaller, if the acceleration due to gravity is more, when the initial velocities and the distance travelled are the same. So, when a body dropped from the same height then it reaches the ground quicker at poles than at the equator.

24. How does the acceleration due to gravity differ from universal gravitational constant?

Sol. Acceleration due to gravity (g) can be defined as the acceleration produced in the motion of a freely falling object due to gravitational force of Earth. [1]

Whereas, universal gravitational constant (G) is defined as the gravitational force between two objects of unit mass each separated by a unit distance from each other placed anywhere in space. [1]

The universal gravitational constant and acceleration due to gravity are related as

$$g = \frac{GM}{R^2}$$

where, M is the mass of Earth and R is the radius of Earth. [1]

25. On the Earth, a stone is thrown from a height in a direction parallel to the Earth's surface while another stone is simultaneously dropped from the same height. Which stone would reach the ground first and why?

Sol. Time taken by both stones, $t = \sqrt{\frac{2h}{g}}$ [1]

Therefore, if we drop down a stone from a height and at same time we throw another stone in horizontal direction, then both stones strike the Earth simultaneously at different places because both stones will fall under the same value of gravitational acceleration. [2]

26. If the distance between two masses be increased by a factor of 6, by what factor would the mass of one of them have to be altered to maintain the same gravitational force?

Sol. As we know, $F = \frac{Gm_1m_2}{r^2}$ ...(i) [1]

According to question,

Distance between two masses be increased by factor 6, $r' = 6r$ [1]

So, $$F = \frac{Gm_1m_2}{(6r)^2} = \frac{Gm_1m_2}{36r^2} \quad \text{[using Eq. (i)]}$$

$$= \frac{F}{36}$$

To maintain same force, one of the mass is to be increased by 36 times. [1]

27. Mention the two gravitational unit of force. Express their values in Newton.

Sol. Refer to page No. 74.

4 Marks Questions

28. How does the weight of an object vary with respect to mass and radius of the Earth. In a hypothetical case, if the diameter of the Earth becomes half of its present value and its mass becomes four times of its present value, then how would the weight of any object on the surface of the Earth be affected?

Sol. Weight of the object,

$$w = mg = \frac{GMm}{R^2}$$

If $D' = \frac{D}{2}$

i.e., $R' = \frac{R}{2}$

and $M' = 4M$ [2]

Now, weight of the object,

$$w' = \frac{GM'm}{(R')^2} \Rightarrow w' = \frac{G4Mm}{(R/2)^2} = \frac{16\,GMm}{R^2}$$

$\Rightarrow \quad w' = 16W$

Thus, weight of the object will become 16 times of its original weight. [2]

29. Two objects of masses m_1 and m_2 having the same size are dropped simultaneously from heights h_1 and h_2, respectively. Find out the ratio of time, they would take in reaching the ground. Will this ratio remain the same, if

(i) one of the objects is hollow and the other one is solid and

(ii) both of them are hollow, size remaining the same in each case? Give reason.

Sol. Height of object A, $h_1 = \frac{1}{2}gt_1^2$

($\because$ initially the objects were at rest, so that the initial velocity will be zero at that place)

and height of object B, $h_2 = \frac{1}{2}gt_2^2$

$\therefore \quad h_1 : h_2 = t_1^2 : t_2^2$ or $t_1 : t_2 = \sqrt{h_1} : \sqrt{h_2}$

(i) Acceleration due to gravity is independent of mass of falling body. So, ratio remains the same. [2]

(ii) If bodies are hollow, then also ratio remains the same i.e. $\quad t_1 : t_2 = \sqrt{h_1} : \sqrt{h_2}$ [2]

30. A ball is thrown with a velocity u m/s. Show that under the free fall, it will fall on the ground with same velocity.

Sol. When the ball is thrown upwards, it will reach certain height (h) and starts falling. At maximum height (h), the final velocity will be (v) = 0.

Maximum height reached by the ball, (acceleration = $-g$).

Using equation, $v^2 - u^2 = 2gh$

$\Rightarrow \quad 0 - u^2 = 2gh$

$\Rightarrow \quad h = \frac{u^2}{2g}$ ...(i) [2]

In second case, when the ball starts to fall, the initial velocity (u) = 0. It will accelerate due to gravity i.e., $a = g$ and reach ground with velocity (say v_2).

Using equation,

$$v_2^2 - u^2 = 2gh, \; v_2^2 - 0 = 2gh$$

$\Rightarrow \quad v_2^2 = 2g\frac{u^2}{2g} \quad \left[\because h = \frac{u^2}{2g} \text{ from Eq. (i)}\right]$

$= u^2 \Rightarrow v_2 = u$

$\therefore$ The ball reaches on the ground with same velocity. [2]

Numerical Based Questions

31. Find the gravitational force of attraction between Moon and a body of unit mass on the surface of Moon.

(Take, mass of the Moon = 7.4×10^{22} kg, radius of the Moon = 1.74×10^6m, $G = 6.67 \times 10^{-11}$ N-m²/kg²)

Sol. Given, mass of the body, $m = 1$ kg

Mass of the Moon, $M = 7.4 \times 10^{22}$ kg

Radius of the Moon, $R = 1.74 \times 10^6$m

$\therefore \quad F = \frac{GMm}{R^2}$ [1]

$$= \frac{6.67 \times 10^{-11} \times 7.4 \times 10^{22} \times 1}{(1.74 \times 10^6)^2} = 1.63 \text{ N}$$ [1]

32. What is the gravitational force between Sun and Earth? (Take, mass of Sun = 1.99×10^{30} kg, mass of Earth = 6×10^{24} kg, $G = 6.67 \times 10^{-11}$ N-m²/kg² and distance between Sun and Earth = 1.49×10^{11}m)

Sol. Given, mass of Sun, $M_s = 1.99 \times 10^{30}$ kg

Mass of Earth, $M_e = 6 \times 10^{24}$ kg

Distance between Sun and Earth, $R = 149 \times 10^{11}$ m

$\therefore \quad F = \frac{GM_s M_e}{R^2}$

$$= \frac{6.67 \times 10^{-11} \times 1.99 \times 10^{30} \times 6 \times 10^{24}}{(1.49 \times 10^{11})^2}$$

$$= \frac{79.64 \times 10^{43}}{2.22 \times 10^{22}} = 3.587 \times 10^{22} \text{ N}$$ [2]

33. A body weighs 25 kg on the surface of the Earth. If the mass of the Earth is 6×10^{24}kg, the radius of the Earth is 6.4×10^6 m and the gravitational constant is 6.7×10^{-11} N-m²kg⁻². Calculate

(i) the acceleration produced in the body

(ii) the acceleration produced in the Earth.

Sol. Given, $M_e = 6 \times 10^{24}$ kg, $m = 25$ kg

$R_e = 6.4 \times 10^6$m and $G = 6.7 \times 10^{-11}$ N-m²/kg²

$\therefore$ Gravitational force, $F = G\frac{M_e}{R_e^2}m$

$$= \frac{6.7 \times 10^{-11} \times 6 \times 10^{24} \times 25}{(6.4 \times 10^6)^2}$$

$= 245.36$ N [1]

(i) $\therefore$ Acceleration produced in the body,

$$a = \frac{F}{m} = \frac{245.36}{25} = 9.81 \text{ m/s}^2$$ [1]

(ii) $\therefore$ Acceleration produced in the Earth,

$$a = \frac{F}{M_e} = \frac{245.36}{6 \times 10^{24}}$$

$= 4.09 \times 10^{-23}$ m/s² [1]

34. Find acceleration due to gravity on the surface of Jupiter using data given below.
(Take, mass of Jupiter, $M = 1.9 \times 10^{27}$ kg and radius of Jupiter, $R = 7.0 \times 10^7$ m)

Sol. Given, mass of Jupiter, $M = 1.9 \times 10^{27}$ kg
Radius of Jupiter, $R = 7.0 \times 10^7$ m
Using formula of acceleration due to gravity,

$$g = \frac{GM}{R^2}$$ [1]

where, $G = 6.67 \times 10^{-11}$ N-m^{2}kg^{-2}

$$= \frac{6.67 \times 10^{-11} \times 1.9 \times 10^{27}}{(7 \times 10^7)^2}$$

$$= \frac{12.673 \times 10^{16}}{49 \times 10^{14}}$$

$$= 0.2586 \times 10^2 = 25.86 \text{ ms}^{-2}$$

Acceleration due to gravity on Jupiter is 25.86 ms^{-2}. [1]

35. (i) Will a sheet of paper fall slower than one that is crumpled into a ball in vacuum? Why?
(ii) Show mathematically that acceleration experienced by an object is independent of its mass.
(iii) Show that value of $g = 9.8$ m/s^2
(Take, $G = 6.7 \times 10^{-11}$ N-m^2/kg^2, $M = 6 \times 10^{24}$ kg, $R = 6.4 \times 10^6$ m)

Sol. (i) Both of them will fall at the same speed because acceleration produced in freely falling bodies is the same for all bodies, irrespective of their shapes or masses. [1]

(ii) Consider a body of mass m on the surface of the Earth, M be mass of the Earth, R be the distance between the body and centre of the Earth (radius of the Earth) and g is the acceleration due to gravity. Let F be the force acting on the body.
According to Newton's second law of motion,

$$F = mg \quad \text{...(i)}$$

According to Newton's law of gravitation,

$$F = G\frac{M \times m}{R^2} \quad \text{...(ii)}$$ [1]

From Eqs. (i) and (ii), we get

$$mg = G\frac{M \times m}{R^2}$$

$\therefore g = \frac{GM}{R^2}$, thus g is independent of the mass of the body. [1]

(iii) $$\therefore g = \frac{GM}{R^2} = \frac{6.7 \times 10^{-11} \text{N - m}^2 \text{ kg}^{-2} \times 6 \times 10^{24} \text{kg}}{(6.4 \times 10^6 \text{m})^2}$$

$$= \frac{6.7 \times 6}{6.4 \times 6.4} \times \frac{10^{-11+24}}{10^{12}} = 0.981 \times \text{N/kg}$$

$$= 9.81 \text{ m/s}^2 \approx 9.8 \text{ m/s}^2$$

Thus, the value of $g = 9.8$ m/s^2. [1]

36. A body is dropped from a height h. What is its height above the ground after 2 s of its fall?
(Take, $g = 10$ m/s^2)

Sol. Given, initial velocity, $u = 0$, time taken, $t = 2$ s, acceleration due to gravity, $a = g$

$$\therefore \quad h = ut + \frac{1}{2}gt^2 = 0 + \frac{1}{2} \times 10 \times (2)^2 = 20 \text{ m}$$ [2]

37. An object is thrown vertically upwards to a height of 12 m. Calculate its
(i) velocity with which it was thrown upwards
(ii) time taken by the object to reach a height of 12 m.

Sol. Given, $h = 12$ m, $v = 0$, $g = -9.8$ m/s^2; $u = ?$, $t = ?$

(i) $\therefore \; v^2 - u^2 = 2gh \Rightarrow 0 - u^2 = 2 \times (-9.8) \times 12$

$\Rightarrow \quad u = 15.33$ m/s [1]

(ii) $\therefore \quad v = u + gt$

$\Rightarrow \quad t = \frac{u}{g} = \frac{15.33}{9.8} = 1.56$ s [1]

38. To find the height of a bridge over a river, when a stone is dropped freely in the river from the bridge. The stone takes 2 s to touch the water surface in the river. Calculate the height of the bridge from the water level. (Take, $g = 9.8$ m/s^2)

Sol. Given, initial velocity of the stone, $u = 0$
Time taken, $t = 2$ s
Acceleration due to gravity, $g = 9.8$ m/s^2
Height of the bridge, $h = ?$ [1]
Using equation, $h = ut + \frac{1}{2}gt^2$ [1]

$$= 0 \times 2 + \frac{1}{2} 9.8 (2)^2 = \frac{1}{2} \times 9.8 \times 4 = 19.6 \text{ m}$$ [1]

Thus, the height of bridge above the water level is 19.6 m. [1]

39. A stone is thrown vertically upward with an initial velocity of 40 m/s. Taking $g = 10$ m/s^2, find the maximum height reached by the stone. What is the net displacement and the total distance covered by the stone?

Sol. Given, initial velocity, $u = 40$ m/s
Final velocity becomes zero, i.e. $v = 0$ (at maximum height)
From third equation of upward motion,

$$v^2 = u^2 - 2gh$$

$$(0)^2 = (40)^2 - 2 \times 10 \times h$$

$$0 = 1600 - 20h$$

$$\Rightarrow \quad h = \frac{1600}{20} = 80 \text{ m}$$

$\therefore$ Maximum height reached by the stone = 80 m. [1]
After reaching the maximum height, the stone will fall towards the Earth and will reach the Earth's surface covering the same distance.
So, distance covered by the stone = 80 + 80 = 160 m.
Displacement of the stone = 0. [1]

Because the stone starts from the Earth's surface and finally reaches the Earth's surface again, i.e. the initial and final positions of the stone are same. [1]

40. A car falls off a ledge and drops to the ground in 0.5 s. Find

(i) the speed on striking the ground,

(ii) its average speed during 0.5 s and

(iii) height of ledge from the ground.

(Take, $g = 10\ m/s^2$)

Sol. Given, initial velocity, $u = 0$, time taken, $t = 0.5$ s, acceleration due to gravity, $g = 10\ m/s^2$

(i) $\therefore\ v = u + gt = 0 + 10 \times 0.5 = 5\ m/s$ [1]

(ii) $\therefore\ v_{av} = \dfrac{u+v}{2} = \dfrac{0+5}{2} = 2.5\ m/s$ [1]

(iii) $\therefore\ h = ut + \dfrac{1}{2}gt^2$

$= 0 + \dfrac{1}{2} \times 10 \times (0.5)^2 = 1.25$ m [1]

41. From a cliff of 49 m high, a man drops a stone. One second later, he throws another stone. They both hit the ground at the same time. Find out the speed with which he threw the second stone.

Sol. For the first stone, $u = 0\ ms^{-1}$ and $h = 49$ m

As we know that, $h = ut + \dfrac{1}{2}gt^2$

$\therefore\ 49 = 0 \times t + \dfrac{1}{2} \times 9.8 \times t^2$

$\Rightarrow\ t^2 = \dfrac{98}{9.8} = 10 \Rightarrow t^2 = \sqrt{10} = 3.16$ s [1]

Thus, first stone would take 3.16 s to reach the ground. The time taken by second stone to reach the ground is one second less than that taken by the first stone as both the stones reach the ground at the same time.

i.e., for the second stone, $t = (3.16 - 1)$ s $= 2.16$ s [1]

For the second stone,

$g = 9.8\ ms^{-2}$, $h = 49$ m, $t = 2.16$ s and $u = ?$

$\therefore\ s = ut + \dfrac{1}{2}gt^2$

$\Rightarrow\ 49 = u \times 2.16 + \dfrac{1}{2} \times 9.8\ (2.16)^2$

$\Rightarrow\ 49 - 22.86 = 2.16u$ or $26.14 = 2.16u$

$u = \dfrac{26.14}{2.16} = 12.1\ ms^{-1}$

Thus, the second stone was thrown downward with a speed of $12.1\ ms^{-1}$. [2]

42. The weight of any person on Moon is about 1/6th of that on Earth. He can lift a mass of 15 kg on the Earth. What will be the maximum weight which can be lifted by the same force applied by the person on the Moon?

Sol. $\because$ Maximum weight which can be lifted $= mg$

$= 15\ kg \times 9.8\ m/s^2 = 147$ N

$\therefore$ Weight which can be lifted on Moon

$= 147\ N \times \dfrac{1}{g_E/6}$ [1]

($\because$ at Moon, acceleration due to gravity is 1/6th to that of Earth)

$= \dfrac{147 \times 6}{9.8} = \dfrac{147}{1.63} = 90$ kg [1]

43. How much would a 70 kg man weight on the Moon? What would be his mass on the Earth and on the Moon? (Take, acceleration due to gravity on the Moon = $1.63\ m/s^2$)

Sol. Let us calculate the weight of the man on the Moon.

Mass of the man on the Moon, $m = 70$ kg

Acceleration due to gravity, $g = 1.63\ m/s^2$

We know that, weight is given by

$W = m \times g = 70 \times 1.63 = 114.1$ N [1]

Thus, the man weighs 114.1 N on the Moon. We know that the mass of a body is constant everywhere in universe. So, the mass of this man would be same on the Earth as well as on the Moon. Hence, the mass will be 70 kg on Earth as well as on Moon. [1]

Section-II

Structured Questions

44. (i) (a) Write the value and unit of gravitational constant. [3]

(b) Find gravitational force of attraction between two bodies of mass $m_1 = 1$ kg and $m_2 = 1$ kg separated by 1 m distance from each other.

(ii) (a) What is acceleration due to gravity? How is it related to the weight of an object?

(b) Write the value and unit of acceleration due to gravity. [3]

(iii) Write four facts regarding gravitational force. [4]

Sol. (i) (a) From the Newton's law of gravitation, we get

$F = \dfrac{Gm_1m_2}{r^2} \Rightarrow G = \dfrac{F \times r^2}{m_1m_2}$

$\Rightarrow\ G = \dfrac{Nm^2}{kg^2}$ or Nm^2kg^{-2}

The value of G is 6.67×10^{-11}. [1½]

(b) Given, $m_1 = 1$ kg, $m_2 = 1$ kg

$r = 1$ m

From Newton's law of gravitation, $F = \dfrac{Gm_1m_2}{r^2}$

$= 6.67 \times 10^{-11} \times \dfrac{1 \times 1}{1^2} = 6.67 \times 10^{-11}$ N [1½]

(ii) (a) The rate at which the velocity of a freely falling body increases, is called the acceleration due to gravity. In other words, it is the acceleration produced in a freely falling body due to the gravitational force of attraction of the Earth.

It is related with weight as $w = mg$. [1½]

(b) According to Newton's law of gravitation,

$$F = \frac{GMm}{r^2} \quad \ldots(i)$$

According to Newton's second law of motion,

$$F = ma \quad \ldots(ii)$$

From Eqs. (i) and (ii), we get

$$\frac{GMm}{r^2} = ma \Rightarrow a = \frac{GM}{r^2}$$

Here, $a = g = \frac{GM}{r^2}$

The value of acceleration due to gravity (g) is 9.8 and its unit is m/s^2. **[1½]**

(iii) Four facts regarding gravitational force

(a) It is always attractive. **[1]**

(b) It is directly proportional to the product of the masses. **[1]**

(c) It is inversely proportional to the square of separation between them, i.e., it obeys the inverse square law. Thus, by doubling the separation between the two masses, the force of attraction between them is reduced to one-fourth. **[1]**

(d) It is significant between heavenly bodies, but is insignificant between ordinary bodies because of small magnitude of G. **[1]**

45. (i) (a) What are different gravitational units of force?

(b) Write equations of a body falling freely from rest with height h. **[3]**

(ii) Differentiate between mass and weight. **[3]**

(iii) A ball is thrown vertically upwards from the top of a building of height 25 m with an initial velocity 15 ms^{-1}. Taking $g = 9.8$ ms^{-2}, calculate

(a) the height to which it will rise before returning to the ground.

(b) the velocity with which it will strike the ground.

(c) the total time of journey. **[4]**

Sol. (i) (a) In MKS system, the gravitational unit of force is kilogram force (kgf).

One kilogram of force is the force due to gravity on a mass of 1 kg.

i.e., 1kgf = 9.8 newton

In CGS system, the gravitational unit of force is gram force (gf).

One gram force is the force due to gravity on mass of 1 g.

1gf = 980 dyne. **[1½]**

(b) Equations of a body falling freely from rest ($u = 0$) are

(i) $v = gt$

(ii) $h = \frac{1}{2}gt^2$

(iii) $v^2 = 2gh$

where, v = final velocity

h = height

g = acceleration due to gravity

t = time **[1½]**

(ii) The difference between mass and weight is given below

Mass	Weight
1. It is a measure of the quantity of matter contained in the body at rest.	1. It is the force with which the Earth attracts to a body towards its centre.
2. It is a scalar quantity	2. It is a vector quantity
3. Its SI unit is kg.	3. Its SI unit is newton (N)
4. It is measured by a physical (or beam) balance	4. It is measured by a spring balance which is calibrated to read in newton.
5. It is constant for a body and does not change with the change in place.	5. It is not constant for a body, but varies from place to place due to change in the value of g.

[3]

(iii) Given, $u = 15$ ms^{-1} (upwards)

Height of building, $h = 25$ m

(a) At the highest point, $v = 0$

For upward journey, from relation

$$v^2 = u^2 - 2gh \Rightarrow 0 = u^2 - 2gh$$

or $$h = \frac{u^2}{2g} = \frac{(15)^2}{2 \times 9.8} = \frac{225}{19.6} = 11.47 \text{ m}$$ **[1]**

(b) While returning from the highest point $u = 0$, total height travelled = 11.47 + 25 = 36.47 m

Let v be the velocity with which it strikes the ground. Then from relation,

$$v^2 = u^2 + 2gh$$

$$v^2 = 0 + 2 \times 9.8 \times 36.47$$

$$v^2 = 715 \Rightarrow v = 26.73 \text{ ms}^{-1}$$ **[1]**

(c) If the ball takes time t_1 to go to the highest point from the top of the building, then for upward journey, from relation

$$v = u - gt$$

$$0 = 11.47 - 9.8t_1$$

$$\Rightarrow \quad t_1 = \frac{11.47}{9.8} = 1.17 \text{ s}$$

Now, for the downward journey from the highest point, if the ball takes time t_2 to reach the ground, then $u = 0$, $v = 26.73$ ms^{-1}, from relation $v = 4 + gt$

$$\Rightarrow \quad t_2 = \frac{26.73}{9.8} = 2.72 \text{ s}$$

Hence, total time of journey $t = t_1 + t_2$

$= 1.17 + 2.72 = 3.89$ s **[2]**

Chapter Assessment

1 Mark Questions

1. Newton's law of gravitation is a universal law, because it
   (a) acts on all bodies and particles in the universe
   (b) acts on all the masses at all distances and not affected by the medium
   (c) is always attractive
   (d) All of the above
2. The gravitational force between two point masses m_1 and m_2 at separation r is given by $F = k\frac{m_1 m_2}{r^2}$. The constant k
   (a) depends on system of unit only
   (b) depends on medium between masses only
   (c) depends on both (a) and (b)
   (d) is independent of both (a) and (b)
3. As we go from the equator to the poles, the value of g
   (a) remains the same (b) decreases
   (c) increases (d) decreases upto a latitude of 45°
4. In vacuum, all freely falling objects have the same
   (a) speed (b) velocity (c) acceleration (d) force
5. An object falling freely from rest reaches ground in 2 s. If acceleration due to gravity is 9.8 m/s^2, the velocity of the object on reaching the ground will be
   (a) 9.8 m/s (b) 4.9 m/s (c) 19.6 m/s (d) zero

2 Marks Questions

6. A ball is thrown vertically upwards with a velocity of 25 m/s. If g is 10 m/s^2, then calculate
   (i) height that it reaches and
   (ii) time taken to return back.
7. What would happen, if the value of g becomes zero?
8. (i) What do you mean by free fall?
   (ii) State the universal law of gravitation.
9. Write the formula for magnitude of gravitational force between the Earth and an object on the surface of the Earth.
10. Explain the meaning of the following statement "1 kgf = 9.8 N."
11. How are g and G related?
12. Does a tennis ball bounce higher on Mount Everest than on ground of Mumbai when dropped from height h? Give reason.
13. The Earth and Moon are attracted to each other by gravitational force. Does the Earth attract the Moon with a force that is greater than or smaller than or equal to the force with which the Moon attracts the Earth? Why?
14. How does the force of gravitation between two objects change, when distance between them is reduced to half?

Structured Questions

15. (i) Compare the weight of an object, whose mass is 1 kg at points A and B on the surface of Earth. **[3]**

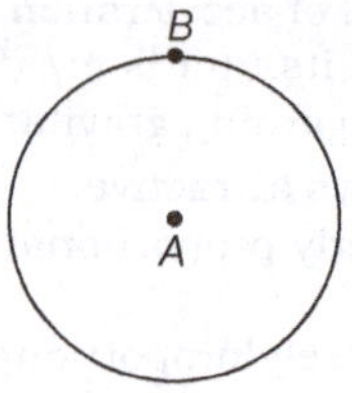

(ii) Two bodies of masses 3 kg and 12 kg are placed at a distance 12 m as shown in figure. A third body of mass 0.5 kg is to be placed at such a point that the force acting on this body is zero. Find the position of that point. **[3]**

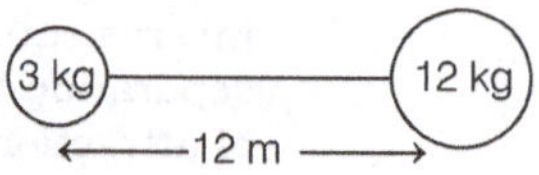

(iii) (a) According to universal law of gravitation, every object in this universe attracts every other object. Explain, why then a table and a chair lying in the same room do not collide with each other?
(b) An object is thrown vertically upwards to a height of 12 m. (I) Calculate its velocity with which it was thrown upwards and (II) time taken by the object to reach a height of 12 m.
(c) Write the SI unit of gravitational constant. **[4]**

16. (i) A rocket of mass 1000 kg is launched from Earth. Calculate the force of attraction acting on it, when it reached the height of 1 km above the surface of Earth. (Take, mass of Earth = 5.96×10^{24} kg and radius of earth = 6.37×10^6 km) **[3]**

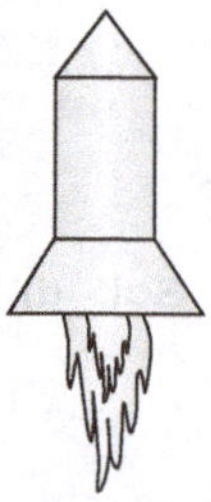

(ii) (a) Which force keeps the Moon in a uniform circular motion around the Earth?
(b) Suppose gravity of the Earth suddenly becomes zero, then which direction will the Moon begin to move, if no other celestial body affects it?
(c) The Earth is acted upon by gravitation of the Sun, even then it does not fall into the Sun. Why? **[3]**

(iii) The radius of the Earth at the poles is 6357 km and the radius at the equator is 6378 km. Calculate the percentage change in the weight of a body, when it is taken from the equator to the poles. **[4]**

For Solutions Scan the Code

Olympiad Section*

Brain Teasing Questions of Olympiad Pattern

1 The weight of a body is the force with which a body is attracted by the Earth towards its centre. What is the weight of an object at the point A shown in figure?

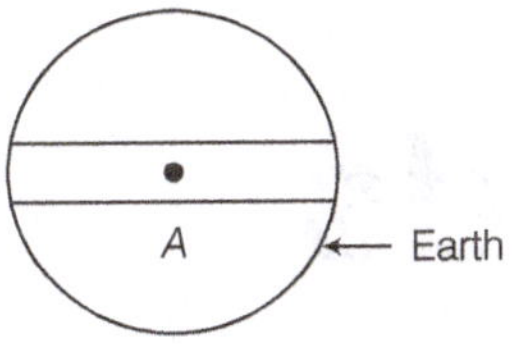

(a) Zero
(b) Infinite
(c) R times the weight at the surface of the Earth
(d) $1/R^2$ times the weight at the surface of the Earth

2 Two spheres of masses 100 kg and 900 kg each of radius 10 m and 20 m respectively, are touching each other, then the gravitational force acting between them is

(a) 6.67×10^{-9} N (b) 9.67×10^{-10}N
(c) 10×10^{-12} N (d) 9×10^{-11} N

3 Consider the following diagrams.

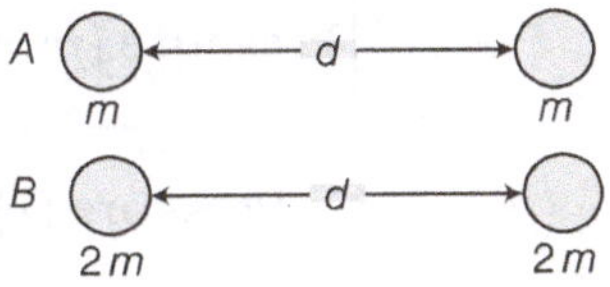

If the gravitational force for system A is F, then what will be the gravitational force for system B?

(a) $\frac{1}{4}F$ (b) $4F$ (c) $\frac{1}{2}$F (d) Unchanged

4 A mass of 1g is separated from another mass of 1g by a distance of 1 cm. How many g-wt of force exists between them?

(a) 8×10^{-13} g-wt (b) 7×10^{-13} g-wt
(c) 1.0×10^{-11} g-wt (d) 2×10^{-9} g-wt

5 Two bodies weighing 50 kg and 10 kg are kept at a distance 5 m apart. If the distance between them is increased by 5 m, then the value of percentage change in force is

(a) 75% (b) 50% (c) 45% (d) 30%

6 An apple falls from a tree because of gravitational force of attraction F_1 between the Earth and apple. If F_2 is the magnitude of force exerted by apple on the Earth, then

(a) $F_1 >> F_2$ (b) $F_2 >> F_1$
(c) $F_1 > F_2$ (d) $F_1 = F_2$

7 If the diameter of Earth becomes two times of its present value and its mass remains unchanged, then how would the weight of an object on the surface of the Earth be affected?

(a) Weight would become one-third
(b) Weight would become one-fourth
(c) Weight would become one-fifth
(d) Weight would become one-sixth

8 If the radius of the Earth shrinks by 4% and there is no change in its mass, then acceleration due to gravity, which depends on mass and radius will change. By how much does the value of g change?

(a) 2% (b) 4% (c) 16% (d) 8%

9 What will be the acceleration of the bodies in the below system, assuming that only gravitational force acts between them?

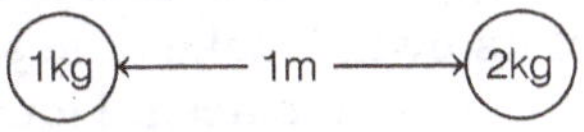

(a) 1.33×10^{-10}m/s^2 and 6.67×10^{-11}m/s^2
(b) 1.33×10^{-11} m/s^2 and 6.25×10^{-11}m/s^2
(c) 5.36×10^{-11}m/s^2 and 5.26×10^{-11}m/s^2
(d) 3.011×10^{-11}m/s^2 and 5.26×10^{-11}m/s^2

10 Astronomers have discovered a planet orbiting a nearby star. It is estimated that the mass of this planet is 16 times that of our Earth and its density is one-fourth of the Earth's density. Assume that planets are spheres of uniform density. If your weight on the Earth is 1000 N, then your weight on this planet would be

(a) 5000 N (b) 1000 N
(c) 2000 N (d) 4000 N

11 The ratio of radii of two planets P and Q is x and the ratio of their densities is y. Find the ratio of the acceleration of free fall on P to that on Q in terms of x and y.

(a) xy (b) x^2y (c) $x+y$ (d) $x-y$

Answers

1. (a) **2.** (a) **3.** (b) **4.** (b) **5.** (a) **6.** (d) **7.** (b) **8.** (d) **9.** (a) **10.** (b) **11.** (a)

* *These questions may or may not be asked in the examination, have been given just for additional practice required for olympiads Scholarship Exams etc. For detailed explanations refer Page No. 215.*

CHAPTER
05

Fluids

SYLLABUS

• Change of pressure with depth (including the formula $p = h\rho g$) • Transmission of pressure in liquids • Atmospheric pressure. • Buoyancy • Archimedes' principle • Floatation • Relationship with density • Relative density • Determination of relative density of a solid.

Fluid is a substance that flows under the action of an applied force and does not have a definite shape of its own. It takes the shape of that vessel in which it would be placed. Liquids and gases are collectively known as **fluids.**

In this chapter, we will be studying the various types of fluid pressure with their applications in different areas. Alongwith it, we will also study famous Archimedes' principle that shows the relationship between the upward force when an object is immersed into the fluid and the weight of the object.

Thrust and Pressure

The force or push acting on an object perpendicular to its surface is called **thrust**. Its effect depends on the area on which it acts. The thrust exerted by a body on a surface is equal to the weight of the body. Its unit is same as that of force, i.e. the SI unit of thrust is **newton** (N) and CGS unit is **dyne**. Its gravitational unit in MKS system is kgf and in CGS system is gf. Also, 1 kgf = 9.8 N and 1gf = 980 dyne. It is a **vector** quantity.

The thrust acting perpendicularly on a unit area of the object is called **pressure.**

$$\text{Pressure } (p) = \frac{\text{Force } (F)}{\text{Area } (A)} = \frac{\text{Thrust}}{\text{Area}}$$

$$\therefore \quad \text{Pressure } (p) \propto \frac{1}{\text{Area } (A)}$$

So, (i) When area increases ⇒ Pressure decreases

(ii) When area decreases ⇒ Pressure increases.

Its SI unit is N/m^2, which is also called **pascal (Pa)** named after the scientist **Blaise Pascal**. It is a **scalar** quantity.

$$1 \text{ Pa} = 1 \text{ N/m}^2$$

One pascal is defined as the pressure exerted on a unit surface area by a force of one newton (N) acting normally on it.

CGS unit of pressure is dyne cm^{-2}.

where, 1 dyne cm^{-2} = 0.1 Nm^{-2}

Other units 1 bar = 10^5 Nm^{-2}

or 1 Nm^{-2} = 10 dyne cm^{-2}

1 torr = 1 mm of Hg

1 atm = 760 torr

From the formula of pressure, it is clear that the pressure exerted on a surface depends upon the two factors

(i) area on which force is applied

(ii) magnitude of applied force

Example 1. Force of 200 N is applied to an object of area $4\,m^2$. Find the pressure.

Sol. Here, force, $F = 200$ N and area, $A = 4\ m^2$

Now, pressure $(p) = \dfrac{\text{force}(F)}{\text{area}(A)} = \dfrac{200}{4} = 50\ N/m^2$

Example 2. A woman is wearing sharp-heeled sandal (stilettos). If the mass of woman is 60 kg and the area of one heel is $1\ cm^2$, find out the pressure exerted on the ground, when the woman stands on just one heel. (Take, $g = 10\ m/s^2$)

Sol. Given, mass, $m = 60$ kg, $g = 10\ m/s^2$

Area of heel, $A = 1\,cm^2 = 10^{-4}\,m^2$

Force, $F = mg = 60 \times 10 = 600$ N

Pressure, $p = \dfrac{F}{A} = \dfrac{600}{10^{-4}} = 6 \times 10^6\ N/m^2$

Some Daily Life Applications of Pressure

Some of the daily life applications of pressure are given below as

(i) The handles of bags, suitcase, etc., are made broad, so that pressure exerted by the hand is less and it is easier to lift them.

(ii) Buildings are provided broad foundations, so that the pressure exerted on the ground becomes less.

(iii) Railway tracks are laid on cement or iron sleepers, so that the pressure exerted by train is spread over the larger area and thus, becomes less.

(iv) Pins, needles and cutting tools are provided sharp pointed ends, so that with minimal efforts, a large pressure can be exerted.

(v) Pressure on ground is more when a man is walking than when he is standing because in case of walking the effective area is less.

(vi) The tractors have broad tyres, so that there is less pressure on the ground and they do not sink into comparatively soft ground in the field.

Density

Mass per unit volume of a substance is known as its density.

$$\text{Density} = \frac{\text{Mass of the substance}}{\text{Volume of the substance}} \quad \text{or } \rho = \frac{m}{V}$$

It is a scalar quantity and represented by letter ρ (rho) or *d*.

The SI unit of density is **kilogram per metre cube** (kg/m^3)

and CGS unit of density is **gram per cubic centimetre** ($g\,cm^{-3}$)

$$1\ kg\,m^{-3} = 10^{-3} g\,cm^{-3}$$

Effect of Temperature on Density

Most of the substance expands on heating and contract on cooling but the mass of the substance remains unchanged. Therefore, density of most of the substances decreases with rise in temperature and increases with decrease in temperature.

Water is an exception due to its uneven expansion. When water is cooled, it contracts upto 4°C and after that it expands below 4°C to 0°C. Thus, the density of water is maximum at 4°C which is equal to $1\ g/cm^3$ or $1000\ kg/m^3$.

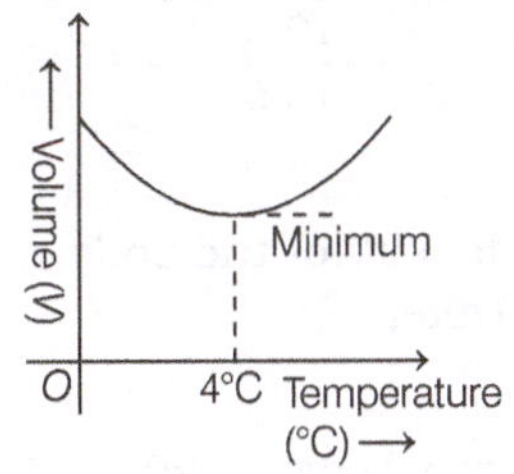

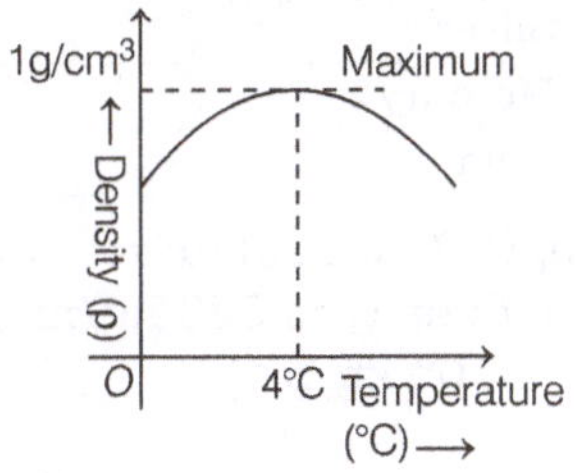

Relative Density

The ratio of the density of a substance to the density of water at 4°C is known as relative density.

Relative density of a substance (RD)

$$= \frac{\text{Density of the substance } (\rho_1)}{\text{Density of water } (\rho_2)} \quad \text{... (i)}$$

In other words, we can say that, relative density of a substance

$$= \frac{\text{Mass of the substance } (m_1)}{\text{Volume of the substance}} \times \frac{\text{Volume of water}}{\text{Mass of water } (m_2)} \quad \text{... (ii)}$$

$$\left(\because \text{Density} = \frac{\text{Mass}}{\text{Volume}}\right)$$

Since, the relative density is a ratio of similar quantities, so it has no unit.

In case of same volume, from Eqs. (i) and (ii), we get

$$\text{RD} = \frac{\rho_1}{\rho_2} = \frac{m_1}{m_2}$$

The relative density of a substance expresses the heaviness (or density) of the substance in comparison to water. By saying that relative density of an iron is 7.8, we mean that iron is 7.8 times as heavy as an equal volume of water.

Density of some common substances

Substance	Density (in g cm^{-3})
Wood (pine)	0.50
Petrol	0.80
Turpentine	0.87
Ice	0.92
Olive oil	0.92
Pure water (at 4°C)	1.00
Sea water	1.02
Glycerine	1.26
Glass	2.5
Aluminium	2.70
Iron	7.86
Copper	8.92
Silver	10.5
Mercury	13.6
Gold	19.3

Example 3. Calculate relative density of the body whose density is 520 kg/m^3. (Take, $\rho_{water} = 10^3\ kg/m^3$)

Sol. Relative Density (RD) $= \dfrac{\text{Density of body}}{\text{Density of water}} = \dfrac{520}{1000} = 0.52$

Pressure Exerted by a Liquid Column

Consider a liquid of density ρ is kept in a cylindrical vessel as shown in figure. To calculate the pressure at a depth h below the free surface of liquid XY, we consider an imaginary cylinder of liquid of cross-sectional area A. The pressure on the surface B will be due to the weight of liquid column above B.

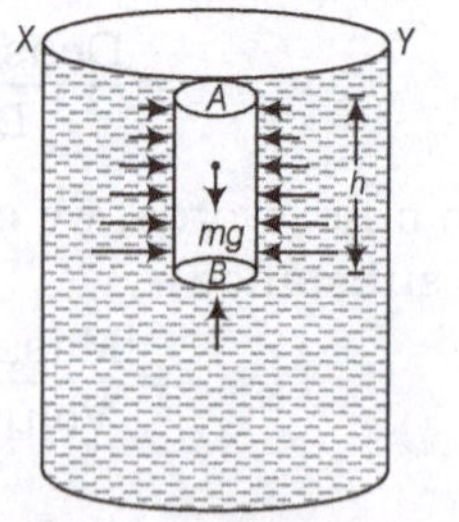

Pressure at a depth in liquid

Then, weight of liquid cylinder acting downwards,

$$w = m \times g = \text{volume} \times \text{density} \times g = Ah\rho g$$

where, ρ is the density of the liquid, if the liquid cylinder is in equilibrium.

So, the force acting on the surface B

$$= \text{weight of liquid column} = Ah\rho g$$

Now, the pressure on surface B,

$$p = \frac{\text{Force}}{\text{Area}} = \frac{Ah\rho g}{A} \Rightarrow \boxed{p = h\rho g}$$

Hence, the pressure difference depends on the vertical height below the free surface of liquid, density of the liquid and the acceleration due to gravity.

There is also atmospheric pressure acting on the free surface of liquid.

So total pressure, $\boxed{p = p_a + h\rho g}$

Thus, the pressure p at a depth below the surface of a liquid open to the atmosphere is greater than atmospheric pressure by an amount ρgh.

At a particular place on earth's surface, g is constant, therefore the liquid pressure at that point depends on height of the liquid column and density of the liquid.

Note The excess pressure above the atmospheric pressure is usually called **gauge pressure** and the total pressure is called **absolute pressure**.

Example 4. A swimmer experiences the pressure while swimming in a lake, then what is the pressure on a swimmer 10 m below the surface of a lake? (Take, $p_a = 1.01 \times 10^5$ Pa)

Sol. Here, $h = 10$ m, $\rho = 1000\ kg/m^3$ and $g = 10\ m/s^2$

$$p = p_a + \rho gh = 1.01 \times 10^5 + (1000 \times 10 \times 10)$$
$$= 2.01 \times 10^5 \simeq 2 \text{ atm}$$

Example 5. At a depth 1000 m in an ocean,

(i) what is the absolute pressure?

(ii) what is the gauge pressure?

(iii) find the force acting on the window of area 20 cm × 20 cm of a submarine at this depth, the interior of which is maintained at sea-level atmospheric pressure. (The density of sea water is $1.03 \times 10^3\ kgm^{-3}$ and $g = 10\ ms^{-2}$)

Sol. (i) We know that, $p = p_a + \rho gh$

$$p = 1.01 \times 10^5 + 1.03 \times 10^3 \times 10 \times 1000$$
$$p = 104.01 \times 10^5 \text{ Pa}$$
$$= 104 \text{ atm}$$

(ii) Gauge pressure, $p_g = p - p_a$

$$p_g = \rho gh = 1.03 \times 10^3 \times 10 \times 1000$$
$$p_g = 103 \times 10^5 \text{Pa} \approx 103 \text{ atm}$$

(iii) The net force acting on the window by gauge pressure can be given as,

$$\Rightarrow \quad F = p_g A = 103 \times 10^5 \times 0.04$$
$$= 4.12 \times 10^5 \text{N}$$

Laws of Liquid Pressure

Laws of liquid pressure are as follows

(i) If a liquid is at rest, then the pressure exerted is same at all points on a horizontal plane.

(ii) Pressure at a given point inside the liquid is directly proportional to the density of the liquid.

(iii) Pressure for different liquids is different at the same depth.

(iv) Pressure is same in all directions and at all points in a horizontal plane at a given depth.

Some Daily Life Consequences of Pressure in Liquid

Some daily life consequences of pressure in liquid are as given below

1. Broadness of Base of a Dam

Since, water pressure increases with depth. Therefore, the wall of a dam is made thicker at the bottom because a thicker wall can withstand a greater pressure exerted by the water at greater depth.

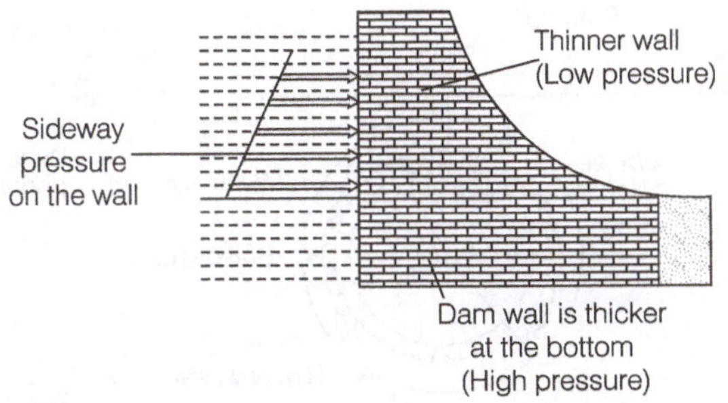

2. Divers use Special Protective Suit for Diving in Sea

When sea divers go deep inside the sea, pressure exerted by the liquid increases much more than that of divers blood pressure. To protect divers from this extreme pressure of liquid, they have to wear protective suits.

Note Pressure in a liquid is independent of area of cross-section.

Check Your LEARNING...

1 Is pressure a vector quantity?
2 Why railway tracks are laid on cement sleepers?
3 Is the pressure at same depth is different for different liquid?
4 What is the effect of density on the pressure?
5 A column of water 40 cm high supports a 30 cm column of an unknown liquid. What is the density of the liquid?

Ans. 1.33×10^3 kg m^{-3}

6 Divers use special protective suits for diving in sea, why?

Pascal's Law (Transmission of Pressure in Liquids)

It states that, whenever an external pressure is applied on any part of a fluid contained in a vessel, it is transmitted undiminished and equally in all directions.

Experimental Demonstration of Pascal's Law

Take a glass flask having narrow holes, through which fluid can come out from its sides and bottom. The flask is provided with an air-tight piston at its mouth as shown in figure.

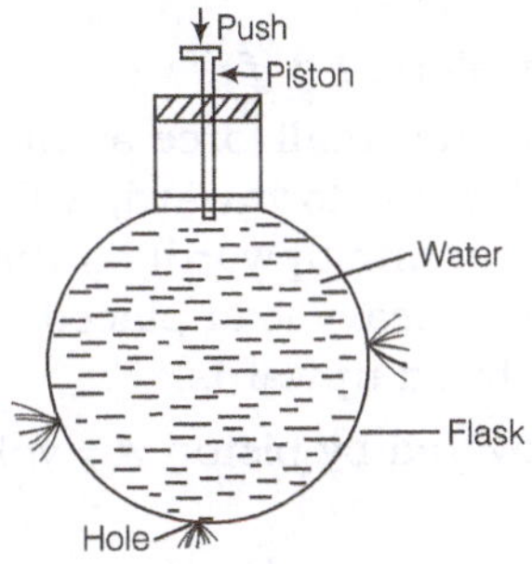

Demonstration of Pascal's law

Fill the flask with water. Now, push the piston down into the flask gently. It is observed that water comes out with the same pressure through each hole. This shows that the pressure applied to the enclosed liquid is transmitted equally in all directions everywhere inside the liquid.

Applications of Pascal's Law

Some applications of Pascal's law are as given below

1. Hydraulic Lift (or Hydraulic Jack)

It is used to lift heavy loads. It is a force multiplier. It consists of two cylinders C_1 and C_2 connected to each other by a pipe E. These cylinders are fitted with water-tight frictionless pistons of different cross-sectional areas. Smaller piston has cross-sectional area a while bigger one has A. These cylinders and the pipe contain a liquid.

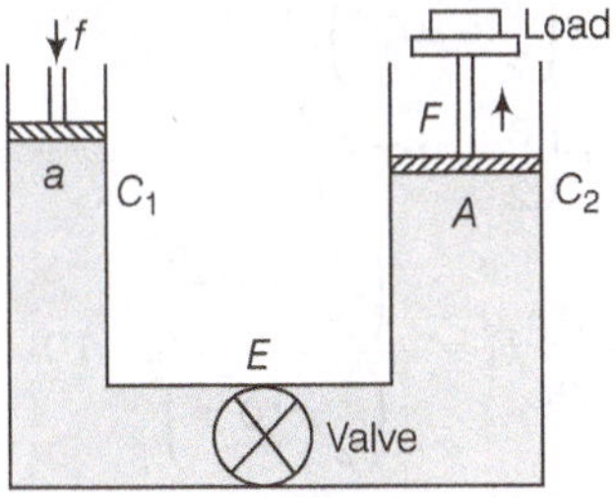

Hydraulic lift

Suppose a downward force f is applied on the smaller piston of cross-sectional area a, then pressure exerted on the liquid,

$$p = \frac{f}{a}$$

According to Pascal's law, this pressure p is also transmitted to the larger piston of cross-sectional area A, then upward force on larger piston C_2,

$$F = p \times A = \frac{f}{a} \times A = \frac{A}{a} \times f$$

$\therefore$ Upward force on a larger piston, $F = \frac{A}{a} f$

or, $$\frac{F}{f} = \frac{A}{a}$$

As $A > a$, therefore, $F > f$.

This shows that the small force applied on the smaller piston (acting downward) will appear as a very large force (acting upward) on the larger piston. As a result of it, a heavy load placed on the larger piston is easily lifted upwards.

Now, volume covered by piston A = volume covered by piston a

$\Rightarrow$ $$AL = al \Rightarrow \frac{l}{L} = \frac{A}{a}$$

$\because$ $$A > a \Rightarrow l > L$$

$\Rightarrow$ Distance moved by effort > Distance moved by load

Example 6. Two syringes of different cross-sections (without needles) filled with water are connected with a tightly fitted rubber tube filled with water. Diameters of the smaller and larger pistons are 1.0 cm and 3.0 cm, respectively.

(i) Find the force exerted on the larger piston when a force of 10 N is applied to the smaller piston.

(ii) If the smaller piston is pushed in through 6.0 cm, how much does the larger piston move out?

Sol. (i) Here, $A_1 = \pi\left(\frac{D_1}{2}\right)^2$, $A_2 = \pi\left(\frac{D_2}{2}\right)^2$

$$A_1 = \pi\left(\frac{1}{2} \times 10^{-2}\right)^2,$$

$$A_2 = \pi\left(\frac{3}{2} \times 10^{-2}\right)^2$$

$$\therefore \quad F_2 = \frac{A_2}{A_1} F_1 = \frac{\pi\left(\frac{3}{2} \times 10^{-2}\right)^2}{\pi\left(\frac{1}{2} \times 10^{-2}\right)^2} \times 10$$

$$F_2 = 90\text{ N}$$

(ii) Volume covered by the movement of smaller piston inwards is equal to volume moved outwards due to the larger piston.

$$\therefore \quad L_1 A_1 = L_2 A_2$$

$$L_2 = \frac{A_1}{A_2} L_1 = \frac{\pi\left(\frac{1}{2} \times 10^{-2}\right)^2}{\pi\left(\frac{3}{2} \times 10^{-2}\right)^2} \times 6 \times 10^{-2}$$

$$L_2 = 0.67 \times 10^{-2}\text{ m} = 0.67\text{ cm}$$

Atmospheric pressure is common to both pistons and has been ignored.

2. Hydraulic Brakes

They are used in big vehicles like trucks, cars, etc.

The working of the hydraulic brakes is also based on the Pascal's law. It consists of a tube T containing brake oil. One end of the tube is connected to the wheel cylinder having two pistons P_1 and P_2.

These pistons are then connected to the brake shoes S_1 and S_2, respectively. The other end of tube is connected to master cylinder fitted with the piston P.

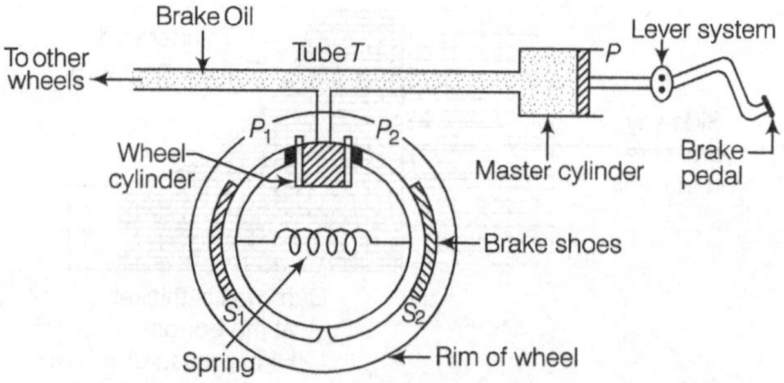

Construction details of hydraulic brakes

The piston P is connected to the brake pedal through the lever system. The area of cross-section of the wheel cylinder is greater than that of master cylinder. The arrangement is shown in figure. When the brake pedal is pressed, the lever system operates, the piston P is pushed, pressure applied on brake oil by piston P is transmitted to pistons P_1 and P_2 in accordance with Pascal's law.

The pistons (P_1 and P_2) push the brake shoes away from each other, so they press against the inner rim of the wheel and retard the motion. Therefore, a small force applied on the brake pedal produces large thrust on the wheels. When pressure on the wheel pedal is released, the brake shoes return to their normal positions due to pulling force of spring.

3. Hydraulic Press (Bramah Press)

It is a machine that has a bed or a plate in which the metallic material is placed, so that it can be crushed, straightened or moulded.

It also works on the principle of Pascal's.

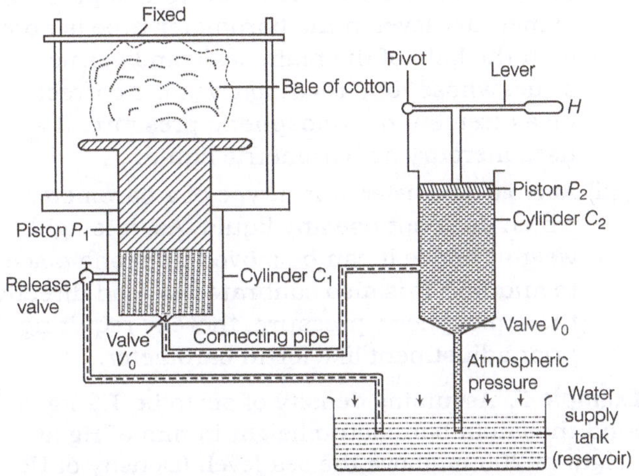

Hydraulic press

Here, the force applied on the fluids by the small cylinder (C_2) results in a large force when pushed in the master cylinder (C_1). The hydraulic press is mostly used for industrial purpose, where a large pressure is required for compressing metals into thin sheets.

The other common uses of the hydraulic press are as follow

(i) For crushing of metallic material.
(ii) For extracting juices from fruits and vegetables.
(iii) For sword making.

Note For hydraulic machines, effort is less than the load. But, the distance moved by the effort is more than the distance moved by the load. i.e. Work done by effort = Work done by load

Thus, Mechanical Advantage (MA) $= \frac{\text{load}}{\text{effort}} > 1$

and Velocity Ratio (VR) $= \frac{\text{Distance moved by effort}}{\text{Distance moved by load}} > 1$

Hence, hydraulic machines act like force multiplier.

Atmospheric Pressure

The gaseous envelope surrounding the earth is called Earth's atmosphere. The pressure exerted by the atmosphere is called atmospheric pressure.

The force exerted by air column on a unit area on the earth's surface is equal to the atmospheric pressure, it is denoted by p_a.

The value of atmospheric pressure on the surface of the earth at sea level is called 1 atmosphere (1 atm), it is nearly about $1.013 \times 10^5 N/m^2$.

Demonstration of Atmospheric Pressure by Collapsing tin can experiment

Take an empty tin can and pour some water in it. Now, heat this water in the open can until it boils. Gradually, the steam occupies the entire space in can and pushes the air out from the tin can. Now, seal it tightly with a stopper and simultaneously remove the flame. Then, pour some cold water over the tin can. It is observed that the tin can collapses inwards as shown in figure.

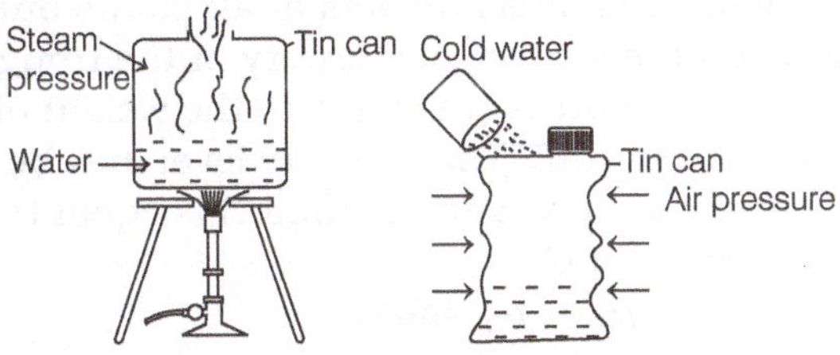

This is due to the fact that on pouring cold water, the steam inside the tin can condenses and a partial vacuum is created. Now, the air pressure outside the tin can exceeds the vapour pressure inside the tin can. Consequently, the tin can collapses due to excess atmospheric pressure.

Measurement of Atmospheric Pressure

Atmospheric pressure at a place is measured by an instrument called **barometer**.

Commonly used barometers are

(i) Simple barometer
(ii) Fortin's barometer
(iii) Aneroid barometer

Mercury Barometer (Simple Barometer)

An Italian scientist **Evangelista Torricelli** (1608-1647) first devised a simple barometer using mercury as the barometric liquid.

It consists of a long glass tube closed at one end and filled with mercury which inverted into a trough of mercury. We find that mercury column in the tube has height of about 76 cm above the mercury level in the tube, at normal temperature and pressure.

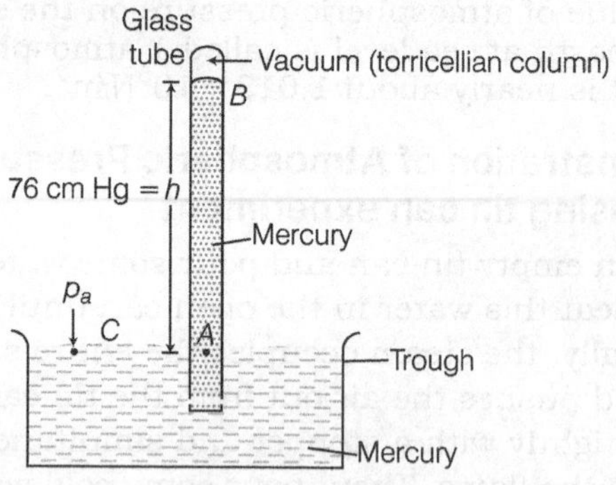

Mercury barometer

Explanation and Working of Simple Barometer

The atmospheric pressure acts at all points outside the tube on the surface of mercury in the trough. On point *A*, the pressure is due to the weight of mercury column *AB*. The mercury level in tube is stationary when pressure at point *A* is equal to pressure at point *C*.

i.e. $$p_A = p_C = \rho g h$$

where, h is the height of mercury column, it is also known as **barometric height.**

If the pressure in atmosphere increases, then the pressure at point *C* also increases and mercury flows from trough into the tube, thereby vertical height of mercury column increases to equalise the pressure at points *A* and *C*. On the other hand, the height of mercury column decreases when atmospheric pressure decreases.

Thus, the barometric height gives the measure of atmospheric pressure.

Advantages of using mercury as barometric liquid over ordinary fluids is given below

(i) Mercury neither wets nor sticks to the glass tube, hence it gives an accurate reading.

(ii) Due to its shining and opaque nature, it can be easily seen while taking reading.

(iii) As, the vapour pressure of mercury is negligible, therefore the vapours in the torricellian vacuum (a vacuum formed above the column of mercury in a mercury barometer) does not affect the barometric height.

Demerits of simple barometer are as follows

(i) There is no protection for the glass tube.

(ii) It is difficult to move barometer from one place to another place.

(iii) A scale cannot be fixed into the tube, so the chance of errors in the measurement are more.

The above demerits have been removed by following barometer

(i) **Fortin Barometer** It is a modified version of simple barometer. For accurate measurement, a vernier scale is provided which slides over the main scale by using the screw *R*. The position of mercury level in the barometer tube is noted with the help of the main scale and vernier scale, whose total reading gives the correct measurement of atmospheric pressure. It also uses mercury as barometric liquid.

(ii) **Aneroid Barometer** It is a type of a barometer which does not use any liquid. As, it is light weight, hence it can be moved from one place to another. It is also calibrated to read directly the atmospheric pressure, thereby requiring no prior adjustment like fortin barometer.

Example 7. Assuming density of air to be 1.2 kg/m^3. Find the fall in barometric height in mm of Hg at a height of 200 m above the sea level. (Density of Hg = 13.6×10^3 kg/m^3)

Sol. Given, density of air, $\rho_a = 1.2 \text{ kg/m}^3$

Height of air, $h_a = 200 \text{ m} = 200 \times 10^3 \text{ mm}$

Density of Hg, $\rho_m = 13.6 \times 10^3 \text{ kg/m}^3$

$\therefore$ Fall in atmospheric pressure, $p = \rho_a g h_a$

$$\therefore \text{Fall in height of Hg} = \frac{p}{\rho_m g} = \frac{\rho_a g h_a}{\rho_m g}$$

$$= \left(\frac{\rho_a}{\rho_m}\right) h_a$$

$$= \frac{1.2}{13.6 \times 10^3} \times 200 \times 10^3$$

$$= 17.65 \text{ mm of Hg}$$

Atmospheric Pressure: Common Manifestation and Consequences

1. Sucking Soft Drinks with a Straw

When we suck the drinks with a straw, air inside the straw goes into the lungs due to which air pressure inside the straw decreases. The atmospheric pressure at the surface of drinks becomes more than pressure inside straw. Thus, drinks move up into our mouth.

2. Filling of Syringe with a Liquid

Similarly, when the syringe plunger is pulled up, air inside the barrel moves upward. And due to excess atmospheric pressure at the surface of liquid, the liquid moves upward and fills the syringe.

Similar cases happen in

(i) action of rubber suckers and

(ii) filling of ink into a fountain pen.

Variation of Atmospheric Pressure with Altitude

As, we go to higher altitudes such as top of mountains, inside an aeroplane at higher altitude, etc., the atmospheric pressure is found to decrease.

Following are the reasons due to which atmospheric pressure decreases at higher altitudes

(i) Density of air decreases at higher altitudes.

(ii) Decrease in height of the air column above us.

Our atmosphere consists of different parallel air layers. Each layer experiences a pressure on it due to the weight (or thrust) of above air column. Therefore, as the height of air column decreases and so thrust exerted by the air column also decreases. As a result, at altitude atmospheric pressure decreases.

As we move up, the density of air layers decreases because the lower layer is more compressed as compared to upper layers. Due to this decrease in density, the atmospheric pressure also decreases.

A variation between the altitude and pressure/density is shown in the graph given below.

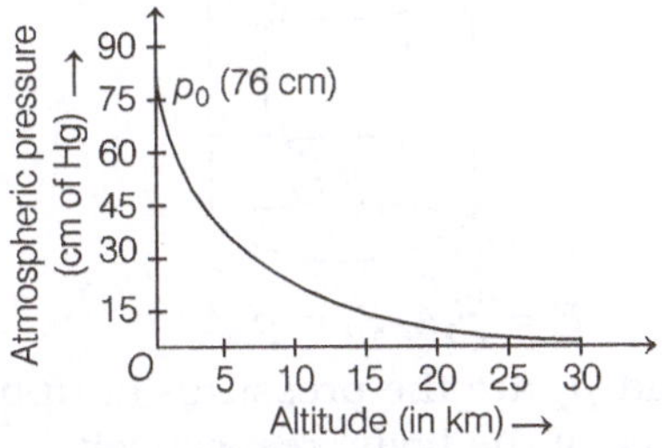

Note The decrease in density of air with altitude is not linear. It is rapid at low altitude but slow at high altitude.

Applications of Atmospheric Variations

There are following applications of atmospheric variations.

(i) **Weather Forecasting** The atmospheric pressure decreases as the temperature or the presence of moisture increases. Thus, with the help of change in atmospheric pressure, we can know about the weather in advance. Barometer is used in determining the change in weather.

(a) If the barometric height at a place suddenly falls, it indicates coming of a storm or a cyclone.

(b) If barometric height gradually falls, it indicates possibility of rain.

(c) A sudden rise in barometric height indicates an extremely dry weather.

(d) A gradual increase in barometric height indicates dry weather.

(ii) **Altimeter** Altitude can be determined based on the measurement of atmospheric pressure. The greater the altitude, lower the pressure. A device which can be used to measure the altitude is known as altimeter. It is used in most aircraft and skydivers use wrist-mounted altimeter to know the exact altitude.

Check Your LEARNING...

1. State Pascal's law.
2. What are hydraulic machines?
3. Give three applications of Pascal's law.
4. What is the value of 1 atm?
5. What is the effect of height on atmospheric pressure?

Buoyancy and Buoyant Force

The tendency of a liquid to exert an upward force on an object immersed in it, is called buoyancy. Even, gases also exhibit the property of buoyancy.

An upward force which acts on an object when it is immersed in a liquid is called **buoyant force.** It is also called **upthrust.**

Cause of Upthrust

We know that when a fluid (either liquid or gas) is at rest, it exerts pressure at all points and in all directions to the walls of container in which it is kept. It increases with the depth inside fluid.

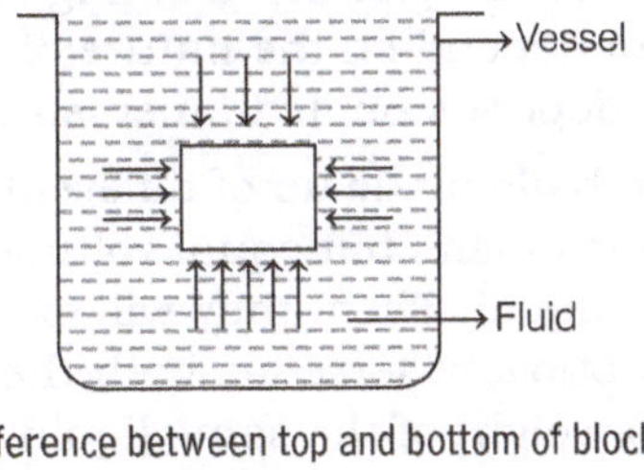

Pressure difference between top and bottom of block is upthrust.

When a body, say a block, is immersed in a liquid, the pressure exerted on the bottom surface is greater than the top surface because the bottom surface is at a greater depth.

This pressure difference causes a net upward force which is called upthrust. However, the thrust on the side walls of body get neutralised as they are equal in magnitude and opposite in direction.

Note When a thin sheet (lamina) is immersed in a liquid, it sinks because of its own weight since liquid exerts negligible upthrust on it.

Characteristic Properties of Upthrust

Following are the three characteristic properties of upthrust

(i) Larger the volume of the body submerged in the fluid, greater would be the upthrust.

(ii) The force acting vertically upward, i.e. upthrust acts at the centre of buoyancy, i.e. centre of gravity of displaced fluid.

(iii) For different fluids with same volume of body inside the fluids, more the density of fluid, greater would be upthrust on it.

Factors Affecting Buoyant Force

The magnitude of buoyant force depends on the following

1. Density of the Fluid

The liquid having higher density exerts more upward buoyant force on an object than another liquid of lower density. This is the reason, why it is easier to swim in sea-water in comparison to normal water, because sea-water has higher density. Hence, it exerts a greater buoyant force on the swimmer than the fresh water having lower density.

2. Volume of Object Immersed in the Liquid

As the volume of solid object immersed inside the liquid increases, the upward buoyant force also increases.

The magnitude of buoyant force acting on a solid object does not depend on the nature of the solid object. It only depends on its immersed volume.

e.g. When two balls made up of different metals having different weighs but equal volume are fully immersed in a liquid. Then, they will experience an equal upward buoyant force, as both the balls displace equal weight of the same liquid due to their equal volumes.

Archimedes' Principle

This principle states that when an object is fully or partially immersed in a liquid, it experiences a buoyant force or an upthrust, which is equal to the weight of liquid displaced by the object. i.e.

Buoyant force or upthrust acting on an object = Weight of liquid displaced by the submerged part of the object

Even gases like air, exert an upward force or buoyant force on the objects placed in them. It is buoyant force or upthrust due to displaced air which makes a balloon rise in air.

Applications of Archimedes' Principle

Archimedes' principle is used in

(i) designing ships and submarines,

(ii) lactometer (used to determine the purity of milk),

(iii) hydrometer (used for determining the density of liquid) and

(iv) determining the relative density of a substance.

Explanation of Archimedes' Principle

Consider a cylindrical body of height h which is immersed in a fluid. The upward force (F_2) on the bottom of the body is more than the downward force (F_1) on its top.

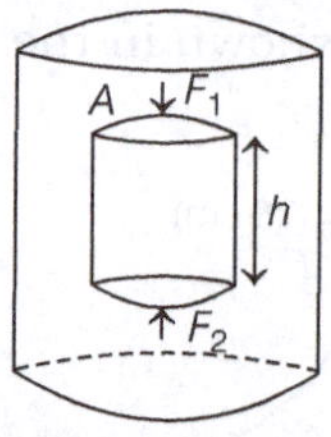

i.e. $$F_1 = p_1A,\ F_2 = p_2A$$

where, p_1 and p_2 are the pressures at upper face and lower face of the body, respectively.

The resultant upward force on the body exerted by the fluid is equal to $F = F_2 - F_1$

or $$F = (p_2 - p_1)A = h\rho gA = mg$$

$[\because p_2 - p_1 = \rho hg$ and $m = Ah\rho]$

Thus, the upward force or upthrust exerted by the fluid on the body is equal to the weight of the displaced fluid.

Example 8. If an iron object is immersed in water, it displaces 8 kg of water. How much is the buoyant force acting on this iron object in newton? (Take, $g = 10\,m/s^2$)

Sol. According to Archimedes' principle, the buoyant force acting on this iron object will be equal to the weight of the water displaced by this iron object.

We know that, weight (w) = $m \times g$

Here, mass of water, $m = 8$ kg

Acceleration due to gravity, $g = 10\,m/s^2$

On putting values, $w = 8 \times 10 = 80$ N

Since, the weight of water displaced by the iron object is 80 N, therefore, the buoyant force acting on the iron object (due to water) will also be 80 N.

Example 9. A body whose volume is 100 cm^3 weighs 1 kgf in air. Find its weight in water.

Sol. Given, volume, $V = 100\,cm^3 = 100 \times 10^{-6}\,m^3 = 10^{-4}\,m^3$

Weight in air = 1 kgf

Weight of water displaced = $mg = \rho Vg$

$$= 1000 \times 10^{-4} \times 9.8\,N$$

$$= \frac{1000 \times 10^{-4} \times 9.8}{9.8}\,kgf \quad [\because 1\,kgf = 9.8\,N]$$

$$= 10^{-1}\,kgf = 0.1\,kgf$$

$\therefore$ Weight of the body in water = 1 kgf − 0.1 kgf = 0.9 kgf

Example 10. A sealed can of mass 700 g has a volume of 500 cm^3. Will this can sink in water? (Take, density of water is 1 g/cm^3)

Sol. Mass of can, $m = 700$ g

Volume of can, $V = 500\,cm^3$

$\therefore$ Density of can, $\rho = \frac{m}{V} = \frac{700}{500} = 1.4\,g/cm^3$

Since, density of the can is greater than the density of water, so the can will sink in water.

Determination of Relative Density of a Solid Substance by Archimedes' Principle

When a solid is immersed completely in water, the ratio of weight of solid in air to the loss of weight when immersed completely in water is called its relative density.

$$\text{i.e. RD} = \frac{\text{Weight of solid in air}}{\text{Loss of weight in water (or upthrust)}} = \frac{w_1}{w_1 - w_2}$$

Using Archimedes' principle, we know that

$$\text{RD} = \frac{\text{Mass of solid}}{\text{Mass of water displaced by the solid}}$$

$$= \frac{\text{Weight of solid}}{\text{Weight of water displaced by the solid}}$$

$$= \frac{\text{Weight of solid}}{\text{Loss in weight of the solid in water (or upthrust)}}$$

$$= \frac{\text{Weight of solid}}{\text{Weight of solid in air} - \text{Weight of solid in water}}$$

i.e. $$\text{RD} = \frac{w_1}{w_1 - w_2}$$

Determination of Relative Density of a Liquid by Archimedes' Principle

When a body is taken which is heavier than both the liquid and water and also insoluble in them, then by using Archimedes' principle,

Relative density

$$= \frac{\text{Weight of the liquid displaced by the body}}{\text{Weight of the water displaced by the body}}$$

$$= \frac{\text{Weight of the body in air } (w_0) - \text{Weight of the body in liquid } (w_1)}{\text{Weight of the body in air } (w_0) - \text{Weight of the body in water } (w_2)}$$

$$= \frac{w_0 - w_1}{w_0 - w_2}$$

Law of Floatation

According to this law, an object will float in a liquid if the weight of object is equal to the weight of liquid displaced by it. Mathematically it is expressed as

Weight of object = Weight of liquid displaced by it

Floating or Sinking of Objects in Liquid

When an object is put in a liquid, then following two forces act on it

(i) Weight (w) of the object which acts in downward direction, i.e. it tends to pull down the object and

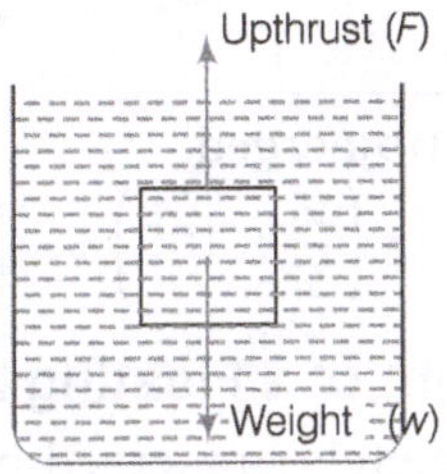

(ii) Buoyant force (upthrust, F) which acts in upward direction, i.e. it tends to push up the object.

Whether an object will float or sink in a liquid, depends on the relative magnitudes of these two forces which act on the object in opposite directions.

There are three conditions of floating and sinking of objects as follows

(i) If $w > F$, i.e. the buoyant force or upthrust exerted by the liquid is less than the weight of the object, then the object will sink in the liquid.

(ii) If $w = F$, i.e. the buoyant force is equal to the weight of the object, then the object will float just below the surface of the liquid.

(iii) If $w < F$, i.e. the buoyant force is more than the weight of the object, then the object will float partially above and partially below the surface of the liquid.

Objects having density less than that of a liquid, float on the liquid. Objects having greater density than that of liquid, sink in the liquid. The density of most of the substances decreases with the increase in temperature.

Relation Between the Density of Liquid, Density of floating Body and Submerged Volume of floating body

As we know,

Weight of the body, $w = V_1 \rho_s g$ ...(i)

where, V_1 = volume of the body,

ρ_s = density of the body

and g = acceleration due to gravity.

And the weight of the liquid displaced by the body or buoyant force, $F_B = V_2 \rho_l g$ ...(ii)

where, V_2 = volume of the liquid displaced

and ρ_l = density of the liquid.

Now, according to the principle of floatation,

$$w = F_B$$

From Eqs. (i) and (ii), we get

$$V_1 \rho_s g = V_2 \rho_l g$$

$$\Rightarrow \boxed{\frac{V_1}{V_2} = \frac{\rho_l}{\rho_s}} \Rightarrow \frac{V_2}{V_1} = \frac{\rho_s}{\rho_l}$$

$\Rightarrow$ % of volume submerged

$$= \left(\frac{V_2}{V_1} \times 100\right)\% = \left(\frac{\rho_s}{\rho_l} \times 100\right)\%$$

Apparent Weight of a Floating Body

If a body is completely immersed in a liquid, its effective weight gets decreased. The decrease in its weight is equal to the upthrust on the body.

Hence, the apparent weight of the body is given as

$$w_{app} = w_{actual} - \text{upthrust}$$

$$\Rightarrow \boxed{w_{app} = w_{actual}\left(1 - \frac{\rho_l}{\rho_s}\right)}$$

where, ρ_s = density of body

and ρ_l = density of liquid.

Special Cases

Three possibilities may now arise

(i) If $\rho_s < \rho_l$, then in this condition, the upthrust applied by the fluid will be greater than the weight of the body. This means, the released body comes up to the fluid surface till the upthrust becomes equal to the weight of the body. At this point, the body floats and partially immersed in the fluid.

(ii) If $\rho_s = \rho_l$, then the upthrust of the liquid balances the weight of the body.
Hence, the body will float which is completely submerged just below the surface of the fluid.

(iii) If $\rho_s > \rho_l$, then the upthrust of the liquid is less than the weight of the liquid, i.e. it is not sufficient to balance the weight of the body, so the body sinks.

Applications of the Principle of Floatation

Some applications of the priniciple of floatation are as given below

1. Submarines

A submarine is a fish shaped water tight boat that sinks by taking water into its ballast tanks.

Each submarine consists of a ballast tanks. If the submarine has to submerge, these tanks are filled with water, which makes the density of submarine greater and hence it sinks. If the submarine has to be surfaced, ballast tanks are blown with compressed air and it expel the water out. Thus, the density of submarine is less than water and it floats on the surface.

2. Ships

Ships are made of materials denser than water but it still floats in water due to the fact that the shape of a ship or boat is made such that it displaces a weight of water equal to its own weight. The volume of ship is much larger as compared to the volume of the material with which it is made.

A ship has to travel in different areas in seas which have different densities. As a consequence, it sinks more in less density water than the water with more density. Therefore, they are marked with white lines on its side, known as **Plimsoll line**. This line indicates the safe limit for loading the ship in water. A ship is not allowed to be loaded further when its Plimsoll line (load line) is crossed.

3. Balloons

Balloon filled with hydrogen rises up in the air. It is due to the fact that the hydrogen filled balloon weight is less than the weight of air displaced by the balloon. Thus, the upthrust force is greater than its weight. These balloons do not rise up infinitely as because the density of air decreases as we go up in the air. When the weight of air displaced by balloon becomes equal to the weight of the balloon, then it does not experience any upward force and it becomes stationary.

4. Icebergs

The density of ice ($0.917\ g\ cm^{-3}$) is less than the density of sea water ($1.03\ g\ cm^{-3}$). Thus, the upthrust of sea water is greater. A big iceberg floats with a large volume inside the water, so that its weight is compensated by the buoyant force acting on it. It has been found that only about 10% of the volume of icebergs is above the sea and 90% volume is present inside the water.

Example 11. An iceberg floats in fresh water with a part of it outside the water surface. Calculate the fraction of volume of iceberg which is below the water surface. (Take, density of ice = $917\ kg\ m^{-3}$ and density of fresh water = $1000\ kg\ m^{-3}$)

Sol. Let V_1 be the total volume of iceberg and V_2 be the volume below water, then for the equilibrium of iceberg,

Weight of iceberg = Weight of water displaced by immersed part of iceberg

or $V_1 \times 917 \times g = V_2 \times 1000 \times g$

$\therefore$ Fraction of volume of iceberg below water =

$$\frac{V_2}{V_1} = \frac{917}{1000} = 0.917$$

Thus, 0.917 part of volume of iceberg will be below water.

Check Your LEARNING...

1 A body whose volume is 500 cm^3, weighs 2 kgf in air. Calculate its weight in water. *Ans.* 1.95 kgf

2 How does boat float in water?

3 Which device is used to determine the density of liquid?

4 How does the apparent weight of the floating body changes in a liquid?

5 How much will a body of 70 N weigh in water, if it displaces 200 mL of water? *Ans.* 68.04 N

QUiCK Revision

- **Thrust** is the force or push acting on an object perpendicular to its surface. Its SI unit is newton (N).
- The handles of bags, suitcase, etc., are made broad, so that the small pressure is exerted by the hand to lift them.
- The density of a substance is defined as mass per unit volume.

$$\text{Density } (\rho) = \frac{\text{Mass of the substance } (m)}{\text{Volume of the substance } (V)}$$

- The **relative density** of a substance is the ratio of its density to the density of water at 4°C.
- **Pascal's law** states that whenever external pressure is applied on any part of a fluid contained in a vessel, it is transmitted undiminished and equally in all directions.
- Hydraulic machines work on the principle of Pascal's law.
- The pressure exerted by the atmosphere is called atmospheric pressure.

$$1 \text{ atm} = 1.013 \times 10^5\ N/m^2$$

- Altimeter is used in aircraft and by skydivers to know the exact altitude.
- **Buoyant force** is an upward force which acts on an object when it is immersed in a liquid. It is also called **upthrust**.
- According to the **Archimedes' principle** when an object is fully or partially immersed in liquid, it experiences a buoyant force or upthrust which is equal to the weight of displaced liquid by the object.
- Archimedes' principle is used in ship, submarines, lactometer and hydrometer.
- According to **law of floatation**, an object will float in a liquid, if the weight of an object is equal to the weight of liquid displaced by it.

Chapter Practice

1 Mark Questions

1. A girl stands on a box having 60 cm length, 40 cm breadth and 20 cm height in three ways. In which of the following cases, pressure exerted by the girl will be
(a) maximum when length and breadth form the base
(b) maximum when breadth and height form the base
(c) maximum when height and length form the base
(d) the same in all the above three cases

Sol. (*b*) Now, according to question, when base is formed by breadth and height, area will be minimum and so pressure will be maximum.

2. The pressure inside a liquid of density ρ at a depth h below its surface, is
(a) $\frac{h}{\rho g}$ (b) $h\rho g$ (c) $\frac{\rho}{hg}$ (d) $\frac{hg}{\rho}$

Sol. (*b*) The pressure exerted by a liquid of density ρ at depth h is $p = \rho hg$
where, g is the acceleration due to gravity.

3. At which point of vessel, pressure is minimum?

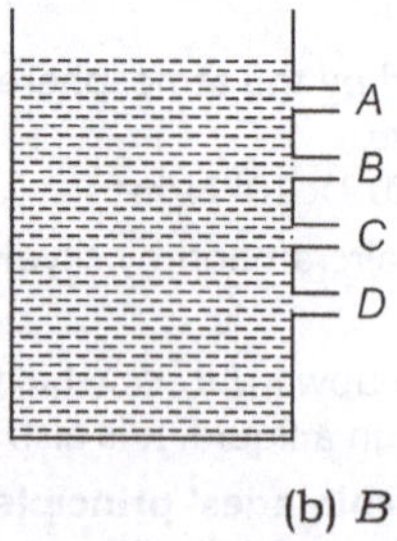

(a) A (b) B
(c) C (d) D

Sol. (*a*) As we know, pressure exerted by liquid is directly proportional to the height of the vertical column. Therefore, pressure at point A is minimum and at point D, pressure is maximum.

4. Why the dam of water reservoir is thick at the bottom?
(a) Quantity of water increases with depth
(b) Density of water increases with depth
(c) Pressure of water increases with depth
(d) Temperature of water increases with depth

Sol. (*c*) The dam of water is thick at the bottom because due to maximum depth, the pressure of water is maximum at bottom and to bear this maximum pressure dam should be thick at the bottom.

5. The diagram as shown in figure is a device which make use of the principle of transmission of pressure.

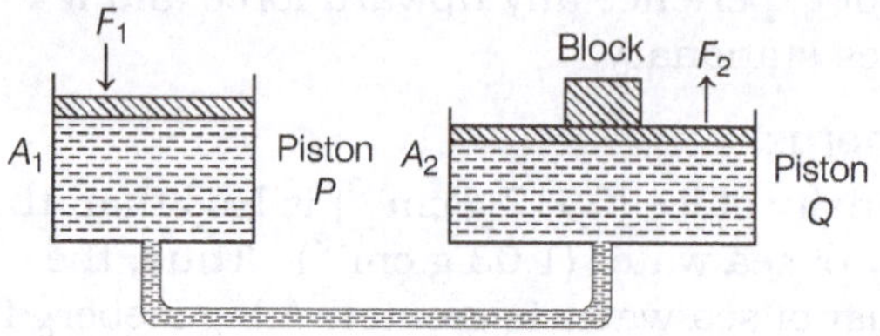

Which of the following is correct about the forces F_1 and F_2?
(a) $F_1 = F_2$ (b) $F_1 > F_2$
(c) $F_1 < F_2$ (d) $F_1 F_2 = 1$

Sol. (*c*) As shown in figure, $A_2 > A_1$
$\Rightarrow$ $F_2 > F_1$ ($\because$ pressure is constant)

6. What is the name of the device which transmits pressure in order to do work?
(a) Hydrostatic paradox
(b) Altimeter
(c) Pascal vessel
(d) Hydraulic machine

Sol. (*d*) Hydraulic machine is used to transmit pressure in order to do work.

7. Suppose the narrow piston's area is 5 cm^2 and wide piston's area is 50 cm^2, if the weight of block is 1800 N. The magnitude of force to lift the block in hydraulic machine would be
(a) 1800 N (b) 18000 N
(c) 18 N (d) 180 N

Sol. (*d*) We know that, $\frac{F_2}{F_1} = \frac{A_2}{A_1}$

Here, $F_2 = 1800$ N, $A_2 = 50$ cm^2 and $A_1 = 5$ cm^2

$$\therefore \quad F_1 = F_2\left(\frac{A_1}{A_2}\right) = 1800 \times \frac{5}{50}$$
$$F_1 = 180 \text{ N}$$

Hence, the force required to lift the block is 180 N.

8. Which of the following statement is incorrect about the transmission of pressure in liquid?
(a) Hydraulic machine acts as a force multiplier.
(b) The pressure applied on smaller piston is smaller than the pressure applied on larger piston.
(c) The transmission of pressure in liquid is based on the Pascal's law.
(d) The effort made by hydraulic machine is always less than the load.

Sol. (*b*) All the statements are correct except the statement in option (b) which can be corrected as the pressure applied on smaller piston is equally transmitted to the larger piston.

9. The unit of atmospheric pressure is
(a) torr (b) pascal
(c) bar (d) All of these

Sol. (*d*) The atmospheric pressure can be measured in different units other than N/m^2, which are pascal (Pa), torr and bar.

10. The device used to measure atmospheric pressure is
(a) Mercury barometer
(b) Aneroid barometer
(c) Fortin barometer
(d) All of the above

Sol. (*d*) The device used to measure atmospheric pressure is called barometer. The commonly used barometers are simple (mercury barometer), Aneroid barometer and Fortin barometer.

11. Consider the following two statements.
I. The atmospheric pressure increases with the increase in altitude.
II. The decrease in density of air causes a non-linear decrease in atmospheric pressure.
Choose the correct option.
(a) I is correct
(b) II is correct
(c) Both I and II are correct
(d) Neither I nor II is correct

Sol. (*b*) Statement II is correct.
While Statement I can be corrected as the atmospheric pressure decreases with the increase in altitude due to decrease in the height of air column and decrease in density of air.

12. When a ball is fully immersed in a liquid, its weight get decreased. It happens due to
(a) gravitational force (b) magnetic force
(c) buoyant force (d) friction force

Sol. (*c*) When a ball is fully immersed in a liquid, its weight decreases due to buoyant force.

13 An object is put one by one in three liquids having different densities. The object floats with $\frac{1}{9}$, $\frac{2}{11}$ and $\frac{3}{7}$ parts of their volumes outside the liquid surface in liquids of densities d_1, d_2 and d_3, respectively. Which of the following statement is correct?
(a) $d_1 > d_2 > d_3$ (b) $d_1 > d_2 < d_3$
(c) $d_1 < d_2 > d_3$ (d) $d_1 < d_2 < d_3$

Sol. (*d*) In a liquid of higher density, more part of the object remains outside the liquid. Since, the order of part of their volume outside the liquid ∝ densities of liquid

$$\because \quad \frac{1}{9} < \frac{2}{11} < \frac{3}{7}$$

Thus, the order of densities in increasing order is

$$d_1 < d_2 < d_3$$

14. A large ship can float, but a steel needle sinks because of
(a) mass (b) volume
(c) density (d) None of these

Sol. (*d*) This concept is explained by Archimedes' principle which states that when a body is fully or partly submerged in a fluid, a buoyant force from the surrounding fluid, acts on the body.

15. Which of the following is correct about the fact that bodies like stones and metals sink in water?
(a) They have higher density compared to water.
(b) They have lesser density compared to water.
(c) They have the same density as that of water.
(d) None of the above

Sol. (*a*) Bodies like stones and metals sink in water because they have higher density as compared to water.

16. A body of weight w is floating in a liquid. Its apparent weight will be
(a) equal to w (b) less than w
(c) zero (d) greater than w

Sol. (*c*) When a body is floating in a liquid, then its apparent weight becomes zero.

2 Marks Questions

17. Why is it difficult to hold a school bag having a strap made of thin and strong string?

Sol. It is difficult to hold a school bag having a strap made of a thin and strong string because the area under the strap is small. Hence, large pressure is exerted by the strap on the fingers or shoulders. Due to the large pressure, the strap tends to cut the skin and hence pain is caused.

18. What do you mean by the term fluid pressure?

Sol. The pressure exerted by fluids (both liquids and gases) due to its weight in all the directions is called fluid pressure. Both solid and fluid pressure are different.

19. Why do solids exert pressure only in downward direction but fluids in all directions?

Sol. As we know, solids exert thrust or force only due to its weight by Earth, but fluid exerts force due to its random motion in all directions. So, fluid exerts pressure in all directions but solid does not.

20. What are the laws of liquid pressure?

Sol. The laws of liquid pressure are as follows
(i) In a liquid at rest, pressure is same at all points on a horizontal plane.
(ii) Pressure inside liquid is directly proportional to density of liquid. [1+1]

21. What is gauge and absolute pressure?

Sol. The excess pressure above the atmospheric pressure is usually called gauge pressure and the total pressure is called absolute pressure.

22. Why does the pressure exerted by water on a diver at a depth inside the sea is different than inside the river?

Sol. At a certain depth inside the sea, the pressure acting on the body of divers will be more than inside the river at same depth as the density of seawater is higher than river water.

23. The blood pressure in human is greater at the feet than at the brain. Give reason.

Sol. As we know, pressure p is directly proportional to the depth h. Since, the height of blood column in the human body is more at feet than at brain. So, the blood exerts more pressure at the feet than at the brain.

24. Why multi-storeyed building has water tanks placed at a greater height?

Sol. This is because, the greater the height of the water tanks, more will be the pressure of the water in taps of the houses. Therefore, for good supply of water, the tanks are placed at good height, from where the supply of water has to be made.

25. What is the principle involved in the hydraulic lift?

Sol. The principle involved in the hydraulic lift is the Pascal's law which states that the pressure applied in any part of liquid column is transmitted undiminished and equally in all directions.

26. What do you mean by atmospheric pressure?

Sol. The gaseous envelope surrounding the Earth is called Earth's atmosphere. The pressure exerted by the atmosphere is called atmospheric pressure. The value of atmospheric pressure on the surface of the Earth at sea level is called 1 atmosphere (1 atm), it is equal to 1.013×10^5 N/m^2.

27. Give two consequences of atmospheric pressure.

Sol. The two consequences of atmospheric pressure are as follows

(i) Sucking a drink with a straw

(ii) Filling of syringe with a liquid [1 + 1]

28. Why are straws used to drink soft drinks?

Sol. When we suck the drinks with a straw, air inside the straw goes into the lungs due to which air pressure inside the straw decreases. The atmospheric pressure at the surface of drinks become more than the pressure inside of straw. Thus, drinks move up into our mouth.

29. Why are the cabins of aeroplanes flying at high altitudes pressurised?

Sol. When an aeroplane takes OFF, it suddenly gains height, due to which the pressure outside it decreases rapidly as compared to the pressure of the oxygen dissolved in the blood of human bodies. Due to this pressure difference, the fine capillaries of nose may burst and bleeding may start. Therefore, in order to protect from these bursting, the pressure needs to be maintained at ground level. Hence, the cabins of the aeroplanes are pressurised.

30. Why does the nose start bleeding at higher altitudes?

Sol. At higher altitudes, atmospheric pressure decreases. Hence, the pressure difference between atmospheric pressure and the pressure of oxygen in the blood increases. Due to this pressure difference, nose bleeding starts at higher altitudes.

31. Explain why liquid does not come out from dropper till its bulb is not pressed?

Sol. As, the air pressure on outlet and the pressure in bulb are equal. So, liquid does not come out but when bulb is pressed its pressure increases and liquid starts coming out of the dropper.

32. Name the given instrument and why it is used?

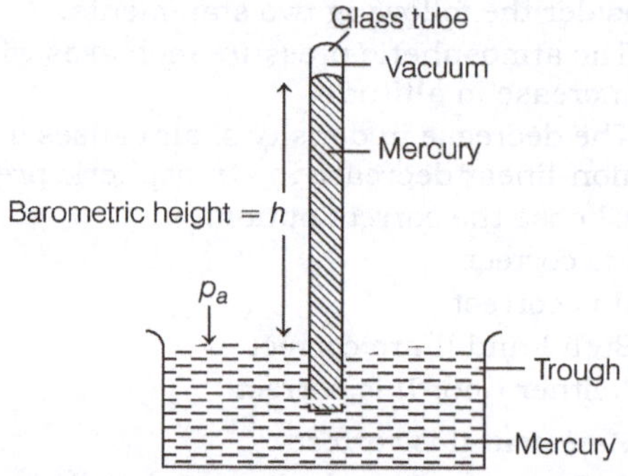

Sol. The given instrument is a simple barometer or mercury barometer. It is used to measure the atmospheric pressure with the help of vertical height of mercury column above the mercury level in the trough to the level in tube.

33. How fortin barometer removed the demerits of a simple barometer?

Sol. Fortin barometer is a modified version of simple barometer. For accurate measurement, a vernier scale is provided which slides over the main scale by using a screw. The position of mercury level in barometer tube is noted with the help of the main scale and vernier scale, whose total reading gives the correct measurement of atmospheric pressure. It also uses mercury as barometric liquid.

34. What is an altimeter? State its principle.

Sol. An altimeter is a device used in an aircraft to measure its altitude.

The principle of altimeter is that, with an increase in the height above the sea level, the atmospheric pressure decreases. Thus, a barometer that measures the atmospheric pressure can be utilised in order to measure the altitude of a place above the sea level.

35. How the scale of altimeter is calibrated?

Sol. The scale of the altimeter is calibrated in terms of height of ascent with height increasing towards left because the atmospheric pressure decreases with increase of height above the sea level.

36. Why does a block of plastic released under water, come upto the surface of water?

Sol. The upthrust or buoyant force acting on the block of plastic by the water is greater than the weight of the plastic block. So, plastic block comes upto the surface of water.

37. A small block is held under water in a tall jar as shown in figure.

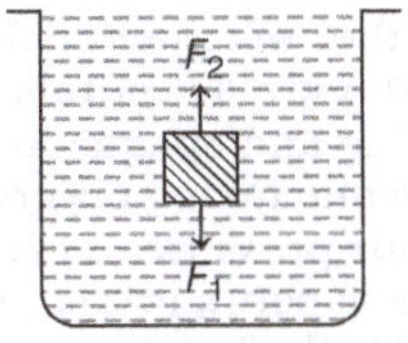

The two forces F_1 and F_2 are acting on the block. Name these forces.

Sol. The force F_1 represents the weight of the block in downward direction and force F_2 represents the upthrust on the block due to water.

38. Give two characteristic properties of upthrust.

Sol. The upthrust has the following characteristic properties.

(i) Larger the volume of body submerged in a fluid, then greater is the upthrust.

(ii) For same volume inside the fluid, more the density of fluid, greater is the upthrust.

39. Define relative density. Give its mathematical form.

Sol. The relative density of a substance is the ratio of its density to that of water at 4°C.

Relative density of a substance

$$= \frac{\text{Density of the substance}}{\text{Density of water at } 4^\circ \text{C}}$$ [1]

In other words,

Relative density of a substance

$$= \frac{\text{Mass of the substance}}{\text{Volume of the substance}} \times \frac{\text{Volume of water}}{\text{Mass of water}}$$ [1]

$$\left[\because \text{Density} = \frac{\text{Mass}}{\text{Volume}}\right]$$

40. Give the relation among volume of submerged part of a floating body, the densities of liquid and the body. Explain the meaning of symbols used.

Sol. The relation between volume of submerged part of a floating body, the densities of liquid and the body is given as

$$\frac{V'}{V} = \frac{\rho_s}{\rho_l}$$

where, V' = volume of immersed part of body,

V = total volume of body,

ρ_s = density of body

and ρ_l = density of liquid.

41. Give reason why there is no change in level of water on melting a floating piece of ice.

Sol. When a floating piece of ice melts into water, it contracts by the volume equal to the volume of ice piece above the water surface while floating on it. Hence, the level of water does not change when the ice floating on it melts.

42. Why an unloaded ship is filled with sand at its bottom?

Sol. An unloaded ship floats with its very small volume inside water. As a result, its equilibrium is unstable. So, it may get blown over on its side by strong winds. Therefore, sand or stones are loaded at its bottom to make the equilibrium of ship stable.

3 Marks Questions

43. (i) State the SI units of thrust and pressure.

(ii) In which situation we exert more pressure on ground, when we stand on one foot or on the both feet? Justify your answer.

Sol. (i) The SI unit of thrust is newton (N). The SI unit of pressure is N/m^2 or pascal (Pa). [1]

(ii) We exert more pressure on ground when we stand on one foot than the both feet, as the area of one foot is half than that of two feet and $p \propto \frac{1}{A}$. [2]

44. How volume of the object immersed affects the buoyant force?

Sol. As, the volume of solid object immersed inside the liquid increases, the upward buoyant force also increases. The magnitude of buoyant force acting on a solid object does not depend on the nature of the solid object. It only depends on its volume.

45. Why does a nail sink in water while a piece of cork floats on it?

Sol. The weight of water displaced by a nail is less than its own weight, so it sinks in water. Whereas, a piece of cork displaces water more than its own weight, so it floats on water. Also, the density of cork is less than the density of iron.

46. Give the use of

(i) Lactometer (ii) Hydrometer.

(iii) Altimeter

Sol. (i) **Lactometer** It is used for determining the purity of milk. [1]

(ii) **Hydrometer** It is used for determining the density of liquids. [1]

(ii) **Altimeter** It is used to measure the altitude of an aircraft. [1]

47. There are four balls *A*, *B*, *C* and *D* which displace 10 mL, 24 mL, 15 mL and 12 mL of a liquid respectively, when immersed completely. Which ball will undergo the maximum apparent loss in weight?

Sol. As the volume of solid object immersed in a liquid, an buoyant force acts on the object in upward direction. The magnitude of the force depends on the volume displaced by the object. As the ball *B* displaces maximum volume of 24 mL, therefore ball *B* will undergo maximum apparent loss in weight.

48. When you immerse an empty plastic bottle in a bucket of water, it comes above the surface of it. Why does this happen? How can it remains immersed in water and why?

Sol. When we immerse an empty plastic bottle in a bucket of water, the upward force (upthrust or buoyant force) exerted by water on the bottle is greater than its own weight. Therefore, it comes above the surface of it. To keep the bottle completely immersed, an external force which is equal to the difference between the upward force and the weight of the bottle must be applied on the bottle in downward direction. This is because the upthrust on the bottle due to water must be balanced.

49. If the density of a body is 800 kg/m^3. Will it sink or float when dipped in a bucket of water? (Take, density of water = 1000 kg/m^3)

Sol. Since, its density is less than that of water. According to the Archimedes' principle, if the density of body is less than the density of liquid, then the upthrust applied by the fluid will be greater than the weight of the body. Hence, it will float.

50. State the law of floatation.

Sol. Refer to text on page 93

51. Explain the following
(i) A dam has broader walls at the bottom than at the top.
(ii) A sharp tip is provided at the end of a pin.
(iii) It is easier to cut with a sharp knife than with a blunt one.

Sol. (i) Since, water pressure increases with depth. Therefore, the walls of a dam is made thicker at the bottom because a thicker wall can withstand a greater pressure exerted by the water at greater depth. [1]

(ii) Pins, needles and nails are provided with a sharp tip, so that the area of contact between the pin and the given surface would be least. Thereby, on applying minimal effort, it would be able to exert high pressure on the surface and hence will easily penetrate through it. [1]

(iii) Because sharp knife has lesser area of cross-section. Hence, with lesser force more pressure is exerted and thus it becomes easy to cut through sharp knife. [1]

52. State Pascal's law and give its two applications.

Sol. Refer to theory (Page 87).

4 Marks Questions

53. Write a short note on hydraulic brakes.

Sol. Refer to theory (Page 88).

54. Draw a well labelled diagram of hydraulic press and write its various uses.

Sol. Refer to theory (Page 89).

55. Why mercury is used as a barometric liquid?

Sol. Advantages of using mercury as barometric liquid are as follows
(i) Mercury neither wets nor sticks to the glass tube, due to which it gives accurate reading.
(ii) As it is shining and opaque in nature, it can be easily seen while taking observations.
(iii) As, the vapour pressure of mercury is negligible, therefore the vapours in the torricellian vacuum does not affect the barometric height.
(iv) Its density is very high having low vapour pressure. Thus it stays in the column without affecting the barometric height.

56. Two holes are made in a sealed oil can. Explain why?

Sol. Following are the reasons
(i) Liquid flows from higher pressure to lower pressure.
(ii) When sealed can is tilted after making hole, some oil comes out and pressure inside can decreases. So, no further oil comes out.
(iii) The second hole facilitates the air flow.
(iv) When another hole is made, then air enters through upper hole and oil comes out from lower hole, due to the pressure difference.

57. What is upthrust? Write its SI unit. Name the factors on which upthrust depends.

Sol. An upward force which acts on an object when it is immersed in a liquid is called buoyant force or upthrust. Its SI unit is newton (N). [2]
Upthrust depends upon the
(i) volume of the body submerged in the fluid.
(ii) density of the liquid. [2]

58. Explain the determination of relative density of a solid and liquids using Archimedes' principle (denser/lighter than water).

Sol. Refer to theory (Page 93).

59. What do you mean by apparent weight of floating body? State the possibilities when a body can sink or float in liquid.

Sol. Refer to theory (Page 94).

60. Two different bodies are completely immersed in water and undergo the same loss in weight. Is it necessary that their weights in air should also be the same? Justify your answer.

Sol. No, this is because the two bodies have undergone the same loss in weight on completely immersing in water due to their equal volumes, not due to their equal weights. So, they may have different weights in air.

61. Find experimentally the relation between pressure and depth of a liquid from the surface.

Sol. Take a cylindrical thin vessel, make some holes at different heights in the vessel. Mark the holes *P*, *Q*, *R*, *S*. Fill up the vessel with a liquid (say water). [1]

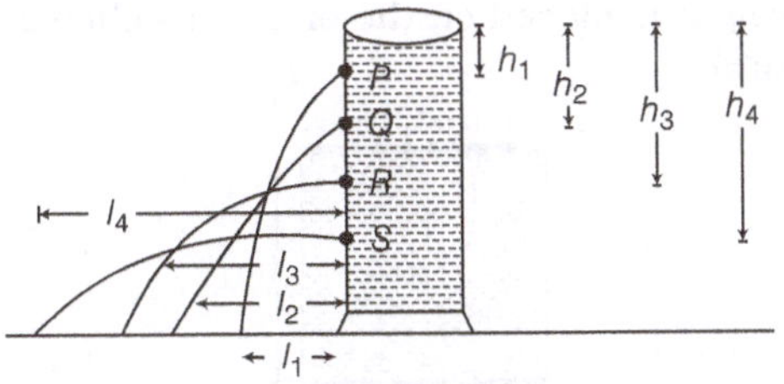

[1]

It is observed that the horizontal range of water coming out is minimum for water coming out of hole *P*. Similarly, the horizontal range of water coming out from hole *S* is maximum as its depth is maximum from surface. This gives the relation that, pressure is directly proportional to the depth of liquid from surface. [2]

62. Draw a diagram illustrating the principle of hydraulic lift and briefly explain its action.

Sol. Refer to theory (Page 87 and 88).

63. Write a note on the 'variation of atmospheric pressure with altitude'.

Sol. Refer to theory (Page 91).

64. How does the weather forecasting takes place? What is the relation between atmospheric pressure and weather forecasting?

Sol. Refer to theory (Page 91).

65. Give four applications of Archimedes' principle.

Sol. Refer to theory (Page 92).

66. How does the submarine works? Explain its working.

Sol. Refer to theory (Page 94).

Numerical Type Questions

67. Express standard atmospheric pressure in (i) Nm^{-2} (ii) bars (iii) torr

Sol. As we know,

(i) Standard atmospheric pressure = 76 cm of Hg

Also, pressure $(p) = \rho hg$

where, $h = 76$ cm $= 0.76$ m

$\rho(Hg) = 13.6 \times 10^3 kgm^{-3}$, $g = 9.8\ ms^{-2}$

$\Rightarrow$ 1 atm $= 0.76 \times 13.6 \times 10^3 \times 9.8$

$= 1.013 \times 10^5\ Nm^{-2}$ [1]

(ii) $1\ Nm^{-2} = 10^{-5}$ bar

$\Rightarrow$ 1 atm = 1.013 bar = 1013 millibar [1]

(iii) 1 torr = 1 mm of Hg

$\Rightarrow$ 1 atm = 760 mm of Hg = 760 torr [1]

68. Find the force acting on an area of $0.5\ m^2$ which will produce a pressure of 50 Pa.

Sol. Here, area, $A = 0.5\ m^2$ and pressure, $p = 50$ Pa

We know that, $p = \frac{F}{A}$

Force, $F = p \times A$

$= 50 \times 0.5 = 25$ N [2]

69. A cube each of side 10 cm is placed inside a liquid. Calculate the thrust exerted by the liquid on any face, if the pressure at the face of cube is 5 Pa.

Sol. Given, $p = 5$ Pa

Area of the cube, $A = 10\ cm \times 10\ cm$

$= 100\ cm^2 = 100 \times 10^{-4}\ m^2$

$\therefore$ Thrust exerted by the liquid on the face of the cube,

$F = p \times A$

$= 5 \times 100 \times 10^{-4}$

$= 5 \times 10^{-2}$ N [2]

70. The two thigh bones (femurs), each of cross-sectional area $10\ cm^2$ support the upper part of a human body of mass 40 kg. Estimate the average pressure sustained by the femurs.

Sol. Given, $A = 20 \times 10^{-4}\ m^2$ ($\because$ 2 thigh bones)

$F = 40$ kg - wt $= 400$ N ($\therefore g = 10\ m/s^2$)

$p_{av} = \frac{F}{A} = \frac{400}{20 \times 10^{-4}}$

$= 2 \times 10^5\ N/m^2$ [2]

71. If two forces in the ratio 5 : 9 act on two areas in the ratio 10 : 3, then find the ratio of pressure exerted.

Sol. Ratio of areas = 10 : 3, i.e. $A_1/A_2 = 10/3$

Ratio of forces = 5 : 9, i.e. $F_1/F_2 = 5/9$

Ratio of pressures $= \frac{p_1}{p_2} = \frac{F_1}{A_1} \times \frac{A_2}{F_2}$ [1]

$= \frac{F_1}{F_2} \times \frac{A_2}{A_1} = \frac{5}{9} \times \frac{3}{10} = \frac{1}{6}$

Therefore, the ratio of pressures is 1 : 6. [1]

72. Which of the two will exert more pressure : 80 kg mass on $10\ m^2$ or 40 kg mass on $4\ m^2$?

Sol. Pressure exerted by 80 kg mass on $10\ m^2$

$= \frac{80 \times 9.8}{10} = 78.4\ Nm^{-2}$ $\left(\text{As, } p = \frac{F}{A} = \frac{mg}{A}\right)$

Pressure exerted by 40 kg mass on $4\ m^2$

$= \frac{40 \times 9.8}{4} = 98\ Nm^{-2}$

So, the second body (40 kg) will exert more pressure. [2]

73. A 50 kg girl wearing high heels shoes balances on a single heel. The heel is circular with a diameter 1.0 cm. What is the pressure exerted on the horizontal floor?

Sol. Given, mass of girl, $m = 50$ kg

Diameter of circular heel $(2r) = 1.0$ cm

$\therefore$ Radius, $r = 0.5$ cm $= 5\times10^{-3}$ m

Area of circular heel, $A = \pi r^2$

$= 3.14\times(5\times10^{-3})^2 \text{m}^2 = 78.50\times10^{-6} \text{m}^2$ [1]

$\therefore$ Pressure exerted on the horizontal floor,

$$p = \frac{F}{A} = \frac{mg}{A} = \frac{50\times9.8}{78.50\times10^{-6}}$$

$= 6.24\times10^6$ Pa [1]

74. A boy weighing 40 kgf is wearing shoes with heel of area of cross-section 10 cm^2, while a girl weighing 25 kgf is wearing sandals with heel of area of cross-section 0.5 cm^2. Compare the pressure exerted on ground by their heels when they stand on heel of one foot.

Sol. Given, $F_1 = 40$ kgf, $A_1 = 10\text{ cm}^2 = 10\times10^{-4}\text{ m}^2$

$\therefore$ Pressure exerted by the boy, $p_1 = \frac{F_1}{A_1}$

$$= \frac{40}{10\times10^{-4}} = 4\times10^4 \text{ kgf m}^{-2} \quad ...(i)$$ [1]

Also, $F_2 = 25$ kgf, $A_2 = 0.5\text{ cm}^2 = 0.5\times10^{-4}\text{ m}^2$

$\therefore$ Pressure exerted by the girl, $p_2 = \frac{F_2}{A_2}$

$$= \frac{25}{0.5\times10^{-4}} = 50\times10^4 \text{ kgf m}^{-2} \quad ...(ii)$$ [1]

Hence, from Eqs. (i) and (ii), we get

$$\frac{p_2}{p_1} = \frac{50\times10^4}{4\times10^4} = \frac{25}{2} = 25:2$$ [1]

75. The relative density of silver is 10.8. The density of water is 10^3 kg/m^3. What is the density of silver in SI unit?

Sol. Relative density of silver $= 10.8$

$$\text{Relative density of silver} = \frac{\text{Density of silver}}{\text{Density of water}}$$ [1]

$$10.8 = \frac{d_s}{10^3 \text{ kg/m}^3}$$

$d_s = 10.8\times10^3$ kg/m^3 [1]

76. The density of the atmosphere at sea level is 1.29 kg/m^3. Assume that it does not change with altitude, then how high would the atmosphere extend?

Sol. Given, $\rho = 129$ kg/m^3, $g = 9.8$ m/s^2, $h = ?$

As, $p = \rho g h$

$1.01\times10^5 = 1.29\times9.8\times h$

$$h = \frac{1.01\times10^5}{1.29\times9.8} = 7989.24 \text{ m} \approx 8 \text{ km} = 8 \text{ km}$$ [2]

77. What is the pressure on a swimmer 10 m below the surface of a lake?

Sol. Given, $h = 10$ m, $\rho = 1000$ kg/m^3 and $g = 10$ m/s^2

We know that,

$p = p_a + \rho g h = 1.01\times10^5 + 1000\times10\times10$

$p = 2.01\times10^5$ Pa

$\Rightarrow p \approx 2$ atm [2]

78. A container of area 0.02 m^2 is filled with water. Find the pressure at the bottom of the container, if a weight is placed on the piston (as shown in the figure).

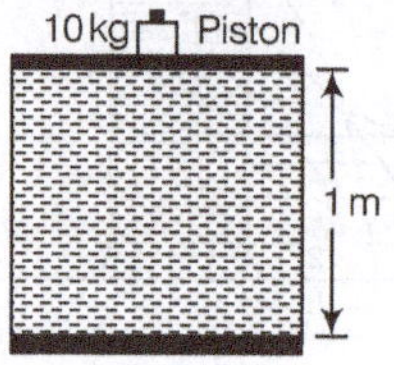

Sol. The pressure at the bottom is given by

$$P = \frac{mg}{A} + \rho g h = \frac{10\times9.8}{0.02} + 10^3\times9.8\times1 = 14.7 \text{ kPa}$$ [2]

79. During blood transfusion, the needle is inserted in a vein where the gauge pressure is 2000 Pa. At what height must the blood container be placed, so that blood may just enter the vein? (Use the density of whole blood from table)

Sol. Given, gauge pressure, $p = 2000$ Pa

Density of whole blood, $\rho = 1.06\times10^3$ kg/m^3

$g = 9.8$ m/s^2 [1]

Let the container be placed at height h metre.

Pressure exerted by the blood, $p = h\rho g$ [1]

or $$h = \frac{p}{\rho g} = \frac{2000}{1.06\times10^3\times9.8}$$

$= 0.193$ m ≈ 0.20 m

80. A hydraulic automobile lift is designed to lift cars with a maximum mass of 3000 kg. The area of cross-section of the piston carrying the load is 425 cm^2. What will be maximum pressure would the smaller piston have to bear?

Sol. Given, maximum mass that can be lifted, $m = 3000$ kg

Area of cross-section, $A = 425\text{ cm}^2 = 4.25\times10^{-2}\text{ m}^2$

$\therefore$ Maximum pressure on the bigger piston,

$$p = \frac{F}{A} = \frac{mg}{A}$$

$$= \frac{3000\times9.8}{4.25\times10^{-2}} = 6.92\times10^5 \text{ Pa}$$ [1]

According to Pascal's law, the pressure applied on an enclosed liquid is transmitted equally in all directions.

$\therefore$ Maximum pressure on smaller piston = Maximum pressure on bigger piston

$p' = p = 6.92\times10^5$ Pa [1]

81. A solid floats in water with (2/3)rd of its volume below the surface of water. Calculate the density of solid.

Sol. Let the density and volume of solid be ρ and V, respectively.

$\therefore$ Weight of solid $= V\rho g$

Volume of solid in water $= \frac{2}{3}V$

$= $ Volume of water displaced

Weight of the water displaced $= V'\rho' g = \frac{2}{3}V \times 10^3 \times g$

$\because$ Weight of body = Weight of water displaced

or $V\rho g = \frac{2}{3}V \times 10^3 g$

$\Rightarrow \rho = \frac{2}{3} \times 10^{-3} = 666.67 \text{ kg m}^{-3}$ **[3]**

82. The volume of 50 g of a substance is 20 cm^3. If the density of water is 1 g cm^{-3}, will the substance float or sink?

Sol. Given, mass of substance, $m = 50$ g

Volume of substance, $V = 20 \text{ cm}^3$

$\therefore$ Density of substance,

$$\rho = \frac{\text{Mass}}{\text{Volume}} = \frac{50}{20} = 2.5 \text{ g cm}^3$$

i.e. the density of the substance is greater than the density of water, so it will sink in the water. **[2]**

83. (i) A cube of side 5 cm is immersed in water and then in saturated salt solution. In which case, will it experience a greater buoyant force ? If each side of the cube is reduced to 4 cm and then immersed in water, what will be the effect on the buoyant force experienced by the cube as compared to the first case for water ? Give reason for each case.

(ii) A ball weighing 4 kg and of density 4000 kg/m^3 is completely immersed in water of density 10^3 kg/m^3. Find the force of buoyancy on it. (Take, $g = 10$ ms^{-2})

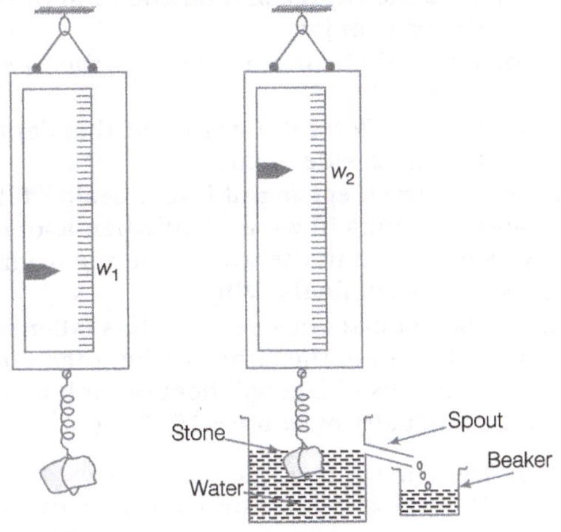

Sol. (i) Buoyant force, $F = V\rho g$

Buoyant force depends upon volume and density since, saturated salt solution have higher density than the water. So, in saturated solution, cube will experience a greater buoyant force.

If each side of the cube is reduced to 4 cm, the volume of cube will decrease less. So, buoyant force will be less than as compared to the first case for water. **[1 + 1]**

(ii) The magnitude of the buoyant force depends on the density of the fluid.

Volume of solid $= \frac{\text{Mass}}{\text{Density}} = \frac{4}{4000} = \frac{1}{1000} \text{ m}^3$ **[1]**

Buoyancy, $F = V\rho g$

$= \frac{1}{1000} \times 1000 \times 10 = 10 \text{ N}$ **[1]**

84. A body weighs 65 g in air, 60.5 g in water and 56 g in a liquid. Calculate the relative density of the liquid.

Sol. Loss in weight of the body in water

$= 65 - 60.5 = 4.5 \text{ g}$

Loss in weight of the body in liquid

$= 65 - 56 = 9 \text{ g}$

$\therefore$ Relative density of the liquid

$$= \frac{\text{Loss of weight in liquid}}{\text{Loss of weight in water}} = \frac{9}{4.5} = 2$$ **[2]**

85. Ishita noted down the following observations in her notebook.

(i) Weight of the stone in air = 280 g-wt

(ii) Weight of the stone in pure water = 240 g-wt

(iii) Weight of the stone in salty water = 190 g-wt

Find the relative density of salty water.

Sol. Relative density of salty water

$$= \frac{\text{Loss in weight in salty water}}{\text{Loss in weight in pure water}}$$

$$= \frac{280 - 190}{280 - 240} = \frac{90}{40} = \frac{9}{4} = 2.25$$ **[2]**

86. (i) When a golf ball is lowered into a measuring cylinder containing water. The water level rises such that volume marker indicates 40 cm^3, when the ball is completely submerged. If the mass of ball in air is 44 g, calculate its density.

(ii) A 0.5 kg sheet of tin sinks in water but if the same sheet is converted into a boat or a box, it floats. Give reason.

Sol. (i) Mass of ball, $m = 44$ g

Volume, $V = 40 \text{ cm}^3$

Density, $\rho = \frac{m}{V} = \frac{44}{40} = 1.1 \text{ g/cm}^3$ **[1]**

(ii) The density of tin is higher than that of water, so the sheet of tin sinks in water. But when the same sheet of tin is converted into a boat or box, a lot of air is trapped in the boat or box. Then, the average density of boat or box made of tin sheet becomes lower than that of water. Therefore, it floats in water. **[2]**

87. A piece of copper floats in mercury. Given that the density of copper is 4.2×10^3 kg m^{-3} and that of mercury is 13.6×10^3kg m^{-3}. Calculate the fraction of volume of an copper piece that remains outside the mercury.

Sol. Fraction of copper piece that remains inside mercury, $\frac{V'}{V}=\frac{\rho}{\rho'}=\frac{4.2\times 10^3}{13.6\times 10^3}=0.31$

Fraction of copper piece that remains outside mercury $=1-0.31=0.69$ [2]

Section II

Structured Questions

88. (i) Give three consequences of atmospheric pressure. [3]

(ii) What does the weather forecast states, if

(a) air is humid and Hg falls suddenly?

(b) air pressure rises steeply?

(c) our pressure falls gradually? [3]

(iii) With the help of an example, show that a body loses its weight when it immersed in a liquid. [4]

Sol. (i) The three consequences of atmospheric pressure are as follows

(a) Sucking soft drinks with a straw

(b) Filling of syringe with a liquid

(c) Action of rubber suckers [3]

(ii) (a) It indicates storm or cyclone.

(b) It indicates weather is dry.

(c) It indicates the possibility of rain. [3]

(iii) Tie a small stone with the hook of spring balance as shown in Fig. (a). The spring of the balance stretches due to the weight of the stone. The pointer attached with the spring shows the weight of the stone in the air. Let this weight be w_1. Now, dip the stone in the water as shown in Fig. (b). We find that, the extension of the string decreases and the pointer attached to the spring shows the weight of the stone as w_2. [3]
This weight (w_2) of the stone in water is less than the weight (w_1) of the stone in air.
Thus, we conclude that a body (say a stone) loses its weight immersed in a liquid. [1/2]

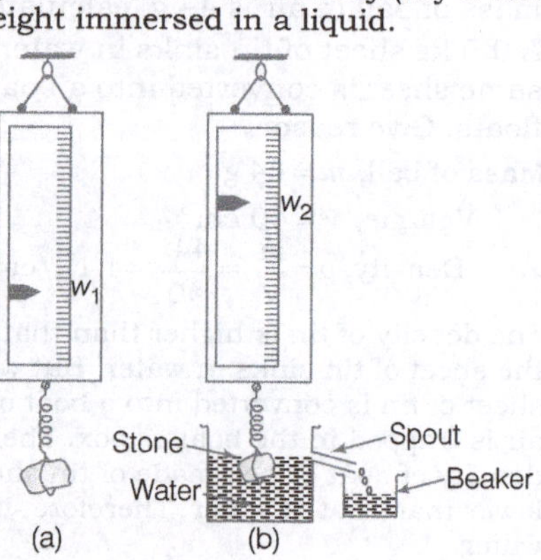

(a) (b) [1/2]

89. (i) (a) Distinguish thrust and pressure.

(b) Why is it easier to swim in sea-water than in river water? [3]

(ii) State the three laws of liquid pressure. [3]

(iii) A body weighs 450 gf in air and 310 gf when completely immersed in water. Find

(a) the volume of the body

(b) the loss in weight of the body

(c) the upthrust on the body

State the assumption made in part (i). [4]

Sol. (i) (a) **Thrust** The total perpendicular force exerted by a body on any surface in contact with it, is called thrust.

Pressure The thrust acting per unit area of a surface is called pressure. [2]

(b) It is easier to swim in sea-water because sea-water exerts more upthrust on the body than the river water. [1]

(ii) The three laws of liquid pressure are

(a) Pressure at same depth is different for different liquid. [1]

(b) Pressure is same in all directions and at all points in a horizontal plane at a given depth.[1]

(c) Pressure at a given point is directly proportional to the density of liquid. [1]

(iii) Given, weight of the body in air = 450 kgf
Weight of the body in water = 310 kgf
Density of water = 1 g cm^{-3}

(a) Volume of the body = Density of water × Loss in weight
$=1\times(450-310)=140$ cm^3

(b) Loss in weight = Weight of the body in air − Weight of the body in water
$=450-310=140$ gf

(c) Upthrust on the body = Loss in weight = 140 gf
Assumption made is density of water is 1 g cm^{-3}. [4]

90. (i) A jar contains a fluid of density d upto a height h. The acceleration due to gravity is g and the atmospheric pressure is p_0.

(a) Give the expression for the total pressure at the base of jar. [3]

(b) What will be the pressure at the free surface? [3]

(c) Give the lateral pressure at this depth on the inner side of jar. [4]

(ii) When a fresh egg is put into a beaker filled with water, it sinks in water. But when a lot of salt was dissolved in the water, the egg begins to rise and then floats. Why?

(iii) A cubical object of side 4 cm has fallen in a well. If mass of the cube is 2 kg, then state whether this object will float or sink in water. (Take, density of water = 1000 kgm^{-3})

Sol. (i) (a) Total pressure at the base of jar = Atmospheric pressure + Pressure due to liquid column

$p = p_0 + hdg$ [1]

(b) Pressure at free surface is equal to atmospheric pressure. [1]

(c) Lateral pressure at this depth on the inner side of jar = hdg. [1]

(ii) On dissolving a lot of salt in water, the density of salt solution becomes much more than pure water. Due to its much higher density, the salt solution exerts much more upward buoyant force on the egg, making the egg rise and then float. [3]

(iii) Given that,

Mass of the object, $m = 2$ kg

Side of cube = 4 cm = 0.04 m [$\because$ 1 m = 100 cm]

Since, volume of cube = $(\text{side})^3$

$\therefore$ Volume of the object, $V = (0.04 \text{ m})^3 = 0.000064 \text{ m}^3$

As we know that,

$$\text{Density} = \frac{\text{Mass of the object}}{\text{Volume of the object}}$$

$$\Rightarrow \text{Density} = \frac{2}{0.000064} \text{ kgm}^{-3} = \frac{2000000}{64} \text{ kgm}^{-3} = 31250 \text{ kgm}^{-3}$$

Here, density of the object (i.e. 31250 kgm^{-3}) is greater than the density of water (i.e. 1000 kgm^{-3}).

Therefore, the object will sink in water. [4]

91. (i) When a gas bubble is released at the bottom of a lake, it grows in size and rises to the surface of lake. Give reason. [3]

(ii) (a) Which system is shown in given diagram?

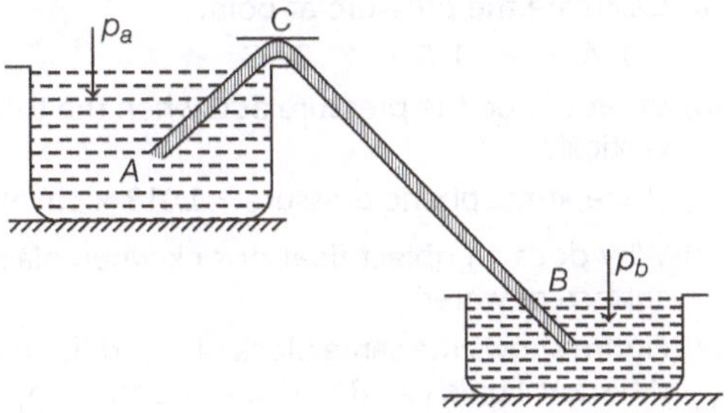

(b) Explain the working of above system. [3]

(iii) A ball filled with air has a volume of 500 cm^3. Calculate the minimum force applied by a child to put it completely inside the water. (Take, $g = 10 \text{ ms}^{-2}$) [4]

Sol. (i) A gas bubble released at the bottom of a lake grows in size as it rises to the surface of lake because at the bottom of the lake, the total pressure exerted on bubble is the sum of pressure due to water column and the atmospheric pressure. As the gas bubble rises, because of the decline in the depth, the pressure due to water column declines. According to Boyle's law, pV is equivalent to constant. Hence, the bubble grows in size because the pressure decreases. [3]

(ii) (a) The given figure shows the siphon system.

(b) Water is supplied from a higher level to a lower level using a siphon system. To transfer water from higher level vessel to lower level vessel, first air is sucked out from the lower end B of the rubber tube. As a result the pressure inside the tube decreases and becomes less than the atmospheric pressure. Due to excess pressure at A, water rises in the tube through the end A and reach level C, then water flows down to the lower level B. [3]

(iii) Given that,

Volume, $V = 500 \text{ cm}^3 = 500 \times 10^{-6} \text{ m}^3$,

$g = 10 \text{ ms}^{-2}$, $F = ?$

Force required to put the ball inside the water

= Buoyant force

= Weight of water displaced = mg ...(i)

Now, we know that,

Mass of water = Density of water × Volume

$m = \rho V$

On substituting this value in Eq. (i), we get

Force $= \rho V g$

$= (1000 \text{ kg m}^{-3}) \times (500 \times 10^{-6} \text{ m}^3) \times (10 \text{ ms}^{-2})$

$= 1000 \times 500 \times 10^{-6} \times 10 \text{ N} = 5 \text{ N}$

$\therefore$ Minimum force applied by a child to put the ball completely inside the water is 5 N. [4]

Chapter Assessment

1 Mark Questions

1. A body will experience minimum upthrust when it is completely immersed in
(a) turpentine (b) water (c) glycerine (d) mercury

2. A body of density ρ sinks in a liquid of density ρ_l. The densities ρ and ρ_l are related as
(a) $\rho = \rho_l$ (b) $\rho < \rho_l$ (c) $\rho > \rho_l$ (d) $\rho = \frac{1}{\rho_l}$

3. Pressure at any point inside a liquid contained in a vessel is
(a) proportional to density
(b) inversely proportional to density
(c) proportional to square root of density
(d) proportional to square of density

4. The Bramah press working is based upon
(a) Newton's laws (b) Archimedes' principle
(c) Boyle's law (d) Pascal's law

5. A cork floats while the nail sinks in water. Which of the following statements is the reason for the same?
(a) Weight of cork is less than buoyant force while weight of nail is greater than buoyant force.
(b) Weight of cork is greater than buoyant force while weight of nail is less than buoyant force
(c) Weight of cork and nail is less than buoyant force.
(d) Weight of cork and nail is greater than buoyant force.

2 Marks Questions

6. A ship made of an iron floats on water but an iron needle sinks. Explain, why?

7. Why does a balloon collapse when air is removed from it? Explain.

8. Give some applications of Pascal's law.

9. A boy gets into a floating boat
(i) what happens to the boat?
(ii) what happens to the buoyant force on the boat?

10. How is it possible to lift a heavy object in water with ease?

11. Why does a body lose weight when immersed in a liquid?

12. (i) Why a wide steel belt is provided over the wheels of an army tank?
(ii) Write down an equation that defines density.

13. Name the factors on which barometric height depends.

14. How does the liquid pressure on a diver change if
(i) the diver moves to the greater depth and
(ii) the diver moves horizontally.

15. You find your mass to be 42 kg on a weighing machine. Is your mass more or less than 42 kg?

Structured Questions

16. (i) (a) What do you mean by buoyancy? Which type of liquid applies greater buoyant force on a body inside it?
(b) Relative density of silver is 19.3. The density of water is 10^3 kg/m^3. What is the density of silver in SI unit? **[3]**

(ii) You have a bag of cotton and an iron bar, each indicating a mass of 10 kg when measured on a weighing machine. In reality, one is heavier than other. Can you say which one is heavier and why? **[3]**

(iii) A tube of length 200 cm filled with a liquid of density 0.90×10^3 kg m^{-3} as shown in figure, is placed inclined with the vertical such that the level A of liquid in the tube is at a vertical height of 100 cm from its lowest point C. There is a point B in the tube below the point A at a vertical depth 60 cm.

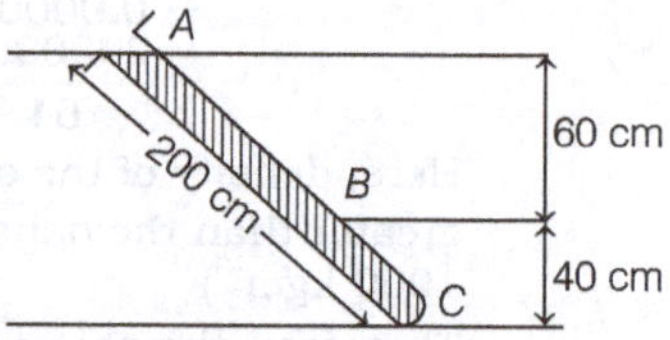

(a) Calculate the pressure at point
I. A II. B III. C
(b) What will be the pressure at C when the tube is made vertical?
(Take atmospheric pressure = 1.013×10^5 Nm^{-2}) **[4]**

17. (i) Why does an object float or sink when placed on the surface of water? **[3]**

(ii) Figure shows the same block of wood floating in three different liquids A, B and C of densities ρ_1, ρ_2 and ρ_3 respectively. Which liquid has the highest density? Give reason for your answer.

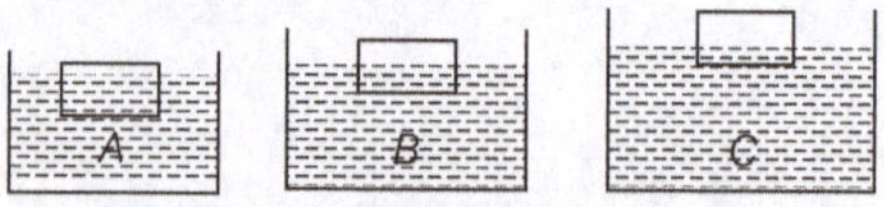

[3]

(iii) A solid of mass 600 g has volume 450 cm^3, then
(a) what is the density of this solid?
(b) what will be the mass of water displaced by this solid?
(c) find the relative density of the solid.
(d) will it float or sink in water? **[4]**

For Solutions Scan the Code

Olympiad Section*

Brain Teasing Questions of Olympiad Pattern

1 A cylinder of certain mass is held in vertical position. If the height of the cylinder is 10 cm and radius of cross-section is 4 cm, such that the pressure acting on its bottom surface is 21560 Nm^{-2}. Then, the value of mass of cylinder is

(a) 11.06 kg (b) 20.01 kg
(c) 19.01 kg (d) 2765.7 kg

2 An alloy made of two metals (Au and Cu) and the Cu weight 200 gwt in air and 160 gwt in water. If densities of metals Au and Cu are 20 $g\,cm^{-3}$ and 4 $g\,cm^{-3}$ respectively, then the value of percentage of mass of each metal present is

(a) 25%, 75% (b) 30%, 70%
(c) 40%, 60% (d) 10%, 90%

3 A block of wood floats in a liquid of density 0.8 cm^{-3} with one fourth of its volume submerged. In oil, the block floats with 60% of its volume submerged the density of

(i) wood and (ii) oil are respectively

(a) 0.2 g-cm^{-3}, 2 g-cm^{-3}

(b) 200 kg-m^{-3}, $\frac{1000}{3}$ kg-m^{-3}

(c) 1000 kg-m^{-3}, 200 kg-m^{-3}

(d) None of the above

4 In the arrangement shown below, a block of 2800 kg is in equilibrium on applying a force of 45 N, then density of the liquid is

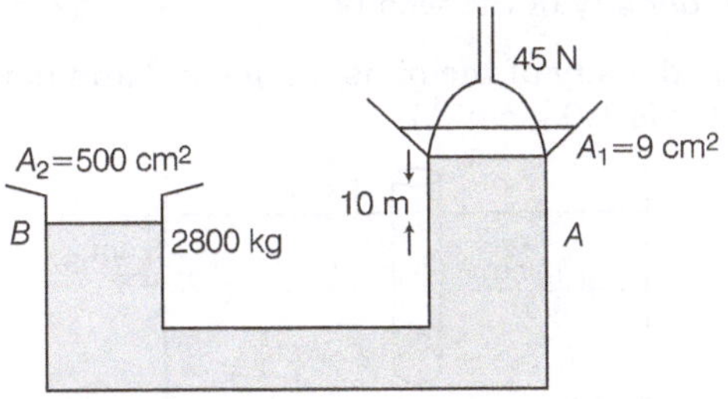

(a) 5089 kg-m^{-3} (b) 6089 kg-m^{-3}
(c) 5020 kg-m^{-3} (d) 9269 kg-m^{-3}

5 At what depth in an ocean with a bubble of air have one-fourth of the volume, if it will be reaching the surface? (Take, atmospheric pressure = 76 cm of Hg and density of Hg = 13.6 g cm^{-3})

(a) 3100.8 cm (b) 4134 cm
(c) 6000 cm (d) 8000 cm

6 A metal cube is found to float in a liquid of density 2 g cm^{-3} with $\frac{1}{2}$ cm of its vertical side above the liquid. On placing a weight of 144 g over its top, it just submerges in the liquid. The specific gravity of the metal cube

(a) $\frac{23}{12}$ (b) $\frac{27}{12}$
(c) $\frac{29}{12}$ (d) $\frac{31}{12}$

7 A cone of height 16 cm and volume 2948 cm^3 floats in a liquid of density 3.2 g cm^{-3}, such that its base lies below the surface of the liquid. If the area of cross-section of conical region above the liquid surface is 6 cm^2, then the density of the cone is

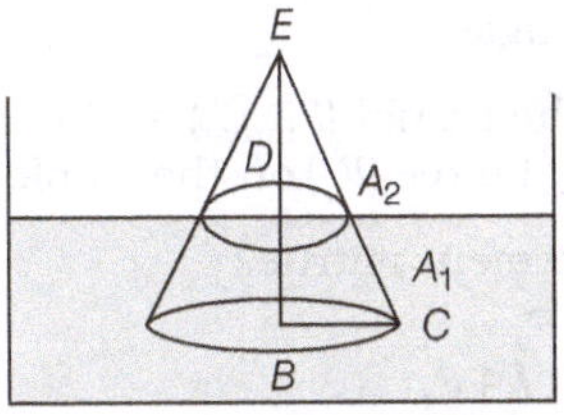

(a) 3.193 g cm^{-3} (b) 4.193 g cm^{-3}
(c) 5.192 g cm^{-3} (d) 4.921 g cm^{-3}

8 A 'U' tube contains oil, carbon tetrachloride and water as shown in the figure. The density of oil is 0.8 g cm^{-3} and that of carbon tetrachloride is 1.6 g cm^{-3}. If oil and water surfaces are at the same level, then the height of the water column is

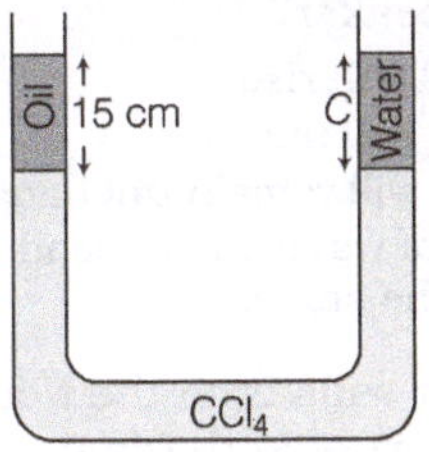

(a) 12 cm (b) 40 cm
(c) 10 cm (d) 15 cm

9 A jet in water travelling at a velocity of 20 ms^{-1} hits a wall normally. Calculate the pressure on the wall if the water does not bounce back. (Density of water (ρ) = 1.0×10^3 kg m^{-3})

(a) 8.0×10^5 Pa (b) 4.0×10^5 Pa
(c) 2.0×10^5 Pa (d) 2.0×10^{-4} Pa

10 A sky crane was used for the landing of the Mars explorer 'Curiosity'

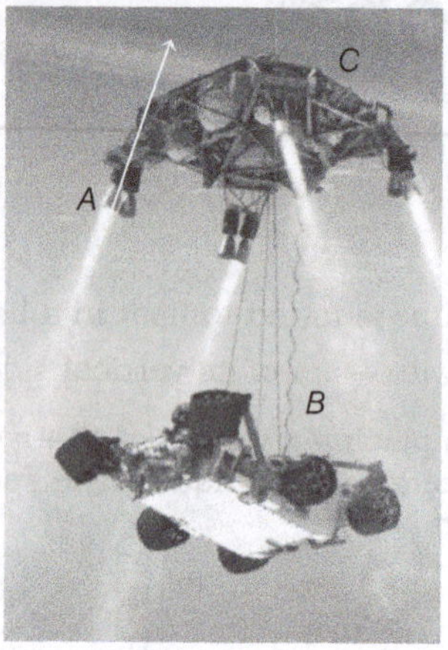

The four exhausts expel combustion gases that hold the crane at a constant height before landing. The four exhausts are arranged in an oblique arrangement. In figure you can see the thrust exerted on the crane by the gas from exhaust *A*. The thrust of the gas ejected from the other exhausts have the same magnitude and operate at the same angle.

Compare the thrust (F_{thrust}) at *A* to the gravitational force (F_g) on the whole system.

Which statement is true?

(a) $F_{thrust} = F_g$
(b) $F_{thrust} = 1/4\, F_g$
(c) $F_{thrust} < 1/4F_g$
(d) $F_{thrust} > 1/4\, F_g$

11 A piece of ice with a stone (denser than water) embedded inside, is kept in a vessel containing water. Size and mass of the stone is such that the stone - ice combination is floating on water. When the ice melts, what will happen to the level of water in the beaker?

(a) Water level will rise
(b) Water level will fall
(c) Water level will remain unchanged
(d) Final level of water will depend upon actual density of the stone.

12 A supertanker sails from the North Sea, via a river, to the port of Rotterdam.

Which statement about the draft (i.e. how deep a ship lies in the water) is true when the ship sails form the sea into the river?

(a) The tanker will have a deeper draft in the river.
(b) The tanker will have a shallower draft in the river.
(c) The draft will remain the same.
(d) The draft depends on the air pressure.

13 A floating iceberg in seawater as shown in the figure below of is extremely dangerous because most of the ice is below the surface.

This hidden ice could damage a ship that is still a considerable distance from the visible ice. Estimate what fraction of the iceberg lies below the water level if the density of seawater is 1030 kg/m^3 and the density of iceberg is 917 kg/m^3.

(a) 0.352 (b) 0.756 (c) 0.781 (d) 0.890

14 An oil layer which is 9 cm deep lies above a depth of water. A uniform cylinder of wood of length 25 cm is floating vertically upright in the two liquids as shown in the diagram. If 5 cm of the wooden cylinder lies above the oil surface, what is the density of the wood?

(The density of the oil is 0.9 g cm^{-3} and density of water is 1.0 g cm^{-3}.)

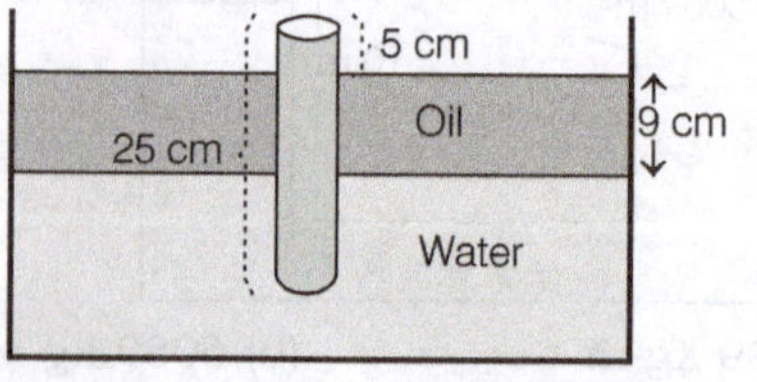

(a) 0.76 g cm^{-3} (b) 0.66g cm^{-3}
(c) 0.80g cm^{-3} (d) 0.70g cm^{-3}

15 A submarine if floating on water half submerged (position A). It is then lowered to position B where it sits for a while. Later the submarine is taken to position C and submarine waits there before it is finally taken to the rest position at the bottom of the sea, which is position D. Assume that density of water and value of g is same everywhere.

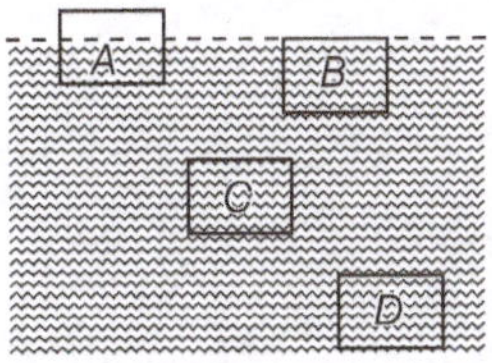

Which of the following is correct for buoyancy force at the 4 places?

(a) $F_A < F_B = F_C = F_D$
(b) $F_A < F_B < F_C < F_D$
(c) $F_A < F_B = F_C < F_D$
(d) $F_A = F_B = F_C = F_D$

16 Figure given below shows a small boat containing some iron balls, floating on a still lake. These iron blocks are now dropped into the lake. Select the wrong statement.

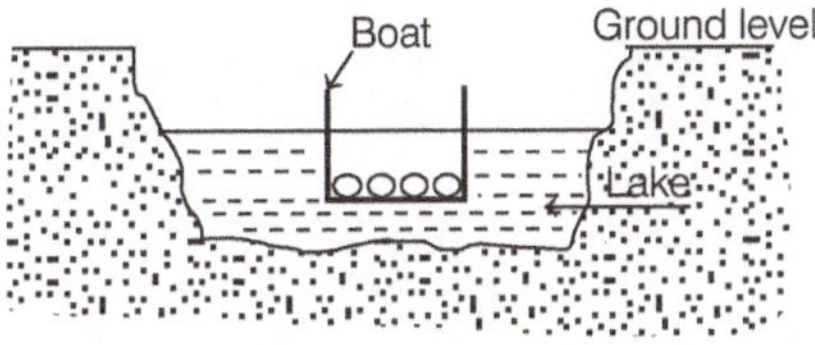

(a) Level of the lake will fall with ground reference.
(b) The boat will rise with water reference.
(c) Level of the boat will rise with ground reference.
(d) Water level will not change from the ground reference.

Answers

1. (d)	**2.** (a)	**3.** (b)	**4.** (a)	**5.** (b)	**6.** (a)	**7.** (a)	**8.** (a)	**9.** (b)	**10.** (d)
11. (b)	**12.** (a)	**13.** (d)	**14.** (a)	**15.** (a)	**16.** (d)				

* *These questions may or may not be asked in the examination, have been given just for additional practice required for olympiads Scholarship Exams etc. For detailed explanations refer Page No. 216.*

CHAPTER

06

Heat

SYLLABUS

• Concepts of heat and temperature. • Anomalous expansion of water; graphs showing variation of volume and density of water with temperature in the 0 to 10°C range.
• Hope's experiment and consequences of Anomalous expansion.

Heat given to a substance, changes the temperature of the body. Hence, heat and temperature both are inter-related to each other. In this chapter, we will study the concept of heat, temperature and its measurement, thermal expansion and anomalous behaviour of water.

Concept of Heat and Temperature

Heat

It is the form of energy which flows from hotter body to colder body by virtue of temperature difference, when bodies are kept in contact. The process of transfer of heat is a non-mechanical process, i.e. there is no mechanical work involved in the process of heat transfer. The amount of heat is measured in joule (SI unit). Another widely used unit for the heat is calorie, where

$$1 \text{ cal} = 4.186 \text{ J}$$

1 calorie is equal to the amount of heat energy required to raise the temperature of 1g of water from 14.5°C to 15.5°C.

Similarly, 1 kilocalorie is equal to the amount of heat energy required to raise the temperature of 1kg of water from 14.5°C to 15.5°C.

$$1 \text{ kcal} = 1000 \text{ cal}$$

The CGS unit of heat is erg, where $1 \text{ J} = 10^7$ erg.

Theory of Heat

According to this theory, all substances (solids, liquids and gases) are made of molecules. These molecules are in the state of continuous, random motion which provide some kinetic energy to the molecules of the body. The heat possessed by the body is the total internal energy of the body which is the sum of kinetic energies of all individual molecules of the body due to translational, vibrational and rotational motion of the molecules.

Temperature

It determines the degree of hotness or coldness of a substance. It is a fundamental physical quantity. Its SI unit is kelvin (K).

Another units of temperature are celsius (°C) and fahrenheit (°F).

Temperature of a body is measured by a device called **thermometer.**

Conversion of Temperature From One Scale to Another

The temperature on celsius and fahrenheit scales are related as

$$\frac{T_C}{5} = \frac{T_F - 32}{9}$$

or

$$T_F = 32 + \frac{9}{5} T_C$$

The temperature on celsius and kelvin scales are related as

$$T = 273 + T_C$$

The relationship between these different scales of temperature is given below as

$$\frac{T_C - 0}{100} = \frac{T_F - 32}{180} = \frac{T - 273}{100}$$

where, T_C = temperature on celsius scale,
T_F = temperature on fahrenheit scale,
and T = temperature on kelvin scale.

Some Important Points about Temperature

These are as follows

(i) Temperature determines the direction of flow of heat, when two bodies at different temperature are placed in contact.

(ii) The amount of heat energy contained by an object depends on its mass, temperature and the nature of material of the object.

(iii) The temperature of 0K is called absolute zero temperature.

(iv) Negative temperature is not possible on kelvin scale.

Thermal Equilibrium

When two bodies having different temperature are kept in contact with each other, then heat flows from the body of higher temperature to the body of lower temperature, till the temperatures of both of them become equal.

The state, when there is no flow of heat between two bodies is called thermal equilibrium. e.g. A hot tea kept in a room becomes cold because heat moves from hot tea (hot object) to surroundings (cold object as compared to tea).

Differences between Heat and Temperature

Heat	Temperature
It is a energy that is transferred from one body to another as the result of difference in temperature.	It is the measure of degree of hotness or coldness of a body, expressed in terms of any of several arbitrary scales, like celsius, fahrenheit and kelvin.
SI unit of heat is joule (J).	SI unit of temperature is kelvin (K).
It is not a fundamental quantity.	It is a fundamental quantity.
Heat has ability to do work.	Temperature can only be used to measure the degree of heat.
The amount of heat loss by any hotter body is equal to the heat gained by colder body.	The fall in temperature of hotter body may not be equal to temperature rise in colder body.
Heat is measured by the principle of calorimetry.	Temperature is measured by a thermometer.

Check Your LEARNING...

1. Calorie is the unit of which physical quantity?
2. How many joules are in 1 calorie of heat? *Ans.* 4.186 J
3. What is the SI unit of temperature?
4. Give a formula for the conversion of temperature between celsius and fahrenheit scale.
5. Convert 37°C into fahrenheit. *Ans.* 98.6 °F

Thermal Expansion

When heat is supplied to the material, its dimensions (length, area and volume) change due to change in its temperature. The phenomenon of changing in dimensions of an object due to heat supplied, is known as thermal expansion.

There are three types of thermal expansion, which are as follows

(i) Linear expansion

(ii) Areal (or superficial) expansion

(iii) Volumetric (or cubical) expansion

Due to the definite shape of solids, it can be expanded, linearly, areally and volumetrically. Expansion in length of a body due to increase in its temperature is **linear expansion,** whereas expansion in area due to increase in temperature is called **areal** or **superficial expansion** and expansion in the volume of the body due to increase in temperature is called **volumetric expansion.**

Fluids do not have definite shape but have definite volume, so they only show cubical or volumetric expansion.

Anomalous Behaviour of Water

In the case of fluids, with the rise of temperature, the volume increases. Therefore, the density decreases. But water shows an anomalous behaviour, as it contracts on heating between the temperature 0°C to 4°C. When water is cooled below the room temperature (i.e. normal temperature), the volume of given amount of water decreases.

Until its temperature reaches to 4°C, the volume decreases (and hence density increases). So, it is clear that water has maximum density (and hence minimum volume) at 4°C.

The figure shows the variation of volume of 1 kg of water with temperature (°C).

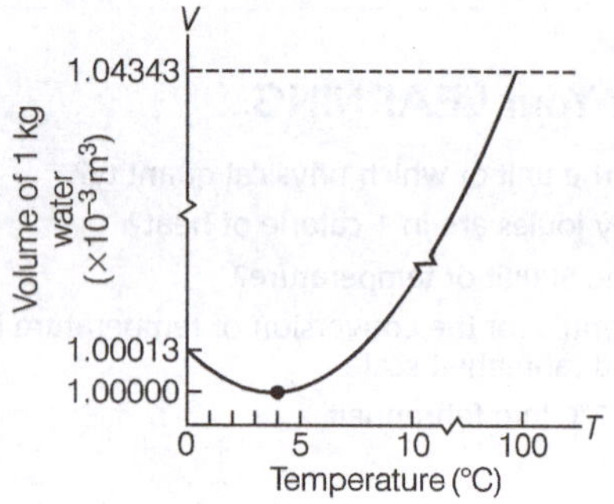

Abnormal behaviour of water

And the curve given below shows the variation of density of water with respect to temperature from 0°C to 10°C.

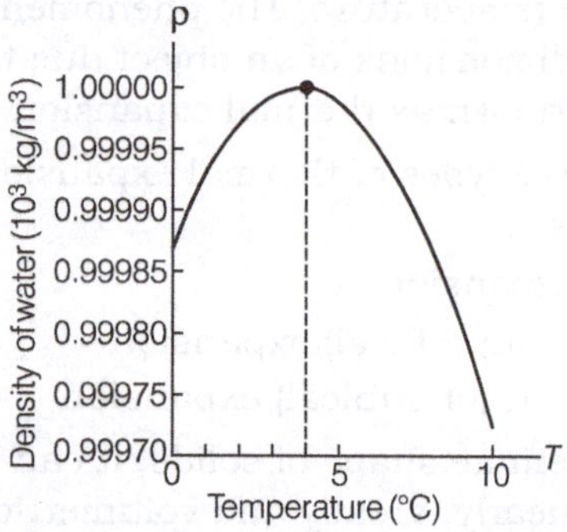

Variation of density of water w.r.t. temperature

Note Other substances show the anomalous behaviour i.e. silver iodide from 80°C to 141°C and silica below -80°C.

Demonstration of Anomalous Expansion of Water : Hope's Experiment

Scientist TC Hope in year 1805 devised an arrangement, known as **Hope's apparatus** to demonstrate the anomalous behaviour of water.

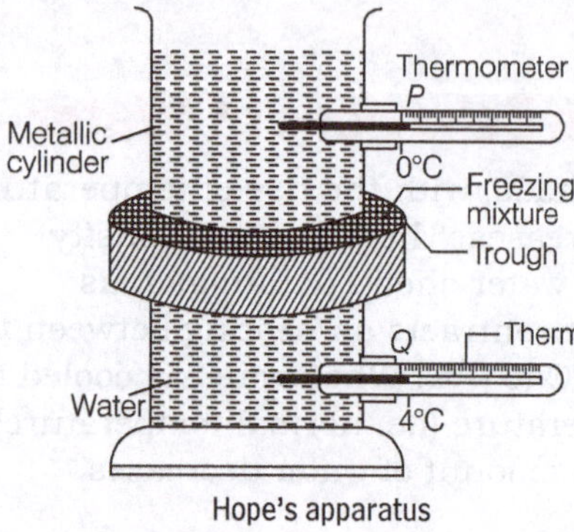

Hope's apparatus

Construction

It consists of a long cylindrical jar with two opening side, one near the top and the other near the bottom to fit thermometers. Two thermometers T_1 and T_2 are fitted air tight on the two openings of the cylindrical jar as shown in figure.

The cylindrical jar is filled with water. The cylindrical trough at the central portion of the jar is filled with a freezing mixture of ice and common salt.

Working and Observations

(i) In the beginning, both the thermometers show the same reading, say 14°C.

(ii) As the trough is filled with the freezing mixture, the water in the central portion of the jar loses heat energy and becomes cooled.

(iii) Due to this, the volume of water in central portion decreases and density increases. As a result, the denser layers of water move downwards, displacing the lighter layers of water there towards central portion.

(iv) Thermometer T_1 near the top shows a rapid fall in temperature till it reaches 4°C. At 4°C, the density of the water in this part of the jar is maximum.

(v) Denser water remains in the lower portion. Now, water in the central portion of the jar cools to below 4°C. Due to the anomalous expansion of water, it begins to expand.

(vi) The water in central portion moves upward, due to which thermometer T_2 shows a rapid fall in temperature, however the temperature of water in lower portion is remained 4°C.

(vii) The temperature of water in upper portion of the jar continues to decrease gradually below 4°C. Thus, the final temperature recorded by thermometer T_1 is 0°C and thermometer T_2 is 4°C. The figure shows the variation in temperature by T_1 and T_2 thermometers, w.r.t. time.

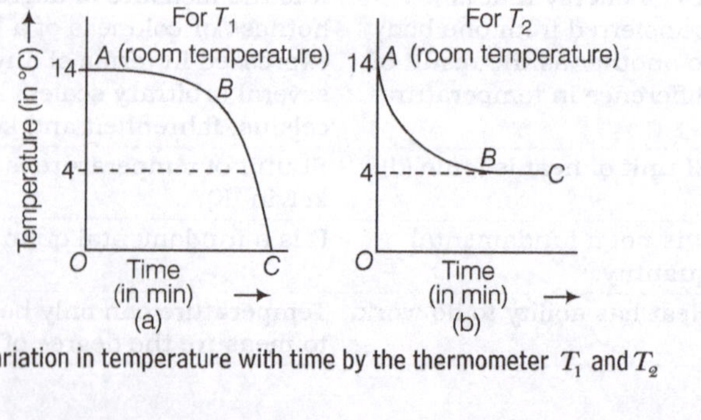

Variation in temperature with time by the thermometer T_1 and T_2

Conclusion

(i) Water expands on cooling from 4°C to 0°C.

(ii) Water contracts on heating from 0°C to 4°C.

So, behaviour of water expansion between 0°C to 4°C is **anomalous.**

Consequences of Anomalous Expansion of Water

(i) **The anomalous expansion of water helps the aquatic organisms able to survive in very cold weather**

In winters, when atmospheric temperature falls to 0°C or below it, the surface water of lakes or other water bodies turns into ice. When temperature of water at the surface falls to 4°C, water contracts and its density increases.

Thus, the layer of water at 4 °C will settle down at bottom followed by 3°C to 0°C. Top layer of water is at 0°C, in the form of ice. The less density of ice than that of water makes it to float on the water and due to its poor heat conductivity, it does not allow to exchange the temperature in and out of it. So, the water below the ice layer does not freeze and marine animals remain alive and move freely near the bottom.

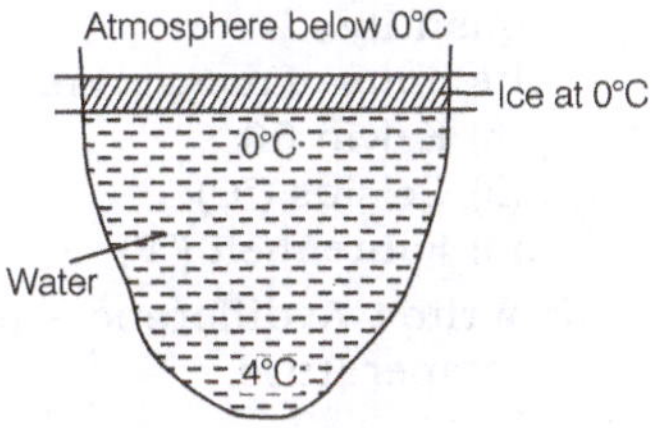

Formation of ice of the surface water of pond

(ii) **The anomalous expansion of water is responsible for the water pipe lines to burst**

Generally, in winters, as the atmospheric temperature starts falling below 4°C, water in pipe lines expands and exerts a very large pressure on the pipes which cause bursting of pipes.

(iii) **The anomalous expansion of water is responsible for destroying of crops during very cold nights**

Plants died up due to expansion of the frozen water in capillary tube of plants and due to this, crops are destroyed. In order to save plants against it, fields are filled with water.

Check Your LEARNING...

1. When heat is supplied to a material, its dimension is changed. Why?
2. Water is cooled from 4°C to 0°C, will it contract or expand?
3. At what temperature, density of water is maximum?
4. How many thermometers are used in Hope's apparatus?
5. Which property of water is responsible for the bursting of water pipes in winter at some places?

QUiCK Revision

- **Heat** It is the form of energy that is transferred from one part of a system to another part or from one system to another by virtue of temperature difference only.
- SI unit of heat is **joule**, **calorie** and **kilocalorie** are also other units of heat.
  1 calorie = 4.186 joules ≈ 4.2 joules
- **Temperature** It is the measure of degree of hotness or coldness of a body. It determines the direction of flow of heat.
- SI unit of temperature is **kelvin (K)**, **celsius (C)** and **fahrenheit (F)** are also used to measure temperature.
- **Thermal expansion** It is the increase in size of a substance on heating.
- **Anomalous expansion of water** Water is a substance which on heating from 0°C to 4°C contracts i.e., volume decreases (or density increases). On heating further above 4°C, the volume increases and hence density decreases. This is the anomalous expansion of water.
- **Hope's experiment** is used to demonstrate the anomalous expansion of water.
- The anomalous expansion of water helps the aquatic organism to survive in very cold weather.
- Water pipe lines are burst in winter due to anomalous behaviour of water.
- In cold nights, crops are destroyed due to anomalous expansion of water.

Chapter Practice

Section-I

1 Mark Questions

1. Which of the following is not the unit of heat?
(a) calorie (b) erg (c) torr (d) joule

Sol. (c) Torr is not the unit of heat, it is the unit of pressure.

2. Choose the correct statement about heat.
(a) Heat flows from colder body to hotter body.
(b) The amount of heat energy in a body depends on its temperature.
(c) Heat is the degree of hotness or coldness of the body.
(d) Heat determines the direction of flow of temperature.

Sol. (b) Heat is a form of energy that flows from hotter body to colder body. The amount of heat energy in a body depends on its temperature while temperature is the degree of hotness or coldness of the body and it also determines the direction of flow of heat.

3. Water shows an anomalous behaviour
(a) at 0°C (b) at 4°C
(c) above 4°C (d) between 4°C and 0°C

Sol. (d) Water shows an anomalous behaviour between 4°C and 0°C, as it expands with decreasing temperature.

4. The density of water is maximum at
(a) 0°C (b) 100°C (c) 4°C (d)273°C

Sol. (c) Water has maximum density at 4°C.

5. Which of the following graph shows the correct variation of an anomalous behaviour of water with temperature?

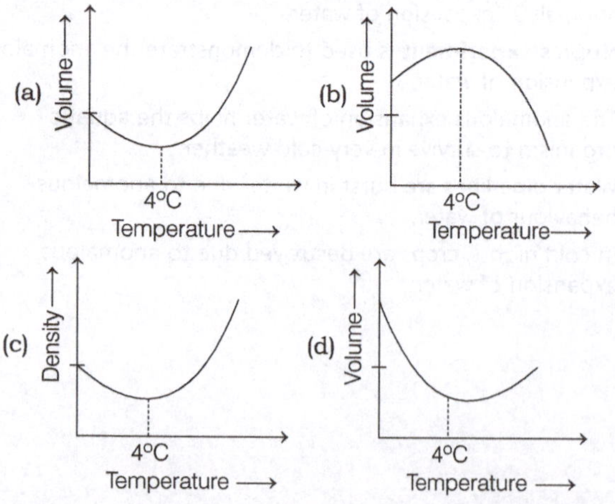

Sol. (a) **For details,** Refer to theory Pages 111 and 112.

2 Marks Questions

6. What do you mean by heat?

Sol. Heat is a form of energy which is transferred from one part of a system to another part or from one system to another by virtue of temperature difference only.

7. How can we say that, one body is hotter than other? Give a term to find out the degree of hotness. Write its units of measurement also.

Sol. Temperature determines the degree of hotness or coldness of a substance. It is a fundamental quantity.
Its units of measurement are [1]
(i) Kelvin (K)
(ii) Celsius (°C)
(iii) Fahrenheit (°F) [1]

8. Write two differences between heat and temperature.

Sol. Refer to text on page No. 111.

9. Two bodies P and Q have quantity of heat 1000 J and 100 J and their respective temperatures are 90°C and 24°C. Both of them are kept in contact. How does the heat flow between them?

Sol. Flow of heat does not depend on heat contained by the body. Flow of heat is due to temperature difference only.
So, heat will flow from body P to Q, as the temperature of body P is more than that of body Q. [1+1]

10. What do you mean by thermal expansion, write its types?

Sol. Thermal expansion of a substance is the change in its size with the change of temperature.
It is of three types
(i) Linear expansion (ii) Areal expansion
(iii) Volumetric expansion [1+1]

11. Write a short note on anomalous behaviour of water.

Sol. Refer to theory, Pages 111 and 112.

12. Write any two substances other than water that also show anomalous behaviour.

Sol. The substances other than water that show the anomalous behaviour are
(i) silver iodide from 80°C to 141°C, [1]
(ii) silica below –80°C. [1]

13. How crops are destroyed due to the anomalous behaviour of water?

Sol. Refer to theory Page 113

3 Marks Questions

14. How can you say that heat is a form of energy?

Sol. From the kinetic theory of matter, it is clear that the molecules of water have greater energy than those of ice and the molecules of steam have greater energy than those of water.

When we supply heat to a block of ice to convert it into water, we increase the energy of its molecules. As, it is clear that the supplying heat to a substance increases the energy of that substance. Hence, we can say that heat is a form of energy. [2+1]

15. If a given mass of water is heated from 0°C to 10°C, sketch the volume-temperature graph to show the behaviour of water.

Sol. The temperature-volume graph is shown below as

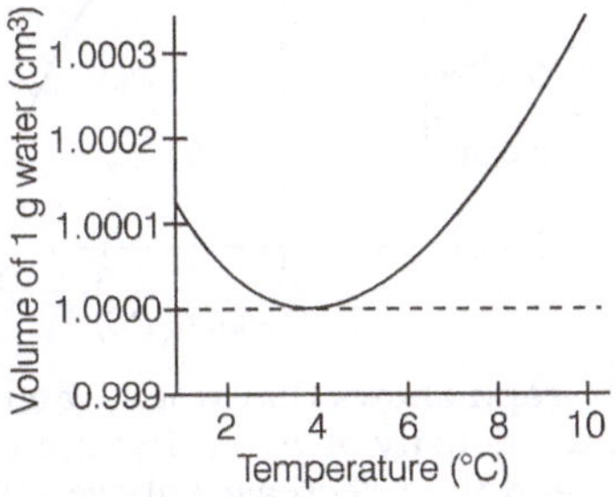

[1]

The above graph shows that the volume of water first decreases on heating it from 0°C to 4°C and then increases on further heating it from 4°C to 10°C. Thus, water has minimum volume at 4°C. [2]

4 Marks Questions

16. Give answers of the following

(i) Why telegraph wires are given enough sag?

(ii) Why the soft drink bottles are made of thick glass?

Sol. (i) Since, wires made up of metal and metal contracts, when temperature falls. Therefore, telegraph wires are kept loose so that they may not break on contraction in winters. [2]

(ii) In soda water/soft drink bottle some gases remain in it, when it is packed. During summers, the temperature of the gas increases due to which gas expands (volume expansion of gas) and exerts a large pressure on the wall and cap of the bottle. If the glass of the bottle is not sufficiently thick and strong, it may cracked down to expansion force. [2]

17. How does the anomalous expansion of water help in preserving the aquatic life during every cold weather?

Or

How do fish survive in frozen lakes?

Or

How are aquatic animals able to survive inside a frozen pond?

Sol. In winter, when atmospheric temperature falls to 4°C, then, the water at the surface of ponds and lakes cools and contracts. Thus, it becomes denser and sinks to the bottom. In this process, the light water from the bottom rises to the top. This process continues till all the water of the pond reaches at 0°C. When temperature of the upper surface of water falls below 4°C, its density decreases and it remains on the surface. [2]

This continues till temperature drops to 0°C. Top layer of water is at 0°C, in the form of ice. The less density of ice than that of water makes it to float on water. Since, ice is a poor conductor of heat, it prevents the transfer of heat from the water of the lake below the layer ice and thus helps in keeping the water under the layer of ice at 4°C. Consequently, the fish and other aquatic creatures survive in water bodies, though their surface has frozen into ice. [2]

Numerical Type Questions

18. Convert 40 J into calories. [2]

Sol. We know that,

$$1 \text{ cal} = 4.18 \text{ J} \approx 4.2 \text{ J}$$

$$\therefore \quad 40 \text{ J} = \frac{40}{4.2} \text{ cal} = 9.52 \text{ cal}$$

19. Two temperature scales A and B are related by $\frac{A-42}{110} = \frac{B-72}{220}$. At which temperature, two scales have the same reading? [2]

Sol. We have, by the given relation between the temperature scales A and B as,

$$\frac{A-42}{110} = \frac{B-72}{220}$$

So, for the two scales to have the same reading $A = B$ and so $\frac{A-42}{110} = \frac{A-72}{220}$, which yields $A = 12$.

20. The freezing point on a thermometer is marked as −20°C and the boiling point as 130°C. A temperature of human body (34° C) on this thermometer will be read as how much degree? [2]

Sol. Given, freezing point = −20°C, boiling point = 130°C

$$T_c = 34° \text{ C}$$

As, $$\frac{\text{Temp} - \text{FP}}{\text{BP} - \text{FP}} = \text{Constant}$$

$$\therefore \quad \frac{T_c - 0}{100 - 0} = \frac{T - (-20)}{130 - (-20)}$$

So, on this thermometer 34°C will read as

$$T = -20 + \frac{150}{100} \times 34 = 31°\text{C}$$

21. The temperature of a body on kelvin scale is found to be xK. When it is measured by fahrenheit thermometer, it is found to be x°F, then what is the value of x? [2]

Sol. We know that,
$$\frac{F-32}{9}=\frac{K-273}{5}$$
$$\Rightarrow \frac{x-32}{9}=\frac{x-273}{5}$$
$$\Rightarrow x=574.25$$

22. The reading of both thermometers on celsius and fahrenheit are in the ratio 2:5. What is the temperature of both? [2]

Sol. Given, $\frac{T_C}{T_F}=\frac{2}{5}$
$$\Rightarrow T_F=\frac{5}{2}T_C$$
$$\therefore \frac{T_C}{100}=\frac{(5/2)T_C-32}{180}$$
$$\Rightarrow 9T_C=\frac{25}{2}T_C-160$$
$$T_C=45.71°\text{C}$$

Section-II

Structured Questions

23. (i) Is 'touching' a proper method to measure the hotness of an object? Explain with example. [3]
(ii) Draw a graph showing the variation of density of water with temperature. [3]
(iii) Demonstrate the anomalous behaviour of water with the help of an experiment. [4]

Sol. (i) No, touching is not a proper method to measure the hotness of an object. [1]

Illustration Take three vessels *A*, *B* and *C* and fill tap water in them. Heat vessel *A* slightly and put some ice cubes in vessel *C*. Now, put the three vessels side by side. Put your right hand in vessel *A* and left hand in vessel *C* for about two minutes. [1]
Now, put both the hands in vessel *B*. Your right hand feels that the water in vessel *B* is cold, while your left hand feels that it is warm. This example explains that the feeling on touching depends on our condition. Same object may feel warm or cold depending on the temperature of our hand. [1]

(ii) The density-temperature graph is shown below as

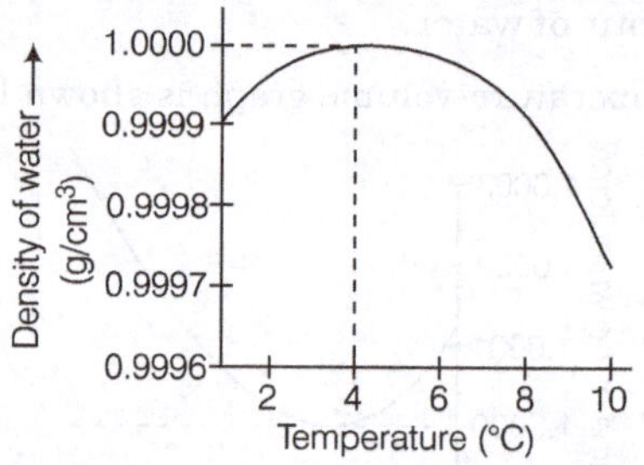

[3]

The above graph shows that when water is heated from 0°C, the density of water first increases from 0°C to 4°C and then decreases above 4°C. Thus, the water has maximum density at 4°C.

(iii) Refer to theory Pages 111 and 112. [4]

Chapter Assessment

1 Mark Questions

1. The value of 1 J equals to
(a) 1 kcal (b) 4.18 cal
(c) 0.24 cal (d) 1 cal

2. The SI unit of temperature is
(a) fahrenheit (b) joule
(c) kelvin (d) celsius

3. Choose the correct statement about the behaviour of water.
(a) Water shows an anomalous behaviour.
(b) Water shows contractive behaviour below 4°C.
(c) Water shows expandable behaviour above 4°C.
(d) All of the above are correct.

4. In the process of freezing of lake, the formation of ice takes place first at
(a) the bottom (b) the top
(c) the middle (d) everywhere

2 Marks Questions

5. Two bodies at different temperature are placed in contact. State the direction in which heat will flow.

6. Define temperature and write its SI unit.

7. At what temperature, the density of water is maximum? State its value.

8. Why do fruits and vegetables get damaged during severe frost?

9. Write the formula for conversion of temperature from
(i) celsius to kelvin scale and
(ii) fahrenheit to celsius scale.

Structured Questions

10. (i) State the volume changes observed, when a given mass of water is heated from 0°C to 10°C. Sketch a volume-temperature graph to show the behaviour. **[3]**
(ii) A given mass of water is cooled from 10°C to 0°C. State the volume changes observed. Represent these changes on a volume-temperature graph. **[3]**
(iii) (a) Explain Hope's experiment to show the anomalous expansion of water.
(b) Write two consequences of the anomalous expansion of water. **[4]**

11. (i) Deep pond of water has its top layer frozen during winter. State the expected temperature of water layer
(a) just in contact with ice
(b) and at the bottom of pond. **[3]**
(ii) Give answers of the following
(a) Why taps left dripping is sub-zero temperature during extremely cold season?
(b) Why are hilly rocks burst during severe frost? **[3]**
(iii) Describe an experiment to show that water has maximum density at 4°C. What important consequences follow from this peculiar property of water? Discuss the phenomenon in nature. **[4]**

For Solutions Scan the Code

Olympiad Section*

Brain Teasing Questions of Olympiad Pattern

1 Gap left between the ends of two railway lines in a railway track is due to
(a) linear expansion (b) areal expansion
(c) cubical expansion (d) None of these

2 Exposed water pipes lagged with straw in winter in hilly areas to
(a) expand water
(b) contract water
(c) maintain the water temperature above 0°C
(d) maintain the water temperature below 4°C

3 Soft drink bottles are not filled completely
(a) to avoid the bottle from bursting
(b) to avoid the bottle from spilling out
(c) Both (a) and (b)
(d) Neither (a) nor (b)

4 Fruits and vegetables get damaged during severe frost due to the
(a) bursting of the cells (b) bursting of the tissues
(c) contraction of cells (d) None of these

5 Arrange the various layers of ice and water in an ice covered pond.
(a) 4° C→ 3° C→ 2° C→ 1° C→ 0° C (water) → 0° C (ice)
(b) 0° C (ice) → 0° C (water) → 1° C→ 2° C→ 3° C→ 4° C
(c) – 4° C (ice) → –3°C (ice) → –2° C (ice) → 1° C (ice) → 0° C (ice) → 0° C (water)
(d) All of the above

6 Two blocks *A* and *B* are placed as shown in the figure.

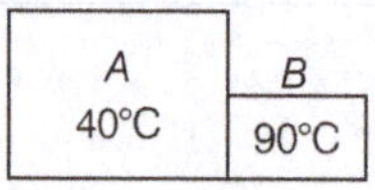

Heat flows
(a) remains constant (b) from *A* to *B*
(c) from *B* to *A* (d) Cannot say

7 Water firstly heated from 4°C to 8°C, then cooled from 8°C to 0°C and again heated from 0°C to 4°C. Which of the following is correct?
(a) Water will initially expand and lastly contract.
(b) Initially contract and lastly expand.
(c) Expand throughout the process.
(d) Contract throughout the process.

8 On keeping the two bodies in contact, if there is no exchange of heat between them, the bodies are said to be
(a) anomalous (b) in thermal equilibrium
(c) Both (a) and (b) (d) Neither (a) nor (b)

9 Thermal expansion occurs in
(a) solid only (b) Both solid and liquid
(c) Both liquid and gas (d) solid, liquid and gas

10 There is a slight temperature difference between the water fall at the top and the bottom because
(a) potential energy of water at top of the fall gets converted into heat kinetic energy at the bottom of the fall
(b) potential energy of water remains same throughout the fall
(c) kinetic energy of water at top of the fall gets converted into heat potential energy at the bottom of the fall
(d) None of the above

11 A circular metal washer is uniformly heated. Select the correct statement.
(a) Both its external and internal diameters increase.
(b) Its external diameter increases and internal diameter decreases.
(c) Its external diameter is unchanged and internal diameter decreases.
(d) Its external diameter increases and internal diameter is unchanged.

12 Fig. 1 shows metallic disc with a hole at its centre. Which one of the figure from Fig. 2 to 5 schematically shows the how disc will appear after it is uniformly heated?

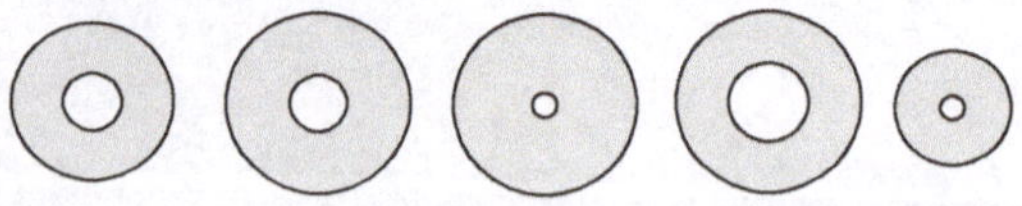

Fig. 1 Fig. 2 Fig. 3 Fig. 4 Fig. 5

(a) Fig. 2 (b) Fig. 3 (c) Fig. 4 (d) Fig. 5

Answers

1. (a)	2. (d)	3. (a)	4. (c)	5. (b)	6. (c)	7. (a)	8. (b)	9. (d)	10. (a)
11. (a)	12. (c)								

* *These questions may or may not be asked in the examination, have been given just for additional practice required for olympiads Scholarship Exams etc. For detailed explanations refer Page No. 218.*

CHAPTER 07

Energy Flow and Sources of Energy

SYLLABUS

- Energy flow in an Ecosystem.
- Sources of Energy .
- Greenhouse effect and Global warming.

Energy is an essential requirement of our lives. No activity in our daily lives can be undertaken without the use of energy, sun is the ultimate source of energy for Earth, all the sources of energy that are available on the Earth are directly or indirectly developed from solar energy. All the energy received by earth from Sun is utilised in different ways.

Energy Flow in an Ecosystem

An **ecosystem** is the structural and functional unit of biosphere, which has a large community of living organisms (plants, animals and microbes) in a particular area. It consists of two components

(i) **Biotic component** This includes producers, consumers and decomposers.

(ii) **Abiotic component** This includes light, heat, rain, humidity, inorganic and organic substances.

All the interacting organisms in an area together with the non-living constituents of the environment form an ecosystem. e.g., a lake, a field or a forest.

All biotic activities need energy for their existence such as plants, animals and humans all depend on the flow of energy among them. In an ecosystem both the matter and the energy are conserved.

Sun is the most significant source of energy for all ecosystems. The Sun radiates its energy in all directions and only a small portion of this energy is received by the Earth, which is utilised in different ways. Plants absorb most of the solar energy falling on them and produce their food by photosynthesis, so they are called **producers**.

Food Chain

It is a linear network of living organisms in a community through which energy is transferred in the form of food i.e., it describes relationship of organisms about 'who eats whom'. The food prepared by plants is transferred to different organisms through food chain.

Types of Food Chains

The choice of habitat classifies food chains into following two parts

(i) **Terrestrial Food Chain**

It is the food chain present on land.

e.g., Grass → Insect → Snake → Hawk

(ii) **Aquatic Food Chain**

It is the food chain in different water bodies.

e.g., Phytoplankton → Zooplankton→ Fish → Shark.

The simplest food chains operating in nature are represented in the figure below

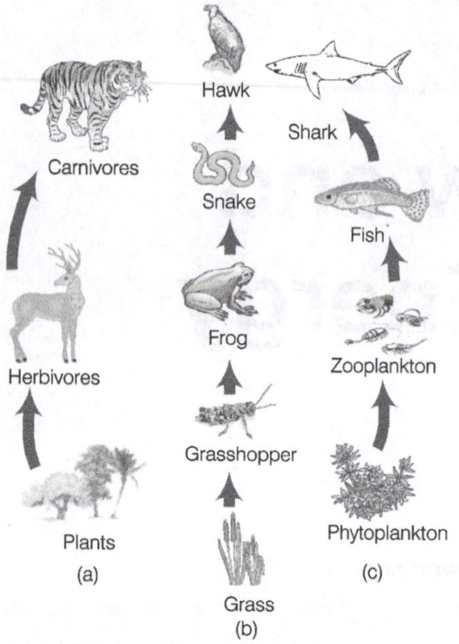

Food chains in nature (a) in forest, (b) in grassland and (c) in ocean

Trophic Levels

The transfer of food or energy takes place through various steps or levels in the food chain. These levels are known as trophic levels.

The producers (autotrophs) are at the **first trophic level**. They utilise the solar energy and make it available for consumers (heterotrophs). The herbivores or the primary consumers are at the **second trophic level,** small carnivores or secondary consumers are at the **third trophic level** and large or the tertiary consumers form the **fourth trophic level.**

Energy Flow in Trophic Levels

In an ecosystem, energy is accumulated by the primary producers and is transferred through food chain to different **trophic levels.** This phenomenon is called **energy flow.** It is linear or **unidirectional** and there is no recycling to previous level. The flow of energy in an ecosystem can be understood in the following steps

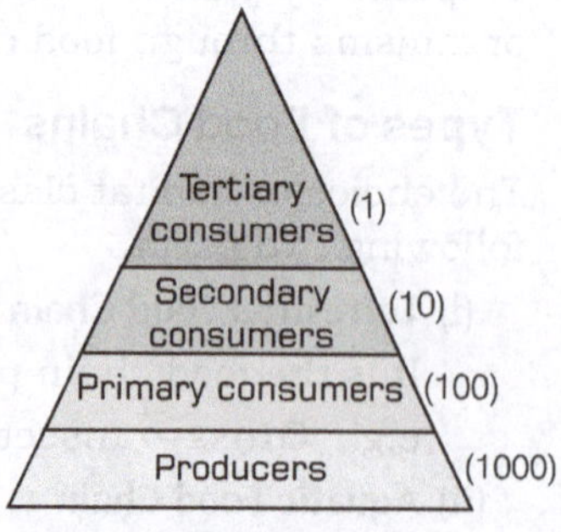

Trophic levels

- The green plants in a terrestrial ecosystem capture about 1% of the energy of sunlight that falls on their leaves and convert it into food energy.
- The green plants are then eaten by primary consumers, a major amount of energy is lost as heat and some amount of energy goes into digestion and in doing work and rest goes towards growth and reproduction. An average of 10% of the energy of food eaten is turned back into its own body and made available for the next level of consumers. This is known as the **10% law** (Lindeman; 1942).
- Therefore, 10% can be taken as the average value for the amount of organic matter i.e., present at each step and reaches to the next level of consumers.
- Since, only a little energy is available for the next level of consumers, food chains generally consist of three or four steps. The loss of energy at each step is very large. So, little usable energy remains after four trophic levels.

Food Web

It is the interconnection of different food chains, which correlate at various trophic levels operating in an ecosystem. Each organism is generally eaten by two or more other kinds of organisms which in turn are eaten by several other organisms. So, instead of a straight line food chain, the relationship can be shown as a series of branching lines creating a food web.

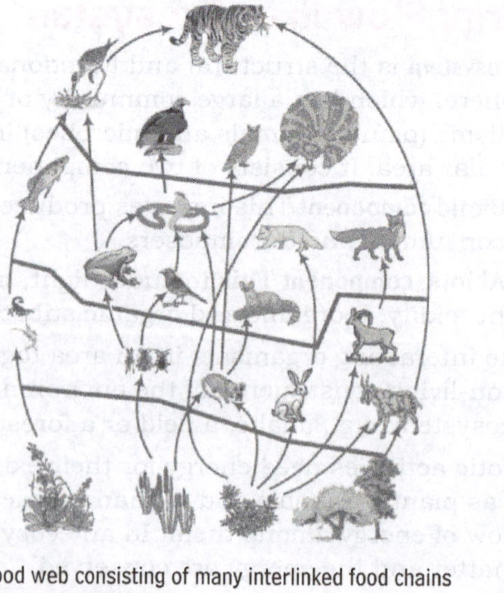

Food web consisting of many interlinked food chains

Applications of Laws of Thermodynamics in Energy Flow

The energy flow in an ecosystem is governed by the first and second laws of thermodynamics. The first law of thermodynamics states that energy can neither be created nor be destroyed, it is only transformed from one form to another. In an ecosystem, the solar energy is converted to chemical energy by plants during photosynthesis. This energy is transferred from herbivores to carnivores. The second law states that no energy transfer is 100% efficient.

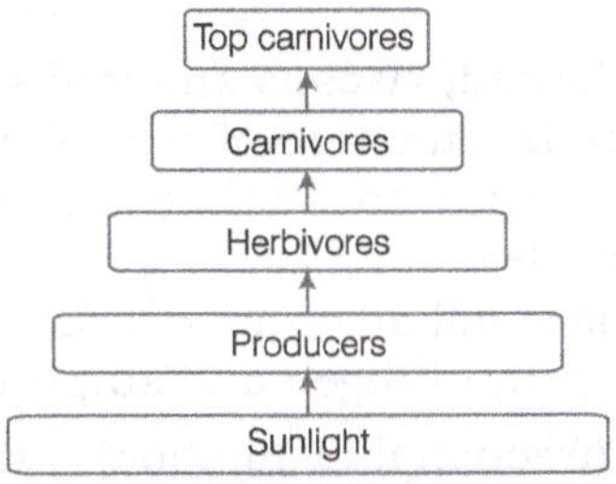

Flow of energy in an ecosystem

From the above diagram, it is clear that flow of energy is unidirectional. The energy that is captured by autotrophs, does not revert back to the solar input. Also, the energy which passes to the herbivores, does not come back to autotrophs. Thus, a portion of the transferred energy always changes to useful form in accordance with the second law of thermodynamics.

Check Your LEARNING...

1 Define ecosystem.
2 Write the components of ecosystem.
3 What is the most significant source of energy in ecosystem?
4 How many trophic levels are there in food chain?
5 Give an example of aquatic food chain.
6 How can you say that the flow of energy in ecosystem is linear?

Sources of Energy

A system which is capable of providing energy in a convenient form at a steady rate over a long period of time is called source of energy.

The different sources of energy are sun, wind, fossil fuels, energy from rivers (energy from falling water, run of the river), ocean (tides, waves, geothermal), nuclear energy, etc.

A good source of energy can be characterised by the following factors

(i) **Safe and Convenient to Use** Electricity and LPG are the most common, safe and easy to use sources of energy for household purposes. In the same time, nuclear energy can be used only by highly trained engineers with the help of nuclear power plants. Nuclear energy cannot be used for our household purposes.

(ii) **Easy to Transport** Coal, petrol, diesel, LPG, etc., can be easily transported from the places of their production to the consumers with the help of trucks and other vehicles.

(iii) **Easy to Store** LPG can be easily stored in a cylinder and can be kept in a home conveniently.

(iv) **Large Amount of Work per unit Volume or Mass** LPG is better resource than coal because more energy is generated by the same mass or volume of LPG than that of coal.

(v) **Economical** A good source of energy should give more amount of energy for lesser cost.

Classification of Sources of Energy

Different sources of energy can be classified as

(i) **Renewable Sources of Energy** These are those sources of energy which are being produced continuously in nature and are inexhaustible. These are also called **non-conventional** or **alternative source of energy.**

e.g., Solar energy, wind energy, hydro energy, bio-fuels (such as wood, bio-gas and alcohol), hydro energy from ocean (tidal energy, sea waves energy and ocean thermal energy).

Advantages of renewable sources of energy are given below

(a) These sources will last as long as the Earth receives light from the Sun.

(b) These sources are freely available in nature.

(c) These sources do not cause any pollution.

(ii) **Non-renewable Sources of Energy** These are those sources of energy which have been accumulated in nature over a long time and cannot be quickly replaced. These sources of energy will be exhausted one day. These are also called **conventional sources of energy.**

e.g., Fossil fuels such as coal, petroleum, natural gas and fissionable materials, etc.

Disadvantages of non-renewable sources of energy are given as below

(a) Due to their extensive use, these sources are depleting rapidly.
(b) It is difficult to discover and exploit new deposits of these sources.
(c) These sources are a major cause of environmental pollution.

Differences between the Renewable Sources of Energy and Non-renewable Sources of Energy

Renewable Sources	Non-renewable Sources
These are the sources of energy which are being produced continuously in nature.	These are the sources of energy which have been accumulated in nature over a long time and cannot be quickly replaced.
These are also called non-conventional sources of energy.	These are also called conventional sources of energy.
These sources are inexhaustible in nature.	These sources are exhaustible in nature.
These are pollution free.	These are the cause of pollution.
These sources can be regenerated.	These sources cannot be regenerated.

Non-Renewable Sources of Energy

Fossil Fuels

Fossil fuels are remain of prehistoric plants and animals which got buried deep inside the earth millions of years ago and changed into fuel due to excess heat and high pressure inside the earth.

The energy of fossil fuels is in fact the solar energy which was trapped by natural processes a very long time ago. Coal, petroleum and natural gas are the major fossil fuels which we are using today. The process of formation of fossil fuels is called **fossilisation.**

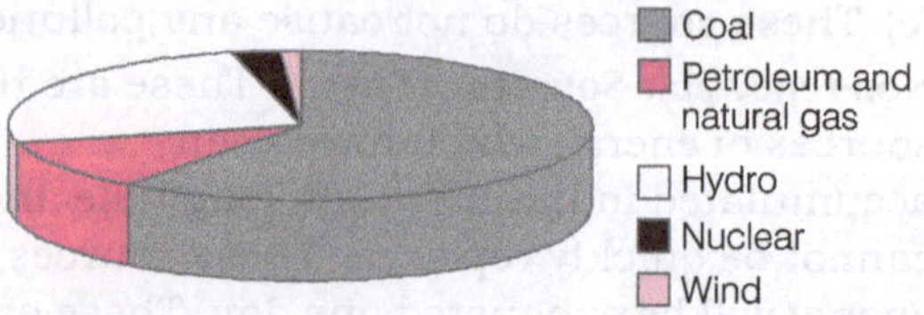

Pie-chart showing the major sources of energy for our requirements in India

Coal

It is a naturally occurring black material which is a mixture of carbon and compounds of carbon containing hydrogen, nitrogen, oxygen and sulphur. It is a major source of energy. It is found in coal mines.

Uses of coal are as follows

(i) It is used as a fuel for heating purposes in homes and in industry.
(ii) It is used as a fuel in thermal power plants for producing electricity.
(iii) It is used in the manufacturing of coke, fuel gases like coal gas, synthetic petrol and synthetic natural gas.
(iv) It is used to make coal tar.

Petroleum

It is a dark coloured, viscous and foul smelling crude oil which is a mixture of several solid, liquid and gaseous hydrocarbons mixed with water, salt and Earth particles.
It also contains small amounts of other compounds containing oxygen, nitrogen and sulphur.

After refining (fractional distillation) many major fractions are obtained such as petroleum gas, petrol, kerosene oil, diesel, lubricating oil, paraffin wax and bitumen (asphalt).

Uses of petroleum are as follows

(i) In transportation for running the vehicles.
(ii) In power stations, where diesel and gasoline are used in gas turbines to produce electricity.
(iii) For heating and lighting purposes.
(iv) As lubricants, for smooth running of all types of machines.
(v) Both petro-chemical and chemical industries uses petroleum byproducts as raw material.

Petroleum gas is a mixture of three hydrocarbons i.e. butane (C_4H_{10}), propane (C_3H_8) and ethane (C_2H_6). However, its main constituent is butane. If it is liquefied under pressure, then it is known as liquefied petroleum gas (LPG).

Characteristics of LPG are as follows

(i) It has very high calorific value and is neat and clean domestic fuel.
(ii) It burns with smokeless flame and thus does not cause pollution.
(iii) It does not produce any poisonous gas on combustion.
(iv) It is easy to handle and convenient to store in cylinders after mixing a strong smelling substance called ethyl mercaptan (C_2H_6SH), the leakage of this gas can be easily detected.

Natural Gas

It is an another source of heat energy. It mainly consists of methane (CH_4) (about 97%) and small quantities of ethane (C_2H_6) and propane (C_3H_8).

Uses of natural gas are as follows

(i) When natural gas in liquid form is subjected to high pressure, we get Compressed Natural Gas (CNG) which is used as fuel in vehicles like cars, buses and trucks. It is a good alternative to petrol and diesel because it does not cause any air pollution. It is an eco-friendly fuel.

(ii) It is used for cooking food, heating water, manufacturing fertilisers and to produce electricity.

Disadvantages of Fossil Fuels

The disadvantages of fossil fuels are as follows

(i) These are non-renewable sources of energy and once used cannot be renewed.

(ii) The fossil fuel reserved in the Earth are limited and may get exhausted soon.

(iii) Burning of fossil fuels releases acidic oxides which lead to acid rain which affects our water and soil resources.

(iv) Greenhouse gases like CO_2 (carbon dioxide) are released on burning of fossil fuels and causes air pollution.

(v) Fossil fuels are not burnt completely. They leave ashes after burning.

Note New reserves of fossil fuels are not being formed now because the necessary conditions for them, do not exist any more. So, fossil fuels are classified as non-renewable sources of energy.

Controlling of Pollution Caused by Fossil Fuels

The pollution caused by burning of fossil fuels can be reduced by increasing the efficiency of the combustion process. It can also be done by using various techniques to reduce the escape of harmful gases and ashes into the surroundings. Along with the direct use of fossil fuels for various purposes like cooking and transport, these are majorly used for generating electricity.

Note

- In thermal power plant, fossil fuels are burnt everyday to produce heat energy, which is converted into electrical energy.
- Carbon tax is a tax which is levied on the carbon content of fuels.

Check Your LEARNING...

1. What does it mean that a source of energy is renewable or non-renewable?
2. What is difference between petroleum gas and natural gas?
3. Natural gas is preferred over petrol or diesel, why?
4. Why should we avoid the use of fossil fuels as sources of energy?

Renewable Sources of Energy

Energy from Falling Water

The kinetic energy of flowing water or the potential energy of water at height is a traditional source of energy. The power plants which convert the potential energy of flowing water into electricity are called hydro power plants. Electricity being produced by these power plants is called **hydroelectricity.**

Flowing water possesses kinetic energy, which can be used to rotate the blades of a turbine. The turbine rotates the shaft of a generator to which it is connected and this generates the electricity.

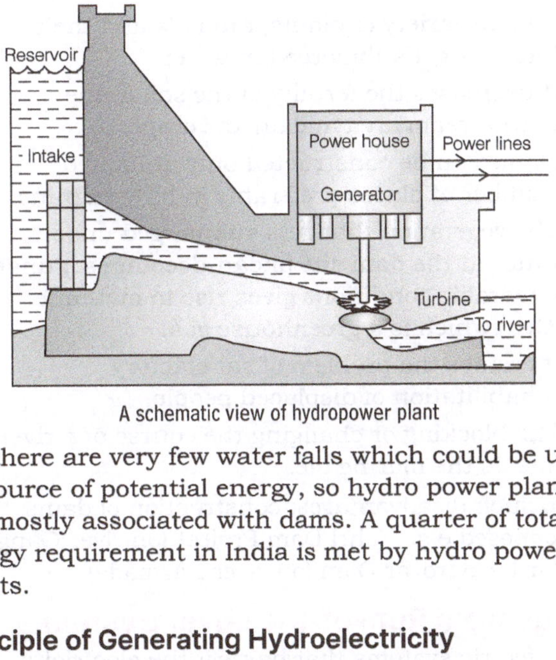

A schematic view of hydropower plant

As, there are very few water falls which could be used as source of potential energy, so hydro power plants are mostly associated with dams. A quarter of total energy requirement in India is met by hydro power plants.

Principle of Generating Hydroelectricity

The water flowing in a river is collected in a high rise dam, constructed on the river to obstruct the flow of water.

Since, water is collected at a significant height above the ground level, the **kinetic energy** of flowing water is converted into **potential energy**. This potential energy of stored water in a dam is then converted into kinetic energy of flowing water. The water from the high level is carried through the pipes to turbine located near the bottom of the dam, which is connected to the electric generator. When the water turbine rotates, then the armature of the generator also rotates rapidly and generates electricity.

Advantages of Hydroelectricity

The advantages of hydroelectricity are as follows

(i) It does not cause any environmental pollution.
(ii) The moving water needed for the purpose is available free of cost.
(iii) Water is a renewable source, which will never get exhausted. Each time when it rains, reservoir of dams gets refilled.
(iv) The construction of dams on rivers also helps in controlling floods and in irrigation.

Disadvantages of Hydroelectricity

The disadvantages of hydroelectricity are as follows

(i) Construction of dams may lead to ecological damage.
(ii) A large variety of plants, animals and their habitats get submerged in water.
(iii) It decreases the fertility of the soil in the downstream area and affects crops.
(iv) Dams can be constructed only at limited number of places preferably in hilly terrains.
(v) The vegetation that gets submerged under water at the dam site (mean-decompose) under anaerobic conditions gives rise to methane (CH_4) which is a greenhouse gas.
(vi) It creates the problem of satisfactory rehabilitation of displaced people.
(vii) The blocking or changing the course of a river affects the marine life.

Due to such disadvantages, construction of dams were opposed e.g., Tehri Dam Project (on river Ganga) and Sardar Sarovar Dam (on river Narmada).

Energy from Run-of-the-River System

Hydroelectric systems that harvest the electricity from flowing water in rivers to generate electricity in the absence of a large dam or reservoir are called **run-of-the-river system**.

Water from a river is guided down to the electricity generating house through a penstock. Here, the running water drives a turbine, running a generator to produce electricity. This used water is then fed back to the river downstream.

Advantages

Advantages of run-of-the-river system are as follows

(i) Run-of-the-river hydroelectric plants do not have reservoirs, thus there is no emission of methane by the decomposition of organic matter, as in the reservoir of conventional hydropower plants.
(ii) The people living near the river and existing habitats are not flooded as there is no reservoir.

Disadvantages

Disadvantages of run-of-the-river system are as follows

(i) The amount of power generated depends on the flow speed of river and is less during dry summer and freezing winter months.
(ii) Availability of sites for this type of power generation is less.

Bio-mass

The waste material of living things such as cattle dung and dead remains of plants and animals which are used as a source of energy is called bio-mass. It has been a traditional source of energy e.g., wood, crop residue, bagasse (residue of sugarcane after extracting juice) and cow-dung cake are used as fuels for domestic as well as industrial uses. Bio-mass is also utilised to generate electricity. The energy obtained from bio-mass is called **bio-energy**.

Bio-gas

It is a mixture of methane, hydrogen sulphide, carbon dioxide and hydrogen. It is produced by the decomposition of animal waste like animal dung or plant waste in the absence of oxygen (such degradation of organic matter in absence of oxygen is called **anaerobic degradation**).

Since, the starting material is mainly cow-dung, due to this it is popularly known as **gobar gas**.

Composition of Bio-gas

(i) Methane (CH_4) → 65-75% (combustible)
(ii) Carbon dioxide (CO_2) → 20-30% (non-combustible)
(iii) Hydrogen sulphide (H_2S) → traces (combustible)
(iv) Hydrogen (H_2) → 5-10% (combustible)
(v) Nitrogen (N_2) → 2-6% (non-combustible)

Bio-gas Plant

The set up used to produce bio-gas is known as **Bio-gas plant**. This plant has a dome-like structure built with bricks.

The main components of bio-gas plant are shown in the figure below.

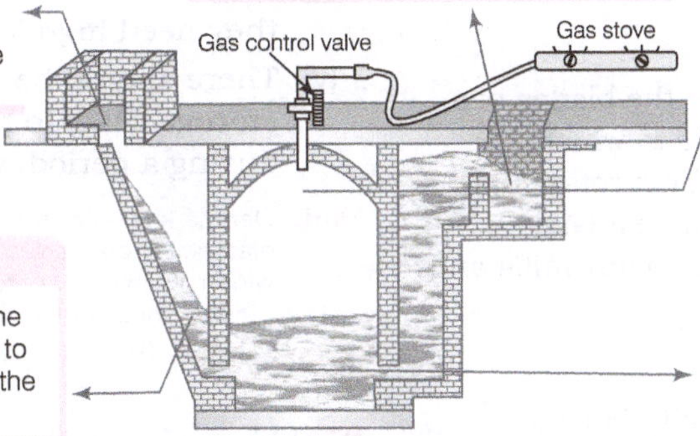

Fixed dome type bio-gas plant

Advantages of Bio-gas

The advantages of bio-gas are as follows

(i) It burns without smoke, therefore causes less pollution.

(ii) Its **calorific value** is high and also used for lighting.

(iii) It is convenient to use and leaves no residue (called a **clean fuel**).

(iv) It gives an excellent method to dispose off wastes which would otherwise create pollution.

(v) The large scale utilisation of bio-waste and sewage material provides a safe and efficient method of waste disposal besides supplying energy and manure.

(vi) It can be supplied directly through pipes.

Note : Calorific value is the heat energy present in the food or fuel. It is determined by the complete combustion of the quantity in food or fuel

Uses of Bio-gas

The uses of bio-gas are as follows

(i) It is used as domestic fuel for cooking as well as in industries.

(ii) It is used to run engines and pumping sets.

(iii) It is used for generating electricity.

Wind Energy

Moving air is called **wind**. As, moving objects possess kinetic energy, so they are capable of doing mechanical work by virtue of their motion. The energy possessed by the wind is due to its high speed.

The Sun rays falling on earth heat different areas of Earth unequally. Due to this uneven heating and rotation of Earth, local convection currents are generated which causes wind to blow.

The kinetic energy of wind is utilised for doing works like

(i) generating electricity

(ii) propelling sail boats in rivers and seas

(iii) in water-lifting pump to pump out water from ground

(iv) grinding grain to obtain flour

(v) rotatory motion of windmill is used to lift water from a well

Windmill

It is a machine which works with the energy of blowing air or wind. It is a structure similar to a large electric fan i.e. erected at some height on a rigid support.

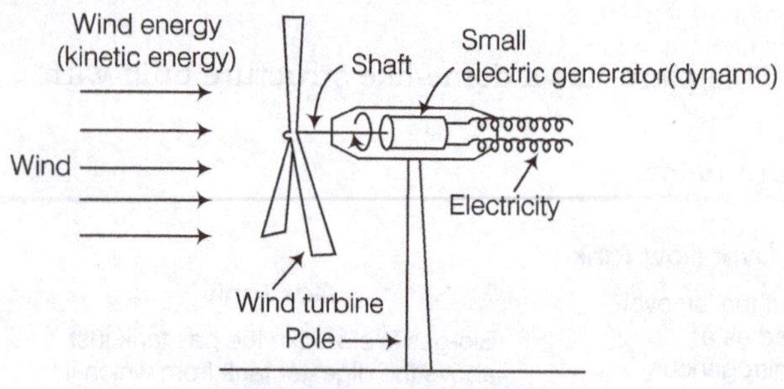

Windmill generating electricity

Principle of Windmill

When the blowing wind strikes across the blades of a windmill, it exerts a force on them due to which, the blades of the windmill start rotating. This rotational motion of the blades can be used to drive a large number of machines like water pumps, flour mills and electric generators.

Wind Generator

Windmill used for generating electricity is called **wind turbine** and the complete set up of generating electricity by using wind energy is called **wind generator.** The wind rotates the blades of a wind turbine which in turn rotates the armature or coil of a small electric generator or dynamo to produce electricity.

Wind Energy Farm

For commercial purposes, a large number of windmills are erected over a large area which is known as wind energy farm. The energy output of each windmill in a farm is coupled together to get electricity on a commercial scale. The wind power potential of India is estimated to be 45000 MW. The largest wind energy farm in India is established near Kanyakumari in Tamil Nadu and can generate 380 MW electricity.

Advantages of Wind Energy

The advantages of wind energy are as follows

(i) It is an environment-friendly and efficient source of renewable energy.

(ii) It requires no recurring expenses for the production of electricity.

(iii) It does not cause any pollution.

Limitations of Harnessing Wind Energy

The limitations of harnessing wind energy are as follows

(i) It can be established only at those places, where wind blows for most of the time of a year.

(ii) The minimum wind speed necessary for satisfactory working of a wind generator is 15 km/h i.e. not always so.

(iii) Wind energy farm requires quite large area of land i.e. nearly 2 hectares land is needed for 1 MW generation of electricity.

(iv) The setting up of wind energy farm is very expensive.

(v) As, the tower and blades are exposed to vagary of nature like rain, Sun, storm and cyclone, they need high level of maintenance.

(vi) There should be some back up facilities (like storage cells) to take care of the energy needs during a period, when there is no wind.

Note Denmark is called the country of winds. More than 25% of their electricity needs are generated through a vast network of windmills. In terms of total output, Germany is the leader while India is ranked fifth in harnessing wind energy for the production of electricity.

Check Your LEARNING...

1 What is the principle of generating hydroelectricity?
2 Write any one negative impact of a hydropower plant on the ecosystem.
3 By which process, bio-gas is produced in a plant?
4 How does bio-gas plant help to reduce the problem of pollution?
5 What is the minimum wind speed necessary for satisfactory working of windmill?

Solar Energy

It is the energy obtained from the Sun. It provides us heat and light. The nuclear fusion reaction taking place inside the Sun keeps on liberating enormous amount of heat and light energy.

A little less than half (47%) of solar energy which falls on the top of the atmosphere reaches the Earth's surface, the rest is refracted back to the space.

Note Solar radiations consist mostly of ultraviolet rays, visible rays and infrared rays. The amount of solar energy received by the earth's surface of 1 m^2 area in one second is called **solar constant**. The value of **solar constant** is 1.34 kJ/m^2s or 1.34 kW/m^2.

Solar Energy in India

India receives solar energy for greater part of the year. In a year, India receives the energy equivalent to more than 5000 trillion kWh. Here, the daily average varies from 4 to 7 kWh/m^2 under clear (cloudless) sky conditions.

Advantages of Solar Energy

The advantages of solar energy are as given below

(i) It does not cause any pollution.
(ii) It is available in abundance in a hot country like ours.
(iii) It is available free of cost.

Limitations of Solar Energy

The limitations of solar energy are as given below

(i) Energy reaching the surface is very much diffused, so direct utility is limited.
(ii) It is not available uniformly all the time and at all the places.
(iii) It is not available at night.
(iv) It is not available on a cloudy day.

Solar Energy Devices

The various devices which are commonly used for harnessing solar energy are called solar energy devices.
e.g., Solar cooker, solar panel and solar cell.

Solar Cell

It is a device which converts solar energy into electrical energy. These cells are made from semiconductors like silicon and germanium. It has the advantage that it is environment-friendly and is also available in abundance but availability of special grade silicon for making solar cell is limited. These cells are also known as **photovoltaic cells.**

Solar cells have no moving parts, require little maintenance and work without the use of any focussing device. This is chief advantage of solar cells. These can be set up in remote and inaccessible places easily, where power transmission is expensive and not commercially viable of solar cell.

Uses of Solar Cells

The uses of solar cells are as given below

(i) It is used in street lighting, traffic signals, water pumps, etc.
(ii) It provides electricity to light houses situated in sea.
(iii) It provides radio and TV transmission to remote areas.
(iv) It is used to operate electronic watches and calculators.
(v) It provides electricity in artificial satellites and space probes like mars orbiters use solar cells as the main source of energy.
(vi) Calculators and many toys are fitted with solar cells.

Solar Panel

When solar cells are arranged side-by-side, connecting each other in such a way that, the total potential difference and the total capacity to provide electric current is much increased, then this arrangement is called solar panel. It provides a much higher power for many practical uses. But the silver required for connecting the solar cells into a panel make this process expensive.

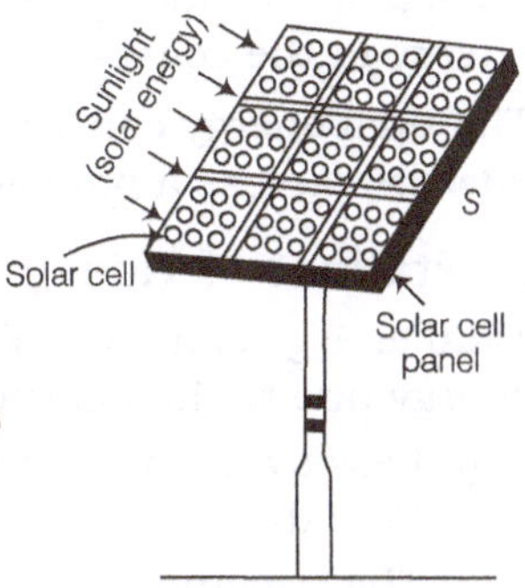

A solar cell panel

Solar Power Plant

It is a device in which heat energy of the sun is used to generate electricity. The principle of solar power plant is that the rays coming from Sun are reflected by a large concave mirror and get concentrated at its focus. These rays contain sufficient energy which can boil water.

A solar power plant consists of a big concave reflectors at their focus, there are water pipes which are painted by black colour. These reflectors concentrate the Sun rays on the pipes that contain water. Due to heat energy of these rays, water starts boiling and steam is generated. Thus, the steam produced helps in rotating the turbine which drives the electric generator. Hence, electricity is produced.

Energy from the Sea

Sea acts as a **renewable source** of energy. The energy from sea is available in different forms. These are explained as below.

Tidal Energy

Due to attraction of moon on sea water, water surface rises and falls, thus the waves are formed. These waves are called **tidal waves** and energy possessed by rising and falling water tides is known as **tidal energy.**

The rise of sea water due to **gravitational pull** of the Moon is called **high tide,** whereas the fall of sea water is called **low tide**. The tidal waves in the sea build up and recede (rise and fall) twice a day.

The enormous movement of water between the high tides and low tides provides a very large source of energy in the coastal areas of the world.

The tidal energy can be harnessed by constructing a **tidal dam** across a narrow opening to the sea.

Limitations of Tidal Energy

Tidal energy is not considered as major source of energy due to the following reasons

(i) Less availability of suitable sites for building tidal dams.

(ii) The rise and fall of sea water during tides is not enough to generate electricity on a large scale.

Wave Energy

Due to the blowing of wind on the surface of ocean very fast sea waves are generated, which have a lot of **kinetic energy** in them.

This energy with the help of various devices can be used to rotate the generator of turbine and electricity is generated.

Wave energy would be a viable preposition only, where waves are very strong.

Ocean Thermal Energy

The water at the surface of the sea or ocean is heated by the Sun, while the water in deeper sections is relatively cold. This difference in temperature is exploited to obtain energy and is known as ocean thermal energy.

The devices used to harness this form of ocean energy are known as **Ocean Thermal Energy Conversion** (OTEC) power plants.

Geothermal Energy

The heat from interior of the earth can be utilised as a source of energy under certain favourable conditions that are created by natural processes. This is known as geothermal energy. It is one of the sources of energy which does not come directly or indirectly from solar energy.

Molten rocks formed in the deeper hot regions of the Earth's crust are pushed upward and trapped in certain regions due to geological changes. These spots are called **hot spots.**

Underground water, when coming in contact of hot spots, gets converted into **steam** due to heat of **molten rocks** (magma) and remains trapped between the rocks, at high pressure. This steam can be used to run turbines connected to electric generators.

Some places where geothermal energy is harnessed; USA, New Zealand, India (Madhya Pradesh).

Energy from Waste

This is the generation of energy in the form of heat or electricity from waste. Each month millions of tonne of waste is produced. Either they become a part of landfill or are exported to third world countries causing huge environmental impact in terms of wild life, ecosystem and to human health. Thus, to cope up with this various technologies aiming, to compress and dispose waste, while attempting the generation of energy from them are being used.

These methods are classified into two categories

(i) **Thermal technologies**

It consists of following methods

(a) **Depolymerisation** In this method, organic compounds are heated at high temperature in presence of water.

(b) **Gasification** It converts carbonaceous substance into CO and some amount of H. The end product is called **synthesis gas** and is considered as a good means of alternate energy.

(c) **Pyrolysis** It employs agricultural waste or organic waste from industries. This process is conducted at high temperature without the use of oxygen.

(d) **Plasma arc Gasification** In this method, a plasma torch is used to ionise gas and thereafter obtain synthesis gas. This process generates electricity while compressing the waste.

(ii) **Non-thermal Technologies** It consists of the methods of anaerobic digestion. In this method, microorganisms are used to destroy the bio-degradable content in the absence of oxygen. This method is widely used at both domestic and commercial levels.

Check Your LEARNING...

1 Why is solar energy considered renewable?

2 Why is the solar cooker box covered with a glass sheet?

3 A solar cell transforms energy of one form into another form. What are these two forms of energy?

4 What is a solar panel?

5 What are the causes of tidal energy?

6 What are the end products of the method of gasification which is a good means of alternate energy?

Nuclear Energy

Energy contained in the nucleus of atom is called **nuclear energy**. It is released during nuclear reaction.

A reaction in which composition of the reacting nuclei changes to form new elements with a simultaneous release of large amount of energy is called a **nuclear reaction**.

Nuclear reactions occur in the following two ways

1. Nuclear Fission

The reaction in which a heavy nucleus splits into two or more smaller nuclei with the evolution of large amount of energy, when it is bombarded with slow moving neutron is called **nuclear fission reaction**.

The fission of an atom of uranium produces 10 million times the energy produced by the combustion of an atom of carbon from coal.

Energy Released in Fission Reactions

In all fission reactions, a small quantity of matter is lost. This lost matter gets converted into energy which is released in any nuclear fission reaction.

The energy (E) obtained due to loss of matter of mass (Δm) is given by the following famous Einstein's equation.

$$E = \Delta mc^2$$

where, c = velocity of light = 3×10^8 m/s.

Nuclear Reactor

It is a device in which nuclear fission can be carried out through a sustained and controlled chain reaction.

Nuclear reactor energy is used to generate steam, which operates on a turbine and turns an electric generator.

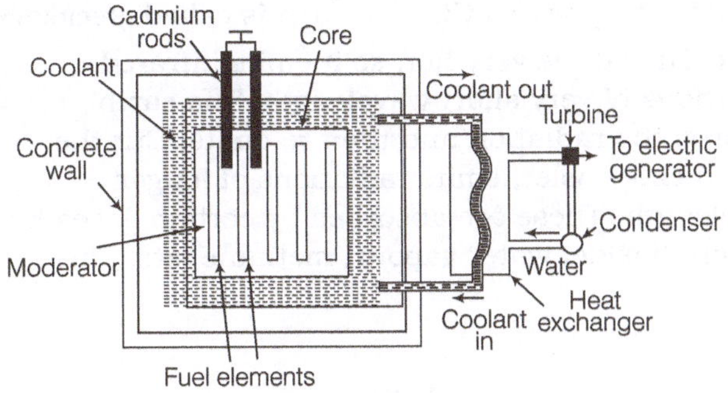

Nuclear power plant

Working

By adjusting **control rods,** the chain reaction can be controlled.

Neutrons produced by α-particle action on polonium
↓
Neutrons slowed down and start fission of $_{95}U^{235}$
↓
Fast neutrons released slowed down by moderator
↓
Again, the neutrons slow down and hence produces fission of $_{92}U^{235}$, thus chain reactions build up

As **water** is used as coolant as well as **moderator.**

Hence,

Coolant takes up the heat produced in the nuclear fission → Passes to water in heat exchanger → Superheated steam is produced → Drives a turbine coupled with an electric generator → From turbine, low pressure steam cooled → Condensed to water → Forced back to steam generator

Uses of Nuclear Reactor

(i) In electric power generation.

(ii) To produce radioactive isotopes for their use in medical, science, agriculture and industry.

(iii) In manufacturing of Pu^{239} which is used in atom bomb.

2. Nuclear Fusion

A reaction in which two or more lighter nuclei fuse to form a heavy nucleus and large amount of energy is released is called nuclear fusion reaction.

Nuclear fusion reaction is responsible for Sun's energy. In the interior of the Sun, two nuclei of hydrogen fuse to form helium and releases large amount of energy in the process.

Conditions for fusion reaction to take place are as given below

(i) High temperature (~ 4-15 million kelvin)

(ii) High pressure (~ 1 million atmosphere)

Because these reactions require a very high temperature, therefore they are called **thermonuclear reactions.**

Hydrogen Bomb

The hydrogen bomb is based on **thermonuclear fusion reaction.** A nuclear bomb based on the fission of uranium or plutonium is placed at the core of the hydrogen bomb. This nuclear bomb is embedded in a substance which contains deuterium and lithium. When the nuclear bomb (based on fission) is detonated, then the temperature of this substance is raised to 10^7 K in a few microseconds. The high temperature generates sufficient energy for the light nuclei to fuse and a devastating amount of energy is released.

Merits of Nuclear Energy

Some merits of nuclear energy are as follows

(i) A tremendous amount of energy can be produced by a very small amount nuclear fuel.

(ii) Nuclear fuel continues to release energy for a long period of time.

Hazards of Nuclear Power Generation

The major hazards of nuclear power generation are as follows

(i) Storage and disposal of spent/used fuels and the uranium continuously decaying into harmful subatomic particles is a big problem.

(ii) Improper nuclear-waste storage and disposal may lead to environmental contamination.

(iii) There is also a risk of nuclear accidents causing due to leakage of nuclear radiation.

Environmental Consequences

We have seen that the exploitation of any energy source causes harm to the environment and its balance. However, the degree of damage caused by the **non-conventional sources** of energy is very less as compared to **fossil fuels**. Hence, it becomes the moral responsibility of every common man on the Earth to look upto the cleanest possible sources of energy.

The environmental consequences of the increasing demand for energy are as follows

(i) The combustion of fossil fuels is producing acid rain and damaging plants (crops), soil and aquatic life.

(ii) The burning of fossil fuels is increasing the amount of greenhouse gas, carbon dioxide in the atmosphere.

(iii) The cutting down of trees from the forest (deforestation) for obtaining fire-wood is causing soil erosion and destroying wildlife.

(iv) The construction of hydro power plants is disturbing ecological balance.

(v) Nuclear power plants are increasing radioactivity in the environment.

Energy Degradation

According to the law of conservation of energy, "energy is neither created nor destroyed, but it is transformed from one form to another". This means, there is 100% transformation of energy in the required final form. But in practice, it has been observed that this transformation is not 100%, rather there is a certain part of energy that gets transformed into some other undesirable form, e.g., sound, heat, etc.

As, this part of energy is not available for productive use, hence it is known as **degraded form of energy.**

Some examples of energy degradation are

(i) When electrical appliances are running with the help of electricity, some part of energy gets converted into heat energy, etc.

(ii) When food is cooked over fire, major part of heat energy is radiated in the atmosphere which is of no use to us.

(iii) No machine gives full efficiency. It means that only a fraction of input energy is used for doing work and rest is get wasted.

Greenhouse Effect

The heating of atmosphere due to the infrared radiation trapped by CO_2 on earth is called **greenhouse effect**. The sun is very hot, so it emits infrared radiations of very short wavelength. The earth absorbs the radiation and then re-emits. But the earth being cooler, emits radiations of longer wavelength. These are absorbed by certain gases like carbon dioxide, water vapour, methane, etc. This effect is called greenhouse effect and the gases are called **greenhouse gases**.

These are carbon dioxide, methane, nitrous oxide, ozone, chlorofluorocarbons (CFCs) etc. They are responsible for heating up of the atmosphere. These gases act like a mirror and reflect back the radiation to the earth.

Higher the concentration of greenhouse gases, the more radiation is being reflected back to the earth. These gases have a average warming effect of nearly 33°C, so that the average temperature on earth's surface is about 15.5°C (or 60°F). If these gases are absent from the earth's atmosphere, the entire heat energy will be radiated in space and then the average temperature on earth would be – 18 °C.

Global Warming

The increase in the average effective temperature near the earth's surface due to an increase in the amount of greenhouse gases in its atmosphere is called global warming.

An increase in average temperature of the earth implies further increase in the amount of greenhouse gases present in its atmosphere, so that they could trap more heat from earth's surface.

Causes of Global Warming

The increase in concentration of greenhouse gases due to various human activities like burning of fossil fuels, industrial growth, clearing of forests, use of automobiles, etc are the main causes of global warming.

Impact of Global Warming in Life on the Earth

Present Consequences

(i) The change in regional climate which has an immediate effect on simple organism and plants.
(ii) The variable changes in the climate in different parts of the world has created difficulties and forced the people and animal to migrate from one place to the other.
(iii) The change in blooming season of different plants.
(iv) The change in the world's ecology.
(v) The increase in the heat stroke deaths.

Future Consequences

With the present rate of increase in the temperature, it is predicted that the average temperature of Earth's surface will become 64°C by the end of the year 2100.
Such a rise in the temperature of the earth might result in

(i) Dislocation and disappearance of plant and animal species.
(ii) Warming of ocean.
(iii) Melting of glaciers and increase in the water level of ocean.
(iv) Shifting in farming region.
(v) Increase in new diseases and health related deaths.
(vi) Changing in regional climate.
(vii) Variable change in the climate.
(viii) Increase in cost of air conditioning.

Ways to Minimise the Impact of Global Warming

To minimise the impact of global warming the following three main measures must be taken.

(i) **Technological Measures** The economic growth and population growth increase the consumption of fuel and hence both are responsible for the release of greenhouse gases. Following are the technological measures
   (a) Use of renewable sources of energy.
   (b) Change of transportation vehicles.
   (c) Use of biochar stoves for cooking.
(ii) **Economic Measures** These arise because of growing industries and deforestation which increase the greenhouse effect. Following economic measures are needed
   (a) Reforestation and sustainable use of land.
   (b) Industries to pay carbon tax.
(iii) **Policy Measures** To check global warming, following are the policy measures taken by government.
   (a) Educating children to live sustainable life style.
   (b) Controlling population.

Check Your LEARNING...

1 What is nuclear fission? Explain with an example.
2 What is nuclear fusion? Explain with an example.
3 Give an example for energy degradation.
4 Which gas is responsible for greenhouse effect?
5 What is meant by global warming?

QUiCK Revision

- **Renewable Sources of Energy** These are the sources of energy which can be reused with their utilisation.
- **Non-Renewable Sources of Energy** Those sources of energy which cannot be reused practically.
- The main source of energy on the Earth is the Sun which has been radiating an enormous amount of energy for nearly 5 billion years and will continue radiating at the same rate for about more than 5 billion years.
- The energy can be harnessed from flowing water, wind, tides bio-gas, nuclear, etc.
- **Greenhouse Effect** It is a natural process in which greenhouse gases trap heat radiated back from earth's surface.
- **Global Warming** It means the increase in the average temperature of the earth and its atmosphere. It happens due to greenhouse effect.

Chapter Practice

Section I

1 Mark Questions

1. Which of the following is not a functional component of an ecosystem?
   (a) Communities (b) Decomposers
   (c) Sunlight (d) Energy flow

Sol. (*d*) The flow of energy is not a functional component of an ecosystem. Energy flow is a consequence of components functioning in an ecosystem.

2. Energy enters in a food chain through
   (a) producers
   (b) primary consumers
   (c) secondary consumers
   (d) tertiary consumers

Sol. (*a*) Energy enters in a food chain through producers which produces food for primary consumers.

3. Choose the incorrect statement regarding energy flow in an ecosystem.
   (a) In an aquatic ecosystem, photo-synthetic plants and bacteria act as producers.
   (b) Primary consumers are also known as carnivores.
   (c) The chemical energy stored in plants is called gross primary production.
   (d) The energy flow in ecosystem is linear.

Sol. (*b*) Primary consumers are herbivores while secondary and tertiary consumers are carnivores.

4. In a food chain, the snake predated a rabbit which feed on fresh green bushes. What percentage amount of the energy accumulated by rabbit, would be acquired by snakes?
   (a) 90% (b) 10%
   (c) 50% (d) 25%

Sol. (*b*) According to Lindeman's 10% energy law, only 10% of the energy is transferred from one trophic level to the next higher trophic level.

5. Which of the following is a non-renewable source of energy?
   (a) Wood (b) Sun
   (c) Fossil fuels (d) Wind

Sol. (*c*) Non-renewable sources of energy are those which are exhaustible and cannot be replaced, once they have been used. Non-renewable sources of energy are also known as conventional sources of energy. The fossil fuels are non-renewable sources of energy, whereas wood, the sun and wind are renewable sources of energy.

6. Which environmental hazard is not contributed by the combustion of fossil fuels?
   (a) Acid rain
   (b) Greenhouse effect
   (c) Destruction of wildlife habitat
   (d) Air pollution

Sol. (*c*) Combustion of fossil fuels does not lead to the destruction of wildlife habitat. However, hydroelectric power projects, acid rain, air pollution and greenhouse effect lead to devastation of wildlife habitat, soil erosion, man made floods, etc.

7. Acid rain happens because
   (a) sun leads to heating of upper layer of atmosphere
   (b) burning of fossil fuels results in the release the oxides of carbon, nitrogen and sulphur in the atmosphere
   (c) electrical charges are produced due to friction amongst clouds
   (d) the earth's atmosphere contains acids

Sol. (*b*) Acid rain happens because of several human activities of polluting the atmosphere. The emission of oxides of carbon, sulphur and nitrogen from the industries, burning of fossil fuels, etc., and also by the natural phenomena such as emission from volcanoes make the water vapour in the cloud more acidic thereby causing acid rain.

8. Fuel used in thermal power plants is
   (a) water (b) uranium (c) biomass (d) fossil fuel

Sol. (*d*) The thermal power plant generates electric power from heat produced by burning fossil fuels i.e. coal and petroleum. Everyday we burn large amount of fossil fuels to generate electricity.

9. In a hydro power plant,
   (a) potential energy possessed by stored water is converted into electricity
   (b) kinetic energy possessed by stored water is converted into potential energy
   (c) electricity is extracted from water
   (d) water is converted into steam to produce electricity

Sol. (*a*) In a hydro power plant, water from the top of the dam is allowed to fall through pipelines over the blades of a turbine at the bottom of the dam. In this process, the potential energy of water changes into its kinetic energy which is transferred to the turbine. The moving turbine rotates the armature of a generator to produce electricity i.e. turbine changes the kinetic energy into electricity. Thus, potential energy possessed by stored water is converted into electricity.

10. Which of the following is employed for harnessing the potential energy of surface water stored in a reservoir?
(a) Thermal power plant
(b) Nuclear power plant
(c) Tidal power plant
(d) Hydroelectric power plant

Sol. (*d*) In a hydroelectric power plant, the kinetic energy of flowing river water is first converted into potential energy. Huge amount of water is stored in a reservoir (dam) and finally, when the stored dam water flows downhill, the stored potential energy of water is harnessed in the form of electrical energy with the help of turbine.

11. Solar energy is the universal source of energy. It is converted into chemical energy by
(a) photovoltaic cells (b) solar cooker
(c) solar concentrators (d) green plants

Sol. (*d*) Solar energy is the universal source of energy that is used by all living organisms for their survival on the Earth. The green plants convert solar energy into chemical energy - food or biomass of plant, by the process of photo-synthesis.

12. Ocean thermal energy is due to
(a) energy stored by waves in the ocean
(b) temperature difference at different levels in the ocean
(c) pressure difference at different levels in the ocean
(d) tides arising out in the ocean

Sol. (*b*) The water at the surface of the sea or ocean is heated by the sun while the water in deeper sections is relatively cold. This difference in temperature between these layers ranging from 10°C to 30°C is exploited to obtain energy. Thus, ocean thermal energy is due to temperature difference at different levels in the ocean.

13. Which one of the following forms of energy leads to least environmental pollution in the process of its harnessing and utilisation?
(a) Nuclear energy (b) Thermal energy
(c) Solar energy (d) Geothermal energy

Sol. (*c*) Solar energy leads to least environmental pollution in the process of its harnessing and utilisation. In nuclear energy, emission of radiation is a high risk for environmental contamination.

In thermal energy, heat produced by burning fossil fuels causes huge environmental pollution. In geothermal energy, noise pollution is created by drilling operations at geothermal sites.

14. The major problem in harnessing nuclear energy is how to
(a) split nuclei
(b) sustain the reaction
(c) dispose of spent fuel safely
(d) convert nuclear energy into electrical energy

Sol. (*c*) The major hazard of nuclear power generation is the storage and disposal of spent or used fuels. Improper nuclear waste storage and disposal result in environmental contamination as well as risk of accidental leakage of nuclear radiation.

It happened in Chernobyl disaster 1986, Fukushima Nuclear disaster 2011 which caused great damage to the living beings and habitates.

2 Marks Questions

15. Give the names of two energy sources that you would consider to be exhaustible. Give reason for your choice.

Sol. Fossil fuels like coal and petroleum are exhaustible. The conditions that existed on the earth and led to their formation, no longer exist today. Thus, the rate at which they are used up today, will lead to their depletion soon.

16. Give any two disadvantages of fossil fuels.

Sol. (i) The fossil fuels are non-renewable sources of energy and once used cannot be renewed. [1]
(ii) Fossil fuels are not burnt completely. They leave ashes after burning. [1]

17. Explain, why fossil fuels are considered as non-renewable sources of energy?

Sol. Fossil fuels are considered as non-renewable sources of energy because they are exhaustible and cannot be replaced quickly.

18. Explain, how does burning of fossil fuels cause water pollution?

Sol. Burning of fossil fuels releases acidic oxides which leads to acid rain and causes water pollution by affecting the water resources.

19. Name two important hydroelectric power projects in India.

Sol. Two important hydroelectric power projects in India are
(i) Bhakra-Nangal Project (Satluj river) [1]
(ii) Hirakund Project (Mahanadi river) [1]

20. How does construction of dams across the river get linked with the production of greenhouse gases?

Sol. The vegetation which is submerged, rots in anaerobic condition and releases large amount of methane (CH_4) in nature which is a greenhouse gas.

21. Give the uses of inlet chamber in the bio-gas plant.

Sol. It connects the mixing tank and the digester tank. It has a slope to ensure smooth flow of slurry into the digester tank.

22. List two practical uses of bio-gas in rural areas.

Sol. The two practical uses of bio-gas in rural areas are as follows
(i) It is used for lighting.
(ii) It is an excellent cooking fuel which burns without smoke.

23. Bio-gas is considered to be a boon to the farmers. Give reasons.

Sol. Bio-gas is considered to be a boon to the farmers, because

(i) it is a source of excellent manure, rich in nitrogen and phosphorus. [1]

(ii) it provides a safe, efficient and profitable disposal method for bio-waste and sewage. [1]

24. What are the limitations of harnessing wind energy?

Sol. Following are the limitations of harnessing wind energy

(i) It can be established only at those places, where wind blows for most of the part of the year. [1]

(ii) The set up of wind farm is very expensive. [1]

25. Name any two energy sources that you would consider to be renewable. Give reasons for your choice.

Sol. Hydro power, as water is replenished by water cycle. Wind power, as wind keeps blowing due to uneven heating of the earth by the sun.

26. Expand OTEC. On which principle is it based?

Sol. The full form of OTEC is Ocean Thermal Energy Conversion. [1]

It is based on exploiting the temperature difference between upper and lower layers of the ocean to harness energy. [1]

27. Name the type of reaction in the sun which produces its energy. List two conditions which are present at the centre of the sun responsible for this reaction.

Sol. Nuclear fusion reaction is responsible for the sun's energy. [1]

It is a reaction in which two nuclei of hydrogen fuse together to form helium under the conditions of high temperature and high pressure to release tremendous amount of energy. [½ + ½]

28. What is a nuclear waste? What are the hazards of nuclear waste to living things?

Sol. The byproducts obtained in a nuclear reaction are called nuclear wastes. These are radioactive wastes and emit radiations (α, β and γ) which may cause skin cancer and severe genetic disorders.

29. Why are we looking at alternative sources of energy?

Sol. We are looking at alternative sources of energy because the fossil fuels cannot be replenished and the rate, at which we are using them, will exhaust them soon.

To meet the rising demand, we have to develop alternative sources of energy.

30. What is energy degradation?

Sol. Refer to theory (Page 130).

31. Can any source of energy be pollution free? Why or why not?

Sol. No source of energy can be pollution free. If any source of energy is exploited or used, it causes environmental pollution. For example, CNG produces greenhouse gases such as carbon dioxide. Hydro power plants disturb the vegetation of that region and destroy the habitat of many plants and animals. The windmills disturb the rainfall pattern of the region. Manufacturing of solar cells also has environmental hazards associated with it.

32. List the causes of increasing energy requirement.

Sol. The causes of increasing energy requirement are

(i) Due to increase population, the number of users is increasing rapidly. Thus, the energy requirement has been increased. [1]

(ii) Improved technology which is more energy dependent. [1/2]

(iii) Increasing wastage of energy forces to exploit more and more sources of energy. [1/2]

33. Describe how ozone present in the atmosphere is important for sustaining life on earth.

Sol. Ozone layer is like a 'blanket' which keeps harmful radiation out and shields the earth from the sun's lethal ultraviolet radiation.

3 Marks Questions

34. Increasing demand of fossil fuels has caused harm to our environments. List its three side effects. Suggest three measures to reduce the consumption of fossil fuels.

Sol. The three side effects of burning fossil fuels are as given below

(i) Air pollution (ii) Global warming

(iii) Acid rain [1½]

The three measures to reduce the consumption of fossil fuels are as below

(i) controlling population.

(ii) using public transport instead of private vehicles.

(iii) using renewable sources of energy. [1½]

35. Why is there so much emphasis on changing over from petrol or diesel driven automobiles to CNG driven vehicles?

Sol. There is so much emphasis on changing over from petrol or diesel driven automobiles to CNG driven vehicles because of the following reasons.

(i) It does not produce smoke.

(ii) On burning CNG it produces CO_2 and water.

(iii) It does not leave unburnt hydrocarbons, lead particulates, etc., which pollute the environment. [1× 3]

36. Give three traditional uses of solar energy.

Sol. The three traditional uses of solar energy are as follows

(i) For drying clothes. [1]

(ii) For obtaining salt from sea water. [1]

(iii) For reducing moisture content in food grains after harvesting. [1]

37. What are the limitations of solar energy?

Sol. The limitations of solar energy are as follows

(i) Energy reaching on the surface of the earth is very much diffused. [1]

(ii) It is not available uniformly all the time and at all the places. [1]

(iii) It is not available in night and cloudy day. [1]

38. If energy in the universe is constant, why is the world yelling out for energy crisis? What does judicious use of energy imply?

Sol. The energy in the universe is constant. However, it is converted into non-usable forms and cannot be converted back into usable forms, it gets wasted. If all the energy available is in non-usable form, we will suffer the crisis for usable form of energy. [1½]

Judicious use of energy implies minimisation of wastage of energy by controlled use of the sources and enabling reuse of energy wherever possible e.g., banning the cutting of the trees, etc. [1½]

39. Describe the three limitations to harness energy from wind?

Sol. Refer to theory (Page 126). [3]

40. What human activities are responsible for the increase of the carbon dioxide?

Sol. Human activities responsible for the increase of the carbon dioxide are as follows

(i) The burning of fuels, deforestation, transportation and industrial production. [1]

(ii) Increase in population. [1]

(iii) Construction of hydro power plant, which is disturbing ecological balance. [1]

41. Plastic production is increasing day-by-day despite of the fact that plastic is harmful for the environment.

Based on the above statement, answer the following.

(i) What are the harmful effects of plastic usage?

(ii) In our day-to-day situation, what are the alternative that we can use instead of plastics?

(iii) What can we learn as a good citizen as in concern for this issue?

Sol. (i) Burning of plastics cause pollution. Plastics cause harm to the cattle/animals, if it enters inside their alimentary canal. [1]

(ii) Paper bags/jute bags can be used instead of plastic bag. [1]

(iii) Every citizen should be discouraged to use plastics as a source of packaging and storing as it is non-biodegradable. [1]

4 Marks Questions

42. Explain the principle, construction and working of hydro power plant.

Sol. Refer to theory (Page 123). [4]

43. Write a note on solar energy. Explain the process by which solar energy can be harnessed directly.

Sol. Refer to theory (Pages 126 and 127). [4]

44. Explain tidal energy, its harnessing and limitations.

Sol. Refer to theory (Pages 127 and 128). [4]

45. Explain the present consequences of global warming.

Sol. Refer to theory (Page 131). [4]

Section II

Structured Questions

46. (i) Hydro energy is an indirect source of solar energy. Justify. [3]

(ii) Write two different ways of harnessing energy from the ocean. [3]

(iii) What are the uses of LPG and natural gas? [4]

Sol. (i) Solar energy is manifested in many forms on the earth, one of which is hydro energy. During water cycle, water flowing in rivers and other water bodies evaporates by the heat of sun, condenses, moves back in upper atmospheric layers and gets replenished back. Thus, energy of flowing water is attributed to the sun. [3]

(ii) The energy can be harnessed from the ocean in the following ways

(a) **Tidal Energy** Due to the gravitational pull of the moon on the spinning of the earth, the level of water in the sea rises and falls, are called high and low tides that can be harnessed by constructing a dam across a narrow opening to the sea. [1½]

(b) **Ocean Thermal Energy** The water at the surface of the sea or ocean is heated by the sun while the water in deeper sections is relatively cold. This difference in temperature is exploited to obtain energy in ocean thermal energy conversion plants. [1½]

(iii) Refer to theory (Pages 122 and 123). [4]

47. (i) Write a short note on run-of-the-river scheme? [3]

(ii) Solar energy can be harnessed directly as well as indirectly. Give two examples of each type. [3]

(iii) Name and explain the methods of generation of energy from waste. [4]

Sol. (i) Refer to theory (Page 124). [3]

(ii) Solar energy is used directly as heat or by converting it directly into electricity e.g., solar cooker (or solar water heater) and solar cell panels. [1½]

Solar energy is used indirectly by converting it into chemical energy (like bio-mass energy), harnessing the energy of wind, sea waves, tides and ocean thermal energy e.g., bio-gas plants and windmills. [1½]

(iii) Refer to theory (Page 128). [4]

48. (i) Write various advantages of bio-gas. [3]

(ii) What are the causes of global warming? [3]

(iii) Define the process of nuclear fission. Write the steps involved in generating electricity in a nuclear reactor. [4]

Sol. (i) Refer to theory (Pages 124 and 125). [3]

(ii) The cause of global warming is the increase in concentration of greenhouse gases in the atmosphere.

(a) The concentration of CO_2 has increased upto 25% due to industrial growth, combustion of fossil fuels, etc. [1]

(b) The concentration of methane has doubled due to agricultural sources such as rice cultivation, animal husbandry, natural gas exploration, burning of bio mass, etc. [1]

(c) The concentration of chloro-fluorocarbon has increased at a rate of 5% per year. [1]

(iii) The reaction in which a heavy nucleus splits into two or more smaller nuclei, with the evolution of large amount of energy, when it is bombarded with slow moving neutron is called nuclear fission.

The steps involved in generating electricity in a nuclear reactor are as follows [2]

(a) The controlled fission of uranium-235 in the nuclear reactor produces a lot of heat energy.

(b) Liquid sodium or CO_2 gas is pumped continuously through the pipes embedded in reactor. Sodium absorbs the heat energy produced in reactor.

(c) The hot sodium is then passed into the coil of heat exchanger containing water. The water absorbs heat from hot sodium and gets converted into steam.

(d) This steam at high pressure is used to rotate the turbine. The shaft of the turbine is connected to the electric generator. When turbine rotates, then its shaft also rotates and drives the generator. The generator, thus produces the electricity. [$1/2 \times 4$]

Chapter Assessment

1 Mark Questions

1. Food chain begins with
(a) respiration (b) photosynthesis
(c) decomposition (d) decay

2. Which of the following is a disadvantage of most of the non-renewable energy sources?
(a) High cost disposal of waste
(b) Unreliability of supply
(c) High running cost
(d) Highly polluting

3. Which of the following is not a greenhouse gas?
(a) CO_2 (b) NO_2 (c) SO_2 (d) CH_4

4. The increase of carbon dioxide gas in atmosphere will cause
(a) decrease in temperature (b) increase in temperature
(c) no change in temperature (d) increase in humidity

5. Which of the following is the result of global warming?
(a) Increase in yield of crops
(b) Decrease in sea levels
(c) Decrease in human deaths
(d) Increase in sea levels

2 Marks Questions

6. Hydro power plants are located near water channels. Give reasons.

7. What are the constituents of bio-gas?

8. When we harness wind energy, we harness solar energy indirectly. Explain, why?

9. What do you mean by waste to energy?

10. Define greenhouse effect.

Structured Questions

11. (i) Electricity generated by hydroelectric power stations are considered to be another form of solar energy. Explain. [3]
(ii) What are the needs to convert waste into energy? [3]
(iii) Explain the principle, construction and working of a bio-gas plant. [4]

12. (i) It is advantageous to convert bio-mass into a bio-gas rather than burning bio-mass directly. Explain, why? [3]
(ii) How greenhouse effect causes global warming? [3]
(iii) What are the expected future consequences of global warming ? [4]

For Solutions Scan the Code

Olympiad Section*

Brain Teasing Questions of Olympiad Pattern

1 Without greenhouse effect, the average temperature of the earth's surface would have been

(a) – 18° C (b) 33°C (c) 0°C (d) 15°C

2 The global warming has resulted in

(a) the increase in yield of crops
(b) the decrease in sea level
(c) the decrease in human deaths
(d) the increase in sea level

3 Which of the following is not a correct consequence of global warming on life on the earth?

(a) No change in blooming season of different plants
(b) The change in world's ecology
(c) Migration of people and animals due to variable changes in climate in different parts of the world
(d) The increase in the heat stroke deaths

4 During winters, we generally prefer to use vaseline. From which substance, do we get vaseline?

(a) Petroleum (b) Coal
(c) Gasoline (d) Kerosene

5 The diagram given below shows nuclear fission in U-235.

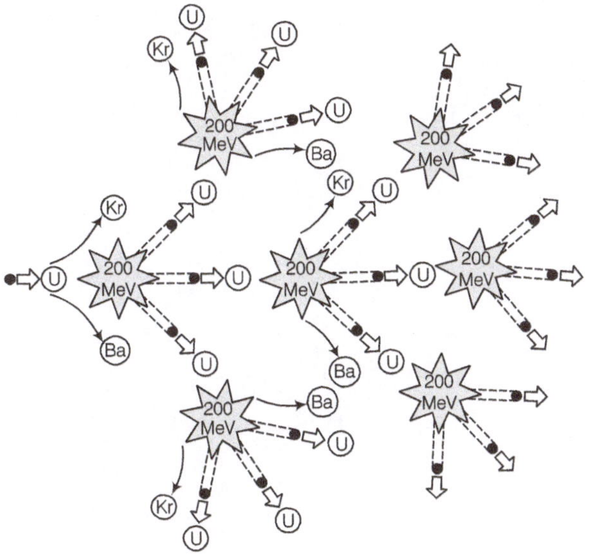

Which of the following observations is not true?

(a) Nuclear fission of uranium is a chain reaction
(b) Each uranium atom produces three more atoms of different kinds
(c) Each neutron splits into three more neutrons
(d) Large amount of energy is evolved during this reaction

6 A diagram of wind mill is given below. Each part is numbered *A*, *B*, *C* and *D*. What is the function of *B*?

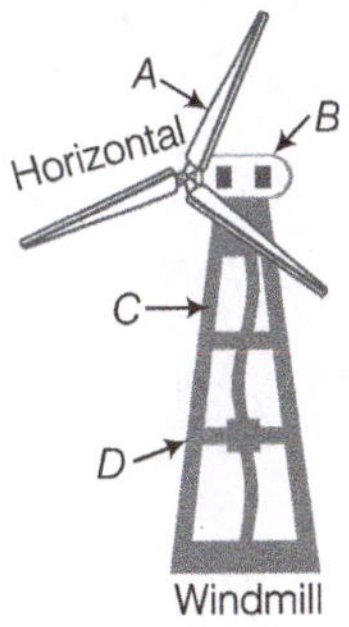

(a) To control the movement of blades
(b) To support the blades
(c) To generate electricity
(d) None of the above

7 In the diagram of solar cooker given below, name the missing part *X*.

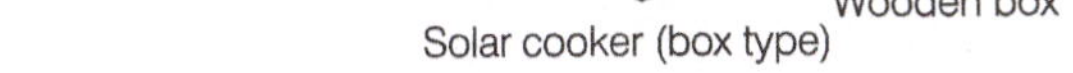

(a) Convex mirror
(b) Concave mirror
(c) Convex lens
(d) Plane mirror

8. A diagram of OTEC (Ocean Thermal Energy Conversion) system is given below. In which part water is converted into water vapours?

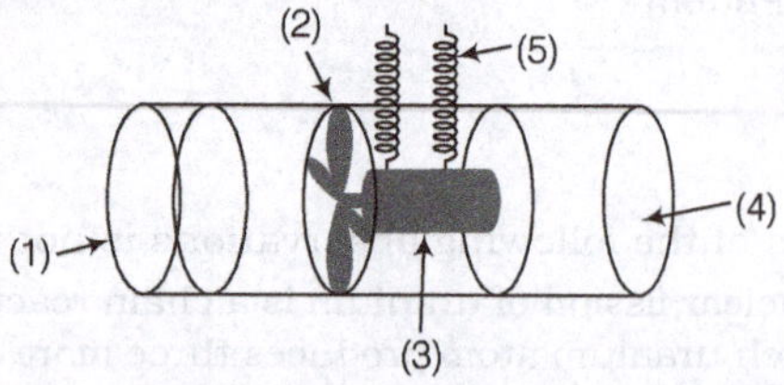

(a) 1 (b) 4 (c) 3 (d) 5

9. If the height of falling water is increased, then more electrical power can be generated in a hydro electric power plant. Why?

(a) More water molecules dissociate into ions.
(b) Temperature of water increases.
(c) Larger amount of potential energy is converted into kinetic energy.
(d) The electricity content of water increases with height.

10. Sugarcane plants are one of the most efficient converters of one form of energy to another form. What type of energy conversion takes place in sugarcane plant?

(a) Biochemical energy to mechanical energy.
(b) Solar energy to chemical energy.
(c) Chemical energy to solar energy.
(d) Solar energy to magnetic energy.

Answers **1.** (a) **2.** (d) **3.** (a) **4.** (a) **5.** (b) **6.** (b) **7.** (d) **8.** (a) **9.** (c) **10.** (b)

* *These questions may or may not be asked in the examination, have been given just for additional practice required for olympiads Scholarship Exams etc. For detailed explanations refer Page No. 219.*

CHAPTER

08

Light

SYLLABUS

(i) Reflection of Light, images formed by a pair of parallel and perpendicular plane mirrors.

(ii) Spherical mirrors. Characteristics of image formed by these mirrors. Uses of concave and convex mirrors (Only simple direct ray diagrams are required).

Light is a form of energy that helps us to see. It is an electromagnetic wave which does not require any medium for its propagation. An object reflects the light rays that fall on it. These reflected light rays, when received by our eyes, make the object visible to us.

Reflection of Light

The phenomenon of bouncing back of light rays in the same medium on striking a smooth surface is called reflection of light. Reflection of light from smooth surface is shown in the figure given below

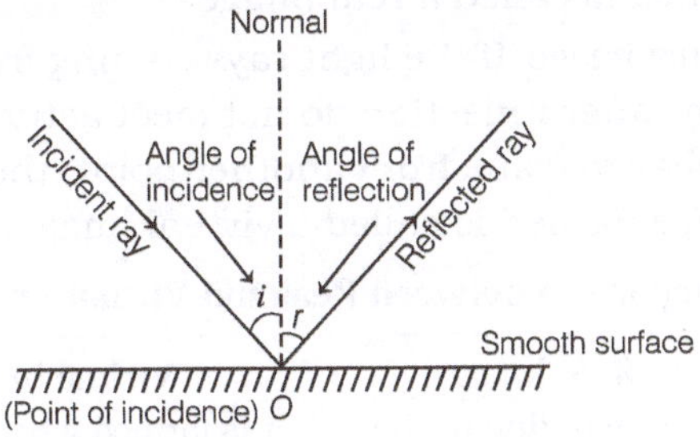

Reflection of light from a smooth surface

Types of Reflection

There are two types of reflection

1. Regular Reflection

The reflection in which parallel light rays are reflected in only one direction and the reflected rays are also parallel to each other is called regular reflection. Regular reflection takes place from smooth surfaces.

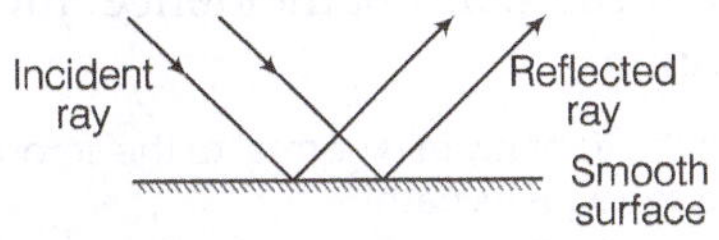

2. Irregular (Diffused) Reflection

The reflection in which parallel light rays reflect in different directions and the reflected rays are not parallel to each other, is called irregular reflection. Irregular reflection takes place from rough or uneven surfaces.

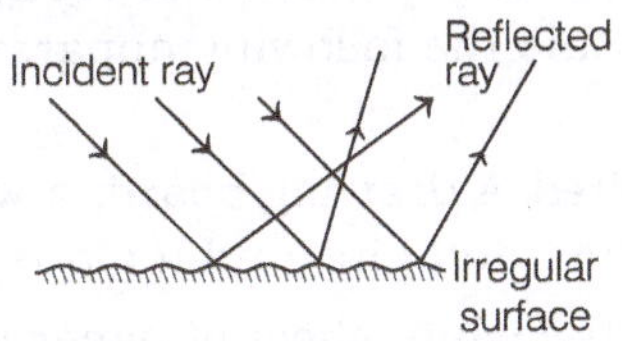

Terms Related to Reflection of Light

The terms used in understanding of reflection of light are as follows

(i) **Reflecting surface** It is a highly polished surface which reflects most of the light rays falling on it.

(ii) **Incident ray** It is that light ray which falls on the reflecting surface.

(iii) **Reflected ray** It is that light ray which bounces back in the same medium by the smooth surface after reflection.

(iv) **Point of incidence** It is the point at which incident ray strikes on the smooth surface.

(v) **Normal** It is a line drawn perpendicular to the reflecting surface and passing through the point of incidence.

(vi) **Angle of incidence** ($\angle i$) It is the angle made by incident ray with the normal.

(vii) **Angle of reflection** ($\angle r$) It is the angle made by reflected ray with the normal.

(viii) **Plane of incidence** It is the plane that contains the incident ray and the normal.

(ix) **Plane of reflection** It is the plane that contains the reflected ray and the normal.

Laws of Reflection

There are two laws of reflection given below as

(i) Angle of incidence is always equal to the angle of reflection.
i.e., $\boxed{\angle i = \angle r}$

(ii) The incident ray, the reflected ray and the normal at the point of incidence, all lie in the same plane.

Note
- When the light ray falls normal to the smooth surface, then it retraces its path.
- The laws of reflection are valid for all the reflecting surfaces.

Experimental Verification of Laws of Reflection

We can perform an experiment to verify the laws of reflection, for this the following apparatus is required.

Apparatus required A drawing board, a white sheet of paper, a few common pins and a plane mirror.

Procedure Pin the white sheet of paper firmly on the drawing board and place the plane mirror on it and trace its outline on the paper. Then, remove the mirror and draw the normal. The normal is the 90° vertical line drawn to the outline of the mirror, now place the mirror again on the outline of the mirror. Next place two pins in a straight line on one side of normal on the white sheet of paper.

Next, place two pins on the other side to the normal in such a way that these two pins are in a straight line with the reflection of the two pins on the other side of the normal.

Now, remove the mirror and the pins and join the pin mark to normal.

It will be seen that the angles which the lines make on both side of the normal will be equal as shown in figure.

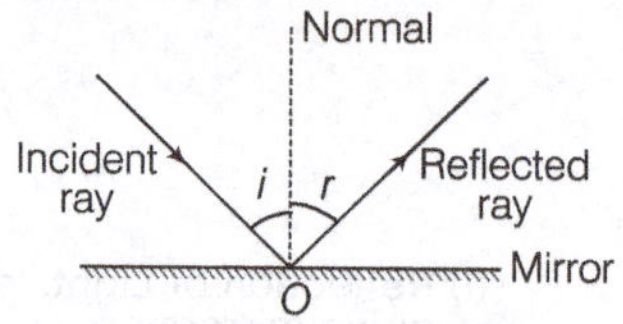

So, if one line represents the incident ray, the ray which is travelling from the source of light and the other line represent the reflected ray, the ray of light which has been reflected. It is proved that the angle which the incident ray makes to the normal i.e., $\angle i = \angle r$ and the incident ray, the reflected ray and the normal, all lie in same plane.

Image

If light rays coming from a point after reflection meet at another point or appear to come from another point, then the second point is called the image of the first point.

Images are of two types

(i) **Real image** If the light rays coming from a point actually meet after reflection, then the image formed is called a real image.

(ii) **Virtual image** If the light rays coming from a point after reflection do not meet actually, but appear to come from another point, then the image formed is called a virtual image.

Comparison between Real and Virtual Images

Real Image	Virtual Image
It is formed, due to the actual intersection of reflected rays.	It is formed when rays after reflection appear to meet when produced backwards.
It can be obtained on the screen.	It cannot be obtained on screen.
Real images are inverted with respect to the object.	Virtual images are erect with respect to the object.

Image Formed by Plane Mirror

If the reflecting surface of a mirror is plane, then the mirror is called a **plane mirror.** Image formed by plane mirror is always virtual.

When the Object is a Point Object

The image of a point object is formed at the point, where rays of light actually intersect or at the point from where they appear to originate. The ray diagram of formation of image I of a point object O in case of plane mirror is shown in the figure.

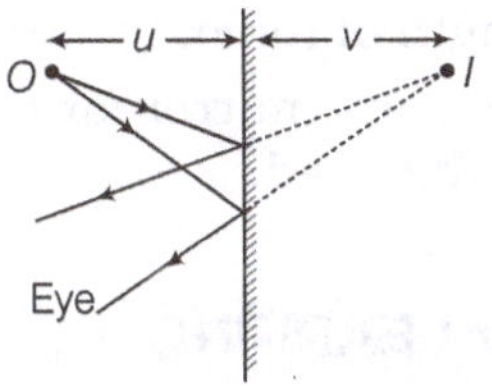

The distance of image from mirror (v) is always equal to the distance of object from mirror (u).

When the Object is an Extended Object

The image formation ($A'B'$) of extended object (AB) by a plane mirror is shown in the figure.

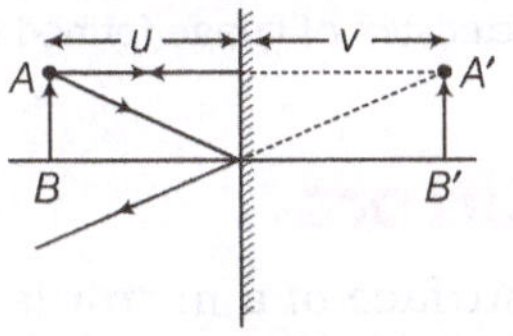

For an extended object, image distance v is equal to object distance u and the size of image is same as that of object. But image formed is erect.

Formation of Image by a Pair of Inclined Plane Mirror

When two mirrors are inclined at a certain angle, then the number of images formed by them, which is given by $n = \frac{360°}{\theta}$

where θ is the angle between the two plane mirrors. Multiple images formed due to multiple reflection because the image formed in one mirror acts as an object for the other mirror.

- If $\frac{360°}{\theta}$ is even, then the actual number of images,

$$n = \frac{360°}{\theta} - 1$$

- If $\frac{360°}{\theta}$ is odd, then the actual number of images,

$$n = \frac{360°}{\theta}$$

Special cases

(i) In case of two plane mirrors parallel to each other, as shown in figure angle θ is equal to zero. So,

$$\text{Number of images} = \frac{360°}{\theta} = \infty \text{ (infinite)}$$

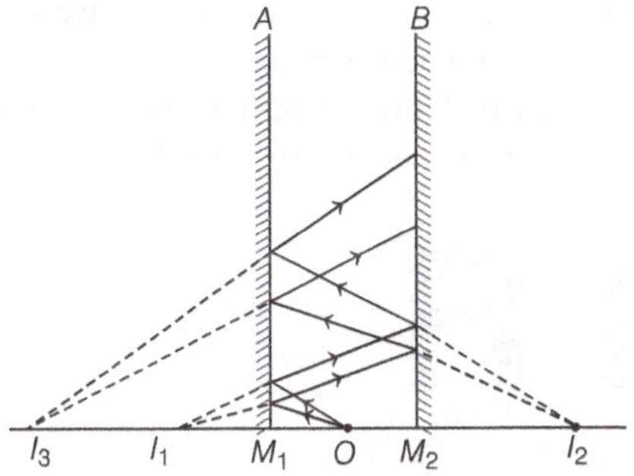

(ii) In case of two plane mirrors inclined at an angle of 90° as shown in figure,

$$\text{So, number of images} = \frac{360°}{90°} - 1 \Rightarrow 4 - 1 = 3$$

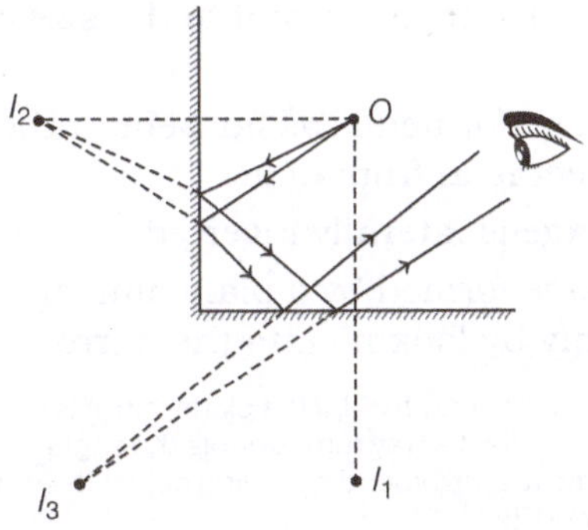

Example 1. The given figure is an overhead view of two plane mirrors inclined at angle θ with an object O placed between them. If you look into the mirrors, you see multiple images of O. If θ equal to (i) 45° (ii) 60° and (iii) 90°, how many images of O would you see?

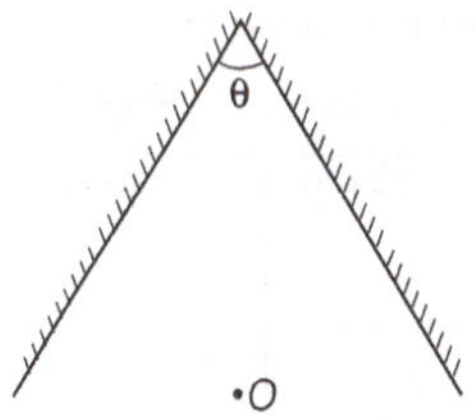

Sol. Use the formula, $n = \frac{360°}{\theta}$ or $\frac{360°}{\theta} - 1$, which gives actual number of images, when $\frac{360°}{\theta}$ is odd or even, respectively.

∴ (i) For $\theta = 45°$, we get $n = 7$

(ii) For $\theta = 60°$, we get $n = 5$

(iii) For $\theta = 90°$, we get $n = 3$

Lateral Inversion

The phenomenon of interchange of left and right sides in the image of an object formed by plane mirror is called lateral inversion.

When you stand in front of plane mirror, left seems to be right and right seems to be left.

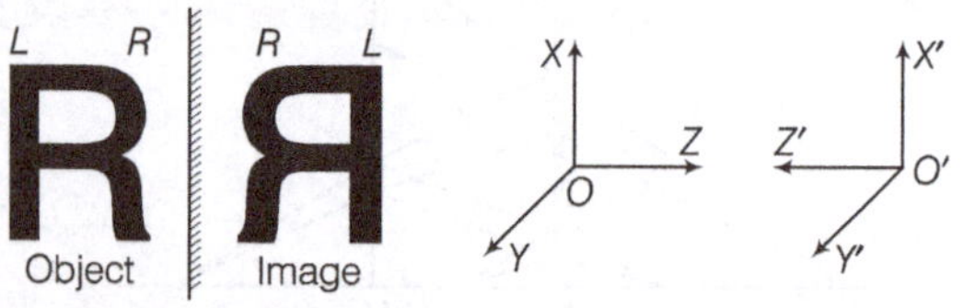

Characteristics of Image Formed by Plane Mirror

Image formed by a plane mirror has the following characteristic properties

(i) It is always virtual and erect.

(ii) The size of image is equal to the size of the object.

(iii) The image formed is as far behind the mirror as the object is in front of it.

(iv) The image is laterally inverted.

(v) The image formed by a plane mirror can be seen only by looking into the mirror.

Note Keeping incident ray fixed, if the plane mirror is rotated by an angle θ, the reflected ray turns double the angle, i.e. 2θ.
If mirror moves with speed v keeping object fixed, image moves with a speed $2v$.

Example 2. A moth at about eye level is 15 cm in front of a plane mirror, you are behind the moth 35 cm from the mirror. At what distance must you focus your eyes to see the image of the moth in the mirror, i.e. what is the distance between your eyes and apparent position of the image?

Sol. The distance between your eyes and apparent position of the image of the moth is

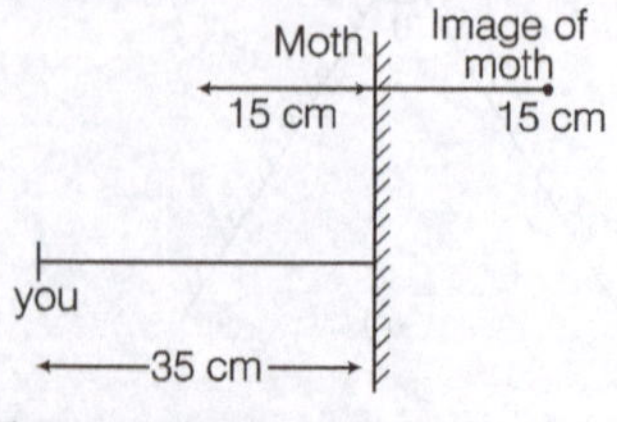

$d = 35\text{ cm} + 15\text{ cm} = 50\text{ cm}$

Uses of Plane Mirror

Few uses of plane mirror are

(i) The most common use of plane mirror is that it is used as looking mirror in dressing room.

(ii) It is used at the corners of a blind curve on highways to enable drivers to see the approaching traffic.

(iii) It is used in instruments such as periscope photocopies, solar cooker, etc.

(iv) It is also used as rear view mirror in vehicles.

(v) It is used in optician's room to increase effective length of room.

(vi) Barber uses plane mirror for seeing the hair at the back of the head.

Check Your LEARNING...

1 Can reflection takes place for any surface? Justify.

2 Can a virtual image obtained on the screen?

3 Write one difference between real and virtual image.

4 Draw a ray diagram to show the image formed by a plane mirror of an extended object.

5 How many images will formed when two plane mirrors are inclined at angle 60° with each other?

6 Write two characteristics of image formed by the plane mirror.

Spherical Mirrors

If the reflecting surface of a mirror is spherical, then the mirror is called a spherical mirror.

Spherical mirrors are of two types

(i) **Convex mirror** The spherical mirror with outward curved reflecting surface is called convex mirror. Convex mirror is also called diverging mirror because it diverges all the light rays falling on its surface.

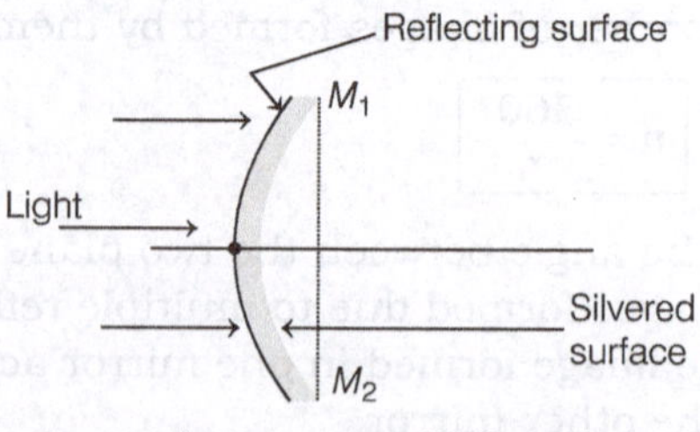

Convex mirror as a part of hollow sphere

(ii) **Concave mirror** The spherical mirror with inward curved reflecting surface is called concave mirror. Concave mirror is also called converging mirror because it converges all the rays falling on its surface.

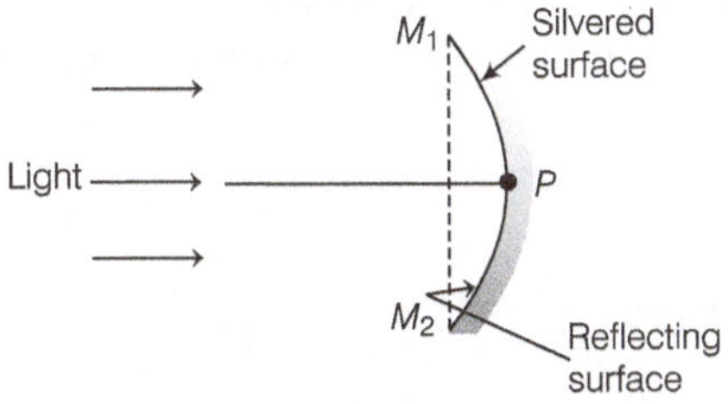

Concave mirror as a part of hollow sphere

Some Definitions Related to Spherical Mirrors

Some definitions related to spherical mirrors are as follows

Centre of Curvature

It is the centre of the sphere of which the mirror is a part. In the figures given below, it is marked by C. In case of concave mirror, the centre of curvature lies in front of it, while in case of convex mirror, the centre of curvature lies behind it.

Radius of Curvature

It is the radius of sphere of which mirror is a part. In the figure, it is shown by *R*.

Pole

It is the mid-point of the reflecting surface of the spherical mirror. In the figure, it is shown by *P*.

Principal Axis

It is the line joining the pole and centre of curvature. In the figure, line passing through *PC* is the principal axis.

Aperture

The diameter of the reflecting surface of spherical mirror is called its aperture. This is that part of the reflecting surface of a mirror which can be exposed to the incident light. It is equal to the straight line distance between two ends of the mirror. In the figure, M_1, M_2 is the aperture of mirror.

Principal Focus of a Spherical Mirror

It is a point on the principal axis of the mirror at which the light rays coming parallel to principal axis after reflection actually meet or appear to be coming from it.

It is represented by *F*. For a concave mirror, the focus is in front of the mirror, while for a convex mirror, the focus is behind the mirror.

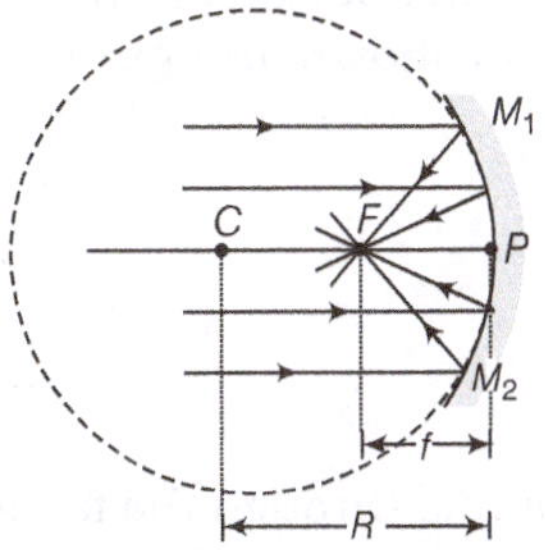

Principal focus for concave mirror

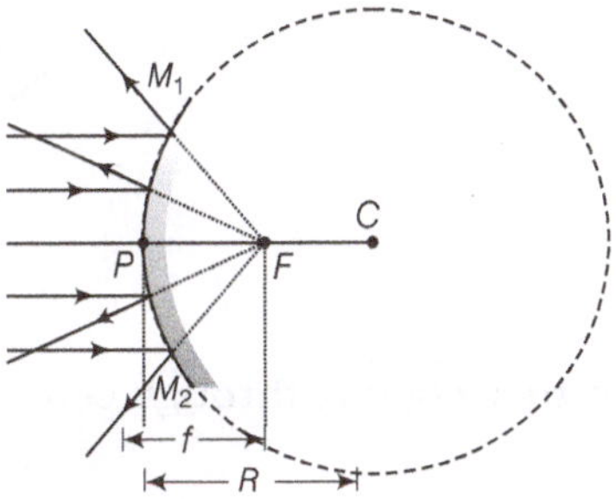

Principal focus for convex mirror

The focus of a concave mirror is real, while the focus of a convex mirror is virtual.

Focal Length

The distance between pole and principal focus of a spherical mirror is called its focal length.
It is represented by f. If the aperture of the mirror is small, then $\boxed{f = R/2.}$

It means that the principal focus of a spherical mirror lies midway between the pole and centre of curvature considering a spherical mirror.

Note
- The plane passing through the focus and perpendicular to the principal axis is called focal plane.
- A line joining any point on the surface of the mirror to the centre of curvature C will be normal to the surface of mirror at that point.

Example 3. A concave mirror is made by cutting a portion of hollow glass sphere of radius 30 cm. Find the focal length of the mirror.

Sol. Given, radius of hollow sphere is 30 cm.

i.e., $R = 30\,\text{cm}$

As, $f = \frac{R}{2}$ (where, f = focal length of the mirror)

$= \frac{30}{2} = 15\,\text{cm}$

Reflection of Light Rays from Spherical Mirror

Reflection of light rays from spherical mirror in different conditions is discussed below

(i) The rays coming parallel to the principal axis pass through the focus after reflection or appear to come from focus as shown in figure.

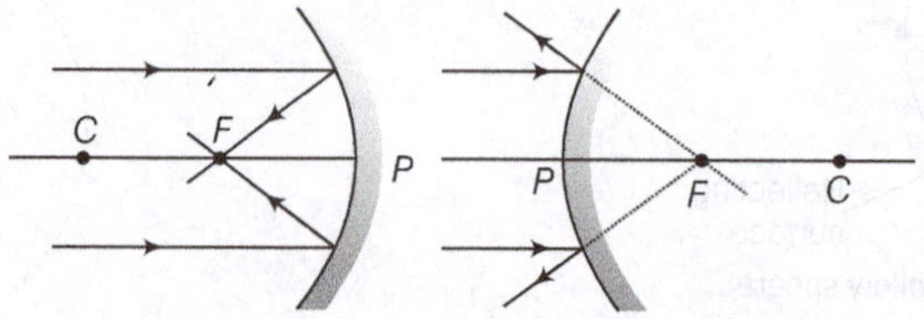

(ii) The rays coming through the focus of mirror or coming towards focus, become parallel to principal axis as shown in figure.

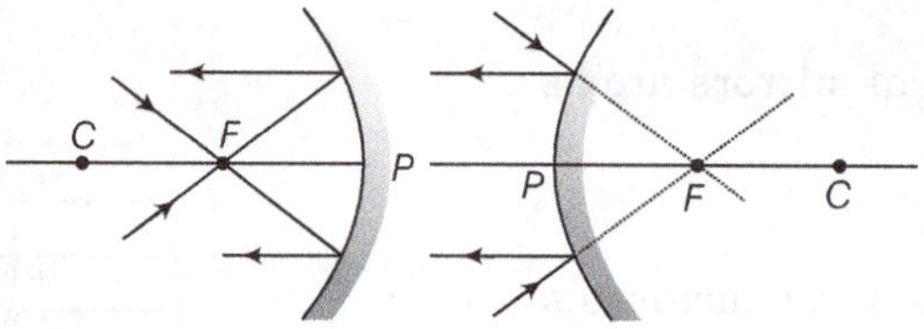

(iii) The light rays coming through centre of curvature or towards centre of curvature, reflect on the same path.

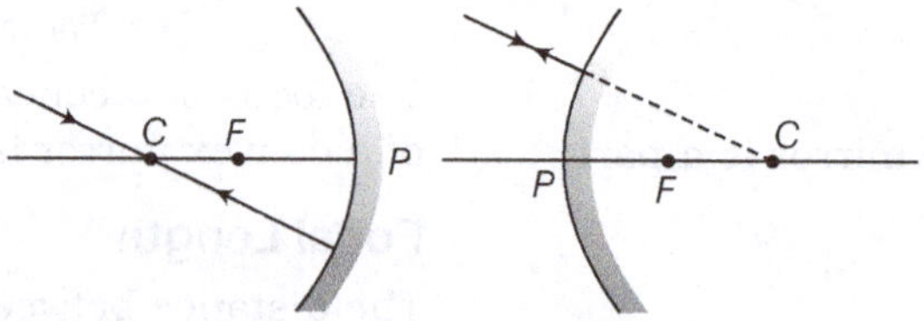

(iv) A ray incident obliquely to principal axis, towards a point *P* on the concave or convex mirror is reflected obliquely, the following laws of reflection are as shown in figure.

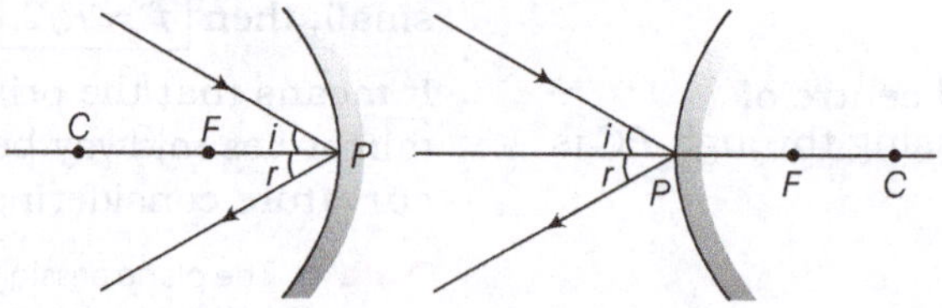

Note : Atleast two incident rays are needed for an image formation.

Image Formation by Spherical Mirror

Image Formation by a Concave Mirror

The table given below illustrates the ray diagram along with the position and nature of image, formed by concave mirror for various positions of the object.

Formation of Image by Concave Mirror for Different Positions of Object

S. No.	Position of Object	Ray Diagram	Position of Image	Nature and Size of Image
(i)	At infinity	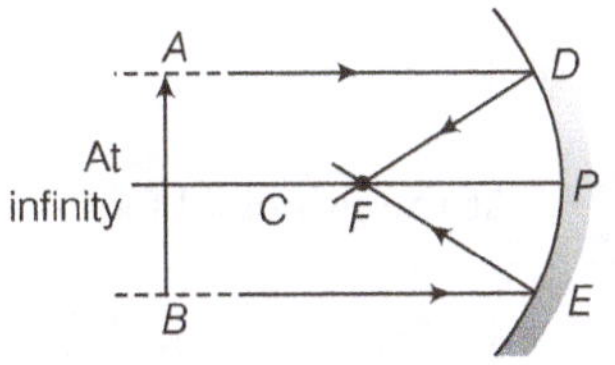	At focus	Real, inverted and extremely diminished in size
(ii)	Beyond the centre of curvature but at finite distance	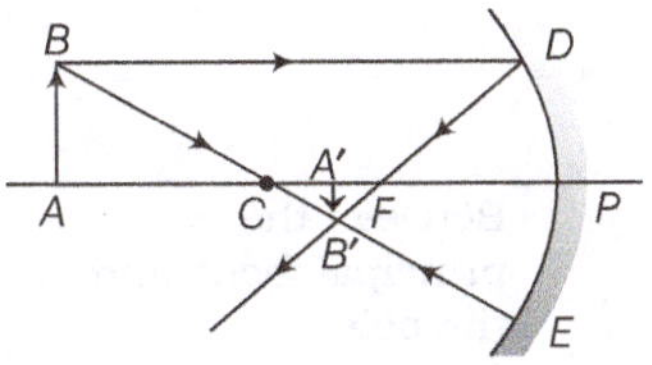	Between focus and the centre of curvature	Real, inverted and diminished
(iii)	At the centre of curvature	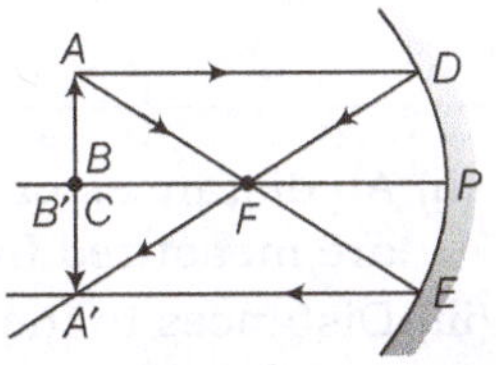	At the centre of curvature	Real, inverted and equal to the size of the object
(iv)	Between focus and centre of curvature	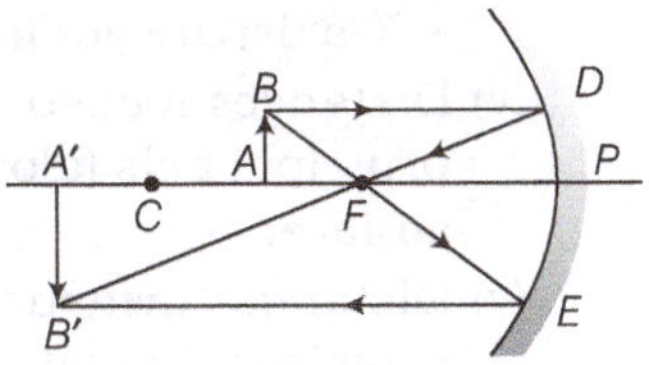	Beyond the centre of curvature	Real, inverted and magnified
(v)	At the focus	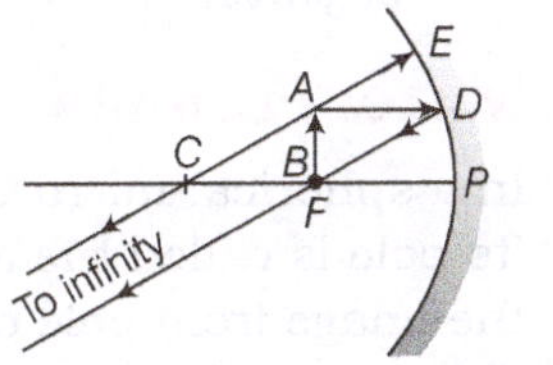	At infinity	Real, inverted and extremely magnified
(vi)	Between the pole and focus	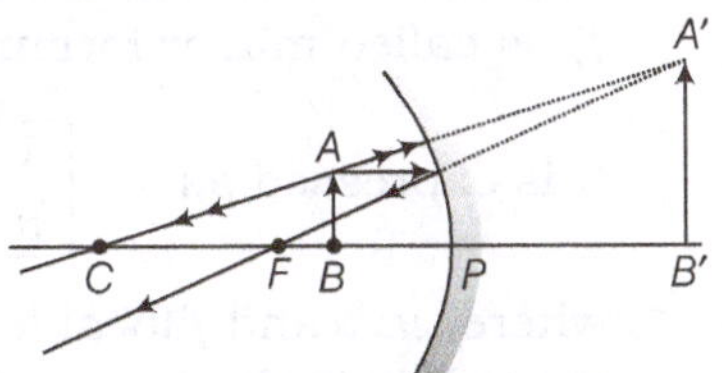	Behind the mirror	Virtual, erect and magnified

Image Formation by a Convex Mirror

For studying the image formed by convex mirror, there are only two positions of the object that are considered. Firstly, when the object is at infinity and the second position is when the object is at a finite distance from the mirror. The table given below illustrates the ray diagrams along with the position and nature of image, formed by convex mirror for the above two positions of the object.

Formation of Image by Convex Mirror for Different Positions of Object

S. No.	Position of Object	Ray Diagram	Position of Image	Nature and Size of Image
(i)	At infinity	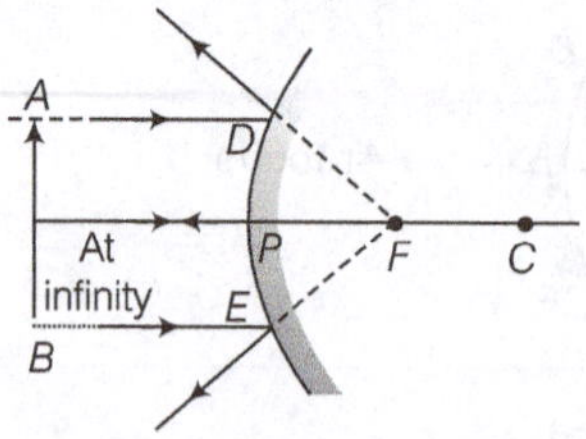	At the principal focus	Virtual, erect and extremely diminished
(ii)	Between infinity and the pole (i.e., at finite distance)	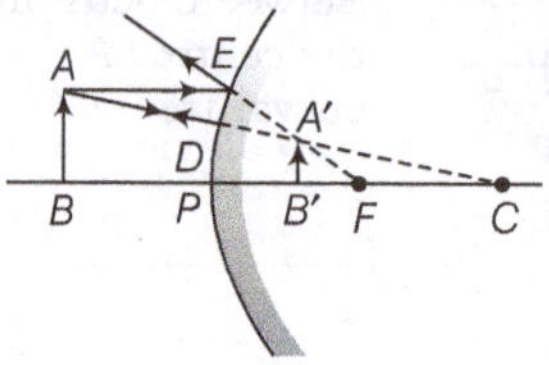	Between the principal focus and the pole	Virtual, erect and diminished

Check Your LEARNING...

1. Which mirror is called a converging mirror?
2. Our face is too far from a convex mirror. What will be the nature of image?
3. What is the nature of image formed by concave mirror when the object is at infinity?
4. Give the nature of image of burning candle placed at the focus of a concave mirror.

Sign Convention for Spherical Mirror

While dealing with the reflection of light by spherical mirrors, we shall follow a set of sign convention called the new cartesian sign convention based on cartesian coordinates. In this convention, the pole (P) of the mirror is taken as the origin.

The principal axis of the mirror is taken as X-axis of the coordinate system.

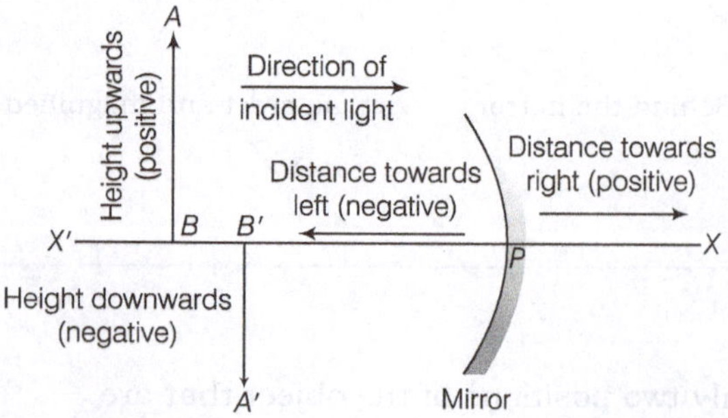

The conventions are as follows

(i) The object is always placed to left of the mirror such that light propagates from left to right.

(ii) All distances parallel to principal axis (X-axis) are measured from the pole of the mirror.

(iii) Distances to the left of pole (along $-X$-axis) are **negative.** Distances to the right of pole (along $+X$-axis) are **positive.**

(iv) Distances measured perpendicularly above the principal axis (along $+Y$-axis) are taken as **positive.**

(v) Distances measured perpendicularly below the principal axis (along $-Y$-axis) are taken as **negative.**

Mirror Formula

In a spherical mirror, the distance of the object from its pole is called the **object distance** (u). The distance of the image from pole of the mirror is called the **image distance** (v). The relation between quantities (u, v and f) is called mirror formula.

It is expressed as $$\boxed{\frac{1}{v}+\frac{1}{u}=\frac{1}{f}}$$

where, u, v and f focal length are to be used according to their new cartesian sign convention.

This formula is valid in all situations for all spherical mirrors and for all positions of the object.

Note Focal length of concave mirror is taken as negative and focal length of convex mirror is taken as positive.

Linear Magnification

The ratio of the height of image to the height of object is called linear magnification. It is represented by m.

i.e., $\boxed{\text{Magnification, } m = \frac{\text{Height of image } (h_i)}{\text{Height of object } (h_o)}}$

or

Magnification is also related to the object distance (u) and image distance (v). It can be expressed as

$$m = -\frac{\text{Image distance}}{\text{Object distance}} = \frac{-v}{u}$$

where, u and v are to be used with their appropriate sign.

Example 4. An object is placed at a distance of 10 cm from a convex mirror of focal length 15 cm. Find the position and nature of image.

Sol. Given, $u = -10$ cm, $f = 15$ cm

By mirror formula, $\frac{1}{v} = \frac{1}{f} - \frac{1}{u} = \frac{1}{15} - \frac{1}{(-10)} = \frac{5}{30}$

$v = 6$ cm from the mirror

Image is formed 6 cm behind the mirror, so image is virtual and erect.

Example 5. An object is placed in front of a convex mirror of focal length 30 cm. If the image is a quarter of the size of object, find the position of the image.

Sol. Given, focal length, $f = +30$ cm

Magnification, $m = \frac{1}{4}$, $v = ?$

We know that, $m = \frac{f - v}{f}$ $\left(\because \text{mirror formula, } \frac{1}{v} + \frac{1}{u} = \frac{1}{f}\right)$

$\Rightarrow \quad \frac{1}{4} = \frac{30 - v}{30}$

$30 = 120 - 4v$

$v = \frac{90}{4} = +22.5$ cm

As, v is positive, therefore a virtual and erect image will be formed on the other side of the object.

Identification of Mirrors

Observing the image produced by a mirror at different positions of object, its nature can be identified.

Following are the ways to identify whether the mirror is plane, convex or concave

(i) If the image formed by the mirror is of same size of object for different positions of object, then the mirror is a **plane mirror**.

(ii) If the image formed by the mirror is diminished for all positions of object, then mirror is a **convex mirror**.

(iii) If the image formed behind the mirror is longer than the object, then the mirror is a **concave mirror**.

Uses of Spherical Mirrors

Some uses of the spherical mirrors are given below

(i) **For concave mirrors**

- These are commonly used in torches, search-lights and vehicles headlights to get powerful parallel beams of light.
- Concave mirrors are used as shaving mirrors to see larger image of the face.
- Dentists use these mirrors to see large images of the teeth.
- Large concave mirrors are used to concentrate sunlight to produce heat in solar furnaces.

(ii) **For convex mirrors**

- These are commonly used as rear view mirrors in vehicles because they always give an erect image and have wider field of view as they are curved outwards.

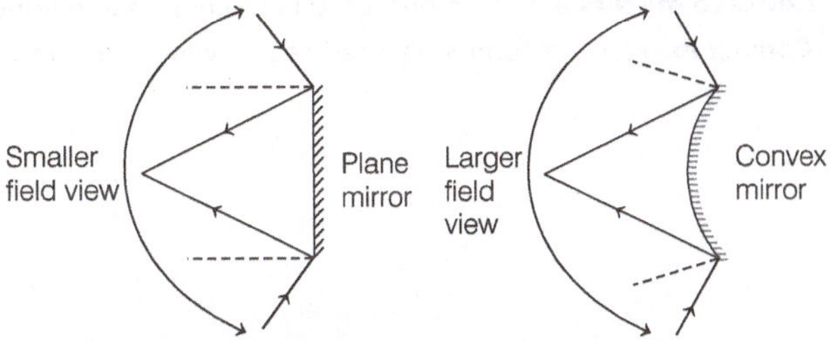

- Big convex mirrors are used as shop security mirrors, the shop owner can keep an eye on the customers to look for thieves and shoplifters among them.

Check Your LEARNING...

1 Write the mirror formula in terms of radius of curvature for a spherical mirror.

2 What is the value of linear magnification (m) when an object is placed at the centre of curvature in front of concave mirror?

3 If $m < -1$, what is the nature of image formed?

4 If the image formed behind the mirror is longer than the object, then what type of mirror it is?

5 Which mirror is used by the dentists to observe teeth?

QUiCK Revision

- **Light** is a form of energy that helps us to see.
- **Reflection** is the phenomenon of change in the path of light without any change in medium.
- **Laws of Reflection**
  (i) Angle of incidence is always equal to the angle of reflection.
  (ii) The incident ray, reflected ray and the normal at the point of incidence, all lie in the same plane.
- If the light rays coming from a point after reflection meet at another point or appear to come from another point, then the second point is called the **image of the first point**.
- If the reflecting surface of a mirror is plane, then the mirror is called a **plane mirror**.
- If the reflecting surface of a mirror is spherical, then the mirror is called a **spherical mirror**.
- Spherical mirrors are of two types
  (i) **Convex mirror**
  (ii) **Concave mirror**
- **Centre of curvature** of a spherical mirror is the centre of the sphere of which the mirror is a part.
- The relation between **focal length** and **radius of curvature** is given by
  $$R = 2f \text{ or } f = \frac{R}{2}$$
- **Mirror formula** is given by $\frac{1}{u} + \frac{1}{v} = \frac{1}{f}$ where u is the object distance, v is the image distance and f is the focal length.
- **Magnification** is the ratio of the size of image to the size of object.
- A **concave mirror** can form real or virtual image depending on the position of the object.
- A **convex mirror** always forms virtual and erect images.
- **Concave mirrors** are commonly used in torches, search lights and vehicles headlights to get powerful beams of light.
- **Convex mirrors** are commonly used as rear view mirror in vehicles.

Chapter Practice

Section-I

1 Mark Questions

1. Which of the following is correct about law of reflection?

(a) $\frac{i}{r}$ = constant (b) $\frac{\sin i}{\sin r}$ = constant

(c) $i + r$ = constant (d) $i = r$

Sol. (*d*) According to the law of reflection, angle of incidence is always equal to the angle of reflection.

2. The image formed by plane mirror is always

(a) real
(b) virtual
(c) virtual and laterally inverted
(d) real and laterally inverted

Sol. (*c*) Plane mirror always forms a virtual, erect and laterally inverted image.

3. Two plane mirrors are placed parallel to each other as shown in figure.

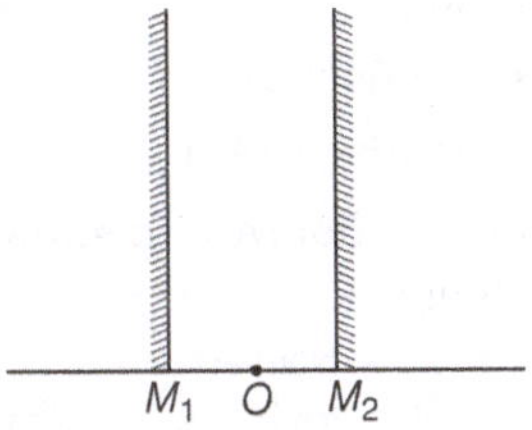

How many images are formed in this mirror arrangement?

(a) infinite (b) 0 (c) 1 (d) 2

Sol. (*a*) When two plane mirrors are placed parallel to each other, then infinite number of images are formed.

4. Choose the correct statement when two plane mirrors placed parallel to each other.

(a) The nature of image formed will be virtual.
(b) Image formed is diminished in size.
(c) No image will be formed.
(d) The image formed will be inverted as of same size as that of object.

Sol. (*a*) The set up of these two plane mirrors will form virtual image as same size as that of object in infinite amount.

5.

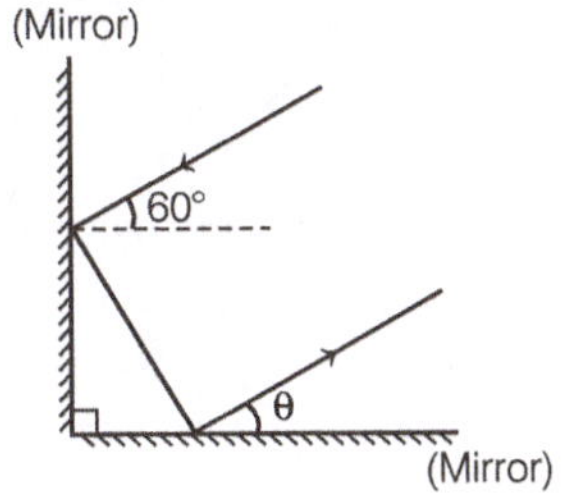

The value of θ in the above figure is

(a) 45° (b) 60°
(c) 90° (d) 30°

Sol. (*b*) According to question,

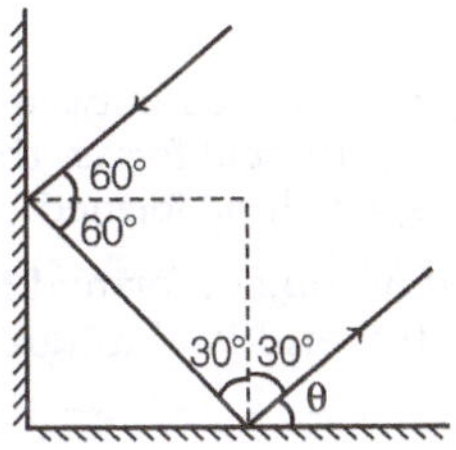

The value of θ is 60°.

6. In a barber's shop, two plane mirrors are placed

(a) perpendicular to each other
(b) parallel to each other
(c) at an angle of 60° between them
(d) at an angle of 45° between them

Sol. (*b*) In a barber's shop, two plane mirrors are placed parallel to each other.

7. The image of an object in front of a convex mirror is formed

(a) at the object itself
(b) at twice the distance of the object in front of the mirror
(c) at half the distance of the object in front of the mirror
(d) behind the mirror

Sol. (*d*) The image of an object in front of a convex mirror is always formed behind the mirror.

8. An incident ray is directed towards centre of curvature of a spherical mirror, the reflected ray

(a) retraces its path
(b) passes through the focus
(c) passes through the pole
(d) becomes parallel to the principal axis

Sol. (*a*) When an incident ray is directed towards the centre of curvature of a spherical mirror, then the reflected ray will retrace the path of incident ray.

9. A real and enlarged image can be obtained by using a

(a) convex mirror
(b) plane mirror
(c) concave mirror
(d) either plane or convex mirror

Sol. (*c*) Concave mirror gives an enlarged and real image when the object is placed between centre of curvature and focus.

10. The image formed by a concave mirror is observed to be virtual, erect and larger than the object, where should be the position of the object?

(a) Between principal focus and centre of curvature.
(b) Centre of curvature
(c) Beyond centre of curvature
(d) Between pole of the mirror and its principal focus

Sol. (*d*) If the object is placed between the pole of the mirror and its principal focus, then virtual, erect and magnified image will be formed.

11. The image of an object formed by the given mirror is real, inverted and is of magnification-1.

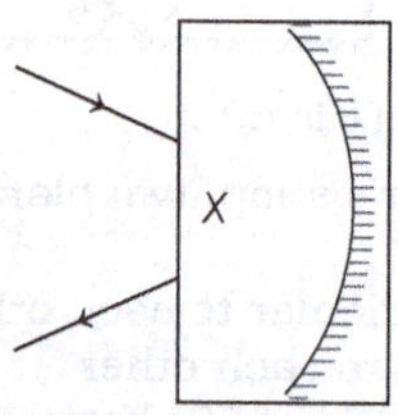

Which mirror is inside the box *X*?

(a) Plane mirror (b) Concave mirror
(c) Convex mirror (d) Diverging mirror

Sol. (*b*) As the image formed is real, so the concave mirror is inside the box *X*.

12. If the image is at the distance of 30 cm from the mirror and magnification is –1, where is the object placed?

(a) – 30 cm (b) – 60 cm
(c) 60 cm (d) 30 cm

Sol. (*a*) Given, $m = -1$, $v = -30$ cm

We have, $m = -\frac{v}{u} \Rightarrow -1 = -\frac{-30}{u}$

$\therefore \quad u = -30$ cm

13. Consider the following statements and choose the incorrect one.

I. Magnification is the ratio of object height to the image height.
II. Magnification is equal to the ratio of object distance to the image distance.
III. Magnification is positive for real and inverted and erect images.

Codes

(a) Only I (b) Only II
(c) Only III (d) All are incorrect

Sol. (*d*) All the statements are incorrect. As, magnification is the ratio of image height to the object height or image distance to the object distance.

Magnification is always negative for real and inverted images and positive for virtual and erect images.

14. Which of the following is the correct ray diagram for image formation?

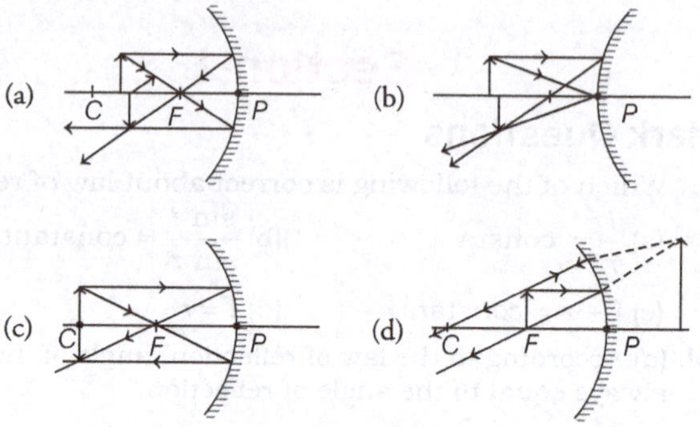

Sol. (*c*) The correct ray diagram is shown in option (c).

2 Marks Questions

15. Give the difference between angle of incidence and angle of reflection.

Sol. **Angle of incidence** It is the angle made by incident ray with normal. **[1]**

Angle of reflection It is the angle made by reflected ray with normal. **[1]**

16. State laws of reflection.

Sol. Refer to theory (Page 142).

17. Draw a labelled diagram to show the laws of reflection of light.

Sol.

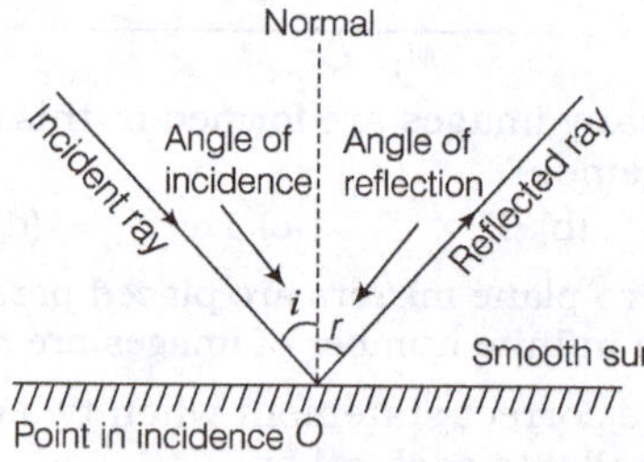

18. The diagram shows an incident ray and normal on a plane mirror. Draw the reflected ray and find the angle between the incident ray and reflected ray.

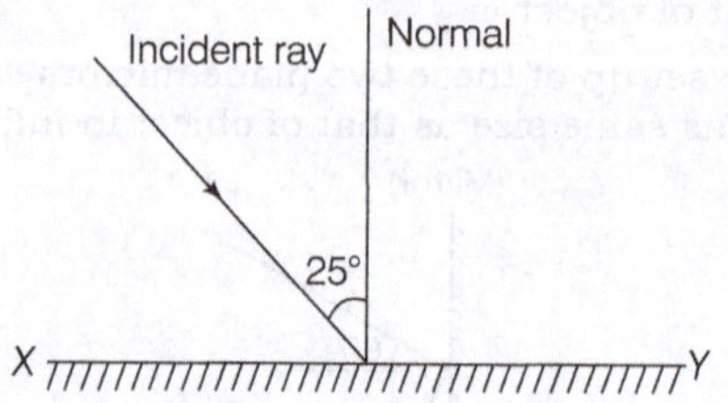

Sol. Angle between the incident ray and reflected ray is 50°.

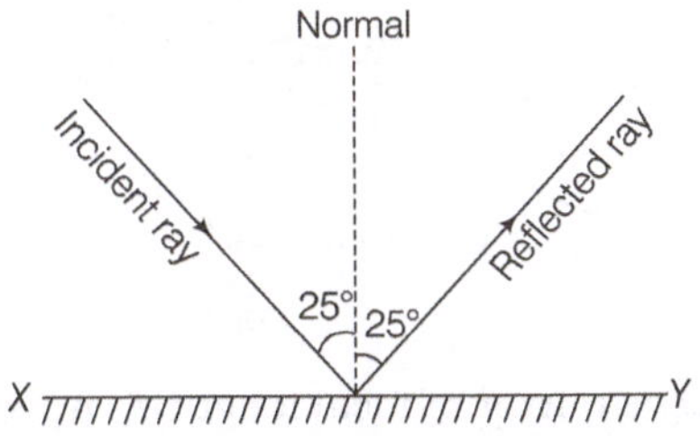

19. When a plane mirror is placed horizontally on levelled ground at a distance of 40 m from the foot of a tower, the top of the tower and its image in the mirror subtend an angle of 90° at the eye. What is the height of the tower?

Sol.

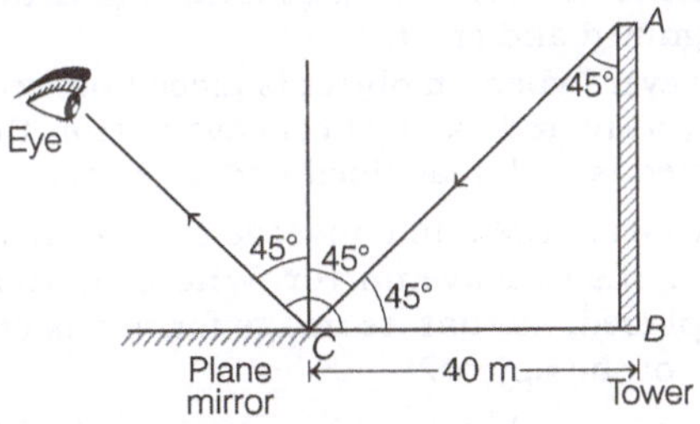

[1]

From geometry of figure, height of tower AB is 40 m.

As, in right angle ΔABC, $\angle CAB = \angle BCA = 45°$

$\therefore \quad CB = AB = 40$ m [1]

20. Give one use of each of the following.

(i) Regular reflection

(ii) Irregular reflection

Sol. (i) Regular reflection helps in the formation of virtual images as in case of plane mirror. [1]

(ii) Irregular reflection helps in illuminating the areas, where light is not falling directly. [1]

21. Give the convenient condition to locate the image formation in case of plane mirror.

Sol. To form an image in case of plane mirror there must be two rays meeting virtually. So that, a virtual [1] image of same size is obtained behind the mirror. [1]

22. An object AB is placed in front of a plane mirror. Draw a labelled diagram to show the formation of image of AB.

Sol.

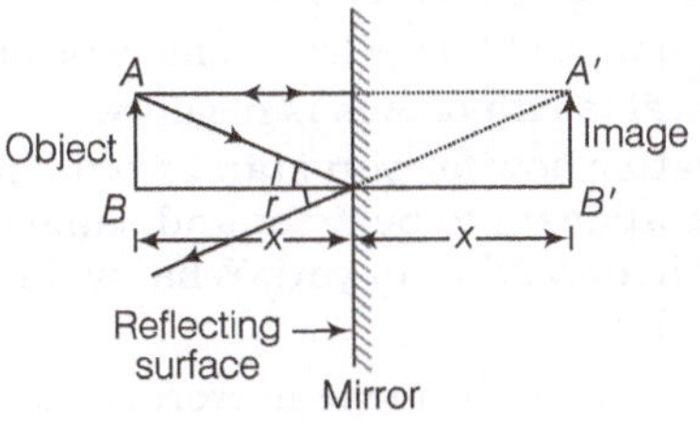

[1]

Image $A'B'$ is virtual, erect and equal in size of the object. [1]

23. Under what condition in an arrangement of two plane mirrors, incident ray and reflected ray will always be parallel to each other, whatever may be angle of incidence? Show the same with the help of diagram?

Sol. When plane mirrors are placed at 90° to each other, then the incident and reflected rays will always be parallel to each other, whatever may be the angle of incidence. [1]

The rays are shown below

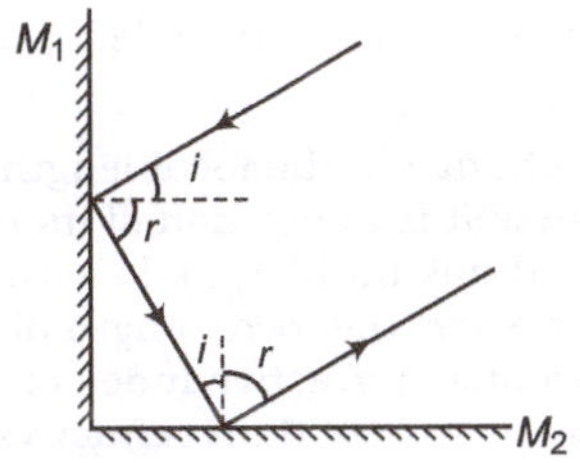

[1]

24. If two mirrors are placed at an angle θ, what will be the number of images formed by the pair of mirror?

Sol. Refer to theory (Page 143).

25. A boy is running towards a plane mirror with a speed of 2 m/s. With what speed the image of the boy approach him?

Sol. The image of the object in a plane mirror is as far behind the mirror as the object is in front of it. Therefore, the image of the boy comes near the mirror through the distance equal to that moved by the boy towards the plane mirror. Hence, the image of the boy will approach him with double his speed i.e., with 4 m/s.

26. A student is standing in the centre of a room. He wants to fix a plane mirror in front of him on a wall. What should be the smallest length of the mirror taken by him, so as to enable him to see full image of the back wall?

Sol. In order to see the full image of the back wall, the student should take the smallest length of the mirror to be one-third of the height of the wall.

27. (i) What do you mean by a divergent beam of light?

(ii) What do you mean by laterally inverted?

Sol. (i) It is a beam of light in which the width of the beam goes on increasing as the rays proceed forward. In this case, the rays spread out from a point. [1]

(ii) In case of image formation by the plane mirror, the left side seems to be right and right side seems to be left. This is called laterally inverted image. [1]

28. What do you mean by lateral inversion? Write the letters of English alphabet which in front of plane mirror do not show lateral inversion.

Sol. When we look through the plane mirror, the left part of the object appears as the right part of the image and *vice-versa*. This is called lateral inversion. The following letters do not show lateral inversion i.e.,

A, H, I, M, O, T, U, V, W, X, Y

29. What will be the nature of image formed by a plane mirror?

Sol. The nature of image formed by a plane mirror is virtual and same size as that of object.

30. What change do you expect in the focal length of a concave mirror and a convex lens, when immersed in water?

Sol. There is no change in the focal length of concave mirror because it is about half of its radius of curvature and has nothing to do with the external medium. However, the focal length of convex lens increases because refractive index of glass with respect to water is less than refractive index of glass with respect to air. **[1 + 1]**

31. A concave mirror of small aperture forms a sharper image, why?

Sol. The rays of light travelling parallel to the principal axis after reflection from a concave mirror meet at a single point, only if the beam of light is narrow or if the mirror is of small aperture. In case, a wide beam of light falls on a concave mirror of large aperture, the rays after reflection from the mirror do not come to focus at a single point. Therefore, it follows that, if the aperture of the concave mirror is small, the image formed will be sharper.

32. Draw a ray diagram showing image formation when object is in between principal focus and pole in case of concave mirror and give nature of image.

Sol. Image formation when object is in between principal focus and the pole.

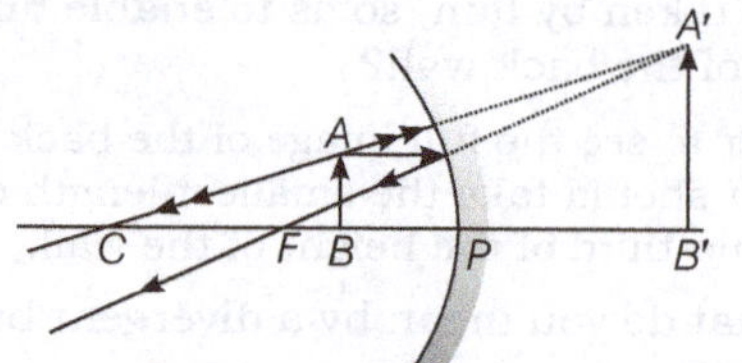

Nature Virtual, erect, magnified and behind the mirror.

33. We wish to obtain an erect image of an object, using a concave mirror of focal length 15 cm. What should be the range of distance of the object from the mirror? What is the nature of image? Is the image larger or smaller than the object? Draw a ray diagram to show the image formation in this case.

Sol. The object should be kept at a distance less than 15 cm from the mirror. The image is virtual and erect. The image is larger than the object. **[1]**

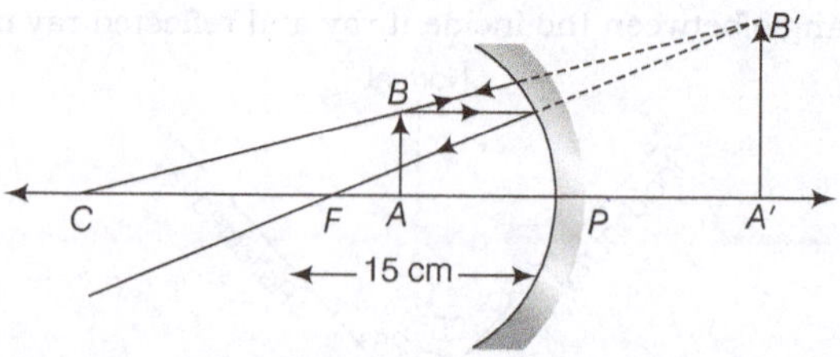

[1]

34. A concave mirror of focal length f can form a magnified, erect as well as an inverted image of an object placed in front of it. Justify this statement stating the position of object with respect to the mirror in each case for obtaining these images.

Sol. When an object is placed between focus and pole of concave mirror, the image formed is virtual, magnified and erect. **[1]**

However, when an object is placed between centre of curvature and focus of concave mirror, the image formed is real, magnified and inverted. **[1]**

35. Rays from the sun converge at a point 15 cm in front of a concave mirror. Where should an object be placed, so that its image formed is equal to the size of the object?

Sol. As we know that for concave mirror, if object is placed at infinity, its image will be formed at focus. Thus, from the question, focal length of given mirror will be 15 cm and for same size of image. In case of concave mirror, object must be placed at centre of curvature. So, when we place the object ($15 \times 2 = 30$ cm) in front of concave mirror we get same size of image.

36. The magnification produced by a plane mirror is +1. What does it mean?

Sol. If magnification is + 1, the image size is same as that of object size. Since, magnification is positive, the image is erect with respect to the object.

37. If the magnification of an image formed by a mirror is positive, what does it mean?

Sol. If magnification of an image formed by a mirror is positive, it means the image formed is virtual.

38. State whether the following are positive or negative when a concave lens forms a virtual image

(i) Distance of image from lens

(ii) Focal length of lens.

Sol. (i) Distance of image from lens is positive. **[1]**

(ii) Focal length of lens is negative. **[1]**

39. No matter how far you stand from a mirror your image appears to be erect and same distance from the mirror as that of you. What will be the type of mirror?

Sol. The mirror will be plane mirror, because it always forms erect and virtual image (where object distance and image distance are equal).

40. If p, q and r denote the object distance, image distance and the radius of curvature respectively, of a spherical mirror, then find out the relation between them.

Sol. From mirror formula, $\frac{1}{f} = \frac{1}{v} + \frac{1}{u}$

We have, $\frac{1}{\frac{r}{2}} = \frac{1}{q} + \frac{1}{p}$ $\left(\because f = \frac{r}{2}\right)$ **[1]**

or $\frac{2}{r} = \frac{p+q}{pq}$ or $\frac{r}{2} = \frac{pq}{p+q}$

$\therefore$ $r = \frac{2pq}{p+q}$ **[1]**

41. The plane mirror and convex mirror form virtual images of objects. Can they produce real images under same circumstances? Explain.

Sol. Yes, a plane mirror and a convex mirror form real images of object, if object is virtual as shown in Figs. (a) and (b). **[1]**

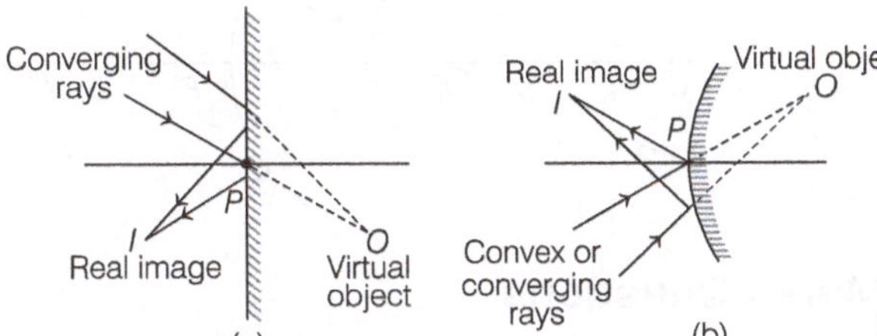

(a) (b) **[1]**

42. What is the nature of the image formed by a concave mirror, when object is placed at centre of curvature?

Sol. The following are the nature of images as follows

(i) The image is also formed at centre of curvature. **[1]**

(ii) The image is real, inverted and of same size as that of object. **[1]**

43. Why do we prefer a convex mirror as a rear view mirror in vehicles?

Sol. As, we know that the field of view of a convex mirror is wider than that of concave mirror, so we prefer convex mirror as a rear view mirror for vehicles.

44. Name the mirror used in the following cases.

(i) Headlight of car (ii) Solar furnace

Sol. (i) Concave mirror is used to get powerful parallel beam of light. **[1]**

(ii) Concave mirror as it can converge light of the sun in a small area. **[1]**

45. Can we change focal length of a given spherical mirror by changing the object distance from the mirror?

Sol. No, we cannot change focal length of a spherical mirror by changing the object distance (u). By changing u, v will change but f will remain the same.

46. A concave mirror is used as a head mirror by ENT specialists. The same mirror can also be used as a shaving mirror. Why?

Sol. A concave mirror converges the ray of light falling on it in a direction parallel to the principal axis, on to its focus. This is the reason that ENT specialists use it as a head mirror. **[1]**

The concave mirror is used as a shaving mirror because when an object is held between the pole and principal focus of a concave mirror which forms a virtual, erect and magnified image of an object. **[1]**

47. (i) What will be the type of mirror when image formed is diminished for all positions?

(ii) Inner curved surface of large shining spoon acts as what type of mirror?

Sol. (i) If image formed is diminished for all positions, the mirror should be convex mirror. **[1]**

(ii) Inner curved surface of large shining spoon acts as concave mirror. **[1]**

3 Marks Questions

48. Draw a labelled diagram to show the image formation of a point object in case of plane mirror. Is the image formed real or virtual?

Sol. Refer to theory (Page 143).

49. Give three uses of a plane mirror.

Sol. Refer to theory (Page 144).

50. (i) What do you mean by a virtual image?

(ii) Define principal focus of a concave mirror.

Sol. (i) Refer to theory (Page 142).

(ii) Refer to theory (Page 145).

51. If the image formed by a mirror for all positions of the object placed in front of it is always erect and diminished, what type of mirror is it? Draw a ray diagram to justify your answer. Where and why do we generally use this type of mirror?

Sol. The mirror is convex mirror.

Ray diagram for formation of images by a convex mirror

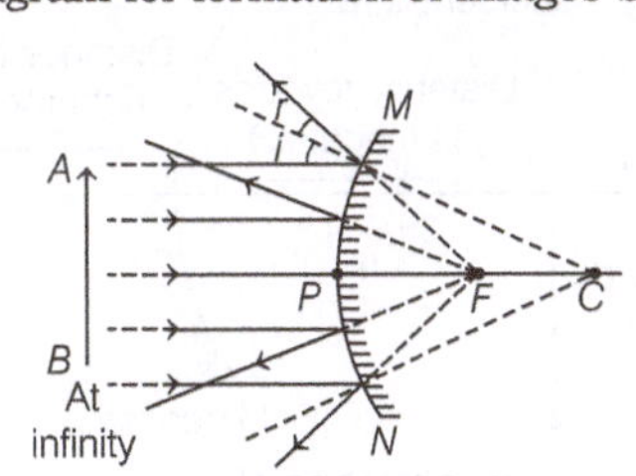

(a) Virtual, erect and highly diminished image at F **[1]**

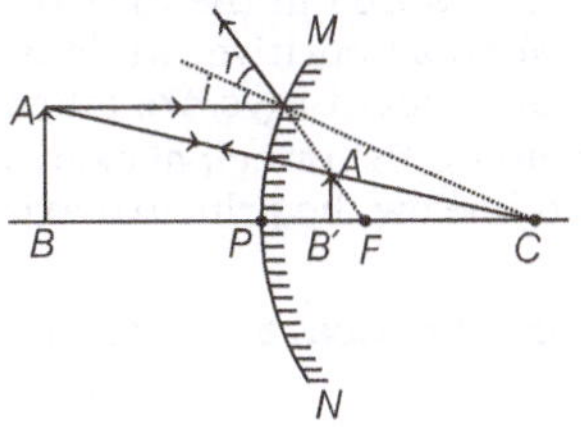

(b) Virtual, erect and highly diminished image between P and F **[1]**

We generally use convex mirrors as rear view mirrors in vehicles to have a wider field of view. [1]

52. Draw a ray diagram showing the image formation by a convex mirror when an object is placed
(i) at infinity
(ii) at finite distance from the mirror.

Sol. (i) The virtual, erect and highly diminished image of the object forms at focus F behind the mirror.

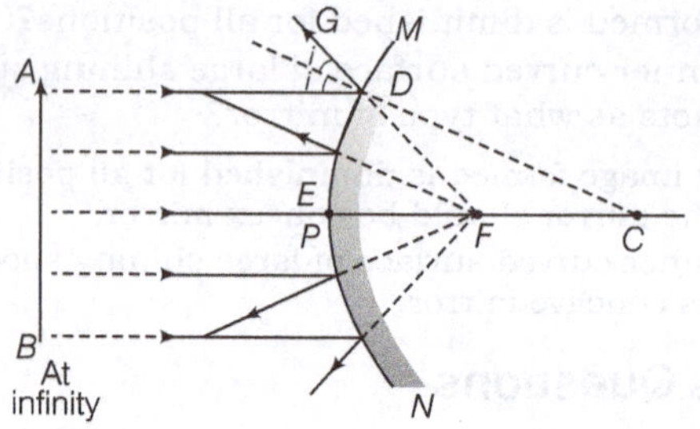

[1½]

(ii) The virtual, erect and diminished image of the object forms between focus F and pole P behind the mirror.

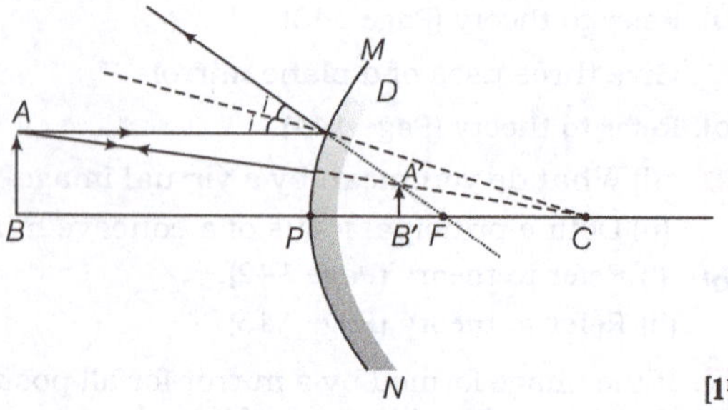

[1½]

53. Discuss the sign convention used in reflection of light.

Sol. Sign conventions

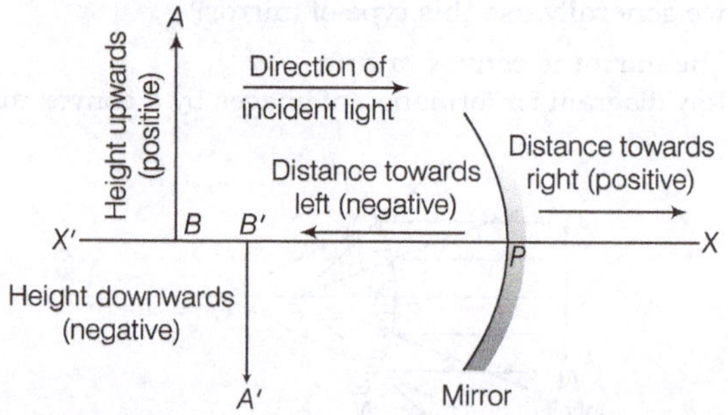

[1]

The following are conclusions that
(i) all distances are measured from the pole.
(ii) distances measured in the direction of incident rays are taken as positive, while in the opposite direction of incident rays are taken as negative.
(iii) distances above the principal axis are taken as positive and below the principal axis are taken as negative. [2]

54. Write the uses of concave mirror and convex mirror.

Sol. Refer to theory (Page 149).

55. (i) Name the type of mirror used in a solar furnace. How is high temperature achieved by this device?
(ii) We wish to obtain an erect image of an object, using a concave mirror of focal length 15 cm. What should be the range of distance of the object from the mirror? What is the nature of image? Is the image larger or smaller than the object? Draw a ray diagram to show the image formation in this case.

Sol. (i) Concave mirror is used in solar furnace. The furnace is placed at the focus of the large concave reflector. The concave reflector focuses the sunlight on the furnace and the high temperature is achieved. [1½]
(ii) The object should be kept at a distance less than 15 cm from the mirror. The image is virtual and erect. The image is larger than the object.

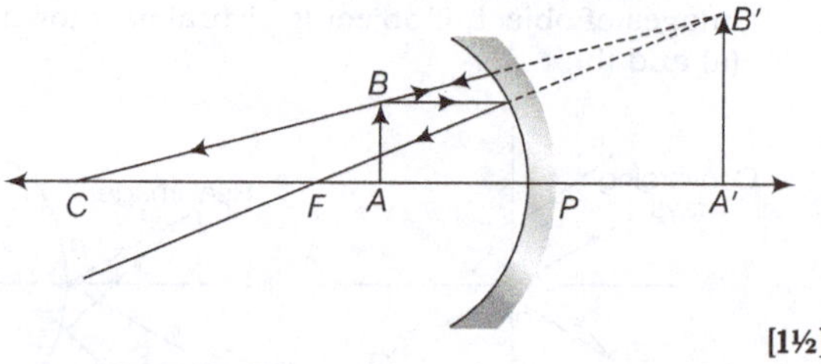

[1½]

4 Marks Questions

56. A student has three concave mirrors A, B and C of focal lengths 20 cm, 15 cm and 10 cm, respectively. For each concave mirror, he performs the experiment of image formation for three values of object distance of 30 cm, 10 cm and 20 cm.
Give reasons for the following.
(i) For the three object distances, identify the mirror which will form an image equal in size to that of object. Find at least one value of object distance.
(ii) Out of the three mirrors, identify the mirror which would be preferred to be used for shaving purpose.
(iii) For the mirror B, draw a ray diagram for image formation for any two given values of object distance.

Sol. (i) When an object is placed at the centre of curvature (i.e., double the distance of focal length) of concave mirror, the image formed is equal in size to that of object. So, for object distance 20 cm, the mirror C with focal length 10 cm is used as

$$u = R = 2f$$
$$= 2 \times 10 \text{ cm} = 20 \text{ cm}.$$ [1]

(ii) For shaving purpose, mirror B (f = 15 cm) would be preferred to form an enlarged and erect image of the face at distance 10 cm. [1]

(iii) (a) For u = 30 cm

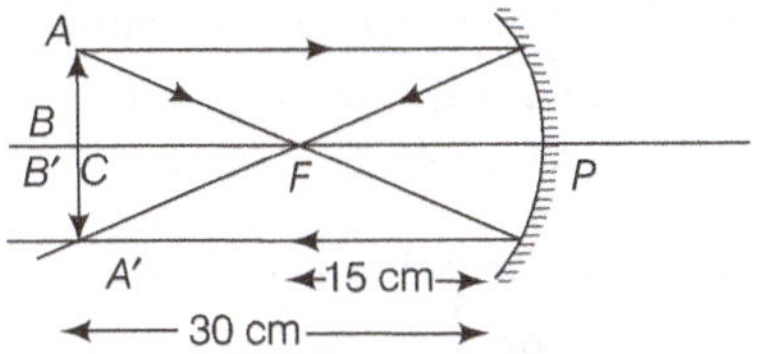

[1]

(b) For $u = 10$ cm,

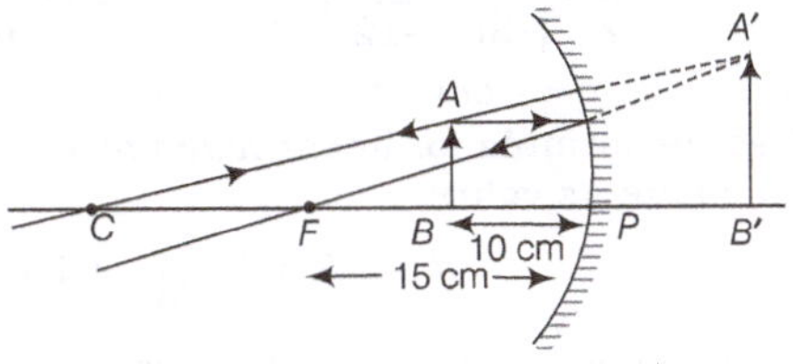

[1]

57. (i) Give the name of the mirror that
(a) can give real as well as virtual image of an object.
(b) will always give virtual and diminished image of an object.
(c) will always give virtual image of same size of an object.
(d) is used by a doctor to examine teeth.
(ii) With the help of a ray diagram, explain the use of concave mirror as solar concentrators.

Sol. (i) (a) The given mirror is concave mirror.
(b) The given mirror is convex mirror.
(c) The given mirror is plane mirror.
(d) The given mirror is concave mirror. [2]

(ii) Ray diagram

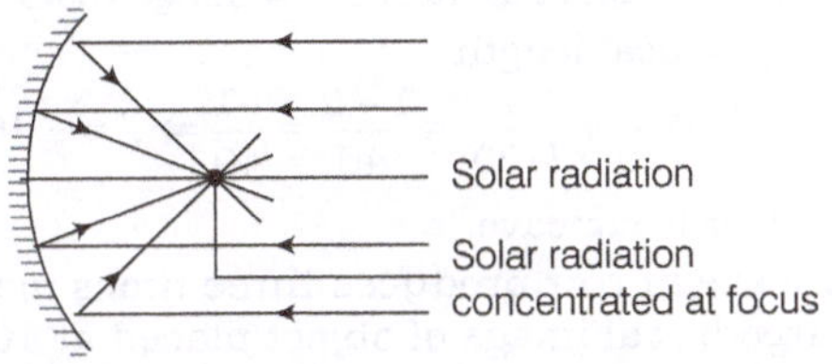

The solar radiation is concentrated at the focus of a concave reflector.

[2]

58. (i) What should be the position of the object when a concave mirror is to be used
(a) as a shaving mirror and
(b) in torches producing parallel beam of light?
(ii) A man standing in front of a mirror, finds his image having a very small head and legs of normal size. What types of mirror are used in designing such a mirror?

Sol. (i) (a) Object should be placed between pole and focus. [1]
(b) At the focus. [1]
(ii) Small head → convex mirror. [1]
Legs of normal size → plane mirror. [1]

59. Write the differences between concave and convex mirror.

Sol. Differences between a concave and convex mirror

Concave Mirror	Convex Mirror
The spherical mirror with inward curved reflecting surface is called a concave mirror.	The spherical mirror with outward curved reflecting surface is called a convex mirror.
The light rays incident on it converge after reflection.	The light rays incident on it diverge after reflection.
The image formed by it is real as well as virtual depending on the position of object.	The image formed by it is always virtual for all positions of the object in front of it.
For an object away from the centre of curvature, the image is diminished, for an object at centre of curvature, the image is of same size and for an object within the centre of curvature, the image is magnified.	The image is always diminished for all positions of the object in front it.

Numerical Type Questions

60. How many images will be formed, if two mirrors are fitted on the adjacent walls and one mirror is fitted on the ceiling?

Sol. Number of images formed by two mirrors is given by

$$N = \frac{360°}{\theta} - 1 = \frac{360°}{90°} - 1 = 3$$ [1]

Also, number of images formed by mirror fitted at the ceiling is 4.

So, total images will be

$$3 + 4 = 7$$ [1]

61. Find the value of radius of curvature of a concave mirror, if its focal length is 10 cm.

Sol. Given, $f = 10$ cm, $R = ?$

$\therefore \quad f = \frac{R}{2} \Rightarrow R = 2f$

$\Rightarrow \quad R = 2 \times 10 = 20$ cm [2]

62. What is the name given to linear distance between the pole and principal focus of a spherical mirror? If this distance is 25 cm, how far is the centre of curvature from the pole of the spherical mirror?

Sol. The linear distance between the pole and principal focus of a spherical mirror is called focal length. [1]
If the focal length of the spherical mirror is 25 cm, then its radius of curvature is

$$R = 2f = 2 \times 25 = 50 \text{ cm}$$

Thus, centre of curvature of a spherical mirror should be at a distance of 50 cm from the pole. [1]

63. If the magnification of a body of size 1 m is 2. What is the size of the image?

Sol. Given, $m = 2$, $h_o = 1$ m, $h_i = ?$

We know that, $m = \frac{h_i}{h_o} \Rightarrow h_i = mh_o$ [2]

$= 2 \times 1 = 2$ m

64. **A convex mirror used for rear view on an automobile has a radius of curvature of 3 m. If a bus is located at 5 m from this mirror. Find the position, nature and magnification of the image.**

Sol. Given, radius of curvature, $R = 3$ m

Distance of the bus, $u = -5$ m

Image of the bus, $v = ?$

Magnification of the image, $m = ?$

We know that, $f = \frac{R}{2} = \frac{3}{2} = 1.5$ m [1]

Using mirror formula, $\frac{1}{f} = \frac{1}{v} + \frac{1}{u}$

$\Rightarrow \frac{1}{v} = \frac{1}{f} - \frac{1}{u} = \frac{2}{3} - \frac{1}{(-5)} = \frac{10+3}{15} = \frac{13}{15}$

$v = \frac{15}{13} = 1.15$ m

$\therefore \quad m = -\frac{v}{u} = -\frac{15/13}{-5} = \frac{3}{13} = 0.23$

The image is virtual, erect and 1.15 m behind the mirror. [2]

65. **A concave shaving mirror is of focal length 50 cm. How far should the mirror be held from the face to produce an image of two fold magnification?**

Sol. $\because m = -\frac{v}{u} = 2$ and $f = -50$ cm

$\Rightarrow \quad v = -2u$ [1/2]

Using the mirror formula, $\frac{1}{u} + \frac{1}{v} = \frac{1}{f}$

$\Rightarrow \frac{1}{u} + \frac{1}{(-2u)} = \frac{1}{f} \Rightarrow \frac{2-1}{2u} = \frac{1}{f} \Rightarrow f = 2u$ [1/2]

$\therefore \quad u = \frac{f}{2} = -\frac{50}{2} = -25$ cm [1]

66. **An object is held 6 cm from a concave mirror of focal length 12 cm. Find the position, nature and magnification of the image.**

Sol. Given, $u = -6$ cm and $f = -12$ cm

Using the mirror formula, $\frac{1}{u} + \frac{1}{v} = \frac{1}{f}$

$\Rightarrow \frac{1}{v} = \frac{1}{f} - \frac{1}{u} \Rightarrow \frac{1}{v} = \frac{1}{-12} - \left(\frac{1}{-6}\right)$

$\Rightarrow \frac{1}{v} = -\frac{1}{12} + \frac{1}{6} \Rightarrow \frac{1}{v} = \frac{-1+2}{12} = \frac{1}{12}$

$\Rightarrow \quad v = 12$ cm [1/2]

As, $\quad m = -\frac{v}{u} = \frac{-12}{-6} = 2$ [1/2]

The image formed is virtual, erect and magnified. [1]

67. **A candle flame is held 3 cm away from a concave mirror of radius of curvature 24 cm. Where is the image formed? What is the nature of the image?**

Sol. Given, object distance, $u = -3$ cm

Radius of curvature, $R = -24$ cm

$\therefore \quad f = \frac{R}{2} = \frac{-24}{2} = -12$ cm, $v = ?$

Apply mirror formula to calculate the value of v.

$\frac{1}{f} = \frac{1}{u} + \frac{1}{v}$ or $\frac{1}{v} = \frac{1}{f} - \frac{1}{u}$

$= \frac{1}{-12} - \frac{1}{(-3)} = \frac{1}{-12} + \frac{1}{3} = \frac{-1+4}{12} \Rightarrow \frac{1}{v} = \frac{3}{12} = \frac{1}{4}$

$\therefore \quad v = 4$ cm [1]

Use the formula for linear magnification (m) to calculate its value.

$m = \frac{-v}{u} = -\frac{4}{(-3)} = +1.33$ [1]

$\therefore$ The image formed is virtual, erect and magnified. [1]

68. **An object 5 cm tall was placed in front of a spherical mirror at 20 cm distance from the mirror. If a virtual image of 10 cm tall was formed behind the mirror, find the focal length of the mirror and the position of the image. Name the type of mirror used.**

Sol. Given, $u = -20$ cm, $h_i = 10$ cm and $h_o = 5$ cm

As we know, $m = \frac{h_i}{h_o} = \frac{10}{5} = 2$

where, h_i = size of image, h_o = size of object, m = magnification.

Also, $m = -\frac{v}{u} \Rightarrow 2 = \left(\frac{-v}{-20}\right) \Rightarrow v = 40$ cm [1]

From mirror formula, $\frac{1}{f} = \frac{1}{v} + \frac{1}{u}$

where, u = object distance, v = image distance and f = focal length.

$\frac{1}{f} = \frac{1}{40} + \frac{1}{(-20)} = \frac{1-2}{40} = \frac{-1}{40} \Rightarrow f = -40$ cm [1]

So, mirror is concave. [1]

69. **A concave mirror produces three times magnified (enlarged) real image of object placed at 10 cm in front of it. Where is the image located?**

Sol. Real image is inverted. So, magnification is negative.

Thus, $m = -3 = \frac{\text{Image size}}{\text{Object size}} = \frac{h_i}{h_o}$

$= \frac{\text{Image size}}{\text{Object size}} = \frac{v}{u}$ (where, v = image distance and u = object distance) [1]

$\Rightarrow -3 = \frac{-(v)}{(-10)}$ ($\because$ object is placed in front of mirror)

$\Rightarrow -3 = \frac{v}{10}$

$\therefore$ Image distance $= -30$ cm

Negative sign shows that image is real, so it will be formed in front of the mirror. [2]

70. **A real image one-fifth the size of an object is formed at a distance of 18 cm from a mirror. What is the nature of mirror? Calculate its focal length.**

Sol. Given, magnification, $m = \frac{-1}{5}$

$v = -18$ cm

$\therefore \quad m = \frac{-v}{u} \Rightarrow \frac{-1}{5} = -\frac{-18}{u}$

$\Rightarrow \quad u = -5 \times 18 = -90$ cm **[1]**

Using mirror formula,

$$\frac{1}{f} = \frac{1}{v} + \frac{1}{u} = \frac{-1}{18} + \frac{1}{(-90)} = \frac{-5-1}{90} = \frac{-6}{90}$$

$f = -15$ cm **[1]**

Thus, real, inverted and smaller image is formed in the concave mirror. **[1]**

71. When an object is placed at a distance of 60 cm from a convex spherical mirror, the magnification produced is $\frac{1}{2}$. Where should the object be placed to get a magnification of $\frac{1}{3}$?

Sol. Distance of first object, $u_1 = -60$ cm

Magnification, $m_1 = \frac{1}{2}$

Distance of second object, $u_2 = ?$

Magnification, $m_2 = \frac{1}{3}$

$$m_1 = \frac{-v_1}{u_1} \Rightarrow v_1 = -m_1 u_1 = \frac{-1}{2} \times (-60) = 30 \text{ cm}$$

Using mirror formula,

$$\frac{1}{f_1} = \frac{1}{v_1} + \frac{1}{u_1} = \frac{1}{30} - \frac{1}{60} = \frac{1}{60} \Rightarrow f_1 = 60 \text{ cm}$$ **[1½]**

Again, $m_2 = \frac{-v_2}{u_2} \Rightarrow v_2 = \frac{-u_2}{3}$

$f_1 = f_2$

$\therefore \quad \frac{1}{f_2} = \frac{1}{v_2} + \frac{1}{u_2} \Rightarrow \frac{1}{u_2} = \frac{1}{f_2} - \frac{1}{v_2}$

$\frac{1}{u_2} = \frac{1}{60} + \frac{3}{u_2} \Rightarrow \frac{1}{u_2} - \frac{3}{u_2} = \frac{1}{60}$

$\Rightarrow \quad \frac{-2}{u_2} = \frac{1}{60} \Rightarrow u_2 = -120$ cm **[1½]**

72. If an object is held at a distance of 60 cm from a convex mirror of focal length 20 cm. At what distance from the convex mirror, should a plane mirror be held, so that images in the two mirrors coincide?

Sol. For convex mirror, $u = -60$ cm, $f = +20$ cm

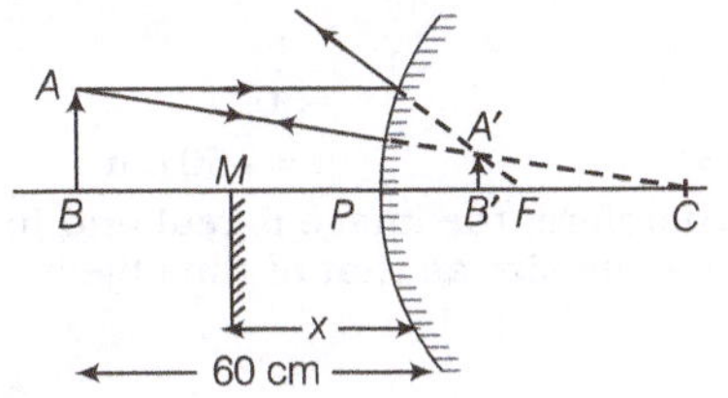

[1]

Using mirror formula, $\frac{1}{v} + \frac{1}{u} = \frac{1}{f}$

$$\Rightarrow \frac{1}{v} = \frac{1}{f} - \frac{1}{u} = \frac{1}{20} - \frac{1}{(-60)} = \frac{3+1}{60} = \frac{4}{60}$$

$v = 15$ cm

$\therefore \quad PB' = 15$ cm **[1]**

Let the plane mirror be held at M such that images in the two mirrors coincide.

As, $\quad BM = MB' = MP + PB' = x + 15$ ...(i)

$BM = \frac{1}{2} BB' = \frac{1}{2}(60 + 15) = 37.5$ ...(ii)

From Eqs. (i) and (ii), we get

$x + 15 = 37.5 \Rightarrow x = 37.5 - 15 = 22.5$ cm **[1]**

Section-II

Structured Questions

73. (i) What are the differences between regular and irregular reflection of light? **[3]**

(ii) Define the following.

(a) Principal axis

(b) Centre of curvature

(c) Aperture of mirror **[3]**

(iii) (a) From the given table, showing object distance and focal length of three concave mirrors, answer the following questions.

S. No.	Object distance (cm)	Focal length (cm)
(i)	30	20
(ii)	10	15
(iii)	20	10

I. Out of three, in which part the mirror will form the image having same size as the object?

II. Which mirror is used as a make-up mirror?

III. (a)Draw the ray diagrams for part I and II.

(b) No matter how far you stand from a mirror, your image appears erect and diminished. Identify the type of mirror. **[4]**

Sol. (i) The differences between regular and irregular reflection are as follows

Regular reflection	Irregular reflection
It takes place on a smooth polished surface.	It takes place on rough surface.
The reflected rays are parallel to each other after reflection.	Reflected rays are not parallel to each other after reflection.
Reflected rays move only in a fixed direction.	Reflected rays can move in any direction.

[1 × 3]

(ii) Refer to theory (Page 145).

(iii) (a) I. The mirror will form an image of same size as that of object in part (iii).

II. In part (ii) concave mirror is being used as a make-up mirror.

III. (a) The ray diagrams are as given below **[1]**

Part I.

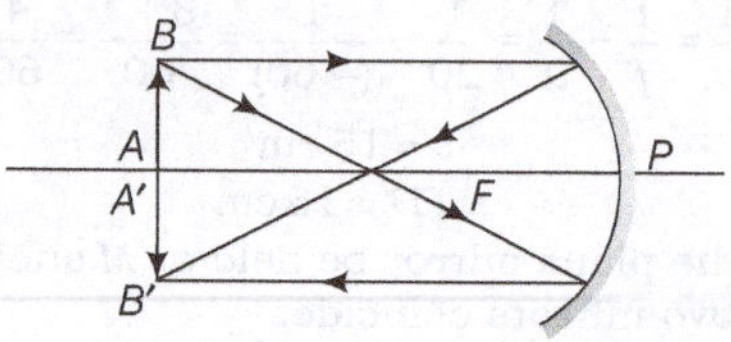

[1]

Part II.

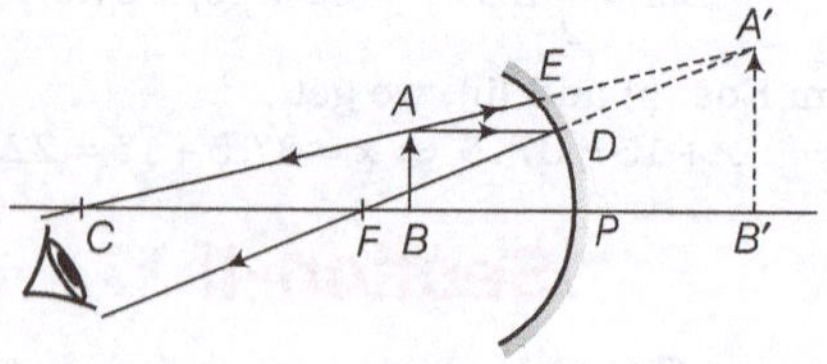

[1]

(b) The mirror is convex mirror. [1]

74. (i) Draw ray diagrams showing the image formation by a concave mirror when an object is placed
(a) at the focus of the mirror
(b) at finite distance from the mirror. [3]
(ii) How can you identify the three types of mirrors without touching? [3]
(iii) A student wants to project the image of a candle flame on the walls of the school laboratory by using a mirror.
(a) Which type of mirror should he use and why?
(b) At what distance, in terms of focal length f of the mirror, should he place the candle flame to get the magnified image on the wall?
(c) Draw a ray diagram to show the formation of the image in this case.
(d) Can he use this mirror to project a diminished image of the candle flame on the same wall? State how, if your answer is yes and why not, if your answer is no. [4]

Sol. (i) (a) Refer to theory (Page 147).
(b) Refer to theory (Page 147). [3]
(ii) Placing an object in front of a mirror and observing the image of the object for different positions.
(a) The image by plane mirror is formed of same size. [1]
(b) An erect and smaller image is formed by convex mirror. [1]
(c) An inverted image of different size beyond focal point and within this point enlarged and erect image is formed by concave mirror. [1]
(iii) (a) He should use a concave mirror. [1]
(b) He should place the candle flame between focus and centre of curvature of the mirror to get the magnified image on the wall. [1]
(c)

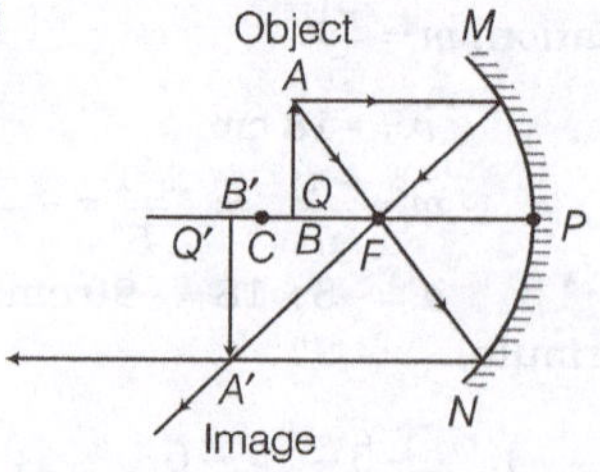

[1]

(d) Yes, when object is located at infinity the diminished image is obtained. [1]

75. (i) A spherical mirror produces an image of magnification – 1 on a screen placed at a distance of 50 cm from the mirror.
(a) Find the distance of the image from the object.
(b) What is the focal length of the mirror?
(c) Draw the ray diagram to show the image formation in this case. [3]
(ii) (a) How can you distinguish between plane mirror, convex mirror and concave mirror by merely looking at the image formed in each case?
(b) Name a mirror that can give an erect and enlarged image of an object. [3]
(iii) For a spherical mirror, we have

$$\frac{1}{v}+\frac{1}{u}=\frac{1}{f}=\frac{2}{R}$$

where, u = distance of an object from pole of mirror,
v = distance of an image from pole of mirror,
f = focal length of mirror
and R = radius of curvature.
We called this formula as mirror formula and is applicable to concave mirror as well as convex mirror.
Using the above formula, answer the following questions.
(a) If we change the value of u by moving an object, then how is focal length f affected?
(b) If the radius of curvature of a spherical mirror is 30 cm. What is its focal length?
(c) Focal length of a mirror depends neither on u nor on v but it depends only on radius of curvature of the mirror. Explain. [4]

Sol. (i) (a) Given, $m = -1$, $v = -50$ cm

$\therefore$ Magnification, $m = \frac{-v}{u}$

$\Rightarrow$ $-1 = \frac{-v}{-50}$

$\Rightarrow$ $u = -50$ cm

Therefore, the image is real and inverted and of same size as that of the object.

∴ Distance of image form the object = 0 **[1]**

(b) Hence, object is placed at centre of curvature,

∵ $R = 50$ cm

∴ $f = \frac{R}{2} = \frac{50}{2} = 25$ cm

As, object distance = image distance = 50 cm **[1]**

(c)

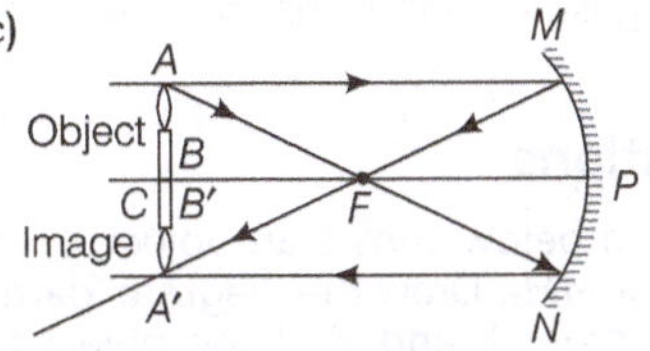

[1]

(ii) (a) By looking into mirror and going close to it, the mirrors can be identified. If image is of same size and erect it is a plane mirror.

If image is of bigger size and erect it is a concave mirror. If image is of smaller size and erect it is a convex mirror. **[2]**

(b) Concave mirror gives erect and enlarged image of an object. **[1]**

(iii) (a) If we change u by moving an object, the distance of an image v changes. But focal length of mirror is not affected. **[1]**

(b) If $R = 30$ cm, then $f = \frac{R}{2} = \frac{30}{2} = 15$ cm **[1]**

(c) Focal length of the mirror is the point where rays actually meet or appears to meet after the reflection. It is half of the radius of curvature. Thus, it does not depend on the distance of object or image. **[2]**

76. (i) A man standing in front of a special mirror finds his image having a small face, big tummy and legs of normal size. What are the shapes of three parts of the mirror? **[3]**

(ii) (a) Under which condition a concave mirror can form an image larger than the actual size?

(b) If position of an object is at infinity, then what will be the position of image?

(c) The image formed is always virtual. What type of mirror it will be? **[3]**

(iii) Draw ray diagrams showing the image formation by a concave mirror when an object is placed

(a) between pole and focus of the mirror

(b) between focus and centre of curvature of the mirror

(c) at centre of curvature of the mirror

(d) a little beyond centre of curvature of the mirror **[4]**

Sol. (i) The upper part of mirror showing smaller face must be convex mirror. **[1]**

The middle part of the mirror showing big tummy must be concave mirror. **[1]**

The lower part of mirror showing normal legs must be plane mirror. **[1]**

(ii) (a) When object is placed between F and P, it will form larger image. **[1]**

(b) Position of image will be at focus. **[1]**

(c) It will be a convex or plane mirror. **[1]**

(iii) Refer to theory (Page 147). **[4]**

Chapter Assessment

1 Mark Questions

1. When the incident ray retraces its path after reflection from a plane mirror, then the angle of incidence is
(a) 45° (b) 90° (c) 60° (d) 0°

2. The radius of curvature of a spherical mirror is
(a) twice the focal length
(b) half the focal length
(c) equal to the focal length
(d) not related to the focal length

3. Which mirror is used for shaving purpose?
(a) Plane (b) Convex
(c) Concave (d) Parabolic

4. Where should an object placed in front of a concave mirror to get a real image of the size of the object?
(a) At the focus of the mirror
(b) At the centre of curvature of mirror
(c) At infinity
(d) Beyond centre of curvature

5. Linear magnification produced by a rear view mirror fitted in vehicles
(a) is equal to one (b) is infinity
(c) is more than one (d) is less than one

2 Marks Questions

6. The angle of incidence for a plane mirror is 30°. What will be the angle between incident and reflected ray?

7. Complete the following ray diagram by drawing suitable rays.

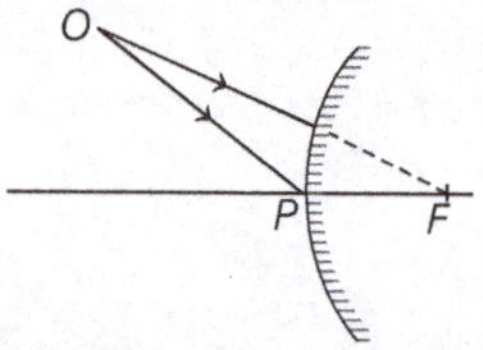

8. Give two differences between real and virtual image.

9. A virtual image cannot be obtained on the screen. This statement appears to be contradictory as we focus a virtual image on to a screen. Justify it.

10. A boy looks his reflection in the concave side of the shining spoon. Is it right side up or inverted? What does he observe, if he looks in the convex side?

11. The magnification for a mirror is -2. How are u and v related?

12. At what distance in front of a concave mirror of focal length 10 cm, an object is placed so that its real image of size five times that of the object is obtained?

13. A concave mirror is a part of hollow sphere of radius 40 cm. What will be the focal length of concave mirror?

14. Explain vehicles in the mirror are closer than they appear. This varnish is printed on the convex mirror outside the driver's side of vehicle. What is the reason behind it?

15. Write a few English alphabet that does not show lateral inversion?

Structured Questions

16. (i) The diagram below shows an object XY in front of a plane mirror MM_1. Draw the diagram, path of two rays from each other X and Y of the object to show the formation of its image. Is the image of XY virtual or real? **[3]**

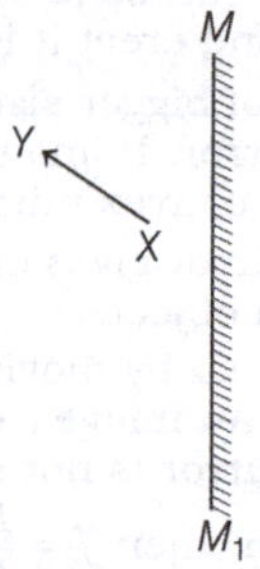

(ii) Name the type of mirror used in the following situations
(a) Headlight of car
(b) Side/rear view mirror of vehicle
(c) Solar furnance **[3]**

(iii) Verify the law of reflection, experimentally. **[4]**

17. (i) Name the mirror shown in figures (a) and (b)

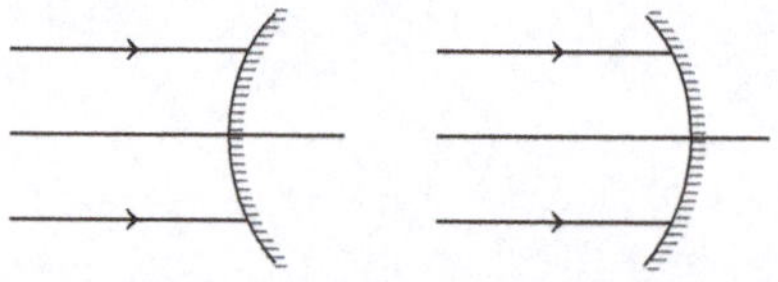

(a) (b)

Draw the reflected rays for the given incident rays in each case and mark focus by the symbol F. **[3]**

(ii) A convex mirror forms an erect image of size one-third the size of object. If radius of curvature of convex mirror is 36 cm. Find the position of the object. **[3]**

(iii) The diagram below shows a convex mirror.

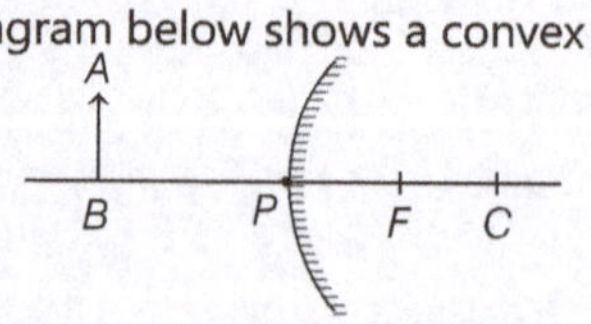

(a) Draw two rays from A and hence locate the position of image of object AB. Label the image $A'B'$.
(b) State two characteristics of the image formed. **[4]**

For Solutions Scan the Code

Olympiad Section*

Brain Teasing Questions of Olympiad Pattern

1 A person stands straight in front of a convex mirror at a distance of 30 m away from it. He sees his erect image whose height is $\frac{1}{6}$th of his real height. What is the focal length of the convex mirror?

(a) 6 m (b) 9 m
(c) 12 m (d) 10 m

2 At an instant, a watch shows time 2 : 35. When seen through the mirror what time will the clock show?

(a) 9 : 25 (b) 10 : 25
(c) 11 : 25 (d) 9 : 25

3 A 2 cm high object is placed at a distance of 32 cm from a concave mirror. The image is real, inverted and 3 cm in size. The focal length of the mirror and the position, where the image formed are respectively

(a) –19.2 cm, –48 cm (b) –40 cm, –18.0 cm
(c) –20 cm, 19 cm (d) –40 cm, –11 cm

4 A girl 160 cm high stands in front of a plane mirror. Her eyes are at a height of 152 cm from the floor. In order to see her full image for minimum length of mirror, where should the lower end of the mirror be placed?

(a) At a height of 4 cm from the floor
(b) At a height of 76 cm from the floor
(c) At a height of 8 cm from the floor
(d) At a height of 84 cm from the floor

5 A man while driving his car observes an ambulance van coming behind from his rear view mirror. In what way is the word AMBULANCE printed in front of van?

(a) AMBULANCE (b) ƎƆNA⅃UBMA
(c) ƎƆNA⅂UBMA (inverted) (d) AMBULANCE (inverted)

6 Raj used a device to focus the image of a distant object on the screen as shown in the figure below. The device should be

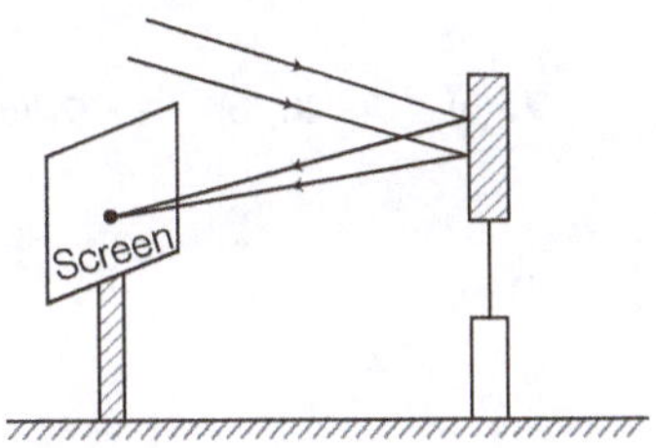

(a) concave mirror (b) convex mirror
(c) plane mirror (d) None of these

7 Trace the path of a ray of light in the following diagram and choose the correct option.

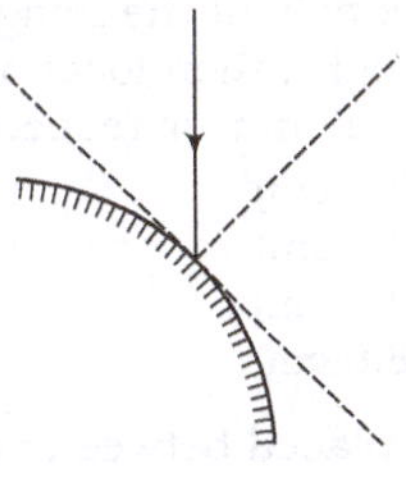

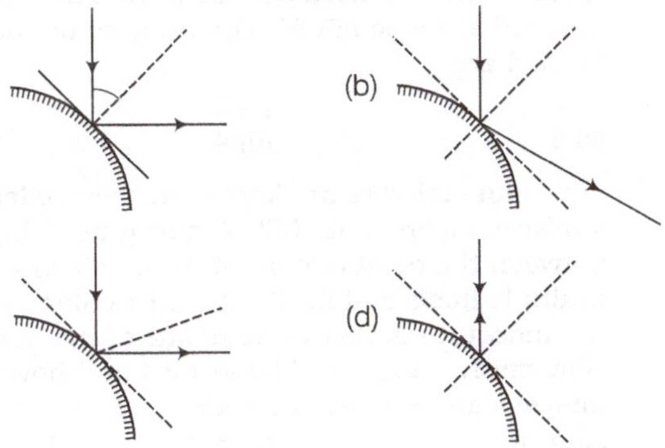

8 From the following diagram, find out the angle of incidence in case of plane mirror. If angle between incident and reflected ray is 75°.

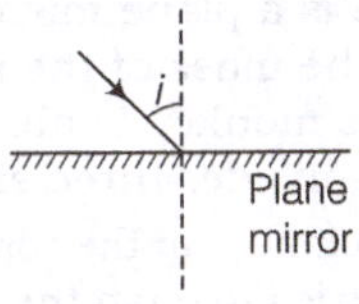

(a) 75° (b) $\left(\frac{75}{2}\right)^\circ$ (c) 180° (d) 90°

9. The diagram shows a patient having her eyes tested. A chart with letters on it is placed behind her and she sees the chart reflected in a plane mirror.

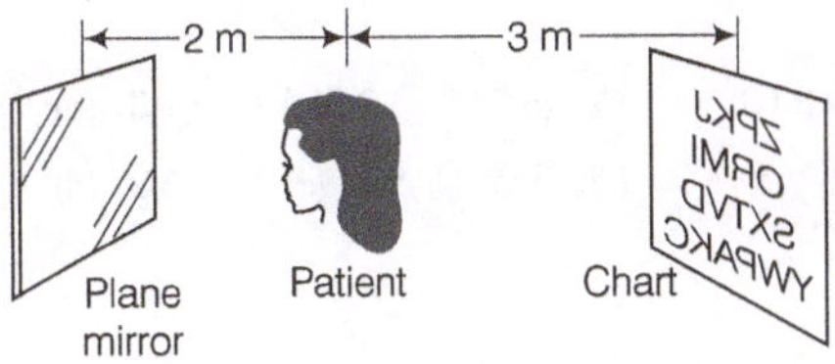

How far away from the patient does the chart seens to be?

(a) 2 m (b) 4 m (c) 5 m (d) 7 m

10 Focal length of a concave mirror is f. In terms of f, the separation between an object and its doubled magnified real image by this mirror is

(a) $\frac{9f}{2}$ (b) $\frac{5f}{2}$

(c) $4f$ (d) $\frac{3f}{2}$

11 An object of height 2.0 cm is placed on the principal axis of a concave mirror at a distance of 12 cm from the pole. If the image is inverted, real and 5 cm in height, then location of the image and focal length of the mirror respectively are

(a) (– 30 cm, + 8.6 cm)
(b) (– 30 cm, – 8.6 cm)
(c) (+ 30 cm, + 8.6 cm)
(c) (+ 30 cm, – 8.6 cm)

12 A light bulb is placed between two plane mirrors inclined at angle of 60°. The number of images formed are

(a) 6 (b) 2
(c) 5 (d) 4

13 Two plane mirrors are kept with their reflecting surfaces inclined at 100°. A mosquito flying in between the combination of these mirrors finds multiple images of itself. At a particular moment the mosquito is very close to one of the mirrors. How many images will be formed and how many images can be mosquito see?

(a) 2, 1 (b) 4, 2
(c) 3, 1 (d) 3, 2

14 A monkey is holding onto one end of a light rope which passes over a frictionless pulley and at the other end there is a plane mirror which has a mass equal to the mass of the monkey. At equilibrium, the monkey is able to see his image in the mirror. Consider three situations

I. The monkey climbs up the rope.
II. The monkey tries to push the rope down.
III. The monkey lets go up the rope.

Under which of the above conditions does the monkey continue to see his image ?

(a) I only (b) II only
(c) III only (d) I, II and III

15 A light source device located on point A produces an incident light which is reflected by a mirror with the configuration as shown in the following figure.

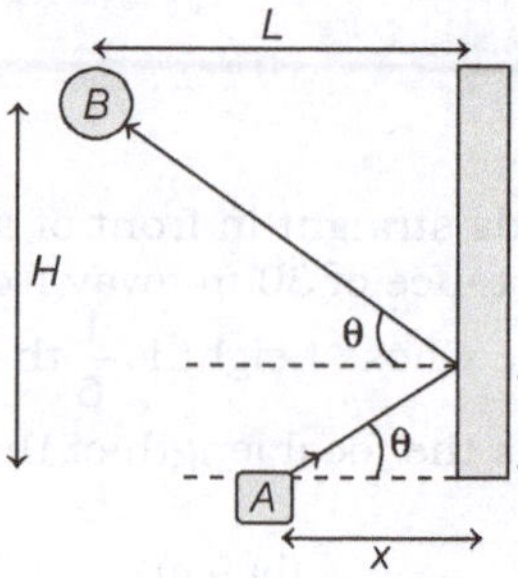

Schematic view of a light both from point A to B.

An object which is located on the point B is aimed to be a target of the reflected light. If the horizontal distance of the object in the point B to the mirror is 2.20 m, vertical distance between A and B (H), and between A and the point of reflection (h) are 1.68 m and 0.430 m respectively. Find the horizontal distance (x) between the light source device (A) and the mirror.

(a) 0.381 m (b) 0.757 m (c) 1.04 m (d) 1.42 m

16 A girl (G) walks into a room along the path shown by the dashed line (see figure). She tries to observe images of small toys numbered 1, 2 and 3 in the plane mirror on the wall.

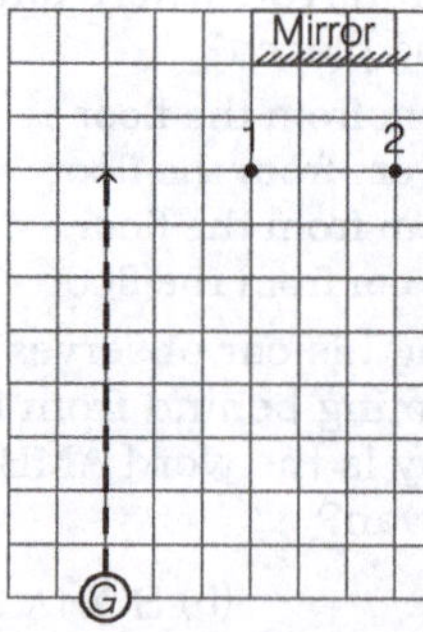

The order in which she will see images of the toys is

(a) 3,2,1 (b) 3, 2 (c) 1, 2, 3 (d) 2, 3

Answers									
1. (a)	**2.** (a)	**3.** (a)	**4.** (b)	**5.** (b)	**6.** (a)	**7.** (a)	**8.** (b)	**9.** (d)	**10.** (d)
11. (b)	**12.** (c)	**13.** (d)	**14.** (d)	**15.** (b)	**16.** (d)				

* *These questions may or may not be asked in the examination, have been given just for additional practice required for olympiads Scholarship Exams etc. For detailed explanations refer Page No. 219.*

CHAPTER

09

Sound

SYLLABUS

• Nature of sound waves, requirement of a medium for sound waves to travel. • Propagation and speed in different media. • Comparison with speed of light. • Infrasonic, sonic, ultrasonic frequencies and their applications.

We hear sound from various sources e.g., from humans, birds, machines, vehicles, TV, radio, etc. Sound is a form of energy which produces a sensation of hearing in our ears. Sound propagates in the form of mechanical waves.

Propagation of Sound in a Medium

The source of sound creates a disturbance in the medium through which it travels. The particles of the medium do not move forward but the disturbance is carried forward. A particle of the medium in contact with the vibrating object is first displaced from its equilibrium position, then it exerts a force on the adjacent particle. As a result of which, the adjacent particle gets displaced from its position of rest. After displacing the adjacent particle, the first particle comes back to its original position. This process continues in the medium till the sound reaches our ear. This is a propagation of sound in the medium.

From the above description, it is clear that particles of the medium vibrate in the direction parallel to direction of propagation of sound wave, so sound waves are longitudinal waves.

Longitudinal Waves

In longitudinal waves, the individual particles of the medium move in a direction parallel to the direction of propagation of the disturbance.

Formation of Compression and Rarefaction in Air

Sound waves are the longitudinal waves, so they move in the air in the form of compression and rarefaction. When a vibrating object moves forward in air, it pushes and compresses the air in front of it, creating a compression which starts to move away from the vibrating object. When the vibrating object moves backwards, it creates rarefaction.

Compression is the part of a longitudinal wave in which the particles of the medium are closer to one another than they normally are and it is the region of high pressure. It is denoted by C.

Rarefaction is the part of a longitudinal wave in which the particles of the medium are farther apart than they normally are and it is the region of low pressure. It is denoted by R.

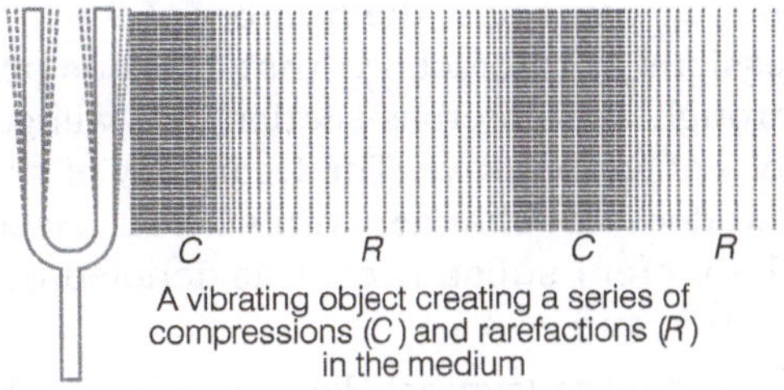

A vibrating object creating a series of compressions (C) and rarefactions (R) in the medium

As the object moves back and forth rapidly, then a series of compressions and rarefactions are created in air. These make the sound waves that propagate through the medium.

Sound Propagation Requires a Material Medium

The substance through which sound travels is called a medium. The medium can be a solid substance, a liquid or a gas. Sound waves being the mechanical wave require a medium to propagate. Thus, a material medium is necessary for the propagation of sound from one place to another, which has following properties

- The medium must be elastic.
- The medium must have inertia.
- The medium should be frictionless.

Note Sound cannot travel in vacuum. Hence, on the moon one cannot hear the sound produced by others.

Some Terms Related to Sound Waves

Wave can be described by its wavelength, frequency, time period, amplitude and speed. Brief explanation of these terms are given below.

1. Wavelength

The distance between the two consecutive compressions (*C*) or two consecutive rarefactions (*R*), is called the wavelength of sound waves. It is the minimum distance in which a sound wave repeats itself.
In other words, it is the combined length of a compression and an adjacent rarefaction. It is represented by a Greek letter lambda (λ). Its SI unit is metre (m).

Note Wave number is the reciprocal of wavelength i.e. $\bar{\nu} = \frac{1}{\lambda}$

2. Frequency

The number of complete waves (or oscillations) produced in one second is called frequency of the wave. It is the number of vibrations that occur per second. If we can count the number of the compressions or rarefactions that cross us per unit time through a given cross-section , we will get the frequency of sound wave. The frequency of a wave is fixed and does not change, even when it passes through different substances. It is denoted by ν (Greek letter, nu).

Its SI unit is hertz (symbol Hz) named in the honour of Heinrich Rudolf Hertz, who discovered photoelectric effect.

1 hertz is equal to 1 vibration per second.

$$1 \text{ kHz} = 1000 \text{ Hz}$$

3. Time Period

The time taken by two consecutive compressions or rarefactions to cross a fixed point is called the time period of the wave.

In other words, the time required to produce one complete wave (or oscillations) is called time period of the wave. It is denoted by symbol *T*. Its SI unit is second (s).

The time period of a wave is the reciprocal of its frequency,

i.e. $$\text{Time period, } T = \frac{1}{\text{Frequency} (\nu)}$$

or $$\text{Frequency} = \frac{1}{\text{Time period}}$$

4. Amplitude

The maximum displacement of the particles of the medium from their original mean positions on passing the sound wave through the medium, is called amplitude of the sound wave. It is used to describe the size of the wave. It is usually denoted by the letter *a*. Its SI unit is metre (m).

The amplitude of a wave is the same as the amplitude of the vibrating body producing the wave.

5. Velocity

The distance travelled by the sound wave in one second is called velocity of the wave or speed of the wave. Under the same physical conditions, the velocity of sound remains same for all frequencies. It is represented by letter *v*. Its SI unit is metre per second (m/s or ms^{-1}).

Displacement-Time Graph

A displacement-time graph shows how the displacement of one point on the wave varies over time.

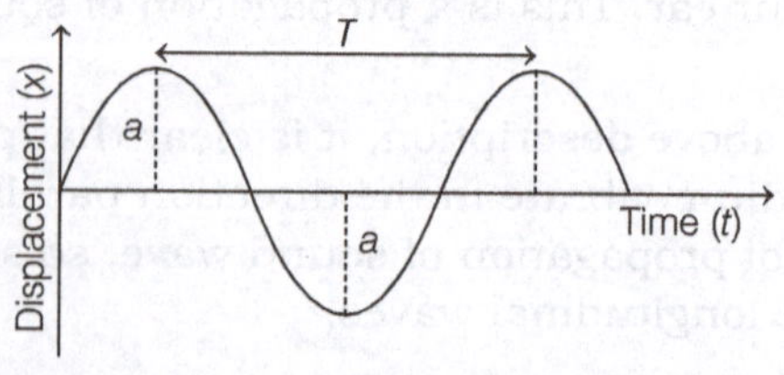

where, *a* is amplitude and *T* is the time period of wave.

Relationship between Wavelength, Wave Velocity and Frequency

$$\text{Wave velocity} = \frac{\text{Distance travelled}}{\text{Time taken}}$$

Suppose distance travelled by a wave is λ (wavelength), in time T, then the wave velocity is given by

$$v = \frac{\lambda}{T}$$

We know that, $f = \nu = \frac{1}{T}$

Therefore, $v = \lambda \times \nu$ or $\boxed{v = \nu\lambda}$

or velocity (speed) = frequency × wavelength

Example 1. A sound wave of length 50 m travels 500 m in 2.5 s. What is the velocity and frequency of sound?

Sol. $\because$ Velocity of sound, $v = \frac{\text{Distance travelled by sound wave}}{\text{Time}}$

$$= \frac{500}{2.5} = \frac{5000}{25} = 200 \text{ m/s}$$

and frequency, $\nu = \frac{v}{\lambda} = \frac{200}{50} \times 100 = 400 \text{ Hz}$

Example 2. A wave pulse of velocity 100 Hz produced on a string, moves a distance of 6 m in 6 ms. Calculate (i) velocity of pulse and (ii) wavelength of pulse.

Sol. Given, distance, $d = 6\text{ m}$, time, $t = 6\text{ ms} = 6 \times 10^{-3}$ s

Frequency, $f = 100$ Hz

(i) $\therefore$ Velocity of pulse, $v = \frac{\text{Distance }(d)}{\text{Time }(t)} = \frac{6}{6 \times 10^{-3}}$

$= 10^3$ m/s

(ii) We know that, velocity of wave pulse,

$$v = f\lambda$$

$\therefore$ Wavelength, $\lambda = \frac{v}{f} = \frac{10^3}{100} = 10$ m

Example. 3. A sound source is producing 2100 wave pulses in 3 s. If the distance covered by a compression and an adjacent rarefaction is 1 m, then find (i) frequency, (ii) wavelength and (iii) speed of sound wave.

Sol. Given, (i) $\because$ number of waves produced in 3 s = 2100

$\therefore$ Number of waves produced in 1 s $= \frac{2100}{3} = 700$

Therefore, frequency of sound wave,

$$f = 700 \text{ Hz}$$

(ii) Wavelength = Distance covered by a compression and an adjacent rarefaction

Therefore, wavelength of sound wave, $\lambda = 1$ m

(iii) Speed of sound wave, $v = f\lambda = 700 \times 1$

$= 700$ m/s

Check Your LEARNING...

1 Write the name of types of waves on the basis of medium.

2 Is water wave a mechanical wave?

3 In the following condition, which one generates transverse wave
(i) wave in string? (ii) sound waves?

4 What is the SI unit of wavelength?

5 What is relationship between velocity, frequency and wavelength of a wave?

6 A wave vibrates up and down 5 times in 0.5 s and it covers a distance of 7 m during this interval. Calculate
(i) frequency of the wave,
(ii) velocity of the wave. *Ans.* 10 Hz, 14 ms^{-1}

Speed of Sound in Different Media

The speed of sound depends on the properties of medium through which it travels. It decreases, when we go from solid to gaseous state. i.e. The speed of sound is more in solids, less in liquids and least in gases (since solids are much more elastic than liquids and gases).

Speed of Sound in Different Media at 25°C

State	Substance	Speed in m/s
Solids	Aluminium	6420
	Nickel	6040
	Steel	5960
	Iron	5950
	Brass	4700
	Glass (flint)	3980
Liquids	Water (sea)	1531
	Water (distilled)	1498
	Ethanol	1207
	Methanol	1103
Gases	Hydrogen	1284
	Helium	965
	Air	346
	Oxygen	316
	Sulphur dioxide	312

Note Speed of sound at 0°C
in air → 331.5 m/s, in water → 1402 m/s and in steel → 6100 m/s

Factors Affecting Speed of Sound in Gas

Following are the factors which affect the speed of sound in gas

(i) **Effect of Density** Speed of sound is inversely proportional to the density of the gas. Therefore, speed of sound decreases with the increase in the density of gas.

(ii) **Effect of Temperature** The speed of sound increases with the increase in the temperature of the gas. This is because as the temperature increases, density of the gas decreases, thereby increasing the speed of sound.

(iii) **Effect of Humidity** The density of the moist air is less than the density of dry air. Therefore, the speed of sound in moist air is slightly greater than in dry air. So, speed of sound increases with the increase in humidity.

(iv) **Effect of Direction of Wind** If the direction of wind is in the direction of propagation of sound, then speed of sound increases. Otherwise, the speed of sound decreases.

Factors not Affecting Speed of Sound

Speed of sound in gas is not affected by the change in

(i) pressure,
(ii) amplitude of wave and
(iii) wavelength or frequency of wave.

Comparison of Speed of Sound with Speed of Light

The speed of sound in air is about 344 ms^{-1} at 22°C and 331 ms^{-1} at 0°C, whereas speed of light in air is $3\times 10^8 ms^{-1}$. Thus, speed of light is much greater than the speed of sound. The sound needs a medium to propagate, whereas light does not.

Consequences of the Large Difference in the Speed of Sound and that of Light

It is observed that during **thunder** and **lightning**, the flash of lightning is seen first and the sound of thunder is heard a little later, although both are produced at the same time in clouds. It is due to the fact that, speed of light is greater than the speed of sound.

Sonic Boom

- When the speed of any object exceeds the speed of sound, it is said to have **supersonic speed**. Many objects such as some aircrafts, bullets and rockets, etc., travel at supersonic speeds. When a sound producing source moves with a speed higher than that of sound, it produces shock waves in air, which carries a large amount of energy. The tremendous air pressure variations caused by the shock waves produce a loud burst of sound, known as 'sonic boom'.
- It produces untolerable loud noise which causes pain in our ears. The shock waves produced by a supersonic aircraft have enough energy to shutter glass and can even damage buildings.

Range of Hearing

The average frequency range over which the human ear is sensitive is called audible range. This range of frequencies are also called sonic sound. For human beings, it is from 20 Hz to 20000 Hz. Children under the age of 5 and some animals, such as dogs can hear upto 25000 Hz. As people grew older, their ears become less sensitive to higher frequencies.

Infrasonic Sound

The sound of frequencies lower than 20 Hz (infrasonic frequency) are known as infrasonic sounds or infrasound, which cannot be heard by human beings. Earthquakes and some animals like whales, elephants and rhinoceroses produce infrasonic sound of frequency 5 Hz. It is observed that some animals get disturbed and start running here and there just before the earthquakes occur. This is because earthquakes produce low frequency infrasound before the main shock waves which possibly alert the animals and they get disturbed.

Ultrasonic Sound

The sounds of frequencies higher than 20000 Hz or 20 kHz are called as ultrasonic sounds or ultrasound which cannot be heard by human beings. Dogs can hear ultrasonic sounds of frequency upto 50000 Hz. This is why, dogs are used for detective work by the police. Monkeys, bats, cats, dolphins, leopards and porpoises can also hear ultrasonic sounds.

Bats can hear ultrasonic sounds having frequencies upto 120000 Hz. Bats, dolphins, porpoises and rats can also produce ultrasonic sounds as well as hear ultrasonic sound.

Properties of Ultrasound

Ultrasounds are high frequency waves, it also has two additional properties as

(i) They travel in a straight line without bending around the corners.
(ii) They can penetrate into matter to a large extent.

Applications of Ultrasound

Some of the important applications of ultrasound are given below

1. In Cleaning Minute Parts of Machines

Ultrasound is used to clean parts located in hard-to-reach-places, such as spiral tubes, odd-shaped machines and electronic components, etc.

Objects to be cleaned are placed in a cleaning solution and ultrasonic waves are sent into the solution. Due to their high frequency, the ultrasound waves stir up the solution. Hence, the particles of dust, grease and dirt vibrate too much, become loose and get detached from the object and fall into the solution. The objects, thus get completely cleaned.

2. In Internal Investigation of Human Body

Ultrasound is used to investigate the internal organs of human body such as liver, uterus and heart, etc.

These waves can penetrate the human body and different types of tissues and get reflected in different ways from a region, where there is a change of tissue's density. In this way, it gives pictures of the inner organs by converting into electrical signals. These pictures or images are then displayed on a monitor or printed on a film. This technique is called **ultrasonography**. It is used for the examination of foetus during pregnancy to detect any growth abnormalities.

Ultrasound is also used for diagnosing heart diseases by scanning the heart from inside. This technique is called echocardiography.

3. In Industries

Ultrasound is used in industry for detecting flaws (cracks, etc.) in metal blocks without damaging them. Metal blocks are used in the construction of big structures like bridges, machines and scientific equipment, etc. The crack can be detected by using ultrasound. This is based on the fact that an internal crack (or hole) does not allow ultrasound to pass through it.

If there is even a small defect, the ultrasound waves get reflected back indicating the presence of the flaw or defect as shown in figure.

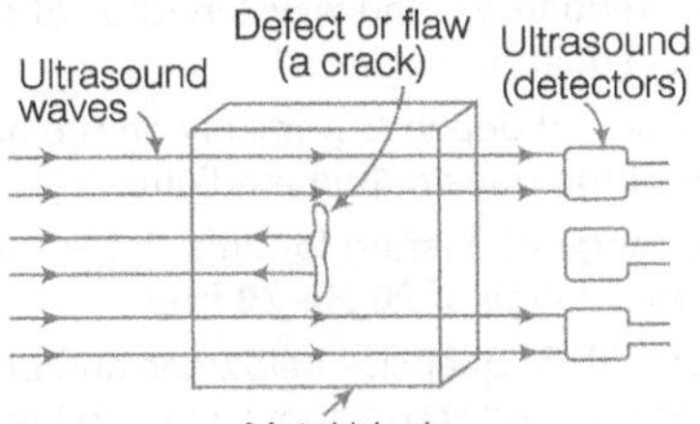

Ultrasound reflected from a part of block, which shows that this metal block has a flaw or defect (like a crack) inside it

4. SONAR

It is abbreviated as Sound Navigation and Ranging. Ultrasonic waves are used to locate and detect objects under water in SONAR because these waves can penetrate water to long distance due to its high frequency.

Use of Ultrasonic Waves by Bats

Bats search out prey and fly in dark night by emitting and detecting reflections of ultrasonic waves. This method used by some animals like bats, tortoises and dolphins to locate the objects by hearing the echoes of their ultrasonic squeaks is known as echolocation.

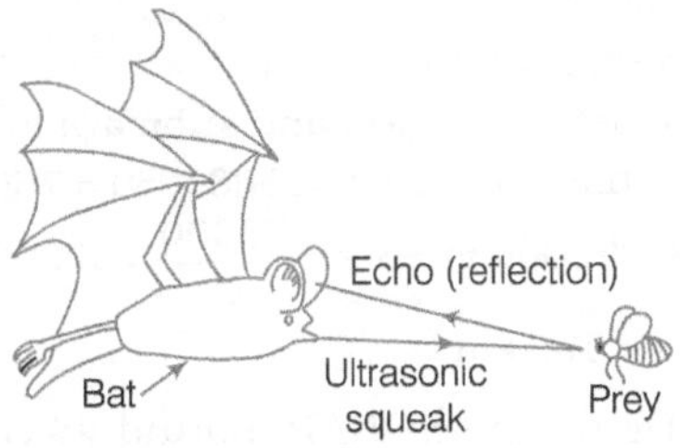

Bats can search their prey in the darkness of night by the method of echolocation

Differences between Ultrasonic Waves and Supersonic Waves

Ultrasonic Wave	Supersonic Wave
These pressure waves of frequency greater than 20000 Hz are called ultrasonic waves.	It refers to the movement of an object with a speed greater than the speed of sound.
The speed of ultrasonic waves is equal to the speed of sound.	A supersonic object moves faster than the sound waves.
The basic properties of ultrasonic waves is same as that of sound waves and these waves are produced by piezoelectric oscillators.	Object moving with a speed greater than sound produces shock waves which ultimately produces a narrow region of high pressure and temperature.
It is widely used in medical diagnosis. It is also used to test flaws in metal, etc.	There is no specific use of sonic boom. But can be used to predict the speed of aircraft whether it is more or less than the speed of sound.

Example. 4. The light from the bomb due to its explosion is seen 3 s before the explosion is heard. If the speed of sound in air is 332 m/s, then find the distance of observer from the place of explosion of bomb.

Sol. Given, speed of sound, $v = 332$ m/s

Time, $t = 3$ s

If d be the distance between the observer from the place of explosion of bomb, then

$$d = v \times t = 332 \times 3 = 996 \text{ m}$$

Since, speed of light (= 3×10^8 m/s) is much greater than the speed of sound =(332 m/s), therefore we can assume that the light takes negligible time and sound takes 3 s to reach the observer.

Example 5. A submarine produces the ultrasonic waves of velocity 1500 ms^{-1} in water. The officer receives signal after 50 s of emission of ultrasonic waves. Find the distance of object which is present at the bottom of sea.

Sol. Given, velocity of ultrasonic waves in water,

$v = 1500 \text{ ms}^{-1}$

Time taken, $t = 50$ s

Distance between object and submarine, $s = ?$

We know that, $d = v \times t = 1500 \times 50 = 75000$ m

As, $2s = 75000 \text{ m} \Rightarrow s = \frac{75000}{2} = 37500 \text{ m}$

$= 37.5$ km

Example 6. Using the SONAR, sound waves are emitted at the surface of water, which after being reflected from bottom of water, are detected. If the time interval from the emission to the detection of the sound waves is 4 s, calculate the depth of the water. (Take, speed of sound in water = 1450 ms^{-1}.)

Sol. Given, time interval from the emission to the detection of the sound wave = 4 s

Time taken by sound waves to travel from surface to bottom, $t = 4/2 = 2$ s

and speed of sound waves, $v = 1450 \text{ ms}^{-1}$

Depth of water $= vt = 1450 \times 2 = 2900$ m

Example 7. In a submarine, equipped with a SONAR, the time interval from the emission to the detection of the sound pulse is found to be 77 s. What is the distance of enemy submarine? (Take, speed of sound in water = 1450 ms^{-1})

Sol. Time interval of transmission and detection, $t = 77$ s

Speed of sound wave in water, $v = 1450 \text{ ms}^{-1}$

Distance travelled by the ultrasound

= 2 × distance between both submarines = $2d$

$2d = v \times t = 1450 \times 77 = 111650 \text{ m} \Rightarrow d = 55825 \text{ m}$

Therefore, the distance of enemy submarine is 55825 m.

Check Your LEARNING...

1 In which medium, the speed of sound is greatest?
2 With the increase in the humidity, does the speed of sound increase or decrease?
3 Why lightning seen before thunder?
4 What is audible range of sound?
5 Which animal generates infrasonic sound?
6 Is supersonic object move faster than the sound?
7 Write the full name of SONAR.
8 Which type of frequency is used by bats for catching their prey?

QUiCK Revision

- **Wave** occurs when a system is disturbed from its equilibrium position and this disturbance travels or propagates from one region of the system to other.
- The waves requiring a material medium for their propagation are called **mechanical waves.**
- According to the motion of medium, particle waves are of two types.
  (i) **Transverse wave**
  (ii) **Longitudinal wave**
- Sound travels as successive **compressions** and **rarefactions** in the medium.
- In sound propagation, it is the energy of the sound that travels and not the particles of the medium.
- Sound cannot travel in vacuum.
- The change in density from one maximum value to the minimum value and again to the maximum value makes one complete oscillation.
- The distance between two consecutive compressions or two consecutive rarefactions is called the **wavelength** (λ).
- The time taken by the wave for one complete oscillation of the density or pressure of the medium is called the **time period** (*T*).
- The number of complete oscillations per unit time is called the **frequency**, $\nu = \frac{1}{T}$.
- The speed v, frequency ν and wavelength λ, of sound are related by the equation $v = \lambda\nu$.
- The speed of sound depends primarily on the nature and the temperature of the transmitting medium.
- The **audible range** of hearing for an average human being is in the frequency range of **20 Hz-20 kHz.**
- Sound waves with frequencies below the audible range are termed **infrasonic** and those above the audible range are termed **ultrasonic.**
- **Ultrasound** has many medical and industrial applications.
- The **SONAR** technique is used to determine the depth of the sea and to locate underwater hills, valleys, submarines, icebergs, sunken ships, etc.

Chapter Practice

Section-I

1 Mark Questions

1. A tuning fork produces sound wave, because it creates
(a) heat (b) light
(c) vibration (d) None of these

Sol. (c) If tuning fork is vibrating, then it produces sound.

2. Which of the following does not produce sound wave?
(a) Drum (b) Birds
(c) TV (d) Microwave oven

Sol. (d) Microwave oven is used to produce electromagnetic wave.

3. Sound travels in air, if
(a) particles of medium travel from one place to another
(b) there is no moisture in the atmosphere
(c) disturbance moves
(d) both particles as well as disturbance travel from one place to another

Sol. (c) When sound travels in air, then only disturbance created by the vibration of particle moves from one place to another.

4. A person is listening to a tone of 400 Hz sitting at a distance of 500 m from the source of the sound, then the time interval between the successive
(a) compressions from the source is 2.5 ms
(b) rarefactions from the source is 3.5 ms
(c) Both (a) and (b)
(d) Neither (a) nor (b)

Sol. (a) The time interval between the successive compressions or rarefactions will be given as

$$\text{Time interval} = \frac{1}{\text{Frequency}} = \frac{1}{400} = 0.0025 \text{ s}$$
$$= 2.5 \text{ ms}$$

5. The frequency of a source of sound is 200 Hz. How many times does it vibrate in 2 min?
(a) 2400 (b) 24000
(c) 24500 (d) 2450

Sol. (b) Given, frequency = 200 Hz

Number of oscillations in 1 s = 200
(Because frequency represents number of oscillations in 1s)
Number of oscillations in 2 min or 120 s
$= 200 \times 120 = 24000$

6. A guitar of frequency 360 Hz makes 120 vibrations. If the velocity of sound in air is 330 m/s, then how much distance is travelled by the sound in air?
(a) 90 m (b) 100 m
(c) 110 m (d) 140 m

Sol. (c) Given, frequency, $\nu = 360$ Hz
Velocity, $v = 330$ m/s
Wavelength, $\lambda = ?$
As, $\lambda = \frac{v}{\nu} = \frac{330}{360} = \frac{33}{36}$ m

$\therefore$ Distance travelled by the sound wave of 120 vibrations $= 120 \times \frac{33}{36} = 110$ m.

7. A man beating a drum in front of a cliff hears the echo after 4 s. What is the distance of man from the cliff, if velocity of sound in air is 330 m/s?
(a) 660 m (b) 500 m (c) 1000 m (d) 0.3 km

Sol. (a) Given, speed = 330 m/s and time = 4 s
As we know that,
Distance, $s =$ Speed $\times$ Time $= 330 \times 4 = 1320$ m
As in 4 s, sound has to travel twice the distance between man and the cliff.
So, distance between man and cliff is
$$\frac{s}{2} = \frac{1320}{2} = 660 \text{ m}$$

8. A tuning fork starts vibrating after colliding a ball as shown below. The tuning fork produces sound of frequency 500 Hz due to its vibration.

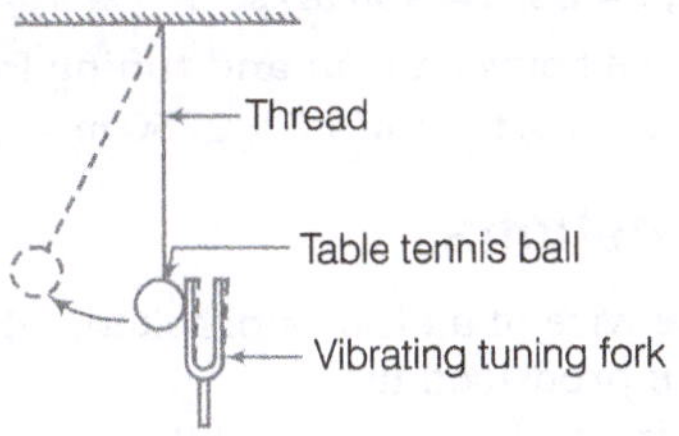

If the wavelength of sound produced by tuning fork due to its vibration is 90 cm, then speed of sound will be
(a) 332 m/s (b) 350 m/s
(c) 450 m/s (d) 380 m/s

Sol. (c) Given, wavelength, $\lambda = 90$ cm $= 0.9$ m
Frequency, $f = 500$ Hz
$\therefore$ Speed of sound wave produced by tuning fork,
$v = f\lambda = 500 \times 0.9 = 450$ m/s

9. Find the value of wavelength, when frequency of vibration is changed to 300 Hz. Take, $v = 450$ m/s.
(a) 1.8 m (b) 0.5 m (c) 1.5 m (d) 2.5 m

Sol. (c) According to given condition,
$v = 450$ m/s and $f = 300$ Hz

$$\therefore \quad \lambda = \frac{v}{f} \quad [\because v = f\lambda]$$
$$= \frac{450}{300} = 1.5 \text{ m}$$

10. Which of the following statement is correct?
(a) Speed of sound is maximum in solids.
(b) Speed of sound is minimum in gases.
(c) Speed of sound is maximum in gases.
(d) Both (a) and (b).

Sol. (d) Speed of sound is greatest in solids, whereas least ingases.

11. Infrasound can be heard by
(a) dog (b) bat
(c) rhinocerose (d) human beings

Sol. (c) Infrasounds are the waves whose frequency is less than 20 Hz. Rhinoceroses communicate using infrasound of frequency as low as 5 Hz.

12. What is the use of SONAR?
(a) To determine depth of sea
(b) To locate sunken ship
(c) To locate underwater hills
(d) All of the above

Sol. (d) SONAR is used to determine the depth of the sea and to locate underwater hills, valleys, submarine, ice bergs, sunken ship, etc.

13. If a man hears a sound of velocity 450 m/s produced by tuning fork in 5 s after colliding the ball, then distance between the man and tuning fork is
(a) 2.5 km (b) 1.5 km (c) 2 km (d) 2.25 km

Sol. (d) Given, $t = 5$ s, $v = 450$ m/s
$\therefore$ Distance between man and tuning fork,
$$d = v \times t = 450 \times 5 = 2250 \text{ m} = 2.25 \text{ km}$$

2 Marks Questions

14. When the wire of a sitar is plucked, what kind of waves are produced in
(i) the wire and (ii) air?

Sol. (i) Transverse waves are produced in the wire. [1]
(ii) Longitudinal waves are produced in air. [1]

15. Give some examples of waves which are the combination of both transverse and longitudinal wave motion.

Sol. If a wave propagates along the surface of a medium, then generally it has both transverse as well as longitudinal components. When such a wave travels through the medium, its particles move either along a circle or an ellipse. [1]

e.g.
(i) Ocean waves in deep water.
(ii) Seismic waves along the surface of the Earth during earthquake. [1]

16. What is sound and how is it produced?

Sol. Sound is a form of energy, which produces the sensation of hearing in our ears. It is produced, when an object is set to vibrate or we can say that vibrating objects produce sound. [2]

17. Why are the longitudinal waves also called pressure waves?

Sol. It is because longitudinal waves travel in a medium as series of alternate compressions and rarefactions i.e., they travel as variations in pressure. Therefore, they are called pressure waves. [2]

18. How does the sound produced by a vibrating object in a medium reach your ear?

Sol. A vibrating object produce sound waves by disturbing the particles in the medium. This disturbance caused by vibration propagates and finally reach our ears. The ear drums in our ears, vibrates as a consequence of the sound and therefore, we hear the sound produced by an object. [2]

19. Explain how sound is produced by your school bell?

Sol. The bell produces the sound when it is struck by a hammer. When the bell is struck by hammer, it starts vibrating. Since, the vibrating objects produce sound which then travels through and then reaches our ears. [2]

20. A tuning fork is producing sound, prove with an activity that sound is produced by it during vibrations.

Sol. Take a tuning fork and vibrate it with a rubber pad. Now, touch the suspended ball gently with the prong of the vibrating tuning fork.

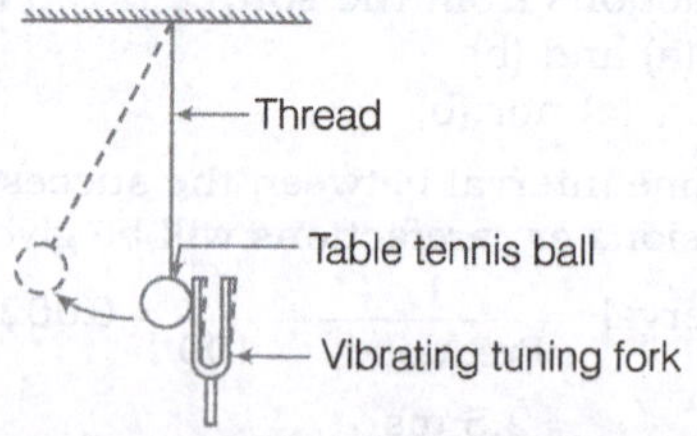

When we touch the ball with tuning fork, a sound will be produced due to vibration of fork and due to the vibration of fork, ball also starts vibrating and comes into motion. So, it proves that sound is produced due to vibrations. [2]

21. Why is sound wave called mechanical wave?

Sol. The sound wave is called mechanical wave because on propagation of sound wave in a medium, the particles of the medium vibrate to and fro about their equilibrium positions parallel to the direction of propagation of the wave. [2]

22. Suppose you and your friend are on the Moon. Will you be able to hear any sound produced by your friend?

Sol. No, I will not be able to hear any sound produced by my friend because the sound waves require some material medium like air to travel. There is no atmosphere or air on the Moon, so the sound produced by my friend will not reach me. Hence, I will not be able to hear. [2]

23. Define the terms wavelength and wave velocity and write their SI units.

Sol. **Wavelength** The distance between the two consecutive compressions (C) or two consecutive rarefactions (R), is called the wavelength of sound waves. It is represented by a Greek letter lambda (λ). Its SI unit is metre (m).

Wave Velocity The distance travelled by the sound wave in one second is called velocity of the wave or speed of the wave. It is represented by letter v. Its SI unit is metre per second (m/s or ms^{-1}) [2]

24. Flash and thunder are produced simultaneously. But thunder is heard a few seconds after the flash is seen. Explain, why?

Sol. The velocity of light is very much greater ($3 \times 10^8 ms^{-1}$) than the velocity of sound (344 ms^{-1}). Therefore, the flash of lightning is seen much before the thunder is heard. [2]

25. Give the uses of infrasonic waves.

Sol. Following are the two uses of infrasonic waves

(i) Infrasonic waves are used in drilling deep well through rocky path. [1]

(ii) It can break up hard rocks more easily than ordinary drill process. [1]

26. What is sonic boom? Explain briefly.

Sol. When an object (e.g. jet, aircrafts) travels with speed greater than that of sound, then this speed is known as supersonic speed. Aircraft at the supersonic speed produces shock waves. The pressure variation in such shock wave leads to sharp and loud sound called sonic boom. [2]

27. What is the range of frequencies associated with (i) infrasound and (ii) ultrasound?

Sol. (i) Sound waves having frequencies less than 20 Hz and greater than zero are called infrasound. [1]

(ii) Sound waves having frequencies more than 20000 Hz are called ultrasound. [1]

28. State the two properties of ultrasound that makes it useful to us.

Sol. The two properties of ultrasound that makes it useful to us are as follows

(i) Ultrasound wave has high energy due to its high frequency. [1]

(ii) A wave having high frequency shows least diffraction, so it propagates on the straight. [1]

29. Why do we hear the sound produced by the humming bees while the sound of vibrations of pendulum is not heard?

Sol. The frequency of vibrations of pendulum is below of 20 Hz (infrasound). We cannot hear infrasound but humming bees produce audible sound which can be heard by human beings. [2]

30. Explain how bats use ultrasound to catch a prey?

Sol. Bats can produce ultrasonic waves by flapping their wings and they can also detect these waves.

The ultrasonic waves produced by a bat spread out. These waves after reflecting from a prey like an insect, reach the bat. Therefore, helping the bat to locate its prey. [2]

31. How are ultrasonic waves different from ordinary sound waves? State two applications of ultrasound.

Sol. Ultrasonic waves have greater frequency than 20000 Hz, thereby having high energy while ordinary sound waves have not that much energy. [1]

Applications of ultrasound are given below

(i) In the treatment of muscular pains.

(ii) In the diagnosis of diseases. [1]

32. What is SONAR? Write two uses of SONAR technique.

Sol. The acronym SONAR stands for Sound Navigation and Ranging. It is a device which uses ultrasonic waves to measure the distance, direction and speed of underwater objects. [1]

Uses of SONAR technique are as follows

(i) It is used to determine the depth of the sea.

(ii) It is used to locate underwater hills, valleys, submarines, icebergs, sunken ships, etc. [1]

33. How is ultrasound used for cleaning?

Sol. Ultrasound is generally used to clean parts located in hard to reach places e.g., spiral tube, odd shaped parts, electronic components, etc. Objects to be cleaned are placed in a cleaning solution and ultrasonic waves are sent into the solution. Due to the high frequency, the particles of dust, grease and dirt get detached and drop out. The objects thus get thoroughly cleaned. [2]

3 Marks Questions

34. (i) By what type of medium, can longitudinal waves be transmitted? Explain it in brief.

(ii) Name the types of waves and two examples associated with compressions and rarefactions.

Sol. (i) Since, longitudinal waves travel in the form of compressions and rarefactions, so they involve changes in the volume and density of medium. As all media, i.e., solids, liquids and gases have elasticity of volume. Hence, these waves (longitudinal waves) can be transmitted through all the three types of media. [1]

(ii) There are two types of waves

(a) Longitudinal waves (b) Transverse waves [1]

e.g. The waves which are formed by consecutive compressions and rarefactions travel along a slinky, when it is pushed and pulled at one end, are the longitudinal waves.
The following figure shows longitudinal waves.

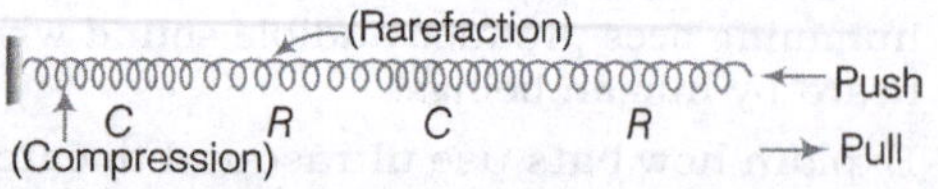

[1]

35. **Describe in details with the help of a diagram, how compressions and rarefactions are produced in air near a source of sound?**

Sol. Refer to (Page 165). [3]

36. **Explain a technique to find the fault in a block of metal using reflection of sound.**

Sol. Ultrasonic waves can be used to detect the fault in a block of metal using reflection of sound.
These waves are allowed to pass through the metal block. Transmitted waves are detected by the detectors. If there is even a small defect, then the ultrasound gets reflected back and does not reach the detector. This is shown in figure below. This indicates the presence of a flaw or defect like crack or hole, etc. [2]

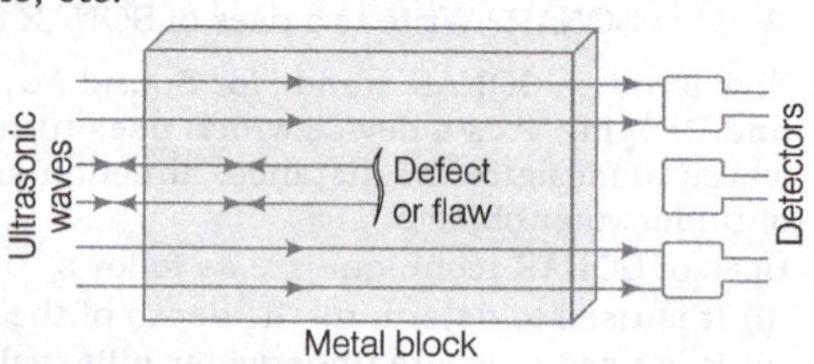

Metal block [1]

37. **(i) Which has shorter wavelength infrasonic or ultrasonic?**
(ii) Can dolphin detect ultrasonic waves?
(iii) Name any one living organism which can detect infrasonic waves.

Sol. (i) Ultrasonic wave has shorter wavelength. [1]
(ii) Yes, dolphin can detect ultrasonic waves. [1]
(iii) Rhinoceros can detect infrasonic waves. [1]

38. **(i) Write two main properties of ultrasound.**
(ii) Mention one application of ultrasound in
(a) industries (b) medical field.

Sol. (i) (a) Ultrasound can travel in a straight line without bending around the corners.
(b) It can penetrate into matter to a large extent. [1½]
(ii) (a) In industries, ultrasound is used to detect cracks and flaws in metal blocks.
(b) In medical field, ultrasound is used to break stones in gall bladder and kidney. [1½]

4 Marks Questions

39. **Write any four characteristics of wave motion.**

Sol. Four characteristics of wave motion are as follows
(i) It is the disturbance which travels forward through the medium and not the particles of the medium. [1]
(ii) Each particle receives vibrations a little later than its preceding particle. [1]
(iii) The wave velocity is different from the velocity of the particles with which they vibrate about their mean positions. [1]
(iv) The wave velocity remains constant in a given medium, whereas particle velocity changes continuously during its vibrations about the mean position. [1]

40. **Draw a curve showing density or pressure variation with respect to distance for a disturbance produced by sound. Mark the position of compression and rarefaction on this curve.**

Sol.

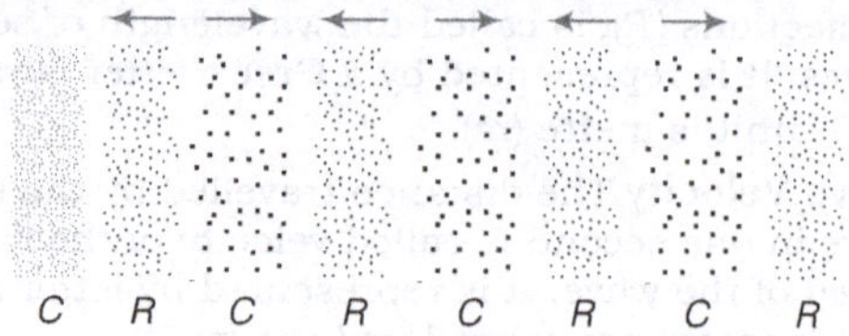

Density variations [1]

Pressure variations [1]

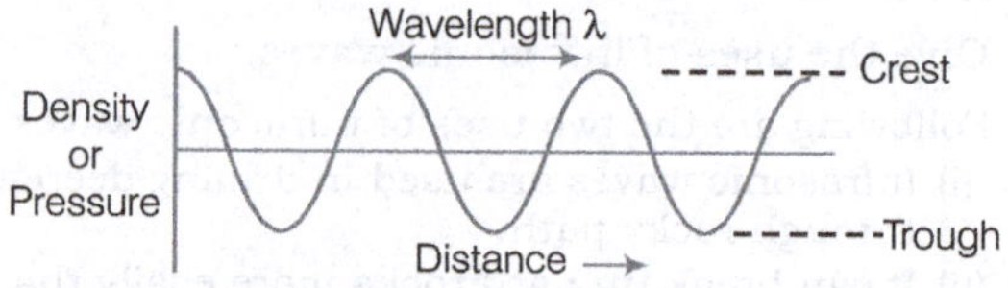

[2]

41. **Define an experiment to show that sound needs a material medium for its propagation.**

Sol. Experiment to show that sound needs a material medium for its propagation is given below.

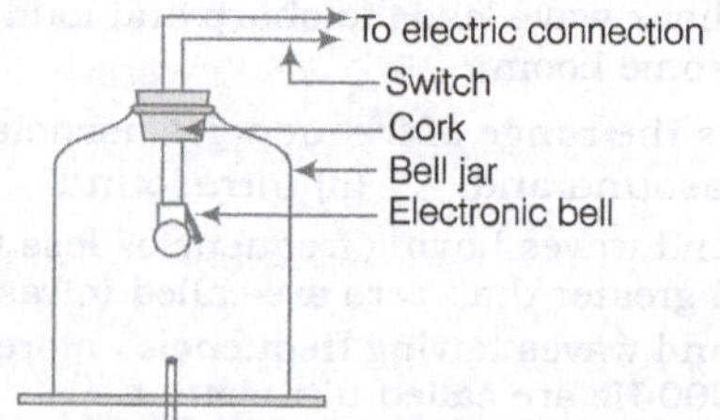

Bell jar experiment showing sound cannot travel in vacuum [2]

Take an electric bell and an airtight glass bell jar. The electric bell is suspended inside the airtight bell jar. The bell jar is connected to a vacuum pump, as shown in the given figure. If you press the switch, you will be able to hear the bell.
Now, start the vacuum pump.

When the air in the jar is pumped out gradually, the sound becomes fainter, although the same current is passing through the bell.

After sometime, when less air is left inside the bell jar, you will hear a very feeble sound. On removal of complete air, no sound is heard.

This confirms that sound needs a material medium for its propagation. [2]

Numerical Type Questions

42. Sound produced by a thunder storm is heard 10 s after the lightning is seen. Calculate the approximate distance of the thunder cloud. (Take, speed of sound = $340\ ms^{-1}$)

Sol. Given, velocity, $v = 340\ ms^{-1}$,

Time, $t = 10$ s, distance, $d = ?$

$\therefore$ Distance d = Velocity (v) × Time (t)

$= 340 \times 10 = 3400\ m = 3.4\ km$ [2]

43. Calculate the wavelength of a sound wave whose frequency is 200 Hz and speed is $440\ ms^{-1}$ in a given medium.

Sol. Given, frequency, $\nu = 200$ Hz, speed, $v = 440\ ms^{-1}$,

Wavelength, $\lambda = ?$

From the relation, $v = \nu\lambda$

$$440 = 200\lambda$$

$$\lambda = \frac{440}{200} = 2.2\ m$$ [2]

44. A person is listening to a tone of 500 Hz sitting at a distance of 450 m from the source of the sound. What is the time interval between successive compressions from the sources?

Sol. The time interval between two successive compressions or rarefactions is equal to the time period of the wave.

$\therefore$ Required time interval = Time period

$$= \frac{1}{\text{Frequency}} = \frac{1}{500} = 0.002\ s$$

$$= 2 \times 10^{-3}\ s = 2\ ms$$ [2]

45. A person has a hearing range from 20 Hz to 20 kHz. What are the typical wavelengths of sound waves in air corresponding to these two frequencies? (Take, the speed of sound in air is $344\ ms^{-1}$.)

Sol. The relation between speed (v), wavelength (λ) and frequency (ν) of a wave, we have

$$v = \nu\lambda \Rightarrow \lambda = \frac{v}{\nu}$$

(i) Here, $v = 344\ ms^{-1}$, $\nu = 20$ Hz

$\therefore$ Corresponding wavelength, $\lambda = \frac{v}{\nu}$

$$= \frac{344}{20} = 17.2\ m$$ [1]

(ii) Here, $v = 344\ ms^{-1}$, $n = 20$ kHz $= 20 \times 10^3$ Hz

$\therefore$ Corresponding wavelength,

$$\lambda = \frac{v}{\nu} \quad [\because nu = n]$$

$$= \frac{344}{20 \times 10^3} = 1.72 \times 10^{-2}\ m$$ [1]

46. Two children are at opposite ends of an aluminium rod. One strikes the end of the rod with a stone. Find the ratio of time taken by the sound wave in air and in aluminium to reach the second child. (Take, speed of sound in air is $346\ ms^{-1}$ and speed of sound in aluminium is $6420\ ms^{-1}$.)

Sol. Let l = length of the rod.

Time taken by the sound to travel through the aluminium rod is given by

$$t_1 = \frac{\text{Distance}}{\text{Speed}} = \frac{l}{v_{Al}}$$

Similarly, time taken by the sound to travel through the air is given by

$$t_2 = \frac{\text{Distance}}{\text{Speed}} = \frac{l}{v_{air}}$$ [1]

$\therefore$ Required ratio, $t_1 : t_2 = \frac{v_{air}}{v_{Al}} = \frac{346}{6420} = \frac{173}{3210}$ [1]

47. The frequency of a source of sound is 100 Hz. How many times does it vibrate in a minute?

Sol. Given, frequency, $\nu = 100$ Hz

From the definition of frequency,

we can say that number of oscillations in 1 s = 100

$\therefore$ Number of oscillations in 1 min or 60 s

$= 100 \times 60 = 6000$

Thus, the source of sound vibrates 6000 times in a minute. [2]

48. Ocean waves of time period of 0.01 s have a speed of $15\ ms^{-1}$. Calculate the wavelength of these waves. Find the distance between a crest and adjoining trough.

Sol. Given, time period of the waves, $T = 0.01$ s

Speed of the waves, $v = 15\ ms^{-1}$

Wavelength of these waves,

$$\lambda = \frac{v}{\nu} \quad (\text{from } v = \nu\lambda)$$

or $$\lambda = v \times T \quad \left(\because \nu = \frac{1}{T}\right)$$

$$= 15 \times 0.01 = 0.15\ m$$ [1]

The distance between crest and adjoining trough $= \frac{\lambda}{2}$

$$= \frac{0.15}{2} = 0.075\ m$$ [1]

49. The given graph shows the displacement *versus* time relation for a disturbance travelling with velocity of $1500\ ms^{-1}$. Calculate the wavelength of the disturbance.

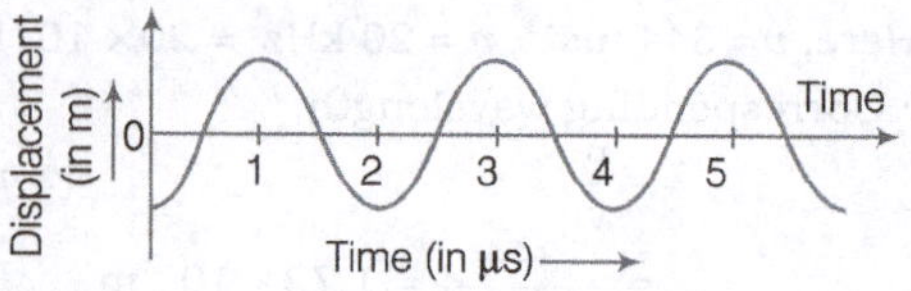

Sol. Given, velocity, $v = 1500\ ms^{-1}$

Time taken in one complete cycle is 2 μs.

$\therefore$ Time period, $t = 2\mu s = 2 \times 10^{-6} s$ **[1]**

$\therefore$ Wavelength, $\lambda = vt = 1500 \times 2 \times 10^{-6}$

$= 3 \times 10^{-3}$ m **[1]**

50. Waves of frequency 100 Hz are produced in a string as shown in the figure. Give its

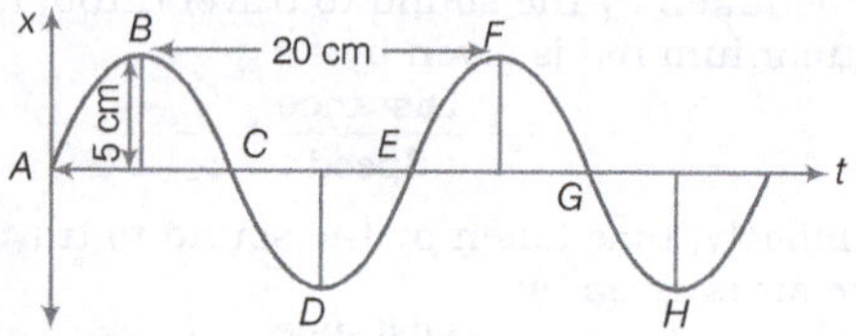

(i) amplitude (ii) wavelength
(iii) velocity (iv) nature

Sol. (i) Amplitude = 5 cm

(ii) Wavelength = 20 cm

(iii) Velocity, $v = \nu\lambda = 100 \times 20 \times 10^{-2} = 20\ ms^{-1}$

(iv) **Nature** It is a transverse wave. **[1×4]**

51. A sound wave has frequency of 3 kHz and a wavelength 45 cm. How long will it take to travel 1.8 km?

Sol. Given, frequency, $\nu = 3$ kHz $= 3 \times 10^3$ Hz

Wavelength, $\lambda = 45$ cm $= 45 \times 10^{-2}$ m

From the relation, speed of wave, $v = \nu\lambda$

$= 3 \times 10^3 \times 45 \times 10^{-2} = 1350$ m/s

Distance to be covered = 1.8 km = 1.8 × 1000 m

= 1800 m **[1]**

$\therefore$ Time taken by the wave to cover the distance of 1.8 km

$= \frac{\text{Distance}}{\text{Speed}} = \frac{1800}{1350} = 1.33$ s **[1]**

52. A sound wave travels at a speed of $339\ ms^{-1}$. If its wavelength is 1.5 cm, what is the frequency of the wave? Will it be audible?

Sol. Given, speed, $v = 339\ ms^{-1}$

Wavelength, $\lambda = 1.5$ cm $= 1.5 \times 10^{-2}$ m

$\therefore$ Frequency, $\nu = \frac{v}{\lambda} = \frac{339}{1.5 \times 10^{-2}} = 22600$ Hz **[1]**

This frequency is greater than 20000 Hz, so it will not be audible. Audible range for human ear is 20 Hz to 20000 Hz. **[1]**

53. A submarine emits a SONAR pulse, which returns from an underwater cliff in 1.02 s. If the speed of sound in salt water is $1531\ ms^{-1}$, how far away is the cliff?

Sol. Total time taken = 1.02 s

$\therefore$ Time taken by the pulse to go from submarine to the cliff is given by $t = \frac{1.02}{2} = 0.51$ s

Speed of sound, $v = 1531\ ms^{-1}$ **[1]**

$\therefore$ Distance of cliff from the submarine = Speed × Time

$= 1531 \times 0.51 = 780.81$ m **[1]**

54. A bat can hear sound at frequencies upto 120 kHz. Determine the wavelength of sound at this frequency. (Take, speed of sound is 344 m/s)

Sol. Given, speed of sound, $v = 344$ m/s

Frequency of sound wave, $\nu = 120$ kHz $= 120 \times 10^3$ Hz

Wavelength of sound wave, $\lambda = ?$

We know that, $v = \nu\lambda$

$\lambda = \frac{v}{\nu} = \frac{344}{120 \times 10^3}$

$= 2.87 \times 10^{-3}$ m **[2]**

Section-II

Structured Questions

55. (i) (a) What is meant by compression and rarefaction of a longitudinal wave?

(b) Give well labelled graphical representation of a longitudinal wave. **[3]**

(ii) When a workman hammers to one end of the long iron pipeline, an observer places his ear on the other end of pipeline. How he can distinctly hear two sounds? Justify your answer. **[3]**

(iii) State the factors on which the speed of sound in a gas depends. **[4]**

Sol. (i) (a) **Compression** It is that part of a longitudinal wave in which the particles of the medium are closer to one another than they normally are.

Rarefaction It is that part of a longitudinal wave in which the particles of the medium are farther apart than normal. **[1½]**

(b)

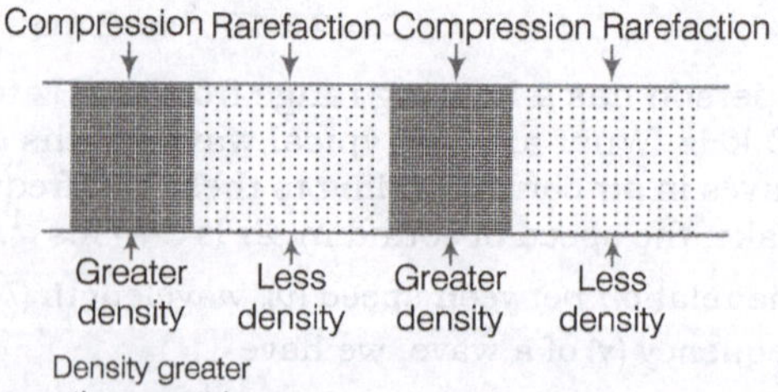

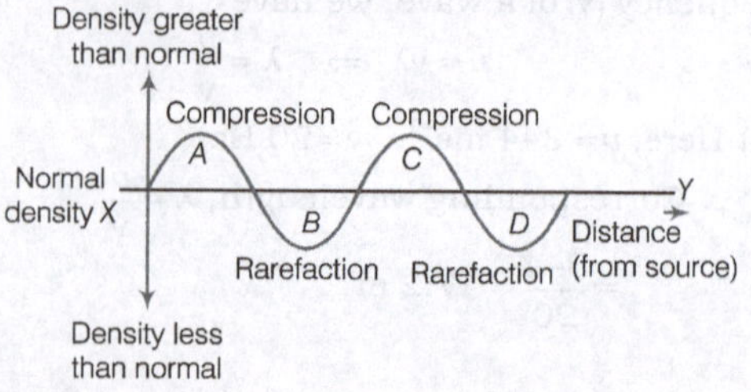

Graphical representation of a longitudinal wave **[1½]**

(ii) Due to propagation of sound through solids such as iron, the sound of hammering to one end will be heard by the observer at the other end of the pipeline. Also, the sound of hammering will be propagated through air to reach the observer. As we know that, sound travels faster in iron than in air. So, the listener hear two sounds. The first one, travelling through the iron pipeline and the second travelling through air. **[3]**

(iii) The speed of sound in a gas depends on the following factors

(a) **Density** At constant pressure, the speed of sound in a gas is inversely proportional to the square root of its density.

i.e., Speed of sound $\propto \frac{1}{\sqrt{\text{Density of gas}}}$ **[1]**

(b) **Temperature** The speed of sound in a gas is directly proportional to the square root of its absolute temperature.

i.e., Speed of sound $\propto \sqrt{\text{Absolute temperature of gas}}$ **[1]**

(c) **Humidity** Speed of sound is greater in humid or moist air than in dry air. **[1]**

(d) **Pressure** Pressure has no effect on the speed of sound in a gas. **[1]**

56. (i) How is it that bats are able to fly at night without colliding with other objects?

(ii) (a) How are ultrasonic waves different from ordinary sound waves?

(b) State two applications of ultrasound.

(iii) Represent graphically by two separate diagrams in each case.

(a) Two sound waves having the same amplitude but different frequencies.

(b) Two sound waves having the same frequency but different amplitudes.

(c) Two sound waves having different amplitudes and also different wavelengths.

Sol. (i) Bats search out prey and fly at night by emitting and detecting reflections of ultrasonic waves. Bats emit high frequency ultrasonic squeaks while flying and listen to the echoes produced by reflection of their squeaks from the obstacle, prey or object in their path. From the time taken by the echo to be heard, bats can determine the distance of the object and can avoid the object by changing the direction without colliding with it. **[3]**

(ii) (a) Ultrasonic waves have greater frequency (more than 20000 Hz). Ordinary sound has lower frequency than ultrasonic wave. **[1]**

Due to their high frequencies, they

I. have high power.

II. can penetrate anywhere to a large extent.

III. are able to travel along well-defined straight paths, even in the presence of obstacles. **[1]**

(b) Applications of ultrasound are

I. To detect the flaw or defect in metal.

II. In the diagnosis of diseases. **[1]**

(iii) (a)

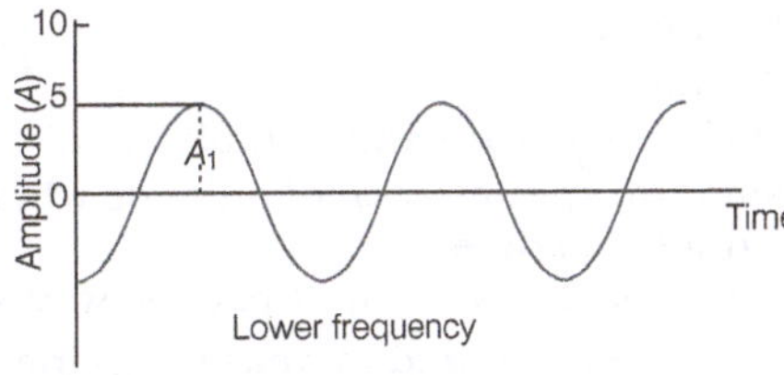

Case (a)

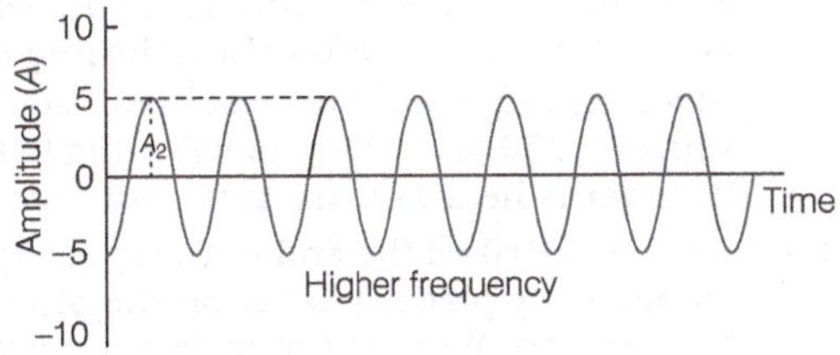

Case (b)

In both cases (a) and (b), amplitude is same and frequencies are different, i.e. ($A_1 = A_2$). **[1½]**

(b)

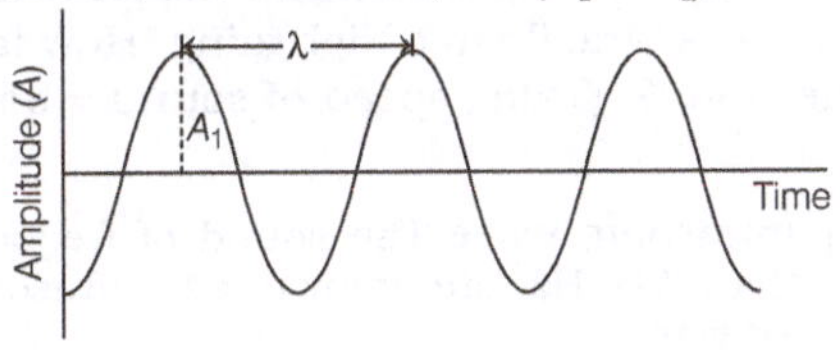

Case (a)

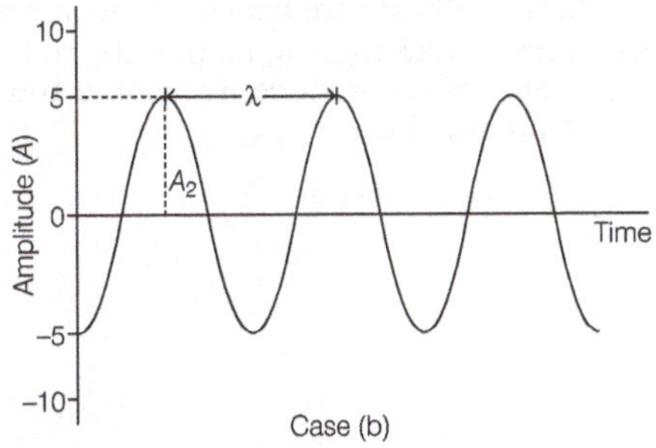

Case (b)

In both the cases (a) and (b), frequency is same and amplitudes are different, i.e. ($A_1 \neq A_2$). **[1½]**

(c)

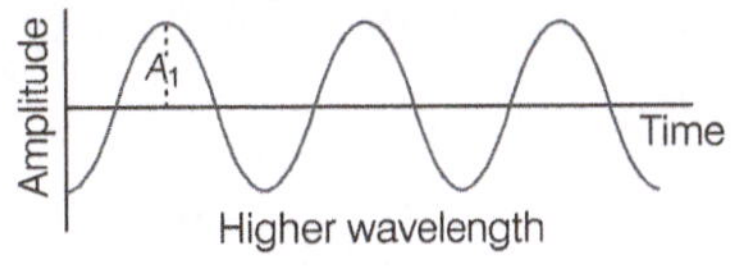

Case (a)

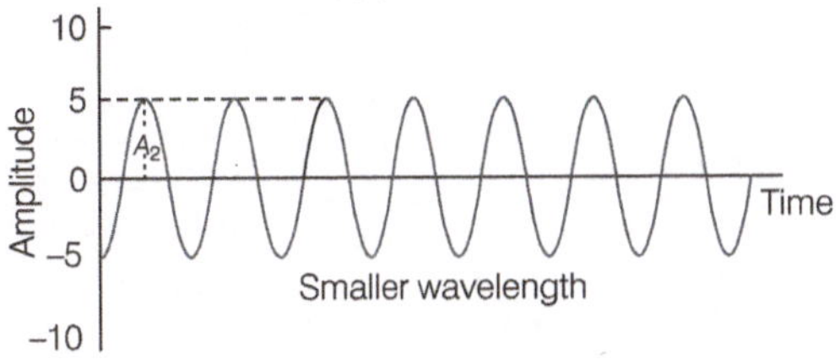

Case (b)

In both cases (a) and (b), amplitudes are different and wavelengths are also different, i.e. $A_1 \neq A_2, \lambda_1 \neq \lambda_2$. [1]

58. (i) (a) Define
(I) infrasonic wave and (II) ultrasonic wave.
(b) Name two species each of animals which can produce and detect
(I) infrasonic waves (II) ultrasonic waves. [4]

(ii) (a) Does speed of sound increase with increase of the humidity of air?
(b) Find the distance of cloud from you, when you hear a thunder 3 s after the lightning is seen. Given, speed of light = 3×10^8 ms^{-1} and speed of sound = 330 ms^{-1}. Why is lightning before the thunder is heard during a thunder storm? [3]

(iii) (a) A person strikes the end of the iron rod with a stone, a boy places his ear on the other end of the iron rod. What is the ratio of time taken by sound wave in air and in iron rod to reach the boy?(Take, v_{iron} = 5950 ms^{-1} and v_{air} = 346 ms^{-1})
(b) On a cloudy day, a thunder sound was heard 14 s after the flash of lightning. How far was the cloud? (Take, speed of sound = 340 ms^{-1}) [3]

Sol. (i)(a) (I) **Infrasonic wave** The sound of frequency lower than 20 Hz are known as infrasonic sound (or wave). [1]

(II) **Ultrasonic wave** The sound of frequency higher than 20000 Hz are called ultrasonic wave. [1]

(b) (I) Animals like whales, elephants and rhinoceroses produce infrasonic sound of frequency 5 Hz. [1]

(II) Dogs can hear and detect ultrasonic wave of frequency upto 50 kHz, while bats upto 200 kHz. [1]

(ii) (a) **Effect of humidity** The density of the moist air is less than the density of dry air. Therefore, the speed of sound in moist air is slightly greater than in dry air. So, speed of sound increases with the increase in humidity. [1½]

(b) Given, time, $t = 3$ s
and speed of sound in air = 330 ms^{-1}
Therefore, the distance from the cloud will be calculated as
Distance = Speed × Time = 330 × 3 = 990 m
As, the speed of light in air (i.e. 3×10^8 ms^{-1}) is much greater than the speed of sound in air (i.e. 340 ms^{-1}). So, this is a reason why, lightning is seen before the thunder is heard during thunderstorm. [1½]

(iii) (a) As we know that, time taken $= \dfrac{\text{Distance}}{\text{Speed}}$

$$\Rightarrow \quad t = \frac{\lambda}{v} \Rightarrow t \propto \frac{1}{v}$$

$\Rightarrow$ t is inversely proportional to $\dfrac{1}{v}$.

$$\therefore \quad \frac{\text{Speed of sound in iron rod}}{\text{Speed of sound in air}} = \frac{t_{air}}{t_{iron}}$$

$$\Rightarrow \quad \text{Ratio} = \frac{t_{air}}{t_{iron}} = \frac{5950}{346} = 17.2:1$$ [1½]

(b) Speed of sound, $v = 340$ ms^{-1}
Time taken by thunder to be heard,

$$t = \frac{d}{v} = 14 \text{ s}$$

$$d = v \times t = 340 \times 14 = 4760 \text{ m}$$

Therefore, the distance of the cloud is 4760 m.[1½]

Chapter Assessment

1 Mark Questions

1. A man can hear the frequency of
   (a) 1 Hz (b) 1 kHz (c) 1 MHz (d) 1 GHz

2. Which of the following factor affect the speed of sound in gases?
   (a) Pressure (b) Temperature
   (c) Both (a) and (b) (d) Neither (a) nor (b)

3. Displacement-time graph and displacement-distance graph of a sound wave is shown in the following figure.

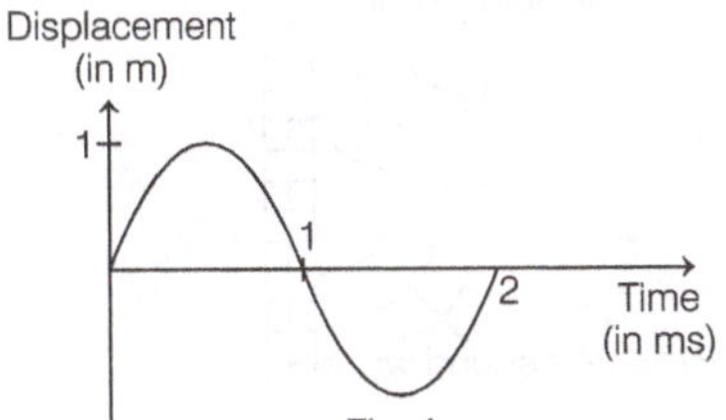

Fig. A

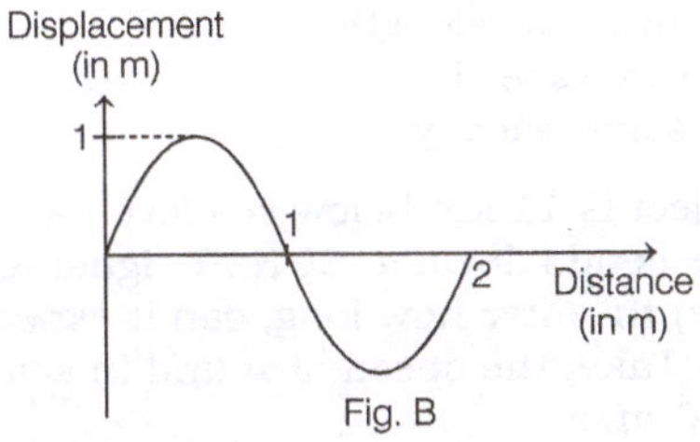

Fig. B

Speed of sound will be
   (a) 332 m/s (b) 500 m/s (c) 1000 m/s (d) 750 m/s

4. Choose the correct statement.
   (a) Speed of sound is more in denser medium than rarer medium.
   (b) Speed of light is less in optically denser medium than optically rarer medium.
   (c) Both (a) and (b).
   (d) Neither (a) nor (b).

5. Speed of sound in air is 340 m/s. If an object is moving in air with supersonic speed, then its speed may be
   (a) 380 m/s (b) 332 m/s
   (c) 340 m/s (d) None of these

2 Marks Questions

6. Give two essential conditions in which sound wave can travel.

7. What is the SI unit of frequency and time period?

8. Arrange the three medium, according to the speed or velocity of sound in each; air, water and solid.

9. Write difference between ultrasonic and supersonic.

10. A sound wave travelling with speed of 240 m/s having wavelength of 3.2 m. Find the value of (i) frequency and (ii) time period of wave.

11. (i) What is the audible range of frequency?
    (ii) For which range of frequencies are the human ears most sensitive?

12. (i) Name one bird which can produce and hear ultrasonic sound.
    (ii) Name the sound of frequencies given below.
    10 Hz, 10 kHz, 10 MHz

13. (i) Write the abbreviation of SONAR.
    (ii) Which part of sound is used in SONAR?

14. A sound wave travels at a speed of 330 ms^{-1}. If its wavelength is 1.5 cm, calculate the frequency of sound wave.

15. Determine the wavelength of an ultrasonic wave of frequency 4.2 MHz. The speed of ultrasonic wave is 1.7 kms^{-1}.

Structured Questions

16. (i) What do you mean by longitudinal wave? With proper diagram, explain the formation of compressions and rarefactions near a source of sound. **[3]**
    (ii) Explain infrasonic sound with suitable familiar examples become of sources producing it. How do some animals, alert at the time of earthquake? **[3]**
    (iii) (a) A radio transmission produces a frequency of 300 kHz. Find its wavelength. (Take, speed of light in air $c = 3.0 \times 10^8$ m/s) **Ans.** 1000 m
    (b) Establish the relationship between speed of sound, its wavelength and frequency. If velocity of sound in air is 340 ms^{-1}, calculate
    (I) wavelength when frequency is 256 Hz and
    (II) frequency when wavelength is 0.85 m. **[4]**

17. (i) What effects occur on the speed of sound in gases due to (a) density, (b) temperature and (c) humidity of the gases. **[3]**
    (ii) (a) Two persons cannot talk with each other on the surface of Moon. Why ?
    (b) The smoke from the gun barrel is seen 4 s before the explosion is heard. If the speed of sound is 342 m/s in air, then calculate the distance of the observer from the gun. **[3]**
    (iii) Write any four differences between ultrasonic and supersonic waves. **[4]**

For Solutions Scan the Code

Olympiad Section*

Brain Teasing Questions of Olympiad Pattern

1 What is the distance travelled by sound in air, when a tuning fork of frequency 256 Hz completes 25 vibrations? (Take, the speed of sound in air is 343 ms^{-1})

(a) 33.49 m (b) 40.00 m
(c) 35.00 m (d) 42 m

2 Ultrasonic sound of frequency 100 kHz emitted by a bat is incident on a water surface, the wavelength of reflected sound and transmitted sound are respectively. (Take, the speed of sound in air = 340 ms^{-1})

(a) 3.4×10^3 m, 1.486×10^{-2}m
(b) 4×10^3m, 5×10^{-2} m
(c) 4.5×10^3m, 1.468×10^{-2}m
(d) 3.4×10^{-3}m, 1.486×10^{-2}m

3 Two waves x and y are taken, such that the distance between their corresponding second and fifth crests of two waves are in the ratio 2 : 7. The ratio of velocities of waves x and y are 3 : 1. The wave that has a greater time period, is

(a) y
(b) x
(c) x and y
(d) None of the above

4 A tuning fork makes 400 vibrations in 2 s in air. If velocity of sound at 0°C is 320 ms^{-1}, then the wavelength of the wave emitted at 27°C is

(a) 1.677 m (b) 1.966 m
(c) 20.99 m (d) 40 m

5 The minimum distance between two particles in same phase is 18 cm. If the velocity of the wave is 36 ms^{-1}, then find the time interval after which the given particle undergoes a phase change of π is

(a) 2.5 ms (b) 2.9 ms
(c) 3.0 ms (d) 4.0 ms

6 A sonar device on a submarine sends out a signal and receives an echo 5 s later. The speed of sound in water, if the distance of an object from the submarine is 3625 m, is

(a) 450 ms^{-1} (b) 490 ms^{-1}
(c) 1450 ms^{-1} (d) 410 ms^{-1}

7 A sonic tape measure is used to measure the length of a room. It measures a time interval of 0.060 s between transmitting a sound pulse and receiving the echo. The speed of sound in air is 330 m/s. How far is the reflecting wall from the tape measure ?

(a) 5.5 m (b) 9.9 m
(c) 11 m (d) 20 m

8 A sound wave is reflected from a brick wall. Compare with the incident wave, the reflected wave has

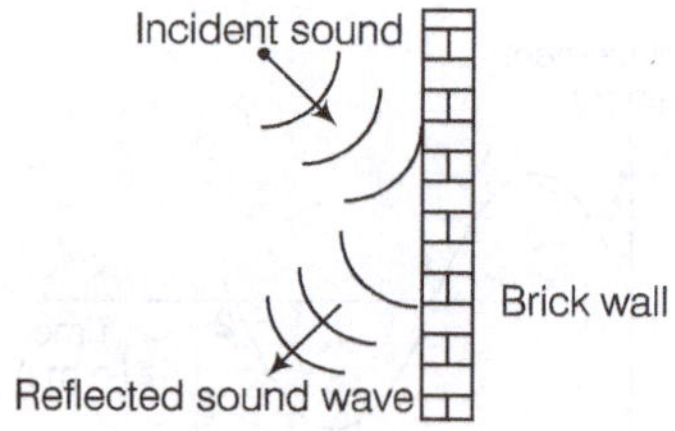

(a) a greater amplitude
(b) a shorter wavelength
(c) the same speed
(d) the same velocity

9 An object is 11 km below sea level. A research vehicle sends down a SONAR signal to confirm this depth. After how long, can it expect to get the echo? (Take, the speed of sound in sea water = 1520 m/s)

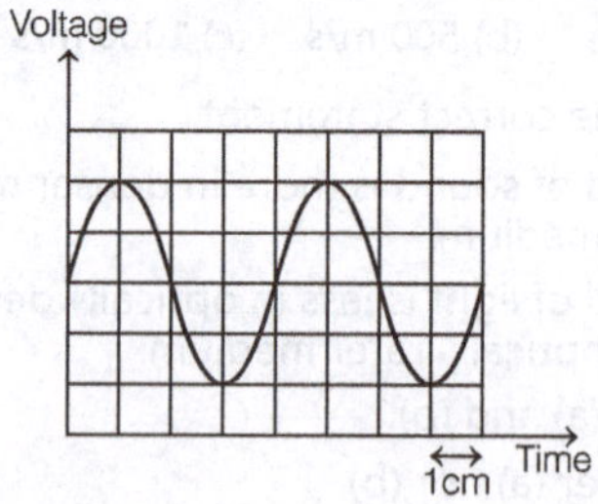

(a) 15.30 s
(b) 14.47 s
(c) 12.20 s
(d) 11.13 s

10 A Cathode Ray Oscilloscope (CRO) is a device which converts electric signals into an active graphical representation on a fluorescent screen. The *X*-axis is always time axis, where the 1 cm is equal to a preset time scale called time base. A sound wave is displayed on the screen of a cathode ray oscilloscope.

The time base of the CRO is set at 2.5 ms/cm.

What is the frequency of the sound wave?

(a) 50 Hz (b) 100 Hz
(c) 200 Hz (d) 400 Hz

11 The difference between the time you see the flash of lightning and the time you hear the thunder is Δt is seconds. Taking the speed of sound in air as 340 ms^{-1} and the speed of light in a vacuum as 3×10^8 ms^{-1}, the approximate distance in kilometers between you and the lightning flash is

(a) $\frac{\Delta t}{2}$ (b) $\frac{\Delta t}{3}$ (c) $\frac{\Delta t}{4}$ (d) $\frac{\Delta t}{5}$

Answers

1. (a)	**2.** (d)	**3.** (a)	**4.** (a)	**5.** (a)	**6.** (c)	**7.** (b)	**8.** (c)	**9.** (b)	**10.** (b)
11. (b)									

* *These questions may or may not be asked in the examination, have been given just for additional practice required for olympiads Scholarship Exams etc. For detailed explanations refer Page No. 221.*

CHAPTER

10

Current Electricity

SYLLABUS

• Simple electric circuit using an electric cell and a bulb to introduce the idea of current (including its relationship to charge) • Potential difference • Insulators and conductors • Closed and open circuits • Direction of current (electron flow and conventional)

Electricity is an indispensable part of life in today's world. It is a controllable and convenient form of energy for a variety of uses in houses, schools, industries, etc. Modern industrial societies are very much dependent on the use of electricity not only for lighting but also for running of factory machinery, information and communication systems, heating, travelling, cooking, entertainment, etc. Electricity have made life faster and easier.

In this chapter, we shall study about electricity and related aspects.

Electric Charge

A charge is a physical quantity which is defined by excess or deficiency of electrons on a body. A body is said to be negatively charged, if it gains electrons. Similarly, a body is said to be positively charged, if it loses electrons.

The total charge acquired by a body is an integral multiple of magnitude of charge on a single electron. This principle is called quantisation of charge.

i.e. charge on any body is $\boxed{q = \pm ne}$

Here, n is an integer having values, $n = 0, 1, 2, 3, 4, ...$

The SI unit of charge is **coulomb** (C).

Charge on one electron, e is -1.6×10^{-19}C and charge on one proton is $+1.6 \times 10^{-19}$C.

Electric Current

It is defined as the rate of flow of electric charge through any cross-section of a wire. It is denoted by I.

If q amount of charge flows through a conductor in t time, then

$$\boxed{\text{Electric current, } I = \frac{\text{Charge } (q)}{\text{Time } (t)} = \frac{ne}{t}}$$

where, n = number of electrons flowing through a conductor.

The SI unit of electric current is **ampere** (A) in the honour of French scientist Andre-Marie Ampere. It is a **scalar quantity**.

When 1 coulomb of charge flows through any cross-section of a conductor in 1 s, then the electric current flowing through it is said to be 1 ampere.

i.e. $$1 \text{ ampere} = \frac{1 \text{ coulomb}}{1 \text{ second}} \Rightarrow 1 \text{ A} = \frac{1\text{C}}{1\text{s}}$$

Smaller units of current are **milliampere** ($1\text{mA} = 10^{-3}\text{A}$) and **microampere** ($1\,\mu\text{A} = 10^{-6}\text{A}$).

Example 1. A current of 150 mA flows around the circuit for 2 min. How much electric charge flows around the circuit in this time?

Sol. Given, current, $I = 150 \text{ mA} = 150 \times 10^{-3} \text{ A} = 0.15 \text{ A}$

Time, $t = 2 \text{ min} = 2 \times 60 \text{ s} = 120 \text{ s}$

$\therefore$ Amount of charge, $q = It = 0.15 \times 120 = 18 \text{ C}$

So, 18 C of charge flow around the circuit.

Example 2. A current of 1A is drawn by a filament of an electric bulb. Find the number of electrons passing through a cross-section of the filament in 16 s.

Sol. Given, $I = 1$ A, $t = 16$ s

Number of electrons = ?

$\because \quad q = It$ and $ne = q$

$\Rightarrow \quad n = \frac{q}{e} \Rightarrow q = 16 \times 1 = 16\,\text{C}$

and $\quad n = \frac{q}{e} = \frac{16}{1.6 \times 10^{-19}} = 10^{20}$ electrons

Direction of Current : Conventional and Electronic

The direction of the flow of positive charges is taken to be the direction of electric current.

Conventionally, the direction of electric current is taken as opposite to the direction of flow of electrons.

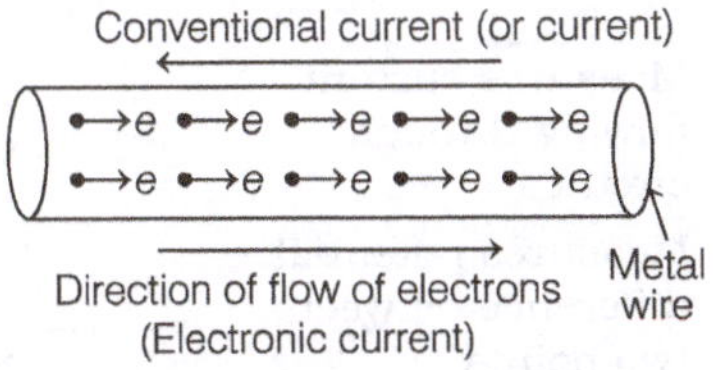

The current will be negative in the direction of flow of electrons.

The rate of flow of electrons in its direction flow is called electronic current in that direction.

Hence, the direction of conventional current (or current) is opposite to the direction of electronic current.

Generally, in laboratory, direct current (DC) source is used to supply electric current or to maintain flow of charge in a circuit.

Direct Current (DC)

The electric current whose direction and magnitude do not change with time is called direct current (DC).

e.g. Current flowing through the cell is direct current.

Sources of Direct Current

The sources which provide direct current (DC) are called sources of direct current. e.g. Cells, Batteries, etc.

Electrical Cell

It is a device which converts chemical energy into electrical energy by maintaining a constant potential difference between its electrodes through chemical reaction. A good cell should have the following requirements

- It should provide a constant current.
- It should be cheap and portable.
- It should have low internal resistance.

There are mainly two types of cells

1. Primary Cells

The cells which give electric current as a result of irreversible chemical reaction are called primary cells. These cells they cannot be used again and again. e.g. Dry cell, voltaic cell, leclanche cell, etc.

2. Secondary Cells or Accumulator

These type of cells give electric current by reversible chemical reaction. The electric energy can be stored in the cell and can be used any time. Secondary cells can be recharged, i.e. can be used again. e.g. Lead or acid accumulator, Ni-Fe or alkali accumulator, Li-H battery etc.

Differences between the Primary Cell and Secondary Cell

Primary Cell	Secondary Cell
In this, chemical reaction is irreversible.	In this, chemical reaction is reversible.
This type of cell cannot be recharged again.	This type of cell can be recharged again and again.
Its internal resistance is high.	Its internal resistance is low.
In primary cells, only chemical energy is converted into electrical energy, when current is drawn.	In these cells, chemical energy is converted into electrical energy while discharging and electrical energy can be converted into chemical energy while charging.
These are light and cheap.	These are heavy and costly as they have combination of cells.

Internal resistance of a cell

It is the resistance, which is present within the battery that resists the flow of current, when connected to a circuit. It depends on the following factors.

(i) It increases on increasing the distance between the electrodes.

(ii) It decreases on increasing the dipped effective area of plates.
(iii) It decreases on increasing the temperature of electrolyte.

Electric Circuit

A closed and continuous path through which electric current flows is known as electric circuit. It has various components including a source of current (a cell or battery), a load (a bulb heater or any other appliances), a switch/key (to open or close a circuit), a fuse, a rheostat (to control the current through the circuit) and connecting wires. The connecting wires are generally made of copper. In an electric circuit, electric current is shown from the positive terminal of the cell through the bulb and ammeter.

Closed and Open Circuits

When the key is closed, the circuit is called **closed circuit**. This means that current would flow through the circuit to operate the device. When the key is opened, the circuit is called **open circuit**. This means that current would not flow through the open circuit.

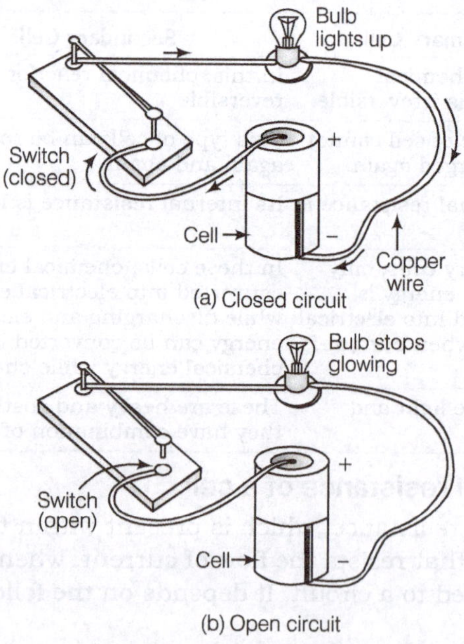

The electric circuit showing actual components like bulb, cell, switch, etc.

Symbols Used in Electric Circuits

Circuit Component	Description	Symbol
Cell	Provides potential difference between two points	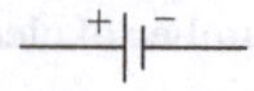
Battery	A combination of two or more cells connected in series	
Connecting wire	Connects different circuit components	——
Bulb	Circuit components	
Resistance	Controls current flowing through circuit	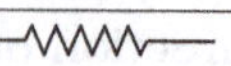
Rheostat	Variable resistance	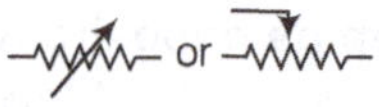
Ammeter	Measures current flowing through circuit	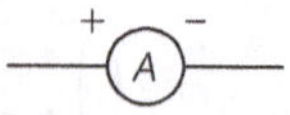
Voltmeter	Measures potential difference between two points	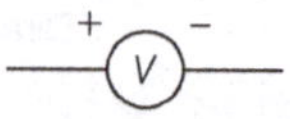
Key open	Open the circuit	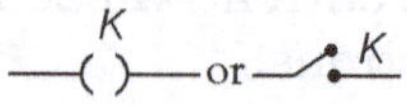
Key closed	Close the circuit	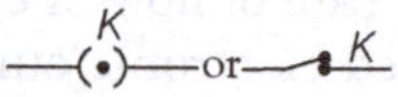
Fuse	Safety device	
Wires joints	–	
Wires crossing without joining		
Galvanometer	Detects presence and direction of current in a wire	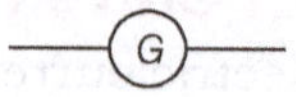
DC generator	Converts mechanical energy into electrical energy (direct current)	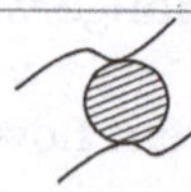
AC generator	Converts mechanical energy into electrical energy (alternating current)	

Simple Circuit Diagram

It is a schematic diagram which represents the relative positions and connections of various circuit components represented by their symbols.

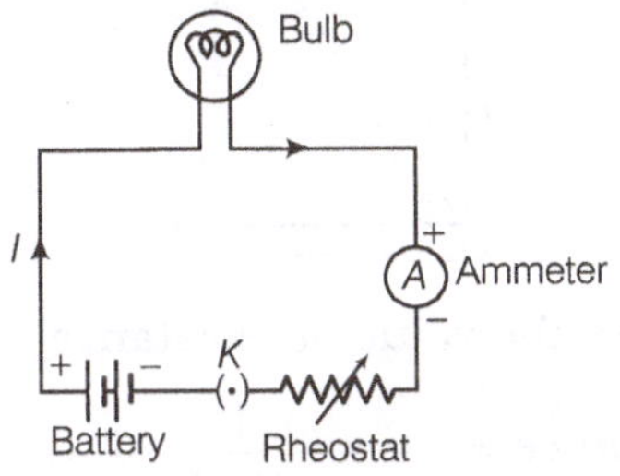

A schematic diagram of an electric circuit comprising of battery, electric bulb, rheostat, ammeter and plug key

Detection of Current

Current can be detected by ammeter and galvanometer as discussed below

Ammeter

It is an electrical device used to measure direction and magnitude of electric current. It is connected in series with circuit. An ammeter has negligible resistance, so it does not change the magnitude of current, when current is passed through it.

Galvanometer

It is an electrical device which is used to detect the presence of weak current or to find its direction. Galvanometer does not give the magnitude of current.

Voltmeter

It is an electrical device used to measure the electrical potential difference between two points in an electrical circuit. It is a high resistance device connected in parallel with the components through which potential to be measured.

Check Your LEARNING...

1. Can a charged particle has charge of 1.5e?
2. When three electrons are flowing for 2 s in a conductor, then what is the value of current in the conductor? (Take, $e = 1.6 \times 10^{-19}$C) *Ans.* 2.4×10^{-19}C
3. Which type of energy is converted into electrical energy in a cell?
4. Is dry cell a primary cell?
5. What do you mean by secondary cell?
6. Draw the circuit symbol of variable resistance.
7. Name the device which is used to detect very small current.

Electric Potential

It is defined as the amount of work done, when a unit charge moves from infinity to a point in electric field.

Electric Potential Difference (ΔV)

It is defined as the work done per unit charge in moving a unit positive charge from point B to point A (or one point to other point).

The SI unit of electric potential difference is volt (V) and is named after Italian physicist Alessandro Volta. It is a **scalar quantity**.

Let W be the work done in moving a charge Q from point B to point A, then the potential difference ($V_B - V_A$) between these two points is given by

$$\boxed{\Delta V = V_B - V_A = \frac{W}{Q}}$$

It can be also given by, $V = \dfrac{W}{Q}$

The electric potential difference between two points is said to be 1 volt, if 1 joule work is done in moving 1 coulomb of electric charge from one point to the other.

Thus, $$1 \text{ volt} = \frac{1 \text{ joule}}{1 \text{ coulomb}}$$

$$\Rightarrow \quad 1\text{ V} = \frac{1\text{ J}}{1\text{ C}} \Rightarrow 1\text{ V} = 1\text{ J/C} = 1\text{JC}^{-1}$$

Small units of electrical potential, $1\text{ mV} = 10^{-3}\text{ V}$

$1\ \mu\text{V} = 10^{-6}\text{ V}$

Large units of electrical potential, $1\text{ kV} = 10^{3}\text{ V}$

$1\text{ MV} = 10^{6}\text{ V}$

Note Earth is considered to be at zero potential.

Example 3. Calculate the potential difference between two terminals of a battery, if 100 J of work is required to transfer 20 C from one terminal of the battery to the other.

Sol. Given, work done, $W = 100$ J

Charge, $q = 20$ C

Potential difference, $\Delta V = ?$

$$\therefore \quad \Delta V = \frac{W}{q} = \frac{100}{20} = 5\text{ V}$$

The potential difference between two points is 5 V.

Example 4. How much work is done in moving a charge of 2C from a point of 118 V to a point at 128 V?

Sol. Given, charge, $q = 2$ C

Potential at point A, $V_A = 118$ V

Potential at point B, $V_B = 128$ V

Work done, $W = ?$

We know that,

Potential difference, $\Delta V = V_B - V_A = 128 - 118 = 10$ V

$\therefore$ Work done, $W = \Delta V \times q = 10 \times 2 = 20$ J

So, the work done in moving the charge is 20 J.

Ohm's Law

This law was given by George Simon Ohm in the 1827 and it gives a relationship between current and potential difference.

According to this law, the electric current flowing through a conductor is directly proportional to the potential difference applied across its ends, provided the physical conditions (such as temperature, dimensions, pressure, etc) remains unchanged.

If V is the potential difference applied across the ends of conductor through which current I flows, then according to Ohm's law,

$$I \propto V$$

or $$I = \frac{1}{R} \times V$$

or $$I = \frac{V}{R}$$

$$\boxed{V = IR}$$

where, R is the constant of proportionality called resistance of the conductor at a given temperature.

The conductors which obey Ohm's law are called **ohmic conductors**, while the conductors which do not obey Ohm's law are called **non-ohmic conductors.**

V-I Graph

The graph between the potential difference (V) and the corresponding current (I), is found to be a straight line passing through the origin.

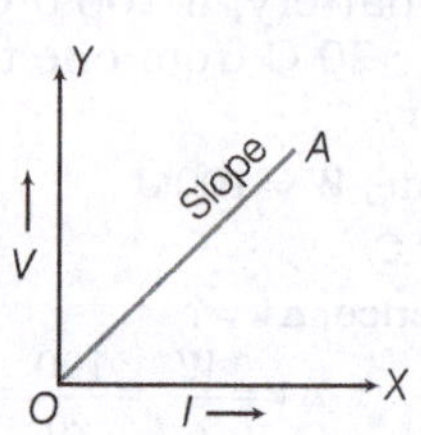

If potential difference (V) is plotted on Y-axis and current (I) on the X-axis, then slope of graph $\left(\frac{\Delta Y}{\Delta X}\right)$ gives the value of resistance.

$\therefore$ Resistance = Slope of V-I graph

If potential difference (V) is plotted on X-axis and current (I) on the Y-axis, then reciprocal of slope of graph

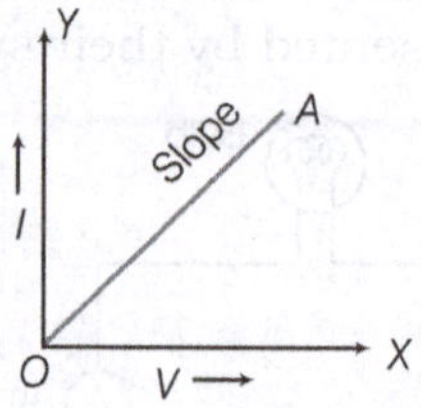

$\left(\frac{1}{\Delta Y / \Delta X}\right)$ gives the value of resistance.

$$\therefore \quad \text{Resistance} = \frac{1}{\text{Slope of } V\text{-}I \text{ graph}}$$

Electrical Resistance

It is that property of a conductor by virtue of which it opposes/resists any flow of charges through it. It arises due to the mutual collisions of free electrons which drift through the conductor towards positive terminal.

Resistance of a conductor is given by $R = \frac{V}{I}$.

The SI unit of resistance is ohm (Ω). Resistance of a conductor is said to be 1 ohm, if a potential difference of 1 volt across the ends of the conductor makes a current of 1 ampere to flow through it.

Thus, $$1 \text{ ohm} = \frac{1 \text{ volt}}{1 \text{ ampere}}$$

$$\Rightarrow \quad 1\,\Omega = \frac{1\text{ V}}{1\text{ A}} = 1 \text{ V/A}$$

Example 5. A resistor allows a current of 0.02 A to flow through it, when there is a potential difference of 10.0 V between its ends. What is its resistance?

Sol. Given, current, $I = 0.02$ A

Potential difference, $V = 10.0$ V

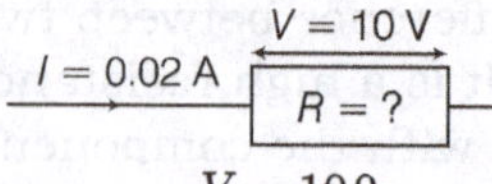

$\therefore$ Resistance, $R = \frac{V}{I} = \frac{10.0}{0.02} = 500\,\Omega$

So, the resistance of the resistor is 500 Ω.

Example 6. The potential difference between the terminals of an electric heater is 75 V, when it draws a current of 5 A from the source. What current will the heater draw, if the potential difference is increased to 150 V?

Sol. Given, potential difference, $V = 75$ V

Current, $I = 5$A

We know that, $R = \frac{V}{I} \Rightarrow R = \frac{75}{5} = 15\,\Omega$

When potential difference is increased to 150 V, then current,

$$I' = \frac{V'}{R} = \frac{150}{15} = 10 \text{ A} \qquad (\because V' = 150 \text{ V})$$

So, the current through the heater becomes 10 A.

Factors Affecting the Resistance of a Conductor

Factors which affects the resistance of a conductor are as follows

(i) The resistance of the conductor is directly proportional to its length l or $\boxed{R \propto l}$.

(ii) The resistance of the conductor is inversely proportional to its cross-section A or $\boxed{R \propto \frac{1}{A}}$.

Hence, $R \propto \frac{l}{A} \Rightarrow \boxed{R = \rho \frac{l}{A}}$,

where, ρ = constant called resistivity.

(iii) The resistance of the conductor depends on the nature of the material of which it is made.

(iv) The resistance of the conductor increases with increase of its temperature.

Conductors and Insulators

Materials can be categorised as conductors and insulators as discussed below

Conductors

The substances or materials which offer very little resistance for the current flowing through them are conductors. e.g. Almost all metals are good conductors of electric current. They have a large number of free electrons.

Insulators

The substances or materials which offer very high resistance to the electric current flowing through them are called insulators. They have almost no free electrons. e.g. Diamond, wood, etc.

Efficient Use of Energy

The use of energy without wasting it degrading the environment is called efficient use of energy. The efficient use of energy can be done by some general practices and by using eco-friendly technology. e.g. By using LED lights in place of electric bulb, a lot of energy can be saved which goes wasted in the form of heat in electric bulb.

Some ways to achieve eco-efficient environment are as follows

(i) Electric cooker should be used instead of ordinary vessel.

(ii) Saving electricity (switch OFF the device, when not in use).

(iii) By reduction in pollution, using those fuels which create very little or no pollution.

(iv) Use of solar water heater instead of LPG for heating water.

(v) Use of solar energy whenever possible.

Social Initiatives

Due to the rapid growth of industries, demand of energy resources are increasing day-by-day.

Urbanisation and industrialisation are causing crisis of energy resources and environmental hazards.

Following initiative should be taken for efficient use of energy

(i) Use of alternative form of energy such as solar energy, biomass energy, geo-thermal energy, wind energy, etc.

(ii) Do not waste energy uselessly. Put OFF all the electric devices whenever not in use.

(iii) Use of public transport should be preferred.

(iv) Replace the incandescent bulbs with CFLs and LED bulbs. It reduces approximately 75% of energy in use.

Check Your LEARNING...

1 What do you mean by 1 volt?

2 Write the relation between electric current and voltage.

3 Define the unit of resistance.

4 A resistor allows a current of 0.05 A to flow through it, when there is a potential difference 12.0 V between its ends. What is its resistance? *Ans.* 240 Ω

5 What happens to the resistance of a wire as its length decreases?

6 What do you mean by efficient use of energy?

7 Write one advantage of LED over incandescent bulbs.

QUICK Revision

- **Electric cell** is a device which converts chemical energy into electrical energy by maintaining a constant potential difference between its electrodes through chemical reaction, in the electrolyte.
- A **charge** is a physical quantity which is defined by excess or deficiency of electrons on a body.
- The rate of flow of electric charge through any cross-section of a wire is known as **electric current**.

  $$\text{Electric current } (I) = \frac{\text{Charge } (q)}{\text{Time } (t)}$$

  SI unit of electric current is **ampere (A)**.
- A closed and continuous path through which electric current flows is known as **electric circuit**.
- **Ammeter** is an electrical device used to measure direction and magnitude of electric current.
- **Voltmeter** is an electrical device used to measure potential difference across any given circuit.
- **Electric potential** at a point in space is defined as the work done in moving a unit positive charge from infinity to that point.

  $$V = \frac{W}{q} \text{ volt}$$
- According to the **Ohm's law**, the electric current flowing through a conductor is directly proportional to the potential difference applied across its ends, provided that physical conditions (such as temperature, dimensions, pressure etc.) remains unchanged.
- **Resistance** is that property of a conductor by virtue of which it opposes/resists any flow of charges through it.
- **Conductors** are the materials which has free electrons and allow current to pass through them.
- **Insulators** are the materials which do not have free electrons and do not allow current to pass through them.

Chapter Practice

Section-I

1 Mark Questions

1. A current of 4.8 A is flowing in a conductor. The number of electrons passing per second through the conductor will be

(a) 3×10^{20} (b) 76.8×10^{20}
(c) 7.68×10^{-19} (d) 3×10^{19}

Sol. (*d*) Given, current, $I = 4.8\,A$, $e = 1.6 \times 10^{-19} C$

We know that, $I = \frac{q}{t} = \frac{ne}{t}$

$\therefore \quad \frac{n}{t} = \frac{I}{e} = \frac{4.8}{1.6 \times 10^{-19}} = 3 \times 10^{19}$

2. The amount of charge provided by the cell per second into the circuit, if 2 A current flows through the circuit, is

(a) 2 C (b) 1 C (d) 4 C (d) 0.2 C

Sol. (*a*) Given, $I = 2\,A, t = 1\,s$

$\therefore$ Charge, $q = I \times t = 2 \times 1 = 2\,C$

3. How many electrons enter into the filament of the bulb per second, if current is 0.2 A? (Take, $e = 1.6 \times 10^{-19}$ C)

(a) 6.25×10^{18} (b) 2.5×10^{18}
(c) 1.25×10^{19} (d) 1.25×10^{18}

Sol. (*d*) Given, $t = 1\,s$, $I = 0.2\,A$

We know that, $I = \frac{ne}{t} \Rightarrow n = \frac{It}{e} = \frac{0.2 \times 1}{1.6 \times 10^{-19}}$

$= 1.25 \times 10^{18}$ electrons/s

4. Electrical cell is a device which converts

(a) electrical energy into mechanical energy
(b) mechanical energy into electrical energy
(c) electrical energy into chemical energy
(d) chemical energy into electrical energy

Sol. (*d*) Electrical cell is a device which converts chemical energy into electrical energy by maintaining a constant potential difference between its electrodes through chemical reaction.

5. Which of the following cell gives electric current by reversible chemical reaction?

(a) Primary cells (b) Secondary cells
(c) Both (a) and (b) (d) Neither (a) nor (b)

Sol. (*b*) Secondary cells give electric current as a result of reversible chemical reaction, whereas primary cells give electric current as a result of irreversible chemical reaction.

6. Which of the symbol is used for fuse in electrical circuit?

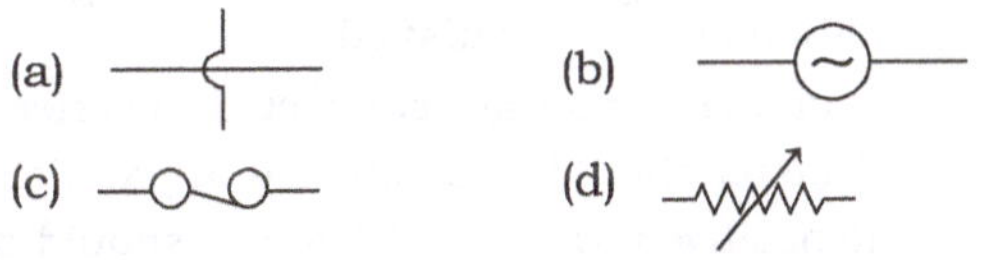

Sol. (*c*)

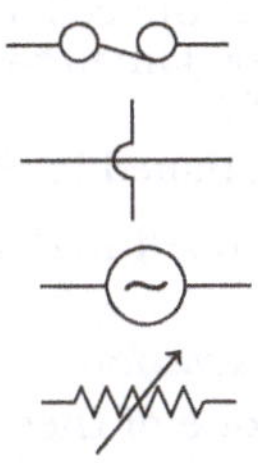

→ Fuse
→ Wires crossing without joining
→ AC generator
→ Rheostat

7. Which one of the following is the correct set-up for studying the dependence of the current on the potential difference across a resistor and why?

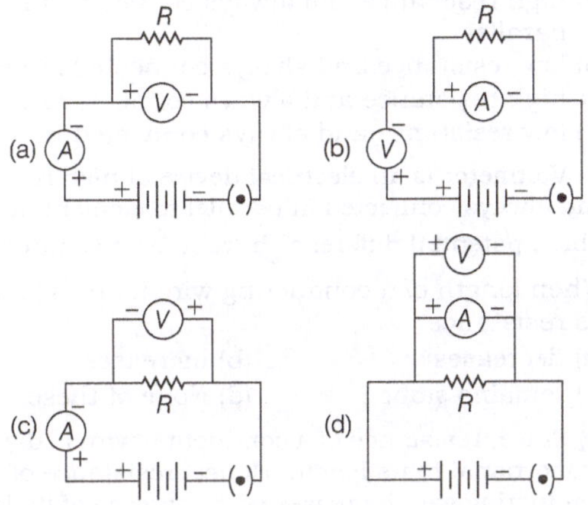

Sol. (*c*) Option (c) represents correct set up for studying the dependence of the current on the potential difference across a resistor because ammeter *A* is connected in series while voltmeter *V* is connected parallel across resistor *R*.

8. Identify the circuit in which the electrical components have been properly connected.

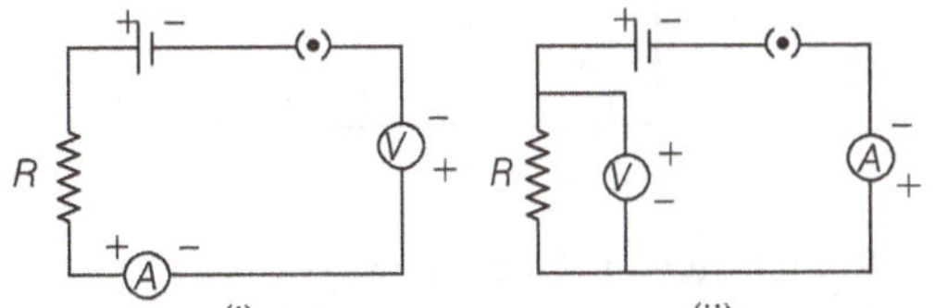

(i) (ii)

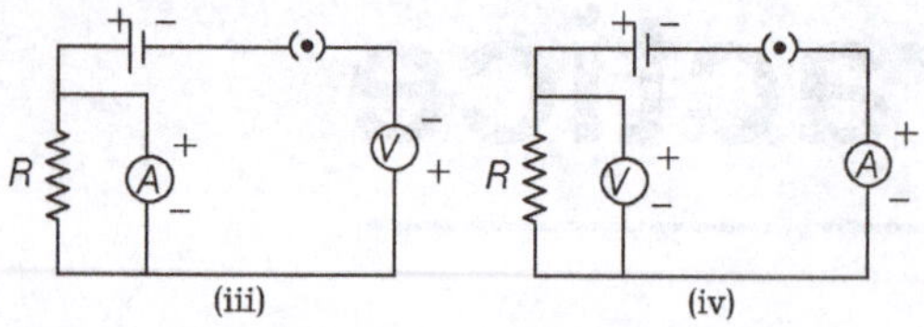

(iii) (iv)

(a) (i) (b) (ii) (c) (iii) (d) (iv)

Sol. (*b*) While identifying the circuit, the following conditions must be satisfied.

- An ammeter is always connected in series.
- Voltmeter should be connected in parallel.
- The positive terminals of *V* and *A* should be joined to positive terminal of the cell and their negative terminals should be joined to the negative terminal of the cell.

Thus, the above conditions are satisfied in case (ii).

9. Which of the following device is used to detect the presence of weak current?

(a) Ammeter (b) Galvanometer
(c) Voltmeter (d) None of these

Sol. (*b*) Galvanometer is an electrical device which is used to detect the presence of weak current.

10. Voltmeter is an electrical device of

(a) high resistance and always connected in parallel
(b) low resistance and always connected in series
(c) high resistance and always connected in series
(d) low resistance and always connected in parallel.

Sol. (*a*) Voltmeter is an electrical device of high resistance and always connected in parallel to element across which potential difference have to be measured.

11. When length of a conducting wire increases, then its resistance

(a) decreases (b) increases
(c) remains same (d) None of these

Sol. (*b*) Since, resistance of a conducting wire is directly proportional to its length. Hence, resistance of a conducting wire increases with increase of its length.

12. Consider the following circuit diagram shown below and answer the following questions.

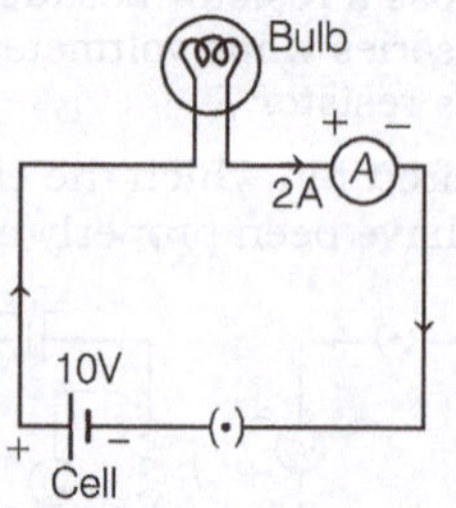

Resistance of the bulb is

(a) 20 Ω (b) 5 Ω
(c) 10 Ω (d) 15 Ω

Sol. (*b*) Given, $V = 10$ V, $I = 2$ A

According to Ohm's law, $V = IR$

$\Rightarrow \quad R = \frac{V}{I} = \frac{10}{2} = 5\,\Omega$

13. The amount of energy consumed by the bulb per second, if potential difference across battery is 10 V and current in the circuit is 1A is

(a) 15 J (b) 10 J
(c) 25 J (d) 20 J

Sol. (*b*) Given, $I = 1$ A, $t = 1$ s, $V = 10$ V

We know that, $V = \frac{W}{q}$

$\Rightarrow \quad W = V \cdot q = VIt \qquad (\because q = It)$

$= 10 \times 1 \times 1 = 10$ J

14. By using LED lights in place of incandescent bulb, a lot of

(a) energy can be saved
(b) energy can be wasted
(c) air pollution can be decreased
(d) None of the above

Sol. (*a*) By using LED lights in place of incandescent bulb, a lot of energy (approximately 75%) can be saved.

2 Marks Questions

15. What is the direction of current: conventional and electronic ?

Sol. Refer to Page 183. [2]

16. Draw the symbol of

(i) plug key open (ii) plug key closed

What does each situation mean?

Sol. (i) 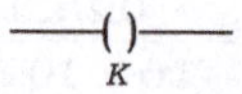 (ii) 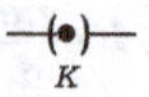 [1]

When plug key is opened, no current flows through the circuit and when plug key is closed, current flows through the circuit. [1]

17. What do the following circuit symbols represent?

(i) 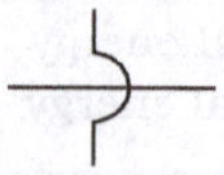 (ii) 

Sol. (i) Wires crossing without joining. [1]

(ii) Fuse [1]

18. Write the name of the symbols used in electric circuits to represent.

(i)  (ii) 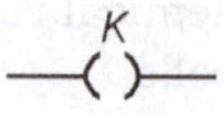

Sol. (i) Bulb [1]

(ii) Open plug key [1]

19. (i) What are the values of mA and μA in terms of A?

(ii) Draw the symbols of battery and rheostat.

Sol. (i) $1\text{ mA} = \frac{1}{1000}\text{ A} = 10^{-3}\text{A}$

and $1\mu\text{A} = \frac{1}{1000000}\text{ A} = 10^{-6}\text{ A}$ [1/2 × 2]

(ii) Symbol of battery

Symbol of rheostat

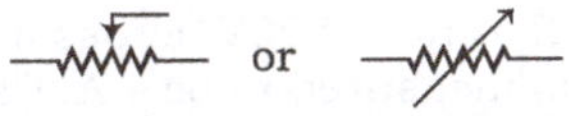

[1/2 × 2]

20. What is an ammeter? How is it connected in a circuit? Draw a diagram to illustrate your answer.

Sol. An ammeter is an instrument used to measure current. It is always connected in series in a circuit. [1]

This is illustrated in the diagram below

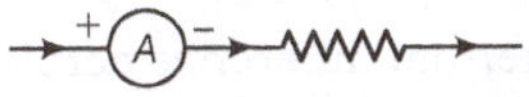

[1]

21. Write the use of galvanometer. Draw its symbol also.

Sol. Galvanometer is an electrical device which is used to detect the presence of weak current or to find its direction. It does not give the magnitude of current.[1]

Its symbol is 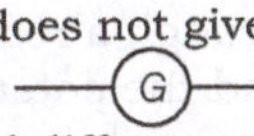 [1]

22. The potential difference between two points in an electric circuit is 1 V. What does it mean? Name a device that helps to measure the potential difference across a conductor.

Sol. The potential difference between two points is 1 V. It means that, if a charge of 1 coulomb is moved from one point to the other, 1 joule of work is required.

The potential difference a conductor is measured by means of an instrument called the voltmeter. [2]

23. What happened when two ends of a metallic wire are connected across the terminals of a cell. In which direction electrons are flowing through the conductors?

Sol. When two ends of a metallic wire are connected across the terminals of a cell, then some potential difference is set up between its end. [1]

Electrons are flowing through the conductors from its lower potential end to its higher potential end. [1]

24. What causes the potential difference between the two terminals of a cell?

Sol. The chemical reaction occurring inside the cell generates excess of electrons at negative terminal and deficiency of electrons at positive terminal. [2]

25. Let resistance of an electrical component remains constant while the potential difference across the two ends of components decreases to half of its former value. What change will occur in the current through it?

Sol. By Ohm's law, voltage is directly proportional to the current i.e. $V \propto I$. [1]

If V becomes half, current flowing through it is also halved. [1]

3 Marks Questions

26. Name the particles responsible for the flow of current in three states of matter.

Sol. There are three states of matter solid, liquid and gas. The particles responsible for the flow of current in three states which are as follows

(i) **Solid** Free electrons present in valence shell. [1]

(ii) **Liquid** Free ions (positive or negative). [1]

(iii) **Gas** Ionised molecules of gases. [1]

27. Differentiate between primary and secondary cells.

Sol. Differences between primary and secondary cells are given below

Primary Cell	Secondary Cell
In this cell, only chemical energy is converted into electrical energy, when current is drawn.	In this cell, chemical energy is converted into electrical energy while discharging and electrical energy can be converted into chemical energy while charging. [1]
This type of cells can not be recharged again.	This type of cells can be recharged again and again. [1]
In this, chemical reaction is irreversible.	In this, chemical reaction is reversible. [1]

28. What do you mean by a complete electric circuit? Draw a labelled diagram of electric circuit.

Sol. A closed and continuous path through which electric current flows is known as electric circuit. It has various components including source of current, resistance, switch fuse, etc. [1½]

For the labelled circuit diagram Refer to Page 184. [1½]

29. Differentiate between conductors and insulators.

Sol. Refer to Page 187. [3]

30. (i) Define 1 volt.

(ii) Plot a graph taking potential difference (V) on X-axis and current (I) on Y-axis. Also, specify the relationship between slope and resistance.

Sol. Refer to Pages 185 and 186. [3]

31. Write the three factors on which the resistance of a conductor depends.

Sol. The factors on which the resistance of a conductor depends are as follows

(i) Length of the conductor.

(ii) Area of cross-section of the conductor.

(iii) Nature of the material of the conductor. [1×3]

32. Read the following information.

Six wires labelled as A, B, C, D, E and F have been designed as per the following parameters.

Wire	Length	Diameter	Materials	Resistances
A	l	$2d$	Aluminium	R_1
B	$2l$	$d/2$	Constantan	R_2
C	$3l$	$d/2$	Constantan	R_3
D	$l/2$	$3d$	Copper	R_4
E	$2l$	$2d$	Aluminium	R_5
F	$l/2$	$4d$	Copper	R_6

Answer the following questions using the above data.

(i) Which of the wires has maximum resistance and why?

(ii) Which of the wires has minimum resistance and why?

(iii) Arrange R_1, R_3 and R_5 in ascending order of their values. Justify your answer.

Sol. (i) Wire C has maximum resistance because it has maximum length and least thickness. [1]

(ii) Wire F has the minimum resistance, since it has least length and maximum thickness. [1]

(iii) $R_3 > R_5 > R_1$

(using relation, $R \propto \frac{l}{A}$ and comparison). [1]

4 Marks Questions

33. In the circuit given below, label the parts P, Q, R and S; and state the function of each part. [4]

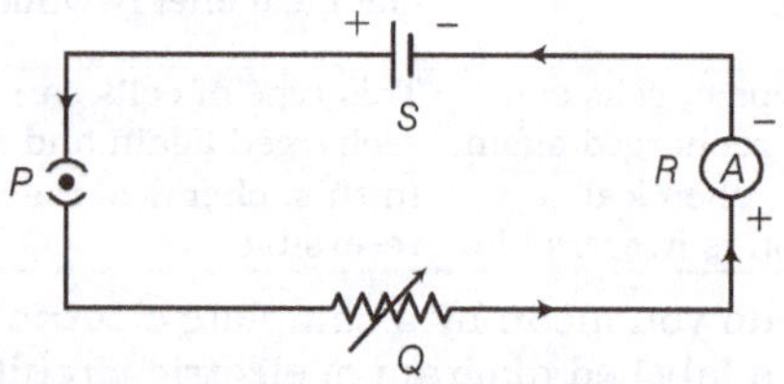

Sol. The circuit components are as follows

$P \rightarrow$ A closed key, which is used to close the circuit.

$Q \rightarrow$ A rheostat, which is used to provide variable resistance in order to control the current flowing through the circuit.

$R \rightarrow$ An ammeter, which measures the current flowing through the circuit.

$S \rightarrow$ A cell, which provides potential difference between two terminals. [1×4]

34. Write a short note on

(i) voltmeter (ii) ammeter

Sol. Refer to Page 185. [4]

35. (i) Write the various units of electric potential.

(ii) Draw a V-I graph for ohmic conductors.

(iii) Write the expression for the resistance of the conductor.

Sol. Refer to Pages 185 and 186. [4]

36. Briefly explain the social initiatives that should be taken to conserve energy and for eco-friendly use of sources of energy.

Sol. Refer to Page 187. [4]

Numerical Based Questions

37. If a charge of 2.5C is first moved from infinity to point P and then to point Q, a work of 10 J and 25 J is done, respectively. Calculate the potential difference between points P and Q.

Sol. Given, $W_1 = 10\text{ J}$, $q = 2.5\text{ C}$, $V_P = ?$, $W_2 = 25\text{ J}$, $V_Q = ?$

Potential at P, $V_P = \frac{W_1}{q} = \frac{10}{2.5} = 4\text{ V}$ [1/2]

Potential at Q, $V_Q = \frac{W_2}{q} = \frac{25}{2.5} = 10\text{ V}$ [1/2]

Potential difference between the points P and Q i.e.,

$V_Q - V_P = 10\text{ V} - 4\text{ V} = 6\text{ V}$ [1]

38. A cell is connected to a bulb which develops a potential difference of 20V across it. The current in the circuit is measured to be 4 A. Calculate the resistance offered by the filament of the bulb to the flow of current.

Sol. Given, potential difference, $V = 20\text{ V}$, current, $I = 4\text{ A}$

According to Ohm's law, $V = IR$

$\Rightarrow \quad R = \frac{V}{I} = \frac{20}{4} = 5\,\Omega$ [2]

39. Find the potential difference across the ends of the wire of resistance 5Ω, when a current 2.5A is flowing through it.

Sol. Given, current, $I = 2.5\text{ A}$, resistance, $R = 5\,\Omega$

As per Ohm's law, $V = IR = 2.5 \times 5 = 12.5\text{ V}$ [2]

40. The current flowing through a resistor connected in an electric circuit and the potential difference applied across its ends are shown in figure.

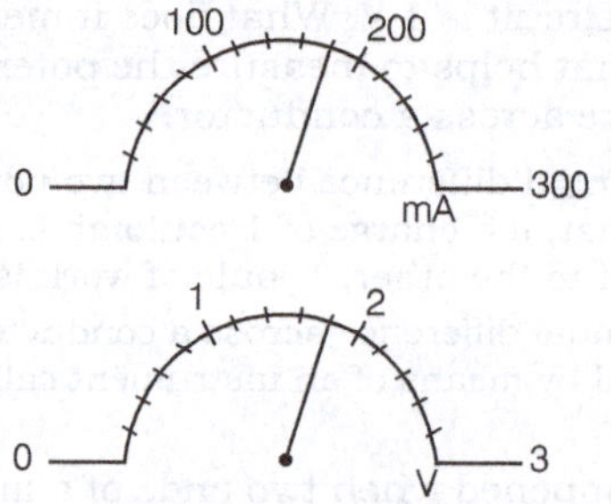

What is the value of the resistance of the resistor?

Sol. Reading from ammeter, $I = 180\text{ mA} = 0.18\text{ A}$

Reading from voltmeter, $V = 1.8\text{ V}$

$\therefore$ Resistance of the resistor, $R = \frac{V}{I} = \frac{1.8}{0.18} = \frac{180}{18} = 10\,\Omega$ [2]

Section-II

Structured Questions

41. (i) What are the requirements that a good cell should have? [3]

(ii) When a charge of 50C is moved from infinity to points X and Y, work is done to do so is 15 J and 20 J, respectively. Calculate potential difference between the points X and Y. [3]

(iii) A child has drawn the electric circuit to study Ohm's law as shown in figure. His teacher told that the circuit diagram needs correction. Study the circuit diagram and redraw it after making all corrections.

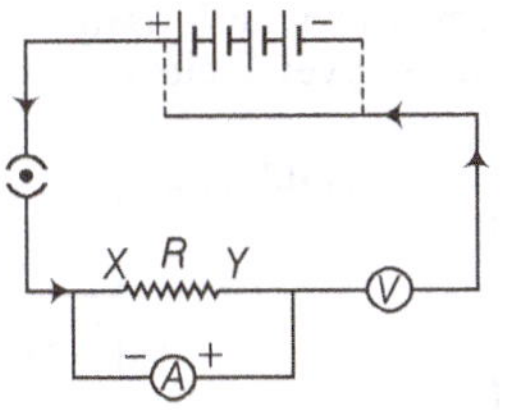

[4]

Sol. (i) A good cell should have the following requirements

(a) It should provide a constant current.

(b) It should be cheap and portable.

(c) It should have low internal resistance. [1×3]

(ii) Given, $W_X = 15\,J$, $W_Y = 20\,J$, $q = 50\,C$, $V_Y - V_X = ?$

∴ Potential difference between points X and Y,

$$V_Y - V_X = \frac{W_Y}{q} - \frac{W_X}{q}$$

$$= \frac{(W_Y - W_X)}{q} = \frac{20 - 15}{50}$$

$$= \frac{5}{50} = \frac{1}{10} = 0.1\text{ V}$$ [3]

(iii) The circuit diagram is not correct because of the following reasons

(a) Ammeter is connected in parallel with R and voltmeter connected in series with it in contrary of the fact that ammeter should be connected in series and voltmeter in parallel. This is so because same current flows in series and same voltage exist in parallel combination.

(b) The current is drawn from negative terminal and enter into the battery at positive terminal which is not possible in one battery circuit.

(c) Cells are connected in series combination in the circuit. [3]

The correct diagram is given as below

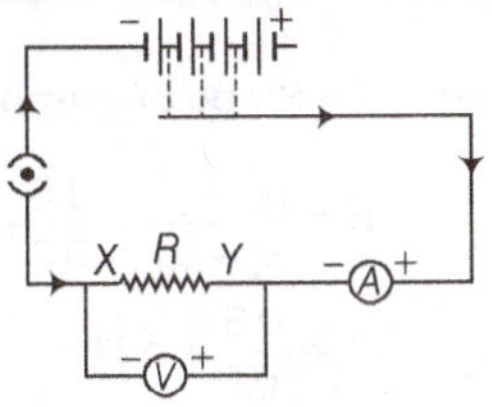

[1]

42. (i) (a) The values of current I flowing in a given resistor for the corresponding values of potential difference V across the resistor are given as below.

I (amperes)	0.5	1.0	2.0	3.0	4.0
V (volts)	1.6	3.4	6.7	10.2	13.2

Plot a graph between V and I and also calculate the resistance of that resistor.

(b) Will current flow more easily through a thick wire or a thin wire of same material, when connected to same source? Why? [4]

(ii) (a) How does the resistance of a wire vary with its area of cross-section?

(b) Out of the two wires P and Q shown below which one has greater resistance? Justify it.

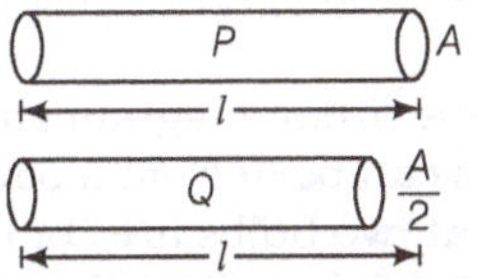

[3]

(iii) (a) A TV set shoots out a beam of electrons. The beam current is 10 μA. How many electrons strike the TV screen in each second? How much charge strikes the screen in 1 min?

(b) Calculate the amount of work done in moving 4 C charge through a potential difference of 4 V? [3]

Sol. (i) (a)

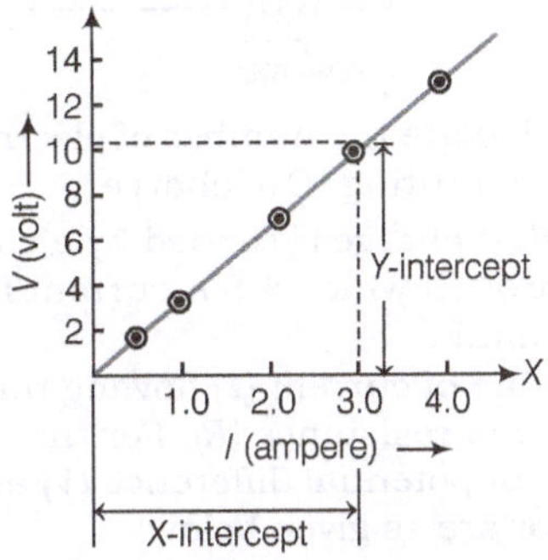

[1]

$$\text{Resistance} = \text{Slope of graph} = \frac{\Delta Y}{\Delta X}$$

$$= \frac{Y\text{-intercept}}{X\text{-intercept}} = \frac{(10.2 - 0)\text{ V}}{(3.0 - 0)\text{ A}} = 3.4\,\Omega$$ [1]

(b) The current will flow more easily through the thick wire. [1]

Resistance is inversely proportional to the area of cross-section. Lesser the resistance more is the current flowing through the wire. [1]

(ii) (a) Resistance is inversely proportional to the area of cross-section of the wire. Thus, if the wire is thick, then resistance is less. If the wire is thin, then resistance is large. [2]

(b) Smaller the area of cross-section, greater will be resistance as $R \propto \frac{1}{A}$. (∵ lengths are same) [1]

So, wire Q has greater resistance.

(iii) (a) Given, current, $I = 10\ \mu A = 10 \times 10^{-6}\ A = 10^{-5}\ A$

Time, $t = 1\,s$

Number of electrons per second, $n = ?$

Amount of charges in 1 min, $q = ?$

Using the relation, $I = \frac{ne}{t}$ (∵ $q = ne$)

$$\Rightarrow n = \frac{It}{e} = \frac{10^{-5} \times 1}{1.6 \times 10^{-19}} \quad (\because e = 1.6 \times 10^{-19} C)$$

$$= 6.25 \times 10^{13}\text{ electrons}$$

$$\therefore \quad q = It = 10^{-5} \times 60 = 600\ \mu C$$ [1½]

(b) Given, charge, $q = 4\,C$

Potential difference, $V = 4\,V$

$\therefore$ Work needed to be done, $W = qV$

$= 4 \times 4 = 16\,J$ [1½]

43. (i) (a) Draw a circuit diagram showing how four bulbs can be lit from a battery of four cells, so that two bulbs are controlled by the same switch while each of the other two bulbs has its own switch.

(b) Redraw the following circuit using appropriate symbols.

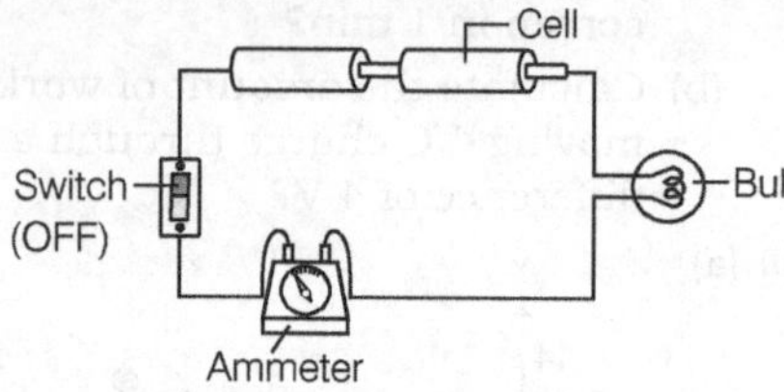

[3]

(ii) (a) Calculate the number of electrons constituting 1C of charge.

(b) What charge is carried by a conductor through which 4.5 A current flows in 1 min? [4]

(iii) The value of current (I) flowing through a given resistor of resistance (R). For the corresponding values of potential difference (V) across the resistor are as given below

V (V)	0.5	1.0	1.5	2.0	2.5	3.0	4.0	5.0
I (A)	0.1	0.2	0.3	0.4	0.5	0.6	0.8	1.0

Plot a graph between current (I) and potential difference (V) and determine the resistance (R) of the resistor. [3]

Sol. (i) (a) The circuit diagram is shown as below

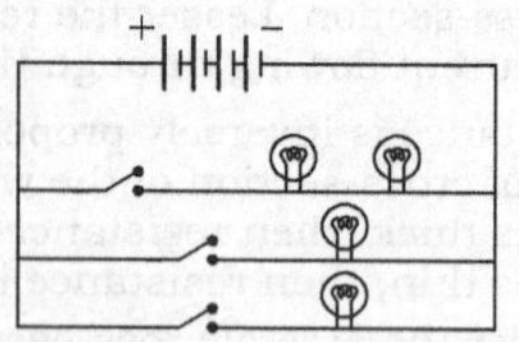

[1½]

(b) The circuit redrawn using appropriate symbols is given below

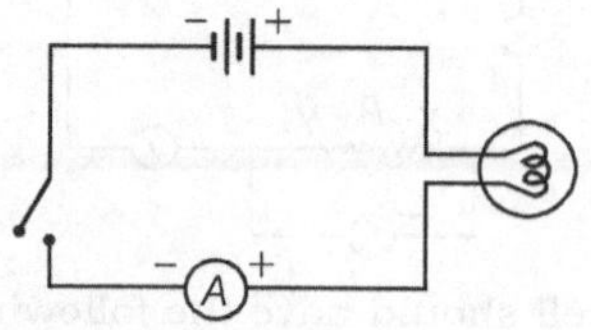

[1½]

(ii) (a) We know that, charge on 1 electron $= 1.6 \times 10^{-19}\,C$

$\Rightarrow 1.6 \times 10^{-19}$ coulomb charge on 1 electron.

$\therefore$ 1 coulomb charge $= \dfrac{1}{1.6 \times 10^{-19}}$

$\simeq 6.25 \times 10^{18}$ electrons [2]

(b) Given, current, $I = 4.5\,A$

Time, $t = 1\,\text{min} = 60\,s$

$\therefore$ Charge carried by a conductor, $q = It$

$= 4.5 \times 60$

$= 270\,C$ [2]

(iii) Scale, At X-axis, 1 div (1 cm) = 0.1 A

At Y-axis, 1 div (1 cm) = 0.5 V

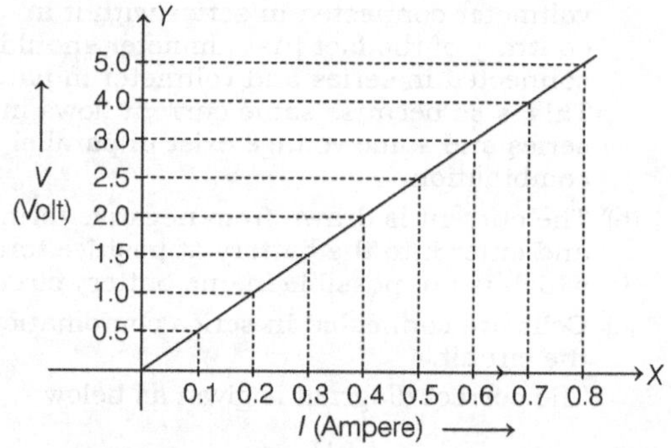

$\therefore$ Resistance, $R = $ Slope of graph $= \dfrac{V}{I}$

$$R = \frac{y_2 - y_1}{x_2 - x_1} = \frac{1.5 - 1.0}{0.3 - 0.2}$$

$$= \frac{0.5}{0.1} = 5\,\Omega$$

[3]

Chapter Assessment

1 Mark Questions

1. If 2 ampere current is flowing through an electrical circuit, then number of electrons passes through the circuit per second is (Take, $e = 1.6 \times 10^{-19}$C)
(a) 6.25×10^{19} electrons
(b) 1.25×10^{19} electrons
(c) 1.25×10^{18} electrons
(d) 3.2×10^{18} electrons

2. Internal resistance of a cell
(a) increases with increasing of area of electrode
(b) decreases with increasing temperature of electrolyte
(c) Both (a) and (b)
(d) Neither (a) nor (b)

3. Which of the following symbol of circuit component is used for changing the current in the circuit?
(a) 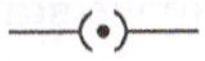
(b) 
(c) 
(d) 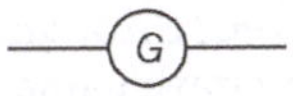

4. If 50 J of work is required to transfer a charge of 10C from one terminal of battery to other, then potential difference between the two terminals of the battery is
(a) 2.5 V
(b) 7.5 V
(c) 10 V
(d) 5 V

5. If the area of cross-section of a conducting wire increases by some ways without changing its length, then resistance of conducting wire will
(a) increase
(b) decrease
(c) remains same
(d) None of these

2 Marks Questions

6. Define 1 ampere of current.

7. How does the resistance of a wire vary, if
(i) area is made half and
(ii) length is made double?

8. Is there any change in current, when a wire of different material of same length and area of cross-section is used? Explain it.

9. Give the resistance of an ideal ammeter. Why does it so?

10. What do you mean by circuit diagram? Draw a schematic circuit diagram of an electric circuit having cell, electric bulb, ammeter and plug key.

11. What is rheostat? Why is the rheostat used in electrical circuit?

12. Mention the factors on which resistance of a conductor depends.

13. What are the advantages of connecting electrical appliances in parallel with the battery instead of connecting them in series?

14. Mention the nature of *V-I* graph for a circuit in which Ohm's law is valid.

Structured Questions

15. (i) (a) How is the direction electric current taken in electric circuit?
(b) Draw the symbol for circuit of component of switch, when it is
I. opened and II. closed. **[4]**

(ii) (a) An electron beam has an area of cross-section 1 mm^2. A total of 5×10^{16} electrons go through any perpendicular cross-section per second. Calculate the current. (Take, charge on electron 1.6×10^{-19} C)
(b) When a car is started it takes 0.5 s and 25 C of charge passes through the coils of starting motor. Calculate the current passing through the motor. **[3]**

(iii) Explain the following questions.
(a) Why is tungsten used almost exclusively for filament of electric lamps?
(b) How does the resistance of a wire vary with its area of cross-section?
(c) Why are copper and aluminium wires usually employed for electricity transmission? **[3]**

16. (i) Due to rapid growth of industries, demands of energy resources are increasing day-by-day. So, what initiative should be taken for efficient used of energy? **[3]**

(ii) Describe the closed and open circuits with proper diagram. **[3]**

(iii) (a) Write any two differences between primary and secondary cells.
(b) What current flows in a resistance of 2 kΩ, when
I. a potential difference of 10 V and
II. a potential difference of 8 mV is applied in turn? **[4]**

For Solutions Scan the Code

Olympiad Section*

Brain Teasing Questions of Olympiad Pattern

1 A potential difference of 400 V is maintained across a conductor of resistance 200 Ω. Calculate the number of electrons flowing through it in 1s. (Take, charge on one electron, $e = 1.6 \times 10^{-19}$C)

(a) 1.25×10^{19}C (b) 2.25×10^{-19}C
(c) 3.00×10^{19}C (d) 4.05×10^{-19}C

2 Calculate the resistivity of the material of a wire 1.5 m long, 0.4 mm in diameter and having a resistance of 3 Ω.

(a) 2.5142×10^{-7} Ωm
(b) 3.153×10^{-7} Ωm
(c) 4.093×10^{-9} Ωm
(d) 2.92×10^{-7} Ωm

3 A resistance of 3 Ω is connected in series with another resistance of 5 Ω. A potential difference of 6 V is applied across the combination. The value of current through the circuit and potential difference across the 3 Ω resistance is respectively,

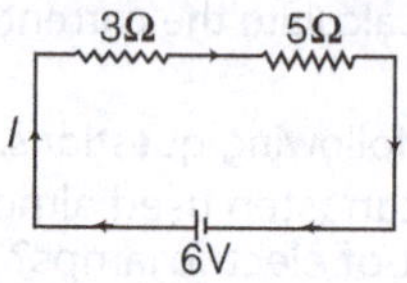

(a) 0.75 A, 2.25 V
(b) 0.90 A, 1.00 V
(c) 0.60 A, 1.25 V
(d) 0.50 A, 2.25 V

4 If an electron revolves in the path of a circle of radius 0.5×10^{-10} m at a frequency of 5×10^{15} cycles/s, then electric current in the circle is

(a) 0.9 mA (b) 0.8 mA
(c) 1.2 mA (d) 2.9 mA

5 In the given circuit diagram, the value of total resistance of the circuit is

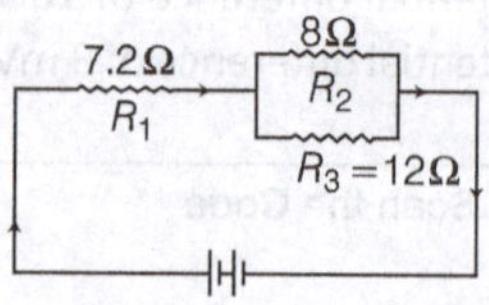

(a) 4.9 Ω (b) 4.2 Ω (c) 12 Ω (d) 6 Ω

6 The circuit diagram shows four identical resistors connected in series with a 12 V battery.

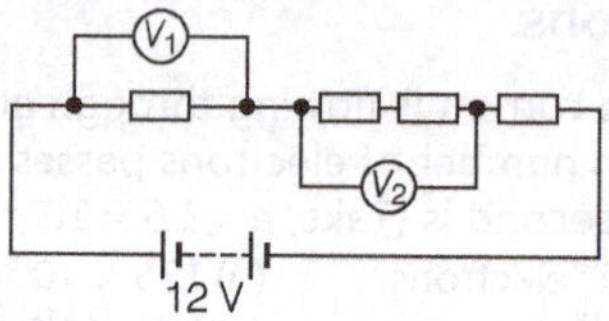

What would be the readings on voltmeters V_1 and V_2?

Voltmeter readings			Voltmeter readings	
	V_1	V_2	V_1	V_2
(a)	1 V	2 V	(b) 2 V	4 V
(c)	3 V	6 V	(d) 4 V	8 V

7 There are two resistors R_1 and R_2 ($R_1 > R_2$) connected through a battery of emf V volt. Choose the correct option regarding the above statement.

(a) When the resistors are connected in series, current through R_2 resistor is more than that of R_1.
(b) They have same potential difference across each resistor, when connected in series.
(c) Resistor R_2 has more current than R_1, when connected in parallel.
(d) They have same current, when connected in parallel.

8 A wire of length 1 m has a resistance of 2Ω, when connected to a cell, the current in the wire is 3 A.

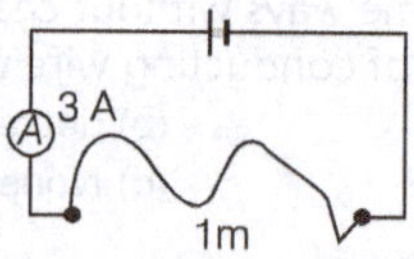

2 m length of the same wire is connected to the same cell.

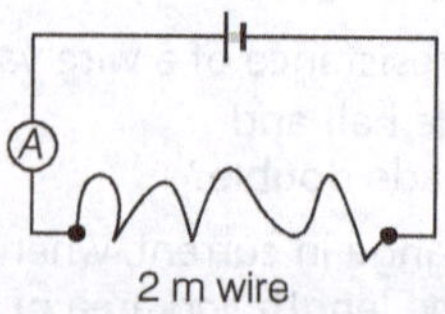

What is the resistance of the wire and the current in it?

	(a)	(b)	(c)	(d)
Resistance	1 Ω	1 Ω	4 Ω	4 Ω
Current	1.5 A	3 A	1.5 A	3 A

9 Which two resistor combinations have the same effective resistance between X and Y?

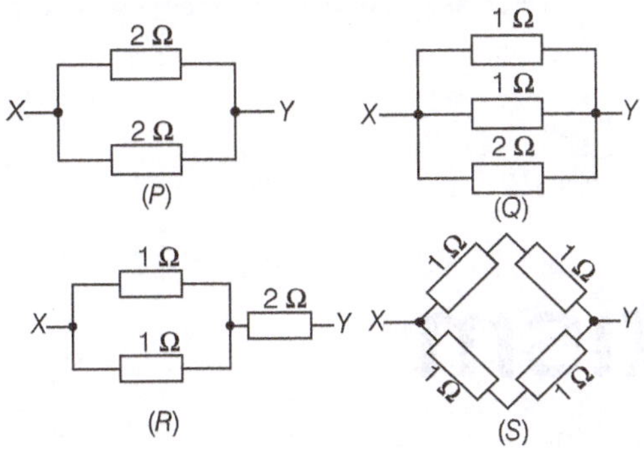

(a) P and Q (b) P and S
(c) Q and R (d) R and S

10 Which circuit could be used to find the resistance of the resistor R?

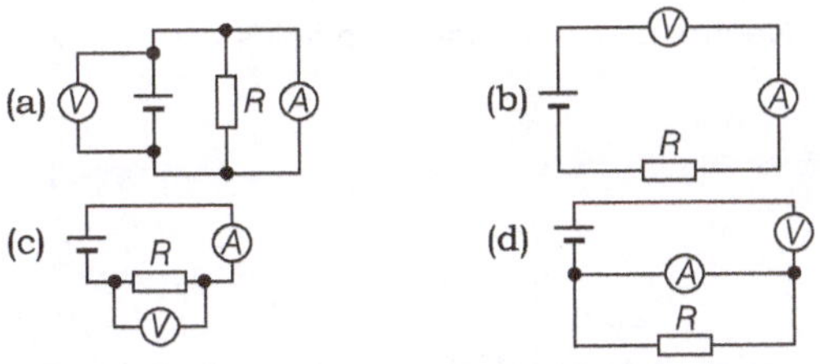

11 A load that has resistance of 10 Ω is to a connected to a constant voltage (120 V) supply. Desired variation in the current through the load is from 3 A to 5 A. The resistance and current range of the rheostat should be

(a) 0-0.36 Ω, 0-5 A (b) 14-24 Ω, 0-3 A
(c) 14-30 Ω, 0-5 A (d) 0-24 Ω, 3-5 A

12 In the circuit depicted in figure, slide S is displaced along variable resistor R towards point X.

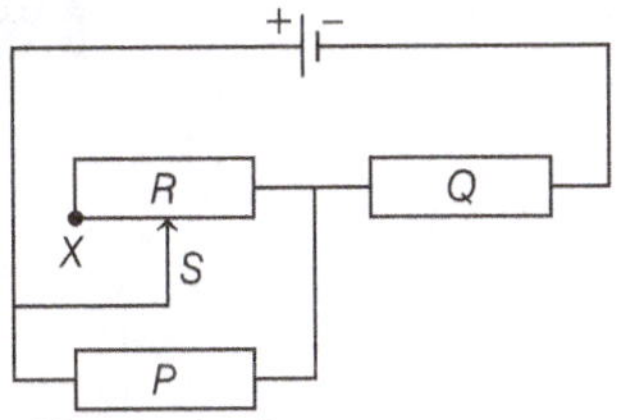

Electric circuit

How does the current passing through resistors P and Q change?

	in P	in Q
(a)	increase	increase
(b)	increase	decrease
(c)	decrease	increase
(d)	decrease	decrease

Answers

1. (a)	**2.** (a)	**3.** (a)	**4.** (b)	**5.** (c)	**6.** (c)	**7.** (c)	**8.** (c)	**9.** (b)	**10.** (c)
11. (c)	**12.** (a)								

* *These questions may or may not be asked in the examination, have been given just for additional practice required for olympiads Scholarship Exams etc. For detailed explanations refer Page No. 222.*

CHAPTER 11

Magnetism

SYLLABUS

- Induced magnetism, Magnetic field of Earth, Neutral points in magnetic fields.
- Introduction of electromagnet and its uses.

A naturally occurring ore of iron (magnetite) attracts small pieces of iron towards itself. The phenomenon of attraction of small bits of iron, steel, cobalt, nickel, etc., towards the ore, is called **magnetism**.

Magnets

A magnet is a naturally occurring or artificial material which attracts iron and its ores.

Magnets are of two types

(i) Natural magnets (ii) Artificial magnets

Natural magnets are generally irregular in shape and weak in strength. On the other hand, artificial magnets have desired shape and desired strength.

A bar magnet, a horse shoe magnet, magnetic needle, compass needle, ball-ended magnet, etc., all are the examples of artificial magnets as shown in figures.

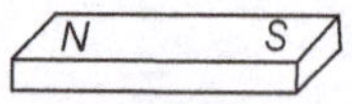

(a) Bar magnet

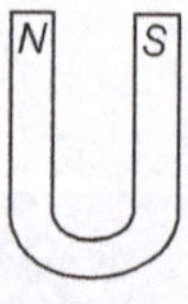

(b) Horse shoe magnet

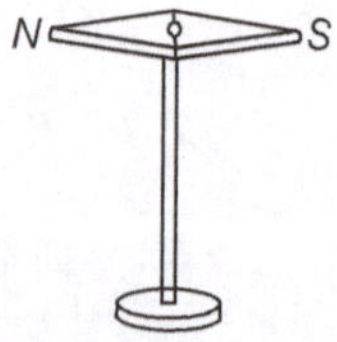

(c) Magnetic needle

(d) Compass needle

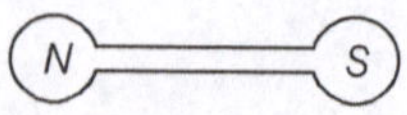

(e) Ball-ended magnet

Different types of magnets

Bar Magnet

A magnet in the shape of a bar is called bar magnet. It has two poles. One pole is designated as North pole and the other as South pole. If a bar magnet is dropped into a pile of iron filings, then the maximum amount of filings get deposited near the ends of the magnet and almost nil in the middle as shown in the figure below.

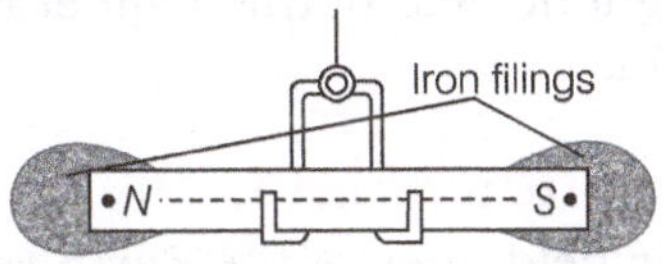

A bar magnet dropped into a pile of iron filings

The pattern suggests that attraction is maximum at the two ends of the bar magnet. These ends are called poles of the magnet.

Properties of a Bar Magnet

A bar magnet possesses the following four properties

(i) **Attractive Property** A magnet attracts the iron or iron made objects towards itself. This property of attraction is called attractive property of a magnet. Attractive property of the magnet is maximum at the ends and minimum at its middle part.

(ii) **Directive Property** If a bar magnet is suspended freely with a silk thread through its centre of gravity in a horizontal plane, then it always points towards North-South direction. The end towards the geographical North direction is North pole and towards geographical South direction is South pole. So, a bar magnet has directive property, since it points in geographical direction. The North and South poles are marked by the letters N and S, respectively.

(iii) **Like Poles Repel and Unlike Poles Attract** When South and North poles of different magnets are brought close to each other, it is found that they attract each other. On the other hand, when two North or two South poles (like poles) are brought close, they repel each other.

(iv) **Poles Exist in Pairs Only** (i.e., non-existence of monopole) Poles of a magnet cannot be separated from a magnet by any means i.e., magnet cannot be separated as North and South poles. If a magnet is cut into two parts, then each part separately has a North pole and South pole.

Magnetism Induced by Bar Magnet on Magnetic Material (Induced Magnetism)

When a magnetic material (soft iron or steel) is placed in contact with magnet, it acquires the properties of magnet. It starts attracting small pieces of iron filings when placed near it.
On carrying the material away from the magnet, its magnetic properties disappear.

It stays magnetised as long as the magnet is in contact with it. This temporary magnetism acquired by magnetic material is called induced magnetism.

The temporary magnetic properties acquired by a magnetic material on placing it in contact with magnet, is called induced magnetism.

The magnetism induced by North pole of the magnet possesses South polarity in the material and *vice-versa*. So, there is always attraction between the magnet and material acquiring induced magnetism, thus, we can say that magnetic induction precedes attraction.

Check Your LEARNING...

1 What are the two types of magnet?
2 What happens when a bar magnet is suspended freely?
3 Where is the magnetism minimum in a bar magnet?
4 Does a single pole of magnet exist in nature?
5 What will happen when the similar poles of two bar magnet brought close?
6 What do you mean by temporary magnetic property of a material due to a magnet?

Magnetic Field

The region surrounding a magnet in which magnetic effect can be experienced i.e., its force can be detected is called magnetic field. Magnetic field is a vector quantity which has both magnitude and direction.

Lines of Magnetic Field

The magnetic field lines (or lines of magnetic field) are a visual and intuitive realisation of the magnetic field. The magnetic field lines in a magnetic field are those imaginary lines which continuously represent the direction of the magnetic field. The tangent drawn at any point on magnetic field line shows the direction of magnetic field at that point.

Properties of Lines of Magnetic Field

The properties of lines of magnetic field (or magnetic field lines) are given below

(i) The magnetic field lines of a magnet form continuous closed loops.

(ii) The tangent to the field lines at a given point represents the direction of the net magnetic field at that point.

(iii) The larger the number of field lines crossing per unit area, the stronger is the magnitude of the magnetic field.

(iv) The magnetic field lines do not intersect, or if they did, the direction of the magnetic field would not be unique at the point of intersection.

(v) Parallel and equidistant magnetic field lines represent a uniform magnetic field.

(vi) Magnetic field lines are crowded near the poles of a magnet, where the magnetic field is strong and are far separated near the middle of the magnet and far from the magnet, where the magnetic field is weak.

(vii) They also behave like stretched elastic rubber strings.

(viii) These lines emerge normally from the magnetised surface.

Earth's Magnetism

In 1600, Sir William Gilbert was the first to suggest that the Earth itself is a huge magnet. Earth behaves like a powerful magnet is placed within it. The magnetic field of the Earth is considered to be arisen due to electrical currents produced by convective motion of metallic fluids (consisting mostly of iron and nickel) in the outer core of the Earth. This is known as the **dynamo effect.**

Evidences of Earth's Magnetic Field

The points given below prove the existence of Earth's magnetic field

(i) A freely suspended magnet always rests in North-South direction. This is possible only if a magnetic force is applied on the magnet which forces it to always rest in North-South direction.

(ii) An iron rod buried inside the Earth along North-South direction becomes a magnet. This is possible, if iron rod is kept near a magnet which induces magnetism in it.

(iii) While drawing the magnetic lines of force of a magnet we get neutral points, where the magnetic field is zero. It is possible only if there exists another magnetic field along with the magnetic field of the magnet in opposite direction.

Earth's Magnetic Field

The magnetic field lines of the Earth resemble that of a hypothetical bar magnet located at the centre of the Earth.

The pole near the geographic North pole (N_g) of the Earth is called the **North magnetic pole** (N_m) and the pole near the geographic South pole (S_g) of the Earth is called **South magnetic pole** (S_m).

Some definitions related to Earth's magnetism are

(i) **Geographic Axis** The straight line passing through the geographical North and South poles of the Earth is called its geographic axis. It is the axis of rotation of the Earth.

(ii) **Magnetic Axis** The straight line passing through the magnetic North and South poles of the Earth is called the magnetic axis.

(iii) **Magnetic Equator** It is the great circle on the Earth perpendicular to the magnetic axis.

(iv) **Magnetic Meridian** The vertical plane passing through the magnetic axis of a freely suspended bar magnet is called magnetic meridian.

(v) **Geographic Meridian** The vertical plane passing through the line joining the geographical North and South poles is called the geographic meridian.

(iv) **Neutral Points** Those points, where the magnetic field of a magnet and Earth's horizontal magnetic field are equal in magnitude but opposite in direction are called **neutral points.** Thus, the net magnetic field at neutral points is zero. If a compass needle is placed at such a point, it can stay in any position.

Uniform Magnetic Field of Earth

The magnetic field of Earth is uniform. The field lines are parallel and equidistant. These lines do not intersect with each other. They are directed from geographic South to geographic North.

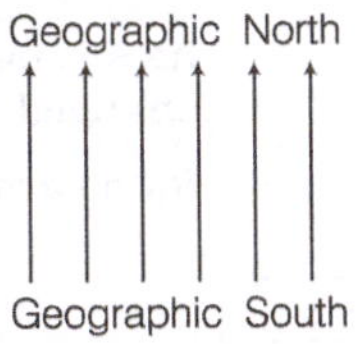

Non-uniform Magnetic Field of a Bar Magnet along with Neutral Points

The magnetic field around a bar magnet is non-uniform. They are not equispaced and parallel.

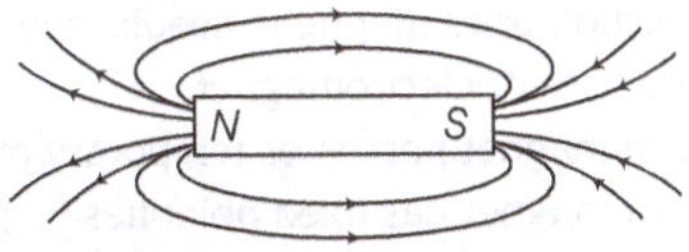

The non-uniform magnetic field lines of a bar magnet placed in the magnetic meridian along with neutral points can be explained for two cases.

(i) **When magnet is placed in magnetic meridian with its North pole pointing towards geographic North.** Magnetic field lines near a bar magnet with the help of compass needle when magnet is placed with its North pole points towards geographical North is given in the figure. Here, fields due to magnet and the Earth are in the same directions at points on the axial line and are in opposite directions at points on the equatorial line. Therefore, the two neutral points X and X' lie on the equatorial line.

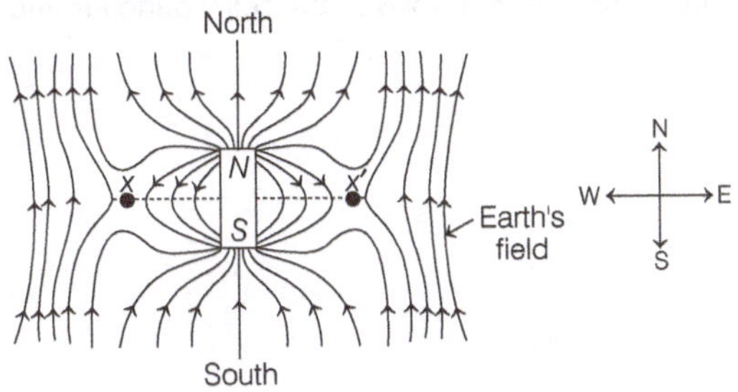

(ii) **When the magnet is placed in magnetic meridian with its South pole points towards geographical North.** The pattern of magnetic field lines near a bar magnet with the help of compass needle when magnet is placed with its South pole pointing towards geographical North is given in the figure below. Here, fields due to the bar magnet and the Earth are in the same direction at points on equitorial lines and are in opposite directions at points on the axial line of the magnet. Therefore, two neutral points Y and Y' lie on the axial line.

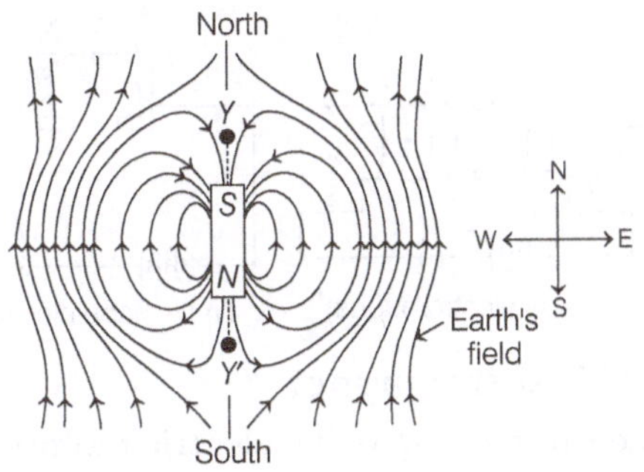

Magnetic Compass

It is a small magnetic needle pivoted at the centre of a small brass or aluminium box which has a transparent glass top.

A magnetic compass is used

(i) to find geographical direction.
(ii) to find direction of a magnetic field.
(iii) to test the polarity of a magnet.

Permanent Magnets and Electromagnets

Permanent Magnets

The substances which at room temperature retain their magnetic property for a long period of time are called permanent magnets. Permanent magnet can be made by placing a rod of magnetic material in a current carrying coil (or solenoid). The magnetic field of the coil (or solenoid) magnetises the rod.

The material used for making the permanent magnet should be such that, its magnetic property is not erased by variations of temperature or minor mechanical damage or stray magnetic fields. Steel is favoured for making permanent magnet.

Electromagnets

Electromagnets are usually in the form of iron core coils (or solenoids).

When current flows through the coil, it becomes magnet when current is switched OFF, then its magnetism disappears.

The electromagnets can be of any shape but usually, they are of two shapes

(i) *I*-shape (or bar) electro-magnet and

(ii) *U*-shape (or horse-shoe) electro-magnet

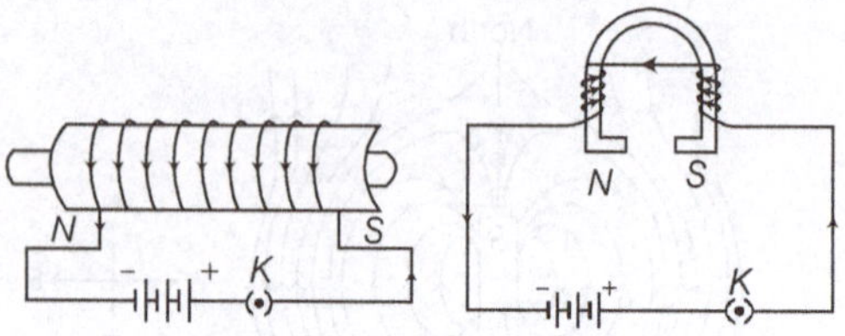

(i) *I*-shape electromagnet (ii) *U*-shape electromagnet

Uses of Electromagnet

It is used in electric bells, electric motors, telephone, diaphragms, loudspeakers and for sorting scrap metal and for extraction in hospitals. Giant electromagnets are used in cranes to lift machinery and other parts.

Differences between an electromagnet and a permanent magnet

Electromagnet	Permanent magnet
It is a temporary magnet.	It is a permanent magnet. i.e., it cannot be demagnetised easily.
Its strength can be changed.	Its strength cannot be changed.
Its polarity can be changed.	Its polarity is fixed.

Check Your LEARNING...

1 How will you find the direction of magnetic field at a point with the help of a magnetic field line at that point?
2 Give any one evidence of existence of Earth's magnetic field.
3 What is the magnetic field at neutral point?
4 In which direction does magnetic needle stay at neutral point?
5 Give any two uses of electromagnet.
6 Which type of magnet possesses temporary magnetism?
7 Which type of magnet has fixed polarities?

QUICK Revision

- **Magnetism** It is the property by virtue of which a substance can attract iron filings. The substance which have this property is called a magnet.
- **Magnetic Compass** It is a device made up of magnet used to find directions of magnetic field.
- Magnetism can be induced by a bar magnet or any magnetic material. This phenomenon is called **magnetic induction.** This property precedes attraction but it is a temporary property.
- **Magnetic Field or Magnetic Field Lines** The region around a magnet, where magnetic force is experienced by magnetic materials is called **magnetic field**. A pictorial representation of the magnetic field around a magnet is called **magnetic field lines.**
- **Neutral Points** The points, where the magnetic field of magnet and Earth's horizontal magnetic field are equal in magnitude but opposite in direction.
- **Electromagnet** It is a temporary strong magnet made from a piece of soft iron when current flows in the coil wound around it. It is used in electric bells, electric motors, loudspeakers, etc.

Chapter Practice

Section-I

1 Mark Questions

1. Consider the following statements.
   I. Like poles always repel to each other.
   II. When a bar magnet is suspended freely in space, then it stays always in North-South direction.
   Choose the correct statement.
   (a) I only (b) II only
   (c) Both I and II (d) Neither I nor II

Sol. (c) When two bar magnets are brought closer to each other, then like poles repel while unlike poles attract to each other.

2. Which of the following is not true with respect to magnetic field lines?
   (a) Magnetic field lines of force are closed and continuous curve.
   (b) Parallel and equidistant magnetic field lines represent a uniform magnetic field.
   (c) Two magnetic field lines of force can intersect only at a single point.
   (d) None of the above

Sol. (c) The magnetic field lines of force do not intersect each other, if they intersect, then direction of magnetic field at the point of intersection will not be unique.

3. Which of the region (*A*, *B* and *C*) represents region of a uniform magnetic field?

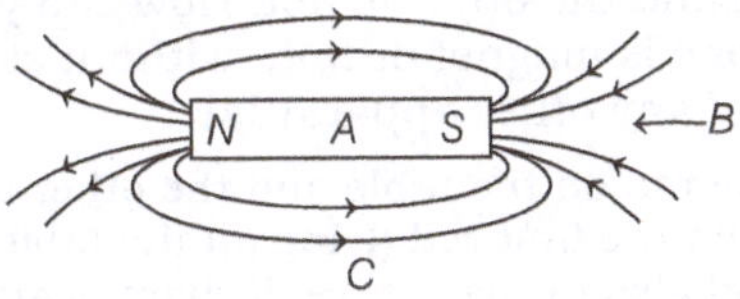

   (a) *A* Only (b) *B* Only
   (c) *A* and *C* both (d) *A*, *B* and *C*

Sol. (a) In the region of a uniform magnetic field, field lines are parallel and equidistant.

4. If B_1, B_2 and B_3 are magnetic field intensity at points *A*, *B* and *C* respectively. Then

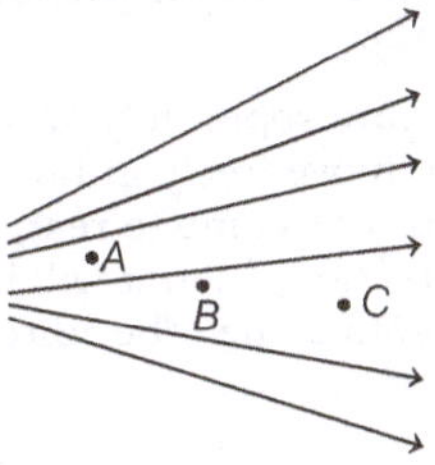

   (a) $B_1 = B_2 = B_3$ (b) $B_1 > B_2 > B_3$
   (c) $B_1 < B_2 < B_3$ (d) None of these

Sol. (b) Magnetic field lines are closest at point *A*. Closer at point *B* and farthest at point *C*, hence $B_1 > B_2 > B_3$.

5. Magnetic field pattern due to a bar magnet is shown below in the diagram. This bar magnet is placed at a place where Earth's magnetic field exists.

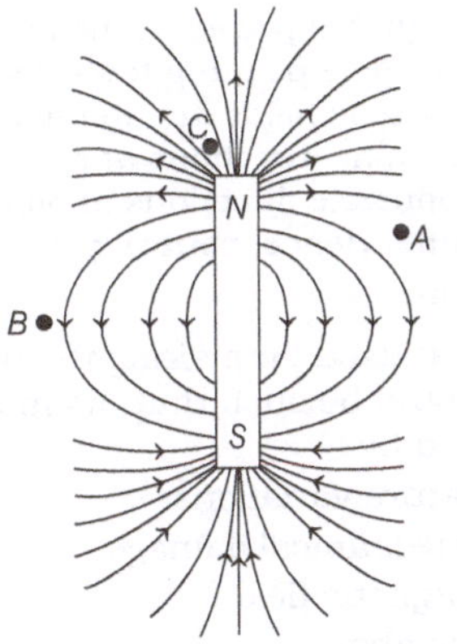

   Magnetic field strength is maximum at point
   (a) *A* (b) *B* (c) *C* (d) *A* and *B*

Sol. (c) Magnetic field strength is maximum at point *C* because maximum number of magnetic field lines passes through this point.

6. Choose the incorrect statements.
   (a) Magnetic field lines meet inside the magnet.
   (b) Magnetic field lines do not pass through the magnet.
   (c) Both (a) and (b)
   (d) Neither (a) nor (b)

Sol. (c) Magnetic field lines pass through the bar magnet and do not meet (cross) with each other.

7. The Earth's magnetic field exists due to
   (a) rotation of Earth.
   (b) convective motion of metallic fluids.
   (c) Both (a) and (b)
   (d) a huge bar magnet inside the Earth.

Sol. (c) Due to rotation of Earth, electrical currents are produced by convective motion of metallic fluids (consisting mostly of iron and nickel) in inner core of Earth which is responsible for Earth's magnetism.

8. Magnetic meridian is the
   (a) horizontal plane in the direction of magnetic field.

(b) horizontal plane in the perpendicular direction of magnetic field.
(c) vertical plane in the direction of magnetic field.
(d) vertical plane in the perpendicular direction of magnetic field.

Sol. (*c*) Magnetic meridian is the vertical plane in the direction of magnetic field.

9. When magnet is placed in the magnetic meridian with its North pole pointing towards geographic North, then neutral points lie on the
(a) axial line of bar magnet
(b) equatorial line of the bar magnet
(c) Both (a) and (b)
(d) Neither (a) nor (b)

Sol. (*b*) When magnet is placed in the magnetic meridian with its North pole pointing toward geographic North, then the magnetic fields due to the magnet and the Earth are in same directions at point on the axial line and are in opposite directions at points on the equatorial line. Hence, neutral point occurs on equatorial line.

10. The material used for making the permanent magnet should be such that, its magnetic property is not erased by
(a) temperature variations
(b) minor mechanical damage
(c) stray magnetic field
(d) All of the above

Sol. (*d*) The material used for making the permanent magnet should be such that, its magnetic property is not erased by temperature variations or minor mechanical damage or stray magnetic fields.

11. Which of the following materials is used for making permanent magnet?
(a) Soft iron (b) Steel
(c) Both (a) and (b) (d) Neither (a) nor (b)

Sol. (*b*) Steel is favoured for making permanent magnet because it can hold magnetic property for a long period of time.

12. Polarity and strength always remain unchanged for a
(a) temporary magnet
(b) permanent magnet
(c) Both (a) and (b)
(d) Neither (a) nor (b)

Sol. (*b*) Polarity and strength always remain same for a permanent magnet.

13. Electromagnets are used in
(a) electric bells (b) electric motors
(c) loudspeakers (d) All of these

Sol. (*d*) **Electromagnet** is a temporary strong magnet made from a piece of soft iron when current flows in the coil wound around it. It is used in electric bells, electric motors, loudspeakers, etc.

2 Marks Questions

14. What are natural magnets? Write down their demerits?

Sol. Natural magnets are pieces of naturally occurring iron ore called magnetite (Fe_3O_4). [1]
They have the following demerits
(i) They have weak magnetism.
(ii) They have irregular shapes. [1]

15. What is an artificial magnet? Write down their merit.

Sol. An artificial magnet is made of hard steel and prepared in laboratory. e.g., A bar magnet, a horse shoe magnet, compass needle, etc., are the examples of artificial magnets. Merit of an artificial magnet is that it can be of desired shape and desired strength.

16. How does the magnetic pole strength of a magnet vary when
(i) it is cut into two equal parts parallel to its length
(ii) it is cut perpendicular to its length

Sol. (i) The magnetic pole strength of new broken magnet is half of the strength of original magnet because both broken part is identical and equal. [1]
(ii) There is no change in magnetic pole strength of new magnet because new magnet is magnetically identical. [1]

17. What is induced magnetism? Define magnetic induction.

Sol. The magnetism acquired by an unmagnetised material when it is brought near (or in contact with) a magnet is called induced magnetism. [1]
The phenomenon of making unmagnetised material to magnetic material temporarily is called magnetic induction. [1]

18. You are given two identical rods in which one is magnet and the other is not. How can you tell which one is magnet or not, without suspending it or use of any other apparatus?

Sol. Take one rod on the table and the other in your hand and touch the first rod (lying on the table) at the ends and also in the centre. If there is attraction at all the three points (i.e., both ends and centre), then rod in your hand is a simple rod. If there is a attraction only at the ends but no attraction at the centre, then the rod on the table is a magnet.

19. You are provided two similar bars in which one is a magnet and other is a soft iron. How will you distinguish between them without the use of any other magnet?

Sol. Suspend these bars separately at its centre of gravity, so that they can move freely in horizontal plane. After sometime, when they come to rest, if the bar stays in North-South direction, then it will be a magnet and the other which (points some other direction) is a soft iron bar.

20. Following figure shows that several soft iron pins can be hung one below the other from the pole of a magnet. What will happen when magnet is removed? Explain.

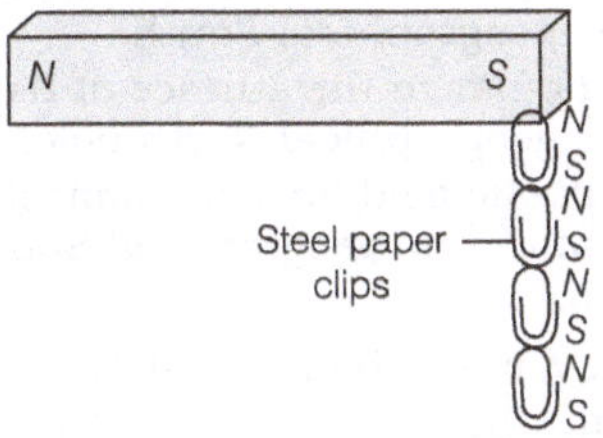

Sol. Soft iron pins are hung with each other by induced magnetism. When magnet is removed, the other pins will fall down because the magnetism in pins vanishes to zero when magnet is removed.

21. Explain, why two magnetic field lines can never intersect each other?

Sol. Two magnetic field lines can never intersect each other because in this condition, there would be two directions of magnetic field at the point of intersection, which can never be possible.

22. What do you mean by the terms (i) magnetic force and (ii) magnetic field?

Sol. (i) According to Faraday, a magnet modifies the space around itself in such a way that if any other magnetic material is brought near to this space, it experiences a force, called magnetic force. [1]

(ii) The region around magnet, where force is experienced by magnetic materials is called magnetic field. [1]

23. What conclusion can be drawn when a compass needle show no deflection at a point?

Sol. If a compass needle shows no deflection at a point in any direction, then it is concluded that,

(i) there are at least two magnetic field nearby and
(ii) the resultant (or net) magnetic field at that point is zero. [1+1]

24. How does a compass help in detecting magnetic field around a magnet?

Sol. When the magnetic compass is placed near the magnet, then it gets deflection. This illustrates the presence of magnetic field around a magnet.

25. Plot the Earth's magnetic field lines in a horizontal plane as obtained by a limited space.

Sol. Magnetic field lines in a horizontal plane due to Earth's magnetic field in a limited place is uniform and parallel running from geographic South to geographic North direction. [1]

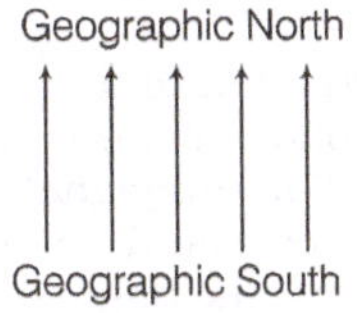

[1]

26. What is an electromagnet? Give one use of it.

Sol. An electromagnet is a temporary strong magnet. It consists of a long insulated copper wire wound around a soft iron core, which attains magnetism due to the flow of current. Giant electromagnets are used in cranes to lift machinery and other parts.

3 Marks Questions

27. What are artificial magnets? How is it usually made? Why are they required?

Sol. Magnets made by man using elements like iron, nickel, cobalt or their mixture with other elements are called artificial magnets. [2]

We require artificial magnet, due to the following qualities

(i) We can design any shape of artificial magnet as per desire. [1/2]
(ii) Its magnetism can be obtained as per requirement. [1/2]

28. What is compass needle? Write its uses.

Sol. Compass needle is a small magnetic needle pivoted at the centre of a small brass or aluminium box with transparent glass top. [1]

Uses of a compass needle are

(i) To find geographic North and geographic South directions.
(ii) To find out polarity of a magnet.
(iii) To find out the direction of magnetic field. [2]

29. What do you understand by poles of a magnet? How will you test its polarity?

Sol. Near the two ends of a magnet there are points, where the magnetic strength is maximum. These are called poles of a magnet. [1]

To test polarity of a magnet, suspend it with a thread through its centre of gravity. So that, it can move freely in horizontal plane. After sometime, it comes to rests. The end directing towards North direction is called North pole and other is South pole. [2]

30. On the basis of effect of magnet, how a magnet can transform energy from one form to another without any permanent loss in their own energy?

Sol. Transformation of energy is taken as

(i) **Mechanical to Mechanical** Such as attraction and repulsion.
(ii) **Mechanical to Electrical** Such as generators.
(iii) **Electrical to Mechanical** Such as motors and and charged particle deflection. [1 × 3]

31. How does an iron bar acquire magnetism when it is brought near to the North pole of bar magnet? Draw a diagram of an iron bar to show its polarity. What will happen when magnet is removed?

Sol. When an iron bar is brought near to the North pole of a bar magnet, it gets magnetised in such a way that the nearer end of iron bar becomes South pole and other end becomes North pole.

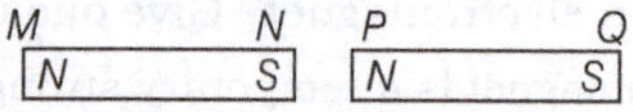

The iron bar PQ is placed near a bar magnet MN. When magnet is removed the induced magnetism in iron vanishes, then it becomes an ordinary piece of iron bar. [3]

32. Comment upon the statement induced magnetism is temporary.

Sol. When an unmagnetised bar is placed near a magnet, the bar becomes a magnet i.e., it acquires the property of attracting iron filings when they are brought near its ends. This is called induced magnetism. [2]

If the magnet is removed, it is seen that all the iron filings which was clung to it falls down. That means the bar loses its magnetism. Hence, we can say that induced magnetism is temporary. [1]

33. Explain the statement, induction precedes attraction.

Sol. When a piece of iron is brought near one end of a magnet, the nearer end of the piece acquires the opposite polarity. Since, unlike poles attract each other, the iron piece is attracted towards the end of the magnet. So, the piece of iron first becomes a magnet and then it is attracted. This explains the statement induction precedes attraction. [3]

34. Show that iron filings which are sprinkled on a sheet of cardboard over a bar magnet take up a definite pattern.

Sol. When we place a bar magnet below a sheet of cardboard and spread some iron filings uniformly over it. Then, the iron filings arrange themselves along the curved lines when cardboard is slightly taped which is shown in the figure below. [2]

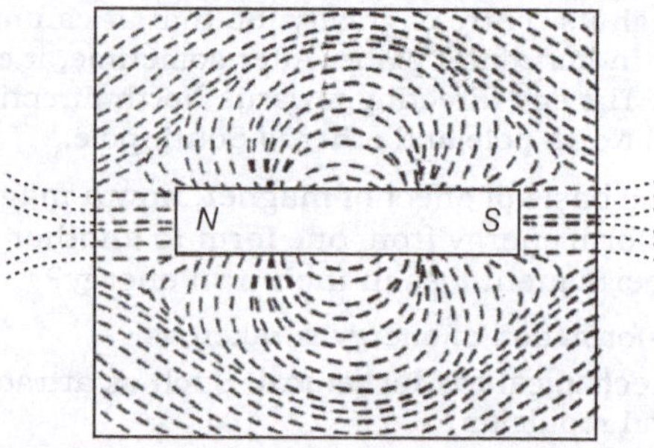

[1]

35. State the evidences of the existence of Earth's magnetic field.

Sol. The existence of Earth's magnetic field is based on the following facts

(i) A freely suspended magnet always rests in geographic North-South direction.

(ii) An iron rod burried inside the Earth along North-South direction, after some days becomes a magnet.

(iii) Neutral points are obtained near a magnet on plotting the magnetic field lines between the Earth's magnet and a bar magnet. [1 × 3]

36. Explain the general shape of Earth's magnetic field lines.

Sol. The Earth's magnetic field lines are

(i) Perpendicular to the surface of Earth, downward near the geographical South.

(ii) Perpendicular to the surface of Earth, upward near the geographical North pole.

(iii) The magnetic field lines are almost parallel near the equator from geographical South to North direction. [1 × 3]

37. What do you mean by neutral points in magnetism?

Sol. Neutral points near a magnet are the points, where resultant of intensity of magnetic field of a magnet and the horizontal component of Earth's magnetic field is zero.

Practically when two different types of magnetic field (one due to Earth and the other due to magnet itself) interfere together, then there may be some points in the field, where compass needle show no deflection. Those points are known as neutral points. [3]

4 Marks Questions

38. In a class room, an ordinary piece of iron bar is placed on the top of a wooden table. Teacher has a bar in his hand and moves her hand below the table near the iron bar. It is observed that ordinary bar moves magically on the table. What conclusion do you draw from this magic?

Sol. The conclusion from this activity are as following

(i) Teacher has strong magnet in his hand.

(ii) Induced magnetism is produced in soft iron bar.

(iii) Opposite poles of magnet attract the bar.

(iv) There is a small force of friction between small iron bar and table top.

(v) Due to induction opposite poles of magnet and iron come close to each other. [4]

39. You are given two identical bar magnets X and Y, one is magnetised and the other is unmagnetised. How can you identify which one is magnetised by using your hands, eyes and brain?

Sol. As we know that, there is zero magnetisation at the centre of the magnet.

Firstly, place magnet X and Y perpendicularly and then magnet Y on X as shown in figure.

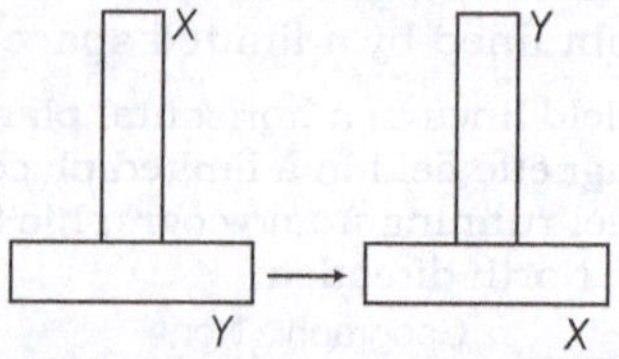

[2]

If there is no attraction in first case and there is attraction in second case, then magnet Y is magnetised and X is unmagnetised. If there is attraction in first case and no attraction in second case, then magnet X is magnetised and magnet Y is unmagnetised. [2]

40. State five properties of magnetic field lines.

Sol. Magnetic field lines possess the following properties
(i) They are directed from the North to South pole of a magnet outside the magnet and from South to North pole inside the magnet.
(ii) They are continuous closed curves.
(iii) The magnetic field lines do not intersect each other.
(iv) Magnetic field is strong at poles. Where lines are crowded and at the middle of the magnet, where magnetic fields is weak and lines are separated.
(v) The uniform magnetic field lines are parallel to each other. The Earth's magnetic field lines in a limited space is uniform. **[4]**

41. Draw the pattern of magnetic field lines near a bar magnet with the help of compass needle
(i) when magnet is placed with its North pole pointing towards geographic North.
(ii) when the magnet is placed with its South pole pointing towards geographic North.
Also, indicate the position of neutral point by marking X.

Sol. Refer to theory (Page 201).

Section-II

Structured Questions

42. (a) Write any three properties of magnetic lines of force. **[3]**
(b) Draw a labelled diagram to make an electromagnet from a soft iron bar AB. Mark the polarity at its ends. Write its uses. **[3]**
(c) How can you locate the position of a pole in a magnet? Explain experimentally. **[4]**

Sol. (a) Three properties of magnetic field lines are
(i) They leave from N-pole and enter at S-pole and continue inside magnet upto N-pole making closed curves.
(ii) The tangent at any point on the lines of field give direction of magnetic field at that point.
(iii) Lines of field are crowded in the region of strong magnetic field, whereas they are widely separated in the region of weak magnetic field i.e., usually at middle of the magnet. **[1 × 3]**

(b) The labelled diagram is shown in the figure below

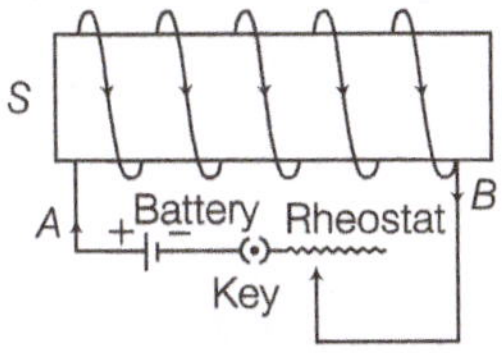

[1]

Here, the polarity at the end A, where the current is clockwise, is South (S), while at the end B, where the current is anti-clockwise, is North (N). **[1]**

The uses of electromagnet are
(i) For separating the iron pieces from debris and ores.
(ii) In several electrical devices such as telegraph, microphone, loudspeaker, etc. **[1]**

(c) For locating the position of pole of magnet, the following procedure is adopted.
(i) Fix up a A-4 sheet on drawing board with the help of thumb pins.
(ii) Place a permanent magnet on the sheet and mark is boundary with pencil.
(iii) Place a compass P near a pole (say it North) and mark the points 1, 2.
(iv) Repeat the step (iii) for new position Q and R; and mark the points 3, 4, 5, 6 at the end of needle and then remove the needle.
(v) Join points in pair (1, 2), (3, 4), (5, 6) and produce towards magnet. **[2]**
We observe the three lines intersect at point N which is position of North pole. Similarly, we can draw the position of South pole. **[2]**

43. (a) Draw labelled diagram to show, how will a bar magnet come to rest when it is suspended by a silk thread from a rigid support in such a way that it can freely swing in horizontal plane? **[3]**
(b) State the properties of a bar magnet. **[3]**
(c) (i) What are the properties of an electromagnet?
(ii) How can we increase the strength of an electromagnet? **[4]**

Sol. (a) A bar magnet will come to rest along geographical North-South direction. With North pole of the magnet towards geographical North direction and South pole of magnet towards geographical South direction.

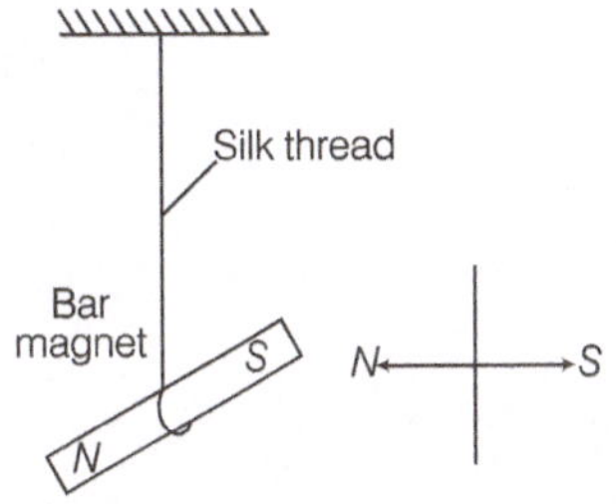

According to diagram, the magnet is not exactly horizontal. The North pole of the magnet is slightly dip downward in northern hemisphere. **[3]**

(b) The properties of a bar magnet are
(i) A bar magnet has directive property.
(ii) It has attractive property i.e., it attracts magnetic materials.
(iii) Poles exist only in pairs i.e., non existence of monopole.
(iv) Like poles repel and unlike poles attract each other. **[3]**

(c) (i) The properties of an electromagnet are
(a) It is a temporary magnet.

(b) Its strength can be changed.

(c) Its polarity can be changed. [3]

(ii) The strength of an electromagnet can be increased by increasing the current through the coil. [1]

44. (a) The unmagnetised iron nails gets attracted to a magnet when brought near to it. Explain the mechanism involved in this phenomenon. [3]

(b) Where are the neutral points situated

(i) when the magnet is placed with its North pole pointing towards geographic North?

(ii) when the magnet is placed with its South pole pointing towards geographic North? [3]

(c) What do you mean by the following terms.

(i) Magnetism

(ii) Magnet

(iii) Pole

(iv) Magnetic or effective length of magnet [4]

Sol. (a) When unmagnetised iron nails are brought near a magnet, the ends of the iron nails which is near to North pole of magnet becomes South pole due to induction. Therefore, the bar magnet by induction magnetises the iron nail which gets attracted by the magnet and clings to it. This magnetised nail magnetises the other nail near it due to the phenomenon called magnetic induction. [3]

(b) (i) If the North pole of bar magnet pointing towards geographic North, the neutral points are situated symmetrical on either side of a magnet at equal distance from the centre in East-West directions. [1½]

(ii) If South pole of a bar magnet pointing towards geographic North, the neutral points are on either side of the magnet at equal distance from the centre in North-South directions. [1½]

(c) (i) **Magnetism** It is the property by virtue of which a substance can attract magnetic materials e.g., soft iron, iron filings, etc.

(ii) **Magnet** Materials which have the property of magnetism are called magnet.

(iii) **Pole** The points inside the magnet near the ends, where the magnetic strength is maximum are called poles of the magnet. The two poles are equal in strength. They are not situated exactly at the ends of the magnet but slightly inside.

(iv) **Magnetic or Effective Length** The distance between two poles of a magnet is called magnetic length or effective length. [4]

Chapter Assessment

1 Mark Questions

1. Which of the following is not the example of an artificial magnet?
   (a) Compass needle (b) Magnetic needle
   (c) Horse shoe magnet (d) None of these

2. Magnetic field pattern due to a bar magnet is shown below. Magnetic field strength is maximum near the region of

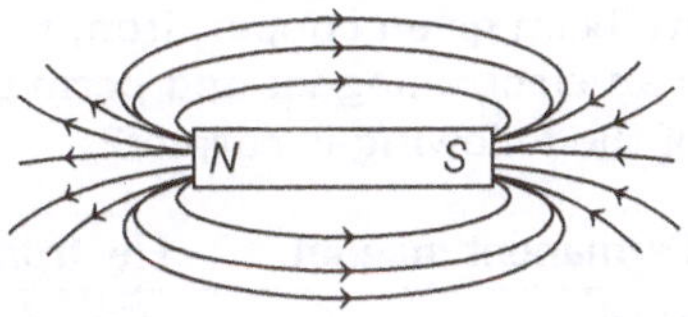

   (a) North pole
   (b) South pole
   (c) Both (a) and (b)
   (d) Neither (a) nor (b)

3. Which of the following is the properties of magnetic field line?
   (a) Magnetic field lines are closed and continuous curves.
   (b) Magnetic field lines never intersect with each other.
   (c) Magnetic field lines are crowded near the poles.
   (d) All of the above

4. Choose the incorrect statement from the following regarding magnetic lines of field.
   (a) The direction of magnetic field at a point is taken to be the direction in which the North pole of a magnetic compass needle points.
   (b) Magnetic field lines are closed curves.
   (c) If magnetic field lines are parallel and equidistant, they represent zero field strength.
   (d) Relative strength of magnetic field is shown by the degree of closeness of the field lines.

5. A freely suspended magnet always stays in
   (a) East-West direction (b) North-South direction
   (c) North-East direction (d) South-West direction

2 Marks Questions

6. Name the magnets shown below.

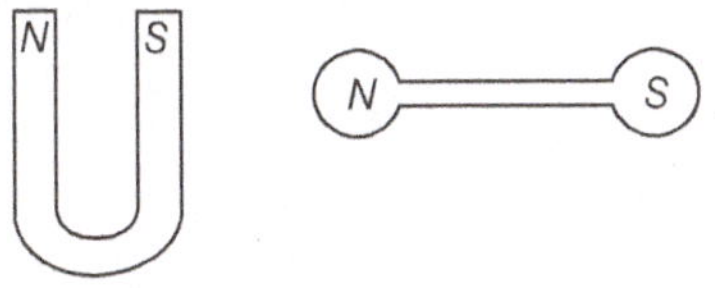

(a) (b)

7. Write any two uses of magnetic compass.

8. Define the terms
   (i) Magnetic equator
   (ii) Magnetic meridian

9. Which types of material are used for making permanent magnet and why?

10. What do you mean by magnetism? How it can be induced?

11. What do you mean by electromagnets?

12. Write the name of the axis about which Earth rotates. Also, define this axis.

13. Draw the magnetic field pattern due to bar magnet.

14. Briefly explain about the cause of Earth's magnetism.

15. What are the two types of magnet? Write one example of each.

Structured Questions

16. (i) Mention any three differences between electromagnet and a permanent magnet. [3]
    (ii) What do you mean by
    (a) attractive and
    (b) directive properties of a bar magnet? Explain briefly. [3]
    (iii) (a) Define magnetic field. Is it a vector quantity or scalar quantity?
    (b) Define magnetic field lines. Why does two magnetic lines of forces not intersect to each other? [4]

17. (i) (a) Draw the I-shape (or bar) electromagnet and U-shape electromagnet.
    (b) Where are giant electromagnets used? [3]
    (ii) Mention any three properties of magnetic lines of force? [3]
    (iii) (a) What are the evidences which prove the existences of Earth's magnetic field?
    (b) Explain the term "Neutral points". [4]

For Solutions Scan the Code

Olympiad Section*

Brain Teasing Questions of Olympiad Pattern

1 The direction of the force on a current-carrying wire placed in a magnetic field depends on

(a) the direction of the current but not on the direction of the field.
(b) the direction of the field but not on the direction of the current.
(c) the direction of the current as well as the direction of the field.
(d) Neither the direction of the current nor the direction of the field.

2 Compass is to be placed near a bar magnet with unknown poles. Outside the magnetic field, the compass needle is pointing towards North as shown below.

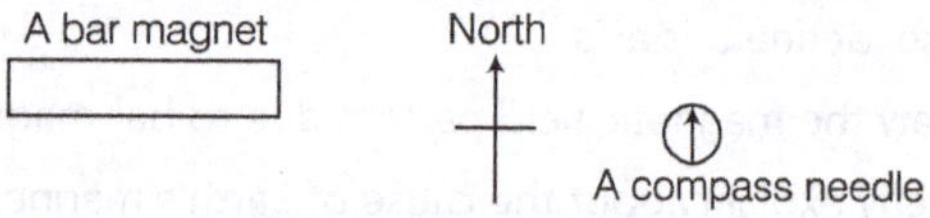

Which of the following is correct?

(a) 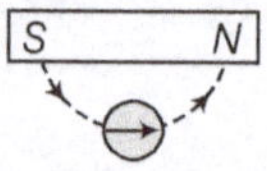

(b) 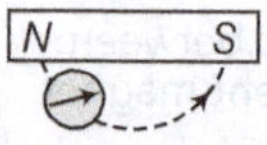

(c) 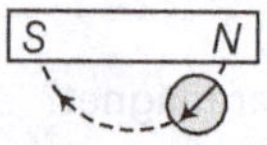

(d) 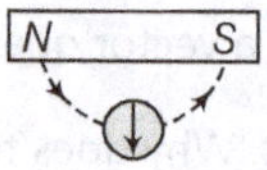

3 A bar magnet is broken into three parts X, Y and Z.

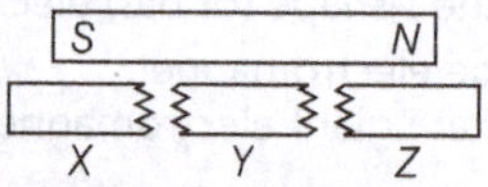

Which diagram show the poles in X, Y and Z?

(a) 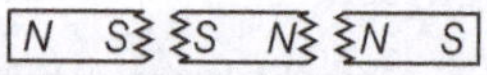

(b) 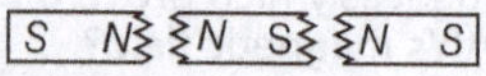

(c) 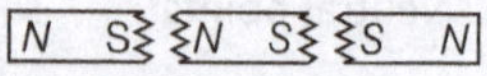

(d) 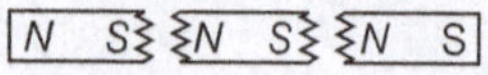

4 Which of the following diagram is correct?

(a) 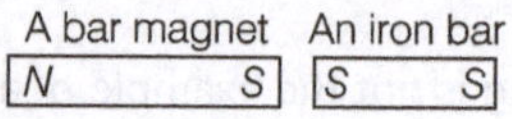

(b) 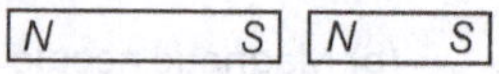

(c) 

(d) 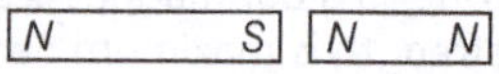

5 You have been given copper, iron, nickel and steel to make an electromagnet and permanent magnet. Which of the following is correct?

	Permanent magnet	Electromagnet
(a)	Steel	Copper
(b)	Copper	Iron
(c)	Steel	Iron
(d)	Iron	Steel

6 Which of the following figure is incorrect for magnetic field lines?

(a) 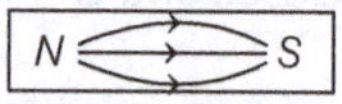

(b) 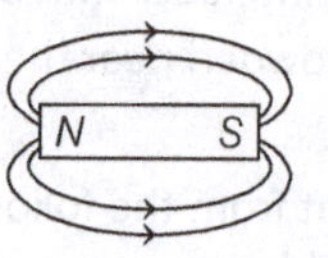

(c) 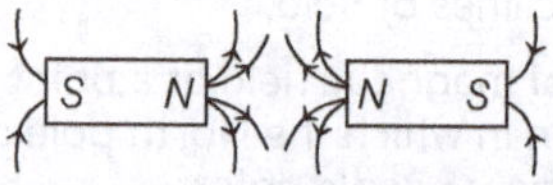

(d) 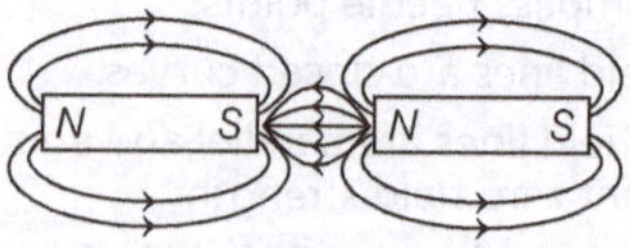

7 The diagram shows a short length of iron placed near the N-pole of a magnet.

Which diagram best represents the resulting magnetic field pattern?

(a) 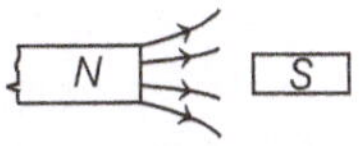

(b) 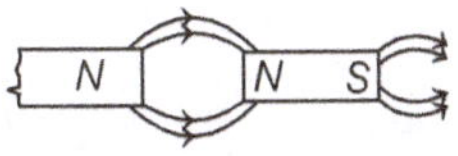

(c) 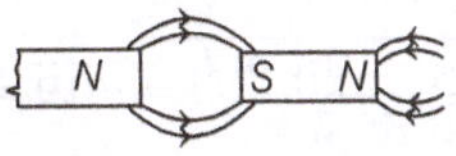

(d) 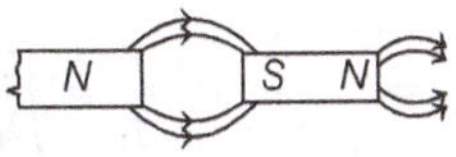

8 Which of the following is not correct for magnetic field lines?

(a) The direction of magnetic field lines outside the magnet is from North pole to South pole.

(b) The direction of magnetic field lines inside the magnet is from South pole to North pole.

(c) The degree of closeness of magnetic field lines tells the relatives strength of magnetic field.

(d) Magnetic field lines never form closed loop.

Answers							
1. (c)	**2.** (c)	**3.** (d)	**4.** (b)	**5.** (a)	**6.** (a)	**7.** (d)	**8.** (d)

* *These questions may or may not be asked in the examination, have been given just for additional practice required for olympiads Scholarship Exams etc. For detailed explanations refer Page No. 223.*

Explanations to Olympiad

Chapter 1. Measurements & Experimentation

1. (*d*) Length, time and mass are fundamental quantities because these are not associated with any other quantities.

2. (*d*) Since, the value of a quantity remains unchanged in various units, so,

$$nu = \text{constant or } n \propto \frac{1}{u}$$

3. (*b*) Given, distance = 11 light min

$$= 11 \times 3 \times 10^8 \times 60$$
$$= 1.98 \times 10^8 \text{ km}$$

4. (*d*) Length, mass and time are fundamental quantities. In mechanics, all the quantities are expressed in terms of these quantities. So, all the options (a), (b) and (c) are correct.

5. (*b*) Given, the speed of bus, $v = 110$ km/h

$\therefore$ In SI unit, $v = \dfrac{110 \times 10^3}{60 \times 60}$ m/s

$$= \frac{1100}{36} \text{ m/s}$$
$$= 30.6 \text{ m/s}$$

6. (*a*) Mass of Earth is 5.98×10^{24} kg

$$1\text{u} = 1.66 \times 10^{-27} \text{ kg}$$

$\therefore$ Average mass of 40 u in kg = $40 \times 1.66 \times 10^{-27}$ kg

Hence, number of atoms in Earth

$$= \frac{5.98 \times 10^{24}}{40 \times 1.66 \times 10^{-27}} = 0.090 \times 10^{51}$$
$$= 9.0 \times 10^{49}$$

7. (*d*) Since, Least count = MS reading – VS reading

20 VS divisions = 16 MS divisions

$$= 16 \text{ mm}$$

$\Rightarrow$ $1 \text{ VS} = \dfrac{16}{20}$ mm

$\therefore$ $\text{LC} = 1 - \dfrac{16}{20} = \dfrac{4}{20} = \dfrac{1}{5} \text{ mm} = 0.2 \text{ mm}$

8. (*d*) Least count

$$= \frac{\text{Pitch}}{\text{Number of divisions on circular scale}}$$
$$= \frac{0.5}{50} = 0.01 \text{ mm}$$

$\therefore$ Diameter of sphere = Main scale reading + (Circular scale coincidence with base line) $\times$ LC

$$= 2 + 25 \times 0.01$$
$$= 2.25 \text{ mm}$$

9. (*c*) Oscillations of a pendulum and rotation of Earth around its axis can be used to measure time. Because both the motions are periodic, which repeats itself after certain interval of time.

10. (*c*) We know that, $T = \dfrac{1}{2\pi}\sqrt{\dfrac{l}{g}} = \dfrac{1}{f}$

$\Rightarrow$ $f \propto \dfrac{1}{\sqrt{l}}$

$\Rightarrow$ $\dfrac{f_2}{f_1} = \sqrt{\dfrac{l_2}{l_1}} = \sqrt{\dfrac{l_1 - 10\% \text{ of } l_1}{l_1}} = \sqrt{0.9} = 0.94$

$\Rightarrow$ $f_2 = 0.94 f_1$

$\therefore$ $\dfrac{f_1 - f_2}{f_1} \times 100 = \dfrac{f_1 - 0.94 f_1}{f_1} \times 100 = 5.1\%$

11. (*b*) In SI system,

Unit of length (l) = m

Unit of velocity (v) = ms^{-1}

Unit of force (F) = kg ms^{-2}

In new system of unit,

Unit of length (l) = 2 m

Unit of velocity (v) = 2 ms^{-1}

Unit of force (F) = 2 kg ms^{-2}

Since, unit of velocity gets doubled due to doubling of length. So, unit of time is unchanged. Since, force gets doubled, so due of doubling of length, here unit of mass remains unchanged.

Linear momentum, L = kg ms^{-1}

Due to doubling of velocity and length its unit gets doubled.

Energy, $E = \text{kgm}^2\text{s}^{-2}$

Due to doubling of velocity and length, its unit becomes four times.

$\therefore$ Only (i), (ii) and (iii) are correct.

Chapter 2. Motion in One Dimension

1. (*a*) Let the distance be s.

Then, according to question, $\dfrac{s}{2}$ distance is covered with speed 3 m/s.

The time taken by the particle,

$$t_1 = \frac{\text{Distance}}{\text{Speed}} = \frac{s/2}{3} = \frac{s}{6}$$

The time taken in first $\dfrac{s}{4}$ distance,

$$t_2 = \frac{s/4}{4.5} = \frac{s}{4.5 \times 4} = \frac{s}{18}$$

The time taken in second half of $s/2$ will be

$$t_3 = \frac{s/4}{7.5} = \frac{s}{4 \times 7.5} = \frac{s}{30}$$

$\therefore$ Total time, $T = t_1 + t_2 + t_3$

$$= \frac{s}{6} + \frac{s}{18} + \frac{s}{30} = \frac{23s}{90}$$

Total distance $= \dfrac{s}{2} + \dfrac{s}{4} + \dfrac{s}{4} = s$

$\therefore$ Average speed of particle $= \dfrac{s}{T} = \dfrac{s}{23s/90}$

$$= \frac{90}{23} = 3.91 \approx 4 \text{ m/s}$$

2. (c) Velocity of man = 10 m/s, distance, s = 48 m

Acceleration of man with respect to bus = Acceleration of man – Acceleration of bus

$$= 0 - 1 = -1\ m/s^2$$

From second equation of motion,

$$s = ut + \frac{1}{2}at^2$$

$$\Rightarrow \quad 48 = 10t - \frac{1}{2}t^2$$

$$\Rightarrow \quad 96 = 20t - t^2$$

$$\Rightarrow \quad t^2 - 20t + 96 = 0$$

$$t^2 - 12t - 8t + 96 = 0$$

$$(t-8)(t-12) = 0$$

$$t = 8\text{ s or } 12\text{ s}$$

8 s is minimum time, so answer will be 8 s.

3. (b) From first equation of motion,

$$v = u + at$$

$$v = at \quad \ldots(i)\ [\because u = 0]$$

So, for first and second stones,

$$v = at_1 \quad \ldots(ii)$$

$$v = at_2 \quad \ldots(iii)$$

On adding Eqs. (ii) and (iii), we get

$$2v = a(t_1 + t_2) \quad \ldots(iv)$$

$$\Rightarrow \quad 2at = a(t_1 + t_2) \quad \text{[from Eq. (i)]}$$

$$\therefore \quad t = \frac{t_1 + t_2}{2}$$

4. (b) According to question, the speed of bullet decreases from v to $v/2$ after travelling 40 cm.

From third equation of motion,

$$a = \frac{v^2 - u^2}{2s} = \frac{\left(\frac{v}{2}\right)^2 - v^2}{2 \times 40}$$

$$a = \frac{-\frac{3}{4}v^2}{80} = \frac{-3v^2}{320}$$

$$\therefore \text{ Distance, } s' = \frac{v^2 - \left(\frac{v}{2}\right)^2}{2a} = \frac{(0)^2 - \left(\frac{v}{2}\right)^2}{2 \times \left(-\frac{3v^2}{320}\right)}$$

$$= \frac{-\left(\frac{v^2}{4}\right)}{-\left(\frac{6v^2}{320}\right)} = \frac{v^2}{4} \times \frac{320}{6v^2}$$

$$= \frac{40}{3}\text{ cm}$$

5. (a) The body is travelling in a straight line with a uniform increasing speed. As, the speed is increasing with time, the graph (a) shows the correct variation in the distance travelled by body.

6. (c) Given, distance of bus

$$= 1\text{ km} = 1000\text{ m}$$

Time, $t = 100$ s

Velocity of bus, $v_b = 10$ m/s

Velocity for overtake, $v = \frac{1000}{100} = 10$ m/s

Let, velocity of scooter = v_s

Both bus and scooter are moving in the same direction.

$$\text{So,} \quad v = v_s - v_b$$

$$10 = v_s - 10$$

$$\therefore \quad v_s = 10 + 10 = 20\ m/s$$

7. (a) When Madhur applies brakes, the acceleration will be in backward direction and speed will be in forward direction. So, velocity and acceleration will act opposite to each other.

8. (d) From figure, there are 11 dots and 10 spaces

The length of the space = $\frac{30}{10} = 3$ cm

The arm is vibrating regularly making 50 dots in one second.

So, the speed of object = $50 \times 3 = 150$ cm/s

9. (a) The stones are thrown under gravity. So, from third equation of falling bodies, $v^2 = u^2 + 2gh$

Here, $u = 0, h = h$

When one of the stone is thrown in upward direction then, $v_1 = 0 + 2(-g)h$

When second stone is dropped in downward direction then, $v_2 = 0 + 2(+g)h$

$$\therefore \quad \frac{v_1}{v_2} = \frac{-2gh}{2gh}$$

$$\therefore \quad \left|\frac{v_1}{v_2}\right| = 1:1$$

10. (a) Let t_1, be the time taken for (1/5) th of total distance and t_2 be the time taken for remaining distance.

$$t_1 = \frac{s}{5v_1},\ t_2 = \frac{4s}{5v_2}$$

Total time, $T = t_1 + t_2$

$$\text{Average speed} = \frac{\text{Total distance}}{\text{Total time}} = \frac{s}{\frac{s}{5v_1} + \frac{4s}{5v_2}} = \frac{5v_1v_2}{v_2 + 4v_1}$$

11. (a) Given, total distance, $s = 100$ m

Acceleration, $a = 1\ ms^{-2}$

Distance covered with acceleration a $(s_1) = 40$ m

Remaining distance $(s_2) = 100 - 40 = 60$ m

Initial velocity, $u = 0$

∴ Time taken to cover 40 m distance,

$$t = \sqrt{\frac{2s_1}{a}} \quad \left(\because s = ut + \frac{1}{2}at^2 = \frac{1}{2}at^2\right)$$

$$= \sqrt{\frac{2 \times 40}{1}} = \sqrt{80}$$

$$= 4\sqrt{5}\text{ s}$$

Velocity for remaining distance, $v = u + at$

$$= 1 \times 4\sqrt{5} \quad (\because u = 0)$$

$$= 4\sqrt{5}\ ms^{-1}$$

$$\text{Time taken, } t' = \frac{s_2}{v} = \frac{60}{4\sqrt{5}} = \frac{15}{\sqrt{5}} = 3\sqrt{5}\text{ s}$$

Total time, $T = t + t' = 4\sqrt{5} + 3\sqrt{5} = 7\sqrt{5}$ s

Time to cover first half, $t_1 = \sqrt{\frac{2s/2}{a}} = \sqrt{\frac{s}{a}} = \sqrt{\frac{100}{1}} = 10$ s

Time to cover second half, $t_2 = T - t_1 = 7\sqrt{5} - 10 = 5.655$

$\therefore \quad t_1 > t_2$

12. (c) The area under the velocity-time graph gives displacement.
After energy impact, the ball rises to a height and then falls back covering some height.
But after consecutive impact, the height decreases.
So, $B = C$ and $D = E$
But $C > D$.

Chapter 3. Laws of Motion

1. (a) The final velocity of mass of water after hitting the metal block is zero.
So, the average change in momentum per second
= initial momentum
$= 1 \text{ kg} \times 5 \text{ m/s} = 5$ kg-m/s
As, this change in momentum occurs during 1s. We may say that the force exerted on the 2 kg block is

$$F = \frac{\text{Change in momentum}}{\text{Time}} = \frac{5}{1} = 5 \text{ N}$$

Hence, by Newton's second law of motion, initial acceleration of the block of mass, $m = 2$ kg is given by

$$a = \frac{F}{m} = \frac{5}{2} = 2.5 \text{ m/s}^2$$

2. (b)

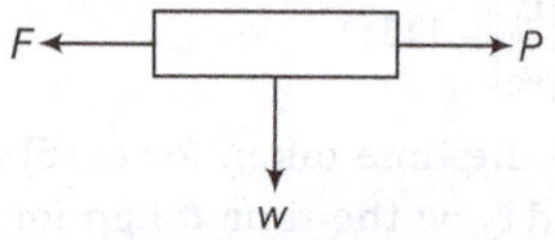

The force P will act in forward direction and force of friction F will act opposite to it in backward direction. The weight of an object will act in downward direction.
So, figure correctly represents the direction of forces.

3. (d) This is because of Newton's third law of motion and gravitation. The weight of the bucket and water will act in downward direction and the force applied by the man will act in upward direction. Due to gravitation, when the rope snaps, bucket falls back in the well.

4. (b) The acceleration due to force 14N,

$$F = ma$$
$$\Rightarrow \quad \frac{F}{m} = a$$
$$\therefore \quad a = \frac{14}{(4+2+1)} = \frac{14}{2} = 2 \text{ m/s}^2$$

The contact force between A and B is used to move the bodies B and C only.

$$\therefore \quad F = ma = (2+1)2 = 3 \times 2 = 6 \text{ N}$$

So, the contact force between A and B is $= 14 - 6 = 8$ N

5. (a) The resultant force acting on the mass will be zero. Because weight of the mass will act in downward direction and force applied by the person through pulley and rope will act in upward direction. So, the resultant force acting on mass will be zero.

6. (a) From graph, the acceleration in ball

$$= \frac{20}{4} \qquad \left(\because a = \frac{v}{t}\right)$$
$$= 5 \text{ m/s}^2$$

The force acting on ball, $F = m \cdot a$

$$= 200 \times 10^{-3} \times 5 = 1 \text{ N}$$

7. (a) Given, mass of ball $= 120 \text{ g} = 120 \times 10^{-3}$ kg
Velocity, $v = 12$ m/s
$\therefore$ Momentum, $p_1 = mv = 120 \times 10^{-3} \times 12$
After turning back, its momentum,

$$p_2 = -120 \times 10^{-3} \times 20 \quad (\because v = 20 \text{ m/s})$$

$\therefore$ Change in momentum, $\Delta p = p_1 - p_2$

$$= (120 \times 10^{-3} \times 12) - (-120 \times 10^{-3} \times 20)$$
$$= 120 \times 10^{-3}(12 + 20)$$
$$= 120 \times 10^{-3} \times 32 \text{ kg-m/s}$$

$$\therefore \quad \text{Force} = \frac{\Delta p}{\Delta t} = \frac{120 \times 10^{-3} \times 32}{0.02} = 192 \text{ N}$$

8. (a) Only the magnetic force acting on the iron box will cause the most extension in spring. Rest of the forces will be balanced among themselves such as weight, elastic force, etc.

9. (b) In regions AB and CD, slope of the graph is constant. i.e. The particle is in uniform motion with constant velocity. It means no force acting on the particle in this region.

10. (b) According to the question, 10 kg mass has an acceleration of 12 ms^{-2}.

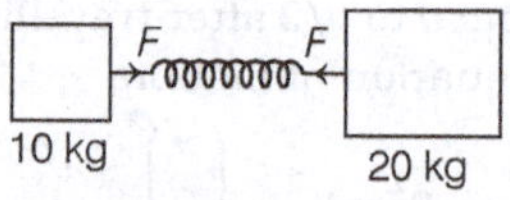

So, force acts on 10 kg mass = mass × acceleration

$$F = m_1 a_1$$
$$F = 10 \times 12 = 120 \text{ N}$$

The reaction of 120 N is applied on 20 kg block by 10 kg black *via* spring.
$\therefore$ Net force acts on 20 kg block,

$$F' = 200 - 120 = 80 \text{ N}$$

Again, $F' = m_2 a_2 \Rightarrow 80 = 20 \times a$ or $a = 4 \text{ m/s}^2$

11. (c) Since, both the vehicles are moving with same kinetic energy. So, their speed will also be same. Also, the retarding force on both is equal. So, they will stop at the same distance.

12. (c) As we know, force, $F = ma \Rightarrow a = \frac{F}{m}$
Since, m is constant, so, $a \propto F$
Hence, the a-t graph of given F-t graph will be as

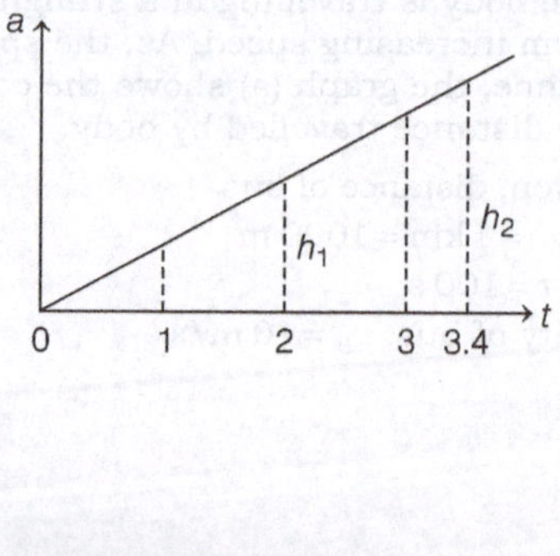

Velocity at 2 s, v_1 = area under graph $= \frac{1}{2} \times h_1 \times t_1$

$$\Rightarrow \quad 7 = \frac{1}{2} \times h_1 \times 2 \Rightarrow h_1 = 7\text{ m}$$

Since, slope of graph will be same, so,

$$\frac{h_1}{t_1} = \frac{h_2}{t_2} \Rightarrow \frac{7}{2} = \frac{h_2}{3.4}$$

$$\Rightarrow \quad h_2 = \frac{3.4 \times 7}{2} = 11.9$$

$\therefore$ Velocity after 3.4 s, $v_2 = \frac{1}{2} \times h_2 \times t_2$

$$= \frac{1}{2} \times 11.9 \times 3.4 = 20.2\text{ ms}^{-1}$$

Chapter 4. Gravitation

1. (*a*) The point *A* is at the centre of the Earth. At centre of Earth, the acceleration due to gravity is zero.

So, the weight of the body at centre i.e., at point *A*,

$$F = m \times 0 = 0$$

2. (*a*)

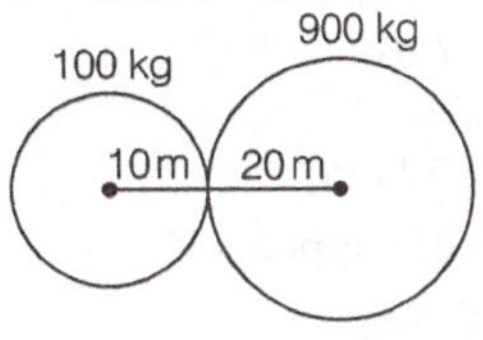

We know that, $F = G\frac{m_1 m_2}{r^2}$

Here, $m_1 = 100\text{ kg},\ m_2 = 900\text{ kg}$

$r = 10 + 20 = 30\text{ m}$

$G = 6.67 \times 10^{-11}\text{ N-m}^2/\text{kg}^2$

The gravitational force between 100 kg and 900 kg spheres,

$$\therefore \quad F = \frac{6.67 \times 10^{-11} \times 100 \times 900}{(30)^2}$$

$$= 6.67 \times 10^{-9}\text{ N}$$

3. (*b*) The gravitational force for system *A*,

$$F = \frac{Gm \times m}{d^2}$$

The gravitational force for system *B*,

$$F' = G \cdot \frac{2m \times 2m}{d^2} = \frac{4Gmm}{d^2}$$

$$\therefore \quad F' = 4F$$

4. (*b*) In MKS system, $F = G \cdot \frac{m_1 m_2}{r^2}$

According to question, $m_1 = m_2 = 1\text{ kg},\ r = 1\text{ m}$

$$\therefore \quad F = 6.67 \times 10^{-11} \times \frac{1 \times 1}{(1)^2}$$

In CGS system, $F = 6.67 \times 10^{-11} \times \frac{10^{-3} \times 10^{-3}}{(10^{-2})^2}$

$$= 6.67 \times 10^{-11} \times 10^{-2}$$

$$= 6.67 \times 10^{-13}\text{ g-wt}$$

$$\approx 7 \times 10^{-13}\text{ g-wt}$$

5. (*a*) Given, $m_1 = 50\text{ kg}$,

$m_2 = 10\text{ kg},\ r_1 = 5\text{ m},$

$r_2 = 5 + 5 = 10\text{ m}$

$$\therefore \quad F_1 = G \cdot \frac{m_1 m_2}{r_1^2} \quad \text{...(i)}$$

and $F_2 = G \cdot \frac{m_1 m_2}{r_2^2} = G \cdot \frac{m_1 m_2}{(2r_1)^2}$ $\quad (r_2 = 2r_1)$

$$= G \cdot \frac{m_1 m_2}{4r_1^2} = \frac{F_1}{4} \quad \text{[from Eq. (i)]}$$

The percentage change $= \left(F_1 - \frac{F_1}{4}\right) \times 100$

$$= F_1\left(1 - \frac{1}{4}\right) \times 100$$

$$= F_1 \times \frac{3}{4} \times 100 = 75\%$$

6. (*d*) Apple and Earth both experience same gravitational force.

i.e. $F_1 = F_2 = \frac{GM_e \cdot M_a}{r^2}$

7. (*b*) $\because \ F = G \cdot \frac{m_1 m_2}{r^2}$

where, m_1 = mass of Earth, m_2 = mass of body

and r = radius of Earth

$$F \propto \frac{1}{r^2}$$

$$\Rightarrow \quad F' \propto \frac{1}{r'^2}$$

$$\because \quad r' = 2r$$

$$F' \propto \frac{1}{(2r)^2} \propto \frac{1}{4r^2}$$

$$F' \propto \frac{1}{4}$$

So, the weight would become one-fourth of initial value.

8. (*d*) As, $g = \frac{GM}{R^2}$

When radius of Earth shrinks by 4 %, then new radius becomes

$$R' = R - 4\%R = \frac{96}{100}R = \frac{24}{25}R$$

$\therefore$ New acceleration due to gravity,

$$g' = \frac{GM}{(R')^2} = \frac{GM}{\left(\frac{24}{25}R\right)^2} = \frac{625}{576}\frac{GM}{R^2}$$

Hence, percentage change in the value of acceleration due to gravity

$$= \frac{g' - g}{g} \times 100\% = \frac{\frac{625}{576}\frac{GM}{R^2} - \frac{GM}{R^2}}{\frac{GM}{R^2}} \times 100\%$$

$$= \left(\frac{625 - 576}{576}\right) \times 100\% \approx 8\%$$

9. (*a*) According to Newton's law of gravitation, the force between two bodies is given by

$$F = \frac{Gm_1 m_2}{d^2}$$

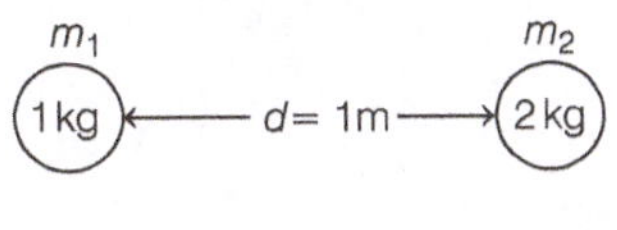

Therefore, $F = \frac{6.67 \times 10^{-11} \times 1 \times 2}{1^2}$

$\Rightarrow \quad F = 2 \times 6.67 \times 10^{-11}$ N

For body of mass 1 kg, force is also given by $F_1 = m_1 a_1$

$\therefore \quad 2 \times 6.67 \times 10^{-11} = 1 \times a_1$

$\Rightarrow \quad a_1 = 1.33 \times 10^{-10} \text{m/s}^2$

For body of mass 2 kg, the force, $F_2 = m_2 a_2$

$2 \times 6.67 \times 10^{-11} = 2 \times a_2$

$\Rightarrow \quad a_2 = 6.67 \times 10^{-11} \text{m/s}^2$

10. (*b*) Given, mass of planet $(M_p) = 16 \times$ mass of Earth (M_e)

Density of planet $\rho_p = \frac{1}{4} \times$ density of Earth (ρ_e)

Since, density $\rho = \frac{\text{Mass } (M)}{\text{Volume } (V)}$

$\Rightarrow \quad V = \frac{M}{\rho}$

$\Rightarrow \quad V_p = \frac{M_p}{\rho_p} = \frac{16 M_e}{1/4 \rho_e}$

$= 64 \frac{M_e}{\rho_e} = 64 V_e \qquad \left[\because V_e = \frac{M_e}{\rho_e}\right]$

$\Rightarrow \quad \frac{4}{3}\pi R_p^3 = 64 \times \frac{4}{3}\pi R_e^3$

$\Rightarrow \quad R_p = 4R_e$

Acceleration due to gravity on planet,

$g_p = \frac{GM_e}{R_p^2}$

$= \frac{G \times 16 M_e}{(4R_e)^2}$

$= \frac{GM_e}{R_e^2} = g_e$

Since, weight $= m \times g$

As, mass of a body is constant and g is same on both. So, the weight will also be same i.e., 1000 N on the planet.

11. (*a*) Density of a planet is given by

$\rho = \frac{3g}{4\pi G r}$

$\therefore \quad \rho_P = \frac{3g_P}{4\pi G r_P}$

and $\quad \rho_Q = \frac{3g_Q}{4\pi G r_Q}$

$\Rightarrow \quad \frac{\rho_P}{\rho_Q} = \frac{g_P}{g_Q} \times \frac{r_Q}{r_P}$

Here, $\frac{r_P}{r_Q} = x$ and $\frac{\rho_P}{\rho_Q} \times y$

$\Rightarrow \quad y = \frac{g_P}{g_Q} \times \frac{1}{x}$

$\therefore \quad \frac{g_P}{g_Q} = xy$

Chapter 5. Fluids

1. (*d*) Given, height of a cylinder = 10 cm = 0.1 m

Radius of cylinder = 4 cm = 0.04 m

Pressure exerted = 21560 N/m^2

As, pressure $= \frac{\text{Force}}{\text{Area}}$

$p = \frac{m \times g}{A}$

$21560 = \frac{m \times 9.8}{2\pi r^2 + 2\pi rh}$

$m = \frac{21560 \times (2\pi r^2 + 2\pi rh)}{9.8}$

$m = \frac{21560 \times 2 \times \pi(r^2 + rh)}{9.8}$

$= \frac{21560 \times 2 \times 22 \times (0.16 + 0.04)}{9.8 \times 7}$

$= \frac{21560 \times 44 \times 0.2}{9.8 \times 7}$

$= \frac{189728}{68.6}$

$= 2765.71$ kg

2. (*a*) Let volume of copper $= V_1$

Volume of gold $= V_2$

Given, density of copper = 4 g/cm^3

Density of gold = 20 g/cm^3

Let m be the mass of copper, then

Volume of copper, $V_1 = \frac{m}{4}$

Volume of gold, $V_2 = \frac{200 - m}{20}$

When immersed in water,

$\rho_w = 1 \text{gcm}^{-3}$

Decrease in weight = upthrust

$(200 - 160)g = (V_1 + V_2)\rho_w g$

$40 = \frac{m}{4} + \frac{200 - m}{20}$

$40 = \frac{5m + 200 - m}{20}$

$\Rightarrow \quad 800 = 4m + 200$

$\Rightarrow \quad 4m = 800 - 200$

$\Rightarrow \quad 4m = 600$

$\Rightarrow \quad m = 150$ g

Copper = 150 g, gold = 50 g

Now, percentage of mass of each metal present is as follows

% of copper $= \frac{150 \times 100}{200} = 75\%$

% of gold $= \frac{50 \times 100}{200} = 25\%$

3. (*b*) Let the volume of the block of wood $= V$

Density of the block of wood $= \rho_w g$

So, the weight of the block $= V\rho_w g$

As, $g = 980 \text{ cms}^{-2}$

The block floats in liquid of density 0.8 gcm^{-3} with $\frac{1}{4}$th of its volume submerged.

So, upward buoyant force acting on the block = weight of the displaced liquid

$$= \frac{1}{4} V \times 0.8 \times g$$

Now, from law of floatation, according to condition of floatation,

$$V \times \rho_w \times g = \frac{1}{4} \times V \times 0.8 \times g$$

$$\Rightarrow \quad \rho_w = 0.2 \text{ g-cm}^{-3} = 200 \text{ kg-m}^{-3}$$

Now, let the density of oil be ρ_{oil} g-cm^{-3}.

The block floats in oil with 60% of its volume submerged.

So, the buoyant force balancing the weight of the block is the weight of the displaced oil

$$= 60\% \times V \times \rho_{oil} \times g$$

Applying condition of floatation,

$$60\% \times V \times \rho_{oil} \times g = V \times \rho_w \times g$$

$$\Rightarrow \quad \frac{60}{100} \times V \times \rho_{oil} \times g = V \times 0.2 \times g$$

$$\Rightarrow \quad \rho_{oil} = 0.2 \times \frac{10}{6} = \frac{1}{3} = 0.33$$

$$= \frac{1000}{3} \text{ kg m}^{-3}$$

4. (*a*) Given, mass of block = 2800 kg

At points *A* and *B*, the pressure p_1 and p_2 will be same, because it is equally transmitted based on Pascal's law.

But to calculate density of liquid, pressure will be

$$p_1 = p_2 + h\rho g$$

$$h\rho g = p_1 - p_2$$

$$= \frac{2800 \times 9.8}{5 \times 10^{-2}} - \frac{45 \times 10^4}{9}$$

$$\rho = \frac{p_2 - p_1}{h \times g} = \frac{5488 \times 10^2 - 5 \times 10^4}{10 \times 9.8}$$

$$= \frac{498800}{98} = 5089.79 \text{ kg/m}^3$$

5. (*b*) According to Boyle's law,

pressure × volume = constant

$$\therefore \quad p_{atm} \cdot V = p_{depth} \cdot \frac{V}{4}$$

$$\Rightarrow \quad p_{depth} = 4 \times p_{atm}$$

$$\text{or} \quad p_{depth} = \rho_{ocean} \times g \times h$$

$$\Rightarrow \quad 4 \times \rho_{mercury} \times g \times 76 = 1 \times g \times h$$

$$\Rightarrow \quad 4 \times 13.6 \times g \times 76 = 1 \times g \times h$$

$$\therefore \quad h = 4134.4 \text{ cm}$$

($\because$ density of mercury = 13.6 g cm^{-3})

6. (*a*) Here, let us suppose that cube has side l in which $\left(l - \frac{1}{2}\right)$ cm is dipped inside the liquid.

$$\therefore \text{ Volume of the cube} = \left[l \times l \times \left(l - \frac{1}{2}\right)\right]$$

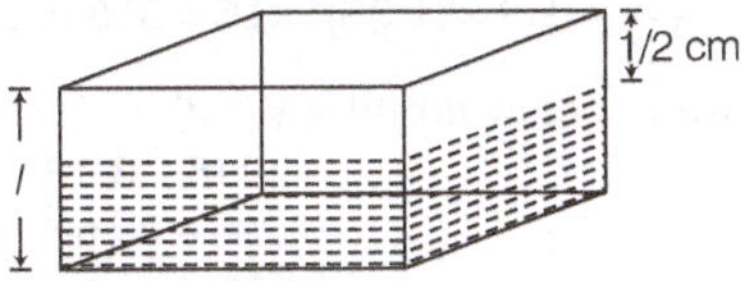

$\therefore$ Mass of the cube $= \rho_{cube} \times l^3$

where, ρ_{cube} is the density of cube.

Now, according to Archimedes' principle mass of the cube is balanced by mass of the liquid *d* is placed

$$\therefore \quad \rho_{cube} \times l^3 = l^2 \times \left(l - \frac{1}{2}\right) \times 2$$

($\because$ density of liquid = 2 gcm^{-3})

$$\Rightarrow \quad \rho_{cube} \times l = \left(\frac{2l - 1}{2}\right) \times 2$$

$$\Rightarrow \quad \rho_{cube} = \left(\frac{2l - 1}{l}\right)$$

When 144 g mass is placed above the top of cube, then

$$(144 + \rho_{cube} \times l^3) \cdot g = l^3 \times 2 \times g$$

$$\text{or} \quad 144 + \frac{2l - 1}{l} \times l^3 = 2l^3$$

$$\text{or} \quad 144 + (2l - 1)l^2 = 2l^3$$

$$\text{or} \quad 144 + +2l^3 - l^2 = 2l^3$$

$$\therefore \quad l^2 = 144$$

$$\Rightarrow \quad l = 12$$

$$\therefore \text{ Density of cube, } \rho_{cube} = \frac{2 \times 12 - 1}{12} = \frac{23}{12}$$

7. (*a*) Here, the volume of a cone is given by

$$V = \pi r_1^2 \frac{h}{3}$$

where, r_1 is the radius of the base of the cone and h is the height.

Now, from the given value, we have

$$\frac{1}{3} \pi r_1^2 \times 16 = 2948$$

$$\Rightarrow \quad r_1 = 13.26 \text{ cm}$$

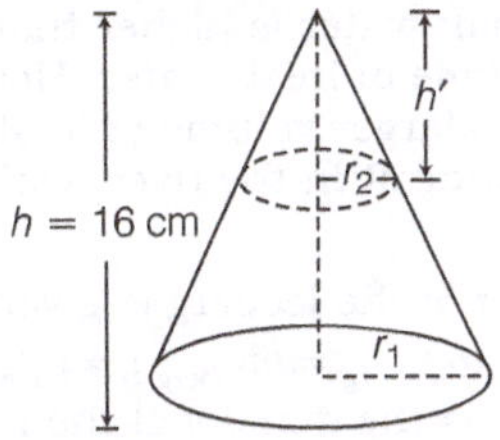

And, the radius of the conical region above the liquid is

$$\pi r_2^2 = 6$$

$$\Rightarrow \quad r_2 = 1.38$$

$\therefore$ The height of the cone above the liquid is

$$h' = \frac{1.38}{13.2} \times 16 = 1.6 \text{ cm}$$

The volume of the cone above the liquid,

$$V' = \frac{1}{3} \pi r_2^2 \times 1.6$$

$= \frac{1}{3} \times 3.14 \times (1.38)^2 \times 1.6 = 3.18\ \text{cm}^3$

Now, volume below liquid $= V - V'$

$= 2948 - 3.18$

$= 2944.8\ \text{cm}^3$

$\therefore$ Density of the cone, $\rho = \frac{2944.8}{2948} \times 3.2 = 3.19\ \text{g cm}^{-3}$

8. (*a*) Given, height of oil column, $h_1 = 15$ cm

Density of oil = 0.8 g/m^3

Height of water, $h_2 = ?$

Density of water = 1 g/cm^3

The CCl_4 (carbon tetrachloride) in both arms of the U-tube are at same level, therefore pressure in both arms will be same.

$\therefore$ Pressure exerted by oil column

= Pressure exerted by water column

$$\therefore \quad p_1 = p_2$$

$$h_1\rho_1 g = h_2\rho_2 g$$

$$\Rightarrow \quad h_2 = \frac{h_1\rho_1 g}{\rho_2 g} = \frac{h_1\rho_1}{\rho_2} = \frac{15 \times 0.8}{1} = 12\ \text{cm}$$

9. (*b*) Given, velocity of water jet, $v = 20\ \text{ms}^{-1}$

Density of water, $\rho = 1 \times 10^3\ \text{kg m}^{-3}$

Pressure on the wall, $p = \rho \times v^2$

$= 1 \times 10^3 \times (20)^2$

$= 4 \times 10^5$ Pa

10. (*d*) Since, the exhausts are arranged in an oblique manner, so the thrust force is pointed diagonally upwards and is larger than its vertical component. The sum of the vertical components of thrust due to four exhausts must be gravitational force F_g. So, the thrust at A and the gravitational force on the whole system are related as $F_{\text{thrust}} > 1/4\ F_g$.

11. (*b*) Since, the stone-ice combination is floating on water, the level of water rises in the vessel. But as the ice melts it need less space inside water and the stone will sink in it due to its greater density. So, the water level in the beaker decreases.

12. (*a*) The density of salty water of sea is higher than the density of fresh water of river, so the buoyancy of a volume of salt water is higher than the buoyancy of the same volume of fresh water. Hence, the tanker will displace a larger volume of fresh water and will have a deeper draft in the river, which contains fresh water.

13. (*d*) The weight of the iceberg is given by

$$w_{\text{iceberg}} = m_{\text{icberg}}\, g = \rho_{\text{iceberg}} V_{\text{iceberg}} g$$

where, ρ_{iceberg} is the density of the iceberg and V_{iceberg} is the whole volume of iceberg. For floating condition, the magnitude of the upward buoyant force must be equal to the weight of the displaced water.

$$w_{\text{water}} = m_{\text{water}}\, g = \rho_{\text{water}} V_{\text{water}}\, g$$

where, ρ_{water} is the density of the water and V_{water} is the volume of displaced water. V_{water} is equal to the volume of the ice beneath the water (the shaded region in the Fig). Since, the system is in equilibrium, the fraction of ice beneath the water's surface can be calculated by

$$\frac{V_{\text{immersed}}}{V_{\text{iceberg}}} = \frac{\rho_{\text{iceberg}}}{\rho_{\text{water}}} = \frac{917}{1030} = 0.890$$

14. (*a*) From principle of floatation, weight of a floating body is equal to the weight of the liquid displaced by its submerged part.

i.e., $$F = \rho_0 V_0 g + \rho_w V_u g$$

$$V_c \rho_c g = \rho_0 V_0 g + \rho_w V_w g$$

$$A n_c \rho_c = \rho_0 A h_0 + \rho_w A h_w$$

$$\Rightarrow \quad 25 \times \rho_c = 0.9 \times 9 + 1 \times 11 \quad [\because h_w = 25 - (9 + 5)]$$

$$\Rightarrow \quad \rho_c = \frac{19.1}{25} \simeq 0.76\ \text{g cm}^{-3}$$

15. (*a*) At position A, the body weight is in equilibrium with the weight of displaced water i.e. the buoyancy force will be equal to the weight of submarine, $F_B > F_A$.

After immersion in a liquid the force on the submarine remains same at all points inside it, i.e.

$$F_B = F_C = F_D$$

$$\therefore \quad F_A < F_B = F_C = F_D$$

But when it is taken to position B, then the buoyancy force will be greater than its weight.

16. (*d*) When iron balls are dropped from the boat, then its weight decreases and so it rises with water reference.

As, the buoyancy force on the boat is reduced. So, the weight of water displaced by the boat also decreases and hence the water level of the lake falls, with ground reference.

Chapter 6. Heat

1. (*a*) Gap left between the ends of two railway lines in a railway track is due to linear expansion in the length of railway lines during summer days. So, the railway lines will not distort.

2. (*d*) Exposed water pipes lagged with straw in winter in hilly areas because of the fact to prevent water from freezing in pipes. In hilly areas, temperature of atmosphere goes down below 0°C. So, water is preserved in pipes at 4 °C because of its abnormal expansion. At 4°C, the density of water is maximum. So, inside the pipe, there will be water available at 4°C.

3. (*a*) Soft drink bottles are not filled completely to prevent the bottle from burst. Because in soft drink, some gases are mixed. To get adjust the expansion in liquid. Some part of bottles are kept empty.

4. (*c*) At the time of severe frost, temperature falls below zero, so the cells of fruits and vegetables contract and get damaged.

5. (*b*) In an ice covered pond, the various layers of ice and water will be in the following series

0°C (ice) $\longrightarrow$ 0°C (water)

Then, temperature will increase to 1°C $\longrightarrow$ 2°C $\longrightarrow$ 3°C and at last, it will be 4°C. At 4°C, the density of water will be maximum. This water will set down in the bottom of pond, so that other animals will survive.

6. (c)

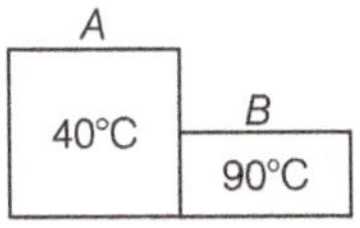

Heat always flows from higher temperature to lower temperature, so heat will flow from 90°C block B to block A at 40°C. They will continue until the temperature of A and B becomes equal.

7. (a) The expansion in water is abnormal, when we heat the water from 4°C to 8°C, it will expand and when we cool from 8°C to 0°C, will contract and again, if we heat from 0°C to 4°C, the density of water at 4°C will be maximum, so it will contract.

8. (b) When two bodies are kept in contact and if there is no exchange of heat between them, the bodies are said to be in thermal equilibrium.

9. (d) When we heat a solid, liquid or gas, the molecules of solid, liquid and gas absorb heat energy, so there will be thermal expansion occur in all the three forms of matter.

10. (a) There is a slight temperature difference between the water fall at the top and the bottom because when water falls, its potential energy converted into heat kinetic energy at the bottom of the fall. The water falls from height (h), so the potential energy of mass m of water will be mgh and converted into heat kinetic energy.

11. (a) The metal on heating expands uniformly through its free surface. So, the circular metal washer on heating its external and internal diameters both increase.

12. (c) Metals on heating expands through its free surface. Hence, metallic disc with a hole is heated uniformly its both surfaces (inner and outer) expand, so the diameter of both the surfaces increase. It is correctly shown in Fig. 4.

Chapter 7. Energy Flow and Sources of Energy

1. (a) Without greenhouse effect, the average temperature of the earth's surface will be below the zero degree i.e. −18°C. The greenhouse gases trap the heat received from the sunlight and therefore increases the temperature of the earth's surface.

2. (d) The temperature of the earth's surface is increasing. So, glaciers are melting which increases the sea level.

3. (a) Due to change in temperature as the consequence of global warming, the season of flower blooming changes. Therefore, option (a) is incorrect and rest are correct consequences of global warming.

4. (a) We get vaseline from petroleum.

5. (b) In nuclear fission,

$${}_0n^1 \longrightarrow {}_{92}U^{235} \longrightarrow {}_{56}Ba^{141} + {}_{36}Kr^{92} + 3\,{}_0n^1 + \text{Energy}$$

So, (b) is correct option.

6. (b) In the diagram of windmill, the part B supports the blades of the fan mounted on the tower. When blades rotates due to wind power, the kinetic energy is converted into other forms of energy to produce electricity.

7. (d) Part X is a plane mirror because in the figure, the sun rays are incident parallel to each other and reflected from the mirror X in parallel beams of light. So, X is plane mirror.

8. (a) In part (1), the water is converted into vapour. This vapour rotates the blades of turbine.

9. (c) If the height of falling water is increased, then the potential energy (which is directly proportional to height) of water also increases which, when converted into kinetic energy gives more electrical power from hydroelectric power plant.

10. (b) In sugarcane plant, the solar energy from the sun is converted into chemical energy to produce sugar.

Chapter 8. Light

1. (a) Given, distance of an object, $u = -30$ m

Height of image $(h') = \frac{1}{6}$th of real height (h)

Magnification, $m = \frac{h'}{h}$

$$\frac{h'}{h} = \frac{-v}{u} \Rightarrow \frac{1}{6} = \frac{-v}{-30}$$

$$v = \frac{30}{6} \Rightarrow v = 5 \text{ m}$$

But, mirror formula, $\frac{1}{f} = \frac{1}{v} + \frac{1}{u} = \frac{1}{5} + \frac{1}{(-30)}$

or $\frac{1}{f} = \frac{1}{5} - \frac{1}{30}$ or $\frac{1}{f} = \frac{6-1}{30}$ or $\frac{1}{f} = \frac{5}{30}$

$$\Rightarrow \quad f = 6 \text{ m}$$

2. (a) For the given case, a mirror diagram can be drawn as

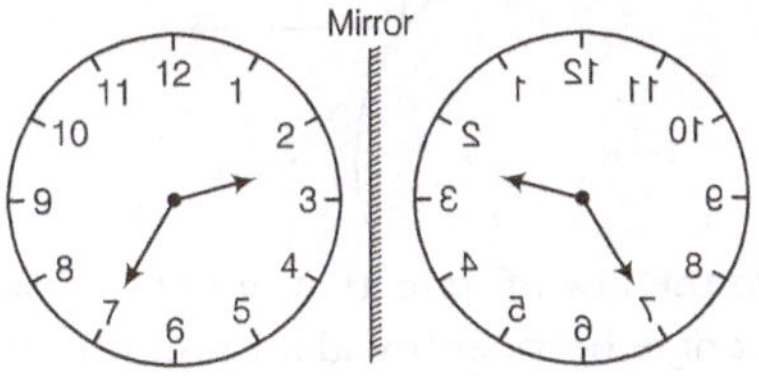

It is clear that from the above diagram, the clock will show the time 2:35 as 9: 25.

3. (a) Given, $h = 2$ cm, $u = -32$ cm, $h' = -3$ cm

Magnification, $m = \frac{h'}{h}$

$$m = \frac{-3}{2}$$

$$\Rightarrow \quad \frac{h'}{h} = \frac{-v}{u}$$

$$\frac{-3}{2} = \frac{-v}{-32}$$

$$\Rightarrow \quad -v = -32 \times \frac{-3}{2}$$

$$-v = 16 \times 3$$
$$v = -48 \text{ cm}$$

Using mirror formula,

$$\frac{1}{v} + \frac{1}{u} = \frac{1}{f} \Rightarrow \frac{-1}{48} - \frac{1}{32} = \frac{1}{f}$$

$$\therefore \quad \frac{1}{f} = \frac{-2-3}{96}$$

$$\therefore \quad f = -19.2 \text{ cm}$$

4. (*b*) To get the full image of an object, the height of plane mirror must be half of the height of object. In question, the eyes of girl is at 152 cm from the floor.

So, the height of mirror $= \frac{152}{2} = 76$ cm from the floor.

5. (*b*) Rear view mirror gets the inverted image of the object behind the car. So, to get the word AMBULANCE it should be printed on van as

ƎƆИA⅃UᗺMA

6. (*a*) The device should be concave mirror to focus the image of a distant object on the screen as shown in the figure below.

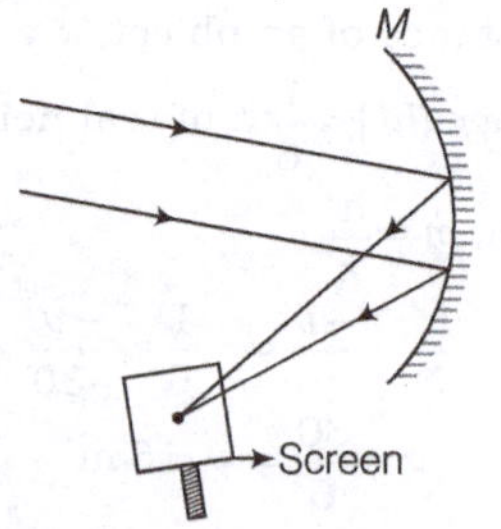

7. (*a*) After reflection from convex mirror, the reflected ray diagram is shown as

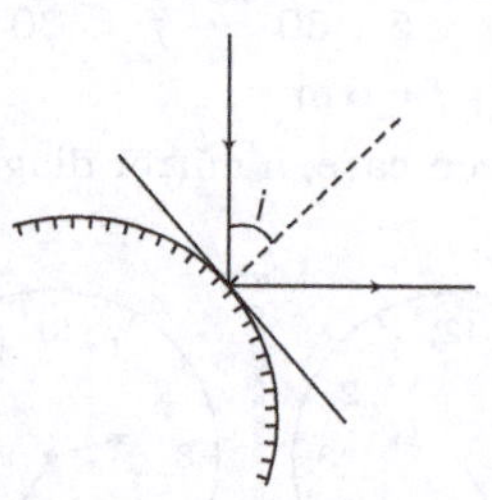

8. (*b*) From the law of reflection of light, $\angle i = \angle r$.

So, the angle between incident and reflected ray

$= 75° = i + r = 2i$

$$\therefore \quad i = \left(\frac{75}{2}\right)^{\circ}$$

9. (*d*) The girl is standing 2 m away from the plane mirror and chart is 3 m away from the girl. The image of letters from the chart formed 2 m away from the eyes of girl is

So, the distance of chart from patient

$= 2 \text{ m} + 3 \text{ m} + 2 \text{ m} = 7 \text{ m}$

10. (*d*) Magnification, $m = -\frac{v}{u}$

Since, image is real. So, it will be inverted.

$$m = -2 = -\frac{v}{u}$$

$$\therefore \quad v = 2u$$

By mirror formula,

$$\frac{1}{v} + \frac{1}{u} = \frac{1}{f}$$

$$\Rightarrow \quad \frac{1}{2u} + \frac{1}{u} = \frac{1}{f}$$

$$\Rightarrow \quad \frac{3}{2u} = \frac{1}{f}$$

$$\therefore \quad u = \frac{3f}{2}$$

$$\therefore \quad v = 2u = 3f$$

$\therefore$ Separation between object and image

$$= v - u = 3f - \frac{3f}{2} = \frac{3f}{2}$$

11. (*b*) Given, $u = -12$ cm

Magnification, $m = -\frac{v}{u} = -\frac{5}{2}$

$$\Rightarrow \quad \frac{-v}{-12} = \frac{-5}{2}$$

$$\Rightarrow \quad v = 30 \text{ cm}$$

Using mirror formula,

$$\frac{1}{v} + \frac{1}{u} = \frac{1}{f}$$

$$\frac{1}{-30} + \frac{1}{-12} = \frac{1}{f}$$

or $\quad f = -8.6$ cm

12. (*c*) Number of images formed,

$$n = \frac{360°}{\theta} - 1$$

$$= \frac{360°}{60°} - 1 = 5$$

13. (*d*) The number of images formed by two inclined plane mirrors are given by

$$n = \frac{360°}{\theta}$$

Here, $\quad \theta = \frac{360°}{100°} = 3.6 \simeq 4$

Since it is even, so the images formed will be $n - 1 = 4 - 1 = 3$.

As, the mosquito is very close to one of the mirrors. So, it can see only two images that are far from its position.

14. (*d*) Since, the mass of plane mirror is equal to the mass of the monkey. So, in case I, both will move up at constant rate and monkey can see his image.

In case II, both will move linearly as downward force and weight are equal. So, the monkey can see his image.

In case III, both will fall freely under gravity and due to equal mass, they cover equal distances in equal time. So, the monkey can see his image.

15. (*b*) From the figure, it can be clearly seen that the angle of incidence is equal to the angle of reflection.

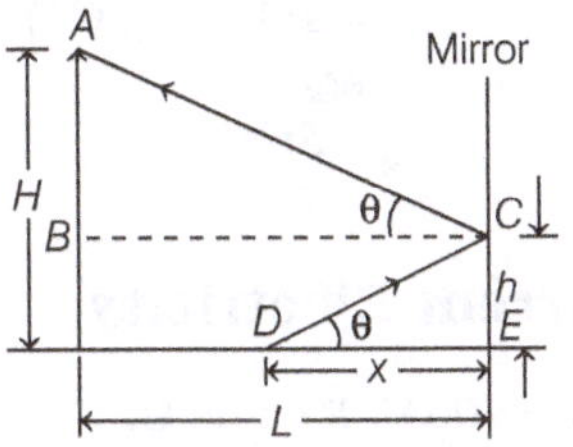

Thus, from ΔABC and ΔDEC, we have

$$\tan\theta = \frac{H-h}{L} = \frac{h}{x} \Rightarrow x = \frac{Lh}{H-h}$$

Here, $H = 1.68$ m, $h = 0.43$ m and $L = 2.2$ m
Substituting these values in above relation, we get

$$x = \frac{2.2 \times 0.43}{1.68 - 0.43} = 0.757 \text{ m}$$

16. (*d*) The ray diagram for given object is shown below

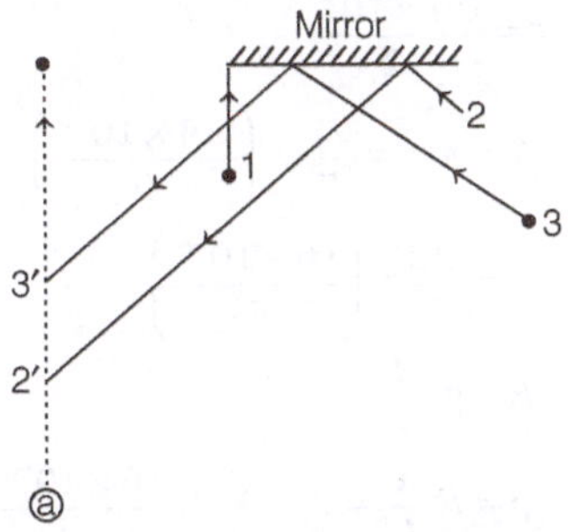

From figure, it can be observed that the image of toy number 1 will never be seen by the girl as it is out of its field of view. So, the girl first sees the image of toy number 2 and then that of toy number 3.

Chapter 9. Sound

1. (*a*) The frequency of tuning fork = 256 Hz, i.e. 256 vibrations are completed in 1 s.

$\therefore$ Time taken to complete 1 vibration $= \frac{1}{256}$

Similarly, time taken to complete 25 vibrations

$$= \frac{1}{256} \times 25$$

$\because$ Distance, $s = v \times t$

Given, $v = 343$ m/s, $t = \frac{25}{256}$

$$s = 343 \times \frac{25}{256}$$

$$= \frac{8575}{256} = 33.49 \text{ m}$$

2. (*d*) Frequency of ultrasonic sound,

$$n = 100 \text{ kHz}$$
$$= 100 \times 10^3 \text{ Hz}$$

Speed of sound in air, $v = 340$ m/s

$\therefore$ The wavelength of reflected sound,

$$\lambda = \frac{v}{n} = \frac{340}{100 \times 10^3}$$
$$= 3.4 \times 10^{-3} \text{ m}$$

Wavelength of sound in air is 3.4×10^{-3} m.

The speed of sound in water, $u' = 1486$ m/s.

$\therefore$ The wavelength of transmitted sound in water,

$$\lambda' = \frac{v'}{n}$$

$$\Rightarrow \quad \lambda' = \frac{1486}{100 \times 10^3} = 1.486 \times 10^{-2} \text{ m}$$

3. (*a*)

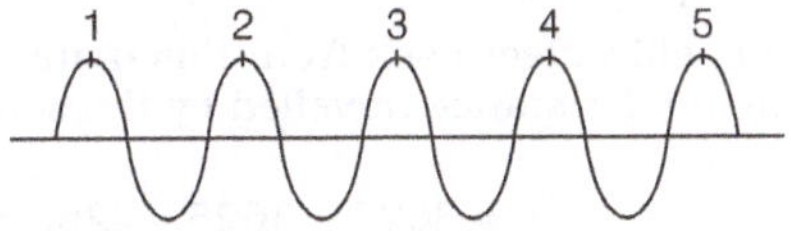

Given, $\frac{v_x}{v_y} = \frac{3}{1}$

We know that, $v = \frac{\lambda}{t}$

$\therefore \quad v_x = \frac{\lambda_x}{t_x}$

and $\quad v_y = \frac{\lambda_y}{t_y}$

$\therefore \quad \frac{v_x}{v_y} = \frac{\lambda_x / t_x}{\lambda_y / t_y}$

$\Rightarrow \quad \frac{3}{1} = \frac{\lambda_x}{\lambda_y} \times \frac{t_y}{t_x}$

$$\frac{v_x}{v_y} = \frac{2}{7} \times \frac{t_y}{t_x}$$

$\therefore \quad \frac{t_y}{t_x} = \frac{3}{1} \times \frac{7}{2} = \frac{21}{2} = 10.5$

$$t_y = 10.5 t_x$$

Hence, wave y has greater time period than wave x.

4. (*a*) Number of vibrations in 2 s = 400

Frequency $= \frac{400}{2} = 200$ Hz

Velocity of sound = 320 m/s

$\therefore$ Wavelength λ = Speed (v) / Frequency (f)

$$= \frac{320}{200} = 1.677 \text{ m}$$

5. (*a*)

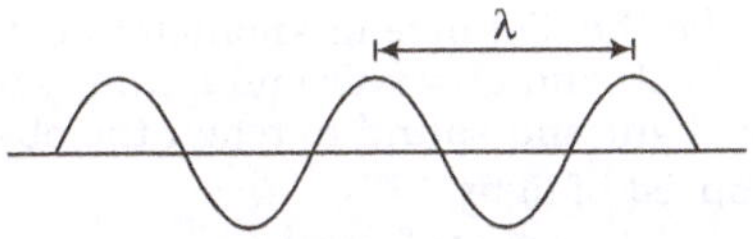

Minimum distance between two particles in same phase $= \lambda = 18 \text{ cm} = \frac{18}{100}$ m

Velocity of wave = 36 m/s

$\because \quad T = \frac{1}{f}$

$\Rightarrow \quad f = \frac{v}{\lambda} = \frac{36 \times 100}{18} = 200$ per second

$\therefore \quad T = \dfrac{1}{200}$

Now, time for a phase change of

$\pi = \dfrac{1}{2}\left(\dfrac{1}{200}\right)$ s

$= \dfrac{1}{400}$ s $= 0.0025$ s

$= \dfrac{25}{10000} = 2.5 \times 10^{-3} = 2.5$ ms

6. (c) The distance of an object from submarine = 3625 m.

Sound will reflect back from this distance to receiver, so the total distance travelled by the sound wave in 5 s

$= 3625 + 3625 = 7250$ m

So, the speed of sound in water,

$v = \dfrac{s}{t} = \dfrac{7250}{5} = 1450$ m/s

7. (b) Total time interval between transmitting a sound pulse and receiving the echo, $t = 0.060$ s.

$\therefore$ Time taken by sound pulse to reach the reflecting wall,

$t' = \dfrac{t}{2} = \dfrac{0.060}{2} = 0.030$ s

Speed of sound, $v = 330$ m/s

$\therefore$ Distance of reflecting wall from the tape measure,

$d = v \times t' = 330 \times 0.030 = 9.9$ m

8. (c) When a sound wave is reflected from a brick wall (hard surface), then amplitude, wavelength and its speed remain same after reflection. But velocity changes due to change in its direction.

9. (b) Speed of sound in sea water, $v = 1520$ m/s

Depth, $d = 11$ km $= 11000$ m

Time taken to reach at object, $t = \dfrac{d}{v} = \dfrac{11000}{1520}$

$= 7.237$ s

Time taken to get echo, $t' = 2t$

$= 2 \times 7.237 = 14.47$ s

10. (b) A pulse converts 4 divisions at 2.5 ms/cm.

So, the time period of signal is

$T = 4 \times 2.5 = 10\text{ms} = 10 \times 10^{-3}$ s

$\therefore$ Frequency, $f = \dfrac{1}{T} = \dfrac{1}{10 \times 10^{-3}} = 100$ Hz

11. (b) Let s be the distance in kilometers between lighting flash and observer and t_1 and t_2 be the time taken by light and sound to reach the observer.

Given, speed of light,

$c = 3 \times 10^8$ ms^{-1}

$= 3 \times 10^5$ kms^{-1}

Speed of sound, $v = 340$ ms^{-1}

$= 0.340$kms^{-1}

Time taken by light, $t_1 = \dfrac{s}{c}$

Time taken by sound, $t_2 = \dfrac{s}{v}$

As per question, $t_2 - t_1 = \Delta t = \dfrac{s}{v} - \dfrac{s}{c}$

$\Rightarrow \quad \Delta t = s\left(\dfrac{1}{0.340} - \dfrac{1}{3 \times 10^5}\right)$

$= s(3 - 3 \times 10^{-6})$

$\approx 3s$

$\therefore \quad s = \dfrac{\Delta t}{3}$

Chapter 10. Current Electricity

1. (a) Given, $V = 400$ V, $R = 200\ \Omega$,

$I = V/R = 400 / 200 = 2$ A

$\therefore \quad I = \dfrac{q}{t} \Rightarrow I = \dfrac{ne}{t}$ $\quad (\because q = ne)$

$n = \dfrac{I \times t}{e} = \dfrac{2 \times 1}{1.6 \times 10^{-19}}$

or $\quad n = \dfrac{20}{16} \times 10^{19} = 1.25 \times 10^{19}$

2. (a) Given, $l = 1.5$ m, $D = 0.4$ mm $= 0.4 \times 10^{-3}$ m, $R = 3\ \Omega$

Radius, $r = \dfrac{0.4 \times 10^{-3}}{2}$

$\therefore \quad A = \pi r^2 = \dfrac{22}{7} \times \left(\dfrac{0.4 \times 10^{-3}}{2}\right)^2$

$= \dfrac{22}{7} \times \left(\dfrac{16 \times 10^{-8}}{4}\right)$

As, $\quad R = \rho \cdot \dfrac{l}{A}$

$\Rightarrow \quad \rho = R\dfrac{A}{l} = 3 \times \dfrac{22}{7} \times \dfrac{16 \times 10^{-8}}{1.5 \times 4}$

$= \dfrac{22 \times 4 \times 2 \times 10^{-8}}{7}$

$= 2.5142 \times 10^{-7}\ \Omega$-m

3. (a) Total resistance of circuit is $R = 3 + 5 = 8\ \Omega$

Potential difference of circuit is 6 V.

Value of current, $I = \dfrac{V}{R} = \dfrac{6}{8} = \dfrac{3}{4} = 0.75$ A

Potential difference of resistance $3\ \Omega$ is $V = IR$

$= 0.75 \times 3 = 2.25$ V

4. (b) Given $r = 0.5 \times 10^{-10}$ m

$f = 5 \times 10^{15}$ cycle/s , $I = ?$

Current $(I) = \dfrac{q}{t} = q \times f = ef \quad \left(\because \dfrac{1}{T} = f\right)$

$= 1.6 \times 10^{-19} \times 5 \times 10^{15}$

$= 8 \times 10^{-4}$ A $= 0.8$ mA

5. (c) Resistances R_2 and R_3 are connected in parallel.

$R_2 = 8\ \Omega, \quad R_3 = 12\ \Omega$

$\dfrac{1}{R_P} = \dfrac{1}{R_2} + \dfrac{1}{R_3}$

$\dfrac{1}{R_P} = \dfrac{1}{8} + \dfrac{1}{12} = \dfrac{5}{24}$

$R_P = \dfrac{24}{5}\ \Omega$

This combination and resistance R_1 is connected in series, then total resistance is

$$R_1 = 7.2\Omega$$

$$R = R_1 + R_P = 7.2 + \frac{24}{5}$$

$$= \frac{72}{10} + \frac{24}{5} = \frac{120}{10} = 12\,\Omega$$

6. (c) Potential difference of each resistor is 3 V, that's why the reading of voltmeter V_1 and V_2 is 3 V and 6 V.

7. (c) Because $R_1 > R_2$, that's why resistor R_2 has more current than R_1, when connected in parallel.

8. (c) When length becomes 2 m, then resistance also becomes twice that means now resistance is 4Ω.

$\therefore \quad V = IR = 2 \times 3 = 6\,V$

The value of current in 2 m length wire can be found from relation as, $R \propto L$

$\therefore$ When $L = 2$ m , $R = 4\Omega$

Thus, current, $I = \frac{V}{R} = \frac{6}{4} = \frac{3}{2} = 1.5$ A

9. (b) In these combinations, circuit P and circuit S has same effective resistance between X and Y.

For *P*,

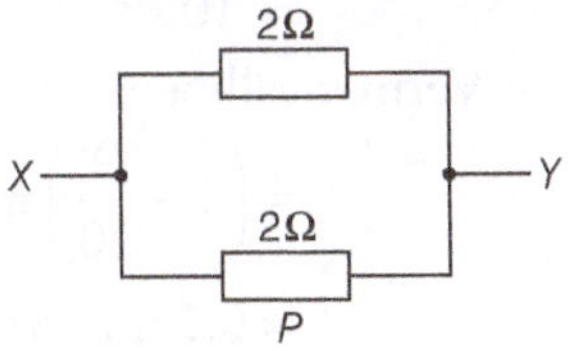

$$\frac{1}{R_P} = \frac{1}{R_1} + \frac{1}{R_2}$$

$$\frac{1}{R_P} = \frac{1}{2} + \frac{1}{2} = \frac{2}{2} = 1\,\Omega$$

For *S*,

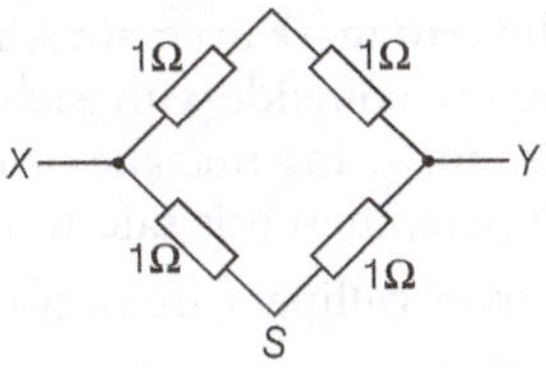

$$R_{S_1} = 1 + 1 = 2$$

$$R_{S_2} = 1 + 1 = 2$$

$$\therefore \quad \frac{1}{R_P} = \frac{1}{R_{S_1}} + \frac{1}{R_{S_2}} = \frac{1}{2} + \frac{1}{2} = \frac{2}{2} = 1\,\Omega$$

10. (c) Circuit (c) is used to find the resistance of the resistor R because voltmeter is connected parallel to the resistor.

11. (c) When 10 Ω load is connected to the circuit, the current supplied by load, $I = \frac{120}{10} = 12$A

The voltage drop for 3A = $3 \times 10 = 30$ V

The voltage drop in rheostat = $120 - 30 = 90$ V

So, the resistance of rheostat = $\frac{90}{3} = 30\,\Omega$

Similarly, the voltage drop for 5A = $5 \times 10 = 50$ V

The voltage drop in rheostat = $120 - 50 = 70$ V

So, the resistance of rheostat = $\frac{70}{5} = 14\,\Omega$

$\therefore$ The resistance and current range of the rheostat should be 14-30 Ω and 0-5 A, respectively .

12. (a) When the slide S is displaced towards X, resistance R increases, thereby decreasing the current in it. As P is connected in parallel to it, so the current passing in resistor P increases. Since, resistors P and R are in parallel, so on increasing R, the equivalent resistance of this parallel combination decreases. So, the current passing through resistor Q increases as overall resistance of circuit also decreases.

Chapter 11. Magnetism

1. (c) The direction of force on a current-carrying wire placed in a magnetic field depends on the direction of the current as well as the direction of the magnetic field. It is decided by certain laws such as Fleming's left hand rule screw law.

2. (c) The North pole of the magnet will repel the North pole of compass and it is shown in figure as

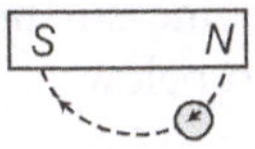

3. (d) When a bar magnet is broken into three parts X, Y and Z.

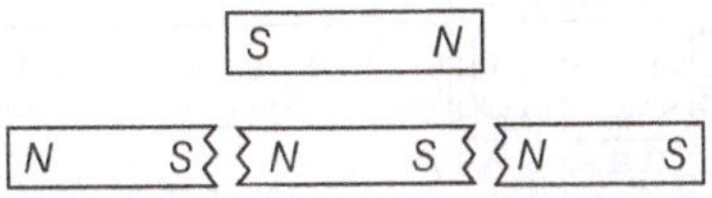

In each piece, N and S-poles are created. Same poles repel and opposite poles attract. So, figure (d) is correct.

4. (b) In diagram (b), in both the pieces of bar magnet opposite poles are shown. In other diagrams, the position of poles is not correctly represented.

5. (a) Steel is used for making permanent magnet because it retains the magnetic properties for a long period of time. Copper wires are used for wrapping on the solenoid for making electromagnet.

6. (a) Magnetic field lines inside the magnet pass from South pole to North pole. Hence, incorrect magnetic field lines are represented by the figure given in option (a).

7. (d) Since, magnetic lines of forces easily enter into iron piece. Hence, nearer end of iron becomes South pole and farther end of iron becomes North pole. Hence, magnetic field pattern is now shown as

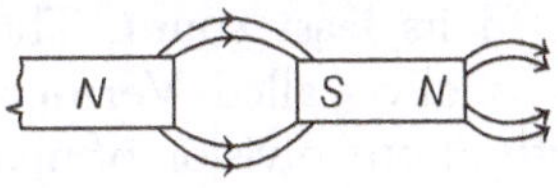

8. (d) Magnetic field lines are closed and continuous curve.

Internal Assessment of Practical Work

Experiment 1

Aim

Determine the least count of the Vernier callipers and measure the length and diameter of a small cylinder (average of three sets)-may be a metal rod of length 2 to 3 cm and diameter 1 to 2 cm.

Apparatus Required

A pair of Vernier callipers, a small cylindrical rod.

Theory

A Vernier callipers is a measuring instrument which is shown in the figure given below

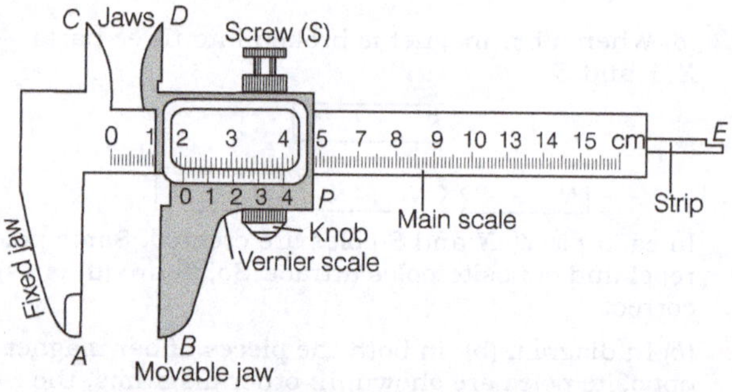

It has two scales, one fixed scale called **main scale** and the other is a sliding scale is called **Vernier scale**. The Vernier scale has ten divisions and the length of these ten divisions made equal to the length of nine divisions on the main scale as shown in figure.

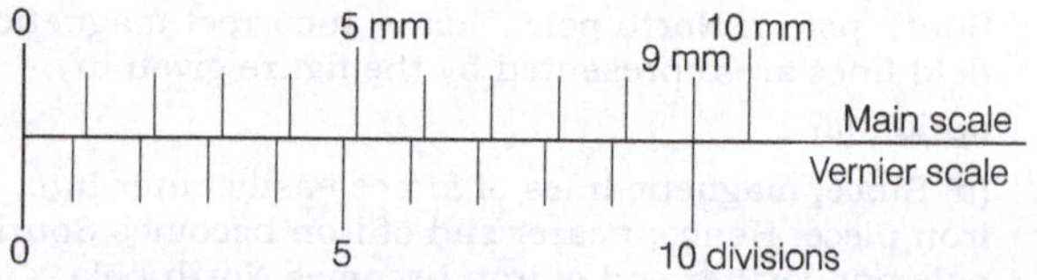

The least distance which can be measured accurately by an instrument is called its **least count**. The least count of Vernier callipers is also called **Vernier constant.** The difference in length of one division of main scale and one division of Vernier scale is called least count of Vernier callipers. i.e.,

Least count of Vernier callipers = Value of one main scale division – Value of one Vernier scale division

According to figure,

10 divisions on Vernier scale = 9 divisions on main scale

1 division on Vernier scale = $\frac{9}{10}$ divisions on main scale.

$\therefore$ Let the value of 1 division on main scale = 1 mm

$\therefore$ 1 division on Vernier scale = $\frac{9}{10}$ mm

Thus, least count of Vernier callipers

$$= \left(1 - \frac{9}{10}\right) \text{mm} = \frac{1}{10}$$

$$= 0.1 \text{ mm or } 0.01 \text{ cm}$$

Zero Error

In the case of Vernier callipers generally, the zero on main scale should coincide with zero on Vernier scale, then the Vernier callipers is said to be **free from zero error.**

But in case both the zero mark on main scale and zero mark on Vernier scale do not coincide with each other due to any defect such as manufacturing mistake or mechanical error in the Vernier callipers, then it is said to have zero error.

Zero error in a Vernier callipers are of two types

1. **Positive Zero Error**

   On coinciding the zeroes on main scale and Vernier scale, if it is found that zero mark on the Vernier scale is on the right hand side of the zero mark on main scale, then it is called positive zero error as shown in figure below.

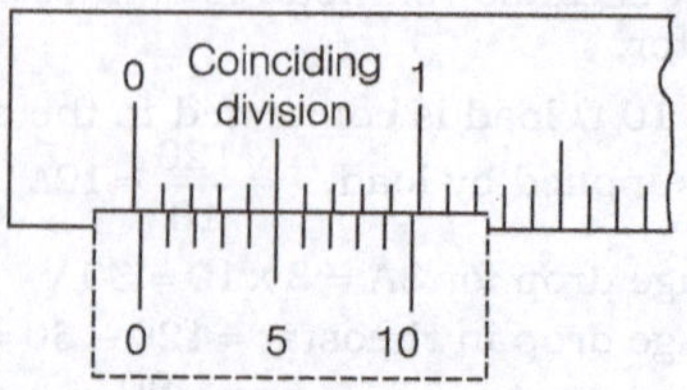

Positive zero error

Positive zero error can be calculated easily by multiplying the number of the Vernier division x (coinciding with any division on the main scale) with the Least Count (LC) of Vernier. i.e., Positive zero error $= +x \times LC$

2. **Negative Zero Error**

If zero mark on Vernier scale lies on the left hand side of the zero mark on main scale, then it is called negative zero error as shown in figure below.

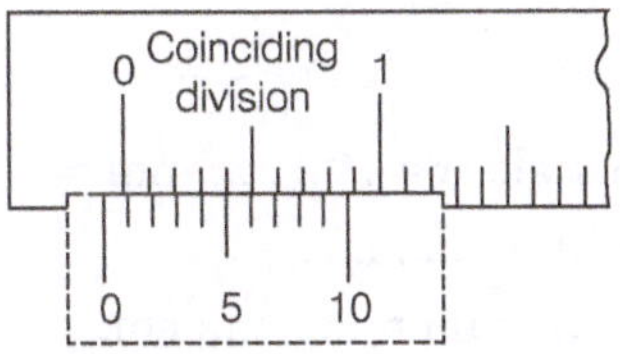

Negative zero error

Let total number of division on Vernier scale $= n$ and coinciding Vernier scale division $= x$

$\therefore$ Difference $= (n - x)$

Negative zero error can be calculated by multiplying the difference $(n - x)$ with the Least Count (LC) of Vernier. i.e., Negative zero error $= -(n - x) \times LC$

Correction

This can be done by subtracting zero error from the observed reading with proper sign (i.e., by subtracting positive zero error or by adding negative zero error as the case may be) and hence correction due to zero error will be done.

Procedure

1. Count the total number of division on Vernier scale (let it be n) and record the value of one division on main scale (let it be x).
2. Calculate the least count of Vernier callipers. It will be $\frac{x}{n}$.
3. Slide the movable jaw of Vernier callipers and bring it in contact with fixed jaw.
4. If zero mark on main scale and that of Vernier scale coincides, the Vernier callipers has no zero error.
5. If zeroes of both the Vernier scale and main scale do not coincides, it means Vernier callipers has zero error, observe whether it is positive or negative zero error and record it with proper sign.
6. Place the given cylindrical rod in between movable jaw and fixed jaw lengthwise in horizontal position as shown in figure below.

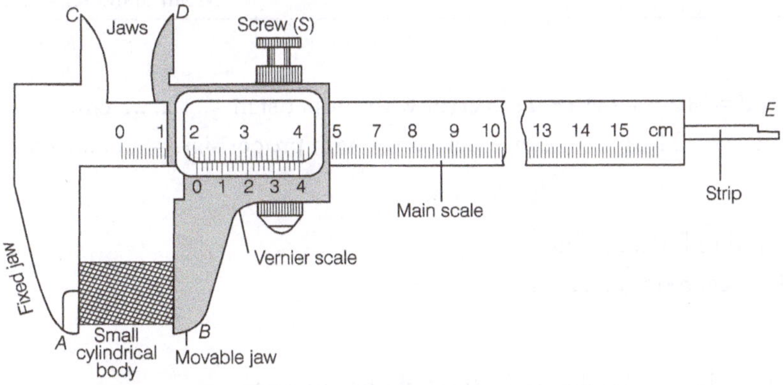

To measure the diameter of small cylindrical body using Vernier calliper

7. Before zero mark on Vernier scale, note down the number of divisions on main scale and multiply this divisions with least count of main scale to get main scale reading.

8. Observe the division on Vernier scale which coincides with any of the division on main scale and multiply this division with least count to get Vernier scale reading.
9. Take at least two more observations to find the mean length of cylindrical rod.
10. Repeat this process by placing the cylindrical rod diameterwise in between fixed and movable jaws in vertical position and measure the diameter of rod at least three times.

Observations

(i) Value of one smallest division on the main scale, x = ... mm = ... cm.
(ii) Total number of divisions on Vernier scale, n = ...
(iii) Least Count of Vernier callipers, LC = ... mm = ... cm.
(iv) Zero error of Vernier callipers = ± .... mm = ± .... cm.

Table : Length of Rod

S. No.	Main scale reading (in cm)	Vernier scale reading (Vernier scale division coinciding with any division of main scale × Least count) (in cm)	Total reading (Main scale reading + Vernier scale reading) (in cm)
1.			
2.			
3.			
4.			
			Mean length = ... cm

Table : Diameter of Rod

S. No.	Main scale reading (in cm)	Vernier scale reading (Vernier scale division coinciding with any division of main scale × Least count) (in cm)	Total reading (Main scale reading + Vernier scale reading) (in cm)
1.			
2.			
3.			
4.			
			Mean diameter = ... cm

Calculations

True length of cylindrical rod = Mean length − Zero error with proper sign = ... cm.
True diameter of cylindrical rod = Mean diameter − Zero error with proper sign = ... cm.

Result

The length of given cylindrical rod = ... cm.
The diameter of given cylindrical rod = ... cm.

Precautions

(i) Both the jaws of Vernier callipers should not be too tight or too loose.
(ii) Reading on main scale and Vernier scale should be taken carefully to avoid error.
(iii) Reading should be taken by placing the rod in different positions between both the jaws of Vernier callipers.

Viva-Voce

Q 1. What is the principle of Vernier callipers?

Ans. The vernier calliper works on the principle of using the alignment of line segments displaced by a small amount to make fine measurements.

Q 2. What do you mean by least count of Vernier callipers?

Ans. The least distance which can be measured by a Vernier callipers is called its least count.

It is the difference of value of one main scale division and value of one Vernier scale division.

Q 3. Who made the device Vernier callipers?

Ans. The device Vernier callipers was made by Pierre Vernier.

Q 4. How may divisions are there on Vernier scale and main scale?

Ans. Both the scales have ten divisions.

Q 5. What is the use of upper jaws (inside jaw) of a Vernier callipers?

Ans. The upper jaw (or inside jaw) of a Vernier callipers are used to measure the inner diameters of rings, cylinder, hollow spheres, etc.

Q 6. Explain the use of lower jaw (outside jaw) of a Vernier callipers.

Ans. The outside jaw or lower jaw are used to measure the thickness of object, e.g. outer diameters of cylinders, spheres, etc.

Q 7. What is the use of thin strip moving behind the main scale?

Ans. The thin strip behind the main scale is used to measure the depths of the cylinders and level of the liquid inside the jars.

Q 8. A Vernier callipers has 25 divisions on Vernier scale which coincide with 24 divisions on main scale. What is least count of this Vernier callipers?

(Take, value of 1 division on main scale = 1 mm)

Ans. The least count of Vernier calliper

$$= \left(1 - \frac{24}{25}\right) \text{mm}$$

$$= \frac{1}{25} \text{ mm} = 0.04 \text{ mm}$$

Q 9. Which scale is sliding scale of a Vernier callipers?

Ans. Vernier scale is sliding scale.

Q 10. Why does the zero of the main scale not coincide with the zero of the Vernier scale sometimes?

Ans. The zero of the main scale does not coincide with the zero of the Vernier scale, when Vernier callipers has an error. This is called zero error of Vernier callipers.

It is of two types

(i) Positive zero error

(ii) Negative zero error

Experiment 2

Aim

Determine the pitch and least count of the given screw gauge and measure the mean radius of the given wire, taking three sets of readings in perpendicular directions.

Apparatus Required

A screw gauge, a thin copper wire.

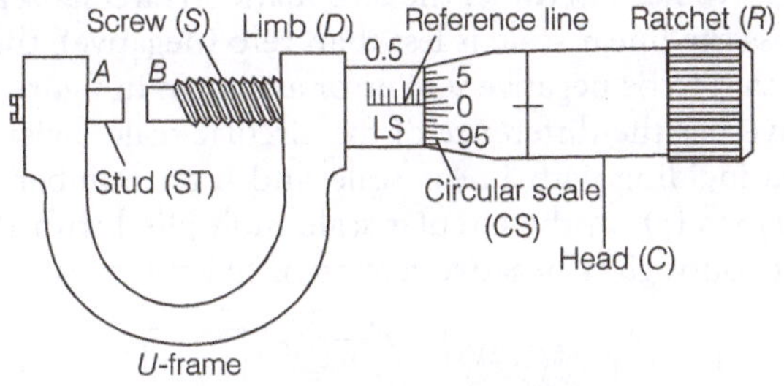

Screw gauge

Theory

The distance moved by the screw during its one complete rotation is equal to the distance between two consecutive threads on a linear scale called **pitch** of screw gauge as shown in figure below.

The least distance which can be measured by a screw gauge is called **least count** of screw gauge.

Least count of screw gauge

$$= \frac{\text{Pitch}}{\text{Number of divisions on the circular scale}}$$

Generally, a circular scale has 100 equal divisions on its head. If screw moves a distance 1 mm on a linear scale, then

least count of screw gauge $= \frac{1}{100}$ mm

$= 0.01$ mm or 0.001 cm

Zero Error

If the zero mark on circular scale coincides with the zero mark on linear scale on bringing the screw in contact with stud A, the screw gauge in this situation is said to be **free from zero error.**

But in case both the zeroes do not coincide with each other, due to any defect like manufacturing defect or any mechanical error, the instrument is said to have zero error. Two types of zero error are found in screw gauge. These are

(i) **Positive Zero Error** If zero mark on circular scale across the linear scale is more than zero (positive), then it is said to be positive zero error as shown in figure. Positive zero error can be obtained by adding the number of circular scale division (x) coinciding with the linear scale which is multiplied with least count of the screw gauge.

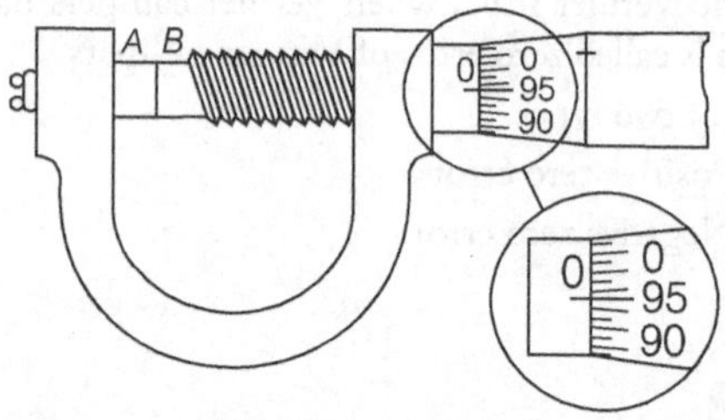

Positive zero error

(ii) **Negative Zero Error** If the zero mark on circular scale across the linear scale is less than zero (negative), then it is said to be negative zero error as shown in figure. It is given as the difference of the circular scale division (x) coinciding with linear scale and total number of divisions (n) on the circular scale multiplied with the least count gives negative zero error of a screw gauge.

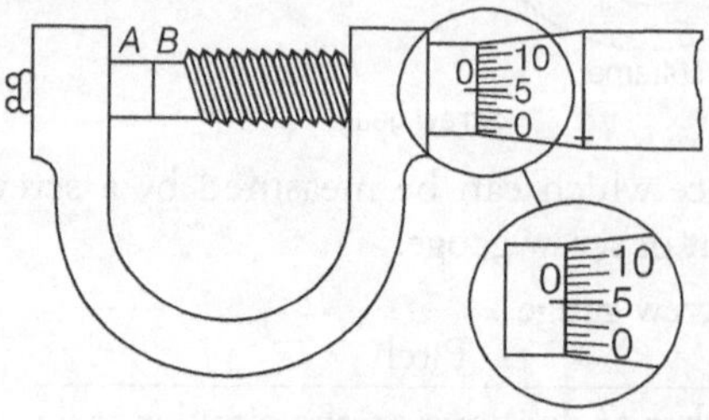

Negative zero error

Zero Correction

This can be done by subtracting zero error from the observed reading with proper sign (i.e., subtracting positive zero error or by adding negative zero error as the case may be).

Procedure

1. Take a screw gauge and find its pitch. To determine the pitch of screw gauge, rotate the screw by five couple rotations and observe the linear distance travelled by screw. Record this observations and determine the pitch of the screw gauge.
2. Determine the least count of the given screw gauge by dividing the pitch by the total number of divisions on the circular scale. Record it.
3. Rotate the screw with the help of ratchet to coincide the stud A and screw head B. If zero on circular scale coincides with zero on linear scale, it means screw gauge has no zero error. If zeroes of both the scale do not coincide with each other, it means there is either positive zero error or negative zero error. Note down this errors with proper sign.
4. Put the copper wire in between stud A and screw head B and move the ratchet clockwise in such a way that the wire is held in between stud A and screw head B.
5. Note down the reading on main scale and circular scale division which coincides with linear scale division. Multiply this circular scale, division by least count of screw gauge and add with reading on the main scale.
6. Repeat this atleast two more times to find out mean diameter of copper wire.

Observation

(i) Value of one smallest division on the main scale = ... mm = ... cm.

(ii) Distance transversed by the screw on giving it five rotations = ... mm = ... cm.

(iii) Pitch of the screw = ... mm = ... cm.

(iv) Total number of divisions on circular scale = ...

(v) Least count of screw gauge

$$= \frac{\text{Pitch of the screw}}{\text{Total number of divisions on circular scale}}$$

= .... mm = ... cm.

(vi) Zero error of screw gauge = ... cm (+ or −).

Table : Diameter of Wire

S. No.	Main scale reading (in cm)	Circular scale reading (Circular scale division coinciding with any division of main scale × Least count) (in cm)	Total reading (Main scale reading + Circular scale reading) (in cm)
1.			
2.			
3.			
4.			
			Mean diameter = ... cm

Calculations

True diameter of given wire = Mean diameter − Zero error with proper sign = ... cm.

The radius of given wire $= \frac{\text{Diameter}}{2}$ = ... cm.

Result

The radius of given wire = ... cm.

Precautions

(i) Hold the copper wire gently in between stud A and screw head *B*.

(ii) Reading should be taken on different places on wire for each observation.

(iii) While taking measurement move the screw in one direction to avoid backlash error.

Viva-Voce

Q 1. What is screw gauge?

Ans. The screw gauge is a device or an instrument which can measure length upto 0.01 mm.

Q 2. What is two main parts of screw gauge?

Ans. Two main parts of screw gauge are

(i) a nut (ii) a bolt or screw.

Q 3. What do you mean by pitch of a screw gauge?

Ans. The distance between two consecutive threads on linear scale of a screw gauge is called pitch of screw gauge.

Q 4. How is the least count of a screw gauge obtained?

Ans. Least count of a screw gauge can be obtained by the formula.

Least Count (LC)

$$= \frac{\text{Pitch of screw}}{\text{Total number of divisions on circular scale}}$$

Q 5. What do you mean by zero error of screw gauge?

Ans. When zero of circular scale does not coincide with the zero of the main scale, when the two studs are joined, screw gauge has zero error.

Q 6. How backlash error is avoided?

Ans. Backlash error is avoided only by turning the screw in one direction.

Q 7. When does the zero error become positive?

Ans. If zero mark on circular scale lies below the zero mark on linear scale, then zero error become positive.

Q 8. How can you change the least count of a screw gauge?

Ans. Least count of screw gauge can be changed by increasing or decreasing the total number of divisions on the circular scale.

Q 9. What is head scale?

Ans. The circular scale of a screw gauge is called head scale.

Q 10. Where does the ratchet attatched to a screw gauge?

Ans. Ratchet is attached to the screw by a spring. Ratchet helps in holding the object which have to be measured between the stud *A* and screw head *B* of the screw gauge.

Experiment 3

Aim

Measure the length, breadth and thickness of a glass block using a meter rule (each reading correct to a mm), taking the mean of three readings in each case. Calculate the volume of the block in cm^3 and m^3. Determine the mass (not weight) of the block using any convenient balance in g and kg. Calculate the density of glass in CGS and SI units using mass and volume in the respective units. Obtain the relation between the two density units.

Apparatus Required

A glass slab (block), a meter rule, a physical balance and a physical weight box.

Theory

The volume of the glass block

= Length × Breadth × Thickness of glass block

or $V = l \times b \times t$

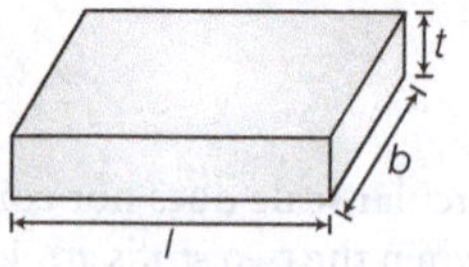

Glass block

The mass per unit volume of the glass block defines its density

i.e., $\text{Density of glass block} = \dfrac{\text{Mass of glass block}}{\text{Volume of glass block}}$

$$\rho = \frac{m}{V}$$

A. To Measure the Length, Breadth and Thickness of a Glass Block

Procedure

1. Take a meter rule and record its least count.
2. Place the scale in contact with glass block as shown in figure. To avoid error due to wear and tear at the zero end, measurement is started other than '0' marked end.

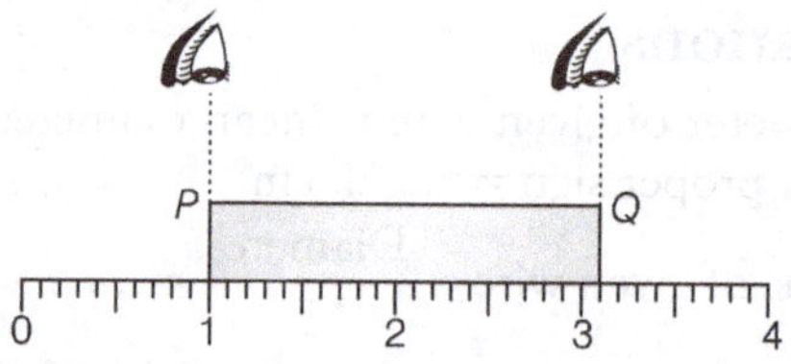

3. To obtain correct measurement of length, subtract the marking observed at end *P* from that observed at other end *Q* (i.e., *Q* – *P*). To avoid parallax error due to thickness of meter rule keep the eye vertically above the end of the glass block as shown in figure.
4. Take two more observations for length of glass block and record them in the table.
5. To measure the breadth (*b*) and thickness (*t*) of the glass block follow the step 3. Take atleast three observations for breadth and thickness; and record it in the table.

Observations

Least count of the meter rule = ... mm = ... cm.

Table: For Dimensions (length, breadth and thickness) of Glass Block

Dimensions	S.No.	Reading on meter rule at end *P* (in cm)	Reading on meter rule at end *Q* (in cm)	*Q* – *P* (in cm)	Mean
Length (*l*)	1.			$l_1 =$	$l = \dfrac{l_1 + l_2 + l_3}{3} =$ ...... cm
	2.			$l_2 =$	
	3.			$l_3 =$	
Breadth (*b*)	1.			$b_1 =$	$b = \dfrac{b_1 + b_2 + b_3}{3} =$ .... cm
	2.			$b_2 =$	
	3.			$b_3 =$	
Thickness (*t*)	1.			$t_1 =$	$t = \dfrac{t_1 + t_2 + t_3}{3} =$ ...... cm
	2.			$t_2 =$	
	3.			$t_3 =$	

B. To Determine the Mass of the Glass Block

Procedure

1. Adjust the levelling screws on which the physical balance is mounted and get the plumb line just above the pointed projection.
2. Raise the beam with the help of lever slowly, such that the pointer after swinging comes to rest exactly on zero mark or swings equally on both sides of zero mark. Otherwise adjust the screw nuts to bring the pointer on zero mark as shown in figure.

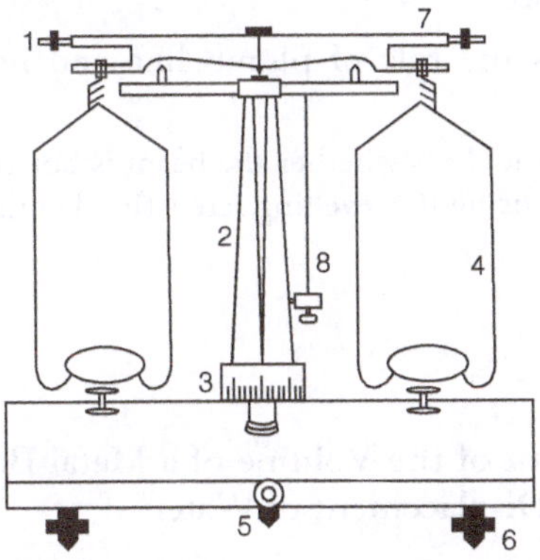

1. Adjusting screw 2. Pillar 3. Ivory scale
4. Weight pan 5. Handle 6. Levelling screw
7. Hanger 8. Plumb line

Physical balance

3. Place the glass block on left hand pan and weights on right hand pan of the physical balance.
4. Raise the beam and check the movement of pointer. To get standard weight the pointer should remain on zero mark.
5. Total sum of all weights kept on right hand pan is the mass (m) of glass block.
6. Take atleast two more observations to find the mean mass of the glass block.

Observations

$m_1 =$ .... g, $m_2 =$ ....g,
$m_3 =$ .... g.

Mean mass of glass block,

$$m = \frac{m_1 + m_2 + m_3}{3} = \text{........g}$$

$$= \frac{\text{.......}}{1000}\ \text{kg} = \text{..............}\ \text{kg}$$

Calculations

Volume of the glass block,

$V = l \times b \times t =$ .... $\text{cm}^3 =$ .... $\times 10^{-6}\,\text{m}^3$

$$\text{Density of glass block} = \frac{\text{Mass}}{\text{Volume}}$$

$$\text{In CGS unit, density} \frac{\text{...... g}}{\text{.......cm}^3} = \text{..............}\ \text{g cm}^{-3}$$

$$\text{In SI unit, density} \frac{\text{...... kg}}{\text{....... m}^3} = \text{..............}\ \text{kg m}^{-3}$$

Result

Density of glass block in CGS unit = ... g cm^{-3}.

Density of glass block in SI unit = ... kg m^{-3}.

Relationship between the CGS unit and SI unit

$$1\ \text{g cm}^{-3} = 1000\ \text{kg m}^{-3}$$

Precautions

1. The pan of the physical balance should be clean, dry and dust free.
2. Put the weight on the pan with the help of forceps gently.
3. Beam should be raised gently without giving jerk.

Viva-Voce

Q 1. How can the volume of a block be calculated?

Ans. Volume of a block is calculated by multiplying its length, breadth and thickness.

Q 2. What are the dimensions of a glass slab (block)?

Ans. The dimensions of a glass block are length, breadth and thickness.

Q 3. How can you measure the length of a glass block using meter rule?

Ans. To measure the length of a glass block using meter rule, we place the meter scale (or rule) in contact with glass block lengthwise, then subtract the marking observed at left hand end from that observed at right hand end of the glass block.

Q 4. What do you mean by the density of a substance?

Ans. The mass of a substance per unit volume is called density of a substance.

Q 5. Write CGS and SI units of density.

Ans. CGS unit of density is g cm^{-3} and the SI unit of density is kg m^{-3}.

Q 6. What are the characteristics of beam balance?

Ans. (i) Both arms of the physical balance must be of equal length.

(ii) Both pans of the physical balance must be of equal mass.

Q 7. Define volume of a block. What are its CGS and SI units?

Ans. Volume of the block is defined as the space occupied by the block. CGS unit of volume is cm^3. SI unit of volume is m^3.

Q 8. How can the density of a substance decrease?

Ans. When a substance is heated, then its density decreases.

Q 9. Why does a jeweller use only physical balance?

Ans. A jeweller needs an accurate measuring instrument to measure small amounts of gold, silver, gems, etc. Therefore, he uses only physical balance.

Q 10. Why is the beam of a physical balance raised gently by the lever?

Ans. The beam of a physical balance is raised gently by the lever to ensure that the pointer swings equally on both sides of the zero mark on the scale.

Q 11. Distinguish between beam balance and spring balance.

Ans. Beam balance is used to measure the mass of an object by comparing it with a standard mass. While spring balance is used to measure the weight of a body at a given place.

Q 12. What is the role of plumb line and how can it adjust?

Ans. Plumb line, lests whether the beam is horizontal. It is adjusted using the levelling screw fitted at the base.

Experiment 4

Aim

Measure the volume of a metal bob (the one used in simple pendulum experiments) from the readings of water level in a measuring cylinder using displacement method. Also, calculate the same volume from the radius measured using Vernier callipers. Comment on the accuracies.

Apparatus Required

A metal bob (or brass bob) with hook, a measuring cylinder (~ 100 cm^2), thread (~ 50 cm), water and a Vernier callipers.

Theory

(i) When a body is immersed completely in water, it displaces water and the volume of water displaced is equal to volume of the body.

(ii) Radius of metal bob can be measured with the help of Vernier callipers and then its volume can be calculated by the formula, $V = \frac{4}{3}\pi r^3$ or $V = \frac{1}{6}\pi d^3$

where, r is the radius and d is the diameter of given spherical metal bob.

A. Measurement of the Volume of a Metal Bob by the Method of Displacement of Water

Procedure

1. Take a measuring cylinder and note its least count.
2. Pour some water into the measuring cylinder and note the level of water in cylinder say $V_1 cm^3$.
3. Tie the given metal bob with a thread and immerse it completely in the water filled measuring cylinder. The level of water now rises as shown in figure. Note down this level say V_2 cm^3.

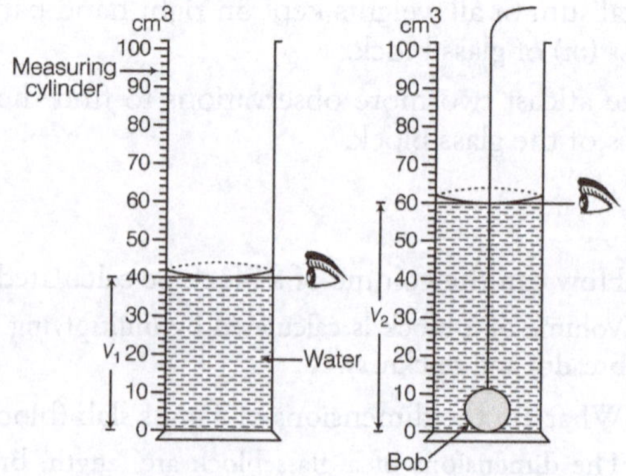

4. Take the difference $(V_2 - V_1)\text{cm}^3$ to get the volume of the given metal bob.

5. Take three more sets of observations by changing the initial level of water in the measuring cylinder and record it. Then, calculate the mean volume of the given metal bob say V cm^3.

Observations

Least count of the measuring cylinder = ... cm^3.

Table: Volume of Bob

S.No.	Initial level of water V_1 (in cm^3)	Final level of water V_2 (in cm^3)	Volume of bob = Volume of water level raised in cylinder $(V_2 - V_1)$ (in cm^3)
1.			
2.			
3.			
4.			
			Mean volume of bob, V = ... cm^3

B. Measurement of the Volume of a Metal Bob by Measuring its Diameter with the help of Vernier Callipers

Procedure

1. Take a Vernier callipers and note the number of divisions on Vernier scale. Let it be n.
2. Note the value of one division on main scale. Let it be x.
3. Calculate the least count of Vernier callipers. It will be $\frac{x}{n}$.
4. Slide the movable jaw of Vernier callipers and bring it in contact with fixed jaw and check, if the zero mark on main scale coincides with the zero mark on Vernier scale, it means that the instrument has no zero error.
5. If both the zero marks on Vernier scale and main scale are not coinciding, observe whether it is positive or negative zero error and record it with proper sign.
6. Fix the metal bob in between two lower jaws as shown in figure.

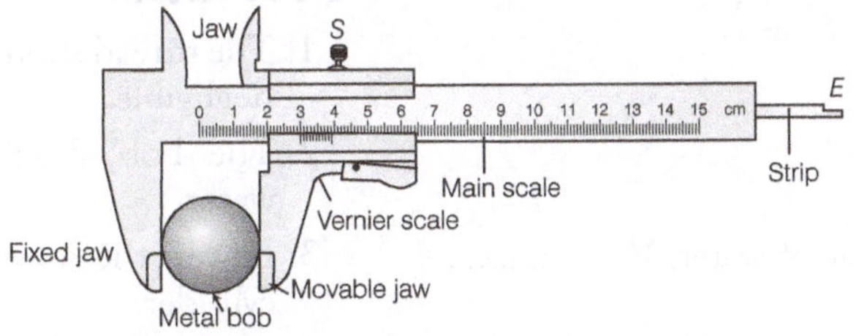

To measure diameter of bob using Vernier callipers

7. Note down the number of divisions on main scale before zero of Vernier scale and multiply this main scale division with least count to get the main scale reading.
8. Note down the division on Vernier scale which coincides with any of the division on main scale and multiply this division with least count of Vernier callipers and add with main scale reading to complete one observation.
9. Repeat the steps 7 and 8 by placing the bob in different places and get atleast three observations to find mean diameter of the metal bob.

Observations

The value of one main scale division, $x =$ .... cm.

Total number of divisions on Vernier scale, $n =$ ....

Least count of Vernier callipers, $\frac{x}{n} =$ .... cm.

Zero error of Vernier callipers = (+ / −) ....

Table: Diameter of Bob

S. No.	Main scale reading (in cm)	Vernier scale reading (Vernier scale division coinciding with any division on main scale × least count) (in cm)	Total reading (Main scale reading + Vernier scale reading) (in cm)
1.			
2.			
3.			
4.			
			Mean diameter, $d =$ .... cm

Calculations

Mean diameter of bob, $d =$ .... cm.

True diameter = Mean diameter − Zero error with proper sign.

Radius of bob, $r = \frac{d}{2} =$ .... cm.

Volume of bob, $V' = \frac{4}{3}\pi r^3 =$ .... cm^3.

Result

The volume of given metal bob

(i) by the method of displacement of water, $V =$ .... cm^3.

(ii) by measuring the radius of the bob using Vernier callipers, $V' =$ .... cm^3.

From above result, it is evident that

(i) volume of bob measured by the method of displacement is correct upto 1 cm^3 while

(ii) volume of the bob calculated by measuring the radius of the bob with the help of Vernier callipers is correct upto 0.01 cm^3, since the least count of Vernier callipers is 0.01 cm.

Hence, measuring the volume of bob using Vernier callipers is more accurate.

Precautions

1. The thread should be thin, so that its volume will be negligible.
2. The bob should be completely immersed into water.
3. Lower the metal bob gently in the measuring cylinder.
4. Eye should be kept at the lowest point of the concave meniscus of water while taking reading of water level in the measuring cylinder.
5. The metal bob should be tightly placed in between the jaws of vernier callipers.

Viva-Voce

Q 1. What do you mean by volume of the metal bob?

Ans. The space occupied by the metal bob is called its volume.

Q 2. Which formula gives the volume of spherical body?

Ans. The volume of spherical body is given by the formula,

$V = \frac{4}{3}\pi r^3$, where r is radius of spherical body.

Q 3. How can you calculate least count of Vernier callipers easily?

Ans. Least count

$$= \frac{\text{Value of one main scale division}}{\text{Total number of divisions on Vernier scale}}$$

Q 4. What are the two methods to measure volume of the given body?

Ans. There are two methods to measure volume of the given body

(i) By the method of displacement of water : When a body is immersed completely in water, it displaces water equal to its own volume.

(ii) By measuring diameter of the given body with the help of Vernier callipers :

In this way, the volume of spherical body is

$$V = \frac{4}{3}\pi r^3 \text{ or } \frac{1}{6}\pi d^3$$

where, r is the radius and d is the diameter of the given spherical body which can be measured with the help of Vernier callipers.

Q 5. Write SI unit of volume.

Ans. SI unit of volume is m^3.

Q 6. To what degree of accuracy can you measure the volume of metal bob by using Vernier callipers to find its diameter?

Ans. To an accuracy of 0.01 cm^3, because using Vernier callipers, the diameter of bob will be measured upto an accuracy of 0.01 cm i.e., equal to least count of Vernier callipers.

Q 7. What is displacement method? Write its one use.

Ans. When a body is immersed completely in water, it displaces an amount of water equal to its own volume. This is called displacement method.

This method is used to measure the volume of a body.

Experiment 5

Aim

Obtain five sets of readings of the time taken for 20 oscillations of a simple pendulum of lengths about 70, 80, 90, 100 and 110 cm; calculate the time periods (T) and their squares (T^2) for each length (l). Plot a graph of L *versus* T^2. Draw the best fit straight line graph. Also, obtain its slope. Calculate the value of g in the laboratory. It is $4\pi^2$ x slope.

Apparatus Required

A metallic bob with hook, fine thread (1.5 m), a laboratory iron stand, a split cork, a stopwatch, a meter scale, a geometry box, a piece of chalk and a pencil.

Theory

Simple pendulum has heavy point mass suspended from a rigid support by means of an inextensible and massless string.

In practical, simple pendulum has a heavy brass bob with hook suspended with the help of a thin strong cotton thread.

Effective length of a simple pendulum is the distance between point of suspension and centre of gravity of the given metallic (brass) bob and it is denoted by L.

To obtain effective length (L) of a simple pendulum by

$$L = l + h + r$$

where, l = length of the thread, h = length of the hook and r = radius of the metallic bob.

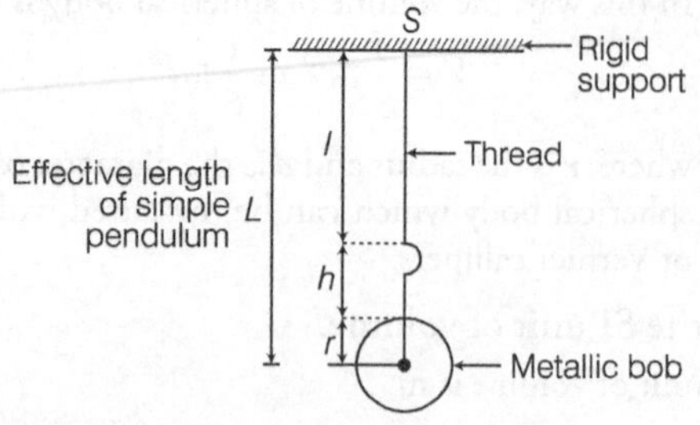

Effective length of a simple pendulum

The motion of the metallic bob from one extreme position to the other and back to the first extreme position is called one oscillation as shown in figure, the motion of the bob from A to B and back to A is one oscillation.

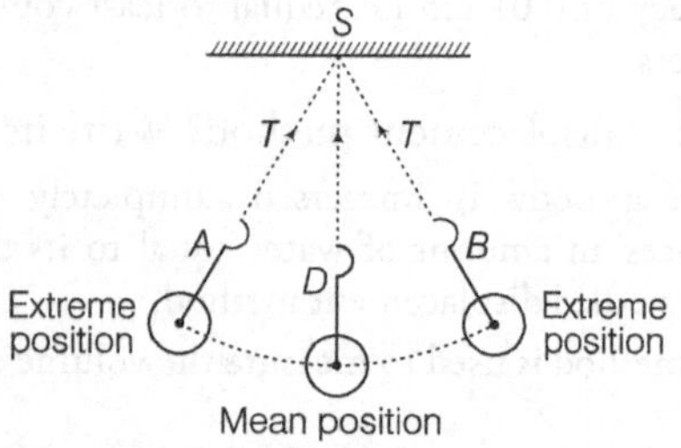

Oscillation of a simple pendulum

Amplitude

The maximum displacement of the bob from its mean position to its extreme position is called **amplitude** of a simple pendulum.

Frequency

The number of oscillations completed by a simple pendulum in one second is called **frequency** and it is denoted by ν. Its SI unit is hertz (Hz).

Time Period

The time taken by the pendulum to complete one oscillation is called its **time period** and it is denoted by T. SI unit of time period is second.

For oscillations of small amplitude, time period of a simple pendulum is given by

$$T = 2\pi\sqrt{\frac{L}{g}}$$

where, L is effective length of the pendulum and g is the acceleration due to gravity.

Measurement of Time Period (T) and their Squares (T^2) for Different Lengths (L) of the Simple Pendulum

Procedure

1. Take a fine cotton thread about 150 cm long and tie its one end with the hook of the bob.
2. Put ink mark on the thread at a distance of 70 cm, 80 cm, 90 cm, 100 cm and 110 cm from the centre of the bob including length of the hook.
3. Take a split cork and pass the thread through the split parts of the cork and fix it firmly in the clamp of iron stand in such a way that lower surface of two half pieces of cork appears as single plane surface. Therefore, the bob hangs freely on the thread.
4. Now, slightly loose the cork, then pull the thread from the upper end slowly to adjust its length upto the first ink mark i.e., 110 cm length of the thread hangs below the surface of the cork. Fix the split cork again as explained in step 3.
5. Place the iron stand near the edge of the table and adjust the position of clamp on the vertical iron, so that the thread hangs in front of the edge of table vertically and the bob is about 2 cm above the ground. Take a piece of chalk and mark cross (×) on the floor which is just below the bob.
6. Take a stopwatch and bring its hands at zero position, then find its least count and record it.
7. Draw a line AB (= 10 cm) with the piece of chalk on the laboratory floor which is parallel to the edge of the table and displace the bob about 3-5 cm along line AB on either side of the cross (×) mark and release it. Now, the pendulum begins to oscillate from A to B and then from B to A. It should be ensured that the pendulum oscillates along the straight line only and not along the circular path.
8. Note the time for 20 oscillations. Take two more observations for the same length to get mean of these observations.
9. Now, change the length to 100 cm by loosening the split cork in clamp and pulling the thread until the next ink mark (i.e., 100 cm) on the thread is reached. Adjust the position of clamp, then tighten it, so that the bob is again about 2 cm above the floor.
10. Similarly, note the time for 20 oscillations which can be found at lengths 90 cm, 80 cm and 70 cm by repeating the steps 8 and 9. Record all observations for different lengths of the thread in a table.
11. Divide the mean time obtained for 20 oscillations by 20 to get time period (T).

Observations

Table : Time Period of the Simple Pendulum for 20 Oscillations

S.No.	Length of the thread with hook $(l+h)$ (in cm)	Effective length, $L=l+h+r$ (in cm)	t_1 (s)	t_2 (s)	t_3(s)	Mean, $t=\frac{t_1+t_2+t_3}{3}$ (in s)	Time period, Observed value of T (in s)	T^2 (in s^2)
1.								
2.								
3.								
4.								
5.								
6.								

Graph of L versus T^2

Plot the graph L *versus* T^2 taking L along Y-axis and T^2 along X-axis.

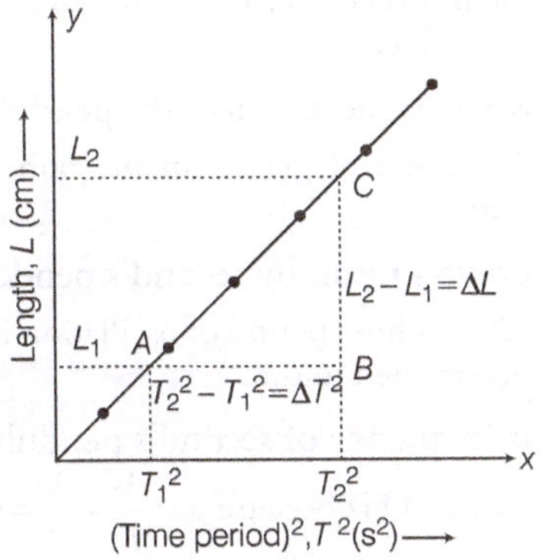

Graph L versus T^2

Calculations

From L-T^2 graph,

$$\text{Slope} = \frac{L_2 - L_1}{T_2^2 - T_1^2} = \frac{BC}{AB} = \ldots\ldots \text{ cm/s}^2$$

The acceleration due to gravity is given by

$$g = 4\pi^2 \times \frac{L}{T^2} = 4\pi^2 \times \frac{BC}{AB}$$

Clearly, $g = 4\pi^2 \times \text{slope} = \ldots\ldots\ldots \text{ cm/s}^2 = \ldots\ldots \text{ m/s}^2$

Result

1. The graph plotted L *versus* T^2 of the simple pendulum is a straight line showing that $T^2 \propto L$.
2. The acceleration due to gravity, $g = 4\pi^2 \times$ slope $= \ldots\ldots\ldots \text{ m/s}^2$.

Precautions

1. The iron stand with long rod and heavy base should be used while doing experiment.
2. Switch OFF the fans while taking observation of the simple pendulum experiment and the laboratory room should be free from air currents.
3. The bob should be displaced gently, so that it may oscillate in a straight line rather than in any conical or spin motion.
4. The oscillations should be of small amplitude (not more than 4 cm).
5. Lower face of the split cork should remain plane.
6. The effective length of the pendulum should be taken from the lower face of the split cork to the centre of the bob.
7. Start counting oscillations by saying zero and stopping the watch at proper position of the bob.

Viva-Voce

Q 1. What do you mean by simple pendulum?

Ans. A heavy metal bob suspended with weightless, flexible and inextensible string from a support is called simple pendulum.

Q 2. What is the value of g at the centre of the Earth?

Ans. Zero

Q 3. Where is the value of g greater, at equator or poles?

Ans. At the poles because the Earth is slightly compressed at poles.

Q 4. What is the approximate value of g at sea level?

Ans. $g = 9.8 \text{ m/s}^2$

Q 5. What is the reason that the amplitude of the simple pendulum is kept small (not more than 4 cm)?

Ans. If the amplitude is large than motion of the simple pendulum will not be simple harmonic and hence $T \neq 2\pi\sqrt{\frac{L}{g}}$

Q 6. Define the following terms.

(i) Amplitude

(ii) Oscillation

(iii) Frequency

(iv) Time period

Ans. (i) **Amplitude** The maximum displacement moved by the pendulum on either side from its mean position.

(ii) **Oscillation** The motion of the pendulum from one extreme position to the other and then back to the original one.

(iii) **Frequency** Frequency of oscillations is defined as the number of oscillations made by pendulum in one second.

(iv) **Time period** Time taken by the pendulum for one complete oscillation is called time period of oscillation.

Q 7. What are the units of frequency?

Ans. Oscillation/second, cycle/sec (cps) or hertz (Hz) are the units of frequency.

Q 8. Give the relation between time period, effective length of a pendulum and acceleration due to gravity.

Ans. Time period is directly proportional to the square root of effective length of a pendulum and inversely proportional to the square root of acceleration due to gravity.

i.e., $$T = 2\pi\sqrt{\frac{L}{g}}$$

Q 9. Can you replace the thread by a rubber band in a simple pendulum experiment?

Ans. No, because it is not inextensible by definition.

Q 10. Can you use a cricket ball in place of the bob?

Ans. No, by definition of simple pendulum the bob must be as small as possible.

Q 11. From where is the length of the pendulum measured?

Ans. From the centre of gravity of the bob to the point of suspension.

Q 12. What do you mean by second's pendulum?

Ans. A pendulum whose period of oscillation is two seconds is called seconds pendulum.

Q 13. What is frequency of second's pendulum?

Ans. 0.5 Hz or (1/2) Hz because $\nu = \frac{1}{T} = \frac{1}{2} = 0.5$ Hz

(as, $T = 2$ s for a second's pendulum)

Experiment 6

Aim

Take a beaker of water. Place it on the wire gauge on a tripod stand. Suspend two thermometers, one with Celsius and the other with Fahrenheit scale. Record the thermometer readings at 5 to 7 different temperatures.

You may start with ice-cold water then allow it to warm up and then heat it slowly taking temperature (at regular intervals) as high as possible. Plot a graph of T_F *versus* T_C. Obtain the slope. Compare with the theoretical value. Read the intercept on T_F axis for $T_C = 0$.

Apparatus Required

A beaker, a stirrer, one Celsius thermometer, one Fahrenheit thermometer, one vertical stand, a burner, a wire gauge, tripod stand and a stopwatch/clock.

Theory

Celsius Scale In Celsius thermometer, the melting point of ice is marked as 0°C and boiling point of water as 100°C. The interval between 0°C and 100°C is divided into 100 equal divisions, on which one division is representing 1°C.

Fahrenheit Scale In Fahrenheit thermometer, the melting point of ice is marked as 32°F and boiling point of water as 212°F.

The interval between 32°F and 212°F is divided into 180 equal division on which one division is representing 1°F.

Relation Between Celsius Scale and Fahrenheit Scale

The relation between the two scales can be obtained by taking the ratio of number of divisions on both the scales i.e.,

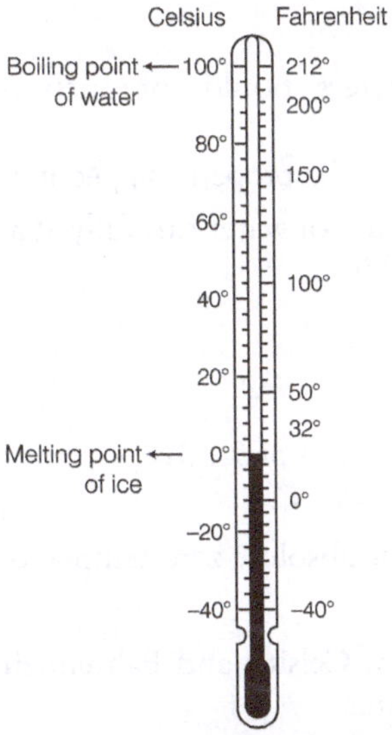

Comparison of Celsius and Fahrenheit scales

$$(T_C - 0)°\,C : (T_F - 32)°\,F :: 100 : 180$$

or $$\frac{T_C - 0}{100} = \frac{T_F - 32}{180}$$

or $$T_F = 1.8\,T_C + 32$$

where, T_C and T_F represent the temperature on Celsius and Fahrenheit scales, respectively.

Procedure

1. Take two thermometers in which one is Celsius scale and other is Fahrenheit scale and record their least counts.
2. Take a beaker and fill sufficient quantity of ice-cold water.
3. Mount these two Celsius thermometer and Fahrenheit thermometer on wooden stand separately and dip them into water beaker as shown in figure. Record the temperature of water with both the thermometers.

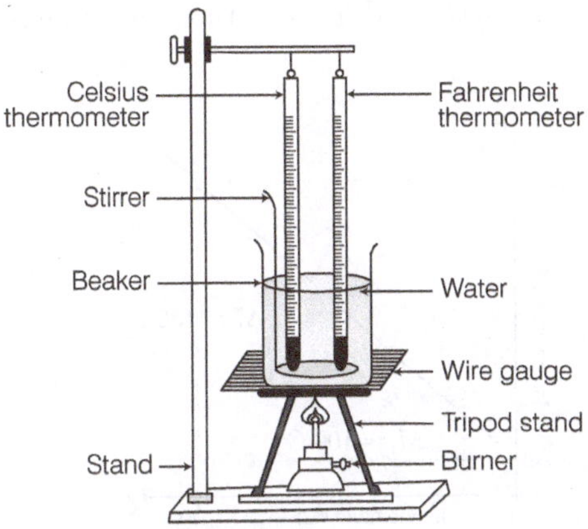

4. Allow the ice-cold water to warm up and reach room temperature, now record the temperature.
5. Now, switch ON burner to start heating of water contained in beaker slowly.
6. Stir the water with the help of stirrer to heat the water uniformly and record the temperature after regular intervals of time.
7. Take 5 to 7 observations.

Observation

Least count of Celsius thermometer = ... °C.

Least count of Fahrenheit thermometer = ... °F.

Table: Readings of Celsius and Fahrenheit thermometers

S.No.	Time (in minutes)	Reading in Celsius thermometer, T_C (in °C)	Reading in Fahrenheit thermometer, T_F (in °F)
1.			
2.			
3.			
4.			
5.			
6.			

Graph of T_F *versus* T_C

Plot a graph for Celsius thermometer reading T_C *versus* Fahrenheit thermometer reading T_F.

Take T_C on X-axis and T_F on Y-axis as shown in figure.

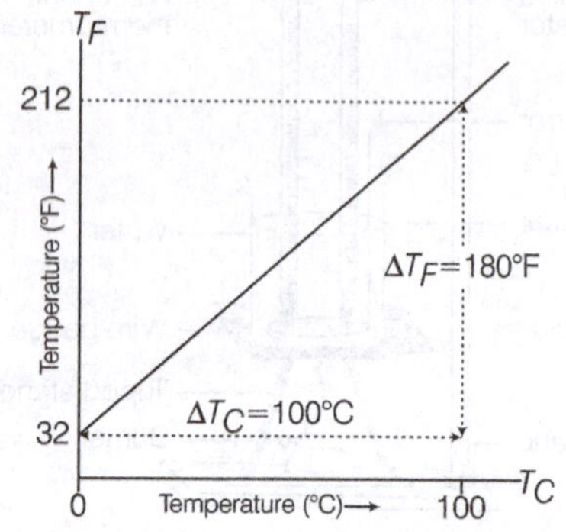

Calculations

Record the value of T_F from the graph when T_C = 0°C. From the $T_F - T_C$ graph, Slope $(= \tan\theta) = \dfrac{\Delta T_F}{\Delta T_C}$ = ...

Result

The value of T_F from the graph when, T_C = 0° C = ...
Theoretically, when T_C = 0° C, T_F = 32°F,
which is exactly same as the calculated value.

Precautions

1. The two thermometers should not touch the base and walls of the beakers.
2. Thermometers should be properly dipped in water.
3. Read the temperature of water carefully at a certain intervals of time and record it.

Viva-Voce

Q 1. How temperature on Celsius scale is related to the temperature on Fahrenheit scale?

Ans. Let T_C and T_F represent the temperature on Celsius and Fahrenheit scales, respectively. Their relation will be

$$T_F = 1.8 T_C + 32$$

Q 2. How many divisions are made between melting point of ice and boiling point of water in a Celsius thermometer?

Ans. There are 100 divisions in a Celsius thermometer between melting point of ice and boiling point of water.

Q 3. At what temperature is Fahrenheit scale equal to Celsius scale?

Ans. At – 40° i.e., –40°C = – 40°F

Q 4. What is the freezing temperature of water?

Ans. The freezing temperature of water is 0°C or 32°F.

Q 5. The boiling point of water is 100°C or 212°F. Is this statement True/False?

Ans. True.

Q 6. The normal human temperature is 36.9°C. What will be this temperature on Fahrenheit scale?

Ans. As we know the relation, $T_F = 1.8\, T_C + 32$

Putting T_C = 36.9°C, we have

$$T_F = 1.8 \times 36.9 + 32$$
$$= 98.42°\text{F}$$

Q 7. What is the absolute zero temperature?

Ans. 0 kelvin

Q 8. Are Kelvin, Celsius and Fahrenheit all measures of temperature?

Ans. Yes

Q 9. Which liquid is used inside the thermometer?

Ans. Mercury

Q 10. What are the properties of thermometric liquid?

Ans. (i) It should not stick to the walls of the glass tube.

(ii) It should have low melting point and high boiling point, so that thermometer can be used for wide range of temperature measurement.

(iii) It should be highly conducting, so that it quickly attains the temperature of the body in contact.

Q 11. Write down the unit of absolute temperature.

Ans. The unit of absolute temperature is kelvin.

Q 12. Define absolute zero temperature.

Ans. The temperature at which molecular motion ceases and average kinetic energy of the molecules becomes zero is called absolute zero temperature.

Experiment 7

Aim

Using a plane mirror strip mounted vertically on a board, obtain the reflected rays for three rays incident at different angles. Measure the angles of incidence and angles of reflection. See if these angles are equal.

Apparatus Required

A plane mirror strip with holder to support the mirror vertically, a white drawing sheet, four thumb pins, awl pins, a pencil, a protractor, a scale (15 cm) and a drawing board (soft wooden).

Theory

When a ray of light falls on a plane mirror obliquely, after striking the mirror, it reflects back into the same medium such that angle of incidence = angle of reflection.

or $\angle i = \angle r$

Procedure

1. Fix the drawing sheet on the drawing board with the help of thumb pins.
2. Draw a horizontal line on drawing sheet say *MN* and in the middle of line *MN* mark point O. From point O, draw a perpendicular line *OP* as shown in figure.

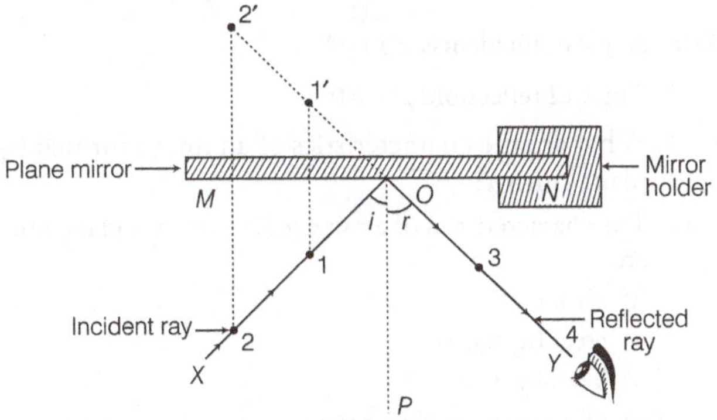

Reflection through a plane mirror

3. Draw a line *OX* at an angle say $\angle XOP = 30°$. Now, place the mirror strip on the line *MN* with the help of mirror holder in such a way that the mirror is held vertically with its polished surface on the line *MN* as shown in figure above.
4. Fix two awl pins vertically (1) and (2) on the line *OX* at separation of about 4 cm, so that the images of two awl pins (1) and (2) are observed as (1′) and (2′).
5. Now, fix two more awl pins (3) and (4) vertically on the line *OY* such that its images appear in a straight line with awl pins (1′) and (2′). Remove the mirror and the awl pins and encircle all the pin prick marks on the sheet with the help of a pencil.
6. Draw a line joining the points (3) and (4) which meets at point O on the line *MN*.
7. Now, the line *XO* is the incident ray and the line *OY* is the reflected ray and $\angle XOP (= 30°)$ is angle of incidence and $\angle YOP$ is the angle of reflection.
8. Take a protractor and measure the angle $\angle YOP$.
9. Take three more observations by changing the angle of incidence $\angle XOP$ = (40°, 50° and 60°).

Observations

Least count of meter scale = ... cm.

Least count of protractor = ... degree.

S.No.	Angle of incidence, $\angle i$ (in degree)	Angle of reflection, $\angle r$ (in degree)
1.	30	
2.	40	
3.	50	
4.	60	

Result

From the observation table, it is evident that angle of incidence = angle of reflection or $\angle i = \angle r$ in each observation, within the limits of experimental error.

Precautions

1. Sharp and pointed awl pins should be used.
2. Keep the awl pins in vertical position such that their tips must lie in a straight line.
3. The plane mirror should be kept fixed during all observations of the experiment.
4. Use sharp pencil to draw a thin line.
5. Measure the angles accurately with the help of protractor.

Viva-Voce

Q 1. State the laws of reflection of light.

Ans. There are two laws of reflection of light

(i) The incident ray, the reflected ray and the normal at the point of incidence all lie in the same plane.

(ii) Angle of incidence is equal to angle of reflection i.e., $\angle i = \angle r$

Q 2. What do you understand by the following terms

(i) Incident ray

(ii) Normal

(iii) Angle of incidence

(iv) Angle of reflection?

Ans. (i) **Incident Ray** A ray of light which falls on the mirror is called an incident ray.

(ii) **Normal** The line drawn perpendicular to the surface of mirror at the point of incidence is called normal.

(iii) **Angle of Incidence** The angle made by the incident ray with the normal is called angle of incidence.

(iv) **Angle of Reflection** The angle between the reflected ray and the normal is called the angle of reflection.

Q 3. How can you make a plane mirror with glass piece?

Ans. When a plane glass piece is silvered on one of its face, then it behaves like a mirror.

Q 4. What will be the direction of reflected ray when a ray of light falls normally on the surface of plane mirror?

Ans. When a ray of light falls normally (i.e., at 90°) to the mirror surface, it reflects back following the same path.

Q 5. When an object is placed in front of a plane mirror, then where is its image formed?

Ans. A virtual image is formed behind the plane mirror and it is as far behind the mirror as the object is in front of the mirror.

Q 6. What are the different types of reflection?

Ans. There are two types of reflection

(i) Regular reflection and

(ii) Irregular or diffused reflection.

Q 7. What type of reflection takes place in a plane mirror?

Ans. Regular reflection

Q 8. Why does a plane mirror cause regular reflection?

Ans. A plane mirror causes regular reflection due to its smooth polished surface.

Q 9. Name any one device based upon the principle of reflection of light by plane mirror.

Ans. Periscope is a device based upon the principle of reflection of light.

Q 10. If you touch your left ear, it appears as if your image has touched the right ear, while looking at your image in a plane mirror. Why?

Ans. It is due to lateral inversion. The right looks left and left looks right inside the mirror.

Q 11. Due to which phenomenon do we see the non-luminous objects?

Ans. We see the non-luminous objects due to diffused or irregular reflection of light.

Q 12. Observe the following figure and find the values of the angle of incidence and the angle of reflection.

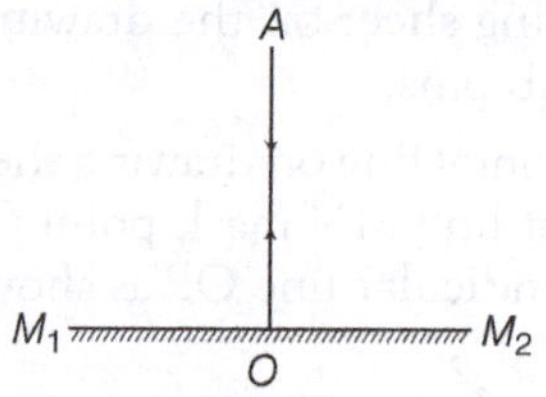

Ans. Angle of incidence, $\angle i = 0°$

Angle of reflection, $\angle r = 0°$

Q 13. What are the characteristics of an image formed by a plane mirror?

Ans. The characteristics of an image formed by a plane mirror are

(i) virtual

(ii) erect (upright)

(iii) laterally inverted

(iv) of same size as the object

(v) the image is at the same perpendicular distance behind the mirror as the object is in front of it.

Experiment 8

Aim

Place three object pins at different distances on a line perpendicular to a plane mirror fixed vertically on a board. Obtain two reflected rays (for each pin) fixing two pins in line with the image. Obtain the positions of the images in each case by extending backwards (using dashed lines), the lines representing reflected rays. Measure the object distances and image distances in the three cases. Tabulate, are they equal? Generalise the result.

Apparatus Required

A plane mirror strip, a drawing board (soft wooden), a mirror holder with vertical groove to support the plane mirror vertically, a white drawing sheet, four drawing (thumb) pins, awl pins, a pencil, a protractor and a meter scale.

Theory

When an object is placed in front of a plane mirror, then the image is formed behind the mirror at a perpendicular distance equal to the perpendicular distance at which the object is placed in front of the mirror.

Procedure

1. Take a white drawing sheet and fix it on the drawing board with the help of thumb pins.
2. Draw a line MN on the sheet and place the plane mirror strip along this line holding vertically in the groove of holder as shown in figure.

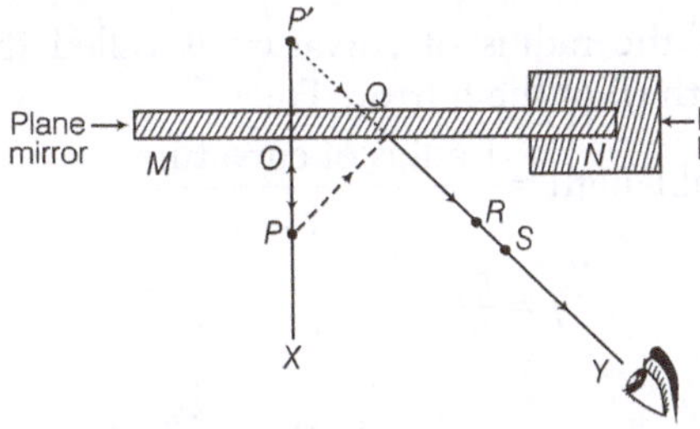

3. Draw a line OX perpendicular to the line MN.
4. Take a point P on the line OX and fix awl pin on point P in such a way that the image of pin point P appears as P′ in the mirror.
5. Now, keep the eye at position Y on the right side of line OX as shown in figure and observe the image of the pin P located behind the mirror at position P′.
6. Fix two awl pins at points R and S in such a way that the tips of these awl pins should appear to be in a straight line P′RSY as shown in figure.
7. Remove the awl pins from points P, R and S; and draw small circles around 'its pin prick', on the sheet with the help of fine pencil.
8. Now, remove the mirror and join the points R and S, then extends it upto Q on the line MN. Similarly, extend the line PO. These two lines will meet at point P′. Join P and Q also by a dotted line.
9. Take a scale and measure OP and OP′; and record it.
10. Repeat the experiment atleast three more times by changing the position of pin P.

Observations

Least count of meter scale = ... cm.

Least count of protractor = ... degree.

S.No.	Perpendicular distance of object *OP* (in cm)	Perpendicular distance of image *OP′* (in cm)
1.		
2.		
3.		
4.		

Result

It is observed that

1. $PO = OP'$ i.e., the image is formed as far behind the mirror as the object is in front of it.
2. $\angle POQ = \angle P'OQ = 90°$ i.e., the line joining the object and the image points is normal to the plane mirror.
3. Geometrically,

   ΔPOQ and $\Delta P'OQ$ are congruent

   i.e., $\Delta POQ \cong \Delta P'OQ$

   $\therefore \quad PO = OP'$, (by CPCT)

Precautions

1. All the awl pins should be placed straight, so that their tips are in a straight line.
2. It should be ensured that the mirror is not displaced from its original position during each observation.
3. Awl pins should be sharp, pointed and clean.

Viva-Voce

Q 1. Identify the incident ray in this experiment.

Ans. *PO* is an incident ray.

Q 2. If *PO* is an incident ray, then what will be its reflected ray?

Ans. Since, ray *PO* falls normally to the plane surface, so its reflected ray will follow the same path in the reverse direction i.e., *OP*.

Q 3. What type of image is formed in this experiment?

Ans. Virtual image is formed in this experiment because this image is formed when the rays reflected from the plane mirror appear to meet when they are extended backwards.

Q 4. What are the uses of plane mirror?

Ans. A plane mirror is used for

(i) looking glass (ii) making periscope

(iii) making kaleidoscope

Q 5. If a person stands at a distance of 15 cm from a plane mirror, what will be the distance between the person and his image when the mirror is moved 8 cm away from him?

Ans.

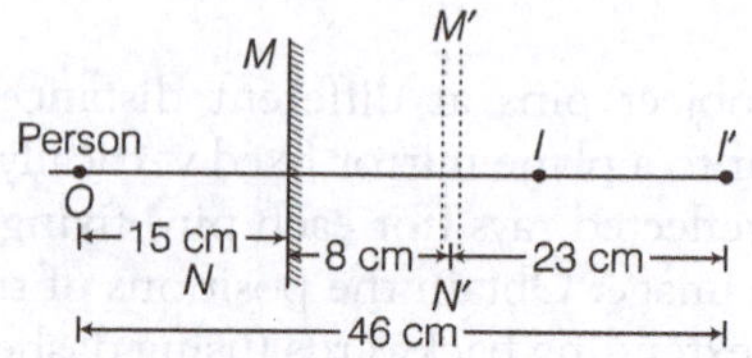

The distance between the person and his image will be 46 cm.

Q 6. State the size of image formed in a plane mirror.

Ans. The size of image formed in a plane mirror is equal to that of object.

Q 7. State the nature of image formed in a plane mirror.

Ans. The image formed in a plane mirror is virtual in nature.

Q 8. If an object is placed at a distance of 5cm from a plane mirror, how far will its image be seen?

Ans. Its image will be seen at a distance of 5 cm behind the mirror when object is placed in front of the mirror.

Experiment 9-A

Aim

Obtain the focal length of a concave mirror (a) by distant object method, focussing its real image on a screen or wall and (b) by one needle method removing parallax. Enter your observations in numbered rows.

Apparatus Required

A concave mirror, a paper sheet, an optical bench with two uprights, one needle, mirror holder and a meter scale.

Theory

(a) When object is at a far distance, image is in the focal plane of the mirror. It is real, inverted and highly diminished.

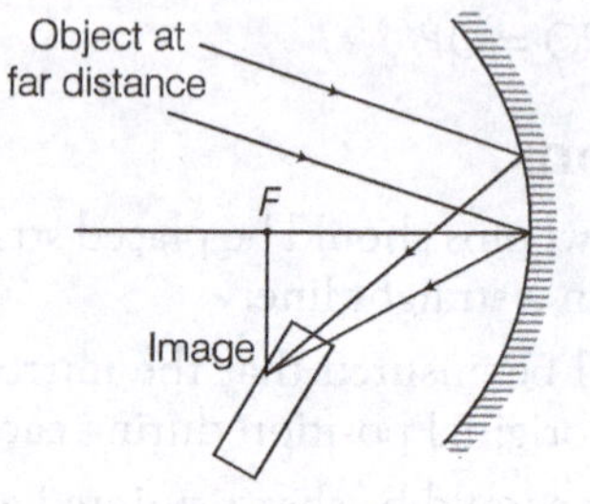

(b) If an object is placed at the centre of curvature (C) of a concave mirror, then its real and inverted image is formed at the centre of curvature (C). This image is formed of same size as that of object. The distance between the centre of curvature and pole of a concave mirror is called radius of curvature (*R*).

Half the radius of curvature is called the focal length (*f*) of the mirror. Thus,

$$\text{Focal length} = \frac{\text{Radius of curvature}}{2}$$

or $$f = \frac{R}{2}$$

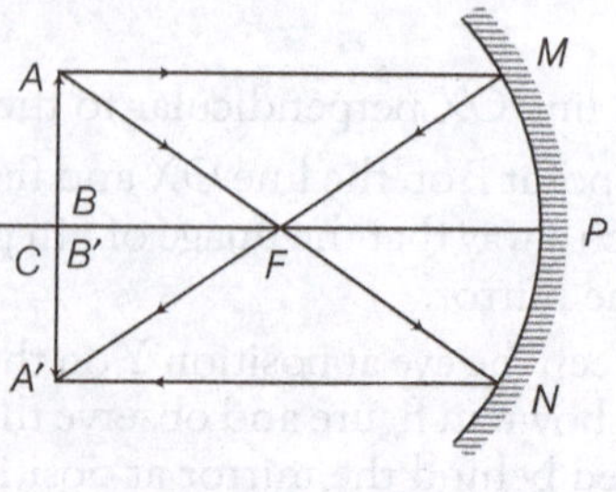

A. Distant object Method

Procedure

1. Take a concave mirror and hold it in your hand.
2. Direct the concave mirror towards a distant object (a tree/ a window / a tall building, etc.) visible through the window of the laboratory from, where sun light enters.
3. Take a sheet of paper in front of concave mirror and adjust the mirror in such a way that a clear and sharp image of a distant object is formed on the sheet of paper.
4. Take a meter scale and measure the distance between the paper sheet and the concave mirror. This is the approximate focal length of the concave mirror.

B. One Needle Method

Procedure

1. Place two uprights on the optical bench, one holding the concave mirror and the other holding optical needle. Place the mirror upright on zero end of optical bench.
2. Take an optical needle called it object needle and mount it in the second upright. Bring this upright in front of mirror upright such that tip of the needle remains at the centre of mirror and its inverted image is seen in the mirror as shown in figure.

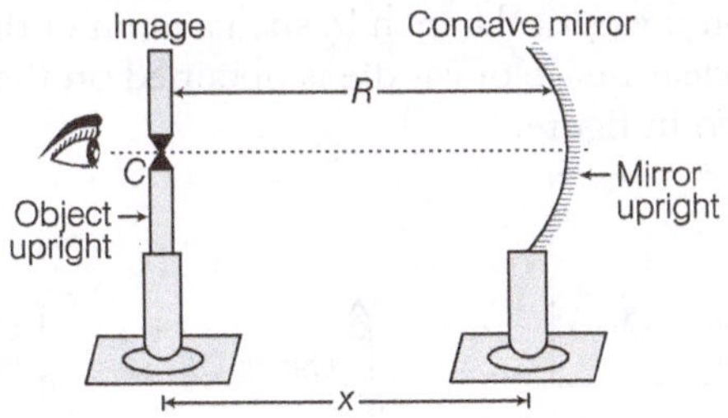

3. Move the object needle near concave mirror to and fro in such a manner that tips of object needle and image needle coincide with each other.
4. Measure the distance between the mirror and the needle and record it. This distance is equal to the radius of curvature (R) of given concave mirror and half of this distance is called focal length of given concave mirror.
5. Take two more observations to find mean focal length of given concave mirror.

Observations

Least count of given meter scale .... cm.

S. NO.	Position of pin from the mirror, x (in cm)	Focal length, $f = \frac{R}{2} = \frac{x}{2}$ (in cm)
1.		
2.		
3.		

Result

The focal length of given concave mirror by

(a) the distant object method = ... cm and

(b) one needle method = ... cm.

Precautions

1. The needle should be sharp and thin.
2. The uprights must be vertical.
3. Keep the tip of needle and centre of concave mirror at the same height.
4. Clean the mirror with cotton cloth before taking observations.

Viva-Voce

Q 1. What is relation between focal length and radius of curvature of a concave mirror?

Ans. Focal length of a concave mirror is equal to half of its radius of curvature.

i.e., $$f = \frac{R}{2}$$

Q 2. Define principal axis.

Ans. Principal axis of a concave mirror (or spherical mirror) is the straight line joining the pole of the mirror to its centre of curvature.

Q 3. What do you understand by focus of a concave mirror?

Ans. The focus of a concave mirror is a point on the principal axis at which the light rays incident on the mirror parallel to the principal axis meet after reflection from the mirror.

Q 4. How will you measure the focal length of a concave mirror?

Ans. Focal length of a concave mirror is measured by calculating distance between pole and focus of the mirror.

Q 5. What do you mean by parallax?

Ans. Parallax is a difference in the apparent position of an object viewed along two different line of sight.

Q 6. What is real image?

Ans. Real image is formed due to actual intersection of reflected rays and it can be obtained on the screen.

Q 7. What is centre of curvature of a concave mirror?

Ans. The centre of sphere of which the concave mirror is a part, is called its centre of curvature.

Q 8. What is pole of a mirror?

Ans. Centre of the mirror is called its pole.

Q 9. Distinguish between real and virtual image.

Ans.

Real Image	Virtual Image
It is formed due to actual intersection of the reflected rays.	It is formed when reflected rays appear to meet.
It is always inverted.	It is always erect.
It can be obtained on the screen.	It cannot be obtained on the screen.

Experiment 9-B

Aim

To determine the focal length of a concave mirror by focussing the image of the illuminated wire gauge attached to a ray box. It could also improvise with a candle and a screen. Enter your observations in numbered rows.

Apparatus Required

An optical bench fitted with a meter rule, three uprights, a concave mirror, a candle, a ground glass screen and a mirror holder.

Theory

When an object is placed beyond the focus of a concave mirror, then its real and inverted image can be obtained.

The distance between the object and the mirror is called object distance and is denoted by u.

The distance between the image and the mirror is called image distance and it is denoted by v. With the help of optical bench fitted with meter rule, we can measure u and v; and then focal length (f) of a concave mirror is obtained by the relation.

$$\frac{1}{f} = \frac{1}{v} + \frac{1}{u} \quad \text{or} \quad f = \frac{uv}{u+v}$$

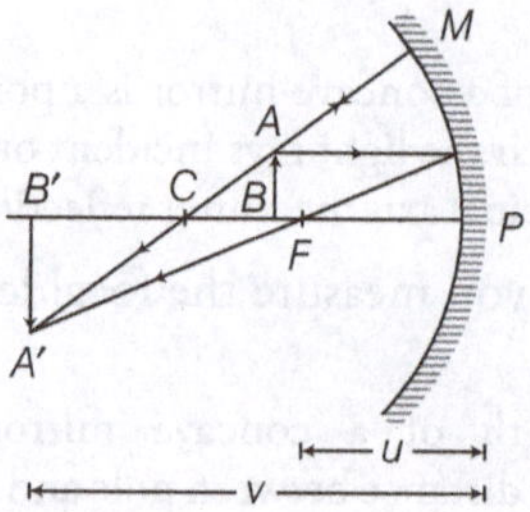

Procedure

1. Place three uprights on the optical bench, holding the concave mirror, the screen and candle.
2. Place a screen mounted on upright at point X and concave mirror mounted on upright at point Y on the optical bench.
3. Mount the candle on the upright and place it in between the screen and concave mirror such that the top of the candle should be at the level of the pole of mirror.
4. The screen should also be adjusted by moving to and fro on the optical bench in such a manner that a sharp and clear image of candle is obtained on the screen as shown in figure.

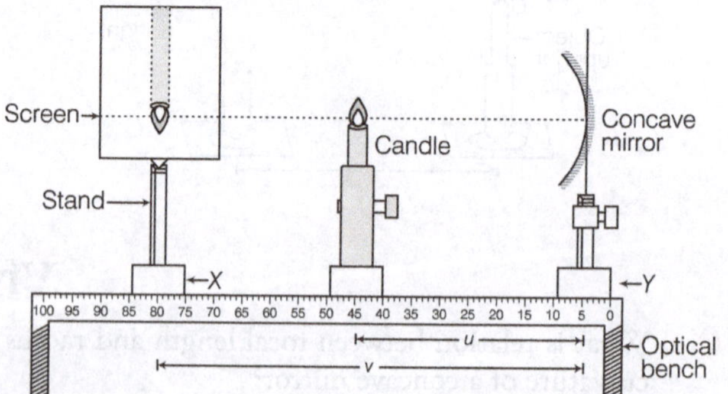

5. Measure the distance between candle and the mirror (say it u cm) and the distance between the screen and the mirror (say it v cm).
6. In this way, take atleast five observations by changing the position of the candle, the screen and the mirror.

Observations

Least count of given meter rule = ... cm.

S.No.	Position of the candle from the mirror, u (in cm)	screen from the mirror, v (in cm)	$f = \frac{uv}{u+v}$ (in cm)
1.			
2.			
3.			
4.			
5.			
			Mean focal length = ... cm

Calculations

By using the formula, $\frac{1}{f} = \frac{1}{v} + \frac{1}{u}$ or $f = \frac{uv}{u+v}$ cm

For each set of observation, the focal length of concave mirror is obtained using this formula. Mean value of f gives more accurate focal length of concave mirror.

Result

The focal length of concave mirror = ... cm.

Precautions

1. A clear and distinct image of candle should be obtained on the screen while taking observations.
2. The pole of mirror, the screen and the flame of burning candle should be kept at the same height in a straight line.
3. While changing the position of candle, the candle stand should be moved slowly on the optical bench.

Viva-Voce

Q 1. What do you understand by a mirror?

Ans. Mirror is a fine polished surface which reflects most of the light rays that are incident on it.

Q 2. Why should a mirror be silvered at the back surface?

Ans. To helps the light rays in reflection, it is needful to be silvered at its back surface.

Q 3. Name materials used for silvering the back surface of a mirror.

Ans. In cheap mirrors, silvering is done by deposition of mercuric oxide.

In good quality of mirrors, silvering is done by deposition of silver nitrate.

Q 4. Define the focal length of a concave mirror.

Ans. The distance between the pole of the concave mirror and its principal focus is called its focal length.

Q 5. What is the focal length of a plane mirror?

Ans. Infinite.

Q 6. Is the mirror formula $\frac{1}{v} + \frac{1}{u} = \frac{1}{f}$ applicable for a plane mirror? Explain.

Ans. Yes, it is applicable.

For a plane mirror, $f = \infty$ and $\frac{1}{f} = 0$.

Mirror formula becomes, $\frac{1}{v} + \frac{1}{u} = 0$

or $\frac{1}{u} = -\frac{1}{v}$ or $v = -u$

Positive sign of v indicates that the image is virtual and is behind the mirror as that of the object in front of it.

Q 7. What kind of mirror is used in a car to view the traffic behind it?

Ans. Convex mirror is used in a car to get wide field of view of the traffic behind it.

Q 8. Why a concave mirror is used as shaving glass?

Ans. It is because when a concave mirror is held near the face i.e., face lies between its pole and focus, an erect and enlarged image of the object (face) is formed. An enlarged image of the face helps in having better shave.

Q 9. Is the focal length of a mirror changed due to (i) change in medium or (ii) colour of light?

Ans. No, since focal length of a mirror does not depend upon the external medium and the wavelength of light.

Q 10. Name the types of mirror that you know.

Ans. There are three types of mirror. These are

(i) Plane mirror (ii) Concave mirror

(iii) Convex mirror

Q 11. Is it possible to obtain a virtual image on the screen?

Ans. No, it cannot be obtained on the screen.

Q 12. What will happen to an image of an object when it is placed at infinity in front of a concave mirror?

Ans. When object is at infinity, then its image will be formed at focus.

Experiment 10

Aim

Connect a suitable DC source (two dry cells or an acid cell), a key and a bulb (may be a small one used in torches) in series. Close the circuit by inserting the plug in the key. Observe the bulb as it lights up. Now, open the circuit, connect another identical bulb in between the first bulb and the cell, so that the two bulbs are in series. Close the key. Observe the lighted bulbs. How does the light from any one bulb compare with that in the first case when you had only one bulb? Disconnect the second bulb. Reconnect the circuit as in the first experiment. Now, connect the second bulb across the first bulb. The two bulbs are connected in parallel. Observe the brightness of any one bulb. Compare with previous results. Draw your own conclusions regarding the current and resistance in the three cases.

Apparatus Required

Two small torch bulbs, two bulb holders, four dry cells of 1.5V each, cell holder, connecting wires, a one way key and a piece of sand paper.

Theory

Series Combination of Resistances In this combination, the resistances are joined end to end. The total resistance of the circuit becomes equal to the sum of resistances which are connected in series. The resultant resistance of the circuit is greater than their individual resistances.

Thus, in series combination, $R_S = R_1 + R_2$

where, R_S is total resistance of the circuit in series combinations.

The current flow in the circuit remains the same.

Parallel Combination of Resistances In this combination, the current flows in more than one path (two path in present case) in the circuit. The value of total resistance of the circuit becomes less than the value of individual resistance connected in the circuit. The current flow will be different in each path, if the resistances are different.

In parallel combination, $\frac{1}{R_P} = \frac{1}{R_1} + \frac{1}{R_2}$

where, R_P is total resistance in this combination.

Procedure

1. Connect all the four cells in series i.e., negative terminal of the first cell with the positive terminal of second cell and the negative terminal of second cell to the positive terminal of third and so on as shown in figure.

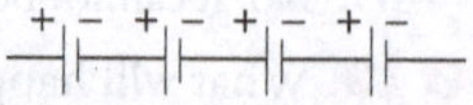

2. After connection of cells, connect a bulb B_1 and a one way key in series with the cells as shown in figure.

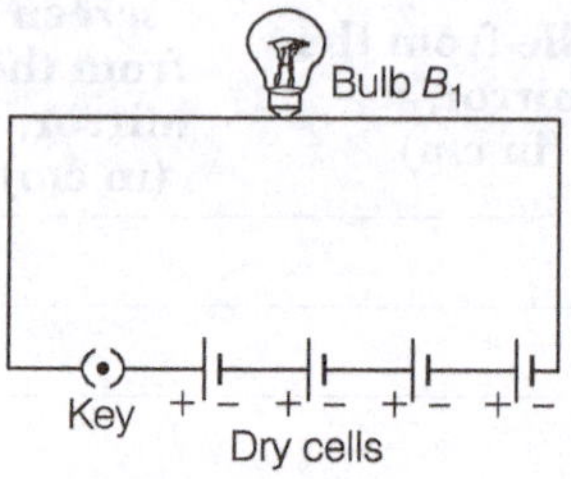

3. Close the key by inserting plug into the key. Now, current begins to flow in the circuit and observe the brightness of bulb B_1.
4. Replace the first bulb B_1 with the second bulb B_2 in the circuit and observe the brightness of the bulb B_2 as shown in figure.

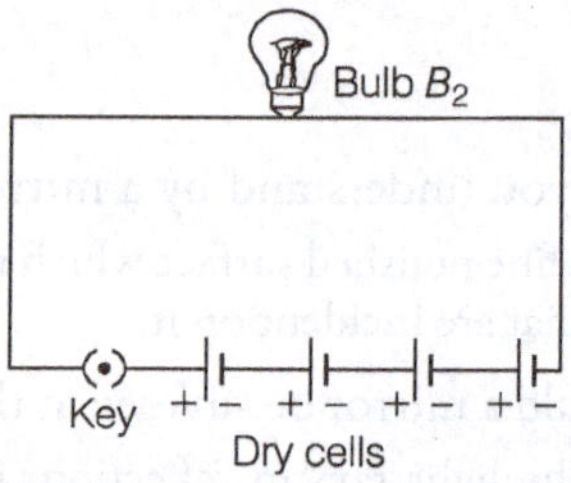

5. Now, connect the bulbs B_1 and B_2 in series and observe their brightness as shown in figure.

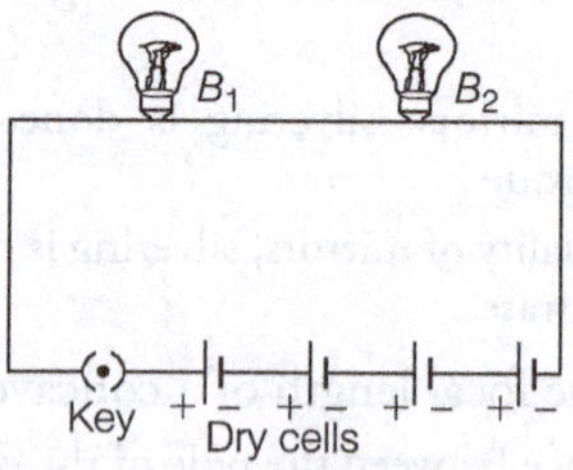

Series combination

6. Now, disconnect the bulbs B_1 and B_2; and reconnect the bulbs in parallel combination as shown in figure given below.

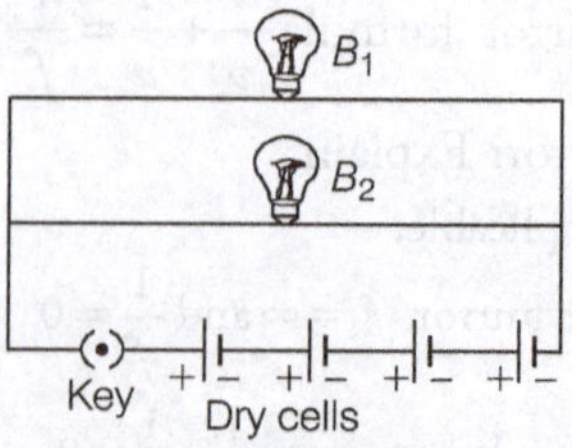

Parallel combination

7. Observe the brightness of bulbs in parallel combination and record in a table.

Observations

S.No.	Bulb (s) in the circuit	Glow of the bulb
1.	B_1	Bright
2.	B_2	Bright
3.	B_1 and B_2 in series connection	Brightness decreases
4.	B_1 and B_2 in parallel connection	Same brightness as of single bulb B_1 or B_2

Result

1. If two or more bulbs are connected in a circuit with a source of emf (electromotive force), then each bulb glows with same brightness due to same current flowing through each bulb. For each identical bulb in the circuit, the resistance will also be same.
2. When two identical bulbs are connected in series, their individual resistance are added up i.e., $R_S = R_1 + R_2$ and current decreases as $i = \frac{V}{R}$ for the same emf. Due to decrease in current in the circuit, the brightness of bulbs connected in series also decreases.
3. If two identical bulbs are connected in parallel, their equivalent (total) resistance decreases as to $R_P = \frac{R_1 R_2}{R_1 + R_2}$.

   The brightness of identical bulbs will be same as was observed in their individual cases because the current divides in this connection and for the same voltage and each bulb draws current as per its specification.

Precautions

1. Plug the key for each observation separately.
2. Connection should be tight.
3. Rub the terminals of the cell and connecting wire with the help of sand paper before connecting in the circuit.

Viva-Voce

Q 1. What are the different types of connection of resistance in a circuit?

Ans. There are two types of connection in a circuit
(i) Series connection and
(ii) Parallel connection

Q 2. When two bulbs are connected in series, what will be their equivalent resistance?

Ans. Equivalent resistance will be greater than individual resistances.
The equivalent resistance will be

$$R_S = R_1 + R_2$$

Q 3. Define electric current.

Ans. The flow of charge per unit time in a circuit is called as electric current.

Q 4. Name the unit of electric current.

Ans. Ampere (A) is the unit of electric current.

Q 5. What do you mean by electric resistance?

Ans. The obstruction offered by the material of wire to the flow of current in a circuit is called an electric resistance.

Q 6. Write down the SI unit of resistance.

Ans. Ohm (Ω)

Q 7. Define potential difference.

Ans. The work done in moving a unit positive charge from one point to the other point in a circuit is called potential difference between the points.

Q 8. When the bulbs are connected in parallel, then what will be their equivalent resistance?

Ans. The equivalent resistance will be

$R_P = \frac{R_1 R_2}{R_1 + R_2}$ which is less than individual resistance of the bulb.

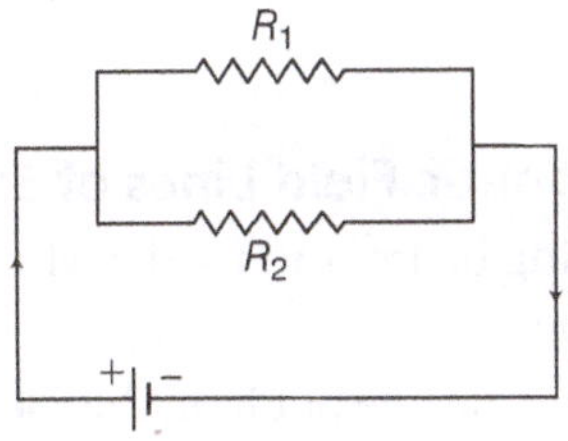

Experiment 11

Aim

Plot the magnetic field lines of Earth (without any magnet nearby) using a small compass needle. On another sheet of paper place a bar magnet with its axis parallel to the magnetic lines of the Earth i.e., along the magnetic meridian or magnetic North-South. Plot the magnetic field in the region around the magnet. Identify the regions, where the combined magnetic field of the magnet and the Earth is (a) strongest, (b) very weak but not zero and (c) zero. Why is neutral point, so called?

Apparatus Required

A magnetic compass, a bar magnet, pencil, drawing board, white drawing sheet, cellotape and eraser.

Theory

Magnetic Field It is the region around a magnet in which a compass needle rests in a particular direction or any other magnet experiences a force of attraction or repulsion.

Magnetic Field Line It is an imaginary, continuous curve which represents the direction of magnetic field at a point.

Geographical Meridian The vertical plane passing through the geographical axis of the earth is called geographical meridian.

Magnetic Meridian The vertical plane passing through the North-South line of freely suspended magnet is called magnetic meridian.

Neutral Point It is the point near the magnet, where the magnetic field due of magnet is equal and opposite to that of the horizontal component of Earth's magnetic field. The Earth has its own magnetic field. Its magnetic lines are parallel to each other. The lines are directed from geographical South to geographical North. If the magnetic field lines are closer, field at that point is strong and if they are far apart, field at that point is weaker.

Procedure

A. To Plot Magnetic Field Lines of Earth

1. Take a drawing board and fix the white sheet of paper with cellotape.
2. Take a compass needle put it on the sheet. Now, observe the direction of compass needle and mark the direction as North and South.
3. Mark the point P on the paper and place the compass such that its South point coincides with the point P.
4. Also, mark point P_1 in front of the North pole as shown in the figure.

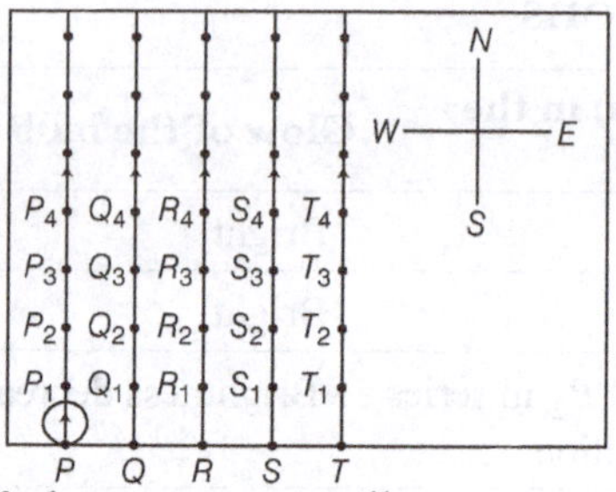

5. Now, shift the compass needle to a new position such that its South pole coincides with P_1 and mark the North pole of compass needle as P_2.
6. Repeat the above process till you reach at the North edge of the paper and join all the points with free hands.
7. Similarly, starting from a South edge of paper mark other points Q, R, S and T.
8. The parallel lines drawn by you, by joining the different points represent direction of magnetic field of the Earth.

B. To plot Magnetic Field Lines of a Bar Magnet Placed in the Magnetic Meridian with its North Pole Pointing Towards the Geographical North

1. Take a drawing board, fix a white sheet on it with cellotape.
2. Draw a line at the middle of the paper. Put the compass needle at the middle of this line.
3. Now, rotate the drawing board till the line drawn on the paper becomes parallel to the compass needle.
4. Take a bar magnet place it on the drawing board such that its North pole pointing towards geographical North as shown in the figure.

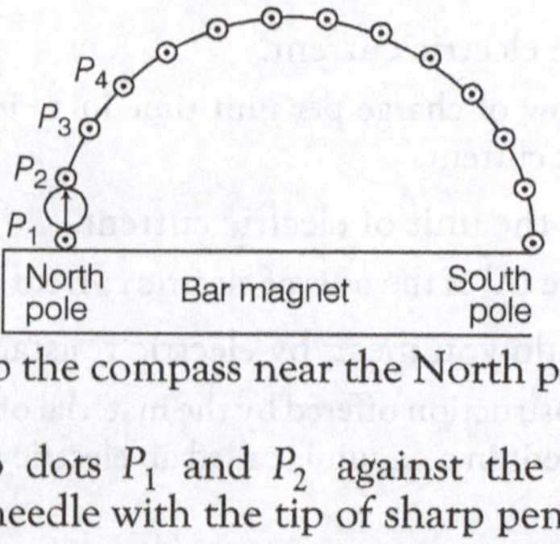

5. Now, keep the compass near the North pole of the bar magnet.
   Mark two dots P_1 and P_2 against the two ends of compass needle with the tip of sharp pencil.
6. Again, move the compass needle, so that its South end lies over point P_2 and mark point P_3 at the North end of compass needle and repeat this process till a point near the South end of the magnet is reached.

Result

1. Total volume of water in measuring cylinder,
$V\ cm^3 = ...\ cm^3$
Weight of this displaced water $= V\rho g$
$= V \times 1 \times 980$
$= 980 V$ dyne = ... dyne
2. Loss in weight of the metal ball when immersed in water $= (W - W_1)$ gf.
$= (W - W_1) \times 980$ dyne

Upthrust, $V\rho g = (W - W_1)$
= .... gf = ... dyne

Precautions

1. Check the spring balance properly.
2. Metal ball must not touch the wall of the eureka can or its bottom.
3. While taking the measurement, the eye should be placed in the line of the pointer of spring balance.

Viva-Voce

Q 1. A piece of iron sinks into water but large ship does not. Why?

Ans. In case of large ship, weight of the water displaced is equal to weight of the ship, so it floats on water but weight of the water displaced by an iron piece is small as compared to weight of the iron, hence it sinks.

Q 2. Why cannot a person sit on the surface of water?

Ans. The average density of a person is larger than water, so weight of person remains larger than the buoyant force.

Q 3. Will a body weight more in air or in vacuum?

Ans. A body weight more in vacuum because in air, there is an upthrust force which results in loss of weight of the body.

Q 4. How does the buoyant force depend on the volume of body submerged in liquid?

Ans. Buoyant force increases on increasing the volume of body submerged in liquid.

Q 5. What do you mean by upthrust force?

Ans. When a body is immersed in a liquid, it exerts an upward force on the body. It is called upthrust force.

Q 6. State Archimedes' principle.

Ans. According to this principle, if a body is partially or completely immersed into liquid, it loses its weight and this loss in weight is equal to the weight of displaced liquid.

Q 7. Why is a force needed to keep a block of dry wood inside water?

Ans. Due to the upthrust force acting upward, a force is needed to keep a block of dry wood inside water.

Q 8. A piece of cork float in water. Why?

Ans. The density of cork is less than the density of water, hence it floats on the surface of water.

Q 9. Name the factor on which buoyant force depends.

Ans. (i) Volume of the submerged body.
(ii) Density of liquid.

Q 10. What is the relation between CGS and SI units of density?

Ans. The relation between CGS and SI units of density is given by

$$1\ g/cm^3 = 10^3\ kg/m^3$$

Q 11. State the principle of spring balance.

Ans. It works on the principle that the extension produced in the length of the spring is directly proportional to the load suspended.

ICSE
SAMPLE PAPER 1
(Fully Solved)

Physics-IX

Time : 2 hrs

Max Marks : 80

General Instructions

1. You will not be allowed to write during the first 15 minutes. This time is to be spent in reading the question paper.
2. The time given at the head of this paper is the time allowed for writing the answers.
3. Attempt all questions from **Section A** and any 4 questions from **Section B**.
4. The intended marks for questions or parts of questions are given in brackets [ ].

Section-A [40 Marks]

(Attempt all questions from this section)

1. Choose the correct answers to the questions from the given options. **[15]**

(i) A ray of light is incident on a smooth surface as shown below. The angle of reflection will be • ***Analysis***

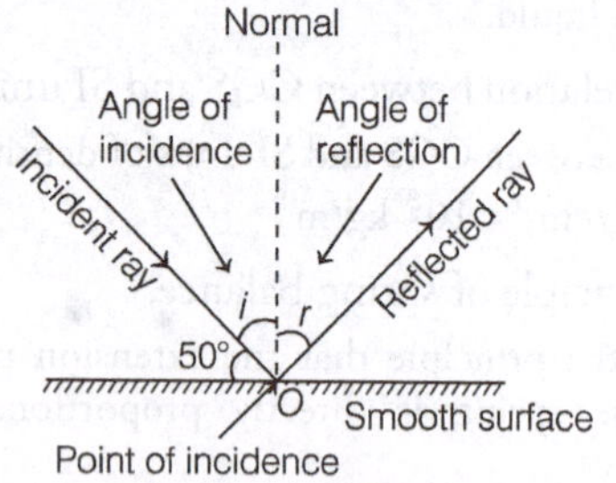

(a) 50° (b) 40°
(c) 90° (d) 10°

(ii) In which of the following frequency ranges is ultrasound found? • ***Recall***

(a) 1 Hz - 1 kHz
(b) 2 kHz - 10 kHz
(c) 11 kHz -20 kHz
(d) 21 kHz -30 kHz

(iii) Which of the following is an example of an artificial magnet? • ***Recall***

(a) Compass needle
(b) Horse-shoe magnet
(c) Magnetic needle
(d) All of the above

(iv) A particle moves in a circular path of radius 14 cm. If it completes one-fourth revolution along the circular path as shown below, then displacement *AB* of the particle is • ***Analysis***

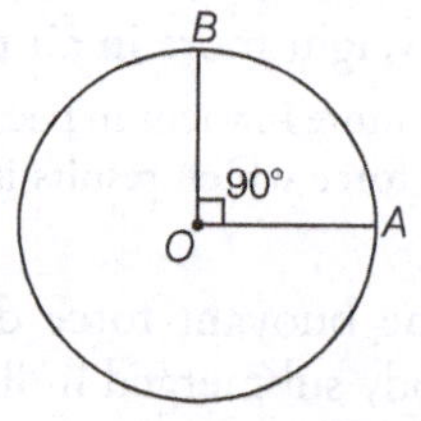

(a) $7\sqrt{2}$ cm (b) $14\sqrt{2}$ cm
(c) $\frac{14}{\sqrt{2}}$ cm (d) $\frac{7}{\sqrt{2}}$ cm

(v) According to the law of reflection, angle of incidence is always equal to the angle of • ***Recall***

(a) reflection (b) refraction
(c) Both (a) and (b) (d) None of these

(vi) Which of the following is a fundamental unit? • ***Recall***

(a) Hertz (b) Metre
(c) Pascal (d) Newton

(vii) A body of mass 60 kg is taken on the surface of moon. If gravitational acceleration on the surface of moon be one-sixth of the gravitational acceleration of the surface of earth, then mass of the body (in kg) on the surface of moon will be (Take, $g = 10\ \text{m/s}^2$) • ***Application***

(a) 6 (b) 60 (c) 600 (d) 100

(viii) **Assertion** (A) The atmospheric pressure decreases as altitude increases.

Reason (R) The weight of the air column above decreases as altitude increases. • ***Understanding and Application***

(a) Both A and R are true and R is the correct explanation of A.
(b) Both A and R are true and R is not the correct explanation of A.
(c) Assertion is false but reason is true.
(d) Assertion is true but reason is false.

(ix) Which of the following is an example of renewable source of energy? • *Recall*
(a) Coal (b) Petroleum
(c) Sun (d) None of these

(x) Which of the following is equivalent to energy? • *Recall*
(a) Heat
(b) Temperature
(c) Both (a) and (b)
(d) Neither (a) nor (b)

(xi) Ships and submarine are designed on the basis of • *Understanding*
(a) Newton's law of gravitation
(b) Archimedes' principle
(c) Kepler's laws
(d) Pascal's law

(xii) A solid object is gently put on a liquid, a buoyant force acts on the solid object is • *Understanding*
(a) uniform in all directions
(b) in vertical downward direction
(c) in vertical upward direction
(d) parallel to the surface of liquid.

(xiii) Mirror used by the dentists to observe teeth is • *Recall*
(a) concave mirror
(b) convex mirror
(c) plane mirror
(d) All of the above

(xiv) Which of the following is transmitted in a wave motion? • *Recall*
(a) Mass (b) Amplitude
(c) Energy (d) A particle

(xv) The relation between electric current and voltage is • *Recall*
(a) $I = VR$ (b) $V = I / R$
(c) $I = V / R$ (d) $V = R / I$

2. (i) Complete the following by chossing the correct answers from the bracket **[6]**
(a) .... [Momentum/Force/Mass] is the measure of inertia. • *Recall*
(b) Thrust and ...... [density of fluid/force/pressure] have the same unit. • *Recall*
(c) A ray of light passing through ...... [focus/pole/centre of curvature] incident on the surface of a spherical mirror is normal to the mirror surface. • *Understanding*
(d) 3 kHz sound can be heard by ...... [dolphins only/human beings only/bats only] • *Recall*
(e) The atmospheric pressure .... [increases/decreases] with rising altitudes as the density of air .... [decreases/increases] • *Application*

(ii) Two bodies P and Q have quantity of heat 1000 J and 100 J and their respective temperatures are 90° C and 24° C. Both of them are kept in contact. How does the heat flow between them? **[2]**

(iii) Draw the symbol of
(a) plug key open (b) plug key closed **[2]**
What does each situation mean? • *Application*

3. (i) A bar magnet is placed between two compasses, as shown in Fig.

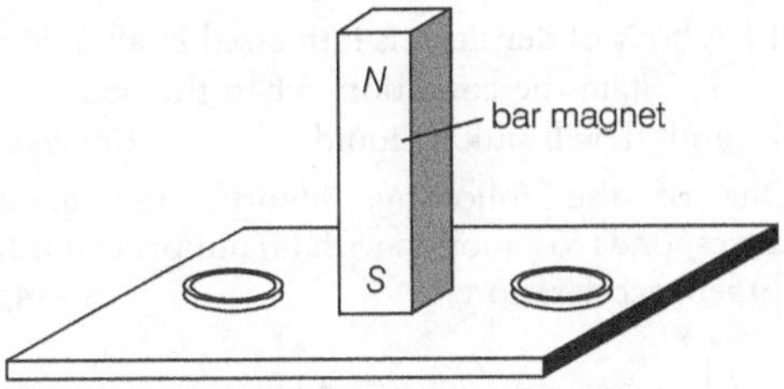

On Fig., draw the needles inside the two compasses and mark the N-pole of both compass needles. **[2]**
• *Understanding and Application*

(ii) A tuning fork is producing sound, prove with an activity that sound is produced by during vibrations. **[2]**
• *Understanding and Application*

(iii) (a) State the SI units of thrust and pressure. **[1]**
(b) In which situation, we exert more pressure on ground, when we stand on one foot or on the both feet? Justify your answer. • *Recall and Understanding* **[1]**

(iv) How does a compass help in detecting magnetic field around a magnet? • *Recall* **[2]**

(v) Imagine what would happen, if the value of g becomes • *Understanding*
(a) 100 times of its present value? **[1]**
(b) $\frac{1}{100}$ times of its present value? **[1]**

(vi) Give one use of each of the following. • *Recall*
(a) Regular reflection **[1]**
(b) Irregular reflection **[1]**

(vii) Fig. shows part of an electric bell. **[3]**

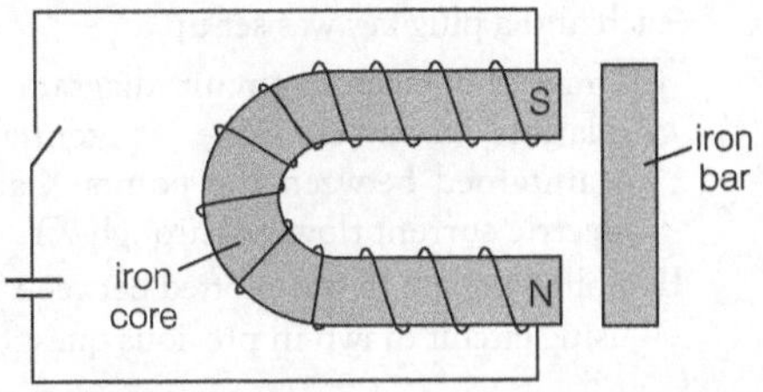

A switch and a cell are in series with a length of wire coiled around an iron core.
The switch is closed and the current in the wire produces a south pole S and a north pole N at the ends of the core, as shown in figure. Magnetic poles are also produced in a small iron bar, placed near to the ends of the core.
(a) On Fig., mark with an N the position of the north pole produced in the iron bar and mark with an S the position of the south pole produced in the iron bar.
(b) State and explain what happens to the iron bar once it is magnetised.

(c) The switch is opened and there is no current in the wire. State what happens to the magnetic poles in the iron bar. • *Understanding and Analysis*

Section-B [40 Marks]

(Attempt any four questions from this section)

4. (i) (a) State Archimedes' principle. • *Recall*

(b) A body of density ρ is immersed in a liquid of density ρ_l. State the condition, when the body I. will float and II. will sink in liquid. • *Understanding* [3]

(ii) Out of the following, identify the graph which corresponds to a motion with (a) uniform retardation and (b) zero acceleration. • *Application*

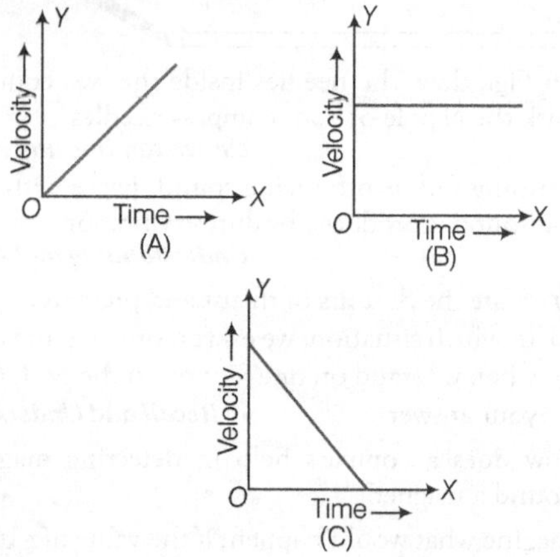

[3]

(iii) (a) Name an instrument that measures electric potential in a circuit. Define the unit of electric current. • *Application* [1]

(b) What do the following symbols represent in a circuit diagram?

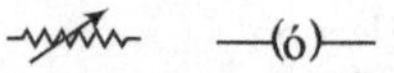

• *Recall* [1]

(c) An electric circuit consisting of a 0.5m long nichrome wire *XY*, an ammeter, a voltmeter, four cells of 1.5 V each and a plug key was set up.

I. Draw the electric circuit diagram to study the relation between the potential difference maintained between the points X and Y and the electric current flowing through *XY*. • *Analysis*

II. Following graph was plotted between *V* and *I* values using circuit drawn in previous question. • *Analysis*

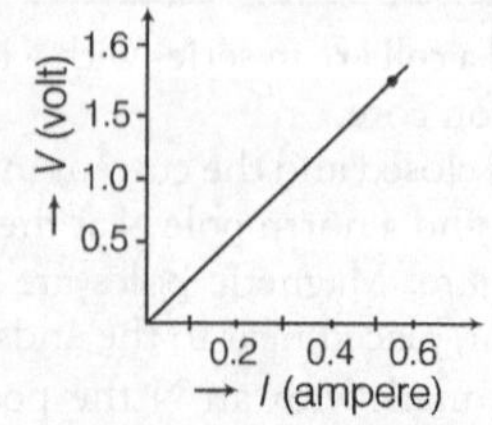

What would be the values of $\frac{V}{I}$ ratio, when the potential difference is 0.8 V, 1.2 V and 1.6 V respectively ? What conclusion do you draw from these values? [2]

5. (i) (a) What is the range of audible sound? • *Recall* [1]

(b) Write two properties of ultrasound which audible sound does not possess. • *Recall* [2]

(ii) Draw ray diagrams showing the image formation by a concave mirror, when an object is placed • *Analysis*

(a) between pole and focus of the mirror

(b) between focus and centre of curvature of the mirror

(c) at centre of curvature of the mirror

(d) a little beyond centre of curvature of the mirror [4]

(iii) Complete the table using the correct terms related to magnetism. The first label is done for you. • *Recall* [4]

Sr. No.	Description	Label
(a)	The region around a magnet where its influence can be felt	Magnetic field
(b)	The imaginary lines used to represent a magnetic field	
(c)	The law that states like poles repel and unlike poles attract	
(d)	The device used to detect the presence of a magnetic field	

6. (i) The speed-time graph for a car is shown in the figure. • *Application*

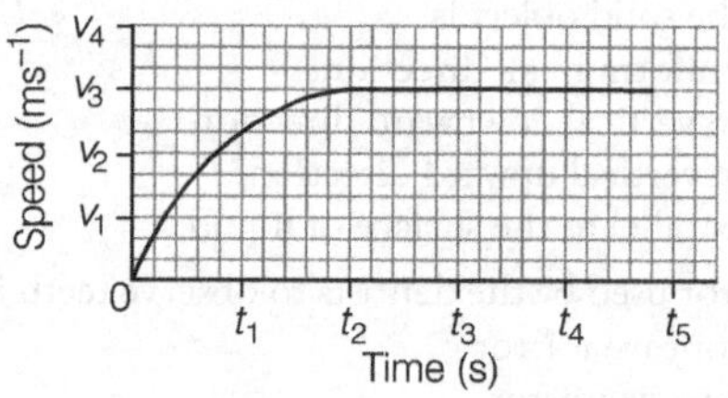

(a) Find how far does the car travel in the first t_2 s. Shade the area on the graph that represents the distance travelled by the car during the period.

(b) Which part of the graph represents uniform motion of the car? [4]

(ii) (a) Define magnetic field. (b) Give two properties of field lines of a bar magnet. • *Recall* [3]

(iii) A 500 kg vehicle moving with a speed of 10 m/s is brought to rest at a distance of 50 m. • *Analysis*

(a) Find the acceleration and time.

(b) Calculate unbalanced force acting on it. [3]

7. (i) (a) Will a sheet of paper fall slower than one that is crumpled into a ball in vacuum? Why?

(b) Show mathematically that acceleration experienced by an object is independent of its mass. • *Analysis*

(c) Show that value of $g = 9.8$ m/s^2

(Take, $G = 6.7\times10^{-11}$ N-m^2/kg^2, $M = 6\times10^{24}$ kg, $R = 6.4\times10^6$ m) [3]

(ii) A ball is thrown vertically upwards with a velocity of 25 m/s. If g is 10 m/s^2, then calculate

(a) height that it reaches,

(b) time taken to return back. [4]

(iii) Two friends Shefali and Anjali make a toy telephone by joining two plastic cups through a long string. They both stand apart. Anjali speaks softly into one cup and Shefali hears by putting her ear in the other cup. Now, Shefali speaks and Anjali listens.

Read the given passage carefully and give the answer of the following questions:

(a) What type of waves are produced by voice of Anjali and Shefali in the air inside the plastic cup? • *Understanding*

(b) What type of waves are produced in the string? • *Application*

(c) Waves of frequency 100Hz are produced in a string as shown in figure. Give its amplitude and wavelength. • *Analysis* [3]

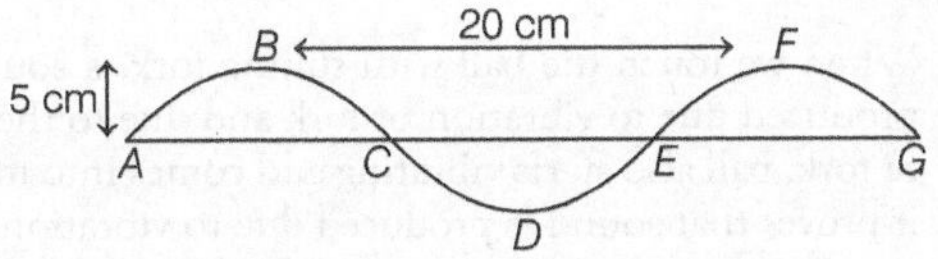

8. (i) Plastic production is increasing day-by-day despite of the fact that plastic is harmful for the environment. • *Analysis*

Based on the above statement, answer the following.

(a) What are the harmful effects of plastic usage? • *Recall*

(b) In our day-to-day situation, what are the alternative that we can use instead of plastics? • *Recall*

(c) What can we learn as a good citizen as in concern for this issue? • *Analysis* [3]

(ii) (a) Which has shorter wavelength infrasonic or ultrasonic? • *Recall*

(b) Can dolphin detect ultrasonic waves? • *Recall*

(c) Name any one living organism which can detect infrasonic waves. • *Application* [3]

(iii) In the circuit given below, label the parts *P*, *Q*, *R* and *S*; and state the function of each part. • *Analysis* [4]

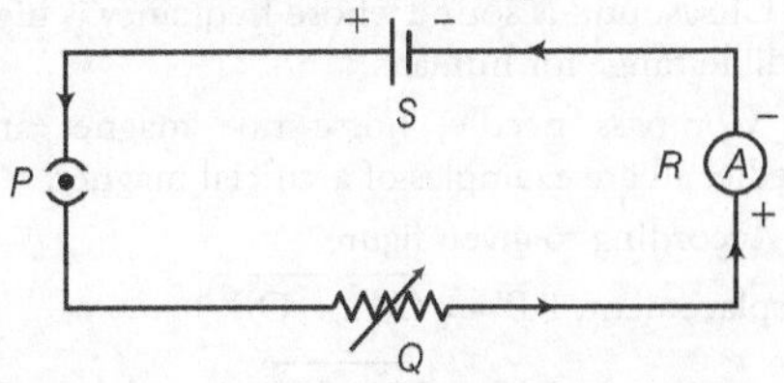

9. (i) Through what type of medium, can (a) the transverse waves and (b) the longitudinal waves be transmitted. Explain in brief. • *Understanding* [3]

(ii) A spherical mirror produces an image of magnification − 1 on a screen placed at a distance of 50 cm from the mirror.

(a) Write the type of mirror. • *Understanding* [4]

(b) Find the distance of the image from the object.

(c) What is the focal length of the mirror?

(d) Draw the ray diagram to show the image formation in this case.

(iii) What do you mean by the following terms.

(a) Magnetism

(b) Magnet • *Recall* [3]

(c) Pole

(d) Magnetic or effective length

(e) Geometrical length of magnet

Answers

1. (i) (*b*) From the given diagram,

$$50 + i = 90^\circ$$

$$\Rightarrow \quad i = 90 - 50 = 40^\circ$$

$\therefore$ Angle of reflection (r) = Angle of incidence $(i) = 40^\circ$

(ii) (*d*) Ultrasound is sound whose frequency is higher than the audible range for humans.

(iii) (*d*) Compass needle, horse-shoe magnet and magnetic needle, all are examples of artificial magnet.

(iv) (*b*) According to given figure.

Displacement, $AB = \sqrt{OA^2 + OB^2}$

$$= \sqrt{14^2 + 14^2}$$

$$= 14\sqrt{2} \text{ cm}$$

(v) (*a*) According to the law of reflection, angle of incidence is always equal to the angle of reflection.

(vi) (*b*) Metre is the fundamental unit of length, whereas hertz, pascal and newton are derived units.

(vii) (*b*) Since, mass of the body remains same on the surface of each planet or satellite, it does not depend on the value of gravitational acceleration.

(viii) (*a*) Atmospheric pressure is caused by the weight of the air above us. As altitude increases, the thickness of the air column decreases, leading to a reduction in the weight exerted on a given surface. This results in lower atmospheric pressure at higher altitude.

(ix) (*c*) Renewable sources of energy are those sources which are never get exhausted with time. Hence, sun is renewable sources of energy.

(x) (*a*) Heat is equivalent to energy while temperature is a measure of degree of coldness or hotness.

(xi) (*b*) Ships and submarine are designed to displace a weight of fluid at least equal to its own weight, which is based on Archimedes' principle.

(xii) (*c*) Buoyant force acts in vertical upward direction.

(xiii) (*a*) Dentists use concave mirrors to see large image of teeth.

(xiv) (*c*) Energy is transmitted in a wave motion.

(xv) (*c*) According to Ohm's law, $I = V / R$.

2. (i) (a) Mass

(b) force

(c) centre of curvature

(d) human beings only

(e) decreases, decreases

(ii) Flow of heat does not depend on heat contained by body. Flow of heat is due to temperature difference only.

$\therefore$ Heat will flow from body P to Q, as the temperature of body P is more than that of body Q.

(iii) (a) 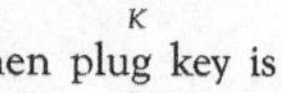 (b) 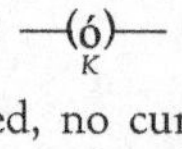

When plug key is opened, no current flows through the circuit and when plug key is closed, current flows through the circuit.

3. (i)

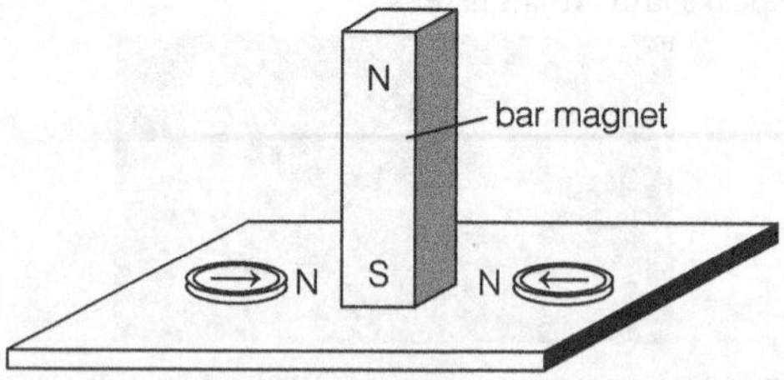

(ii) Take a tuning fork and vibrate it with a rubber pad. Now, touch the suspended ball gently with the prong of the vibrating tuning fork.

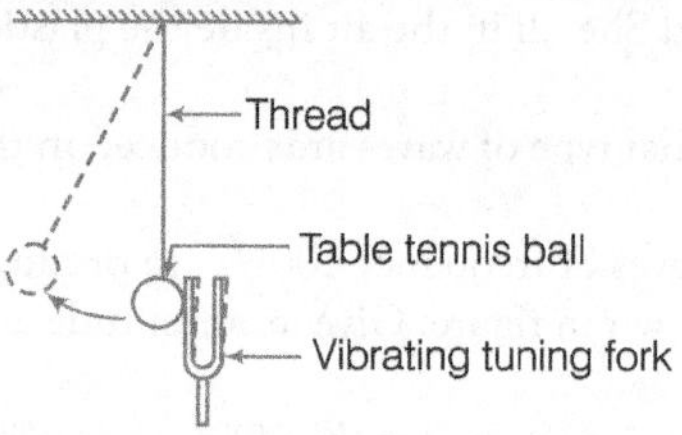

When we touch the ball with tuning fork, a sound will be produced due to vibration of fork and due to the vibration of fork, ball also starts vibrating and comes into motion. So, it proves that sound is produced due to vibrations.

(iii) (a) The SI unit of thrust is newton (N) and pressure is N/m^2 or pascal (Pa).

(b) We exert more pressure on ground when we stand on one foot than the both feet, as the area of one foot is half than that of two feet and $p \propto \frac{1}{A}$.

(iv) The needle of a compass rests in a direction other than the geographic North-South direction, when it is brought near to a space around a magnet, which is called magnetic field of the magnet. This illustrates the presence of magnetic field around a magnet.

(v) (a) Earth's attraction would be so large that you would be crushed to the earth.

(b) We can easily jump to the top of a multi-storey buliding from the ground.

(vi) (a) Regular reflection helps in the formation of virtual images as in case of plane mirror.

(b) Irregular reflection helps in illuminating the areas, where light is not falling directly.

(vii) (a)

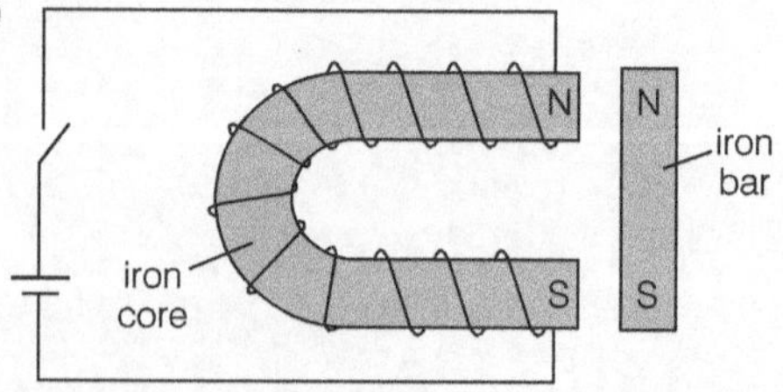

(b) The iron bar moves towards the iron core as unlike poles attract each other.

(c) The iron bar loses its magnetic poles.

4. (i) (a) Archimedes' principle states that, when a body is immersed partially or completely in a liquid, then it experiences a buoyant force or upthrust, which is equal to the weight of the liquid displaced by it.

(b) I. When $\rho < \rho_l$, then in this condition, the upthrust applied by the liquid will be greater than the weight of the body. Hence, the body floats partially immersed in the liquid.

II. When $\rho > \rho_l$, then in this condition, the upthrust of the liquid is less than the weight of the liquid i.e., it is not sufficient to balance the weight of the body, so the body sinks.

(ii) (a) The graph with uniform retardation is shown in graph (C), since in this graph, the velocity of the object decreases uniformly.

(b) The graph (B) corresponds to the zero acceleration because the velocity of body does not change with time.

(iii) (a) An instrument that measures electric potential in a circuit is called voltmeter. The unit of electric current is ampere (A). 1 ampere is constituted by the flow of 1 coulomb of charge through any point in an electric circuit in 1 second.

(b)

Rheostat

Plug key or switch

(c) I. The electric circuit diagram to study the given relation is shown below

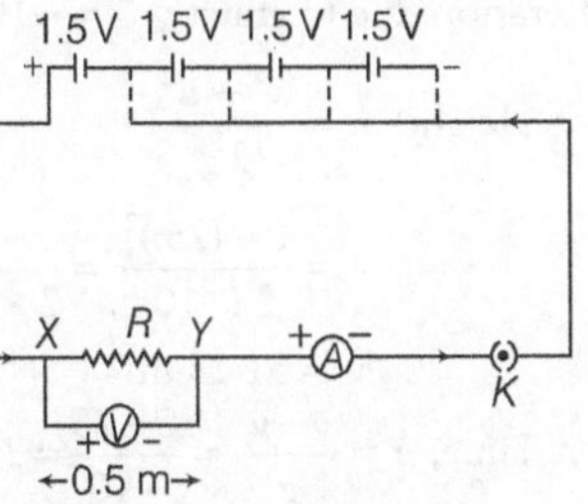

II. Following graph was plotted between V and I values

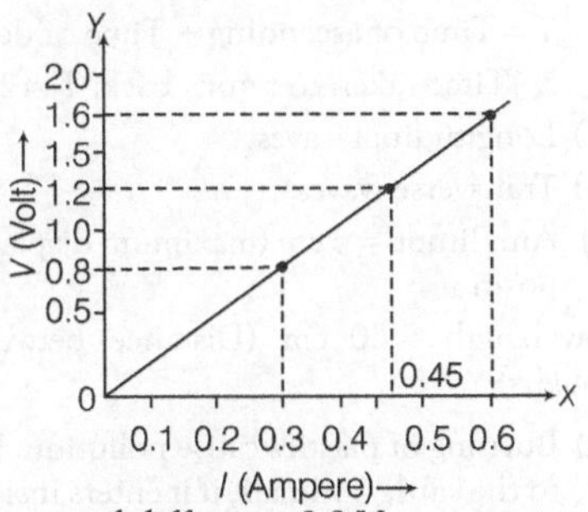

At potential difference 0.8 V,

$$\frac{V}{I} = \frac{0.8}{0.3} = \frac{8}{3} \quad \text{...(i)}$$

At potential difference 1.2 V, $\frac{V}{I} = \frac{1.2}{0.45} = \frac{8}{3}$ ...(ii)

At potential difference 1.6 V, $\frac{V}{I} = \frac{1.6}{0.6} = \frac{8}{3}$ ...(iii)

Conclusion If I be the current through XY resistor and V be the potential difference across it, then the ratio $\frac{V}{I}$ = constant.

$\therefore$ $V \propto I$ and Ohm's law is obeyed.

5. (i) (a) The frequency range of audible sound is 20 Hz to 20000 Hz.

(b) Two properties of ultrasound which audible sound does not possess are

I. The energy carried by them is very high.

II. It does not bend appreciably at the edges of an obstacle because of its small wavelength. This means, it can travel along a well defined straight path.

(ii) (a) The enlarged, virtual and erect image of the object forms behind the mirror.

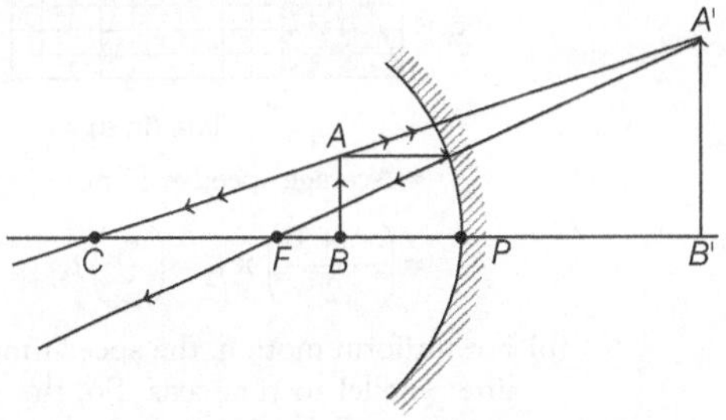

(b) The enlarged, real and inverted image of the object forms beyond centre of curvature.

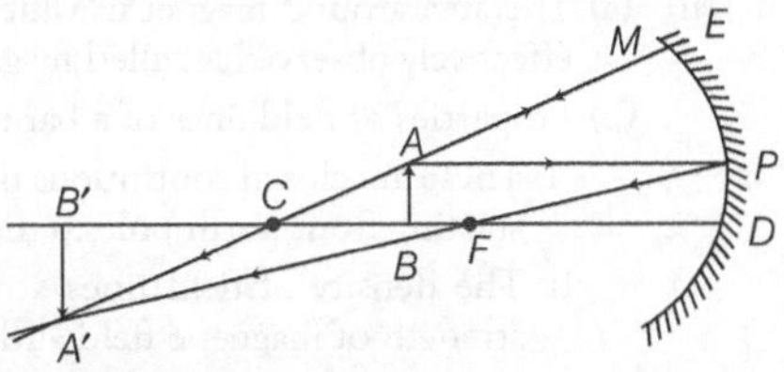

(c) The real and inverted image of the object of equal to the size of object forms at centre of curvature.

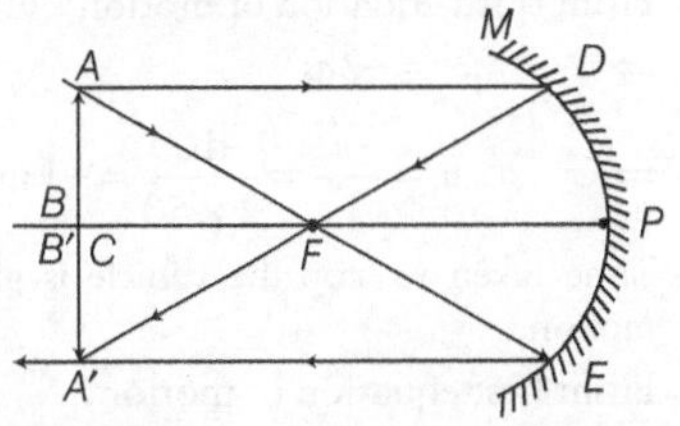

(d) The diminished, real and inverted image of the object forms between centre of curvature and F.

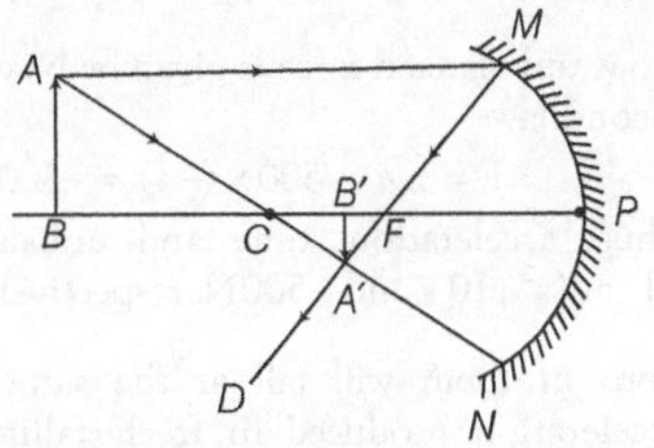

(iii)

Sr. No.	Description	Label
(a)	The region around a magnet where its influence can be felt	Magnetic field
(b)	The imaginary lines used to represent a magnetic field	Magnetic field lines
(c)	The law that states like poles repel and unlike poles attract	Law of magnetic poles
(d)	The device used to detect the presence of a magnetic field	Magnetic compass

6. (i) (a) Distance travelled in t_2 second = Area under speed-time graph

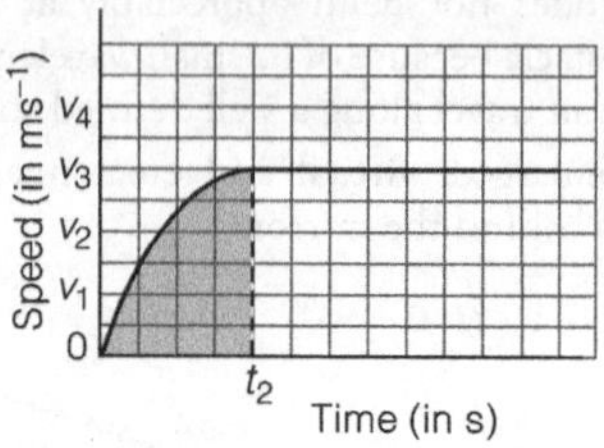

$= \text{Average speed} \times \text{Time}$

$$= \left(\frac{v_3 + 0}{2}\right) \times t_2 = \left(\frac{v_3}{2}\right) t_2$$

(b) For uniform motion, the speed-time graph is a straight line parallel to time axis. So, the straight part of the curve parallel to time axis represents the uniform motion of the car.

(ii) (a) The area around magnet in which its influence can be effectively observed is called magnetic field.

(b) Properties of field lines of a bar magnet are as follows

I. These are closed continuous non-intersecting curves starting from north pole to the south pole.

II. The density of field lines at a point describes the strength of magnetic field at that point.

(iii) Given, mass, $(m) = 500$ kg, initial velocity, $(u) = 10$ m/s, distance, $(s) = 50$ m, acceleration, $(a) = ?$ and force, $(F) = ?$

(a) From third equation of motion, $v^2 = u^2 + 2as$

$$\Rightarrow \quad u^2 = -2as \qquad (\because v = 0)$$

$$\Rightarrow \quad a = \frac{-u^2}{2s} = \frac{-100}{2 \times 50} = -1 \text{ m/s}^2$$

Time taken to stop the vehicle is given by equation of motion.

From first equation of motion,

$$v = u + at \Rightarrow u = -at \qquad (\because v = 0)$$

$$\Rightarrow \quad t = \frac{u}{-a} = \frac{10}{-(-1)} = 10 \text{ s}$$

(b) Now, unbalanced force is given by Newton's second law.

$$\therefore \quad F = ma = 500 \times (-1) = -500\text{N}$$

Thus, acceleration, time and unbalanced force are -1 m/s^2, 10 s and -500N, respectively.

7. (i) (a) Both of them will fall at the same speed because acceleration produced in freely falling bodies is the same for all bodies, irrespective of their shapes or masses.

(b) Consider a body of mass m on the surface of the earth, M be mass of the earth, R be the distance between the body and centre of the earth (radius of the earth) and g is the acceleration due to gravity. Let F be the force acting on the body.

According to Newton's second law of motion,

$$F = mg \qquad \text{...(i)}$$

According to Newton's law of gravitation,

$$F = G\frac{M \times m}{R^2} \qquad \text{...(ii)}$$

From Eqs. (i) and (ii), we get

$$mg = G\frac{M \times m}{R^2}$$

$\therefore \; g = \dfrac{GM}{R^2}$, thus g is independent of the mass of the body.

(c) $\therefore g = \dfrac{GM}{R^2} = \dfrac{6.7 \times 10^{-11} \text{N - m}^2 \text{ kg}^{-2} \times 6 \times 10^{24} \text{kg}}{(6.4 \times 10^6 \text{m})^2}$

$$= \frac{6.7 \times 6}{6.4 \times 6.4} \times \frac{10^{-11+24}}{10^{12}} = 0.981 \times \text{N/kg}$$

$$= 9.81 \text{ m/s}^2 \approx 9.8 \text{ m/s}^2$$

Thus, the value of $g = 9.8$ m/s^2.

(ii) Given, initial velocity, $u = 25$ m/s, final velocity, $v = 0$.

If a body is thrown upwards, then its velocity becomes zero at the maximum height.

Acceleration due to gravity, $g = -10$ m/s^2

(a) $\because$ Height, $h = \dfrac{v^2 - u^2}{2g}$

$$= \frac{0 - (25)^2}{2(-10)} = \frac{-625}{2 \times (-10)}$$

$$h = 31.25 \text{ m}$$

(b) $\because$ Time, $t = \dfrac{v - u}{g} = \dfrac{0 - 25}{-10} = 2.5$ s

Time taken to return back,

T = Time of ascending + Time of descending $= 2t$

$\therefore$ Time taken to return back, $T = 2 \times 2.5 = 5$ s

(iii) (a) Longitudinal waves

(b) Transverse waves

(c) Amplitude = 5 cm (maximum displacement from mean position)

Wavelength = 20 cm (Distance between two crests or troughs)

8. (i) (a) Burning of plastics cause pollution. Plastics cause harm to the cattle/animals, if it enters inside their alimentary canal.

(b) Paper bags/jute bags can be used instead of plastic bag.

(c) Every citizen should be discouraged to use plastics as a source of packaging and storing as it is non-biodegradable.

(ii) (a) Ultrasonic wave has shorter wavelength.

(b) Yes, dolphin can detect ultrasonic waves.

(c) Rhinoceros can detect infrasonic waves.

(iii) The circuit components are as follows

$P \rightarrow$ A closed key, which is used to close the circuit.

$Q \rightarrow$ A rheostat, which is used to provide variable resistance in order to control the current flowing through the circuit.

$R \rightarrow$ An ammeter, which measures the current flowing through the circuit.

$S \rightarrow$ A cell, which provides potential difference between two terminals.

9. (i) (a) Since, transverse waves travel in the form of crests and troughs, so they involve changes in the shape of medium. They can be transmitted through a medium having elasticity of shape. As, solids and liquids have elasticity of shape. Hence, transverse waves can be transmitted through solids and liquids.

(b) Since, longitudinal waves travel in the form of compressions and rarefactions, so they involve changes in the volume and density of medium. As all media, i.e. solids liquids and gases have elasticity of volume. Hence, these waves (longitudinal waves) can be transmitted through all the three types of media.

(ii) (a) The mirror is concave mirror.

(b) Given, $m = -1$, $u = -50$ cm

$\therefore$ Magnification, $m = \dfrac{-v}{u}$

$\Rightarrow \quad -1 = \dfrac{-v}{-50}$

$\Rightarrow \quad v = -50$ cm

Therefore, the image is real and inverted and of same size as that of the object.

(c) The distance between the pole of the mirror and the focal point of a mirror is called the focal length.

(d) Here, object is placed at centre of curvature, so the object distance is equal to the image distance, since screen is placed at distance of 50 cm from the mirror, therefore object distance = image distance = 50 cm

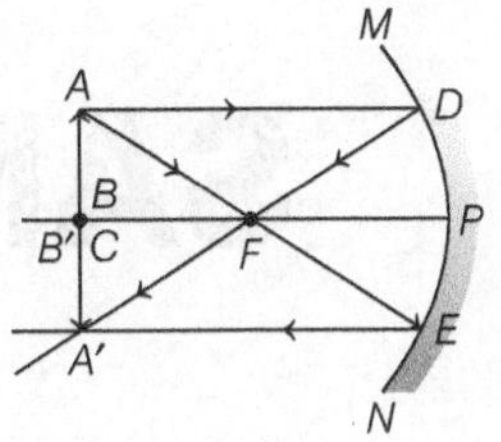

(iii) (a) **Magnetism** It is the property by virtue of which a substance can attract magnetic materials (e.g., soft iron, iron fillings, etc.)

(b) **Magnet** Materials which have the property of magnetism is called magnet.

(c) **Pole** The points inside the magnet near the ends, where the magnetic strength is maximum are called poles of the magnet.

The two poles are equal in strength. They are not situated exactly at the ends of the magnet but slightly inside.

(d) **Magnetic or Effective Length** The distance between two poles of a magnet is called magnetic length or effective length.

(e) **Geometrical Length of magnet** The geometrical length of a magnet is the distance between its end points along its length. Magnetic length of a magnet is approximately 5/6 of its geometrical length.

ICSE

SAMPLE PAPER 2

(Unsolved)

Physics-IX

Time : 2 hrs | Max Marks : 80

General Instructions

1. You will not be allowed to write during the first 15 minutes. This time is to be spent in reading the question paper.
2. The time given at the head of this paper is the time allowed for writing the answers.
3. Attempt all questions from **Section A** and any 4 questions from **Section B**.
4. The intended marks for questions or parts of questions are given in brackets [ ].

Section-A **[40 Marks]**

(Attempt all questions from this section)

1. Choose the correct answers to the questions from the given options **[15]**

(i) A student carries out an experiment and plots the *V-I* graph of three samples of nichrome wire with resistances R_1, R_2 and R_3 respectively, as shown in figure. Which of the following is true? • ***Understanding***

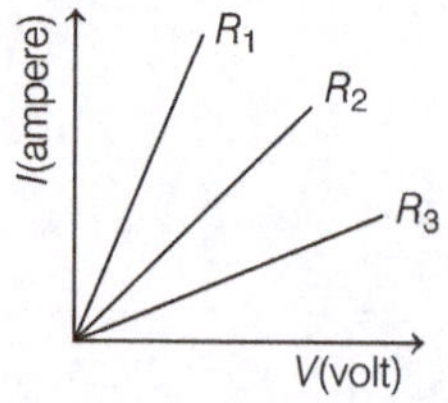

(a) $R_1 = R_2 = R_3$ (b) $R_1 > R_2 > R_3$
(c) $R_3 > R_2 > R_1$ (d) $R_2 > R_3 > R_1$

(ii) Which of the following is not correct with respect to magnetic lines of force? • ***Understanding and Recall***
(a) Magnetic lines of forces are closed curve.
(b) Magnetic lines of forces can intersect to each other.
(c) Magnetic lines of forces emerge from North pole and enter into South pole of a bar magnet.
(d) None of the above

(iii) For an electromagnet, • ***Understanding and Application***
(a) polarity can be changed
(b) strength can be changed
(c) Both (a) and (b)
(d) Neither (a) nor (b)

(iv) m_1 and m_2 are two masses kept at a distance r. If r is increased to double, then gravitational force between the two masses is decreased to • ***Application***
(a) double (b) half
(c) four times (d) one-fourth

(v) Which of the following sound waves is used in SONAR technique? • ***Recall and Understanding***
(a) Infrasonic (b) Ultrasonic
(c) Audible range (d) None of the above

(vi) The given graph shows the displacement *versus* time relation for a disturbance travelling with velocity of 1200 m/s. The wavelength of the disturbance is • ***Application and Analysis***

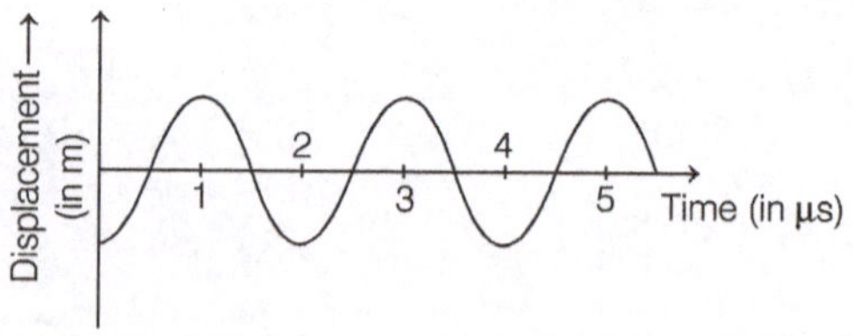

(a) 3.6 mm (b) 1.2 mm
(c) 1.8 mm (d) 2.4 mm

(vii) Least count of vernier calliper is • ***Recall***
(a) 0.01 mm (b) 0.01 cm
(c) 0.01 m (d) 0.01 μ m

(viii) **Assertion** The effect of thrust on sand is larger while standing than lying.
Reason Thrust is a force acting on an object perpendicular to that surface. • ***Understaning***

(a) Both A and R are true and R is the correct explanation of A.
(b) Both A and R are true and R is not the correct explanation of A.
(c) Assertion is false but reason is true.
(d) Assertion is true but reason is false.

(ix) The motion of three cars *A*, *B* and *C* is represented below. Which of the car is travelling fastest? • ***Analysis***

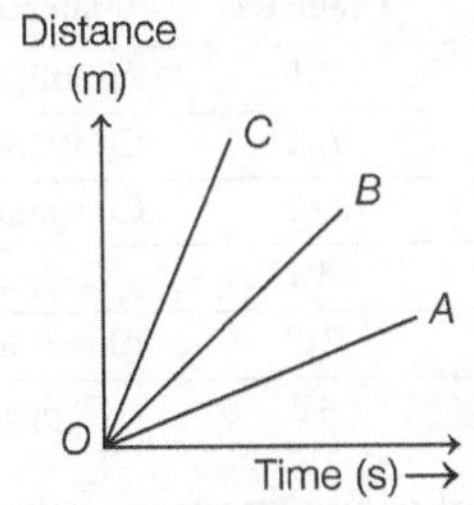

(a) A (b) C
(c) *B* (d) None of these

(x) Gravitational acceleration is maximum at • ***Recall***
(a) poles (b) equator
(c) centre of earth (d) All of these

(xi) An object weighs is 10 N in air. When it immersed fully in water, its weight become 8 N. The weight of water displaced by the object will be • ***Application***
(a) 2 N (b) 10 N
(c) 12 N (d) 8 N

(xii) Thermal expansion occurs in • ***Recall***
(a) solid only
(b) liquid and gas
(c) solid and liquid
(d) solid, liquid and gas

(xiii) Vernier calipers are shown with the jaws closed.

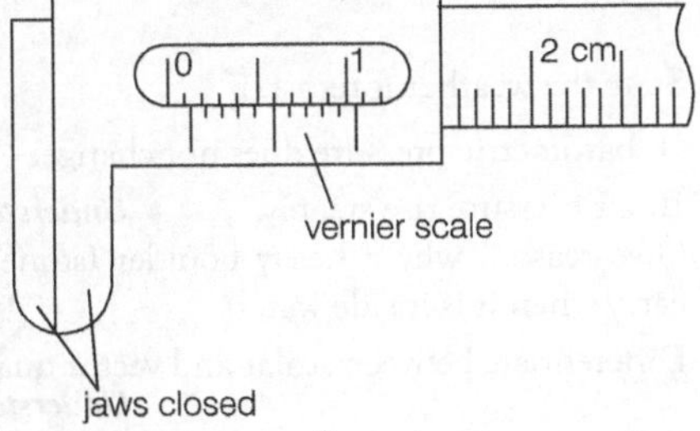

What is the zero error?
(a) 0.04 cm (b) 0.05 cm
(c) 0.14 cm (d) 0.15 cm

(xiv) Gap left between the ends of two railway lines in a railway track is due to • ***Analysis***
(a) linear expansion
(b) areal expansion
(c) cubical expansion
(d) None of these

(xv) The diagram shows a patient having her eyes tested. A chart with letters on it is placed behind her and she sees the chart reflected in a plane mirror. • ***Understanding***

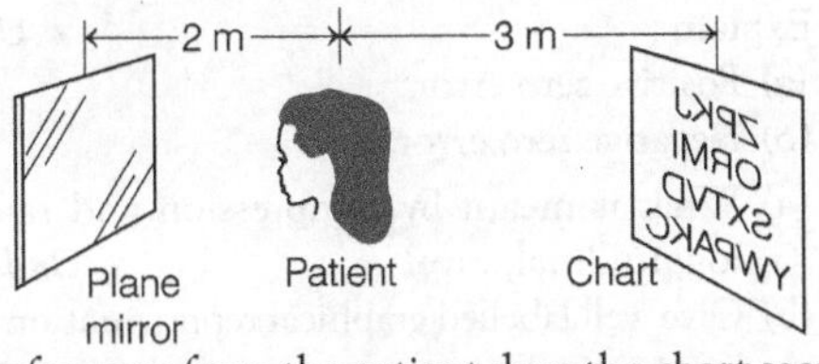

How far away from the patient does the chart seem to be?
(a) 2 m (b) 4 m
(c) 5 m (d) 7 m

2. (i) Complete the following by choosing the correct answers from the bracket **[6]**
(a) The pressure exerted by a liquid at a given depth depends on the .... [density/volume/surface area] of the liquid. • ***Recall***
(b) A body will float in a liquid if its............[density/mass/volume] is less than that of the liquid. • ***Recall***
(c) The buoyant force on an object immersed in a fluid acts in the...............[horizontal/downward/upward] • ***Recall***
(d) The minimum distance required for an echo to be heard in air at room temperature is about...........[11m/17m/21m] • ***Recall***
(e) Action and reaction forces are always........... (equal/unequal) in magnitude and .... (opposite/same) in direction. • ***Recall***

(ii) The plane mirror and convex mirror form virtual images of objects. Can they produce real images under same circumstances? Explain. • ***Analysis* [2]**

(iii) A wave pulse of velocity 100 Hz produced on a string, moves a distance of 6 m in 6 ms. Calculate (a) velocity of pulse and (b) wavelength of pulse. • ***Application* [2]**

3. (i) You are given two identical rods in which one is magnet and the other is not. How can you tell which one is magnet or not without suspending it or use of any other apparatus? • ***Understanding* [2]**

(ii) Write the name of the symbols used in electric circuits to represent. • ***Recall* [2]**

(a)  (b) 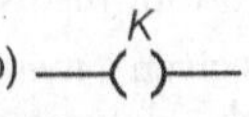

(iii) Complete the path of the ray *AB* over plane mirrors M_1 and M_2 and label all the angles of incidences. **[2]**

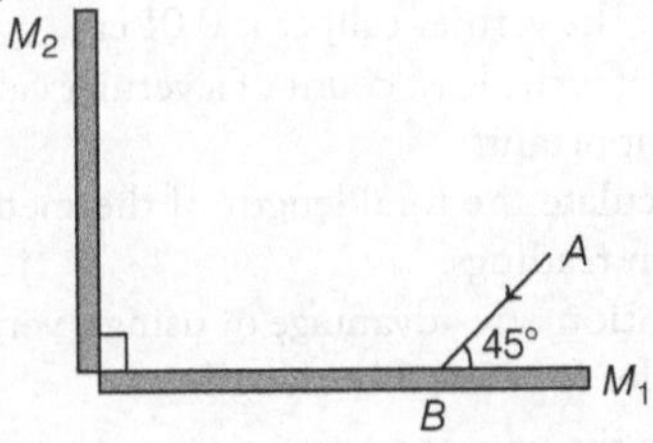

(iv) Interpret force in terms of momentum. Represent the following graphically • ***Understanding and Analysis***
(a) Momentum *versus* velocity, when mass is fixed. **[1]**
(b) Momentum *versus* mass, when velocity is constant. **[1]**

(v) Explain • *Understanding*
(a) Positive zero error **[1]**
(b) Negative zero error **[1]**

(vi) (a) What is meant by compression and rarefaction of a longitudinal wave? • *Understanding* **[1]**
(b) Give well labelled graphical representation of a longitudinal wave. • *Application* **[1]**

(vii) Nikhil Sir was demonstrating an experiment in his class with the setup as shown in the figures below.

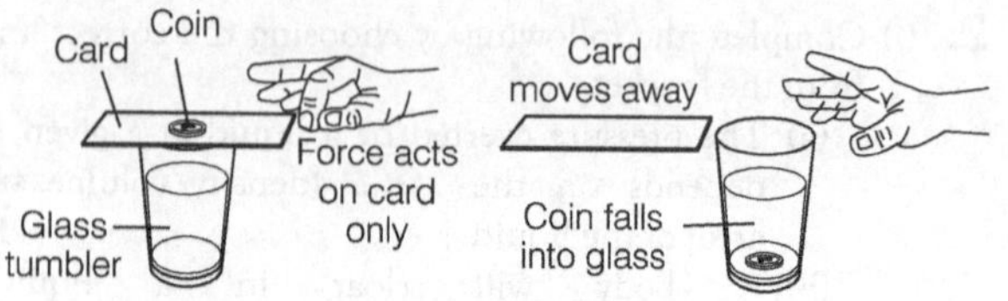

A five rupee coin is set on a stiff card covering an empty glass tumbler standing on a table. He then flicks the card hard with his fingers. • *Understanding* **[3]**
(i) Why does the coin fall into the glass instead of moving with the card ?
(ii) What will happen if the card is pulled slowly instead of flicked?
(iii) If the flicking force is too small, will the coin still fall into the glass? Why or why not?

Section-B **[40 Marks]**

(Attempt any four questions from this section)

4. (i) The following table gives the data about motion of a car

Time (h)	11:00	11:30	12:00	12:30	1:00
Distance (km)	0	20	30	65	100

Plot the graph and
(a) find the speed of the car between 12:00 h and 12:30 h. • *Understanding and Analysis* **[1½]**
(b) What is the average speed of the car? **[1]**
(c) Is the car's motion is an example of uniform motion? Justify. **[1½]**

(ii) Rahul is given a metal rod and asked to measure its length accurately. He uses a vernier caliper and notes the main scale reading as 3.2 cm and the fifth division on the vernier scale coincides with the main scale. The least count of the vernier caliper is 0.01 cm.
(a) What is the least count of a vernier caliper, and why is it important? **[1]**
(b) Calculate the total length of the metal rod using the given readings. **[1]**
(c) Mention one advantage of using a vernier caliper over a ruler for measuring length. • *Application* **[1]**

(iii) (a) Give the uses of a screw gauge. • *Recall* **[1½]**
(b) What is the relation between time period and frequency of a simple pendulum? **[1½]**

5. (i) How long would a force take, if 60 N act on a body of mass 10 kg, so that the body gains velocity of 24 m/s? • *Application* **[3]**

(ii) Draw ray diagrams showing the image formation by a convex mirror when an object is placed
(a) at infinity distance from the mirror, • *Recall* **[2]**
(b) at finite distance from the mirror. **[2]**

(iii) Read the following information.
Six wires labelled as *A*, *B*, *C*, *D*, *E* and *F* have been designed as per the following parameters. • *Analysis*

Wire	Length	Diameter	Materials	Resistances
A	l	$2d$	Aluminium	R_1
B	$2l$	$d/2$	Constantan	R_2
C	$3l$	$d/2$	Constantan	R_3
D	$l/2$	$3d$	Copper	R_4
E	$2l$	$2d$	Aluminium	R_5
F	$l/2$	$4d$	Copper	R_6

Answer the following questions using the above data.
(a) Which of the wires has maximum resistance and why? **[1]**
(b) Which of the wires has minimum resistance and why? **[1]**
(c) Arrange R_1, R_3 and R_5 in ascending order of their values. Justify your answer. **[1]**

6. (i) (a) Define 1 V. • *Understanding* **[1]**
(b) Plot a graph taking potential difference (*V*) on *X*-axis and current (*I*) on *Y*-axis. Also, specify the relationship between the slope and resistance. • *Application* **[2]**

(ii) The circular head of a screw gauge is divided into 100 divisions and the screw moves 2 mm ahead in two revolutions of the circular head. Calculate its (a) pitch and (b) least count. • *Recall* **[3]**

(iii) (a) What are the properties of an electromagnet? • *Understanding*
(b) How can we increase the strength of an electromagnet? **[4]**

7. (i) (a) State the weather forecast, if
I. barometric pressure does not change.
II. air pressure rise steeply. • *Understanding* **[1½]**
(b) Give reason, why a heavy boulder (stone) is easy to carry when it is inside water? • *Analysis* **[1½]**

(ii) (a) Differentiate between scalar and vector quantity. • *Understanding* **[1½]**
(b) A bicycle initially moving with velocity 10 m/s and accelerates for 10 s at rate of 4 m/s^2. Find its final velocity. • *Application* **[1½]**
(c) Why do passengers fall in backward direction, when a train suddenly starts moving on? Give reason. • *Understanding* **[1]**

(iii) (a) Show that the rate of change of momentum = mass × acceleration. • *Understanding* **[1½]**
(b) How does the pressure exerted by a thrust depend on the area of surface on which it acts? **[1½]**

8. (i) (a) Draw a circuit diagram showing how four bulbs can be lit from a battery of four cells, so that two bulbs are controlled by the same switch while each of the other two bulbs has its own switch. • *Applicaiton*

(b) Redraw the following circuit using appropriate symbols. • *Analysis*

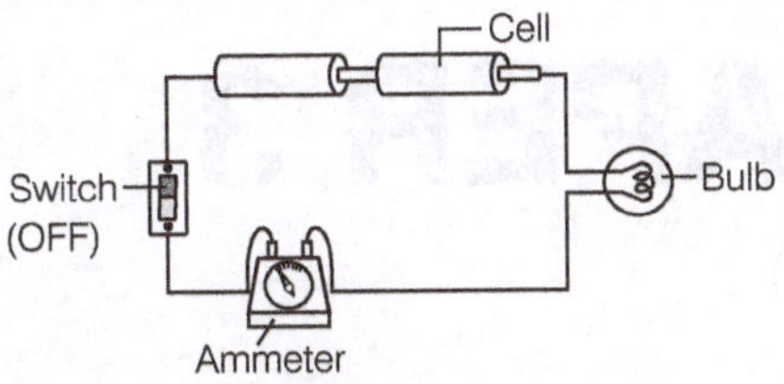

[3]

(ii) (a) Write two main properties of ultrasound. • *Recall* [2]

(b) Mention one application of ultrasound in
I. industries II. medical field. [2]

(iii) (a) A TV set shoots out a beam of electrons. The beam current is 10 μ A. How many electrons strike the TV screen in each second? How much charges strikes the screen in a 1 min? • *Analysis* [1½]

(b) If a charge of 2.5 C is first moved from infinity to point *P* and then to point *Q*, a work of 10 J and 25 J is done, respectively. Calculate the potential difference between points *P* and *Q*. [1½]

9. (i) What is acceleration? How will you express it mathematically? [4]

(ii) Which of the following has more inertia?
(a) A stone and a rubber ball of same size [1]
(b) A bicycle and a train [1]
(c) A five rupees coin and a one rupee coin
Give reason for your answer. • *Analysis* [1]

(iii) Complete the table using the correct terms related to current electricity. The first label is done for you. • *Recall* [3]

Sr. No.	Description	Label
(a)	The SI unit of electric current	Ampere (A)
(b)	The instrument used to measure potential difference	
(c)	The opposition offered by a conductor to the flow of current	
(d)	The SI unit of resistance	

Answers

1. (i) (c) (ii) (b) (iii) (c) (iv) (d) (v) (b)
(vi) (d) (vii) (b) (viii) (b) (ix) (b) (x) (a)
(xi) (a) (xii) (d) (xiii) (c) (xiv) (a) (xv) (d)

2. (i) (a) density (b) density (c) upward (d) 17 m
(e) equal and opposite.
(ii) (a) 10^3 m/s (b) 10 m

4. (i) (a) 70 km/h (ii) 50 km/h

5. (i) $\frac{1}{4}$ s

6. (ii) (a) 0.1 cm (b) 0.001 cm

7. (ii) (b) 50 m/s

8. (iii) (a) 600 μC (b) 6V

ICSE
SAMPLE PAPER 3
(Unsolved)

Physics-IX

Time : 2 hrs | Max Marks : 80

General Instructions

1. You will not be allowed to write during the first 15 minutes. This time is to be spent in reading the question paper.
2. The time given at the head of this paper is the time allowed for writing the answers.
3. Attempt all questions from **Section A** and any 4 questions from **Section B**.
4. The intended marks for questions or parts of questions are given in brackets [ ].

Section-A [40 Marks]

(Attempt all questions from this section)

1. Choose the correct answers to the questions from the given options **[15]**

(i) Which of the following point lies in the region of uniform magnetic field? • ***Recall***

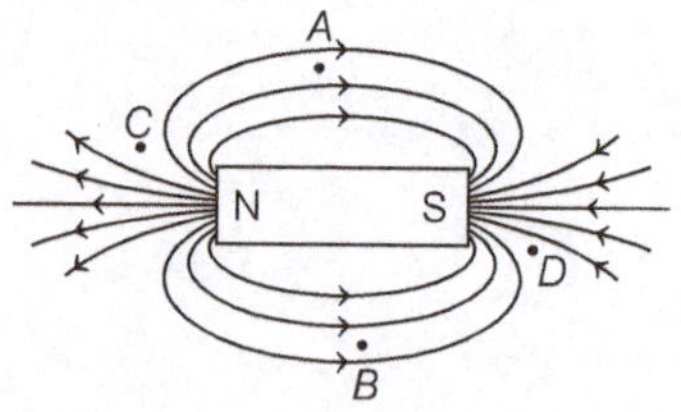

(a) A
(b) B and C
(c) A and B
(d) A, B, C and D

(ii) In a barber's shop, two plane mirrors are placed .... to each other. • ***Application***
(a) perpendicular (b) parallel
(c) Both (a) and (b) (d) None of these

(iii) Which of the following are the example of non-contact forces? • ***Recall***
(a) Gravitational force (b) Electrostatic force
(c) Magnetic force (d) All of these

(iv) Which of the following are non-renewable source of energy? • ***Recall***
(a) Natural gas (b) Coal
(c) Fossil fuel (d) All of these

(v) On moving from equator to pole, acceleration due to gravity • ***Understanding***
(a) increases (b) decreases
(c) remains same (d) None of these

(vi) A ball is thrown vertically upwards with a velocity of 2 m/s. What is the maximum height it reaches ?
[Take, $g = 10 \text{ m/s}^2$] • ***Application and Analysis***
(a) 10 cm (b) 10 m
(c) 20 cm (d) 20 m

(vii) Which among the following is correct? • ***Recall***
(a) Weight is vector quantity
(b) Weight of an object is not constant.
(c) At the centre of the earth, weight of an object become zero
(d) All of the above

(viii) **Assertion** The current flowing through a conductor is directly proportional to the potential difference across its end, provided the temperature remains constant.
Reason The resistance of a conductor changes with temperature variations. • ***Analysis***
(a) Both A and R are true and R is the correct explanation of A.
(b) Both A and R are true and R is not the correct explanation of A.
(c) Assertion is false but reason is true.
(d) Assertion is true but reason is false.

(ix) On increasing the pressure of a gaseous medium, speed of sound • ***Understanding***
(a) increases

(b) decreases
(c) remains unchanged
(d) None of the above

(x) The SI unit of heat is
(a) calorie (b) joule
(c) Both (a) and (b) (d) Neither (a) nor (b)

(xi) The motion of a falling ball towards earth is due to the • *Recall*
(a) weightlessness
(b) gravitational force
(c) acceleration due to gravity
(d) Both (a) and (b)

(xii) Pascal's law states that pressure in a fluid at rest is the same at all points, if • *Understanding*
(a) they are at the same height
(b) they are along same plane
(c) they are along same line
(d) Both (a) and (b)

(xiii) A cell is used to • *Application*
(a) measure current in a circuit
(b) provide current in a circuit
(c) limit current in a circuit
(d) prevent current in a circuit

(xiv) To obtain a magnification of +2 with a concave mirror of radius of curvature 60 cm, the object distance must be • *Understanding*
(a) −90 cm (b) −45 cm
(c) −30 cm (d) −15 cm

(xv) The numerical ratio of displacement to distance for a moving object is • *Recall*
(a) always less than 1
(b) always equal to 1
(c) always more than 1
(d) equal or less than 1

2. (i) Complete the following by choosing the correct answers from the bracket. **[6]**
(a) A body is said to be at rest if it does not change its .... [position/speed/direction] with respect to the surroundings. • *[Recall]*
(b) The force of attraction between any two objects due to their masses is called ....[gravitational force/frictional force/contact force]. • *[Recall]*
(c) When a substance is heated, its molecules move faster, causing it to .... [expand/contract/no change] in size. • *[Recall]*
(d) Vernier calipers are used to measure the ....[length/breadth/diameter] of small objects with higher precision than a regular scale. • *[Recall]*
(e) An object at rest remains at rest, and an object in motion continues to move with the same .... [velocity/speed] and in the same .... [direction/position] unless acted upon by an external force. • *[Recall]*

(ii) A body moves with a velocity of 2 m/ s for 5 s, then its velocity increases uniformly to 10 m/ s in next 5 s. Thereafter, its velocity begins to decrease at a uniform rate until it comes to rest after 5 s.
(a) Plot a velocity-time graph for the motion of the body. • *Application* [1]
(b) From the graph, find the total distance covered by the body after 2 s and 12 s. • *Analysis* [1]

(iii) (a) What are non-contact forces? • *Recall* [1]
(b) How does the distance of separation between two bodies affect the magnitude of the non-contact force between them? • *Understanding* [1]

3. (i) Figure shows an incident ray AO and the normal ON on a plane mirror. The angle which the incident ray AO makes with mirror is 30°. (a) Find the angle of incidence (b) Draw the reflected ray and then find the angle between the incident and reflected rays. • *Analaysis* [2]

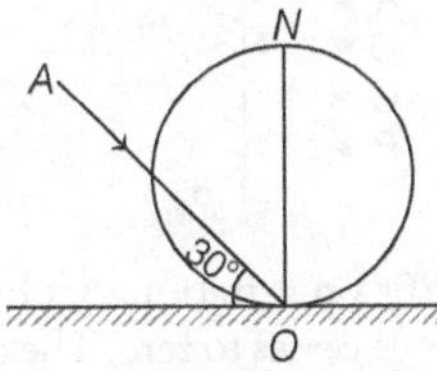

(ii) Give one use of each of the following
(a) Regular reflection • *Applicaton* [1]
(b) Irregular reflection • *Applicaton* [1]

(iii) How does the resistance of a wire vary,
(a) if area is made half • *Applicaton* [1]
(b) if length is made double? • *Applicaton* [1]

(iv) Why we cannot use equation of motion in case of acceleration varies with time? • *Analysis* [2]

(v) (a) What is the audible range of frequency? • *Recall* [1]
(b) For which range of frequencies are the human ears most sensitive? • *Understanding* [1]

(vi) Draw magnetic field lines due to
(a) two unlike poles facing each other • *Application* [1]
(b) two like poles facing each other. • *Application* [1]

(vii) Fig. shows the position of the movable contact when the voltage across the lamp is 12 V and the current in the lamp is 0.25 A. • *Understanding* [3]

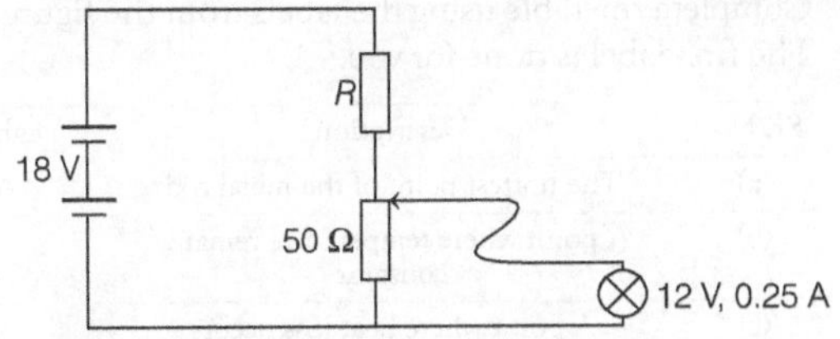

Determine
(a) the current in the 50 Ω resistor,
(b) the current in R,
(c) the potential difference (p.d.) across R,
(d) the resistance of R. • *Understanding*

Section-B [40 Marks]

(Attempt any four questions from this section)

4. (i) (a) How is the direction electric current taken in electric circuit? • *Understanding*

(b) Draw the symbol for circuit of component of switch, when it is • *Recall*

I. opened and II. closed. **[3]**

(ii) State three ways for judicious use of energy. • *Application* **[3]**

(iii) (a) An object O is placed in front of a plane mirror P_1P_2. An observer wants to see its image by keeping his eye at A, B and C. Can he see the image from these points or not? • *Analysis*

(b) Explain with the help of diagram.

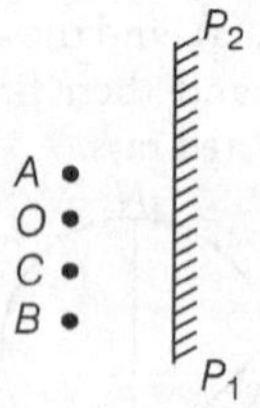

• *Analysis* **[4]**

5. (i) A force acts for 20s on a stationary object of mass 200kg after which the force ceases to zero. The object moves 200m in next 5s. Calculate the • *Application and Analysis* **[3]**

(a) velocity acquired by object

(b) the acceleration produced by force and

(c) magnitude of force.

(ii) A metal rod is heated at one end, and the heat travels through the rod. A student traces the heat flow and marks various points indicating temperature changes and heat transfer. The diagram below represents this scenario. • *Analysis* **[4]**

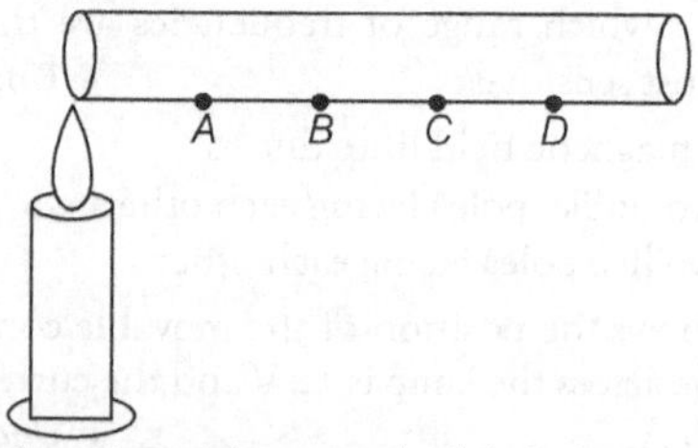

Complete the table using the labels from the figure. The first label is done for you.

Sr. No.	Description	Label
(a)	The hottest point of the metal rod	A
(b)	A point where temperature remains constant	
(c)	A point where heat loss occurs	
(d)	The coldest point of the metal rod	

(iii) Explain the following questions.

(a) Why is tungsten used almost exclusively for filament of electric lamps? • *Understanding* **[1]**

(b) How does the resistance of a wire vary with its area of cross-section? • *Application* **[1]**

(c) Why are copper and aluminium wires usually employed for electricity transmission? • *Understanding* **[1]**

6. (i) Which type of motion represent the following two graphs? Explain briefly. • *Analysis*

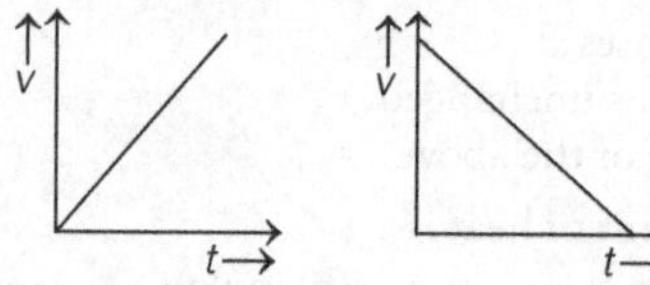

(a) (b) **[3]**

(ii) (a) Distinguish between thrust and pressure. • *Recall* **[1½]**

(b) Why is it easier to swim in sea-water than in river water? • *Application* **[1]**

(c) Given figure represent a jar filled with liquid. Find the net pressure at point A and B.

(Take, ρ = density and g = acceleration due to gravity) • *Analysis* **[1½]**

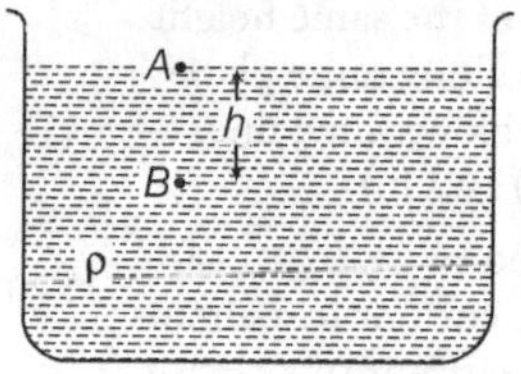

(iii) Define zero error of a Vernier calliper? How do you show by a labelled diagram, the position of the main scale and the Vernier scale in case of two types of zero error? • *Application and Recall* **[3]**

7. (i) (a) Calculate the mass of Earth, if $g = 9.8 \text{ m/s}^2$, $R_{\text{Earth}} = 6400 \text{ km}$ and $G = 6.6 \times 10^{-11} \text{ N-m}^2/\text{kg}^2$. • *Application* **[2]**

(b) Which one will exert more pressure either sea water or river water? Why? • *Understanding* **[2]**

(ii) (a) Define potential difference. • *Recall* **[1]**

(b) If a charge of 2.5 C is first move from infinity to point P and then to point-Q, a work of 10 J and 25 J is done, respectively. Calculate the potential difference between points P and Q. • *Application* **[2]**

(iii) Figure shows a very large plane mirror, inclined at 45° to the horizontal, beneath a pattern on the high ceiling of a hall. • *Analysis*

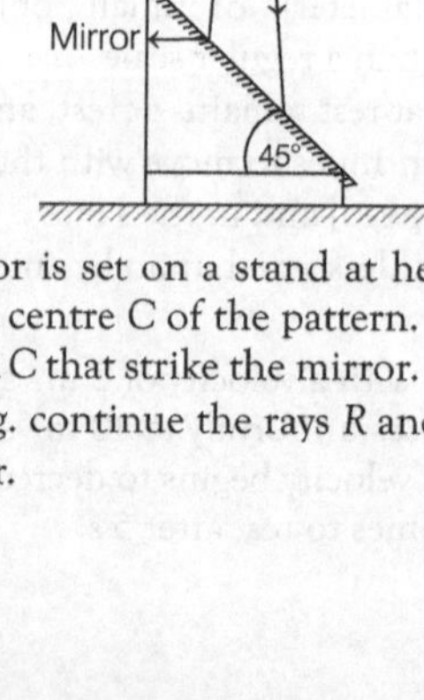

The mirror is set on a stand at head-height immediately below the centre C of the pattern. R and S are two rays of light from C that strike the mirror.

(a) On fig. continue the rays R and S after they strike the mirror. **[1½]**

(b) On figure, show how these rays are used to locate the image of C and mark and label the position of this image with the letter *I* ? [½]

(c) State two characteristics of this image. [1]

Suggest, how the mirror helps visitors to the hall to see the pattern on the ceiling ? [1]

8. (i) A concave mirror forms a virtual image of size twice that of the object placed at a distance 5 cm from it.

Find

(a) the focal length of the mirror • ***Applicaiton*** **[1½]**

(b) position of image. • ***Applicaiton*** **[1½]**

(ii) (a) Draw the I-shape (or bar) electromagnet and U-shape electromagnet. • ***Recall***

(b) Where are giant electromagnets used? • ***Understanding*** **[3]**

(iii) Write the symbols and state the functions of each of the following components in an electric circuit. • ***Recall***

(a) Battery

(b) Resistance

(c) Key open

(d) Connecting wires **[4]**

9. (i) In a hypothetical case, if the diameter of earth becomes double of its present value and mass becomes eight times of present value, then find out the value of acceleration due to gravity of earth.

(Take, present value of $g = 9.8\ ms^{-2}$) • ***Analysis*** **[3]**

(ii) Name the instrument you would use to measure the following • ***Recall***

(a) Diameter of a ball pen

(b) Diameter of a pencil

(c) External/internal diameter of a calorimeter **[3]**

(iii) The distance-time reading of an object is given as follows.

Time (in s)	Distance (in m)
0	0
1	1
2	8
3	27
4	64
5	125
6	216
7	343

(a) What conclusion can you draw about the acceleration? Is it constant, increasing, decreasing or zero?• ***Analaysis***

(b) What do you infer about the force acting on the object? • ***Analysis*** **[4]**

Answers

1. (i) b, (ii) b, (iii) d, (iv) d, (v) a, (vi) c, (vii) d, (viii) b, (ix) c, (x) b, (xi) b, (xii) a, (xiii) b, (xiv) d, (xv) d.

2. (i) (a) position

(b) gravitational force

(c) expand

(d) diameter

(e) velocity, direction

3. (vii) (a) 0.24 A

(b) 0.49 A

(c) 6.0 V

(d) 12.24 Ω

5. (i) (a) 80 m/s (b) 16 m/s^2

(c) 3200 N

6. (i) (a) uniformly accelerated

(b) uniformly retarded

7. (i) (a) 6.08×10^{24} kg

(ii) (b) 6V

9. (i) 19.6 m/s^2